Event-Based Programming

Taking Events to the Limit

Ted Faison

Apress®

Event-Based Programming: Taking Events to the Limit

ISBN-13 (hc): 978-1-59059-643-2 [*Originally published as a hardcover first edition on May 1, 2006.*]

ISBN-13 (pbk): 978-1-4302-4326-7

ISBN-13 (electronic): 978-1-4302-4327-4

President and Publisher: Paul Manning
Lead Editor: Jonathan Hassell
Technical Reviewer: Fernando De Gasperis
Editorial Board: Steve Anglin, Mark Beckner, Ewan Buckingham, Gary Cornell, Morgan Ertel, Jonathan Gennick, Jonathan Hassell, Robert Hutchinson, Michelle Lowman, James Markham, Matthew Moodie, Jeff Olson, Jeffrey Pepper, Douglas Pundick, Ben Renow-Clarke, Dominic Shakeshaft, Gwenan Spearing, Matt Wade, Tom Welsh
Coordinating Editor: Beth Christmas
Copy Editor: Nicole Abramowitz
Compositor: Susan Glinert
Indexer: Ted Faison
Artist: Kinetic Publishing Services, LLC
Cover Designer: Anna Ishchenko

Distributed to the book trade worldwide by Springer Science+Business Media New York, 233 Spring Street, 6th Floor, New York, NY 10013. Phone 1-800-SPRINGER, fax (201) 348-4505, e-mail orders-ny@springer-sbm.com, or visit www.springeronline.com.

For information on translations, please e-mail rights@apress.com, or visit www.apress.com.

Apress and friends of ED books may be purchased in bulk for academic, corporate, or promotional use. eBook versions and licenses are also available for most titles. For more information, reference our Special Bulk Sales–eBook Licensing web page at www.apress.com/bulk-sales.

Any source code or other supplementary materials referenced by the author in this text is available to readers at www.apress.com. For detailed information about how to locate your book's source code, go to www.apress.com/source-code/.

Wisdom is hereditary: You get it from your children.
I dedicate this book to my daughters Giulia, Claudia, and Linda,
who have taught me so much about life.

Contents at a Glance

Contents

About the Author

TED FAISON has more than 25 years of experience in the software industry and has been involved with object-oriented-programming and component-based development since the inception of those technologies. He has worked primarily in the private sector, but has also consulted for the U.S. and Italian governments.

He is a member of the Institute of Electrical and Electronics Engineers (IEEE) and the Association for Computing Machinery (ACM), and an active researcher in the field of software engineering, specializing in component-based software. He currently is a senior software engineer at the Automobile Club of Southern California, where he works on the development of a large .NET distributed system for customer relationship management.

Ted has published numerous papers and given talks at national software conferences. Ted is the author of *Component-Based Development with Visual C#, Borland C++ Object-Oriented Programming*, and *Graphical User Interfaces with Turbo C++*. He has a wide range of interests, including genetics, linguistics, physics, and electronics. He holds a BSEE from California State University, Fullerton.

About the Technical Reviewer

 **FERNANDO DE GASPERIS** is a senior software engineer with more than 20 years of experience in software design and development that spans a wide range of technologies and methodologies. He has led many software development teams successfully in a variety of industries including entertainment, health-care, distribution, logistics, legal, insurance, and financial. Fernando is based in Los Angeles and works as an independent consultant helping companies build solutions based on the Microsoft .NET platform.

Acknowledgments

This book is the result of several years of research, tempered by real-world applications. I wish to thank the many people in academia and the industry who supported me along the way, including Sergio Alvarado (The Aerospace Corporation), Clemens Szyperski (Microsoft), Mike Thornton (Automobile Club of Southern California), Hadar Ziv (University of California, Irvine), and Lech Lakomy (First American Title Company). Special thanks to Fernando De Gasperis (Kelley Blue Book) for his sanity checks and friendship.

Irvine, California

Introduction

Events are by no means a new idea in the software world. They've been around at least since the early 1980s. Smalltalk's Model View Controller paradigm is one of the earliest to use event notifications to keep different parts of a system synchronized with each other. Later graphical user interface (GUI) operating systems, such as Microsoft Windows, are based on an event-driven model, in which applications run passively instead of using their own code to scan the input devices for activity. The operating system uses an event mechanism to notify applications of operator input or other occurrences. Publish-subscribe systems have since become popular, allowing subscribers to sign up to a notification service and get information back using a *push* interaction style. Events really started to go mainstream at the programming language level with the release of Microsoft Visual Basic in the early 1990s. The programming paradigm was based on a window called a form, on which programmers could place UI widgets selected from a toolbox. Programmers could customize the widgets by wiring their events to handlers in the parent form. Borland Delphi, released in early 1995, incorporated the event idea and also added events as new types to Object Pascal, the native Delphi programming language.

What Is an Event-Based System?

A software system is said to be *event-based* if its parts interact primarily using event notifications. In this context, a part is anything containing code, such as a module of functions, an object, or a component made up by classes and objects. Notifications are basically signals sent from one part to another, in response to an event. The focus of this book is not so much on how to structure individual parts internally, but on how to use events and notifications as an interconnection fabric.

Event-Based Architectures Are Better

Before getting too deep in details, a few fundamental questions beg for answers. Why is an event-based approach useful? An event-based system is made up of a collection of independent parts that interact using event notifications. A system designed this way is easier to build, test, and maintain than a traditional one. The larger the system, the greater the benefits of an event-based approach. What problem does an event-based design try to solve? The answer is this: coupling. An event-based design tries to reduce as much as possible the coupling in a system. Coupling creates problems in all phases of a system's life cycle. At design time, changing one coupled part can break others and cause a ripple effect of changes through the rest of the system. Programmers working on coupled parts need to synchronize their activities and are often required to check a whole barrage of changes into the source-control system at once. An even greater problem arises during testing. In a heavily coupled system, developers can only test their code by running the whole system, making it more difficult to isolate behaviors and verify the correct operation of a piece of code. At maintenance time, the smallest change to one part of the system may break code elsewhere in the most unexpected ways.

An event-based system reduces the overall complexity of a system. A side effect is an increase in complexity at the local level. Parts that interact in an event-based system are generally simpler from a coding standpoint, but their operation may be more difficult to understand without seeing the rest of the system.

Coupling is such an important topic that the book devotes the entire first chapter to it. Coupling is a somewhat arcane subject, and some readers may find the first chapter to be a bit theoretical and dry. Fear not! The rest of the book is much lighter, with lots of code samples and practical advice.

Once you start designing an entire system using an event-based approach, it becomes important to have a way to model and document the system. Chapter 6 looks at the various types of diagrams that are available currently for documenting an event-based system. Chapter 7 describes a new type of diagram, known as a *Signal Wiring diagram*, which I've worked with and refined over the years. Developers have used Signal Wiring diagrams to successfully document systems small and large, local and distributed. I've used the diagrams to document systems with more than 2 million lines of code. Readers might find Signal Wiring diagrams to be useful complements of other common diagram types. You can find a Visio stencil with the symbols used in Signal Wiring diagrams in the Source Code area of the Apress Web site (www.apress.com). You can use the stencil with Visio 2000 and later versions.

Sample Code

Many of the topics presented in the book are difficult to explain without examples, so code fragments appear frequently. I've written most of the fragments in C# and VB .NET, but I've used Java and Borland Object Pascal occasionally, where language-specific details are important. Event-based programming contains many facets, and each chapter focuses on specific ones. To see the full picture, you really need to look at complete systems, so I included three case studies at the end of the book. The case studies deal with design issues, alternatives, problems, and solutions, and they tie together many of the concepts and techniques discussed throughout the book. Although the case studies are implemented using C# and VB .NET, none of the ideas presented are language-specific. You can find the sample code in the Source Code area of the Apress Web site (www.apress.com) and also on my personal Web site at www.faisoncomputing.com/publications.htm.

Footnotes

A last note about the footnotes: To make the material easier to read, bibliographic references are called out in footnotes containing a synopsis of the cited work. Appendix B contains a full list of bibliographic references.

CHAPTER 1

■■■

Coupling

Coupling is the single greatest problem in large software systems. By the time you finish reading this book, you'll understand why. Coupling tends to grow throughout a system—like a cancer—as people make changes and additions without proper forethought. The comparison to cancer is appropriate, because if coupling is not kept in check, it can grow to the point of strangling your system. One coupling scenario—circular coupling—is familiar to most programmers. It generally occurs when developers lose control of the design of a system, a situation that often occurs in the last feverish days of development, immediately before deployment, when programmers find themselves adding last-minute fixes and features on the fly. When a group of people adds changes in this manner, the coupling in a system typically gets completely out of hand. Circular coupling can suddenly force you to refactor the system's design, which can be a fairly big problem if you're trying to add a relatively simple feature to a system, perhaps in the maintenance phase with limited time available. Coupling is one of those characteristics that people assume is just part of the system. In reality, you can plan and control coupling, leading to much better and simpler systems. The main reason people turn to event-based programming is to reduce the coupling in a system, so it makes sense to start this book by describing what coupling is, what effects it has, and what you can do to minimize it. Incidentally, in case you're wondering, I'll discuss circular coupling toward the end of this chapter.

Thirty years ago, Stevens, Myers, and Constantine[1] first defined coupling in a software system as *the measure of the strength of association established by a connection from one module to another*. Coupling is frequently cited with another parameter called cohesion. In their paper, Stevens et al. defined cohesion as *the degree of connectivity among the elements of a single module*. Together, coupling and cohesion are important indicators of the quality of a software system. While coupling looks at the external dependencies between modules, cohesion looks at the internal ones of a single module. In the context of event-based systems, the word *module* should be understood as *component*.

In the broadest terms, coupling indicates the presence of interdependencies between classes or components. High-quality software should have a low degree of coupling between its components, because coupling introduces complexity, and complexity makes a system more difficult to understand, test, and maintain. In some sense, you can view coupling as a form of chaos, and attempts have been made[2] to treat coupling like entropy.

Most software systems have a significant amount of coupling between their constituent components, because the designers didn't anticipate coupling as a problem, and therefore didn't invest time in preventing it or dealing with it. Given the problems that coupling causes, it's surprising that today there is no standard way to measure coupling between the various parts of a software system. Coupling has simply become one of those evils that software developers have learned to live with,

---

1. Wayne Stevens, Glenford J. Myers, and Larry Constantine, "Structure Design," *IBM Systems Journal*, May 1974.
2. Mark Shereshevsky, Habbib Ammari, Nicholay Gradetsky, Ali Mili, and Hany H. Ammar, "Information Theoretic Metrics for Software Architectures" (proceedings of the IEEE 25th Annual International Computer Software and Applications Conference, Chicago, IL, October 8–12, 2001).

even though it's clear that coupling introduces a whole set of issues into a system. The larger the system, the bigger the issues.

Given that coupling makes a system more complicated, you might wonder why people design coupled systems in the first place. To understand how coupling creeps in, consider how a typical software system is designed and implemented. Using an object-oriented programming (OOP) methodology, you start by creating classes and relationships to satisfy the system requirements. By the time the design is finished, you have a network of classes, linked in various ways by relationships. Many classes are linked directly or indirectly to practically every other class in the system. Programs designed this way are generally easy to understand, because when a method is called, the source code indicates the name of the class and method. Such programs are also relatively easy to debug, because all the code is present at compile time and you can use a debugger to seamlessly step across a subroutine call, into the called code, and then back to the caller. The compiler provides a great deal of assistance, checking that you pass the correct number and type of parameters in method calls. When developing small systems consisting of a single component, coupling between the classes might not be a major problem, because everything is built and deployed together in a single package. In larger systems that use multiple components, the picture changes, and coupling-related issues often dominate others. If one component is coupled to others, which in turn are coupled to others, you quickly wind up with what is called a stovepipe system. The expression came about several years ago to denote large, monolithic systems, in which none of the system could be used unless all of the code was present. Stovepipe systems are the epitome of nonreusability. To enhance reusability, you should design components with an eye toward the minimization of dependencies on other components.

Axiom 1 The more complex a class or component is, the more decoupled it should be.

A quick note here about the meaning of the word *component*. In this book, a component is a self-documenting binary entity containing classes and/or objects. If you're a .NET developer, a component is basically a .NET assembly.

Axiom 1 might appear to be paradoxical, because the more complex a part is, the more coupled it tends to be with other parts. The point is that coupling introduces complexity, so if a part is complex to start with, due to its internal business logic, then you want to avoid increasing this complexity further with coupling. The following is an immediate consequence of the first axiom:

Axiom 2 Coupling should be introduced into simpler classes and components first.

The idea here is that you don't want to introduce coupling into parts that are inherently complex, unless you have no other choice. Together, you should consider these two axioms the guiding principles of system design. You should do a significant amount of work in the design phase to control where and how much coupling occurs between the various classes and components you create. Even more effort is needed during implementation and maintenance to ensure that the originally planned coupling doesn't grow unnecessarily.

Coupling Is Inevitable

This chapter shows that there are ways to design components to minimize or even eliminate coupling to other components. If you systematically attack the coupling problem when designing each component in a system, you can usually find ways to shift coupling from complex components to simpler ones. But at some point, you reach a point at which no more simplifications are possible, leaving a residual amount of coupling in the system. In the ideal situation, the most complex components are completely decoupled. Only the simplest components are coupled to other components. No amount of refactoring can ever eliminate all the intercomponent coupling, unless you put the entire system into a single component, which takes you back to a stovepipe system. The following theorem describes the inevitability of intercomponent coupling in a multicomponent system:

Theorem 1 It is impossible to build a software system in which all components are completely decoupled from each other.

Informal proof: To function, you must instantiate the classes in each component somehow. In most object-oriented (OO) languages, instantiation entails invoking a class constructor. For example, in languages like C#, Java, and C++, you must use the new operator like this:

```
T2 t2 = new T2();
```

The class in which this instantiation code is located incurs coupling to the class being instantiated. If component C1 contains class T1, which has code to instantiate T2 contained in component C2, then C1 will be coupled to C2, as shown in Figure 1-1.

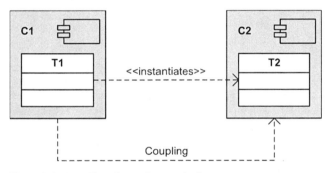

Figure 1-1. *Coupling due to instantiation*

You might try to use reflection to instantiate T2, but you still need to reference a class name (e.g., "C2.T2") in T1's code. The use of class names in T1 would still be a form of coupling between C1 and C2, as you'll see in more detail later in the chapter.

Even if you could completely eliminate coupling due to class instantiation, you'd still have another problem: Once instances are created, they will probably contain calls to other objects. These outgoing calls must be bound to methods of other objects. If you hard-code the name of the methods to call in each class, then each class incurs compile-time coupling to all the objects called, because the source code embeds method names. To avoid compile-time coupling, you might defer binding to run time, using a *Binder* class to connect outgoing calls to methods. The problem is that now the Binder could easily wind up being coupled to every class in the system, so you've merely shifted coupling around in the system. This predicament is somehow reminiscent of the famous words of Abraham Lincoln:

> *You may fool all the people some of the time; you can even fool some of the people all the time; but you can't fool all of the people all the time.*

In a coupling context, you might express the concept like this:

> *You may remove all the coupling from some of the parts; you can even remove some of the coupling from all the parts; but you can't remove all of the coupling from all the parts.*

I'll restate this in more mathematical terms. Given a software system containing n parts

$$\sum_{i=1}^{n} \text{coupling}_i > 0$$

the word *coupling* represents a measurement of some kind between the i-th part and all the other n-1 parts in the system. In the next section, I'll introduce a mathematical symbol to represent coupling. A bit later I'll show how to measure coupling.

An important job during the design phase is to reduce the overall coupling in a system to the lowest level possible. But a problem arises: How do you know when you're finished? In other words, how do you know when coupling is at the lowest level possible? The goal is to ensure that all complex classes and components are entirely decoupled from other components. To accomplish this, and because you know that you can't eliminate coupling completely from a system, you must find ways to shift coupling around in the system until it occurs only in *desirable* places. The rest of the chapter shows ways to accomplish this nontrivial goal.

The Coupling Symbol

Coupling is a kind of dependency between two entities, but no universal symbol exists to represent coupling in software diagrams. Unified Modeling Language (UML) relies on the use of stereotypes to depict relationships. The <<uses>> dependency is often used to indicate a dependency between components, as shown in Figure 1-2.

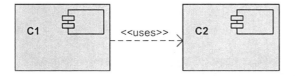

Figure 1-2. *Showing coupling with the UML <<uses>> stereotype*

The diagram simply tells you that C1 *uses* C2. The problem is that there are many ways for C1 to *use* C2, so you have no idea what sort of coupling exists between C1 and C2, or if there is any coupling at all. If there is, does it affect compile time, run time, or both? Is the coupling due to the use of user-defined types or not? Knowing the kind of coupling you're dealing with is not an exercise in futility, because each kind can affect different phases of the software development life cycle in different ways, introducing constraints in the project.

Given the significance of coupling in software systems, I'll use a dedicated symbol to represent coupling in diagrams and logic equations. The symbol is $\propto$. Using this symbol, the previous diagram becomes the one shown in Figure 1-3.

In some math and physics textbooks, the symbol $\propto$ is used to indicate a proportionality relationship. The decision to use this symbol for coupling was not entirely arbitrary, because proportionality is a form of dependency. For readers wishing to reproduce the symbol in their own documents, the coupling symbol is available in the Symbol font in Microsoft Word. The symbol is not a Greek letter and should be read as *coupling* or *is coupled to*. There are several ways in which classes, objects, and components can become coupled, so I'll use subscripts to denote the specific kind of coupling in effect at a given time.

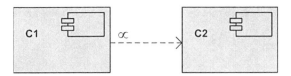

Figure 1-3. *Showing coupling with a special symbol*

Is Coupling Bad?

Yes, coupling is bad, but not all forms of coupling are equal. In the most general terms, duplicated logic, which is a form of coupling, might be considered the worst. Forms of coupling that impact compile time, which I'll call *static*, are probably the next worse. The most benign form of coupling is what I'll call *dynamic*, which occurs only at run time.

The fact is that coupling, in any form, introduces complexity into a system. Different kinds of coupling add different amounts of complexity, but it is undeniable that coupling makes it harder to develop, test, deploy, and maintain software. However, concluding that coupling is the root of all evils in software development would not be correct. For one thing, there are many evils that aren't dependent on coupling. Moreover, coupling isn't really the root of anything. Rather than a cause, it is an effect. It is the consequence of problems introduced at analysis, design, or implementation time.

Consider the main phases in the development life cycle in which coupling introduces complexity. For the purposes of the following discussion, assume a project uses two components, A and B. Coupling between A and B that affects compile time prevents A from being compiled unless B is present. Certain changes to B break the compilation of A, requiring A to be changed together with B. Coupling between A and B that affects run time prevents A from being run unless B is present. Run-time coupling makes it harder to test A, because you must also run B in order to run A. B's presence might complicate the testing scenario considerably, injecting a whole series of issues into the test phase.

Both compile-time and run-time coupling might introduce problems at deployment time, because coupled components might need to be deployed together. If A is from one vendor and B from another, it might be difficult or impractical to package or deploy A and B together. Coupling also complicates work during the maintenance phase. The more coupled A is to B, the more difficult it is to change B without affecting A. The magnitude of the coupling problem grows with the number of components used in a system.

Coupling can also affect the way programmers work.[3] If A and B are statically coupled but under the responsibility of different team members, then the members must work together somehow so that changes to A and B are made at the same time. Once B is checked out of the version-control system and changed, it can't be checked in until A has been suitably changed. A and B must be checked in essentially at the same time. As a consequence, coupled software results in coupled developers and possibly coupled teams.

The Nature of Coupling

It is clear that coupling complicates software one way or another. Just how bad the effects of coupling are depends on where it was introduced in the system and which development phases are impacted by it. I'll discuss the two key phases: build time and run time. Build time includes compilation, linkage, and any other activities required to produce executable code from source code. For interpreted

---

3. James Westland Cain and Rachel Jane McCrindle, "An Investigation into the Effects of Code Coupling on Team Dynamics and Productivity" (proceedings of the IEEE 26th Annual International Computer Software and Applications Conference, Oxford, England, August 26–29, 2002).

languages, these activities occur at run time, so there is no real distinction between build time and run time.

Static Coupling

If the coupling between two items affects build time, the coupling is *static*. If A is statically coupled to B, then B needs to be present in order to build A. To produce A's executable code from source code, some part of B must be present. Exactly which part is required depends on the language being used.

Modern OO languages, like C#, Visual Basic .NET (VB .NET), and Java, merge the declaration and implementation of a class together. During compilation, metadata is added to the executable code. The metadata describes all the types defined in the class, for the benefit of compilers and other software tools. The metadata also makes run-time type identification possible. If you write classes A and B in a language like C# or Java, and A is statically coupled to B, then B's executable code must be present when compiling A. B's source code is of no interest to A at build time or run time.

Older OO languages, like C++ and Object Pascal, separate the declaration of a class from the implementation. If classes A and B are written in C++ or Object Pascal, and A is statically coupled to B, then B's declaration must be present when compiling A. In C++, the class declaration is typically contained in a header file, while in Object Pascal, the declaration is in the same file as the implementation, but in a reserved section.

I use a UML dependency arrow to denote static coupling in diagrams and equations. The arrow is labeled with the symbol $\propto$ subscripted with the word *static*. Figure 1-4 shows an example.

Figure 1-4. *This diagram shows that A is statically coupled to B.*

Static coupling occurs between classes A and B when A contains references to symbols defined in B. A symbol is a name that can indicate anything from a constant to an enumeration to a method to a type declared inside B (such as a field or inner class). The embedding of references to externally defined types is a kind of coupling called *type coupling*. I'll describe type coupling in detail later in this chapter.

Just as static coupling can occur between classes, it can also occur between components. Statically coupled components must always be kept in sync with each other during the development process. Changing one component might break the compilation of other components that are statically coupled to it, requiring you to change those components as well. As a result, changes in one component can produce a ripple of changes throughout the system and involve several members of the development team.

Mathematical Properties of Static Coupling

You can treat all kinds of coupling mathematically, and throughout this chapter, I'll explore significant mathematical properties that apply to coupling. I'll start by focusing on static coupling.

Commutativity

Static coupling is not commutative. To understand why, let class A contain a reference to class B. Class A is statically coupled to class B, because B must be present to compile A. As discussed earlier, the form of B that must be present depends on the language. With languages like C++, you need B's header file. With languages like C#, VB .NET, or Java, you need B's executable code. Regardless of the language, class B is not statically coupled to class A, because class B doesn't contain references to A and can be compiled by itself.

Whether static coupling is transitive or not depends on the type of programming language being used. With languages like C++ that use separate declaration and implementation files for a class, static coupling *may* be transitive. For languages like C# and Java that use a single file for the declaration and implementation of a class, static coupling is not transitive.

Transitivity with Languages That Separate Declarations and Implementations

With languages that separate the class declaration from the implementation, static coupling is transitive, if coupling is due to items in the declaration. To understand why, assume you have three C++ classes: A, B, and C. Each class has a header file and an implementation file. Let's call the header files A.h, B.h, and C.h. Let's call the implementation files A.cpp, B.cpp, and C.cpp. Assume A.h includes the file B.h, and assume B.h includes the file C.h. With this arrangement, A is statically coupled to B, and B is statically coupled to C. When compiling A, the compiler needs to load the header file A.h, which includes B.h. When the compiler tries to load B.h, it discovers that it also has to load C.h. As a result, you need (the header files of) both B and C to be present to build A.

Things change if the coupled items are not in header files but in implementation files. Assume A.cpp (and not A.h) contains a reference to B. It follows that A.cpp must include the file B.h. Assume also that B.cpp (and not B.h) contains a reference to C, so B.cpp needs to include the file C.h. To compile B, you need to have access to C. When you compile A, will B need to be present? Yes, because A.cpp contains a reference to B.h. Will C need to be present? No, because when you compile A, the only file the compiler needs is B.h. There are no references to C in A's code or in B.h.

Transitivity with Languages That Merge Declarations and Implementations

With languages that merge the class declaration and implementation together, static coupling is not transitive. To understand why, let class A be statically coupled to class B, by embedding a reference to class B. Let class B be statically coupled to class C, by embedding a reference to class C. To compile B, you need to have C. To compile A, you need to have B, but not C, because A doesn't reference anything defined in class C. Everything the compiler needs to compile A is contained in the compiled code for B, so C is not necessary.

Dynamic Coupling

Dynamic coupling is a run-time dependency. Given two entities A and B, if A requires B to be present at run time, then A is dynamically coupled to B. To denote dynamic coupling in diagrams and equations, I'll use the symbol $\propto$ subscripted with the word *dynamic*. Figure 1-5 shows an example.

Figure 1-5. *This diagram shows that A is dynamically coupled to B.*

Dynamic coupling occurs between classes A and B when A contains references to executable code or data contained in B. For example, consider the class diagram in Figure 1-6.

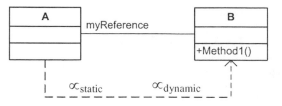

Figure 1-6. *Dynamic coupling is introduced through a direct typed reference.*

In this example, assume class A uses the typed reference named myReference to call B.Method1. Class A is dynamically coupled to B because the executable code for B.Method1 must be present at run time in order to run A. Note that class A is also statically coupled to B, because A references the type B (through the typed reference myReference). It is possible to eliminate the static coupling by separating the interface of B from the implementation of B, as shown in Figure 1-7.

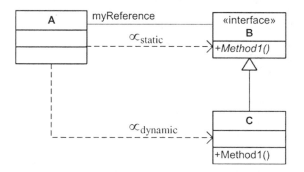

Figure 1-7. *Dynamic coupling is introduced through a reference to an interface of a class.*

Now class A holds a reference to type B, but the executable code for Method1 is in class C, derived from B. If you assume that A.myReference is initialized using a reference received from another object, A will have dynamic, but not static, coupling to C. A will think myReference points to a B object, while it actually points to a C object. Class A doesn't know about the existence of C, and calls C.Method1 through B's interface. Class A is statically coupled to B because the compiler needs to know the layout of type B in order for A to call B.Method1. At run time, C needs to be present, because A calls C's implementation of B.Method1.

Mathematical Properties of Dynamic Coupling

Let's explore the most significant mathematical properties that pertain to dynamic coupling.

Commutativity

Dynamic coupling is not commutative. To understand why, let class A contain a reference to class B. Class A uses the reference to call methods of B. Class A requires class B to be present at run time; otherwise, the executable code for the methods that A calls won't be present and the calls will fail. Class B doesn't require class A at run time, because B doesn't even know that A exists. Therefore, class B is not dynamically coupled to class A.

Transitivity

Dynamic coupling is transitive. To understand why, let class A be dynamically coupled to class B and let class B be dynamically coupled to class C. Assume A uses a typed reference to call a method of B.

When called, B reacts by using a typed reference to call a method of C. Class A requires class B to be present at run time, and class B requires class C to be present at run time. If you remove C at run time, then B is unable to invoke methods of C and fails. If B fails, A also fails. Ergo, class A is dynamically coupled to class C.

Static vs. Dynamic Coupling

Which type of coupling is worse: static or dynamic? The short answer is static coupling, because it manifests itself at compile time. If class A were statically coupled to class B, then changes to B could break the compilation of A. Class A would then need to be changed to make it compilable again. In a large project, changes to one class could break any number of classes that were statically coupled to it, and would require widespread changes throughout the system.

Dynamic coupling is much less a problem during the development phase. If class A were dynamically coupled to class B, then A would only require B in order to run. Since B wouldn't have to be present at compile time, you could change B in any way you want, without ever breaking the compilation of A. Any catastrophes caused by changes to B would only show up when running A.

On the other hand, static coupling is a safer form of coupling than dynamic coupling, from a certain perspective, and here's why: If two classes A and B are statically coupled, the compiler needs B to be available in order to compile A. The compiler is able to type-check any references A makes to items belonging to B, and this type checking can be immensely valuable in finding errors in source code. Dynamic coupling impacts the system at run time, when the compiler is long gone from the scene (at least with compiled languages like C# and Java). Errors related to dynamic coupling show up only at run time.

It's important to remember that the presence of dynamic coupling doesn't preclude static coupling. There is no deterministic relationship between static and dynamic coupling, so two classes might be statically, but not dynamically, coupled. Or they might be dynamically, but not statically, coupled. Or they might be both statically and dynamically coupled.

Coupling Flavors

Coupling can be characterized in any number of ways. The truth is that coupling is a somewhat nebulous concept, and depending on what system parameters are important to you at a given moment, you can slice a system in different ways to expose different kinds and levels of coupling. Eder, Kappel, and Schrefl devised one of the first classifications of coupling in an OO setting.[4] They described three *dimensions* of coupling: interaction coupling, component coupling, and inheritance coupling. They introduced *predicates* to compute degrees of coupling between arbitrary classes in a system. Later, Hitz and Montazeri[5] looked at coupling from the perspective of the level it occurs at (object level and class level). Attempts have been made to integrate the various coupling classification approaches together into a framework[6] with support for formal methods to determine *degrees of coupling* between parts of a system.

In this book, I'll look at the coupling kaleidoscope in yet a different way, identifying three orthogonal *flavors* of coupling that you can treat as dimensions in a mathematical coupling space:

4. Johann Eder, Gerti Kappel, and Michael Schrefl, "Coupling and Cohesion in Object-Oriented Systems" (technical report, University of Klagenfurt, Austria, 1994).

5. Martin Hitz and Behzad Montazeri, "Measuring Coupling and Cohesion in Object-Oriented Systems" (proceedings of the International Symposium on Applied Corporate Computing, Monterrey, Mexico, October 1995).

6. Lionel C. Briand, John W. Daly, and Jurgen K. Wüst, "A Unified Framework for Coupling Measurement in Object-Oriented Systems," *IEEE Transactions on Software Engineering*, January/February 1999.

- *Logic coupling*: This flavor is the least desirable of the three and is also the most abstract and insidious. Logic coupling doesn't impede the software development process, but it can result in run-time errors that are hard to find. Logic coupling often causes headaches during the maintenance phase.

- *Type coupling*: This flavor is probably the most recognizable form of coupling. It arises when one component or class uses a type defined in a different component or class.

- *Signature coupling*: This flavor occurs only at run time and has the potential to completely decouple classes from each other.

In the following sections, I'll cover each flavor in detail, looking not only at some of the mathematical properties that apply to each, but also at programming patterns that allow you to convert one flavor into another.

Logic Coupling

If two classes share information or make assumptions about each other, then they are coupled at the *logic* level. What happens in one class can have an effect on what happens in another—even if the classes share no data or types. Logic coupling is often the result of poor design, poor implementation, or both.

■Definition 1 Logic coupling occurs when information is shared.

To show logic coupling on diagrams, I'll draw a dependency line between the classes, using a double-headed arrow. In Figure 1-8, classes T1 and T2 are logically coupled.

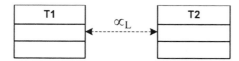

Figure 1-8. *These types are logically coupled.*

As you can see in Figure 1-8, logic coupling is denoted with a dependency line labeled with the symbol $\propto$, subscripted with the letter "L". The arrow is double-headed to symbolize the fact that logic coupling involves mutual coupling. T1 is logically coupled to T2 and vice versa. In the next sections, I'll show you why.

What causes logic coupling? You know that logic coupling results from the sharing of information, but there are different ways for objects to *share* information. A *sharing* relationship is somewhat vague, so I'll need to be much more specific about what I mean.

Let T1 and T2 be two classes. Don't worry whether T1 and T2 are part of the same component or not. There are basically two different ways in which T1 can *share* something with T2, in terms of logic coupling:

- *Algorithmic logic coupling*: This type of sharing is a subflavor of logic coupling where T1 contains an algorithm that is related to an algorithm contained in T2.

- *Literal logic coupling*: This type of sharing is a subflavor of logic coupling where T1 contains a literal value that is also contained in T2 and is used for the same conceptual purpose.

In the following sections, I'll describe each subflavor in more detail. Both have a dynamic nature: They don't induce compilation or other errors at build time. Their effects are felt only at run time.

Algorithmic Logic Coupling

The easiest way to describe algorithmic logic coupling (ALC) is with an example. Let T1 and T2 be two classes. T1 uses an algorithm F to encrypt data, which is then sent to T2. If T2 needs to decrypt the data, it needs a decryption algorithm that I'll call G. It is obvious that the algorithm G is dependent on the algorithm F. If T1 changes the way it encrypts the data, then T2 also needs to change the way it decrypts the data. Class T2 is said to have *algorithmic logic coupling*, or simply *algorithmic coupling*, to T1, as shown in Figure 1-9.

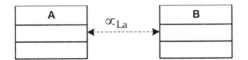

Figure 1-9. *Algorithmic logic coupling between T1 and T2*

As you can see in the diagram, the symbol ∝ is subscripted with the letters "La" to denote ALC. The coupling arrow in the figure is double-headed to indicate that T1 and T2 are mutually coupled. One class doesn't depend on the other; both classes depend on each other. If you change the coupled algorithms in either class, you must change the algorithm in the other class as well (if you want the system to work correctly).

Encryption and decryption algorithms are special cases of a broader set of algorithms called *complementary algorithms*. I need to make a small digression at this point to describe the properties of complementary algorithms and other types of algorithms involved in algorithmic logic coupling.

Complementary Algorithms

It is quite common for classes to be designed in a way that one class produces something that another consumes. Software systems often have many types of producer and consumer classes. Sometimes a class can act as a producer of some type of information, and as a consumer of another type. In the context of coupling, the producer-consumer pattern is important because the producer and consumer algorithms are logically coupled. Before the consumer can consume something, it must know a number of things about the producer, including

- What will be produced?
- When will it be produced?
- How will the information be packaged and formatted?
- How will the information be accessible?

All this meta-information induces algorithmic logic coupling between the consumer and producer algorithms. If the producer changes something in the way it produces information, there is a good chance the consumer will have to be changed as well. Two algorithms are complementary if they work together to accomplish a task or operation. For example, one class might use an algorithm to store data in a buffer, while another class might use a complementary algorithm to read the data from the buffer. The overall operation that the writer and reader accomplish together might be anything, such as getting data from one place to another, making information persistent, making information secure, increasing the performance of the system, and so on.

■**Definition 2** An algorithm G is the complement of an algorithm F if G completes an operation begun by F.

You can find complementary algorithms for any operation that is characterized by two facets or phases. There are many examples, but here are a few:

- Compression/decompression
- Encryption/decryption
- Writer/readers
- Producer/consumers
- Start/stop operations
- Open/close operations

Complementary algorithms are logically conjoined like Siamese twins. They are separate parts of a single logical task. If you change one, you're probably going to have to change the other. Complementary algorithms are designed in terms of each other, so they are intimately coupled, in a logic sense. One is generally useless without the other. Listing 1-1 shows two C# classes, T1 and T2, that contain complementary algorithms.

Listing 1-1. *An Example of Complementary Writer and Reader Algorithms*

```csharp
public class T1
{
  public void WriteMessages(StreamWriter theWriter, ArrayList theMessages)
  {
    // write all the messages
    foreach (string s in theMessages)
      theWriter.WriteLine(s);
  }
}

public class T2
{
  public void ReadMessages(StreamReader theReader, ArrayList theMessages)
  {
    // read all the messages
    while (true)
    {
      string s = theReader.ReadLine();
      if (s == null)
        break;  // end of file
      theMessages.Add(s);
    }
  }
}
```

The method T2.ReadMessages contains an algorithm that is designed to read not just any stream, but streams containing a list of string messages written using the algorithm in T1.WriteMessages. You can say that the algorithm in T2.ReadMessages is the complement of the one in T1.WriteMessages.

Note that the relationship "*is the complement of*" is not commutative. If T2 is the complement of T1, you can't conclude that T1 is the complement of T2. For example, the reader algorithm in this example logically completes the writer algorithm, so the reader is the complement of the writer. The writer is not the complement of the reader, because the writer does not logically complete any operation begun by the reader.

Inverse Algorithms Complementary algorithms are a broad class of algorithms, of which inverse algorithms are a subset. An algorithm can be considered a mathematical function that transforms a system from a certain initial state to a certain final state. Given an algorithm F that transforms a system from the initial state S0 to the final state S1, let there be a complementary algorithm G that transforms the system from the initial state S1 to the final state S0. Mathematically, you could describe algorithms F and G like this:

```
F(S0) = S1
G(S1) = S0
```

You can deduce two things, if G exists: that F is an invertible algorithm, and that G is the inverse of F, if F is applied to the system when the initial state is S0. The following equation shows explicitly that G is the inverse of F:

```
G(F(S0)) = S0
```

This equation tells you that the effect of applying first F and then G to a system in the initial state S0 causes the system to end up in the state S0. You need a simpler way to denote the *is-inverse-of* relationship. In math textbooks, the inverse of a function F is usually called F-1. The problem with this convention, as pointed out by many people over the years, including Feynman,[7] is that it uses the same notation to describe the inverse of F and the reciprocal of F, which is $1/F$. To avoid any confusion in this book, I'll use the function *Inverse* to indicate the inverse of an algorithm. To show that G is the inverse of F, I'll simply use this equation:

```
G = Inverse(F)
```

▓**Definition 3**   Given two algorithms F and G, you can state that G = Inverse(F), for a given initial system state S0, if G(F(S0)) = S0.

You might say that G is the *undo* function of F, because it cancels all effects of applying F to a system in the state S0. It's important to note that if G is the inverse of F for a particular initial system state (S0), it doesn't necessarily follow that G is the inverse of F for *all* possible initial system states. When G can invert F only for a certain subset of the possible initial system states, then G is the *bounded inverse* of F, where the bound denotes the set of system states for which G is able to invert F. For example, if G is able to invert F only for the initial states {S0, S2}, then G is the bounded inverse of F for the set of initial states {S0, S2}. Using mathematical symbols, I'll state this using this formula:

```
G = Inverse_T(F)    where T = {S0, S2}
```

The subscript T is the set of all initial system states for which G is the inverse of F. When G can invert F for any arbitrary initial state, then G is the *unbounded inverse* of G, or simply the *inverse* of F. An unbounded inverse of F, G can be described using this equation, where Sx is an arbitrary initial system state:

```
G(F(Sx)) = Sx
```

Using the Inverse function, you can also write this:

```
G = Inverse(F)
```

---

7.   Richard P. Feynman, "He Fixes Radios by Thinking!," "*Surely You're Joking, Mr. Feynman!" Adventures of a Curious Character* (New York: W. W. Norton & Company, 1984).

There is no subscript to the Inverse function, indicating that G is the inverse of F for all possible initial system states. In the rest of this discussion, assume that G is the unbounded inverse of F. Note that the *is-inverse-of* relationship, being a special case of the *is-complement-of* relationship, is not commutative. The fact that G can invert the results of F doesn't entail that F can invert the results of G. G is a completely different algorithm from F. For all we know, G might not even have an Inverse function.

Symmetric Algorithms Although the relationship *is-the-inverse-of* is not generally commutative, there is a subset of inverse algorithms in which the relationship *is* commutative. I'll call these algorithms *symmetric algorithms*, not to be confused with symmetric key algorithms used in cryptography, which use the same key to encrypt and decrypt data.

If F has an inverse algorithm G, then G is also the symmetric of F if F is the inverse of G. The following definition might be easier to digest:

■Definition 4 Two algorithms F and G are symmetric of each other if F is the inverse of G and vice versa.

If F and G are symmetric, the following two equations apply:

```
G = Inverse(F)
F = Inverse(G)
```

Instead of using two equations, you can make use of a new symmetric function like this:

```
G = Symmetric(F)
```

As with inverse algorithms, you need to specify the initial system conditions for which F and G are symmetric. If they were symmetric only for certain initial states, then you'd say that F and G are *bounded symmetric* algorithms. If the set of initial states included two states S0 and S1, then you'd express this fact with the following expression:

```
G = Symmetric T(F)    where T = {S0, S1}
```

You could express exactly the same symmetry using this expression:

```
F = Symmetric T(G)    where T = {S0, S1}
```

If T isn't specified, it is understood that F and G are *unbounded symmetric algorithms* and are symmetric for all possible initial system states. Symmetry is necessarily a mutual relationship. If F is the symmetric of G, then G must also be the symmetric of F. The property *is-symmetric-to* is generally not reflexive, because it would imply that F is the inverse of itself. The sole case in which F would be the inverse of itself is with a trivial algorithm, which doesn't change the system state.

Symmetric algorithms are common in information systems. For example, consider the algorithms for converting a decimal digit into ASCII and from ASCII to a decimal digit. The algorithms might be coded in C# as in Listing 1-2.

Listing 1-2. *An Example of Symmetric Algorithms*

```
char DigitToAscii(int theDigit)
  {
    // theDigit must be in the range (0..9)
    return (char) (0x30 + theDigit);
  }
```

```
int AsciiToDigit(char theChar)
{
  return (int) theChar - 0x30;
}
```

To prove that DigitToAscii and AsciiToDigit are symmetric, all you have to do is verify that they are inverses of each other for at least one pair of values. You can use the C# code in Listing 1-3 to check value pairs programmatically.

Listing 1-3. *Checking to See If Two Algorithms Are Mutually Symmetric*

```
bool AreFunctionsSymmetric(char theChar, int theDigit)
{
  if (theChar != DigitToAscii(AsciiToDigit(theChar)))
    return false;

  if (theDigit != AsciiToDigit(DigitToAscii(theDigit)))
    return false;

  return true;
}
```

If you find even a single pair of values for which the functions are valid, you can conclude that the functions are at least bounded symmetric functions of each other. In this example, the functions are symmetric over the set of characters in the range {'0'..'9'} and integers in the range {0..9}.

Equipotent Algorithms

As you've seen, complementary algorithms work together as different facets of an overall operation. A completely different class of algorithms, which I'll call *equipotent*, can also introduce ALC. Given two algorithms F and G, and an initial system state S0, F and G are equipotent if they both produce the final state S1.

▮**Definition 5** Two algorithms are equipotent if they achieve the same goals.

Equipotency is expressed using the symbol ≈. To show that F and G are equipotent, you can write

$G \approx F$

Two algorithms F and G might only be equipotent for a certain subset of initial conditions. If so, let's say that G is the *bounded equipotent* of F. You'll need to specify the set of initial system states using the following type of expression:

$F \approx_T (G)$ where T = {S0, S1}

If G produces the same final system state as F for any arbitrary initial system state, then G is the *unbounded equipotent*, or simply the *equipotent* of F.

While complementary algorithms are designed to work in conjunction with each other, equipotent algorithms are designed to actually produce the same results, and therefore represent a duplication of logic. A couple of properties are particularly important. Equipotency is commutative, so if G is the equipotent of F, then F is also the equipotent of G. Equipotency is also reflexive: An algorithm F is always equipotent to itself, so if you duplicate an algorithm verbatim, the two copies are equipotent.

Let's look at an example of equipotent algorithms. Assume a class T1 uses an algorithm F to compute the hash value for a message. If this message is passed to a class T2, and T2 needs to verify the correctness of the message hash, then T2 needs to use an algorithm G that is equipotent to F. In most cases, F and G are exactly the same algorithm, but this might not always be the case. The implementations of F and G might differ, even though they produce the same result. T1 and T2 incur ALC, because changing the algorithm F in T1 requires you to also change the algorithm G in T2, and vice versa.

Note that there is not necessarily a one-to-one relationship between algorithms and functions written in a programming language. You might consider a function to be a single algorithm, but you could also consider each line or a group of contiguous lines to be an algorithm. For example, consider the two functions in Listing 1-4.

Listing 1-4. *Two Methods That Contain Equipotent Algorithms*

```
char commandCode;
char parameters;

void GetSimpleCommand(string theCommand)
{
  commandCode = theCommand[0];
}

void GetLongCommand(string theCommand)
{
  commandCode = theCommand[0];
  parameters  = theCommand[1];
}
```

Although GetSimpleCommand and GetLongCommand contain different code, their first statements, shown in bold text, are designed to do the same thing. You can consider each bold line as an algorithm, so the two methods contain an equipotent algorithm whose purpose is to extract the command code from a command. GetLongCommand contains an additional algorithm to extract the parameters from a command. If the command code position were changed in the command, you would need to change both GetSimpleCommand and GetLongCommand.

Literal Logic Coupling

In Listing 1-4, the two methods contained equipotent algorithms for extracting the command code from a message. To get the command code, the algorithms used a hard-coded literal value to denote the position of the command code in the message. The presence of literals embedded in the code is a special case of logic coupling, called *literal logic coupling* (LLC), or simply *literal coupling.*

In Listing 1-4, LLC was present in two algorithms that were equipotent, but LLC can also occur in complementary algorithms. As an example, assume a system uses a hash table to store values. Each value is associated with a key, which might be a string. A class T1 stores values into the hash table, while a class T2 needs to retrieve them. Clearly, T2 needs to use the same keys as T1 if it wants to obtain the values stored by T1 in the hash table. If T1 stores a value using the code

```
hashtable["MyKey"] = "MyValue";
```

then T2 retrieves the value with the code

```
object myValue = hashtable["MyKey"];
```

Both T1 and T2 embed the literal value "MyKey" to access a particular value in the hash table. If T1 is subsequently changed to use another string for the key of "MyValue", class T2 breaks, in terms of its logic. T2 compiles without any problems, but probably doesn't work correctly. Figure 1-10 shows the coupling graphically.

Figure 1-10. *Literal logic coupling between T1 and T2*

As shown in the diagram, you denote LLC using the symbol $\propto$ subscripted with the letters "Ll", where the second letter is a lowercase L.

Another example shows how LLC might affect a system in which one class T1 sends information to another class T2. Let's assume the system is used in a book library. When a book is checked out, T1 sends a message to T2, describing the book that was checked out. The message might be sent as a string array A, which T1 populates using the following C# code:

```
A[0] = "Frankenstein";
A[1] = "Mary Shelley";
A[2] = "1-593-08005-0";
```

The message contains a sequence of strings. The first element of the message contains the book title, the second contains the author, and the third contains the book's ISBN. In order for T2 to extract meaningful information, T2 needs to know several things about the message, such as

1. The message describes checked-out books.

2. The message contains strings.

3. The strings describe a book title, author, and ISBN, in that specific order.

All this information represents logic coupling between T1 and T2, but the presence of the literal values for the array indices also injects LLC between T1 and T2. T2 might extract data from the message using the following C# code:

```
string title = Message[0];
string author = Message[1];
string isbn = Message[2];
```

A special case of LLC can occur even when no literal values are embedded explicitly in the code, but are implied: This type of LLC occurs when using streams to exchange information. If the writer adds items to the stream, those items have an implicit order in the stream. Although the writer doesn't use literals to indicate where items go in the stream, every item has its place. A class that reads the stream must know the ordering of items in the stream. Streams are a subset of a broader class of shared resources called *implicitly ordered resources*. Any time an implicitly ordered resource is used to send information between two parties, those parties incur literal logic coupling.

It is not uncommon to see literal values embedded in code, but projects that have the same literal value embedded in multiple places contain duplications. You must view duplications as software malignancies, because they generally represent sloppy design or implementation and add unnecessary complexity to the development and maintenance phases. Duplications are problems waiting to happen.

Mathematical Properties of Logic Coupling

Now that you've seen *how* logic coupling can occur, let's explore the most significant mathematical properties that apply to it.

Commutativity

Logic coupling is commutative. There are two forms of logic coupling, so the proof requires looking at each one separately:

- *Literal logic coupling.* Proof: Assume two classes A and B communicate via a shared data structure. Class A uses a literal value x to write data to the structure. The literal x might affect the value written, its format, or its position in the data structure. Let class B use a literal value y to read the value stored by class A in the data structure. If the value of x is changed, A writes the values associated with x in a different way. In order for class B to read the new value correctly, you need to change its y value to make it compatible with x. Conversely, changing y in class B requires you to change x in class A.

- *Algorithmic logic coupling.* Proof: Let Class1 communicate with Class2 via a shared data structure. Class1 writes data in the data structure using an algorithm F, while Class2 reads data from the data structure using an algorithm G. If you change F to write data in a new way, then you also need to change G to read data in the new way. Conversely, if you change G to read data in a new way, then you also need to change F to write the data in the new way.

Transitivity

Logic coupling is transitive. To understand why, let class A contain logic L_a that is coupled to logic L_b contained in class B. Let the logic L_b be coupled to logic L_c contained in class C. If you change the logic L_a, you must change the logic L_b to match the changes. If you change the logic L_b, you must change L_c to match the changes to L_b. As a result, changes to L_a in A require changes to L_c in C, so logic coupling is transitive.

Type Coupling

Type coupling is the most common coupling flavor found in software systems. When developing nontrivial object-oriented software systems, you split the design into a series of classes. The classes collaborate through associations, relationships, and links to implement the system requirements. A typical form of collaboration is through method calls, as shown in Figure 1-11.

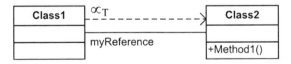

Figure 1-11. *Classes that have type coupling*

The link `myReference` is a reference to an object of type Class2. The reference to Class2 introduces a flavor of coupling that I'll call *type coupling*. Type coupling is designated using the symbol $\propto$ subscripted with an uppercase T. When using `myReference` to call methods in Class2, Class1 uses a statement indicating the name of the method to call. In C#, the statement would be

```
myReference.Method1();
```

Class methods (also called static or shared methods in some languages) might have a class name in place of an instance name. In order to compile Class1, the compiler must have access to Class2 to get a description of the structure of Class2. Class1 is thus *type-coupled* to Class2 and won't be compilable if Class2 is missing.

■**Definition 6** Type coupling occurs when an external type is referenced.

What's an *external* type? Given a type T1, a type T2 is external to T1 if defined outside T1. Type coupling can be static and/or dynamic. To understand when it's static and when it's dynamic, you have to be more specific about what T1 references in T2 and how T1 uses the reference. Type coupling is introduced in two basic situations:

- If T1 creates instances of T2
- If T1 contains references to T2

Each scenario introduces its own subflavor of type coupling, as described in the next sections.

Unambiguous Type Coupling

Assume a type T1 has a reference to a type T2. If T1 uses the reference to create instances of T2, then T1 must have access to T2 at run time in order to invoke the constructor for T2. The form of type coupling that involves type instantiation is called *unambiguous type coupling* (UTC). No type substitutions for T2 (such as types derived from T2) are allowed. Unambiguous type coupling is designated by the symbol ∝, subscripted with the letters "Tu".

There are two common situations in which UTC occurs: between unrelated classes and between related classes. You can consider two classes to be related if one derives directly or indirectly from the other. Figure 1-12 shows an example of UTC between unrelated classes.

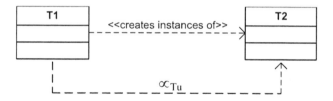

Figure 1-12. *Unambiguous type coupling between unrelated classes T1 and T2*

In this example, T1 is not related to T2, meaning T1 is not derived in any way from T2. If T1 creates instances of T2 using a constructor call, UTC is introduced. In OO languages like C# and Java, constructors are called using the new operator like this:

```
T2 t2 = new T2();
```

The new operator implicitly invokes the constructor for T2. At run time, the executable code for T2 has to be available, because it contains, among other things, the constructor code. You can avoid UTC by having T1 use reflection to instantiate T2, but then T1 must identify the T2 class name "T2". If the name is embedded as a literal in T1's code, then T1 incurs logic coupling to T2.

If T1 and T2 are related through inheritance, T1 implicitly calls the constructor for T2 when T1 is being instantiated. Assume T1 is derived from T2, as shown in Figure 1-13.

In order to create an instance of T1 at run time, you must build an instance of T2 first. In languages like C# and Java, the constructor code for T1 contains a call to the constructor for the base class T2. This call is made to the unambiguous type T2, and no substitutes (e.g., derived classes) are acceptable.

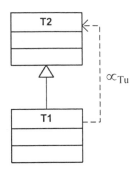

Figure 1-13. *Unambiguous type coupling between T1 and T2, due to inheritance*

K-coupling

K-coupling occurs between two classes Class1 and Class2 when Class2 defines some constant K that Class1 uses explicitly. To show K-coupling on diagrams, I'll use the symbol ∝ subscripted with the letter K. Figure 1-14 shows an example.

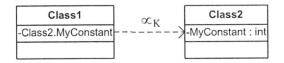

Figure 1-14. *K-coupling between Class1 and Class2*

Listing 1-5 shows a sample C# implementation of Class1 and Class2.

Listing 1-5. *An Example of Classes That Are K-coupled*

```csharp
public class Class1
{
  int i;

  public Class1()
  {
    i = Class2.MyConstant;
  }
}

public class Class2
{
  public const int MyConstant = 5;
}
```

K-coupling is similar to UTC, in that an explicit class name is called out, but now the name of a constant also appears. K-coupling is more benign than unambiguous type coupling, because the compiler can often remove the former but not the latter. To see how, consider what a compiler might do when compiling Class1. When the symbol Class2.MyConstant is found, the compiler needs to have access to Class2 to determine the constant's value. The compiler might then embed the value of MyConstant in the executable code of Class1. At run time, Class1 no longer needs access to Class2, since Class1 already knows the value of Class2.MyConstant.

There are a few caveats with K-coupling. First, the constant appearing in Class1 must be used *by value*, as shown in the previous listing. In some languages, it is possible to access constants also *by reference* (i.e., using a pointer), in which case Class1 won't know the constant's value until the pointer is initialized at run time. If Class1 uses a pointer to get the constant's value, then the coupling between Class1 and Class2 is not considered K-coupling. What type of coupling would it be? The answer depends on the constant's type. If the type is built in, such as integer or Boolean, then Class1 has no compile-time coupling to Class2. If the constant is of a user-defined type, then Class1 is type-coupled to that user-defined type. Listing 1-6 shows a C++ example in which Class1 uses a pointer to a constant integer contained in Class2.

Listing 1-6. *A C++ Example Using a Pointer in Class1 to Reference a Constant in Class2*

```cpp
class Class1
{
  public:
    const int* myValue;
    Class1() {}
};

class Class2
{
  public:
    const int myValue;
    Class2() : myValue(5) {}
};

class MyClass
{
  public:
    MyClass()
    {
      Class1* c1 = new Class1();
      Class2* c2 = new Class2();
      c1->myValue = &c2->myValue;
    }
};
```

Class1 doesn't know anything about Class2, so you can compile and run it without the presence of Class2. You must have Class2 present to compile MyClass. As long as Class1.myValue is initialized to point to an integer value somewhere in the system, Class1 works. Of course, in order for Class1 to work correctly, the pointer needs to point not just to any integer value, but to the *right* value, which is dependent on the system requirements.

As mentioned, K-coupling between T1 and T2 doesn't always occur when T1 references a typed constant defined in T2. K-coupling occurs only when certain types are involved. Exactly which types produce K-coupling depends on the programming language and the compiler. Referencing constants of built-in scalar types like Boolean, integer, float, and char generally causes K-coupling. In C# and VB .NET, all *value types*, which include structures, cause K-coupling. Whether strings qualify for K-coupling depends on how the compiler treats constant strings. Consider this C# example. Assume Class2 defines a constant string like this:

```csharp
public class Class2
{
  public const string MyString = "whatever";
}
```

Assume that Class1 is defined like this:

```
public class Class1
{
  string whatever;

  public Class1()
  {
    string whatever = Class2.MyString;
  }
}
```

The compiler can see that the string value in Class2 is constant. When compiling Class1, the compiler might be able to embed the characters of the string "whatever" somewhere in the executable code of the Class1. If so, then Class1 would be K-coupled to Class2. If the compiler didn't embed the characters in the Class1 code, it might generate code to use a pointer to Class2.MyString, which would then induce unambiguous type coupling between Class1 and Class2.

Ambiguous Type Coupling

If type coupling can be unambiguous, it might not be too surprising to learn that it can also be ambiguous. If a class T1 contains a reference to a class T2, and T1 doesn't create any instances of T2, then T1 has *ambiguous type coupling* (ATC) to T2, as shown in Figure 1-15.

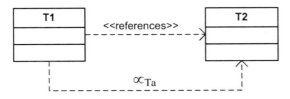

Figure 1-15. *Ambiguous type coupling between T1 and T2*

The symbol ∝ denotes ATC, when subscripted with the letters "Ta". The coupling is called *ambiguous* because the reference in T1 can be set to point to an instance of T2 or to a class derived from T2. The symbol $\propto_{Ta}$ is equivalent to the phrase *ambiguous type coupling*. Figure 1-16 shows T1 using a class T3 derived from T2.

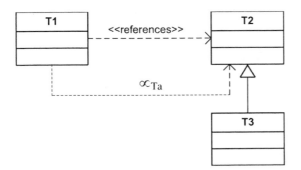

Figure 1-16. *Another example of ambiguous type coupling between T1 and T2*

In order for T1 to use an instance of T3 without creating it, T1 must receive a reference to the T3 instance from another object. T1 might be given a T3 instance as a parameter in a method call. Although T1 has no control over what type of object it gets (there might be several classes derived from T2), it knows one thing: The instance must be of type T2 or a type derived from T2. With ambiguous coupling, T1 needs T2 to be available at compile time. T1 might not require T2 at run time if the compiler is able to *bake* a copy of T2 into T3, meaning that T2's code is embedded somehow inside T3's code.

Platform Coupling

Component software is designed and implemented on top of a component platform, such as the .NET Common Language Runtime (CLR) or the Java Development Kit (JDK). The platform includes built-in components that provide commonly used services, such as memory management, file operations, and graphics primitives. The platform also defines a whole series of built-in types. No meaningful software system can be developed without using at least some of the built-in components and types. Consider the following trivial C# class:

```
class Class1
{
  static void Main(System.String[] args)
  {
    System.Console.WriteLine("Ciao, Mondo");
  }
}
```

Class1 uses the class System.Console, contained in the built-in .NET Framework component called System. Class1 also makes use of the built-in type System.String. Class1 is therefore type-coupled to the classes System.Console and System.String, as shown in Figure 1-17.

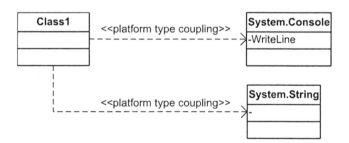

Figure 1-17. *Type coupling between a user-defined class and a platform class*

There is no way to completely eliminate the coupling between Class1 and the built-in classes and types, because the only way to perform standard console I/O in C# is via the System component. You could replace System.String with a user-defined string class, but this wouldn't eliminate any coupling because the effect would only be to change what Class1 is coupled to. You must accept the fact that the coupling between Class1 and the built-in classes is not dependent on bad design, and generally can't be avoided.

The coupling that exists between a class and a built-in type is a special case of type coupling called *platform type coupling*, or simply *platform coupling*. All OO software incurs platform coupling, but the presence of this form of coupling doesn't typically reduce the quality of a software system. The assumption here is that the built-in components and types are stable and well tested; however, this might not always be the case. Java software used to be particularly susceptible to problems caused by platform coupling. In the early Java days, roughly between 1995 and 1998, new versions of the

Java run-time environment were released frequently, adding features like printing, online help, two-dimensional graphics, and others. With each new release, Sun Microsystems deprecated certain methods and introduced others. Software written for a newer version of the run time would sometimes fail with an older version, if it called built-in services that the older version didn't support or that had been changed. The problem was due to the platform coupling between the Java components and the Java run-time components. If the software was developed on one version of the run time and deployed on a different version, there was always the potential for problems. The typical solution was to have users upgrade to the version of the Java run time that the system was written for.

Newer component platforms, such as the .NET Framework, reduce deployment headaches related to run-time version dependencies by embedding information in each component that identifies which version of the component platform it requires. If the required platform is not available, the run time notifies the user and prevents the affected software from running.

Mathematical Properties of Type Coupling

Let's explore the most significant mathematical properties that apply to type coupling.

Commutativity

Type coupling is not commutative. To understand why, let class A contain a reference to class B, while B contains no references to A. Class A is therefore type-coupled to B. You can't compile class A without B, but you can compile B without A.

Whether type coupling is transitive or not depends on the type of programming language being used. With languages like C++ that use separate declaration and implementation files for a class, type coupling *is sometimes* transitive. For languages like C# and Java that use a single file for the declaration and implementation of a class, static coupling is never transitive.

Transitivity with Languages That Separate Declarations from Implementations

With languages that separate the class declaration from the implementation, static coupling is transitive if coupling is due to type references in a class declaration. C++ is an example of a language that uses separate files for class declaration and implementation. Assume you have three C++ classes: A, B, and C. Each class has a header file and an implementation file. Let's call the header files A.h, B.h, and C.h. Let's call the implementation files A.cpp, B.cpp, and C.cpp. Assume A.h contains a reference to class B, and that B.h contains a reference to class C. With this arrangement, A is type-coupled to B and B is type-coupled to C. When compiling A, the compiler needs to load the header file A.h, which references B. When the compiler tries to load the declaration for B in B.h, it discovers the reference to C and must load C.h. As a result, the compiler needs to access the declarations for B and C in order to build A. The implication is that type coupling is transitive.

Things change if the referenced types are not in header files but in implementation files. Assume A.cpp contains a reference to B. It follows that A.cpp needs to include the file B.h. Assume also that B.cpp contains a reference to C, so B.cpp needs to include the file C.h. To compile B, the compiler needs C.h. To compile A, the compiler needs B.h. This time, B.h contains no references to C, so the compiler won't need C. The implication is that, in this scenario, type coupling is not transitive.

Transitivity with Languages That Merge Declarations from Implementations

With languages that merge the class declaration and implementation together, type coupling is not transitive. To understand why, let class A contain a reference to class B, so A is type-coupled to B. Let class B contain a reference to class C, so B is type-coupled to C. To compile B, you need to have C. To compile A, you need to have B, but not C, because A doesn't reference anything defined in class C. Everything the compiler needs to compile A is contained in the compiled code for B.

Signature Coupling

As you've seen, type coupling is related to classes and interfaces, but coupling can occur at a finer level. If you look at the contents of a class, you find fields and methods. It is reasonable to expect that coupling might occur not only at the class level, but also at the field and method level. Fields are really just classes (or scalars) used inside a class, so you can treat coupling to a field exactly like ordinary type coupling.

Methods are a completely different kind of entity from classes. They are not described by a formal type, but by their *signature*. The signature specifies the number and types of parameters that a caller passes to and from a method. When you write a method, you implicitly define its signature. Just as an interface represents the type of an object, so a signature represents the type of a method. As an example, consider the following C# class:

```
public class A
{
  public int GetAge(string theName)
  {
    // ...
  }
}
```

The signature for the GetAge method is

```
int f(string theName)
```

There are three things missing from the signature:

- *The type to which the method belongs*: Signatures describe methods outside the context of classes and interfaces, so they don't specify a class or interface.

- *The method's access qualifier*: The signature doesn't have an access qualifier (e.g., public or private), because qualifiers don't describe the method, but rather the method's accessibility, which is a class-level property.

- *The method name*: The signature doesn't have any particular method name, because signatures are abstract: They don't identify a concrete method. A given signature can apply to any number of methods. The letter "f" is used in the signature above to act as a placeholder for the method name.

In the signature, you can use any word as the method name, including the name of a particular method, so you can also write the signature of GetAge like this:

```
int GetAge(string theName)
```

Any method that takes a single string argument as input and returns an integer has the same signature as A.GetAge.

Now that you know what a signature is, let's see what signature coupling is. This flavor of coupling occurs when one object makes an indirect call to a method in another object. The caller must have a pointer that is initialized at run time to point directly to a method, bypassing any class interfaces of the callee. Figure 1-18 shows two classes that might be involved in signature coupling.

A
-methodReference

B
+Method1()

Figure 1-18. *Two classes with no relationships between them*

Class A has a field called methodReference that is used to make indirect calls to a method. Although the class diagram doesn't show the signature used by A.methodReference, assume the signature is the same as that of B.Method1. The class diagram reveals no information about coupling or other relationships between A and B. Classes A and B are completely decoupled from each other. It is perfectly possible that different people implemented the classes, not predicting that the classes would ever be used together. Assume that at run time there are instances of A and B, called respectively object1 and object2, and that object1.methodReference is initialized to point to object2.Method1, as shown in Figure 1-19.

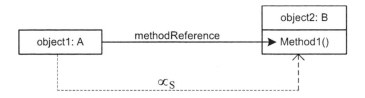

Figure 1-19. *Objects coupled through a method signature*

At run time, object1 becomes signature-coupled to object2, due to the method reference pointing at object2.Method1. The signature used by object1.methodReference must match the signature of object2.Method1.

■**Definition 7** Signature coupling occurs when one object has a reference pointing to a method in another object.

Signature coupling (SC) is designated using the symbol $\propto$ subscripted with an uppercase S, as shown in the previous diagram. When one object is signature-coupled to another, the former requires the latter to be present at run time. The system shown in Figure 1-19 might be implemented using the C# code in Listing 1-7.

Listing 1-7. *A C# Implementation of the Example Shown in Figure 1-19*

```
1    namespace Signature_Coupling.Example1
2    {
3      // declare a reference-to-method type
4      public delegate void SimpleDelegate();
5
6      public class A
7      {
8        // declare a reference-to-method field
9        public SimpleDelegate methodReference;
10
11       // use the reference
12       public void MakeIndirectCall()
13       {
14         // call the method pointed at by
15         // the method reference
16         methodReference();
17       }
18     }
19
20     public class B
```

```
21      {
22        public void Method1()
23        {
24        }
25      }
26
27      public class BuilderBinder
28      {
29        A object1;
30        B object2;
31
32        public BuilderBinder()
33        {
34          object1 = new A();
35          object2 = new B();
36
37          object1.methodReference = new SimpleDelegate(object2.Method1);
38        }
39
40        public void TestSystem()
41        {
42          object1.MakeIndirectCall();
43        }
44      }
45    }
```

Some explanations are in order. On line 4, the code declares a reference-to-method type called SimpleDelegate. C# uses the term *delegate* to represent a reference-to-method type. Other languages have different constructs. For example, Java uses the class java.lang.reflect.Method to support method references.

C# delegates are types that you can use to declare method pointers. The pointer must be initialized before being used; otherwise, it will point to nothing. The code in the preceding listing uses a separate class called BuilderBinder to create instances of A and B. The BuilderBinder also initializes object1.methodReference to point to object2.Method1. In the listing, the delegate is declared outside of all classes, at the namespace level. C# also allows delegates to be declared inside a class, without affecting the signature represented by the delegate.

It is worth reiterating the fact that method references work at the object level, not the class level. Regarding the example, it would be incorrect to say that A.methodReference is initialized to point at B.Method1, because that would imply that class A has some form of coupling to class B, which is not the case.

Getting back to Listing 1-7, object1 uses the methodReference field to call object2.Method1 directly, bypassing the B interface. The variable object1.methodReference doesn't point to an object, but to a method within an object. The method reference introduces signature coupling between object1 and object2, but not between A and B. At build time, there is no relationship whatsoever between A and B, and therefore no coupling. At run time, the BuilderBinder class initializes the method reference on line 37. Later, when object1 calls through methodReference, it doesn't know which object or method is going to be at the other end of the methodReference link. As long as the target method's signature matches the signature expected, the call will succeed, at least at the wire level. The fact that B.Method1 happens to be at the other end of object1.methodReference is completely unknown to class A at compile time, and dependent on the way object1.methodReference was initialized at run time.

When the signature of the method called is the same as the signature expected, then the callee's method is *signature-compatible* with the caller's method reference. Signature-compatibility of a target method obviously doesn't guarantee that the method will produce the expected results. Whether the *right* method is being called, in terms of the system's requirements, is an entirely different story. For the moment, all you care about is whether the method accessed through a method reference is signature-compatible with the reference itself. You can consider signature coupling similar in some ways to the object-level coupling described by Hitz.[8] Signature coupling applies to instances (e.g., objects), not types (e.g., classes).

At run time, you could set `object1.methodReference` to point to any signature-compatible method. That method could be practically anywhere: in object1, in a different instance of A, or in an instance of a different class. The method could be in the same component as the caller, in a different component, or in a different thread. Moreover, at run time you can change repeatedly the method that `object1.methodReference` points to. However, the reference might go to one object on the first call and to a different object on the next call.

Many methods have a signature with a parameter list and/or a return value. If the signature uses only built-in types, then the caller and callee incur platform type coupling to those built-in types. Figure 1-20 shows the platform coupling the String parameter causes in the method's signature.

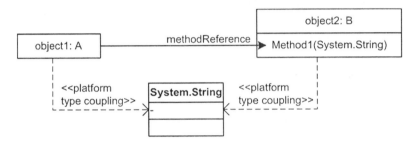

Figure 1-20. *Platform coupling introduced by method parameters*

If the types used in the method signature are user-defined types, then the caller and callee are both type-coupled to the components containing the user-defined types, as shown in Figure 1-21.

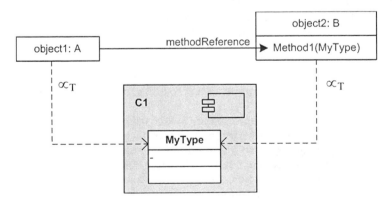

Figure 1-21. *Type coupling introduces user-defined parameters in the target method signature.*

---

8. Martin Hitz and Behzad Montazeri, "Measuring Coupling and Cohesion in Object-Oriented Systems" (proceedings of the International Symposium on Applied Corporate Computing, Monterrey, Mexico, October 1995).

The presence of user-defined types introduces compile-time coupling issues. If MyType is changed, then A and B might be affected, requiring you to change and recompile them. I'll show you more details later in this chapter, in the section titled "Coupling with User-Defined Types."

Signatures As Types

Earlier I stated that signatures are to methods as interfaces are to objects. In other words, signatures are similar to types. Let's look at this parallelism a bit more. Consider a class A that is ambiguously type-coupled to an interface B, as shown in Figure 1-22.

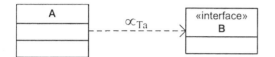

Figure 1-22. *Type coupling between a class and an interface*

A is coupled ambiguously to B, meaning that A can accept an instance of any class that implements B or implements an interface derived from B. Let C be one of these classes. Let's assume that A doesn't create instances of C, but rather receives a reference to C objects from another object I'll call a Builder (not shown in the diagram). Figure 1-23 shows the coupling diagram.

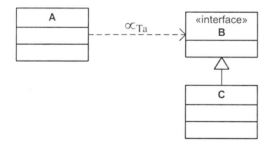

Figure 1-23. *Adding a derived class to the system*

All A knows about the object it receives from the Builder is that the object implements the interface B. Class A treats this object exactly as if it were an instance of B. What is interesting about the diagram is the fact that there is absolutely no coupling between classes A and C. Although A requires B to be present at compile time, it doesn't require C. In fact, A knows nothing about the existence of C.

Let's now compare the coupling between a class and an interface with the coupling between a method reference and a method signature. Assume that class C1 has a method reference that defines a certain signature S1. If you consider the signature a type, you could describe the system as shown in Figure 1-24.

Figure 1-24. *Signature coupling as a form of type coupling*

The method reference in C1 is coupled to S1, causing C1 to be coupled to S1. In the context of coupling, you can treat signatures like types, albeit special types. For starters, signatures don't support inheritance: You can't derive one signature from another, so you can't arrange signatures in a hierarchy. If inheritance doesn't apply to signatures, then signature coupling is always unambiguous. Why? Because if a method reference defines a given signature, you can point it only at methods with that exact signature, since derived signatures are not possible.

To reinforce the notion of signatures as types, consider the way objects use references to typed objects at run time, as shown in Figure 1-25.

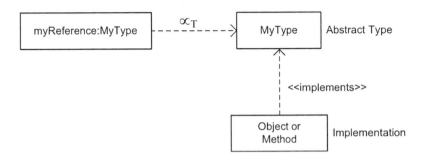

Figure 1-25. *The relationship between a typed object, the type, and the type's implementation*

Assume the item myReference to be a field of a class. If MyType is a class or interface, then at run time you can point myReference at any object that implements the class or interface. If MyType is a signature, then at run time you can point the reference at any method that implements the signature. In both cases, you can use myReference to call a method. In the first case, you can call any method defined by the interface. In the second case, you can only call one method. From this perspective, a signature looks a lot like an interface that only defines one method.

Mathematical Properties of Signature Coupling

Let's explore the most significant mathematical properties that apply to signature coupling. Given the fact that signatures are special types, you can expect the properties of signature coupling to be similar to those of type coupling, while keeping in mind that signature coupling only applies to objects—never to classes.

Commutativity

Signature coupling is not commutative. To understand why, let instA and instB be instances of classes A and B, respectively. Assume class B has a single method and that at run time a method reference in instA is initialized to point to the method in instB. After initialization, instA is signature-coupled to instB, because instA contains a pointer referencing a method of instB. Since there is no reference in instB pointing to any method of instA, there is no signature coupling between instB and instA.

Transitivity

Signature coupling is not transitive. To understand why, let instA, instB, and instC be instances of the classes A, B, and C, respectively. At run time, a method reference in instA is initialized to point to a method in instB, and a method reference in instB is initialized to point to a method in instC. After initialization, instA is signature-coupled to instB, because instA has a reference to a method in instB. Similarly, instB is signature-coupled to instC, because instB has a reference to a method in instC.

You can then deduce that instA is not signature-coupled to instC, because instA has no references to methods in instC.

Coupling Space

Throughout this chapter you've seen various flavors of coupling. If there were only one flavor, then you might be able to measure coupling using a simple number (e.g., 49). The value would tell you how coupled one entity is to another entity. Since there are multiple flavors of coupling, you need to measure the amount of coupling for each flavor separately. There are three basic coupling flavors: logic, type, and signature coupling. Logic coupling has two main subflavors: literal and algorithmic. Type coupling has two main subflavors: ambiguous and unambiguous. Signature coupling has no subflavors.

To measure the coupling of a class, you need to measure the value of the five coupling values: $\propto_{Ll}$, $\propto_{La}$, $\propto_{Ta}$, $\propto_{Tu}$, and $\propto_s$. You can consider these five entities as dimensions in a five-dimensional *coupling space*, and you can treat the space mathematically like a vector space. Because you're dealing with five dimensions, you can't easily represent coupling space on a single graph. You can use two Cartesian planes to show the bidimensional logic- and type-coupling spaces, as shown in Figure 1-26.

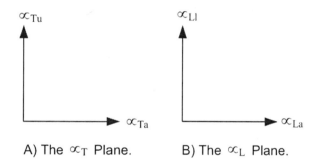

A) The $\propto_T$ Plane.   B) The $\propto_L$ Plane.

Figure 1-26. *The logic- and type-coupling planes of coupling space*

The fifth dimension in coupling space—signature coupling—requires you to graph a single axis, or just a single scalar value. You can use $\propto_{Ll}$, $\propto_{La}$, $\propto_{Ta}$, $\propto_{Tu}$, and $\propto_s$ as unit vectors in your coupling space because, in linear algebra terms, they are *linearly independent*. Given two entities P and Q of a vector space, they are said to be linearly independent if one can't be written as a *linear combination* of the other. In other words, there are no values that added to or multiplied by P can give Q.

How do you measure coupling for each dimension? The previous material in this chapter has provided qualitative information about coupling, but not quantitative. The approach I'll use to measure coupling for a given dimension is to count every single occurrence of coupling in that dimension. For example, in the ATC dimension, you count every ambiguous reference to all external types. If a class T1 has two ambiguous references to class T2 and three to class T3, you would say that T1's ATC value is 5, assuming T1 has no other ambiguous references to other classes. If you find three algorithms in T1 that are logically coupled to three algorithms in T2, you say that T1's ALC value is 3, again assuming T1 has no other logic coupling to other classes. The same approach applies to the other three coupling dimensions.

You get the value of coupling for each dimension by counting coupling occurrences, so the domain for each dimension is the set of all non-negative integers. The value must be zero or greater than zero. For example, the value for $\propto_{Tu}$ might be 0 or 4, but it can't be 1.2 or -5. Let's summarize what you now know about coupling space:

1. It is a discrete space.

2. It is defined only in one quadrant.

A discrete space is not continuous—it includes only specific points. In coupling space, the value of each dimension is restricted to whole numbers. Moreover, those numbers must be non-negative, so the domain for the space is a five-dimensional region in which all coupling values are 0 or positive.

The five components of coupling define a vector, pointing from the origin of coupling space to a specific point. You can compute the magnitude of coupling in the logic- and type-coupling planes using standard vector algebra, as shown in the following two equations.

Equation 1 $$|\propto_L| = \sqrt{\propto_{Ll}^2 + \propto_{La}^2}$$

Equation 2 $$|\propto_T| = \sqrt{\propto_{Tu}^2 + \propto_{Ta}^2}$$

Sometimes you might not be interested in dealing with the individual components of logic and type coupling. All you care about is the magnitude of $\propto_L$ and $\propto_T$. In such cases, you can depict coupling space using a simplified three-dimensional graph, with $\propto_L$, $\propto_T$, and $\propto_S$ as the dimensions, as shown in Figure 1-27.

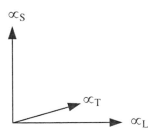

Figure 1-27. *Coupling space, reduced to a three-dimensional space*

The three dimensions are still linearly independent, so you also can consider this simplified space a vector space, like the full five-dimensional space. The overall coupling magnitude is defined as follows:

Equation 3 $$|\propto| = \sqrt{|\propto_L|^2 + |\propto_T|^2 + |\propto_S|^2}$$

The coupling magnitude gives you a basic feel for a class's level of coupling. The magnitudes of the three coupling flavors $\propto_L$, $\propto_T$, and $\propto_S$ are usually more important to know. In most cases, logical coupling is more undesirable than type coupling, and type coupling is sometimes more undesirable than signature coupling. A bit later in the chapter, I'll show you *coupling transforms*, which define ways to convert one coupling flavor into another. Using coupling transforms, you can reduce the amount of coupling in one dimension at the expense of other dimensions, allowing you to custom tailor the kind and amount of coupling a class incurs in each dimension.

Coupling Charts

The previous section showed that coupling is not measured as a simple scalar value, but you can use the magnitude to indicate the overall coupling value. The value itself doesn't tell you *how* a class is coupled; nevertheless, it does give you an overall sense of how coupled something is to other parts of the system. If you had to refactor the most coupled classes in a system, you might compute the coupling magnitude for each of the classes and put them in a table, sorted by magnitude. A class that has a much higher magnitude than average might be trying to accomplish too much, and might need to be split into a series of simpler classes.

To analyze the coupling in a system, a sorted table of magnitudes doesn't give you a good picture of the overall coupling of a system. A better approach is to use a bar chart, in which the vertical axis measures the coupling magnitude, and each vertical bar shows the magnitude of a class. Figure 1-28 shows what the coupling chart might look like for a system containing five classes.

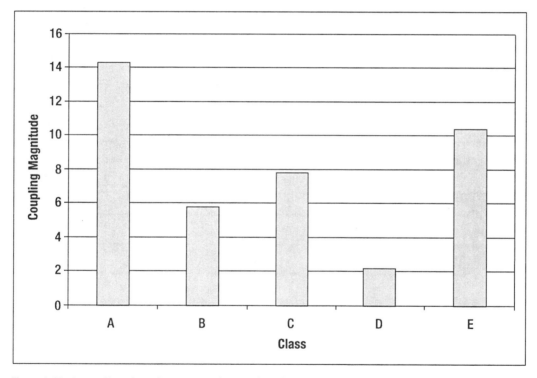

Figure 1-28. *A coupling chart for a system having five classes*

The chart gives you an immediate bird's-eye view of the distribution of coupling in a system. Given that you can distribute coupling in any way among the parts of a system, is there a type of distribution that is better than others? Is there a pattern you should be looking for in a coupling chart? Consider the systems represented by the two coupling charts in Figure 1-29 and Figure 1-30.

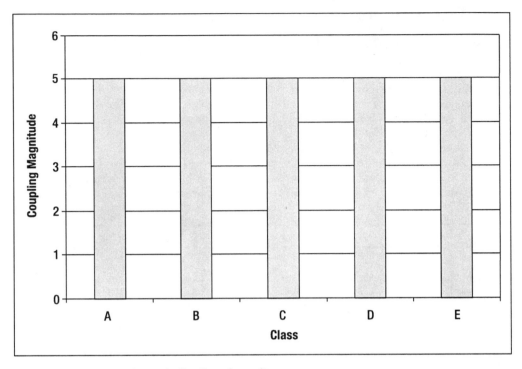

Figure 1-29. *A system with evenly distributed coupling*

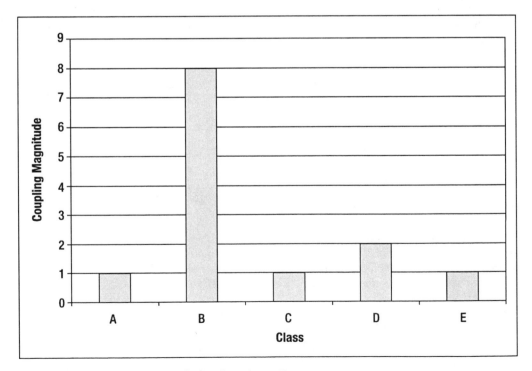

Figure 1-30. *A system with unevenly distributed coupling*

Which distribution is more desirable? It might appear that an even distribution is a good thing, but this is not the case. Remember Axiom 2, stated at the beginning of the chapter: *Coupling should be introduced into simpler classes and components first.* If you distribute complexity unevenly across the components of a system, you could concentrate complexity in some components and keep other components simple. You would then want to offload coupling from the more complex components by transferring it to the simpler ones. As you'll see in later chapters, class factories (which I call Builders in this book) are extremely simple components, whose only task is to create instances of other classes. A Builder incurs unambiguous type coupling to each class or type it instantiates, so Builders tend to be heavily coupled. Using one or more Builders to create all the classes of a system, you could offload a great deal of coupling from the classes that do the heavy lifting in a system. As a result, the coupling chart would show a small number of classes (the Builders) with a very large coupling magnitude. The other classes would have a small amount of residual coupling.

Coupling Diagrams

A coupling diagram shows what is coupled to what, and how. Coupling is shown as a dependency, using the coupling symbols introduced in earlier sections. Figure 1-31 shows the coupling diagram for a simple component system.

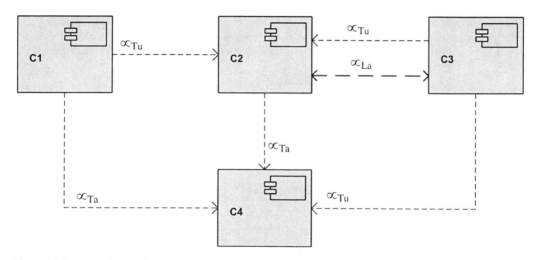

Figure 1-31. *A simple coupling diagram*

Logical coupling is always commutative, so it uses a double-headed arrow. Knowing the exact flavor and subflavor of coupling you're dealing with allows you to spot trouble, such as the occurrence of circular coupling or complicated coupling relationships. By studying a coupling diagram, you can decide where to intervene to alleviate coupling, by applying the coupling transforms described in the next section. When multiple couplings of the same flavor exist between two classes or components, you can show the exact count on coupling diagrams by prefixing the coupling symbol with a count, in parentheses. So you might have a coupling arrow with the legend $(10) \propto_{Ta}$, meaning there are ten separate ambiguous references between one class and another. Figure 1-32 shows a simple example.

Coupling diagrams are useful because they show how coupling propagates through a system. Some coupling flavors are transitive and some aren't. Each flavor has its own impact on a system, so sometimes it is a good idea to draw multiple diagrams for a system, showing only one flavor on each diagram.

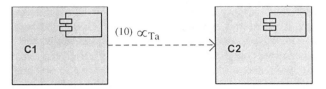

Figure 1-32. *This coupling diagram shows ten ambiguous type references between C1 and C2.*

A particularly interesting coupling diagram is the one that shows static coupling. You know that static coupling affects build time, so classes that are statically coupled might need to be changed simultaneously. If statically coupled classes are assigned to different teams and team members, those teams and team members might have to work in a coordinated fashion; otherwise, changing one class might break the compilation of another. Forcing team members to work this way can be a source of problems, both logistically and interpersonally. The larger the project, the greater the problems. By looking at the static coupling diagram of a system, you can spot couplings that cross team or component boundaries. You might then be able to find ways to refactor the design, to either eliminate the coupling entirely or convert it into a more benign coupling flavor.

Coupling Diagrams As Guides for System Changes

Coupling diagrams are useful during the design phase, but they can also be helpful when making changes to an existing system. Given the coupling diagram of a system, you can use it to determine the best way to introduce changes. Assume a system has the coupling diagram shown in Figure 1-33.

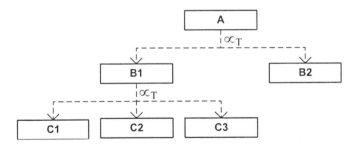

Figure 1-33. *The coupling diagram of a system that needs to be changed*

In the diagram, all the classes are type-coupled. For this example, don't worry whether type coupling is ambiguous or unambiguous. Say you need to add a new feature, requiring C1 to interact with B2. To be more exact, assume C1 needs to call the method B2.DoThis. There are two ways you can add the interaction:

- Using direct method calls
- Using event notifications

Your first impulse might be to have C1 call B2 directly, using a direct method call. The problem is that in the existing design, C1 doesn't have a reference to B2. You know this because the coupling diagram shows no type coupling between C1 and B2. To add a direct method call in C1 to B2, you need to type-couple C1 to B2, which adds complexity to the system. Using event notifications, you could make C1 fire an event that somehow notifies B1 to execute its DoThis method. Adding the infrastructure for the event notification mechanism also adds complexity to the system. Let's look at the two alternatives a bit more in detail.

Using Direct Method Calls

If C1 is to call B2.DoThis, then C1 needs to be type-coupled to the interface implementing DoThis. Assume B2 implements DoThis. You must change the coupling diagram as shown in Figure 1-34.

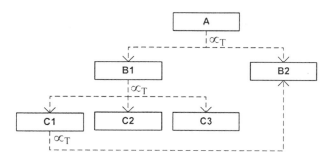

Figure 1-34. *The coupling diagram if C1 calls B2 directly*

The coupling diagram has become more complex, but you might be able to live with this new design. Even so, the diagram should raise a red flag, because it is starting to degenerate from the clean top-down design you started with. Now you have classes at lower levels in the design getting coupled to classes higher up. Coupling from bottom to top could easily introduce circular coupling with future changes, if you're not careful. Every time you make a change that introduces new static coupling, you have to ask yourself if the new coupling is consistent with the goals of the original coupling diagram or not. I would venture to say that the coupling in Figure 1-34 is a degeneration from the coupling in Figure 1-33.

Assume DoThis is published through an interface I1, which B2 implements. The new coupling diagram is shown in Figure 1-35.

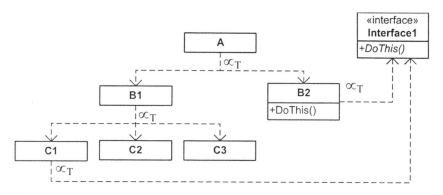

Figure 1-35. *The coupling diagram if C1 calls B2 through a separate interface*

This diagram is an improvement over the previous one, because it adds coupling between C1 and an interface, but you could package this interface in a separate component containing all the user-defined types in the system. Perhaps C1 and B2 are already coupled to this component, so no additional intercomponent coupling is added to the system with the addition of Interface1. I'll discuss user-defined types and their packaging in detail a bit later in the chapter.

Using Event Notifications

You can use event notifications to avoid adding new type coupling between C1 and B2. C1 has to fire an event that you can route to B2. You have to make C2 expose a new event that fires when `B2.DoThis` needs to be called. During the initialization of the system, you must wire C1's event notification to B2. You must change C1 somewhat, but no changes to B2 are necessary, and no coupling needs to be added between C1 and B2. I'll discuss events, event firing, and event notification wiring in later chapters.

Coupling Transforms

The dimensions of coupling space are all linearly independent, but it is nonetheless possible to convert one coupling flavor into another using a *coupling transform*. Mathematically, a coupling transform is a function that maps a point P_0 in coupling space to a new point P_1. Coupling transforms allow you to convert undesirable flavors of coupling into more tolerable flavors. You can never eliminate coupling completely from an entire system, so a coupling transform typically reduces coupling in one dimension at the expense of coupling in one or more other dimensions.

Using transforms, it becomes possible to alter the design of a system and reduce the coupling between its classes and components, assuming you have access to the source code. You could build the coupling transforms described in this chapter into a tool that applies the transforms in an automated way. The resulting system has the same overall functionality as the old one, with less coupling between the parts.

How malignant a certain flavor of coupling is depends often on the characteristics of the software system being built, but the following two statements are generally true:

1. Logic coupling is less desirable than type coupling.

2. Static coupling is less desirable than dynamic coupling.

The first statement is usually true because compilers can't detect logic coupling, at least with current technology. Assume a system has coupled logic in two places, A and B. If you change A but not B, the compiler doesn't help you detect the fact that B is out of sync with A. You'll find the problem later, when you test the system.

The second statement is usually true because static coupling affects build time. If a class A is statically coupled to a class B, then changing B can break the compilation of A. Static coupling forces the teams working on A and B to work in coordination, so changes to A and B are made at the same time.

From the standpoint of flexibility and impact on build time, often the most desirable form of coupling is signature coupling. Although it is possible to convert all forms of coupling into signature coupling, it might not always be advisable to do so, because conversions generally come at the expense of performance, complexity, and loss of compiler type checking.

Logic-Coupling Transforms

As stated on numerous occasions, logic coupling is usually more detrimental to a system than type coupling for two reasons. Logic coupling is often caused by duplications of some sort in the source code, and it is invisible to the compiler.

Duplications are bad, because they complicate the system and make it more difficult to maintain. If a bad piece of code is duplicated in two places, A and B, you need to fix both. Since programmers doesn't usually keep track explicitly of where duplications occur, it is easy for someone to change one of the occurrences, but not all. Since logic coupling is invisible to the compiler, the burden is on the programmers to make sure that a piece of code that is changed isn't associated with a duplicate elsewhere in the system.

Converting LLC to UTC

Literal logic coupling occurs between two classes A and B if those classes both embed their own private copy of a value that is used for the same purpose. Let's look at a simple transform to convert LLC to unambiguous type coupling. Assume A creates a message that B subsequently reads. If A can create different types of messages, there might be a reserved spot in the message designating the message type. A and B might be implemented in C# as shown in Listing 1-8.

Listing 1-8. *Two Classes That Have Literal Logic Coupling*

```
public class A
{
  public void SendVehicleSoldMessage(byte[] theMessage)
  {
    const int MessageTypeIndex = 0;
    const byte VehicleSoldMessage = 15;

    theMessage[MessageTypeIndex] = VehicleSoldMessage;

    // ... write the rest of the message
  }
}

public class B
{
  public void ProcessMessage(byte[] theMessage)
  {
    const int CommandCodeIndex = 0;
    const int CarSoldMessage = 15;

    byte commandCode = theMessage[CommandCodeIndex];
    if (commandCode == CarSoldMessage)
      // ... handle the message
  }
}
```

The coupling diagram for A and B is shown in Figure 1-36.

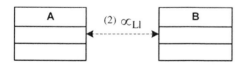

Figure 1-36. *The original logic coupling between A and B*

In Figure 1-36 and subsequent figures in this section, I show coupling magnitudes to highlight how they change after applying a coupling transform. Classes A and B each contain a literal for the messageType value and a literal for the messageType index—hence, the magnitude 2 for the logic coupling value between A and B. The literals are assigned to constants with different names, but this doesn't change the fact that A and B use the literal values for the same purposes (to access the fields of a message). To remove the logic coupling between A and B, one solution is to create a third class C that contains a single copy of the two literals. A and B then reference the common literal values in class C. Figure 1-37 shows the coupling diagram for this new arrangement.

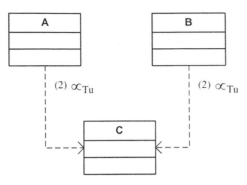

Figure 1-37. *The coupling diagram for A and B, after removing the logic coupling*

As you can see, the logic coupling between A and B is gone, but now A and B have two units each of unambiguous type coupling to the new class C. Why two again? Because class C contains two literals that A and B reference. Listing 1-9 shows the C# implementation of A, B, and C.

Listing 1-9. *The Refactored System, After Eliminating Logic Coupling Between A and B*

```csharp
public class C
{
  public const int MessageTypeIndex = 0;
  public const byte VehicleSoldMessage = 15;
}

public class A
{
  public void SendVehicleSoldMessage(byte[] theMessage)
  {
    theMessage[C.MessageTypeIndex] = C.VehicleSoldMessage;

    // ... write the rest of the message
  }
}

public class B
{
  public void ProcessMessage(byte[] theMessage)
  {
    byte commandCode = theMessage[C.MessageTypeIndex];
    if (commandCode == C.VehicleSoldMessage)
      // ... handle the message
  }
}
```

With the refactoring, you actually increased the magnitude of total coupling in the system. The system originally had two units of LLC. Now the LLC is gone, but there are four units of UTC in the system (two between A and C and two between B and C). Is the new implementation better than the original one? It depends on what metrics you use to define *better*. The original implementation had only two classes, so it had fewer parts, but the parts contained duplicated logic. On the other hand, the new implementation has three classes, but those classes contain no duplicated logic.

The new implementation is probably easier to maintain, if changes are made to the literal values stored in C, because there is only one set of literals in the system instead of two. Classes A and B wind up being unambiguously type-coupled to C, because A and B use constants defined in C. By looking at the example, you can derive the pattern used in this LLC-to-UTC transform.

Pattern for Converting LLC into UTC

If two classes, A and B, contain duplicate literals, do the following:

1. Remove the duplicated values from A and B.
2. Migrate the values to a third class C.
3. Change A and B to use the common values stored in C.

Note that other transforms exist to convert LLC into UTC. For example, you could leave the literal definitions in class A and reference them from class B. Doing so would save you the trouble of creating a third class, but might introduce other problems. For example, if B has LLC with another class D, where would you put the literals shared by B and D? Either in B or D. By introducing a third class C, you have a common place to store all the literals that many other classes might share. The moral of the story is that there is no single transform that is universally *best*.

Converting LLC to ATC

The previous pattern introduced unambiguous type coupling to a third class. A less constraining flavor of type coupling is ambiguous type coupling, so let's see how you might convert LLC to ATC. Assume you start with the same two classes A and B shown in Listing 1-8. I'll continue to use the class approach described in the previous section, using a third class named C. Rather than exposing two constants, C exposes two fields or properties that are initialized using private embedded literals. Listing 1-10 shows a C# implementation.

Listing 1-10. *A New Class to Store the Literal Values That Were Duplicated in A and B*

```
public class C
{
  public int MessageTypeIndex = 0;
  public byte VehicleSoldMessage = 15;
}
```

The class is almost identical to class C in the previous section, but the new implementation stores the literal values in fields instead of constants. As a result, classes A and B need an instance reference (instead of a class reference) for class C, as shown in Listing 1-11.

Listing 1-11. *The New Implementation for Classes A and B*

```
public class A
{
  public C c;  // must be initialized at run time
  public void SendVehicleSoldMessage(byte[] theMessage)
  {
    theMessage[c.MessageTypeIndex] = c.VehicleSoldMessage;
```

```
    // ... write the rest of the message
  }
}

public class B
{
  public C c;  // must be initialized at run time
  public void ProcessMessage(byte[] theMessage)
  {
    byte commandCode = theMessage[c.MessageTypeIndex];
    if (commandCode == c.VehicleSoldMessage)
    {
      // ... handle the message
    }
  }
}
```

The new A and B classes now contain a field of type C. You must initialize this field at run time, but you can point it to an object of type C or derived from C. Since you can use any class derived from C, the type coupling between A and B to C is ambiguous. A separate class Z might initialize the fields in A and B as shown in Listing 1-12.

Listing 1-12. *Using a Separate Class to Initialize A and B*

```
public class D : C
{
  // ...
}

public class Z
{
  void InitializeAandB()
  {
    A a = new A();
    B b = new B();
    D d = new D();

    a.c = d;
    b.c = d;
  }
}
```

The new code binds A and B to an instance of a class D, derived from C. Figure 1-38 shows the coupling diagram between all the classes, after transforming LLC into ATC.

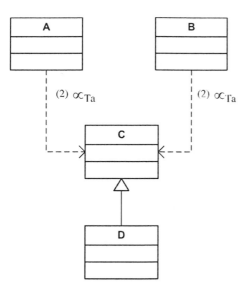

Figure 1-38. *The coupling diagram for A and B, after removing the logic coupling*

As you can see, it's a bit more complicated to transform LLC into ATC, compared to UTC. As in the previous transform, you swap two units of LLC for four units of type coupling, but this time the type coupling is ambiguous. By looking over the example, you can derive the pattern used in this LLC-to-ATC transform.

Pattern for Converting LLC into ATC

If two classes, A and B, contain duplicate literals, do the following:

1. Remove the duplicated values from A and B.

2. Migrate the values as initialized fields into a third class C.

3. Change A and B to access the fields using a reference to C.

4. Initialize the reference to point to an object of type C or derived from C.

There are other ways to transform LLC into UTC. One interesting alternative is to use virtual methods in C to return the value of the literals. Doing so gives derived classes the opportunity to change the literal values by overriding the base class virtual methods.

Converting ALC to UTC

Just as literal logic coupling can be converted into type coupling, so can algorithmic logic coupling. The ALC transforms have many similarities with the LLC counterparts discussed in the previous two sections.

As a practical example of a transform, let A and B be classes that contain complementary algorithms to read and write data in a file. Class A contains the write algorithm, while B contains the read algorithm. The system has one unit of ALC, because A's write algorithm is coupled to one algorithm in B (or, using B's perspective, B's reader algorithm is coupled to one algorithm in A). Although logical coupling is mutual, a single instance of logic coupling has the value 1 (and not 2). Figure 1-39 shows the coupling diagram for A and B.

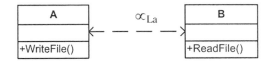

Figure 1-39. *The coupling diagram for A and B, due to complementary algorithms*

Regardless of whether the coupled algorithms are complementary or equipotent, the solution is the same: Package the coupled algorithms in the same class, as shown in Figure 1-40.

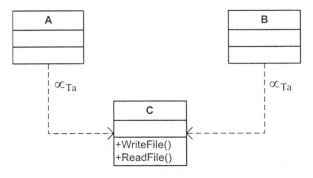

Figure 1-40. *The system after removing the logic coupling between A and B*

The new implementation is probably easier to maintain, because anyone changing the WriteFile algorithm is able to immediately change the ReadFile algorithm as needed. The drawback of the transform is that the new system is slightly more complex than the original one, because it has an additional class. By looking at the example, you can derive the pattern used in this ALC-to-UTC transform.

Pattern for Converting ALC into UTC

If two classes, A and B, contain logically coupled algorithms, do the following:

1. Remove the coupled algorithms from A and B.

2. Migrate the algorithms to a third class C.

3. Change A and B to reference the algorithms in C.

While it is always theoretically possible to eliminate ALC using the transform described, in some cases it might not be practical or advisable. For example, consider a distributed system in which components C1 and C2 are on different computers, connected over the Internet. C1 is on a secure server, while C2 is on client machines that aren't secure. C1 uses a proprietary encryption algorithm to send messages to C2, while C2 never sends data back to C2, as shown in Figure 1-41.

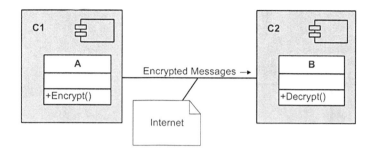

Figure 1-41. *The system after removing the logic coupling between A and B*

To use the ALC-to-UTC transform described, you need to create a third class C and put both the encryption and decryption algorithms in it. The first problem is to decide where class C should live. You have three options:

- In C1
- In C2
- In a separate component C3

The first and second options are out of the question, for security reasons, because they would entail sending data over the Internet in clear text. To see how, let's assume C were placed on the secure computer, in component C1. Class A would call C.Encrypt to encode messages before sending them. When B got the encrypted message, it would have to make a remote procedure call to C.Decrypt, which would return the decrypted message over the Internet. A similar result would occur if you put C in component C2.

Putting class C in a separate component C3 is also problematic, because this third component needs to be accessible to A and B. The connection to C needs to be secure, as shown in Figure 1-42, because it carries both encrypted and unencrypted messages.

In many cases, the necessity of a secure connection between C1/C2 and C3 renders the design impractical, because of its cost or the complexity of the resulting system. Assuming you opt to create a secure connection, you would no longer need the encryption algorithms in the first place. You might realize that the system had originally been designed to use encryption so it could rely on an inexpensive and easily available Internet connection to send messages from A to B. Attempting to package the encryption and decryption algorithms in a common class C is simply not a viable economic alternative.

In this section, I showed how to convert ALC into UTC. I won't show how to convert ALC into ATC using a single transform, because you can achieve the same goal by first converting ALC into UTC, and then converting UTC into ATC. I'll show how to perform the latter conversion in the next sections.

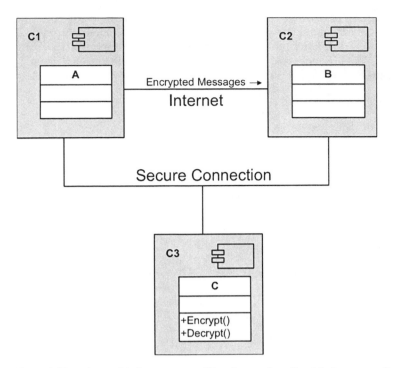

Figure 1-42. *Using a third component C3 to house class C, with the encryption algorithms*

Type-Coupling Transforms

Type coupling is usually easier than logic coupling to deal with in a system, because the compiler can check types to prevent you from making type-related mistakes. For example, if a class A supports the methods M1 and M2, the compiler issues an error if you try to compile code containing a call to A.M3. Also, the compiler tells you if you pass the wrong number or type of parameters in a call to A.M1 or A.M2.

In a type-coupled system, the compiler also protects you from partial changes. For example, if you modify class A by removing M1 or changing the method's signature, you might forget to change all the code that invokes the method. The compiler will refuse to compile some of the code, showing you where the discrepancies are.

Of the two subflavors of type coupling—unambiguous and ambiguous—the latter is often more desirable than the former, because it provides more flexibility, so knowing how to convert UTC into ATC is very important. All forms of type coupling are static in nature. In later sections, I'll show how to eliminate static coupling by converting it into signature coupling, which is dynamic.

Converting UTC to ATC

If a class A references another class B, UTC occurs when A can only work if B itself is present. Classes derived from B are not acceptable to A. As discussed in the section "Unambiguous Type Coupling," there are two most common ways A incurs UTC to B:

1. A is derived from B.

2. A creates instances of B.

In the first case, there really is no way to break the coupling, short of redesigning A. If A is derived from B, it was probably designed that way for a reason. If you didn't design A yourself, you might want to think twice before refactoring A's ancestry. Changing the base class of a class is not something you should attempt without proper forethought, especially if the sole goal is to reduce coupling. Inheritance always causes UTC, and there is no way around it.

In the second case, there are ways to change UTC into ATC. Let's look at a simple example, with a class A that does nothing except create an instance of B and invoke a method. Figure 1-43 shows the class diagram of the system.

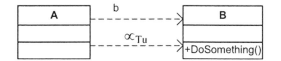

Figure 1-43. *Classes A and B, where A has UTC to B*

Listing 1-13 shows a possible C# implementation of A and B.

Listing 1-13. *A Simple C# Implementation of A and B*

```csharp
public class A
{
  B b;
  public void UseB()
  {
    b = new B();
    b.DoSomething();
  }
}

public class B
{
  public void DoSomething()
  {
    // ...
  }
}
```

Since A calls B's constructor explicitly, B must be present both at compile time and run time, so class A is both statically and dynamically coupled to B. Class A doesn't accept substitutes for class B, such as derived classes. To convert the UTC between A and B into ATC, you must change the design so that A accepts B or a derived class. There are two common strategies, both of which entail the use of a class builder, increasing somewhat the complexity of the system. Two types of builder approaches are possible:

1. Using a reactive builder

2. Using an active builder

Let's look at each approach separately.

Using a Reactive Builder

A builder works in reactive mode if it creates objects on demand and returns them to client objects. The builder is not responsible for deciding *when* to create objects. Reactive builders are similar to the Builder OO design pattern.[9] Figure 1-44 shows how you might use a reactive builder to solve the UTC-to-ATC transform problem.

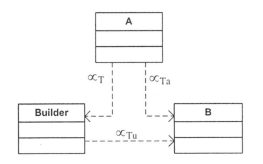

Figure 1-44. *Using a reactive builder to eliminate UTC between A and B*

Class A delegates to Builder the task of creating B objects, so A calls Builder when it needs an instance of B. Is this new design better than the original one? Let's look at the pros and cons. On the pro side, A is less strongly coupled to B than before, because now it has ambiguous coupling instead of unambiguous coupling. Also, the Builder makes the system more flexible, because the Builder might provide A with objects of classes derived from B, which provide features that B didn't provide. On the con side, A is now coupled to two classes: B and Builder. The subflavor of type coupling that occurs between A and Builder depends on whether A instantiates the Builder (causing $\propto_{Tu}$) or A receives a reference to Builder from another object (causing $\propto_{Ta}$).

We're now in a position to state the first Builder pattern for converting UTC into ATC.

Pattern 1 for Converting UTC into ATC

If class A needs to create an instance of class B, you can transform the coupling between A and B from UTC into ATC by using a *reactive builder* as follows:

1. Introduce a Builder class, responsible for instantiating B.

2. Make A call the Builder when it needs an instance of B. The Builder might return an instance of B or a derived class.

Using an Active Builder

It is possible to use a builder in a slightly different manner, without adding to the coupling woes of class A. Looking at the coupling diagram in the previous section, you need to reverse the direction of the coupling relationship between A and Builder, resulting in the coupling diagram shown in Figure 1-45.

---

9. Erich Gamma, Richard Helm, Ralph Johnson, and John Vlissides, *Design Patterns: Elements of Reusable Object-Oriented Software* (Boston: Addison-Wesley Professional, 1995).

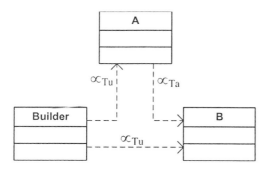

Figure 1-45. *Using an active builder to avoid adding coupling to class A*

When the coupling between A and Builder is reversed, Builder becomes responsible for calling A to provide it with a B object. How does Builder know when to call A? There are two typical cases: at initialization time, or later on demand, when A signals a need for a new B object. I'll discuss both situations in much more detail in Chapter 10, when dealing with the Builder role.

Figure 1-45 is obviously more complex than the original system, so let's look at the pros and cons to decide whether the new design is any better than the original one. The design in Figure 1-45 has less coupling than the design in Figure 1-43, but Figure 1-45 has one additional class (Builder). This new class, in turn, is unambiguously coupled to both A and B. The new design essentially moves to Builder, from A, the burden of unambiguous type coupling to B. It seems you've only reshuffled the coupling around at the expense of extra complexity. Are you just playing musical chairs with coupling, with no tangible benefits for the system? No. The introduction of an active Builder class is often a good solution, and for two reasons. First, Builders are typically very simple classes, providing the sole service of instantiating classes. Remember Axiom 2, stated at the beginning of the chapter: *Coupling should be introduced into simpler classes and components first.* If the Builder class is simpler than class A, you should try to offload as much coupling from A onto Builder. The second reason the Builder approach might be a good idea is because somewhere in the system there might be other classes that are in the same predicament as A: They need to create instances of B. Those other classes could also use your Builder class, so Builder would be the only class in the system with unambiguous type coupling to B. You could also use Builder to instantiate other classes.

As with reactive builders, active builders can provide A with objects of class B or a derived class. A uses whatever object it gets as if it were a B object. The process of converting UTC into ATC can be summarized like this:

Pattern 2 for Converting UTC into ATC

If class A needs to create an instance of class B, you can transform the coupling between A and B from UTC into ATC by using an *active builder* as follows:

1. Introduce a Builder class.

2. Make the Builder create an instance of A.

3. Make the Builder create an instance of B, or a derived class.

4. Have the builder pass a reference to B (or derived class) to the created instance of A.

Converting ATC into Signature Coupling

Signature coupling is a coupling flavor that has a dynamic nature. Given that you can never completely eliminate coupling from a system, signature coupling is sometimes the most desirable flavor of coupling. Given two classes, A and B, assume A has ATC to B due to the fact that A uses a typed reference to invoke a method in B. Figure 1-46 shows the coupling diagram:

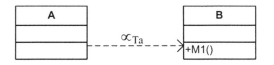

Figure 1-46. *Two classes coupled by ambiguous type coupling*

Listing 1-14 shows a simple C# implementation.

Listing 1-14. *A Simple Implementation, Causing ATC Between A and B*

```csharp
public class A
{
  public void UseB(B theB)
  {
    theB.M1();   // call method of B
  }
}

public class B
{
  public void M1()
  {
      // ...
  }
}
```

Class A doesn't instantiate class B, but instead receives a reference to B from another object. To eliminate the ATC between A and B, you need to remove from A the reference to type B. Instead of class A calling a method through the interface B, make A call B.M1 using a method reference. Use an active Builder to initialize A's method reference, resulting in the coupling diagram shown in Figure 1-47.

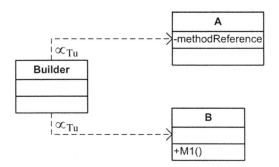

Figure 1-47. *Using an active Builder to eliminate all type coupling between A and B*

In this new design, no coupling of any kind exists between classes A and B. The Builder class is responsible for instantiating both A and B, ergo the unambiguous type coupling in the diagram. After creating the instances of A and B, Builder initializes a.methodReference to point at b.M1. Listing 1-15 shows a simple C# implementation.

Listing 1-15. *Using Signature Coupling to Eliminate ATC Between A and B*

```
public class Builder
{
  A a = new A();
  B b = new B();

  public void InitializeSystem()
  {
    a.methodReference = new A.SimpleMethod(b.M1);
  }
}

public class A
{
  public delegate void SimpleMethod();
  public SimpleMethod methodReference;

  public void UseB()
  {
    if (methodReference != null)
      methodReference();
  }
}

public class B
{
  public void M1()
  {
    // ...
  }
}
```

In the new implementation, you don't have to modify B at all. In class A, you eliminate the use of type B and replace it with a delegate. C# delegates are basically method pointers. In Java, you use a java.reflect.Method object to point at b.M1. Before attempting to make a call through methodReference, class A checks to see if it was initialized. Since A.methodReference isn't initialized at build time, class A must test the field at run time before using it, because class A relies on another class (e.g., Builder) to initialize the field.

By looking over the example, the pattern used to convert unambiguous type coupling into signature coupling can be stated like this:

Pattern for Converting ATC into SC

If a class A uses a typed reference to call a method M1 in a class B, eliminate the ATC between A and B by doing the following:

1. Remove the typed reference from A.

2. Create a public method reference in A, using the signature of B.M1.

3. Create a Builder class to instantiate A and B as objects objA and objB.

4. Make the Builder initialize the method reference in objA to point at objB.M1.

Common Coupling Scenarios

Numerous system architectures and design patterns are in use today. A system architecture that is used over and over again is really just a design pattern, albeit a high-level one. Some patterns have been around since the early days of computing, before the advent of object-oriented programming, but all patterns evolved to solve common problems, with an eye on flexibility and simplicity. Perhaps because many of the patterns were developed in the heyday of object-oriented programming, before packaging and coupling issues gained serious recognition, virtually all patterns introduce coupling in one form or another. You can revisit and tweak most design patterns to minimize or eliminate coupling. In the following sections, I'll discuss some popular designs from a coupling perspective.

Client-Server Coupling

Client-server architectures became popular in the early 1990s as a distributed computing solution. Conceptually, there is nothing about the client-server design pattern that prevents it from being used in a nondistributed system. Although the expression *client-server* is falling out of favor, the architecture is common. Call it what you want, the pattern is simple. It involves a component, called the *server*, which makes its operations available to other components, called *clients*. Figure 1-48 shows the basic arrangement.

Figure 1-48. *A simple client-server system*

In client-server systems, the servers are reactive. Servers don't contact clients, and they do nothing on behalf of clients until they receive a request of some kind. Clients begin interactions with the server by calling server methods or sending messages to the server. The kind of coupling that exists between the client and server depends on how the two interact. Here are two common modes:

1. The client has a reference to an object exposed by the server.

2. The client knows the address of the server.

I'll discuss each case separately.

Client Calls Server Using a Typed Reference

In this case, the client calls methods exposed by a server object. In a distributed system, the object is generally a local server proxy object that encapsulates the communication with the remote server object. The client either has unambiguous or ambiguous type coupling to the proxy, depending on whether the client creates the proxy or simply gets a reference to it from another component. Figure 1-49 shows the coupling if the client creates the proxy object and assigns it to a reference called myReference.

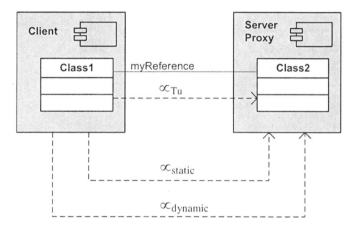

Figure 1-49. *The coupling that occurs if Class1 creates an instance of a Class2 object*

It isn't unusual for a client component to contain classes that interact with multiple server proxy objects. Each client class might wind up being type-coupled to many server proxy objects. Figure 1-50 shows how the coupling chart might look for a system in which the client component has five classes, named C1_1 through C1_5.

If the client classes have a nontrivial amount of logic, you want the classes to have minimal coupling. One solution is to convert the type coupling between client and proxy classes into signature coupling. To do so, you need to introduce a Builder component on the client side. The Builder is responsible for instantiating the server proxy objects. The client classes C1_1 through C1_5 use method references to invoke server methods. The delegates are initialized by the Builder to point to methods of the server proxy objects. The client classes then have zero type coupling to the server proxy classes. The coupling chart for the system might then look something like the one in Figure 1-51.

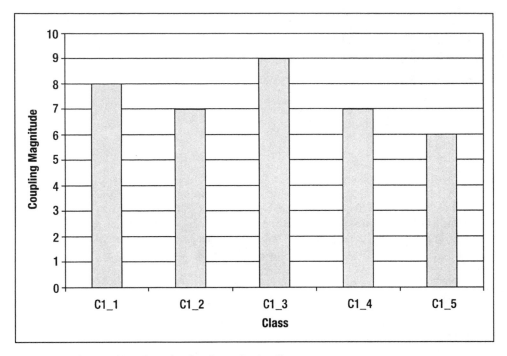

Figure 1-50. *The coupling chart for the classes in the client component*

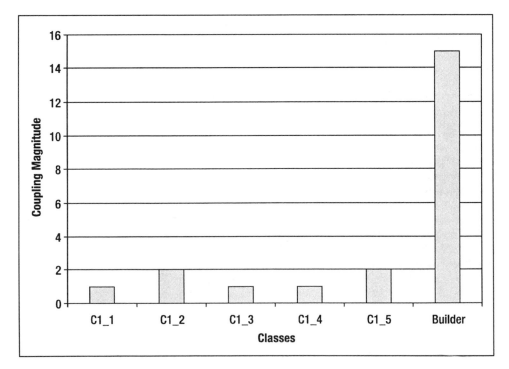

Figure 1-51. *The coupling chart after the introduction of an active Builder*

Since the Builder is the only class in the client that has coupling to the server proxies, the classes C1_1 through C1_5 incur less coupling, making their development and testing simpler.

Client Sends Messages to the Server

In many distributed systems, the client talks to the server over a network connection by sending messages. The server runs a listener process of some kind to process incoming client requests. For this type of system to work, the client obviously must know the address of the server. If the client embeds the server address as an embedded literal in its code, logic coupling exists between the client and the server, as shown in Figure 1-52.

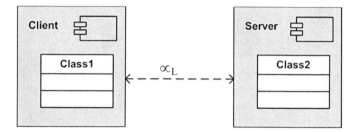

Figure 1-52. *Client talks to server by sending messages.*

There is logic coupling between the client and server, because the two are sharing information (the address of the server). If the client obtains the server's network address from a third component, such as a directory service, the coupling becomes that shown in Figure 1-53.

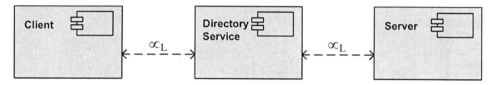

Figure 1-53. *Coupling when client obtains server address from a directory service*

Has the introduction of the directory service component really helped? The client is still logically coupled to something—the directory service instead of the server. The assumption here is that the directory service is a component that is accessed via a well-known system name or a reserved network address. You can use the directory service as a single place to put all the names and addresses of distributed components in the system. Updating the single directory service handles the changing of names and addresses of distributed components. Figure 1-54 shows the typical coupling diagram of a directory service in a system.

The coupling diagram has a star pattern, with the system coupling concentrated on the center component, which in this case is the directory service. Directory services tend to be shrinkwrapped systems, so they are very simple from a development standpoint: They require no programming, although they do need some administrative support. If you consider directory services as simple components, you should concentrate as much coupling on them as possible, if doing so alleviates coupling on more complex components.

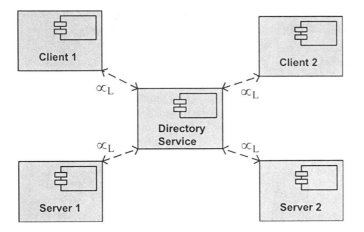

Figure 1-54. *Using a directory service as a focal point of logic coupling*

Without the directory service, you have to go through the entire system after a component changes name or address to update the affected client components. On the other hand, if you change the address of the directory service, you still have to visit all the components that call the directory service, but the name or address of a directory service is much less likely to change than names and addresses of other components in a distributed system.

Parent-Child Coupling

A parent-child relationship occurs typically when one class (the parent) manages lower-level classes (the children). An example might be a Window class that acts as a parent to child *Decorator* classes like status bars, menu bars, and toolbars. Figure 1-55 shows the class diagram.

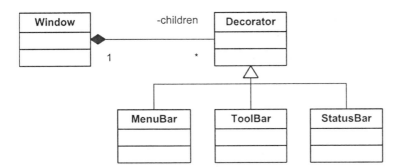

Figure 1-55. *An example of a parent-child relationship*

In parent-child relationships, usually the parent creates instances of the children, so the parent has unambiguous type coupling, and therefore static coupling, to each specific child class. See Figure 1-56.

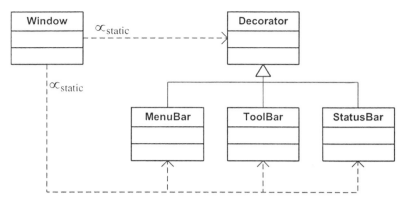

Figure 1-56. *The coupling diagram for the parent-child example*

In this example, the child Decorator class and its derivatives have no coupling to the parent Window class. The parent class is statically coupled to all the child classes, so the parent requires all the child classes to be present at compile time. This coupling can become a problem when there are many types of children, because a change in any of the children could break the compilation of the parent. To reduce coupling, you can introduce a separate active Builder object to handle the instantiation of the child classes. Once a child object is created, the Builder can hand it over to the parent Window object. With the Builder, the coupling between parent and child classes is substantially reduced, as shown in Figure 1-57.

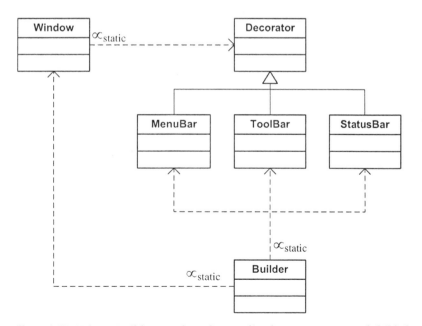

Figure 1-57. *Using a Builder to reduce the coupling between parent and child classes*

With the presence of the Builder, there is no longer any static coupling between the parent and child classes, and the class Window only requires the single class Decorator to be present at build time. It is the Builder class that now assumes static coupling to the parent and child classes, resulting in a coupling chart that might look like Figure 1-58.

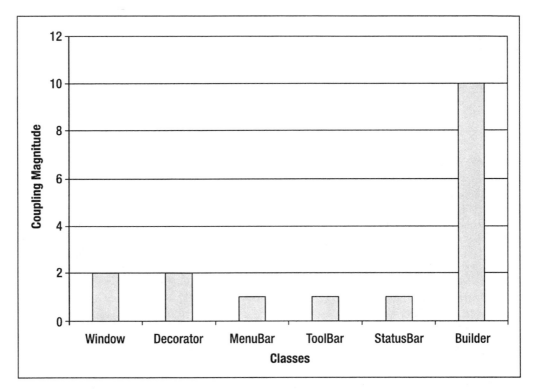

Figure 1-58. *The coupling chart after the introduction of a Builder*

The chart shows that the Window and Decorator classes have a small amount of coupling, while the Builder has a large amount. The graph doesn't show coupling for the derived Decorator classes, because this example demonstrates coupling only on the parent class, which is the Window class.

This presence of a Builder is often a good way to reduce parent-child coupling, because a Builder is usually an extremely simple class, containing little or no business logic, while the parent class is probably much more complex. In many cases, the Builder might interact with the child classes simply by calling their constructors and no other methods. According to Axiom 1, introduced at the beginning of the chapter, it is better for a simple class to be coupled than a complicated class.

In some parent-child relationships, the parent and child can be of the same type. For example, a TreeNode class, used to represent the nodes of a UI Tree control, can act recursively as a parent to child nodes that are also TreeNode objects, as shown in Figure 1-59.

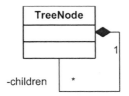

Figure 1-59. *A parent that has children of the same type*

In Figure 1-59, coupling is obviously not a problem in this case, since there is only one class involved.

Circular Coupling

In the previous section, the child Decorator classes had no reference back to the parent. There are cases in which children need access to the parent, and the common way to achieve this is by equipping each child with a reference to the parent, as shown in Figure 1-60.

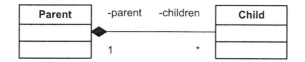

Figure 1-60. *A parent-child relationship with children having references to the parent*

A potentially problematic consequence of adding a reference from the children to the parent appears if you look at the design's coupling diagram, shown in Figure 1-61.

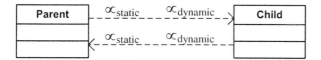

Figure 1-61. *Bidirectional static coupling between parent and children*

The problem is that the Parent requires the Child to be present at build time, but the Child also requires the Parent to be present at build time. The Parent and Child classes have *circular coupling*. If both classes are part of the same component, you might be able to compile the component, but some languages and compilers don't allow circular coupling under any conditions. For example, if you implement the system using C++, you might have two header files called Parent.h and Child.h that contain the class declarations. However, Parent.h would need to include Child.h and vice versa, resulting in a circular file reference. Some C++ compilers refuse to compile either class.

The problem gets worse if Parent and Child are packaged in separate components, as shown in Figure 1-62.

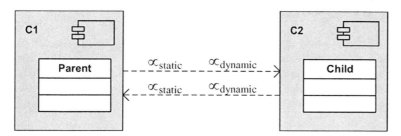

Figure 1-62. *Circular coupling between components*

C1 is circularly coupled to C2, so neither component is independently deployable. If the components are developed using a language that merges class declaration and implementation together, such as C# and Java, you have an even bigger problem. C1 requires C2's executable code to be present at build time, and C2 has the same requirement on C1, so neither component is even buildable. You must either refactor the system's packaging, putting the Parent and Child classes in the same component (assuming your compiler can deal with circular coupling), or you need to refactor the design of the Parent and Child classes at a deeper level.

When you keep the Parent and Child classes in separate components, there are two common ways to break the circular coupling between them: using interfaces and using signature coupling. I'll discuss each separately.

Breaking the Circle Using Interfaces

If the Child class needs to interact closely with the Parent class, in the sense that it needs to call several Parent methods, an interface approach might be appropriate. The idea is to refactor the parent as the implementation of an interface, and to package the interface in a third component, as shown in Figure 1-63.

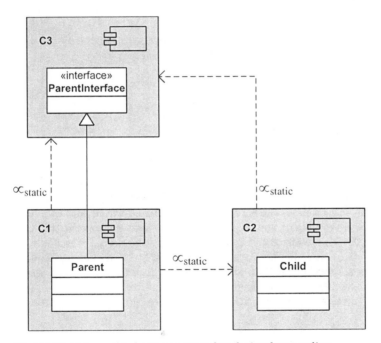

Figure 1-63. *Using a third component to break circular coupling*

The diagram shows that C1 is coupled to C2, but not vice versa. Both C1 and C2 are coupled to C3, but C3 is not coupled to anything. Due to the structure of the coupling, this new design imposes a strict build order: first C3, then C2, and then C1. To avoid unambiguous type coupling between Child and Parent, which would result in static coupling between Child and Parent, the Parent class must pass a reference to itself, typed as an InterfaceParent, to the Child class. Listing 1-16 shows a simple implementation.

Listing 1-16. *Breaking Circular Parent-Child Coupling Using an Interface*

```
// In C3
public interface ParentInterface
{
  //...
}

// In C2
public class Child
{
  ParentInterface parent;

  public Child(ParentInterface theParent)
  {
    parent = theParent;
  }
}

// In C1
public class Parent : ParentInterface
{
  Child child;

  public Parent()
  {
    child = new Child(this);
  }
}
```

The use of an interface to decouple the Parent class from the Child is reminiscent of the observer design pattern. The Child is the subject that the Parent creates and wishes to receive notifications from. The Child is implemented with the ability to make outgoing calls through the interface ParentInterface. The Parent supplies this interface to the Child and receives callbacks, which now might be considered event notifications.

By adding one more component to the design, it is possible to completely eliminate the static coupling between the Parent and Child classes. A separate Builder component is required, whose job is to create instances of the Child and pass them to the Parent. You must refactor the Child class to implement an interface, which you could package in C3, along with InterfaceParent, as shown in Figure 1-64.

The decoupling between the Parent and Child classes has come at the expense of a new component containing a Builder. Although the system is more complex in terms of the number of components, the development of each component is much simpler. The Builder typically contains only code to create instances of Child objects, passing them to the Parent. Component C3 contains only interfaces, with no implementation, so C3 is also very simple. The only complexity remains in the Parent and Child classes, which you can now compile—and even run—separately from each other.

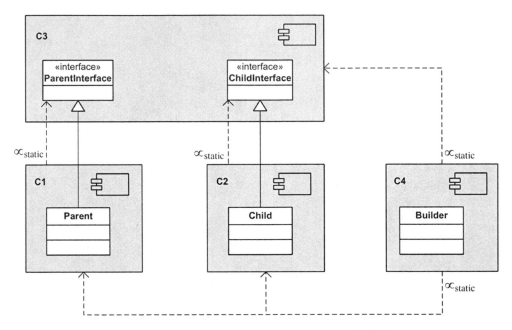

Figure 1-64. *Eliminating all static coupling between the Parent and Child classes*

Breaking the Circle Using Signature Coupling

Signature coupling relies on indirect method calls through a method pointer (which, as mentioned numerous times, is called a *delegate* in the .NET world). An outgoing call made through a method pointer is called an *untyped object call*, also known as a *callback* in some contexts. The caller doesn't know the type of the object being called and doesn't use interfaces to call methods.

You don't need to introduce a separate Builder class to use method references to break circular coupling between the Parent and Child. You can have the Child class expose one method pointer for each Parent method it needs to call. When creating a Child object, the Parent object initializes all the Child method pointers to point to methods in the Parent object. Using this design, you obtain the coupling diagram in Figure 1-65.

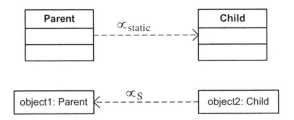

Figure 1-65. *Using untyped object calls to break circular coupling between parent and child*

There is no static coupling from the Child class back to the Parent class. Child objects call back to the Parent object using the method pointers that the Parent initialized at run time. Because there is static coupling between the Parent and Child, the order of compilation is Child first, then Parent. At run time, there is only signature coupling between the Child and Parent objects.

You can remove all static coupling between the Parent and Child by using a separate Builder class that creates Child objects on behalf of the Parent. Both the Parent and Child call each other through method pointers, and the Builder is responsible for initializing those method pointers. Figure 1-66 shows the static coupling diagram. Figure 1-67 shows the signature-coupling diagram.

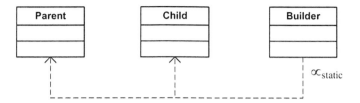

Figure 1-66. *The static coupling introduced by a Builder*

Figure 1-67. *The signature coupling between the Parent and Child objects*

Listing 1-17 shows how you might implement the Parent, Child, and Builder classes in C#.

Listing 1-17. *Using a Builder to Remove All Static Coupling Between Parent and Child*

```csharp
public class Builder
{
  public Parent parent;
  public Child child;

  public Builder()
  {
    // build the parent and child objects
    parent = new Parent();
    child = new Child();

    // bind parent and child together
    parent.OnSetVisible += new Parent.EventVisible(child.Show);
    child.OnModified += new Child.EventModified(parent.UpdateScreen);
  }
}

public class Parent
{
  public delegate void EventVisible();
  public event EventVisible OnSetVisible;

  public void ShowChild()
  {
```

```
      if (OnSetVisible != null)
        OnSetVisible();
    }

    public void UpdateScreen()
    {
      // redraw the screen and show the child
      ShowChild();
    }
  }

public class Child
{
  public delegate void EventModified();
  public event EventModified OnModified;

  public void DoSomething()
  {
    // notify the parent that we were modified
    if (OnModified != null)
      OnModified();
  }

  public void Show()
  {
    // show the child on the screen...
  }
}
```

The Parent and Child classes use .NET *event* properties to expose *delegates*. As mentioned, .NET delegates are basically method references. The Builder initializes the method references of the Child to point to Parent methods and vice versa. In Java, instead of using event properties, you could use reflection, with class java.lang.reflect.Method to encapsulate method references.

Coupling with User-Defined Types

User-defined types (UDTs) are extremely important in OO systems, because they contain the bulk of the business logic of the system. The problem is that UDTs often increase the type coupling in a system. Consider the interaction shown in Figure 1-68, in which T1 and T2 are arbitrary UDTs.

Figure 1-68. *An interaction between arbitrary types*

From the perspective of coupling, it doesn't matter whether the interaction transfers data or control from T1 to T2. The interaction is generally implemented in one of the following three ways:

1. *T1 sends a message to T2*: If the message contains a UDT, then both T1 and T2 have to know the UDT, because T1 must serialize the UDT, and T2 must deserialize it. Both T1 and T2 are therefore type-coupled to the UDT.

2. *T1 calls a T2 method through T2's interface, using the notation* object.method: Regardless of the signature of the T2 method being called, T1 is type-coupled to T2 (which is a UDT), because T1 uses T2 at build time.

3. *T1 calls a T2 method indirectly, using a method reference*: If the method signature references a UDT, then both T1 and T2 need to know that UDT, because T1 must identify the UDT in the outgoing call to T2, while T2 must know what the incoming UDT is. Hence, both T1 and T2 are type-coupled to the UDT.

The first case is straightforward, but the other two need additional discussion.

Coupling Due to Interfaces

Object-oriented programming is hinged on the notions of class and interface. Objects are entities that expose their behaviors through an interface. Clients wishing to invoke a class method typically do so by using a typed pointer or reference, using the object.method notation. In many OO languages, given a class T2 with a method M1, a client can invoke M1 using notation of the form

myT2Object.M1();

The symbol myT2Object is a reference to an object of type T2 and must be initialized at run time. If a class T1 uses the preceding notation to invoke methods of T2, then T1 is necessarily type-coupled to T2. If T1 and T2 are contained in different components C1 and C2, those components are statically coupled, as shown in Figure 1-69.

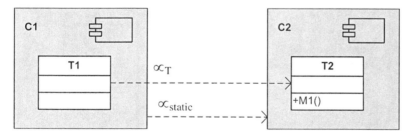

Figure 1-69. *The coupling caused by the use of interfaces in outbound calls from T1 to T2*

Using the object.method notation to call a method forces the caller to have a certain familiarity with the callee, because the caller specifies at build time which T2 method to call. Although interface-based calls entail type coupling, interfaces form the basis for contract-based programming, a powerful OO programming technique. Classes that expose an interface can define formal contracts, stating the preconditions, the postconditions, and the side effects of each method call. Tools can then verify contract compliance, signaling, and violations.

Most interfaces in nontrivial software systems are user-defined. Making outbound calls through a user-defined interface T invariably type-couples the caller and the callee to the component defining T. Assume a simple system contains a component C1 with a class T1 that uses the object.method notation to call a class T2 contained in a component C2. Also assume that T2 implements the interface T, and that T defines only a single method M1 that takes no parameters and returns none. The coupling in this system between C1 and C2 is due solely to the use of the interface T in the method call. From a packaging standpoint, T can be defined in only three places:

1. In C1, requiring C2 to be statically coupled to C1

2. In C2, requiring C1 to be statically coupled to C2

3. In a separate component C3, requiring both C1 and C2 to be statically coupled to C3

Figure 1-70 shows the system coupling if the interface T is defined in C1.

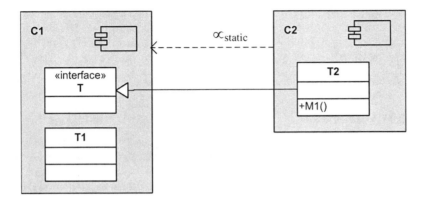

Figure 1-70. *Static coupling when T is packaged with T1*

Figure 1-71 shows the system coupling if T is packaged in C2.

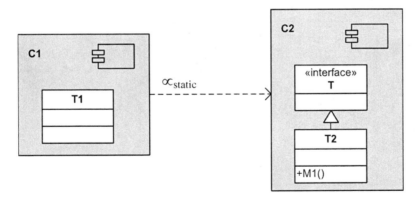

Figure 1-71. *Static coupling when T is packaged with T2*

When the interface T is packaged with T2, the presence of the interface doesn't help reduce coupling between C1 and C2. T1 can call T2 directly through T2's interface without introducing further coupling.

Figure 1-72 shows the system coupling if T is packaged in a separate component C3.

In all cases, static coupling is present. Assuming the method being called (M1) has no user-defined types in its signature, there is only way to eliminate the static coupling between C1 and the component containing T: by eliminating the interface reference in T1's outgoing call. The solution is to make T1 call T2 indirectly, using a method reference that points directly at a method, as described in the section titled "Signature Coupling."

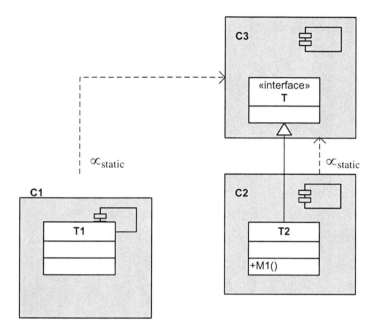

Figure 1-72. *Static coupling when T is packaged separately from T1 and T2*

Coupling Due to Method Parameters

When making an intercomponent method call, the presence of user-defined types in the method signature introduces type coupling. Assume a method has the following signature:

```
void MyMethod(UDT1)
```

Assume the caller is in the class T1 and the method being called is in T2. Figure 1-73 shows the static coupling that occurs in the system.

Careless packaging of user-defined types can result in a morass of intercomponent static coupling, which might end up looking something like the diagram in Figure 1-74.

With such a complex coupling diagram, the system is going to have constraints in the order in which components must be built. Changes to one component might require you to rebuild several components. Moreover, changes in the system could unexpectedly introduce circular static coupling, which might require you to refactor the system packaging and some of the classes.

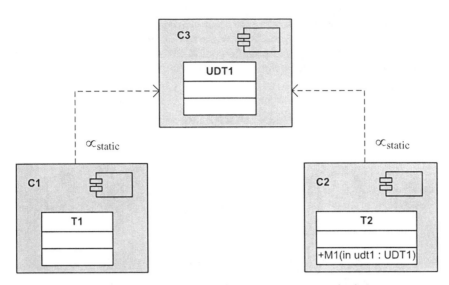

Figure 1-73. *The static coupling introduced by user types in a method signature*

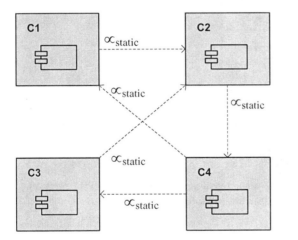

Figure 1-74. *Complex static coupling among components, due to careless packaging*

To keep coupling diagrams clean, you can package together all UDTs used in more than one component. In a system with lots of components, the static coupling to the UDT component assumes a star shape, as shown in Figure 1-75.

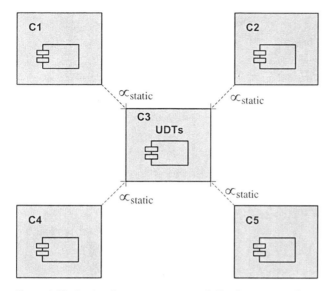

Figure 1-75. *Packaging common user-defined types together*

The diagram tells you that changes to C3 require you to rebuild all the other components, but changes to C1, C2, C4, and C5 don't impact any other components. An ideal system has a star-shaped static coupling diagram, with the user-type component at the center. The system would require C3 to be built first. You could then build the remaining components in any order.

Summary

Coupling is one of those subjects that many people find terribly boring. The problem might stem from the fact that for most people, the word "coupling" isn't specific. Hopefully, the material presented in this chapter has helped you understand the various facets of coupling. Knowing what coupling is and what effects it has, you might be inclined to spend time in your next project thinking about ways to design and partition your code to keep coupling under control. After all, a system with minimal coupling is much easier to develop, test, and maintain.

■ ■ ■

CHAPTER 2

Events and Notifications

$\sf T$alking about events can sometimes be confusing, because people use the word *event* in different ways in different software contexts. For example, graphical user interface (GUI) operating systems use *events* to interact with applications. Applications must be written to conform to an *event-driven* model, doing nothing until an event occurs. When the OS determines that an event of interest to an application has occurred, the OS notifies the program. In this context, the information is sent using procedure calls, with additional parameters telling the application what type of event occurred, such as movement of the mouse or the pressing of a key on the keyboard. The application is free to take any action it wants in response to the event *notification*—including nothing.

Another use of the word *event* is in the context of concurrent programming. Programs set and reset *events*, which are process synchronization primitives such as semaphores and mutual exclusions (mutexes). Events are basically flags that one process can set and another can read.

A popular OO design pattern, called the *subject-observer* pattern, is based on events. The pattern is used when an object, called the *observer*, is interested in knowing about events that occur in another object, called the *subject*. The observer tells the subject which events it is interested in. When the subject detects one of these events, it sends an event notification to the observer, often by calling one of the observer's methods. A subject can theoretically have any number of observers.

Programming languages also use the word *event* to denote actions or entities of various kinds. In .NET components, events are associated with *delegates*, *event variables*, and *handlers*. In Java, events are associated with *event sources*, *event objects*, and *event listeners*. When used alone in a Java context, the word *event* usually indicates the object passed as an argument from an event source to an event listener. You can organize these events into a hierarchy with specialized event types derived from general ones, forming an event *type system*.

Defining Events and Notifications

In ordinary language, an event is an occurrence of some kind, while a notification is a message informing the recipient that something (presumably important) has happened. In the software context, the definitions of events and notifications are inextricably bound, with one being defined in terms of the other. Events are a cause; notifications are an effect.

▓Definition An event is a detectable condition that can trigger a notification.

▓Definition A notification is an event-triggered signal sent to a run-time–defined recipient.

The *condition* that is associated with an event might be based on any number of predicates—for example, that today is Tuesday, that the time is 10:30 a.m., or that my cat licked his left front paw for the seventh time in the last five minutes. The detection of the condition must be associated with a notification. Software systems detect all sorts of conditions. Of all those conditions, the only ones I'll call *events* are those that can trigger a notification.

Let's analyze a bit more what is and is not in the definitions. For starters, a condition must be detectable to be called an event. For example, consider the following C# code snippet:

```
void DoSomething()
{
  for (int x = 0; x < 10; i++)
    Console.Out.Write("hello");
}
```

The loop prints a string 10 times to the output console. For each iteration, the control variable x has a different value. According to the definition of event, can you consider the condition in which x assumes the value 3 to be an event? No, because the condition is not detectable in the code. When x assumes the value 3, nothing special happens. Let's add some code to detect the condition:

```
void DoSomething()
{
  for (int x = 0; x < 10; x++)
  {
    if (x == 3)
      Console.Out.Write("hello");
  }
}
```

Is the condition an event now? The answer is still no. Although the condition is detectable, no notification mechanism is associated with the condition. The code prints a string, but it doesn't use a notification to do so. The call to Console.Out.Write is not a notification, because the callee is identified at compile time. The caller always knows who the callee is. Let's change the code again:

```
public delegate void Updater(string theMessage);
public Updater xHasValueThreeHandler;

void DoSomething()
{
  for (int x = 0; x < 10; i++)
  {
    if (x == 3)
      if (xHasValueThreeHandler != null)
        xHasValueThreeHandler ("Third iteration");
  }
}
```

Now you can say that the condition (in which x assumes the value 3) is an event. The previous code introduced a new *delegate* type named Updater. In C#, delegates are basically pointers to methods. The code uses the type Updater to define a field called xHasValueThreeHandler. You can initialize this field at run time to point to any method of any class, as long as the method accepts a single string parameter and returns void. At compile time, there's no way to know if xHasValueThreeHandler will point to a method or not, so you must test the field before using it to ensure that it has been initialized to point to something. When the event is detected, a notification is sent in the form of a call to the method pointed at by xHasValueThreeHandler, if such a method exists.

Let's look at notifications in more detail. A notification is essentially a signal sent when an event occurs. The signal can be sent in two basic ways: by transferring data or by transferring execution control.

When the signal transfers data, the signal is a message written to a resource that is shared by the sender and receiver. The shared resource might be a network connection, shared memory, an OS service, a pipe, a computer, or something else. The message can be anything from a single value to a formatted message with fields describing the event. The fields might include a sender identifier, a message identifier, a time stamp, a priority value, or other information related to the event. In order for the notification to have an effect, the receiver must monitor the shared resource and be able to detect any new data written to it.

When the signal transfers execution control, the signal is sent as a procedure call. Depending on the relative locations of the sender and receiver, the procedure call might be local or remote. The signal is the call itself, with optional data passed as parameters or returned values. Figure 2-1 shows the steps involved in the production of a notification:

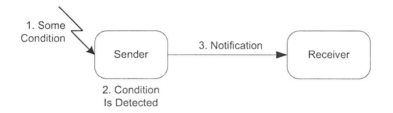

Figure 2-1. *Notifications as signals sent from one place to another*

The receiver doesn't necessarily have to do anything when it receives a notification. What it does is not the concern of the sender. In Figure 2-1, the arrow shows the direction of travel of the signal. Although the arrow *usually* shows the direction of data flow, this isn't always the case. For example, if a notification is delivered with a procedure call, the called method might have no input parameters and return a value. In this case, the direction of data flow would be in the opposite direction of the notification.

Notifications can be sent pretty much anywhere, limited only by their implementation strategy. Notifications can cross process boundaries, machine boundaries, and even network boundaries. Notifications sent by one component sometimes trigger events in others, producing a sequence of notifications and events that propagate through a system in a chain reaction. One component's notifications are another component's events, as shown in Figure 2-2.

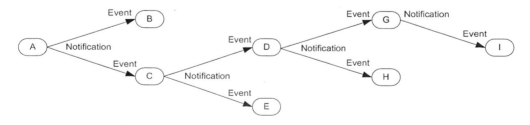

Figure 2-2. *Notifications and events in a chain reaction*

OO languages often provide built-in support for notifications based on procedure calls. In C#, VB .NET, and Delphi Object Pascal, the procedure to call is known as the *event handler*. The sender stores a reference to the event handler in a variable. As mentioned earlier, .NET languages such as C# and VB .NET use a new built-in type called a *delegate* to hold the references to event handlers. These delegates can store references to multiple event handlers. Object Pascal uses a simple pointer that can only reference one event handler at a time.

In .NET languages and Object Pascal, the sender calls the event handler without using a class or interface reference. Receivers are not required to implement any specific interface; therefore, receivers are called *untyped*. In contrast, in the JavaBeans event model, event listeners are *typed*. To receive a certain type of event, a listener must implement a specific interface. The sender uses a reference to this interface to call one of the methods of the receiver. When notification delivery is based on typed receivers, type coupling is introduced between the sender and the receiver. The sender not only identifies the interface of the callee, but it also chooses which method of that interface to call. Both decisions must be made at compile time, but the identity of the object called isn't determined until run time, when the sender's reference-to-interface is initialized.

A Brief History of Events

Events have been around for quite some time in software systems, although under different names. I'll summarize some of the most important developments.

Distributed systems started using event-oriented models in the 1970s. The first systems used shared memory, starting with a centralized shared memory model in multiprocessing systems.[1] The memory represented the rendezvous area for senders and receivers. Processors communicated by posting messages to the shared memory. Distributed shared memory models, with systems interconnected by network connections,[2] provided better performance and resilience to failures.

The Model-View-Controller design pattern[3] developed in the Smalltalk world is probably the first paradigm to display a clear event-based architecture. Events were used to maintain synchronization between the data (model) of a system and observers (views) of the data. The relationship between the model and views was later generalized as the subject-observer design pattern,[4] popularized in the 1990s.

Researchers in the artificial intelligence (AI) community used the shared memory model to support the *blackboard* paradigm.[5] AI processes collaborated in a multiprocessing system to interpret data. Some processes acted as producers of information and would post messages on the blackboard. Other processes would keep an eye on the blackboard contents, taking any messages that were related to their field of expertise.

In the mid-1980s, the Actors system[6] became one of the first multiprocessing systems to use events in the modern sense. Concurrent processes interacted using a pattern-oriented broadcasting

1. W. Wulf, E. Cohen, W. Corwin, A. Jones, R. Levin, C. Pierson, and F. Pollack, "HYDRA: The Kernel of a Multiprocessor Operating System," *Communications of the ACM*, June 1974.
   R.J. Swan, A. Bechtolsheim, Kwok-Woon Lai, and John Ousterhout, "The Implementation of the Cm* Multi-Microprocessor" (proceedings of the National Computer Conference, Dallas, TX, June 1977).
2. Brett D. Fleisch, "Distributed Shared Memory in a Loosely Coupled Distributed System," *Proceedings of the ACM Workshop on Frontiers in Computer Communications Technology* (New York: ACM Press, 1987).
3. Glenn E. Krasner and Stephen T. Pope, "A Cookbook for Using the Model-View-Controller User Interface Paradigm in Smalltalk-80," *Journal of Object-Oriented Programming*, August/September 1988.
4. Erich Gamma, Richard Helm, Ralph Johnson, and John Vlissides, *Design Patterns: Elements of Reusable Object-Oriented Software* (Boston: Addison-Wesley Professional, 1995).
5. Barbara Hayes-Roth, "A Blackboard Architecture for Control," *Artificial Intelligence*, July 1985.
   Robert Engelmore and Tony Morgan, *Blackboard Systems* (Boston: Addison-Wesley Professional, 1988).
   Vasudevan Jagannathan, Rajendra Dodhiawala, and Lawrence S. Baum, *Blackboard Architectures and Applications (Perspectives in Artificial Intelligence)* (Burlington, MA: Academic Press, 1989).
6. Gul Agha, *ACTORS: A Model of Concurrent Computation in Distributed Systems* (Cambridge, MA: The MIT Press, 1986).

mechanism, based on late-bound procedure calls. Around the same time, a number of rule-based systems were developed, such as Darwin.[7] These systems were based on communicating objects that used messages in an event-oriented manner.

In the meantime, starting in the late 1970s, module interconnection languages (MILs) gained favor. The first one was MIL75.[8] MILs seek to describe the modules that make up a system, using a formal grammar. MILs describe the interfaces of modules and the connections between modules, without regard to how the modules are implemented internally. Work on MILs continued into the 1990s. Polylith[9] used a MIL to specify connections between inputs and outputs. Polylith employed a *software bus* as an interconnection and integration medium. ToolBus[10] is a more recent example of a system using a software bus. Components known as *tools* are connected to the ToolBus, used as a multiprocessing message-dispatching infrastructure. Tools interact by sending and receiving messages over the ToolBus.

GUIs also have incorporated events in various degrees and fashions. In the early 1980s, GUI operating systems started taking hold, first with the Apple Macintosh, then with Microsoft Windows and MIT's open source X Window System. Applications developed for these operating systems are event-driven. Rather than containing their own input message-processing loop, applications are *reactive*, doing basically nothing until the operating system notifies them of input by sending event messages. All events are sent to an application's common event handler. Events include an identifier, telling the application what event occurred, plus optional data about the event.

In the late 1980s, a number of people worked on software integration systems, which were essentially frameworks for connecting modules or programs together. The Field system[11] was one of them. It used string-based messages as events to integrate windows and other tools together to implement a multiwindowed software development environment. The system was based on a centralized message subscription/notification facility. Tools, such as a source-code editor, could subscribe to certain types of messages, such as mouse messages. Notifications could be both synchronous and asynchronous.

In the 1990s, Architecture Description Languages (ADLs) became popular. ADLs can be viewed as an incarnation of MILs, but they're oriented more toward components and their connections. Examples of ADLs are Rapide,[12] Wright,[13] C2,[14] and ACME.[15] Many ADLs deal directly with events, considering them first-class citizens. For example, Rapide supports the concept of sets of causal events, in which each event can provoke one or more events in a set. Rapide uses the term *poset* (for *partially ordered set*) to identify a group of related events.

---

7. Naftaly H. Minsky and David Rozenshtein, "A Software Development Environment for Law-Governed Systems," *ACM SIGPLAN Notices*, February 1989.

8. Frank DeRemer and Hans Kron, "Programming-in-the-Large Versus Programming-in-the-Small," *IEEE Transactions on Software Engineering*, June 1976.

9. James M. Purtilo, "The Polylith Software Bus," *ACM Transactions on Programming Languages and Systems*, January 1994.

10. Jan A. Bergstra and Paul Klint, "The Discrete Time ToolBus: A Software Coordination Architecture," *Science of Computer Programming*, July 1998.

11. Steven P. Reiss, "Connecting Tools Using Message Passing in the Field Environment," *IEEE Software*, July/August 1990.

12. David C. Luckham and James Vera, "An Event-Based Architecture Definition Language," *IEEE Transactions on Software Engineering*, September 1995.

13. Robert Allen and David Garlan, "Formalizing Architectural Connection" (proceedings of the 16th International Conference on Software Engineering, Sorrento, Italy, May 1994).

14. Nenad Medvidovic, Richard N. Taylor, and E. James Whitehead, Jr., "Formal Modeling of Software Architectures at Multiple Levels of Abstraction," (proceedings of the California Software Symposium, Los Angeles, CA, April 1996).

15. David Garlan, Robert Monroe, and David Wile, "ACME: An Architectural Interconnection Language" (technical report, Carnegie Mellon University, Pittsburgh, November 1995).

The 1990s marked the period in which major software vendors started marketing event-oriented programming languages. In 1991, Microsoft launched Visual Basic (VB), an important milestone in the history of event-oriented languages. It was the first widely used language with built-in support for events, which were based on untyped procedure calls. VB events were initially limited to GUI controls, such as forms, radio buttons, and checkboxes. VB defined a set of events for each type of control. The system made it very easy for programmers to add event handlers. Although somewhat limited, VB introduced the concept of event-based programming to millions of people and dramatically simplified the task of building user interfaces for the Windows platform. Borland took the event idea from VB and developed a Pascal version, called Delphi. Borland had made its fortune with a product called Turbo Pascal, and the company developed an object-oriented Pascal for the Delphi product. The new Object Pascal language, like VB, also uses procedure calls to deliver events.

Also in the 1990s, distributed component models became popular. The first was the Object Management Group's (OMG's) Common Object Request Broker Architecture (CORBA) in 1991. Some years later, the CORBA Event Service and CORBA Notification Service specifications were added.[16] CORBA events are based on the notion of *event channels*, which carry notifications from a source to a target, both of which are CORBA objects. CORBA supports asynchronous interactions, with provisions for load balancing and recovery. Notification payloads are described using OMG interface definition language (IDL). All CORBA specifications are given in terms of abstract interfaces. Implementation details are left to vendors.

Microsoft introduced Distributed Component Object Model (DCOM) in the mid-1990s. DCOM was an attempt to scale the Component Object Model (COM) architecture to distributed systems, but has since been replaced by the .NET Framework. The .NET Framework is an ambitious enterprise by Microsoft to create a cross-language run-time environment for local and distributed systems. The .NET Framework is a component-based technology that overcomes many of the limitations of Microsoft's COM and DCOM architectures, which developers consider too complicated. The .NET Framework includes support for events, remote procedure calls, and messaging services.

Another significant component model is Sun's JavaBeans. Initially a model for local systems, it was extended into an environment, known as Java 2 Platform, Enterprise Edition (J2EE), to support distributed systems. J2EE includes support for transactions as well as message queuing through the Java Message Service (JMS) API.

During the 1990s, a number of systems were proposed to overcome limitations of the three major component models (CORBA, JavaBeans, and COM). One limitation was incompatibility between them. Components built with one model couldn't interoperate with other models. Several bridging frameworks arose, in the form of model-to-model bridges, such as Iona's COM-to-CORBA bridge COMet.[17] Integration frameworks go beyond the bridging idea, attempting to create a homogeneous environment for disparate component models. For example, the Vienna Component Framework[18] is an environment that uses special *façade* components to support the interoperability of the three major models.

The three major models had several other shortcomings, including lack of support for rapid application development (RAD). Espresso[19] was a Java-based system designed to support tool-based visual composition and Internet distribution. Espresso components interacted exclusively using event notifications. Components could be wired together in an integrated development environment

---

16. CORBA Event Service Specification, www.omg.org/technology/documents/formal/event_service.htm, 2001.

17. Ronan Geraghty, Sean Joyce, Tom Moriarty, and Gary Noone, *COM-CORBA Interoperability* (Upper Saddle River, NJ: Prentice Hall, 1998).

18. Johann Oberleitner, Thomas Gschwind, and Mehdi Jazayeri, "The Vienna Component Framework Enabling Composition Across Component Models" (proceedings of the 25th International Conference on Software Engineering, Portland, OR, May 2003).

19. Ted Faison, "Interactive Component-Based Software Development with Espresso" (technical report, www.faisoncomputing.com/espresso/Introduction.pdf, 1997).

supporting visualization of a system at various levels of abstraction—from the contents of a single component all the way up to the layout of an entire system.

Messaging services, also known as message queues or store-and-forward systems, are used in distributed systems for the reliable delivery of messages, which can be considered in many ways as notifications. Messaging services started receiving widespread interest in the mid-1990s. Messaging services use a central message queuing server[20] that acts as a notification server for messages in a distributed system. Several commercial queues are available, including IBM WebSphere MQ (formerly MQSeries), TIBCO Rendezvous, Microsoft Message Queuing (MSMQ), and others. In message queuing systems, client programs send messages to the queuing server, with information regarding the intended recipients and (optionally) the quality of service (QoS) desired. The QoS might specify things such as support for transactions and delivery of return receipts. Messages are persisted locally on the message queue server, typically in a database or in disk files. Delivery is attempted according to a message priority scheme. If the addressee is offline or not available, delivery is attempted repeatedly until a limit is reached, such as a timeout.

The history of events and event-based systems (EBSs) is very rich and includes a large number of people, papers, and products. Due to the limited space available in this book, I have described only the most significant ones. My apologies to the people and projects that I was forced to omit. For another look at the history of event-based systems and current trends, I recommend reading the paper by Eugster.[21]

Nomenclature and Semantics

Before getting too wrapped up in details regarding events, I need to introduce some of the terminology used in EBSs. Distributed systems tend to use different terms and expressions than local (nondistributed) systems, and all the major event-oriented component infrastructures use their own expressions.

Let's start with the terminology used in this book. As mentioned earlier, an event is the detection of a condition, triggering a signal that is sent to interested parties. The entity that is able to detect events is called the *event publisher*, the *event source*, or simply the *sender*. The entity that receives notifications is called the *event subscriber*, the *event handler*, the *notification target*, the *notification receiver*, or simply the *receiver*. The act of sending the notification signal is also called *sending a notification* or *firing the event*. Any data passed with the notification is called the notification *payload*. Before an event can be fired, there must be receivers. The act of establishing a receiver is called *subscription* or *registration*.

Distributed systems use different terms and expressions. As mentioned earlier, EBSs are also called *publish-subscribe* systems. Publishers are components or objects that can detect events and send notifications. Subscribers are components or objects that receive notifications. In order for a subscriber to receive notifications, the subscriber must register by *subscribing* to the publisher. When dealing with publish-subscribe systems that include middleware systems, I'll sometimes use the term *event* to refer to incoming notifications from upstream, because many middleware systems consider incoming signals as events.

An orthogonal nomenclature is also in widespread use in distributed systems that use message servers. These systems often go by the names *message-oriented middleware* (MOM), *store-and-forward systems*, *message-based systems*, and others. Notifications are called *messages*, because they often consist of pure data packets sent over a network connection. Instead of *firing events*, these systems *send messages*. Entities that register to interact with the server are called *clients*. Clients can

---

20. Burnie Blakeley, Harry Harris, and Rhys Lewis, *Messaging and Queuing Using the MQI* (Columbus, OH: McGraw-Hill, 1995).
21. Patrick Th. Eugster, Pascal A. Felber, Rachid Guerraoui, and Anne-Marie Kermarrec, "The Many Faces of Publish/Subscribe," *ACM Computing Surveys*, June 2003.

both send and receive messages. The server might actually consist of multiple servers arranged in some way. The network of servers is usually referred to as *the server*, when you're not interested in the server topology.

OO languages use their own lexicon with events. The .NET Framework describes events like this: *An event is a message sent by an object to signal the occurrence of an action.*[22]

There are two problems here. First, there is the confusion between events and notifications. The definition applies to notifications, not events. This confusion is common. People often use the word *event* when they are really talking about a notification, probably because what the sender calls a notification can be considered an event by the receiver.

The second problem is the word *action*, which is a bit misleading. An event might be triggered simply by the passage of time, which is hardly an action. In any case, the definition implies that .NET Framework notifications are messages, meaning they carry data of some sort. The .NET Framework documentation describes events as being *raised* or *sent* by the *event sender* and received by the *event target*, also called the *event consumer*. The notification payload is called the *event data*. In order to receive notifications, the event must be *wired* from the sender to the target. The method invoked in the consumer during the course of event firing is called an *event handler*.

In JavaBeans lingo, events are defined differently: *Events are objects sent from event sources to event listeners.* JavaBeans events are essentially the payloads of notifications. During registration, listeners are *added* to event sources. Listeners are said to *handle* events by providing methods that are invoked when the event source fires the event.

In Delphi Object Pascal, the definition is a bit more abstract: *An event is a mechanism that links an occurrence to some code.*[23] Here again, there is confusion. The definition alludes to both events and notifications.

In C++, there is no definition for the word *event*, as C++ predates the recognition of events as essential interaction mechanisms. C++ programmers today are likely to use the word *callback* when talking about events. A callback is the method called in a receiver during event notification.

CORBA technology uses yet another lexicon. In the CORBA event model, event sources and targets are known as event *suppliers* and *consumers*, respectively. Events travel over *channels*, which represent the abstract path from supplier to consumer. CORBA uses services to deliver events. The Event Service was introduced first and is used in systems where event filtering and customizable QoS are not necessary. The CORBA Notification Service is an extension of the Event Service, providing filtering and QoS.

Event Subscription

Event subscription is the process of linking an event publisher to an event subscriber. When a subscriber subscribes to an event, it essentially signs up to receive future notifications from the publisher. Event publishers are usually capable of detecting several types of events and sending different types of notifications. During the subscription process, the subscriber must identify the type of event it is interested in. The publisher stores the subscriber's subscription. Any time an event is detected, the publisher sends a notification to the subscriber of the event.

A publisher exposes the list of events it can detect. It exposes the list by *publishing* the events, which usually means that the events are made visible through interfaces, properties, or methods of some type. Publishers must be prepared to deal with the situation in which an event has no subscribers. Publishers must therefore possess a certain amount of intelligence to check for the existence of subscribers before trying to send notifications.

---

22. Events and Delegates, http://msdn.microsoft.com/library/default.asp?url=/library/en-us/cpguide/html/cpconeventsdelegates.asp, 2004.

23. "What are events?," online help documentation for Borland Delphi 5, 1997.

A subscriber can usually subscribe to multiple types of events from the same publisher. Conversely, an event can have multiple subscribers. When the event is detected, the publisher notifies each of the subscribers. The order in which subscribers are notified depends on a variety of factors. I'll spend more time on events with multiple subscribers in Chapter 3.

In order to receive notifications, a potential subscriber must apply to the publisher for a subscription. In the simplest of systems, subscribers and publishers are connected directly. Subscribers subscribe directly by sending a subscription request to the publisher. The request must identify the subscriber, and the request can also contain other information, such as which types of events the subscriber is interested in, the subscriber's priority, and so on.

The Subscription Process

The subscription process includes everything that happens in order for a subscriber to become subscribed to one or more event notifications. The subscription process occurs at run time, never at compile time. If a subscription were made at compile time, you wouldn't call it a subscription and you wouldn't consider the interaction to be event-based. The subscription process can occur several ways, based on the arrangement of the publisher, the subscriber, and ancillary objects.

In the simplest arrangement, called the *direct-delivery model*, the subscriber submits subscriptions directly to the publisher. The publisher fires events directly to the subscriber, as shown in Figure 2-3.

Figure 2-3. *Subscriptions in a direct-delivery system*

In larger systems, publishers might need to handle large numbers of subscribers or provide notification features that are computationally intensive. In such systems, a middleware system is often allocated to offload the event source from the notification overhead. Subscribers don't interact directly with the event publisher; they interact only with the middleware. Figure 2-4 shows the arrangement, called the *indirect-delivery model*, in which P represents a publisher, M represents a middleware system, and S represents a subscriber.

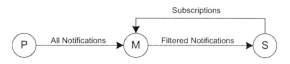

Figure 2-4. *Subscriptions in an indirect-delivery system*

With indirect-delivery systems, the subscriber sends subscription requests to the middleware system, which then assumes the responsibility of filtering and routing notifications to the subscriber. The middleware might receive notifications for all the events published by P, but only those that satisfy subscription criteria are sent to subscribers.

When it is important for subscribers to not be coupled to publishers or middleware, a different subscription process can be used: Instead of the subscriber requesting subscriptions itself, a separate *binder* agent makes the request. You can use binders in both direct- and indirect-delivery systems, as shown in Figure 2-5 and Figure 2-6.

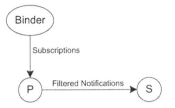

Figure 2-5. *Using a binder with the direct-delivery model*

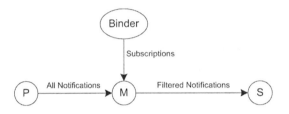

Figure 2-6. *Using a binder with the indirect-delivery model*

The binder takes its name from the fact that it provides the publisher with a *binding* to the subscriber for each notification identified in a subscription. The binder is coupled to both the publisher and the subscriber, while the subscriber is often completely decoupled from both the binder and the publisher and can be developed and tested on its own.

Subscription Models

The subscription model is based on how the subscriber identifies the events of interest. There are many ways to categorize subscription models. For example, JEDI[24] identifies four categories, called *subscription approaches*: channel subscriptions, subject subscriptions, content subscriptions, and event combination subscriptions. Each identifies the events of interest to the subscriber in a different way.

Many systems allow subscribers to be organized into *groups*.[25] The group is an entity that subscribes to certain events. Subscribers need only to specify which group or groups they are members of. The notion is similar to people signing up to newsgroups. Each newsgroup implicitly defines certain types of messages, so people determine the types of messages they get by choosing a newsgroup rather than defining specific message types.

The subscription models I use in this book appear in the hierarchy shown in Figure 2-7.

---

24. Gianpaolo Cugola, Elisabetta Di Nitto, and Alfonso Fuggetta, "The JEDI Event-Based Infrastructure and Its Application to the Development of the OPSS WFMS," *IEEE Transactions on Software Engineering*, September 2001.

25. Daniel J. Barrett, Lori A. Clarke, Peri L. Tarr, and Alexander E. Wise, "A Framework for Event-Based Software Integration," *ACM Transactions on Software Engineering and Methodology*, October 1996.

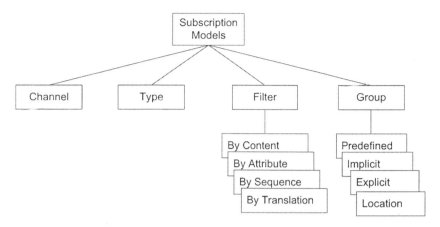

Figure 2-7. *The hierarchy of subscription models*

The four basic subscription models are *channel*, *type*, *filter*, and *group*. A *channel* denotes the physical or abstract construct through which notifications are sent to subscribers. A channel might be an outgoing procedure call, a network connection, a UML component port, or something else. Subscriptions by *type* are commonly used in direct-delivery EBSs developed with a component model (such as JavaBeans, .NET, or Delphi Object Pascal) that supports events or notifications as OO types. Filtered subscriptions use a *filter* to accept or reject notifications based on various criteria. A *group* represents a collection of subscribers that share the same subscription. Group subscriptions are useful when many subscribers are interested in getting the same notifications. The group would be associated to the proper channel or channels with the appropriate filters.

Channels

You can think of notification channels like television channels: Once you select a channel, you get all the programs broadcast on that channel. Event publishers can use any number of channels. If they use just one, then all notifications are sent on that one channel. More commonly, publishers define multiple channels and use an internal mapping algorithm to associate notifications to channels. Some publishers define a different channel for each type of possible notification.

A channel denotes the physical or abstract construct through which event notifications leave the publisher. In direct-delivery models, it is the responsibility of the event publisher to establish a mapping between events and channels. In indirect-delivery models, the notification middleware might be responsible for establishing the mapping. A channel can provide notifications for a single event or a group of events, as shown in Figure 2-8, Figure 2-9, and Figure 2-10.

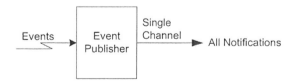

Figure 2-8. *A single channel carrying all notifications*

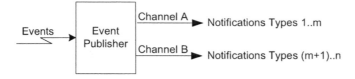

Figure 2-9. *Channels carrying multiple types of notifications*

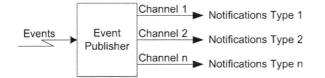

Figure 2-10. *Channels carrying one type of notification*

The event-to-channel mapping, also called *channelization*, can also be related to notification content. The need for channelization arises often when notifications contain textual information. For example, a news service might expose different channels for international news, local news, weather news, and so on, as shown in Figure 2-11.

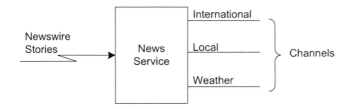

Figure 2-11. *Channels associated with content types*

The news service would need to extract information from incoming newswire stories and determine which channel to assign the story to. There can be a substantial amount of processing involved in determining which channel a notification belongs to. Large systems often use a separate system to handle the job, splitting the job of event detection and channelization, as shown Figure 2-12.

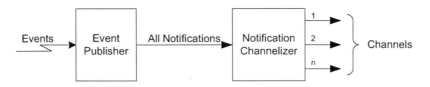

Figure 2-12. *Using a separate system to channelize notifications*

The event publisher detects events, while the channelizer uses an internal algorithm to route notifications to the proper channel.

Types

When talking about subscription models based on *types*, you need to be careful about what you mean with the word *type*, because the word is heavily overloaded in the software context. What is the *type* of an event?

In the JavaBeans event model, the event type refers to the object passed to an event listener's handler method. The event type is really the *payload type*. Several type-based notification systems organize event types this way, including the Cambridge Event Architecture[26] and Hermes.[27] In the .NET Framework event model, events are properties exposed by event publishers. Each event property represents a different event type. For example, a Button component might expose the three properties Clicked, Moved, and Resized. Delphi Object Pascal event types are similar. CORBA event types refer to the interfaces through which event producers call consumers.

Conceptually, a certain amount of overlap exists between channel-based and type-based subscriptions. Many systems associate channels with types, so that each channel relates to notifications of a given type. However, a channel can also carry many types of notifications, so type-based subscriptions are generally more selective and deterministic than channel-based ones.

Filters

Filter-based subscriptions are necessary when the subscriber wants only a subset of the notifications available. The subscriber specifies a filtering expression, and the publisher applies the filter to all the notifications generated. Those that aren't rejected by the filter are sent to the subscriber. When the filtering effort is relatively light, the publisher can often handle both the filtering and notification jobs, as shown in Figure 2-13.

Figure 2-13. *Filtered notifications*

You can also use filters in conjunction with channels. In this case, the subscription identifies both the filtering expression and the channel identifying the notifications to filter. See Figure 2-14.

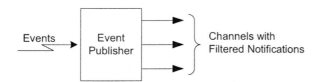

Figure 2-14. *Filtered notifications sent on diffferent channels*

---

26. Jean Bacon, Ken Mood, John Bates, Richard Hayton, Chaoying Ma, Andrew McNeil, Oliver Seidel, and Mark Spiteri, "Generic Support for Distributed Applications," *IEEE Computer*, March 2000.

27. Peter R. Pietzuch and Jean Bacon, "Hermes: A Distributed Event-Based Middleware Architecture" (proceedings of the International Conference on Distributed Computing Systems, Vienna, Austria, July 2002.

Filtering can be quite expensive computationally. In EBSs that support large numbers of subscribers or complex filtering, a dedicated system can perform filtering, as shown in Figure 2-15.

Figure 2-15. *Using a dedicated system to channelize and filter notifications*

To reduce the loading of the channelizing/filtering service, you can use a separate system to split notifications into channels, as shown in Figure 2-16.

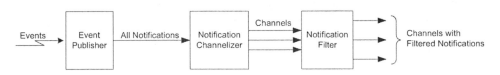

Figure 2-16. *Using separate systems to channelize and filter notifications*

Some systems use a special *subscription language* to specify filtering. Regardless of how the filtering criterion is specified, the effect of filtered subscriptions is to reduce the volume of notification traffic toward the subscriber. A notification can be associated with multiple filters, each specified by different subscribers, so notifications might have to be processed multiple times and using different filters in order to satisfy all subscribers.

Content Filtering

Content-based subscriptions apply to systems in which notifications always carry a payload representing the content. The subscription somehow describes what content is of interest. The notification system then applies the filter to the content of all incoming notifications. Only notifications that aren't rejected by the filter are sent on to subscribers. Using the news client example again, a content-based subscription model could allow the client to register only for news stories that contain a certain sequence of words, a regular expression, or a set of words.

A significant problem with content filtering is its computational cost: It is usually necessary to parse much (or even all) of a notification's payload to filter it properly and determine whether it passes the filtration criterion. Content filtering is feasible in systems with a small number of subscribers, but it can require substantial hardware resources in larger systems, such as Internet-scale ones. Gryphon,[28] JEDI,[29] and Siena[30] are examples of large-scale, content-based notification systems.

As a refinement of content-based filtering, Kulik[31] describes a hybrid content-based filtering model that relies on IP multicasting managed at the router level. Special systems called *match-structure*

---

28. Rob Strom, Guruduth Banavar, Tushar Chandra, Marc Kaplan, Kevan Miller, Bodhi Mukherjee, Daniel Sturman, and Michael Ward, "Gryphon: An Information Flow Based Approach to Message Brokering" (technical report, Hawthorne, NY, IBM T.J. Watson Research Center, 1998).

29. Gianpaolo Cugola, Elisabetta Di Nitto, and Alfonso Fuggetta, "The JEDI Event-Based Infrastructure and Its Application to the Development of the OPSS WFMS," *IEEE Transactions on Software Engineering*, September 2001.

30. Antonio Carzaniga, David S. Rosenblum, and Alexander L. Wolf, "Design and Evaluation of a Wide-Area Event Notification Service," *ACM Transactions on Computer Systems*, August 2001.

processors sit between publishers and multicast routers. The routers act as a distributed notification system. Processors read incoming messages and generate a header known as a *match-structure* that lets the routers determine the list of subscribers.

Attribute Filtering

In many systems, it is possible to classify events using a set of attributes. These attributes can be considered part of an n-dimensional *attribute space*. An attribute-based subscription identifies notifications of interest by specifying constraints in the attribute space. Attribute-based filtering also goes by different names in the literature, such as *topic-based* or *subject-based* filtering.

There are two fundamental types of attribute filters: those that work with preclassified events and those that must classify events on the fly, according to some criteria. The first type, also known as *source-side filtering*, requires the event source to add attributes to the event content. To simplify processing at the subscriber end, attributes are usually put in a special section of the notification payload, such as a header. The header might be expressed using Extensible Markup Language (XML) or a series of name-value pairs.

The second type of attribute filter puts the attribute extraction burden on the notification service, based on the event's content, history, traffic patterns, or other. If the attributes are based on keywords found in the content, the notification service must parse the content of every notification, which is computationally expensive. An even worse situation occurs when the attributes are based on event history or event patterns. Consider a stock exchange notification service that sends out real-time stock transactions. If a subscriber wants to be informed when the volume of a certain stock exceeds a certain value, an attribute-based subscription would be necessary. But to support the subscription, the notification service might need to parse every stock transaction, identifying the stock type and the number of shares involved. The service would also need to maintain internal state information to keep track of the total volume of shares handled of a given stock. Only when the volume hit the threshold set by the subscriber would a notification be sent. Clearly, such a system would be inefficient, expensive, and difficult to scale.

Attribute-filtering performance can be very good when the attributes are clearly defined in a content header. Such attribute-based filtering can have good enough performance to be used in embedded systems.[32] As an example of attribute filtering, consider a news server that receives stories classified by headline, date, author name, country, and name of the originating newswire service. The system's attribute space would have the dimensions {headline, date, author, country, wireService}. When specifying a filter, the subscription would use an expression that might look something like this:

```
(date: today) and (wireService: Reuters) and (location: Congo)
```

Attribute-based expressions are conceptually equivalent in many ways to the WHERE clause in a SQL query. Jin and Strom[33] describe a notification system that uses a relational database model to support SQL-like attribute-based filtering.

31. Joanna Kulik, "Fast and Flexible Forwarding for Internet Subscription Systems" (proceedings of the Second International Workshop on Distributed Event-Based Systems, San Diego, CA, June 2003).

32. Carlos Mitidieri and Jörg Kaiser, "Attribute-Based Filtering for Embedded Systems," (proceedings of the Second International Workshop on Distributed Event-Based Systems, San Diego, CA, June 2003).

33. Yuhui Jin and Rob Strom, "Relational Subscription Middleware for Internet-Scale Publish-Subscribe" (proceedings of the Second International Workshop on Distributed Event-Based Systems, San Diego, CA, June 2003).

Sequence Filtering

Subscribers might only be interested in a certain sequence of events. Subscriptions for sequence filters must identify the events in a sequence and their temporal constraints. Each event in a sequence can be further qualified by attribute, channel, or content restrictions. When events occur that fit the sequence filter, a notification is sent to the subscriber. Event sequences are also known as *composite events* in some systems, such as the Cambridge Event Architecture.[34] For example, a weather news subscriber might issue notifications of type freewayTrafficAlert, precipitation, and freewayCondition. A subscriber might be interested in getting freewayCondition notifications for freeway 405 in Southern California, but only if the freeway has traffic problems and it's raining. The subscriber would need to subscribe to freewayCondition notifications, but only those regarding freeway 405. To get the notifications only in the situations of interest, a sequence filter might be defined with an expression like this:

```
(freewayTrafficAlert.route: 405) and
(freewayTrafficAlert.date: today) and
(precipitation.location: california.southern) and
(precipitation.time.hour > now.hour - 6) and
(precipitation.amount > 0)
```

You could also use a sequence filter to reduce often-occurring notifications by specifying a cutoff frequency. For example, even if a notification occurs at the rate of three per second, a subscriber might only be interested in getting them once a minute. The subscription would use a filter specifying the maximum frequency of 1/60 Hz for the given notification.

Sequence filtering generally requires the management of internal state for each subscriber, which can result in a substantial amount of overhead for the filtering service. The filter state might be required to track the notification history for a given subscriber, such as the number and type of notifications already sent in a designated period of time.

Translation Filtering

Translation filters, also known as *message transforming functions*,[35] allow the following kinds of translations:

- *Notification content*: The filter might convert the content from one language to another or change the format of any dates found into a specific format. This type of filtering is obviously expensive, because it generally requires the entire payload to be processed.

- *Notification type*: This kind of filtering can be used to exclude specific types of notifications. Say a channel carries notifications related to events of type n1, n2, and n3. You could use a translation filter to block notification types that weren't of interest. You can also use notification type filtering to convert types. For example, a subscriber might wish for notifications of type n1, n2, and n3 to be converted to type n4, perhaps because the subscriber considers the three types to be equivalent.

- *Notification sequence*: This type of filtering is also known as *composite event detection*. The idea is to send a notification when a certain sequence of events has occurred. For example, a subscriber might want to be sent a notification n1 when events e1, e2, and e3 occur in a row and within five minutes of each other. In order to keep track of past occurrences of events, a translation filter needs to be stateful and maintain a separate state for each subscriber, which obviously can be computationally expensive in the presence of many subscribers.

---

34. Jean Bacon, Ken Mood, John Bates, Richard Hayton, Chaoying Ma, Andrew McNeil, Oliver Seidel, and Mark Spiteri, "Generic Support for Distributed Applications," *IEEE Computer*, March 2000.
35. Daniel J. Barrett, Lori A. Clarke, Peri L. Tarr, and Alexander E. Wise, "A Framework for Event-Based Software Integration," *ACM Transactions on Software Engineering and Methodology*, October 1996.

Groups

When subscribers sign up for the same events and use the same filters, it can be advantageous to use grouping to simplify the subscription and notification-delivery process. Groups act like virtual subscribers and can have an arbitrary number of members, including none. Figure 2-17 shows three members A, B, and C, in a group.

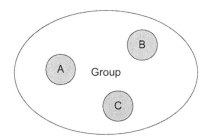

Figure 2-17. *Subscribers organized into a group*

A subscriber belonging to a group receives all the notifications the group is subscribed to. A subscriber might belong to multiple groups. Who determines which group or groups a subscriber belongs to? It depends on the system, but three general cases are possible:

- *The publisher*: This might determine the subscriber group based on something it knows about the subscriber, such the subscriber's name, role, age, or country.

- *The notification infrastructure*: This might determine the group based on the subscriber's connection speed, the node address, and so on. An important case is based on the subscriber's physical location. If the notification infrastructure defines *service areas* for different geographic areas or network nodes, the system might use this information to determine which notifications to send a subscriber.

- *The subscriber*: This might determine the group by specifying the group explicitly in the subscription, or indirectly by signing up for the same events as other subscribers.

A number of notification systems rely on groups, such as ISIS.[36] In general, there are no constraints on which events a group subscribes to, so groups may have an overlap in the notifications they specify, as shown in Figure 2-18.

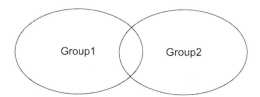

Figure 2-18. *Overlapping groups*

---

36. Kenneth P. Birman, "The Process Group Approach to Reliable Distributed Computing," *Communications of the ACM*, December 1993.

Members who belong to overlapping groups could receive duplicates of certain notifications, depending on the implementation. Groups can also contain other groups, recursively to any depth, as shown in Figure 2-19.

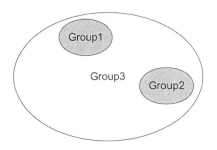

Figure 2-19. *Groups of groups*

The contained groups can conceivably have overlapping subscriptions, which could cause members of Group3 to receive duplication notifications.

Predefined Groups

Predefined groups are those that are defined by an event publisher or notification service. For example, a notification service for diagnostics events of a banking network might predefine three groups: administrator, supervisor, and technician. Each group would come with a built-in subscription for certain types of notifications. Members joining such groups can't change the group's subscription, but members wanting additional notifications beyond those provided by the group might be able to add their own private subscriptions.

Implicit Groups

Implicit groups are those that are set up automatically when two or more subscribers request the same subscription. The event publisher or notification service handling the subscription can use an optimized delivery mechanism to notify members of the group. Subscribers are generally not aware that they belong to an implicit group.

Explicit Groups

Explicit groups must be created at run time through a system-dependent operation. You can associate a group with any number of subscriptions. Once you create an explicit group, subscribers can join it as members. A group acts like a virtual middleware system, with its own subscriptions and list of subscribers. You can use such groups to classify subscribers in any number of ways, such as by role (e.g., administrator, supervisor, guest), creditworthiness (e.g., excellent, good, bad), and so on. A system using explicit groups must identify a policy for managing groups. Most systems identify a special administrator to set up and administer groups, barring normal subscribers from doing so.

Location Groups

In some systems, subscribers are connected to a network of middleware systems, as shown in Figure 2-20.

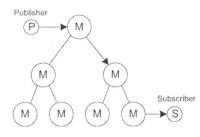

Figure 2-20. *A subscriber connected to a network of middleware systems*

The middleware systems are often situated in different geographic areas, and the middleware to which a subscriber is connected identifies the location of the subscriber. You can then associate each middleware with a predefined group, whose subscriptions determine the types of notifications sent to a subscriber. Such *location groups* are important, especially if subscribers are mobile. For example, a system could use location groups to distribute traffic information to wireless receivers in cars. Cars would only receive notifications pertinent to their location.

Subscription Policies

Subscriptions have a life cycle: They can be created, administered, and canceled. A subscription policy identifies who has the right to change subscriptions and how subscriptions behave over a given period of time. For example, a policy might issue subscriptions that are valid per a specific lease period, after which they expire. Such subscriptions could be useful when sending messages to users by e-mail. If a person never responds, the system could assume the person is not interested in the messages or has closed the e-mail account. In such cases, the person's subscription would expire at some point. The expiration policy might be based on criteria other than time, such as the total number of messages sent to a subscriber or the number of responses the subscriber sent. Other aspects defined in a policy are related to the following:

- Can subscriptions be changed?
- Can subscriptions be canceled?
- How many different subscriptions can a subscriber have?

When a subscription is changed or canceled, a certain amount of latency can exist between the time the change request is sent and the time the event publisher receives and processes it. During this time, which is often variable and related to system load, the publisher might send notifications that the subscriber is no longer interested in. The subscription policy should address this issue as well.

Summary

In this chapter, I provided a quick history and overview of events and notifications. Many people who develop "event-based" programs are unaware of the extensive amount of work and the number of people involved in making events what they are today. Contrary to popular belief, events were not invented by Microsoft for Visual Basic back in the early 1990s. However, Visual Basic is probably the first product that opened up the world of event-based programming to the masses. The adoption of the event-based model in Visual Basic is what made that product so much easier to work with, compared to other products and technologies of the day.

CHAPTER 3

■ ■ ■

Notification Delivery

Notification delivery refers to the process of getting a notification from an event publisher to a subscriber. The complexity of the process depends on a number of issues, such as the distance of the subscribers from the event publisher, the presence of middleware components, and the delivery protocol used. Understanding the pros and cons of the various issues is important, because simple choices can have profound, and perhaps unexpected, effects on the operation of an EBS. Think of notifications like cars on a freeway system, or like nerve impulses in the human central nervous system. If those cars or signals have trouble getting to their destinations, there are going to be problems at different levels. Different types of traffic patterns require specific event notification architectures. To decide which notification architecture is best for a system, you need to answer the following questions, among others:

- Should notification delivery use a centralized architecture or a point-to-point one?
- When are shared resources better than procedure calls for delivery?
- Is a messaging server useful?
- Should distributed shared memory be used?
- How scalable is a given architecture?

Several commercial middleware components are available to handle notification dissemination and delivery, so you might not want to implement a notification architecture from scratch if a solid commercial product is available.

Delivery Protocols

In all but the simplest systems, you can use an indirect-delivery model to get notifications from the publisher to subscribers. In distributed systems, the notification system has a layered architecture, with processes or systems on different layers. The higher layers contain publishers and subscribers, intermediate layers contain notification routing and processing middleware, and the lowest layer handles the physical transport of notifications from a sender to a receiver. Figure 3-1 shows the basic idea.

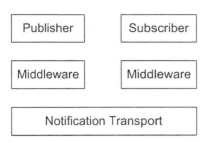

Figure 3-1. *The layered architecture associated with distributed EBSs*

The delivery protocol describes the rules governing the interaction between the top and middle layers. Recall from Chapter 2 that a notification is a signal carrying an optional payload. Delivery protocols define how the notification signals and their payloads are sent and received, from the perspective of the publishers and subscribers. You might think there is an almost infinite number of ways to send and receive signals in a software system, but at the most basic level, there are only two fundamental techniques:

1. By transferring data

2. By transferring control

The first technique sends data, and the second technique transfers execution control. The first technique requires a resource that the sender writes data to. The resource must be accessible to the receiver, so it is called a shared resource. This resource is the conduit connecting the sender to the receiver. The second technique uses procedure calls. Each technique gives rise to a number of specialized protocols, as shown in Figure 3-2.

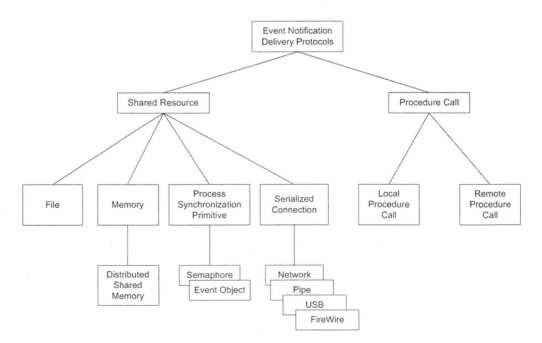

Figure 3-2. *The basic notification delivery protocols*

Shared resource protocols also have several variants based on the type of resource that is shared between the notification sender and receiver. Shared resource (SR) and procedure call (PC) protocols are not entirely orthogonal, in terms of what they transfer. While shared resources only allow data to be transferred, procedure calls allow both execution control and data to be transferred.

Delivery Using Shared Resources

If two processes need to exchange data, there must be some kind of connection between them. When the connection is a resource, the resource acts as a rendezvous point for the sender and receiver. The sender writes data to the resource, and the receiver reads the data. Figure 3-3 shows the basic arrangement.

Figure 3-3. *Sending notifications through a shared resource*

When dealing with the shared resource delivery model, it is common to use the word *message* to denote the notification payload. When associated with publish-subscribe systems, messages are also called *message notifications*, to underscore their relationship with events.

The arrows in Figure 3-3 denote the direction of travel of the notification signal and its associated message. The sender uses a *push* action to write the data to the shared resource. The receiver generally uses a *pull* action to read the message from the resource. The event delivery is typically asynchronous, because the sender and receiver run in different thread or process spaces. Here's a common scenario: The sender writes something to the shared resource, continuing with its work without blocking. Some time later, the receiver detects the data and processes it. In some cases, the receiver sends a response message back to the sender, indicating the outcome of the first operation. In the response phase, the sender and receiver reverse roles.

Shared resources include many types of hardware configurations. Historically, shared memory and shared files were the first to be used. Shared memory is still widely used in multiprocessor machines today. Multiple processors and/or processes are given access to a *global* memory, which they can use to exchange information with other processes. File sharing is also used, but suffers from extremely poor performance compared to memory sharing. Even so, a number of commercial application integration technologies are based on file sharing.

Interprocess synchronization primitives, such as semaphores and event objects, represent another type of shared resource. Primitives can be harnessed to send notifications easily: When the sender wishes to send a notification, it sets the state of a primitive, which the receiver must monitor. The receiver detects the state change and takes appropriate action. No data need be exchanged: The notification can be just a pure signal, represented by the setting of the synchronization primitive.

Most distributed systems today rely on networks to connect the various systems together. The network connection can be considered a shared resource. Interprocess pipes are similar to network connections, but are generally much faster and more reliable. But while pipes are usable only between processes running under the same OS, network connections can also connect different machines together, regardless of OS considerations.

Shared resource delivery protocols are common in distributed systems and are asynchronous in nature. They have a distinct advantage over procedure call protocols, in the form of safety: No transfer of execution control is involved, so the receiver's longevity doesn't affect the sender. The sender and receiver usually run concurrently, often on different machines. The sender can write data without blocking. If the receiver misbehaves or crashes, the sender won't be affected directly and may not even know about the receiver's problem.

The shared delivery model provides a built-in level of security, because the sender and receiver generally have no access to each other's local data. Moreover, in many cases, the shared resource can act as a buffer, allowing the system to function even if the sender and receiver aren't running at the same time. If the receiver is not present when a notification is sent, the shared resource can maintain the notification until the receiver reads it later.

All shared resource protocols work in the same conceptual way: The sender writes data to the resource, and the receiver reads it. But there are differences that arise in the details, depending on what type of shared resource is used. In the following sections, I'll explore each type of resource in more detail.

Shared Files

Files make it very easy to share data. When the sending and receiving processes are on the same machine and that machine has a file system, the implementation is straightforward. A naïve implementation might go something like this: The sender creates a file, writes a notification to it, and then closes the file. The receiver periodically checks for the existence of the file. When the file is detected, the receiver opens it, reads its contents, and then deletes the file. This type of design has a significant drawback: Once the sender has saved the notification in the file, it can't send any more files until the receiver processes and deletes the shared file. To overcome this problem, there are two solutions:

1. Use multiple shared files.

2. Append notifications to an existing file.

To use multiple files, you could use a simple numbering scheme to generate unique filenames, such as name1, name2, and name 3. The scheme would restart the number sequence when it reaches a limit number. To use this approach, the sender and receiver would only need to agree on the numbering scheme. The collection of numbered files acts as a virtual notification queue. Both the sender and receiver need to maintain counters, indicating the next file number to use. Figure 3-4 shows the timing details.

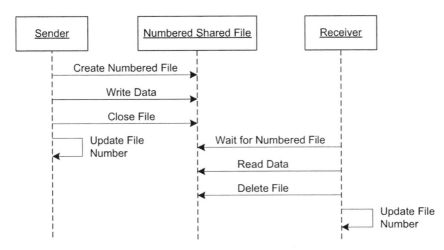

Figure 3-4. *Using a series of numbered files to send notifications*

To append notifications to a single shared file, the sender must obtain an exclusive read-write lock on the file before appending data to it. Before reading data, the receiver would also need to obtain an exclusive read-write lock on the file. Figure 3-5 shows the timing details.

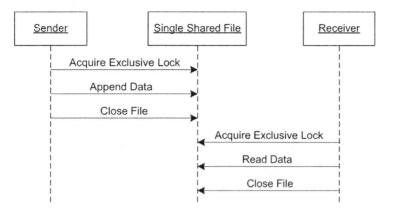

Figure 3-5. *Using a single file to send notifications*

You can also use shared files to pass notifications even when the sender and receiver are on different machines. Some systems use a separate file server, which is usually a network addressable machine. Networked file systems make the location of the file transparent to the sender and receiver. The only requirement is that both the sender and receiver have network access to the machine.

Shared files are somewhat popular in application integration frameworks, such as Sun's ToolTalk[1] and IBM's WebSphere Business Integration Connect.[2]

Shared Memory

One of the earliest types of shared resource used in distributed systems was shared memory (SM). Shared memory is effective in multiprocessor systems, where processor modules are physically packaged together with a common shared memory module. Most systems are implemented using a backplane into which printed circuit boards (PCBs) are plugged, as shown in Figure 3-6.

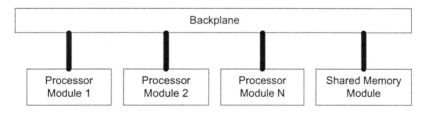

Figure 3-6. *Processor and memory modules in a multiprocessor system*

The backplane carries the signals of a multiprocessor system bus. The VMEbus[3] is an example of a multiprocessor bus. Each PCB contains one or more CPUs with local memory. One or more

---

1. Sun's "ToolTalk User's Guide," http://docs-pdf.sun.com/801-6647/801-6647.pdf.
2. "IBM WebSphere Business Integration Connect: Architecture Overview," www-3.ibm.com/software/integration/wbiconnect/library/doc/wbic420/pdf/architecture.pdf.

PCBs contain the shared memory, which is mapped into the local address space of all the processors. The various processors compete for control of the system bus, which is the only resource through which they can access the shared memory. If all the processor modules are similar, and they all have equal rights to control of the system bus, the system is called a symmetric multiprocessor (SMP). SMPs use a memory access architecture called Uniform Memory Access (UMA), so-called because the speed of access to the shared memory is the same for all processors.

In order for multiple processors to cooperate peacefully in the same box, there must be a mechanism for preventing *bus contention*. Contention occurs when two or more processors try to control the bus at the same time, and can cause a system to fail in unpredictable ways, at both the hardware and software levels. All multiprocessing buses define hardware rules to prevent bus contention. A properly designed card for a particular bus contains hardware that abides by the appropriate bus rules.

The prevention of bus contention is not sufficient to ensure proper operation of a shared memory system. A mechanism must exist that allows each processor to lock a data structure from concurrent alteration by other processors. The mechanism is often based on software flags. Each lockable data structure is associated with a flag. When a processor wants exclusive access to a data structure, it must set the associated software flag. Before doing so, it must wait for the flag to be cleared, indicating no one else is using it. As soon as the flag is tested and found cleared, the processor can set it. There is a serious potential problem here: After each bus read or write cycle, the bus controller might give control of the bus to a different processor, so between the time a processor finds a cleared flag and the time it sets the flag, another processor might have obtained bus control, if only briefly, and modified the flag. If the other processor was waiting for the same flag to become cleared, the two competing processors might interfere with each other. Figure 3-7 shows the timing details.

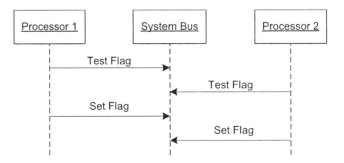

Figure 3-7. *Competing processors interfering with each other*

Right after Processor 1 tests the flag and finds it clear, Processor 2 does the same thing. Since both find the flag clear, they both set it and think they have exclusive access to the associated data structure. The problem is caused by the fact that between the test and set operations, the bus controller changed briefly, allowing an interleaved test operation by Processor 2.

Multiprocessing buses provide so-called *atomic test-and-set* bus cycles to prevent this type of interference. When a processor assumes hardware control of the bus for such a cycle, the processor executes both the test and set operation in the same bus cycle. You can prevent interference between competing processors in other ways, but atomic test-and-set cycles are probably the simplest and safest. As long as all the processors in the system respect the software locks in shared memory, everyone gets along. You can use software flags to lock any portion of shared memory, from a single data structure to the entire memory.

---

3.   VMEbus specifications, www.vita.com.

When using shared memory to send notifications, an area of memory is set aside to handle the notification payload. The area must be associated with a lock, so the sender and receiver don't try to modify it at the same time. The area must accommodate at least one notification, but may be large enough to hold many in a buffer. Figure 3-8 shows the timing of the operations performed by the sender and receiver.

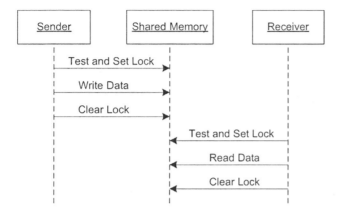

Figure 3-8. *The timing of operations when sending a notification through shared memory*

When the sender wishes to send a notification, it must wait for the software lock to be clear. When it is, the sender uses an atomic test-and-set operation to set the lock. Next, the sender writes the notification payload to the locked area. It might write multiple notifications at this time. When done writing, the sender clears the software lock.

Some time later, the receiver checks the notification area of shared memory. If a notification is found to be present, the receiver must wait for the software flag to be clear, then use an atomic test-and-set operation to set the lock. Next, the receiver reads one or more notifications and then clears the software lock.

The entire arrangement requires that it be possible, by examining the contents of the shared data structure, to determine if it contains notifications or not. When the sender acquires the software lock, it must check to see if the notifications previously sent have been processed; otherwise, it might overwrite them. When the receiver handles a notification, it removes the notification from the shared data structure by clearing the memory used. The cleared state of the data structure indicates the absence of notifications.

But what if the sender wished to send a notification whose values were all zero or null? Such a payload would set the shared memory to a state that was essentially the cleared state. The next time the receiver checked the shared memory, it wouldn't recognize the presence of a new notification, because the memory would look like a cleared data structure, containing no notification. The system essentially uses the shared data structure for two purposes: to control data flow between sender and receiver, and to hold the data being transferred. The system described only works if the signals used to control data flow are distinguishable from ordinary data. Such systems are said to use *in-band* signaling to control the flow of notifications from sender to receiver.

Getting back to notification delivery using shared memory, you can consider the set of all possible shared data structure values as a communication band. If the system never uses certain values in the data structure with ordinary notifications, those values can be reserved for signaling purposes between sender and receiver. If the shared data structure values contain no reserved values, a separate data structure (which is *out-of-band*, relative to the notification data structure) is required. I'll discuss out-of-band systems in a later section, when dealing with semaphores.

ABOUT IN-BAND SIGNALING

The expression *in-band signaling* is borrowed from telecommunication systems, in which control signals are sent along with (in the same communication *band* as) regular data. Touch-tone telephones are a common example of in-band systems. The dialing buttons generate special tones, which are sent in the same channel as voice. The tones are control signals, while voice is considered data. The system uses special combinations of tones for each digit. The combinations were developed to make them easily recognizable from the typical sounds that a telephone connection carries. When touch-tone dialing was being researched decades ago, there were two camps of engineers: those that supported in-band signaling and those that supported out-of-band signaling. The latter system used a separate channel to transfer dialing tones. With such systems, people wouldn't hear tones in the headset when they pressed buttons. In-band systems are cheaper to implement, but out-of-band systems are more secure. When it came time to choose the implementation to use for the telephone system, economics prevailed over security.

Distributed Shared Memory

Shared memory systems don't scale well, because both the system bus and the shared memory become bottlenecks when the number of processors increases. For large systems, Distributed Shared Memory (DSM)[4] is better. DSM systems scale better and also preserve a simple computing model for end-user processes. Figure 3-9 shows a conceptual view of DSM.

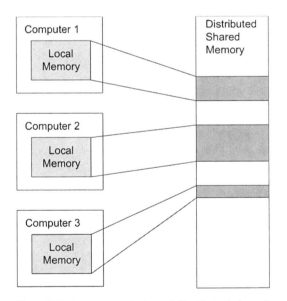

Figure 3-9. *A conceptual view of distributed shared memory*

Each system participating in a DSM system can map part or all of its local memory into the distributed shared memory, accessible to all participants. Conceptually, DSM is similar to virtual memory, and end-user processes can access any portion of DSM without needing to know where the

---

4. Jelica Protic, Milo Tomasevic, and Veljko Milutinovic, "Distributed Shared Memory: Concepts and Systems," *IEEE Parallel And Distributed Technology,* Summer 1996.

physical memory is located. Indeed, several DSM implementations work at the virtual-memory paging level: When an end user requests memory that is located elsewhere, a page fault occurs at the hardware level, causing the missing data to be fetched.

To improve efficiency, some DSMs use data replication, where copies of data can be made on each participating computer. Replication systems are useful for shared data that is read-mostly. When the data is write-mostly, replication becomes counterproductive, because all the copies must be kept in sync after one is changed.

Tuple spaces, such as those used in Linda[5] for parallel processing, are architectures based on a DSM model. Tuples are sets of values that can be read/written from a common store.

Some systems support access to DSM data at the language level. For example, Objective Linda[6] and JavaSpaces[7] have special message-like language constructs that can be used to read and write to DSM directly. JavaSpaces allows entire serialized Java objects to be read/written to DSM.

Semaphores

Semaphores offer a high-performance way of firing events across thread or process boundaries on the same machine. Semaphores are operating-system kernel objects designed for process and thread synchronization. Contrary to other types of shared resources, semaphores are pure signaling mechanisms: They allow no data to be passed from sender to receiver. Since no data can be passed, there is no way to use a single semaphore directly for more than one type of event notification.

Dutch computing pioneer Edsger Dijkstra first described semaphores, which use an internal counter to control process synchronization. The counter's value is intended to represent the number of *available resources* that the semaphore is coordinating access to. When there is only one resource, a binary semaphore can be used that restricts the counter values to 0 and 1.

Semaphores support only two operations: *signal* and *wait*. Semaphores are initialized with the internal counter set to 0. A process that makes a resource available can call the *signal* operation, which increments the semaphore counter. A process that needs the resources can call the *wait* operation, which tests the counter value. If the value is greater than 0, it is decremented and the calling process continues to run. If the value is 0, the calling process is blocked until another process calls the semaphore's signal operation. Figure 3-10 shows a semaphore used to synchronize two processes.

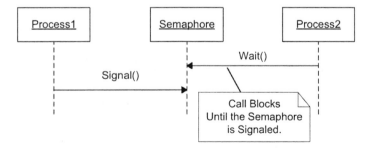

Figure 3-10. *A typical semaphore use*

---

5. David Gelernter, "Generative Communication in Linda," *ACM Transactions on Programming Languages and Systems*, January 1985.
6. Thilo Kielmann, "Object-Oriented Distributed Programming with Objective Linda," (proceedings of the First International Workshop on High Speed Networks and Open Distributed Platforms, St. Petersburg, Russia, June 1995).
7. Eric Freeman, Susanne Hupfer, and Ken Arnold, *Javaspaces Principles, Patterns, and Practice* (Boston: Addison-Wesley Professional, 1999).

The wait operation's test-and-decrement action is atomic, meaning that once it has started, it can't be interrupted. Being *atomic* (in other words, *indivisible*) guarantees that the decrement action occurs immediately after the test, before another process is allowed to run. Semaphores generally allow multiple processes to wait for signals, so semaphore implementation typically maintains a First In, First Out (FIFO) list of blocked processes. When the semaphore gets signaled, a process is removed from the list and allowed to resume execution.

THE ORIGIN OF SEMAPHORE NOTATION

Semaphores in the classic literature use Dijkstra's original notation. The *signal* operation is called V, from the Dutch word *verhogen* (*to increment*). The *wait* operation is called P, from the Dutch word *proberen* (*to test*).

Although semaphores were originally designed to solve a mutual exclusion problem (requiring process synchronization), you can also use them to send notifications. Actually, from a certain perspective, process synchronization operations *are* event notifications. When a process calls a semaphore's wait operation, it is waiting for an event to occur, which might be the availability of a shared resource, but could also be any other type of occurrence. When a process wishes to fire an event, it does so by signaling the semaphore. Figure 3-11 shows this event-oriented view of semaphores.

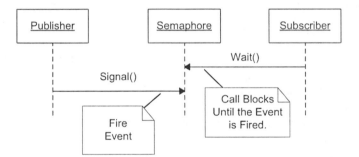

Figure 3-11. *Using semaphores as a shared resource to deliver notifications*

One problem with semaphores is in dealing with multiple subscribers. You might make the event source signal the semaphore once for each subscriber present, but this approach wouldn't prevent one subscriber from *stealing* notifications from others. Notifications could be stolen in the following scenario. Assume there were two subscribers, A and B. When sending a notification using the semaphore, the event source would call the *signal* operation twice—once for each subscriber. Assume A was already waiting for this notification, blocked on the semaphore, and that B hadn't called the semaphore's *wait* operation yet because it was busy doing its own thing. When the event source fired the event, A would be released from its blocked state and would be free to call the semaphore's *wait* operation again. Assume the event source signaled the semaphore again to deliver the notification to B. If A called the *wait* operation again before B got around to calling wait for the first time, A would find the semaphore signaled and would cause the semaphore counter to be decremented 0, thus stealing the notification from B. Once B called the semaphore's wait operation, it would be blocked and would need to wait for the semaphore to become signaled again.

A better approach in handling multiple subscribers is for the subscription mechanism to allocate a separate semaphore for each subscriber. The event sender then keeps track of all the semaphores using an internal collection. When firing an event, the event source signals each semaphore in the collection.

Semaphores are somewhat special shared resources, because they are operating-system kernel objects. You shouldn't use semaphores in large numbers, so it would be a bad idea to design a system that uses thousands of them to handle notifications delivery.

Out-of-Band Channels

Not all shared resources allow a notification payload to be sent. The semaphores described in the previous section are a good example. Semaphores let you send a signal, but no other data. With such shared resources, you can use a separate delivery channel to send a payload. This secondary channel is called an *out-of-band* channel. Out-of-band channels are used in all sorts of communication systems, such as television broadcasts and prerecorded DVDs, which use a dedicated data channel to carry subtitles and program information, separated from the main video or audio channels.

When using an out-of-band channel for payload delivery, the notification signal is carried over one channel and the payload is carried on a separate channel, as shown in Figure 3-12.

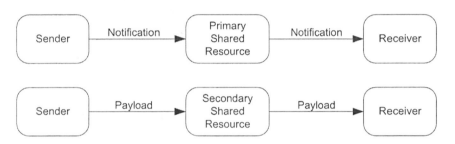

Figure 3-12. *Using a second shared resource for out-of-band payload delivery*

When using this dual shared resource approach, the sender first writes the necessary notification payload data to the secondary shared resource and then signals the semaphore that acts as the primary shared resource. The semaphore releases waiting receivers, which can then read the notification payload data from the secondary shared resource, as shown in Figure 3-13.

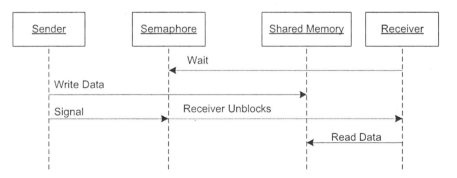

Figure 3-13. *Using a secondary shared resource to pass out-of-band data with a notification*

Using semaphores to coordinate access to a shared resource like memory is not a new idea, of course. What is new is the way you look at what is happening. From the perspective of event-based systems, you consider semaphores to be a communication channel for notifications. You can consider shared memory to be a secondary channel carrying the event notification payload. The semaphore not only acts as the primary signaling channel, but it also protects the secondary channel from concurrent access by the notification sender and receiver.

Serialized Connections

A data structure has been *serialized* when it has broken down into a sequence of bytes, often called *octets*. Serialized data are suitable for transmission through various means. A serialized connection is one that transfers serialized data. Some serialized connections, like streams and pipes, typically transfer data one octet at a time. Other connections, particularly those that use physical wires and cable, transfer data one bit at a time. Examples of such bit-oriented connections are network, modem, and USB connections.

Serialized connections represent the most common type of shared resource used to send notifications. Considering connections as shared resources might seem strange, but it makes sense if you consider the fact that the sender writes data on one side, and the receiver reads data from the other, as shown in Figure 3-14.

Figure 3-14. *A serialized connection as a shared resource*

A serialized connection can be considered a queue, with the sender adding data at one end and the receiver removing data concurrently at the other. This model abstracts away all the physical transmission characteristics of the connection. However, there are two important things you should always keep in mind about serialized connections:

1. Connections might not be reliable.

2. The transmission latency might be unpredictable.

If the sender and receiver are processes running in the same box, communicating over a pipe is fairly reliable. Just keep in mind that reliable does not mean infallible. You should consider connections unreliable if the sender and receiver are not physically packaged together. For example, if the sender and receiver are in different countries and communicate over an Internet connection, the connection is probably not going to be extremely reliable.

The transmission latency of a connection is related to two key parameters: the amount of traffic in the system and the system's bandwidth. When using complex connection infrastructures—which networks are—the transmission latency can be totally unpredictable. Anyone who has surfed the Web knows that some pages can take a much longer time to download than others. As traffic piles up at hot spots in the network, delays occur while the networking infrastructure struggles to process the backlog of messages over a system with finite bandwidth.

When the sender and receiver are in different computers in different places, the sender might not know whether the receiver is online. Even if the receiver is online, it might be too busy to accept incoming data, or the data might arrive faster than the receiver can handle it. For these situations, middleware components like message queues can be helpful.

Regardless of the physical details of the connection medium, all serialized connections conceptually transfer data the same way, as shown in Figure 3-15.

The marshaling/unmarshaling processes transfer objects from one address space into another. When the transfer entails the use of a serialized connection, the marshaling process also serializes the object, while the unmarshaler deserializes them on the other end. Omitted from the previous figures are software layers related to networking. From this point of view, the networking software is transparent. Of course, you need to consider certain aspects of the underlying protocol when designing a notification system. For example, TCP uses a built-in mechanism for resending messages that become garbled in the transmission, while UDP uses no such mechanism.

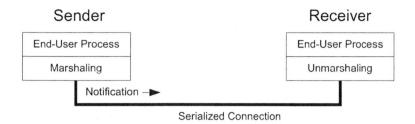

Figure 3-15. *Sending notifications using serialized connections*

Note that I don't include remote procedure calls in the serialized connection protocol described here, although they do use a connection. The reason is due to the semantics of procedure calls, which are profoundly different from shared resource semantics. Recall that procedure calls transfer *execution control* from sender to receiver. Shared resources are used only to transfer *data* from sender to receiver. The receiver must be able to look at the message and determine, from its contents or its origin, what to do with it.

Delivery Using Procedure Calls

Shared resource delivery protocols are widely used in large systems, particularly those designed for lots of publishers and/or subscribers. For smaller systems, especially those in which events are exchanged by components running in the same process space, a procedure call delivery protocol is often more appropriate. Instead of transferring data from the sender to the receiver, execution control (and possibly also data) is transferred.

The procedure call delivery model is attractive because it is simple to implement: The plumbing is built into all major component platforms, often with support for both synchronous and asynchronous calls. Figure 3-16 shows an event source using a procedure call to send a notification to a receiver.

Figure 3-16. *A notification delivered using a procedure call*

The arrow in Figure 3-16 shows the direction of travel of execution control, not the direction of data transferred by the notification. All procedure calls are natively synchronous at the machine level: The caller blocks until the callee returns. If the caller returns when it's completely done, the computing model is synchronous, but if the callee returns immediately after scheduling a background thread to handle the call, the computing model is asynchronous. Synchronous models are much more popular, because they are simpler to deal with: They don't introduce concurrency issues, since the system is only doing one thing at a time. Sometimes you want multiple things to happen at the same time, so you might need to use an asynchronous model. To do so, you must use concurrent code on the caller side, the callee side, or both.

When sending notifications with procedure calls, the procedure call itself represents the notification signal. Procedure calls might or might not have parameters. If they do, the arguments represent the notification's payload. The payload also includes data returned from the callee. Although notifications usually push information from the sender to the receiver, they can also pull information.

When sending notifications using procedure calls, the caller makes an indirect call using a reference initialized at run time. The caller doesn't know in advance (at compile time) who the callee will be. The reference used for the call can be of two kinds:

1. A type reference
2. A method reference

In the first case, the caller knows the type of the callee. The caller's reference specifies the callee's type by interface or class. The caller calls a predetermined method of this interface or class. For example, the caller might have a reference to an interface called `IComparer`. When firing an event, the caller might call the referenced object's `Compare` method.

In the second case, the caller knows nothing about the callee's type and only has a reference to one of the callee's methods. For example, the caller might reference a method with this signature:

```
bool f(int, string)
```

The caller doesn't know the name of this method, which object the method is associated with, or what the method does. It just knows the method's signature. Procedure calls as a notification delivery protocol have a number of interesting features, regardless of whether they use type references or method references:

- They offer a simple computing model.
- They allow data to be passed from caller to callee and vice versa.
- They support a simple error-handling model, using exceptions.

The caller can pass any number of parameters to the callee. Parameters passed by reference allow the callee to return values to the caller. The callee can also affect changes through side effects, such as by changing a global object. Component models like .NET, JavaBeans, and Object Pascal support an exception-based, error-handling model. Callees can signal errors by throwing exceptions, which the caller can catch.

While procedure calls are certainly easy to use, they also have drawbacks, which might preclude them from being used in many situations. The main disadvantages are

- The caller and callee must be running simultaneously.
- With synchronous calls, the caller is vulnerable to failures or delays in the callee.
- There are security issues related to data safety.
- Parameter passing requires marshaling, which might be expensive.

The first problem generally only applies to distributed systems. When making a call, the caller relies on the fact that the callee is online and running. This might not always be the case. The second problem is due to the fact that the caller is blocked while the callee executes. If the callee is slow or dies, the caller is affected. The third problem, data safety, arises when parameters are passed. If the parameters are passed by reference, or contain references, the callee might have access to objects in the caller's space. Malicious or misbehaving callees could unexpectedly change variables in the caller's space. The last problem, marshaling overhead, should be considered when parameters are passed by reference. In this case, the system must set up a proxy object in the callee's space, which connects back to the referenced object on the caller's side. Apart from security concerns, there is a nontrivial run-time performance hit to support calls by reference.

When delivering notifications with procedure calls, using remote procedure calls (RPCs) instead of local procedure calls (LPCs) makes a big difference in performance and reliability. RPCs are often routed over a network connection, using protocols like Simple Object Access Protocol (SOAP) and Remote Method Invocation (RMI). Apart from the networking overhead, such as marshaling and serialization/deserialization, remote calls are much more likely to fail than local ones, due to networking problems or unavailability of the callee.

Local Procedure Calls

LPCs are used when the sender and receiver are in the same thread or process space, and offer excellent performance. The reason is simplicity: For the caller, making an LPC is as simple as saving the call's return address and some parameters on the stack and issuing a low-level *call* instruction. Returning from an LPC is even faster, because there are no parameters to push on the stack, only some minor stack cleanup work.

LPCs are not only fast, but they're also extremely reliable compared to RPCs and other delivery protocols. Because the caller and callee are part of the same process, the callee is guaranteed to be running whenever the caller is running. LPCs are often the best protocol when sending notifications to objects in the same process space as the sender.

Remote Procedure Calls

When the sender and receiver live in different process spaces, RPCs can be used to deliver the notification. Delivering notifications using RPCs is really a special case of shared resource delivery. The procedure call is converted into a packet of data, routed over a shared resource (which is typically a network connection), and delivered to the remote receiver. From the point of view of the sender and receiver end-user processes, the RPC protocol makes everything work *as if* a procedure call had taken place, as shown in Figure 3-17.

Figure 3-17. *An event notification delivered using a remote procedure call*

The direction of the arrow shows the direction in which execution control is conceptually transferred. The most common type of network connection today relies on TCP/IP. To handle incoming RPCs, the receiver must have a service listening to traffic on a specific TCP/IP socket. The RPC protocol provides message serialization/deserialization and parameter marshaling/unmarshaling. The sender may or may not block while the call is in progress, depending on the implementation.

The network connection takes care of transporting the data back and forth over the connection. There are a number of RPC standards, based on different wire protocols. For example, SOAP[8] generally uses HTTP; DCE RPC[9] and Microsoft RPC use TCP or UDP; CORBA[10] uses Internet Inter-ORB Protocol (IIOP); and Java RMI[11] uses HTTP or IIOP.

---

8. Don Box, David Ehnebuske, Gopal Kakivaya, Andrew Layman, Noah Mendelsohn, Henrik Frystyk Nielsen, Satish Thatte, and Dave Winer, "Simple Object Access Protocol (SOAP) 1.1," www.w3.org/TR/2000/NOTE-SOAP-20000508/, 2000.

9. The Open Group, "DCE 1.1: Remote Procedure Call," www.opengroup.org/onlinepubs/009629399/toc.pdf, 1997.

10. Object Management Group, "Common Object Request Broker Architecture: Core Specification," www.omg.org/docs/formal/02-12-06.pdf, 2002.

11. Ann Wollrath and Jim Waldo, "Trail: RMI" (technical report, http://java.sun.com/docs/books/tutorial/rmi/).

Notification Architectures

The notification architecture describes the infrastructure used to get event notifications from the event publisher to the subscriber. There are two basic architectures: direct delivery and indirect delivery. The latter has two derivatives, as shown in Figure 3-18.

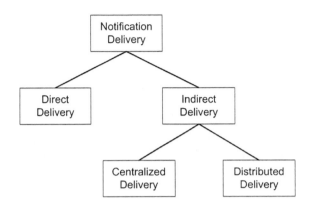

Figure 3-18. *A taxonomy of event notification architectures*

Notification architectures can also be classified using different aspects, such as the presence of middleware, support for mobile subscribers, and support for unicast and multicast operations. The classification shown in Figure 3-18 is based on the type of path used to disseminate notifications in a system. The approach is somewhat similar to the one described by Meier and Cahill.[12]

Direct Delivery

With a direct-delivery architecture, also known as *point-to-point* (PTP), there is no central notification service, and each event publisher assumes the responsibility for delivering events directly to subscribers.

With direct delivery, no middleware components exist between the event publisher and the subscriber. The publisher has direct and immediate control over every notification sent to the subscribers, as shown in Figure 3-19.

Figure 3-19. *The direct-delivery notification model*

In the figure, P is the publisher and S is the subscriber. The obvious advantage of this architecture is simplicity. When the publisher and subscriber are in the same process space, direct delivery is by far the most efficient notification architecture. The disadvantage is lack of scalability, because the publisher must handle the overhead of sending notifications to all subscribers. If there are many subscribers, the publisher's performance is adversely affected. At a limit, the overhead of sending notifications can completely overwhelm the publisher. To keep the overhead at a minimum, most publishers sacrifice QoS features like reliable delivery, prioritized delivery, and transaction support, in favor of speed.

---

12. Rene Meier and Vinny Cahill, "Taxonomy of Distributed Event-Based Programming Systems," *The Computer Journal*, June 24, 2005.

Peer-to-Peer Delivery

Peer-to-peer (P2P) systems[13] gained fame in the late 1990s with Internet programs like ICQ and Napster. P2P systems are based on a decentralized distributed architecture, in which *peers* connected to the Internet can share resources with each other directly. In a P2P system, peers can act as traditional clients and servers simultaneously. As clients, they can request resources from other peers. As servers, they can provide resources to other peers. P2P is about sharing. If one takes the view that notifications are sharable resources, in the sense that any publisher's notifications can be of interest to any number of other subscribers, then a decentralized direct-delivery notification architecture can be considered a P2P system, as shown in Figure 3-20.

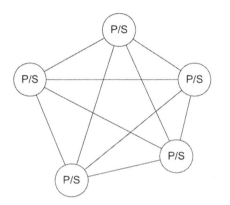

Figure 3-20. *A peer-to-peer direct-delivery notification model*

All nodes in the figure can act both as event publishers and subscribers. Each node maintains a routing table, referencing discovered nodes in relative vicinity. The discovery process begins when a node attempts to connect to the network. At this time, the *connectee* must locate a host that is already a node in the network. Once it finds a host, the connectee adds it to its own routing table. A new discovery process is launched every time a node needs to find new nodes. When a node A needs to find another node B, it sends out special search requests to nearby nodes, which propagate the requests through the network. Once the node B is found, node A updates its own routing table by adding B. Because P2P systems manage their own routing, which is completely separate from the lower-level network routing, P2P systems are also known as *overlay networks*. They function as a sort of high-level network superimposed (overlaid) on a lower-level network (such as the Internet).

The true power of P2P systems lies in their scalability. P2P systems have been shown to support not thousands, but millions, of nodes simultaneously, as demonstrated by popular file sharing programs like Morpheus[14] and Kazaa.[15] This level of scalability is achieved thanks to the decentralized, fault-tolerant, and adaptive nature of P2P systems. P2P systems not only continue to work when a node fails or disconnects, but they work routinely with such failures, as peers appear and disappear from the network.

13. Dejan SMilojicic, Vana Kalogeraki, Rajan Lukose, Kiran Nagaraja, Jim Pruyne, Bruno Richard, Sami Rollins, and Zhichen Xu, "Peer-to-Peer Computing" (HP Labs technical report, www.hpl.hp.com/techreports/2002/HPL-2002-57R1.html, 2002).

14. "Morpheus (computer program)," http://en.wikipedia.org/wiki/Morpheus_(computer_program), 2003.

15. "Peer-To-Peer (P2P) and How Kazaa Works," www.kazaa.com/us/help/glossary/p2p.htm, 2003.

A P2P substrate is used in a number of group communication systems, including Tapestry,[16] Chord,[17] and Pastry.[18] Also of interest is Scribe,[19] which is a P2P notification system built on top of Pastry, making it a second-order overlay network. Although P2P notification systems are still relatively new, many people expect them to become the dominant architecture for Internet-scale notification systems.

Indirect Delivery

With indirect-delivery architectures, publishers send notifications to a middleware system, which then takes responsibility for notifying subscribers. The middleware components serve as decouplers, because publishers and subscribers no longer talk to each other directly. In the literature, middleware components go under a variety of names, including *notification services*, *event services*, *messaging services*, *message-oriented middleware* (MOM), and others. Middleware components offer a host of services to event publishers, such as reliable delivery, various types of QoS, complex subscription filters, and support for mobile subscribers. This last feature has become of great interest, with the rise in popularity of wireless systems. Rendezvous-Notify[20] is an example of system-supporting mobile subscribers.

In indirect-delivery architectures, notification delivery is almost always asynchronous. Notifications are generally textual in nature, so they often are called *messages*. Messages may contain human-readable text, XML data representing the serialized data of complex objects, or other. The event publisher sends messages to the middleware system, which then takes care of delivering them to the appropriate subscribers. The publisher uses a *fire-and-forget* approach, because it doesn't need to block while messages are being delivered by the middleware. The publisher continues with its chores, without waiting for any replies.

The presence of middleware between the publisher and subscriber makes it possible to decouple the two, both in space and time. Spatial decoupling alludes to the fact that the publisher and subscriber have no points in common. They are not connected directly in any way. In some cases, publishers are not even aware of the existence of subscribers, and vice versa. Time decoupling refers to the fact that publishers and subscribers don't need to be running at the same time. If a subscriber is off-line when a notification is sent to it, middleware systems can save the notification in a local store and attempt to deliver it when the subscriber becomes available at a later time.

Centralized Delivery

A centralized-delivery architecture is conceptually similar to a city's postal system: When you acquire residence in the city, you notify the local post office of your name and address. When letters arrive at the post office with your name and address, the post office delivers them to you. For letters mailed

16. Ben Y. Zhao, John Kubiatowicz, and Anthony D. Joseph, "Tapestry: An Infrastructure for Fault-tolerant Wide-area Location and Routing" (technical report, University of California, Berkeley, Berkeley, CA, April 2001).

17. Ion Stoica, Robert Morris, David Karger, M. Frans Kaashoek, and Hari Balakrishnan, "Chord: A Scalable Peer-to-peer Lookup Service for Internet Applications" (proceedings of the ACM SIGCOMM Conference, San Diego, CA, August 2001).

18. Antony Rowstron and Peter Druschel, "Pastry: Scalable, decentralized object location and routing for large-scale peer-to-peer systems" (proceedings of the IFIP/ACM International Conference on Distributed Systems Platforms, Heidelberg, Germany, November 2001).

19. Antony Rowstron, Anne-Marie Kermarrec, Miguel Castro, and Peter Druschel, "Scribe: The Design of a Large-Scale Event Notification Infrastructure" (proceedings of the Third International Workshop on Networked Group Communications, London, UK, November 2001).

20. Sasu Tarkoma, Jaakko Kangasharju, and Kimmo Raatikainen, "Client Mobility in Rendezvous-Notify" (proceedings of the Second International Workshop on Distributed Event-Based Systems, San Diego, CA, June 2003).

in the city, the postal service acts as a centralized notification system: It picks up mail that is sent to you and delivers it to your address. The sender doesn't need to know how to physically get to your address. All he or she needs to know is your postal address. E-mail services use the same conceptual model.

The middleware systems used in centralized-delivery architectures may use one computer or multiple computers. When using one middleware system, the simplest layout is probably the hub-and-spoke arrangement, shown in Figure 3-21.

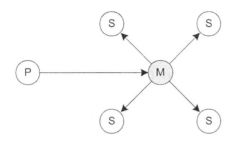

Figure 3-21. *The hub-and-spoke structure of centralized-delivery systems*

In the figure, P is an event publisher, S is a subscriber, and M is the middleware. Other types of arrangements are possible, besides the one shown. For example, JEDI[21] uses a hierarchical arrangement of dispatching middleware servers.

There are two basic types of middleware components used in centralized-delivery models: those based on notification services and those based on messaging services. The main difference is in who determines the recipients. In the former case, the notification service does, while in the latter case, the event publisher does.

Notification Services

Notification services use a true publish-subscribe model. Notification services are also sometimes called event services in the literature. In order to receive notifications, subscribers must send a subscription request to the middleware. The middleware manages the subscription itself, without informing the event publisher. When the publisher sends a notification to the middleware, the latter determines who the recipients are by looking at each subscriber's subscription. A subscriber receives all those notifications that satisfy the subscription criteria. To subscribers, the middleware appears as an event publisher, because it hides the actual event publisher. Systems using notification services generally use a push-push approach: The event publisher pushes notifications to the middleware, which then pushes them to the appropriate subscribers.

Messaging Services

Messaging services are in widespread use today. They act as middleware between senders and receivers, and are based on internally managed message queues. Messages are sent by writing them to the queue associated with the intended recipient, as shown in Figure 3-22.

---

21. Gianpaolo Cugola, Elisabetta Di Nitto, and Alfonso Fuggetta, "The JEDI Event-Based Infrastructure and Its Application to the Development of the OPSS WFMS," *IEEE Transactions of Software Engineering*, September 2001.

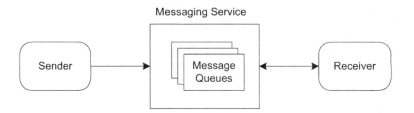

Figure 3-22. *Sending messages using a messaging service*

When a message is posted to a queue, the messaging service subsequently (and therefore asynchronously) delivers the message to the recipient associated with the queue. Most messaging services allow a queue to be associated with only one recipient, precluding multicasting. To send the same message to multiple destinations, the sender must post the message to multiple queues.

Recipients must be set up with the messaging services to receive messages posted to a specific queue, so recipients can be viewed as the *owners* of the queue. Although recipients usually own only one queue, they can own more than one. Any number of senders can write to the same queue, as shown in Figure 3-23.

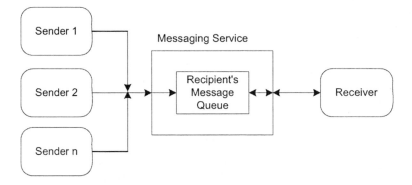

Figure 3-23. *Multiple senders writing to the same queue*

The messaging service manages all access to the queues by senders and recipients, preventing concurrency problems when senders and recipients try to access the same queue at the same time. Messaging services support *point-to-point* delivery, because any sender can send messages to any recipient connected to the service. The burden of choosing which recipients a message should go to is on the message sender, not the messaging service, because it is the sender that chooses which message queue it writes to.

Messaging services are often considered hybrid publish-subscribe systems. Parties wishing to receive messages must *register* with the messaging services, using a procedure that is akin to a subscription. The registration process doesn't usually include a filter, and messaging servers rarely have the capability or responsibility to filter messages.

Systems using messaging services can use both push-push and push-pull delivery approaches, as shown in Figure 3-22 and Figure 3-23 by the double-headed arrows on the recipient end. The push-push approach is similar to the one used with notification services: The publisher pushes messages to the middleware, which pushes them to the recipients.

With the push-pull approach, the subscribers must fetch messages from the middleware. This approach can work in two ways:

1. The messaging service notifies a client that a message has arrived. The subscriber then retrieves (pulls) the message from the messaging service.

2. The subscriber periodically polls the messaging service to see when messages are available. Once messages are detected, the subscriber retrieves them from the messaging service.

Messaging services are commonly used to integrate components across multiple platforms and servers. Examples of commercial messaging services are IBM WebSphere MQ, BEA WebLogic, and Microsoft MSMQ. I'll describe these and others in more detail in Chapter 5.

Centralized-delivery systems are pretty much the *de facto* standard for medium-sized, commercial, event-based distributed systems. By using redundant failover servers, you can build centralized-delivery systems with any desired degree of resilience to single points of failure. Regardless of whether a system uses notification services or messaging services, the advantage of centralized delivery is that it offers good scalability compared to direct delivery.

Distributed Delivery

When a system is designed for a really large number of publishers and/or subscribers, such as in Internet-scale systems, a single centralized middleware infrastructure can become a bottleneck. The solution is to create multiple middleware components that distribute the notification load among them. The distributed-notification delivery model is the most powerful type of architecture. It's also the most complex and expensive, making it a good choice only for the largest of systems.

The simplest distributed-delivery system uses two middleware components, connected together as shown in Figure 3-24.

Figure 3-24. *A simple distributed-notification system*

As in previous figures, P is a publisher, M is a middleware component, and S is a subscriber. Each middleware component can support multiple publishers and subscribers. The two middleware components are interconnected, allowing any publisher to send notifications to any subscriber. You can connect middleware components together in a string to support increasing numbers of subscribers, as shown in Figure 3-25.

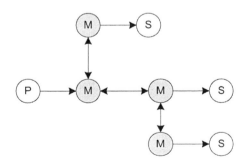

Figure 3-25. *Chaining multiple middleware components in a string topology*

You can also draw a string arrangement as a tree, which gives a hierarchical flavor to the structure. Items near the middle of a string tend to show up in higher positions in the hierarchy. Items at the end of the string are terminal elements in the hierarchy. Figure 3-26 shows a simple hierarchy of middleware components.

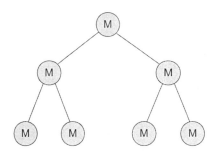

Figure 3-26. *Middleware systems arranged hierarchically*

Each node has one parent, except for the root node. Publishers and subscribers can be connected to any middleware component, which routes notifications through the hierarchy to deliver them to the proper subscribers. In order to route things correctly, the middleware components need to share a certain amount of information regarding the subscriptions, subscribers, and publishers they handle. This information serves to keep all the middleware components in sync with each other. If the middleware components aren't properly synchronized, notifications might be lost, delivered in the wrong order, or delivered multiple times. Care has to be taken when designing the synchronization messages to avoid loading the network excessively; otherwise, the networking overhead to manage the distributed middleware could overwhelm the network, defeating the purpose of using multiple middleware components. An example of a notification system using hierarchical middleware components is JEDI.[22]

The drawback of simple tree topologies is vulnerability to single-point failures. Given two arbitrary nodes, there is only one path through the network that connects them. If the root node or a node near it failed, a large number of publishers and subscribers could be affected. One solution is to use extra links between the middleware components. Figure 3-27 shows a redundant system using three middleware components.

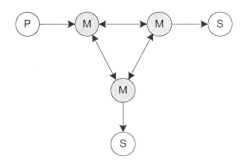

Figure 3-27. *Using redundant connections for improved availability*

22. Gianpaolo Cugola, Elisabetta Di Nitto, and Alfonso Fuggetta, "The JEDI Event-Based Infrastructure and Its Application to the Development of the OPSS WFMS," *IEEE Transactions of Software Engineering,* September 2001.

Using this new arrangement, each middleware has two links with its neighboring middleware systems, so the network is resilient to single-link failures. But vulnerability to middleware failures still exists. If one of the middleware components fails, notification traffic might not reach all intended subscribers.

Most large-scale distributed-notification systems today use the Internet as the backbone connecting the middleware systems, which may be distributed across a wide geographic area, as shown in Figure 3-28.

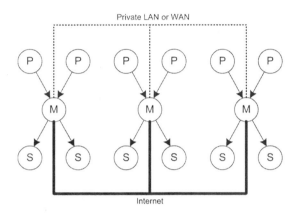

Figure 3-28. *The distributed-notification delivery model*

Publishers and subscribers can connect to any of the middleware components. Any subscriber can receive notifications from any publisher. The middleware components might also have private LAN or WAN connections among them to handle things like replication, failover, and load balancing.

Distributed-notification systems can usually continue to operate, albeit with a certain loss of service, in the presence of failures in the Internet or in the LAN/WAN. Distributed-delivery architectures can give excellent performance in systems with a large number of subscribers, publishers, or both. The obvious drawbacks are complexity and cost. Developing a distributed network of middleware components that is scalable and resilient to failures is not an easy task, and is beyond the scope of this book.

Delivery Synchrony

Many people think of EBSs as large, distributed, asynchronous systems, with middleware components handling messages and notifications, running independently of event publishers. While EBSs certainly can be asynchronous, they don't have to be. For one thing, not all EBSs use middleware, and even those that do might have reasons to prefer synchronous delivery. Moreover, not all EBSs are distributed, or even large. In small systems, synchronous delivery is often preferred. Synchronous delivery has two important advantages: The delivery order of notifications is predictable, and the systems are cheaper and easier to build.

Another consideration is that not all the notifications in a system need be delivered using the same synchrony. For example, in a distributed system, notifications between systems might use asynchronous delivery, while those between objects in the same system might use synchronous delivery. In the following sections, I'll describe both types of timing, showing the pros and cons of each.

Synchronous Delivery

When a notification is delivered synchronously, the sender blocks while the receiver is busy processing the notification. Synchronous delivery is used most often with notifications sent via procedure calls. The reason is simplicity, because the mechanics of blocking are built into the procedure call substrate.

The simplest way to achieve synchronous delivery is with an LPC. Since a call transfers execution control to the callee, the caller is forced to block until the callee returns. LPCs are *natively* synchronous, because it takes extra work to make them asynchronous.

RPCs are similar to LPCs from the viewpoint of the programs using them, because all the inter-process plumbing details are basically transparent to the caller and callee. Under the covers, there are all sorts of networking protocols at work, with proxies, stubs, marshaling, and other hideous gunk that application-level programmers prefer to know little about.

When delivering notifications using shared resources, true synchronous delivery is not possible, since the sender and receiver are generally in separate processes running concurrently. By resorting to a simple stratagem, it's possible to make a notification appear to have been delivered synchronously, from the perspective of the sender. To produce blocking, a secondary shared resource is required to notify the sender when the receiver has finished processing the notification. This design pattern uses a sequence of reads and writes to emulate a single synchronous operation. Figure 3-29 shows the details.

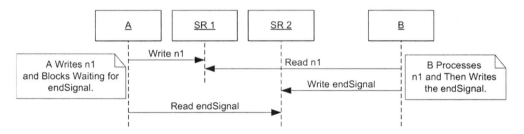

Figure 3-29. *Using a secondary shared resource to unblock the sender of a synchronous notification sent using a shared resource*

Two shared resources are used—one (SR 1) for the *forward* notification, from A to B, and one (SR 2) for the *return* notification, from B to A. A writes the n1 notification to SR- and then blocks, waiting for B to send some kind of endSignal, denoting completion and also returning optional data from the n1 notification handler.

Asynchronous Delivery

Asynchronous delivery is commonly used in distributed systems, in which the sender and receiver are in different process spaces or machines. The sender sends a notification without blocking and continues on while the receiver is busy handling the notification. There are two main scenarios, in terms of the overall interaction between sender and receiver:

1. The sender doesn't care about the outcome of processing in the receiver.

2. The sender does care about the outcome of processing in the receiver or needs to know when the receiver has finished handling the notification.

In the first case, called a *fire-and-forget notification*, the sender doesn't need to get information back from the receiver. In the second case, the sender needs to be informed when the receiver has finished handling the notification. In the return notification, the receiver can furnish status information, indicating the results of its processing. Figure 3-30 shows an example, in which the completion signal is delivered using a synchronous procedure call.

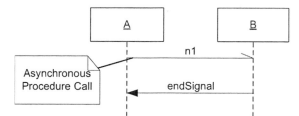

Figure 3-30. *Asynchronous notification with completion signaling, based on procedure calls*

When notification delivery is based on shared resources, two resources are used—one for the forward and one for the return notification, as shown in Figure 3-31.

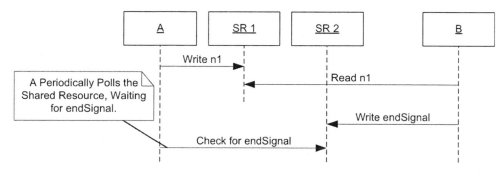

Figure 3-31. *Asynchronous notification with completion, based on shared resources*

Figure 3-31 is similar to Figure 3-30. The difference is that in Figure 3-31, A doesn't block while waiting for the endSignal to return. A is free to continue with its internal processing, and it periodically checks the shared resource to see if the endSignal is available.

Delivery Fanout

The word *fanout* is borrowed from the digital-logic world, where it indicates the maximum number of inputs an output signal can be connected to. With hardware logic, fanout is a function of input and output impedances, but such details are beyond the scope of this book. In the software world, fanout denotes the maximum number of receivers a sender is capable of sending a notification to. There are two important cases of fanout:

1. One

2. More-than-one

When the fanout is one, the event notification is said to be *unicast*: The notification can only be sent to one receiver. If a second receiver subscribes, it generally preempts an existing subscription, effectively stealing the notification from the prior subscriber.

When the fanout is more than one, the event notification is said to be *multicast*: The notification can be sent to multiple subscribers. The upper limit of subscribers supported is implementation-dependent and often not defined. Note that the fanout only indicates the number of subscribers that *can be* supported, not the number of actual subscribers present. A multicast notification might have zero, one, or more actual subscribers.

There are two basic ways to handle multicasting: at the network level and at the application level. Network-level multicasting has been available for several years. It relies on IP multicasting,[23] which is handled at the networking packet level by routers. While early IP multicasting was based on a broadcast model, reliability was addressed by later protocols, such as SRM[24] and RMTP.[25] IP multicasting is based on the notion of group addresses, which identify an address space of members. When a datagram is sent to the group address, all members receive it. There are two problems regarding the use of IP multicasting to handle one-to-many delivery:

1. Not all commercial Internet Service Providers support it.

2. It requires members to join/leave multicast groups, at the IP address level.

An alternative to network-level multicasting is application-level multicasting, which builds the multicasting infrastructure into the applications that participate in a distributed system.

When using procedure calls to deliver notifications, the simplest technique is to have the sender handle the multicasting directly. The technique is only adequate for systems in which the number of recipients is predictably very low. The sender typically uses a collection to store the references to objects or methods to call. When sending multicast notifications, the sender iterates over the collection, firing an event to each subscriber. The firing order usually corresponds to the order in which subscriptions were received. Several component models, including .NET, JavaBeans, and Delphi Object Pascal, use this model.

A more complicated approach, adequate for large and very large systems, can be used in systems that have a peer-to-peer architecture. The participants form an overlay network system, distributing the task of multicasting among themselves to optimize network utilization. Examples include NICE,[26] Herald,[27] Tapestry,[28] Pastry,[29] and Scribe.[30] In Scribe, for example, any peer can create a group. Other peers can join this group, and peers can join any number of groups. When the group peer receives a notification, it handles the job of multicasting it to the other peers in the group.

---

23. Stephen E. Deering and David R. Cheriton, "Multicast Routing in Datagram Internetworks and Extended LANs," *ACM Transactions on Computer Systems*, May 1990.

24. Sally Floyd, Van Jacobson, Ching-Gung Liu, Steven McCanne, and Lixia Zhang, "A Reliable Multicast Framework for Lightweight Sessions and Application Level Framing," *IEEE/ACM Transactions on Networking*, December 1997.

25. John C. Lin and Sanjoy Paul, "A Reliable Multicast Transport Protocol" (proceedings of IEEE INFOCOM'96, San Francisco, CA, March 1996).

26. Suman Banerjee, Bobby Bhattacharjee, and Christopher Kommareddy, "P2P and Multicast" session, "Scalable Application Layer Multicast" (proceedings of the 2002 conference on Applications, Technologies, Architectures, and Protocols for Computer Communications, Pittsburgh, PA, August 2002).

27. Luis Felipe Cabrera, Michael B. Jones, and Marvin Theimer, "Herald: Achieving a Global Event Notification Service" (proceedings of the Eighth Workshop on Hot Topics in Operating Systems, Elmau/Oberbayern, Germany, May 2001).

28. Ben Y. Zhao, John Kubiatowicz, and Anthony D. Joseph, "Tapestry: An Infrastructure for Fault-tolerant Wide-area Location and Routing' (technical report, University of California, Berkeley, Berkeley, CA, April 2001).

29. Antony Rowstron and Peter Druschel, "Pastry: Scalable, decentralized object location and routing for large-scale peer-to-peer systems" (proceedings of the IFIP/ACM International Conference on Distributed Systems Platforms, Heidelberg, Germany, November 2001).

30. Antony Rowstron, Anne-Marie Kermarrec, Miguel Castro, and Peter Druschel, "Scribe: The Design of a Large-Scale Event Notification Infrastructure" (proceedings of the Third International Workshop on Networked Group Communications, London, UK, November 2001).

Quality of Service

Quality of Service (QoS) basically defines a number of added-value options that a delivery system can make available to users. In the QoS context, a *service* refers to a level of assurance regarding some aspect of notification delivery. Before going too far, keep in mind that most notification systems in current use offer little or no support for QoS.

There are a number of different QoS categories, some of which are beyond the scope of this book. I'll focus on those most likely to be of interest to people working with event-notification delivery systems, looking at the following categories:

- Reliability
- Priority
- Timing
- Throughput
- Order

The first category—reliability—affects all notifications. The next three affect only those notifications that were queued on the notification server, if the service couldn't deliver notifications as fast as they were arriving. The last category—order—sometimes conflicts with the other categories. Let's look at each category more in detail.

Reliability

This category indicates how *hard* a notification service should try to deliver a notification. For example, if the recipient is offline when delivery is attempted, what should be done? The following are common options, listed in increasing order of reliability:

- *At least once*: Delivery is attempted once, under normal circumstances. If the recipient is not online, the notification is lost. There are situations in which delivery might not be attempted at all. For example, if the recipient is offline, notifications are stored in a queue. If the queue fills up before the recipient goes online, notifications might have to be discarded without attempting delivery.

- *Exactly once*: The notification service guarantees to attempt delivery, but only once. This option doesn't imply certain delivery. If the recipient never goes online, it will never get the notification.

- *At most, n times*: Delivery is attempted repeatedly, up to n times. After each attempt, the service generally waits for a certain amount of time before trying again. Some services might try pinging recipients at some interval to discover when they go online.

- *Best effort*: The delivery service keeps trying to send a notification until either a retry limit is reached or a timeout condition occurs. As with the previous option, retries are generally attempted after a predetermined delay.

- *Certified delivery*: None of the previous options specify what happens when a delivery fails. The publisher might be led to believe that everything worked fine. With certified delivery, a confirmation of delivery is returned to the publisher through a designated channel linking the notification service back to the publisher. Because successful delivery is usually the norm and not the exception, certified delivery can also be set up to only report delivery failures, saving valuable bandwidth and computing resources.

The first four options fall under the heading *fire-and-forget*, because the sender doesn't know if and when a notification is delivered. For all options, delivery is assumed to occur using a reliable protocol, such as TCP, that can detect and correct transmission errors. Keep in mind that none of the reliability options *guarantees* delivery.

Priority

When you mail a letter, you have the option of choosing a delivery priority, such as overnight delivery or special delivery. Similarly, you can assign notifications a priority level. The level is usually just an integer value, chosen from some range. For example, priorities might be in the range (1..10), with 1 the highest priority and 10 the lowest. As long as the delivery system can keep up with the publisher in sending notifications, priorities have no effect. If notifications can't be delivered fast enough, or if the recipient goes offline, the notifications will have to be queued, and only then will the prioritization order become significant. When scanning the queue for the next notification to send, the delivery service must select the highest-priority item. If there are many with the same priority, a scheme must be supplied to choose which one goes first. FIFO order is generally the norm.

Priorities have been used in embedded systems to support *soft* and *hard* real-time delivery.[31] In many situations, priorities are used to select which type of notification to send. For example, consider a system that has the capability to send out the following types of notifications: textual news headlines, audio news, and video webcasts. Each type essentially has its own information space, but you can use priorities to decide which type should be sacrificed if there are insufficient transmission resources to handle them all at peak times. When notifications are given priorities, the system designer's intention is to change the delivery order. If causal order is important in a system—and it often is—priority QoS attributes shouldn't be set.

Timing

Timing constraints are used to indicate the timing window within which a notification must be delivered. If delivery can't be completed within this time, the notification is considered undeliverable and discarded. You can define the window in relative or absolute terms. In relative terms, the window indicates a length of time within which delivery must occur, such as 10 seconds. In absolute terms, the window can indicate both a starting and ending time. The starting time indicates the earliest delivery time allowed. Since notifications are normally delivered as quickly as possible, start times are rarely used. The end time specifies when the delivery should be completed by, such as 13:21:54.9.

Throughput

Throughput indicates how much information a subscriber gets in a given period of time. In theory, subscribers should get all the notifications directed to them. In practice, there can be reasons to not allow all notifications to be delivered, such as insufficient bandwidth. A delivery service might offer different prices for various levels of service, with the intention of billing the customer according to the requested throughput. A high throughput might require special communications hardware or dedicated notification servers. Throughputs might be expressed in messages/hour, bytes/hour, or other units.

---

31. Joerg Kaiser, Cristiano Brudna, and Carlos Mitidieri, "A Real-Time Event Channel Model for the CAN-Bus" (proceedings of the "Workshop on Parallel and Distributed Real-Time Systems," 17th International Symposium on Parallel and Distributed Processing, Nice, France, April 2003).

Order

This category relates to the previous three and is significant only if a notification service can't keep up with the publisher and is forced to queue notifications. When choosing the next notification to send from the queue, the service needs to know what criterion to use. The following are common ones:

- *Any*: The order is not important. If no other QoS services are specified, FIFO order is the default ordering.

- *FIFO*: Notifications are delivered on a first-come, first-served basis, disregarding constraints related to priority, timing, and throughput.

- *Priority*: Notifications are delivered in order of priority.

- *Deadline*: The notifications with the nearest expiration time are delivered first.

QoS can be supported at different levels. For example, the priority might be used at the notification service level to choose a faster transmission channel at the communication level. QoS services are not orthogonal, and it is possible to specify QoS in a conflicting way. For example, using a low priority with a very short expiration time might cause notifications to be lost.

Supporting QoS requires a certain amount of computing power, so QoS is usually available only if a dedicated notification service is used to handle delivery. QoS is not supported in nondistributed systems built with technologies like JavaBeans and .NET, in which the event source is responsible for notification delivery.

Transactions

In some situations, it might be necessary for a group of notifications to be considered atomic, or indivisible. The intent is to either have all or none of the notifications processed, because processing only some of them would leave the system in an invalid state. There are two important cases in which groups of notifications occur:

1. With one receiver

2. With multiple receivers

Figure 3-32 shows the two cases graphically.

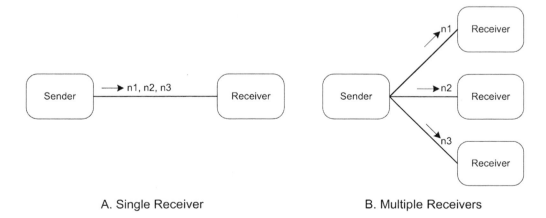

A. Single Receiver   B. Multiple Receivers

Figure 3-32. *Notifications to be processed as a group*

In the single-receiver case, you don't want the recipient to process any of the notifications unless it gets all of them. In the multiple-receiver case, you might not want any of the recipients to process their notification unless all the receivers got their notifications. For example, you might want the receiver that gets the n1 notification to wait until the other two receivers get the n2 and n3 notifications, before processing n1. You can also combine the two cases together, if you send multiple notifications to multiple receivers.

To handle such atomic groups of notifications, you can use transactions, which have been used for years with databases and other systems. Although transactions aren't normally included under the QoS heading in most notification services, they should be, because they can be thought of as an added service offered by the delivery system.

The following is a simple example of how you might use transactions: In a banking application, let there be two notifications associated with Withdrawal and Deposit events. When transferring money between accounts, you could send a Withdrawal notification to one and a Deposit to the other. By wrapping the two notifications in a transaction, you can prevent unexpected failures from disrupting the finances of the bank's customers.

The question at this point is how to implement transactions. At the notification level, there are no standards, but one thing is essential: The communication protocol between the sender and receiver must be able to detect transmission failures. The single subscriber case is not too difficult to implement. What you need to do is create special notifications to designate transactional commands. The notifications might be called BeginTransaction, CommitTransaction, and RollbackTransaction. In the single-subscriber case in Figure 3-32, you would wrap the notification sequence (n1, n2, n3) in a transaction by using the sequence (BeginTransaction, n1, n2, n3, CommitTransaction), as shown in Figure 3-33.

Figure 3-33. *Using transactions with a single receiver*

Using transacted deliveries like this, the subscriber would have to buffer all notifications received after a BeginTransaction, executing them only after a CommitTransaction was received. If the sender detected a failure of some kind after sending BeginTransaction but before sending Commit-Transaction, it could send a RollbackTransaction, causing the subscriber to disregard the previous notifications that were part of the transaction.

Distributed Transactions

Distributed transactions, involving multiple receivers, are more complicated because you have to make sure two things happen:

1. All recipients get the intended notifications.

2. All recipients get the CommitTransaction command.

Because failures could occur after giving some of the receivers the CommitTransaction command, it is necessary to use a multistage commit process. A common approach is to use a two-phase commit process. Assume a sender needs to send notifications as part of a single transaction to three receivers, as shown back in Figure 3-32. All multistage commit approaches require the presence of a separate process (called the *transaction coordinator*) to coordinate the overall transaction. The sender instructs the transaction coordinator when to start a new transaction. The sender then sends notifications to each receiver, but the receivers don't process them immediately. When the sender instructs the transaction coordinator to commit the transaction, the coordinator starts the two-phase commit process by doing the following:

1. The coordinator asks if each receiver would be able to commit the notifications received but not processed yet.

2. If all receivers answer affirmatively, the coordinator sends a CommitTransaction command to each receiver. If even one of the receivers answers negatively, the coordinator sends a RollbackTransaction command to each receiver.

Two-phase commits are not infallible and have the potential to leave the system in an undetermined state if a failure occurs at certain critical points in the commit process. For example, the coordinator might have received a collective affirmative answer for the first phase of the commit. During the second phase, one of the receivers might die after some of the receivers already performed their commit. Dealing with this type of failure scenario and others requires adding complexity to the commit phase, the details of which are beyond the scope of this book.

Delivery Order

When notifications reach their final destinations, they might arrive out of order, with respect to the order in which they were sent. There are several factors that can change the order, including propagation latency, system loading, and QoS ordering.

In EBSs, the delivery order of notifications is often very important, because the whole system relies on notifications to maintain its internal state. If notifications arrive in the wrong order, there is a possibility the system won't behave correctly. One of the problems you face in EBSs is that notification paths are not known at compile time, so you don't have the luxury of compiler errors telling you if you connected two components in ways that might affect the notification order. EBS designers must be familiar with the ways in which notifications can be sent, and understand the consequences and tradeoffs involved in their choices.

When dealing with delivery order, it is very important to keep the notion of event separate from that of notification. Events are not notifications. Events trigger notifications. One event may trigger one or more notifications, or none. When showing events and notifications in the diagrams in the following sections, I'll use the letters e and n to designate them, respectively. I'll number events according to their order of occurrence. I'll number notifications as the events that triggered them. For example, the event $n2$ is the notification sent as a result of the detection of event $e1$. With multicast notifications, it is necessary to distinguish the various individual notifications sent following a single event, so I'll add a dot followed by a sequence number. For example, the notification $n1.2$ indicates the second multicast notification produced by $e1$.

Causal Order

Of all the ways in which notifications can be ordered, the most important one is *causal order*, which indicates that notifications reach their destinations ordered in the same way as the events that triggered them. When dealing with causality, it is important to understand what I mean by *event order*. Events in the real world can occur at any time. If a software system is waiting for certain conditions to occur, there is going to be a difference between the time a condition occurs and the time it is detected as an event. For example, assume three conditions occur in the order e1, e2, e3. If the system uses a loop to check for each event, it might detect e3 first, then e1 and e2, as shown in Figure 3-34.

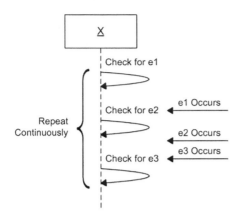

Figure 3-34. *Detecting events in the wrong order*

After X checks for e1, that event occurs, so it is missed. The same thing occurs for e2, so X misses detecting the first two events, because they occur after their presence is checked in the polling loop. Object X does catch the third one, though. A bit later, the loop repeats, and the first two events are detected. To avoid detecting events out of order, the system could avoid polling and rely on real-time hardware detection. Each time a condition occurs, it generates an interrupt, causing the appropriate interrupt service routine to be called to trigger the event detection. But you're still not out of the woods. While servicing the interrupt for the first event, other events can occur, so you must take care to ensure the capture of events that occur while another event is being handled. The details are beyond the scope of this book.

Notifications sent from a sender might trigger events in the receivers. If notifications are delivered using procedure calls, each notification could directly invoke the appropriate event-handler method, ensuring that the various handlers are invoked in the same order as the incoming notifications. But here again there is a potential problem regarding how to handle the incoming notifications that are concurrent, produced from callers in different processes or threads. For the purposes of this discussion, I'll consider the event order to be the order in which the events are detected, without worrying if the detected order reflects the real order.

A common ordering problem occurs with multicast event notifications. Consider the example in Figure 3-35.

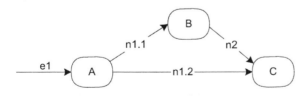

Figure 3-35. *A system using multicast notifications*

Object A detects event *e1* and consequently sends a multicast notification, first to B and then to C. Object B treats the arrival of *n1.1* as an event (which you can call *e2*), producing the notification *n2* sent to C. An important issue is this: Does *n1.2* reach C before or after *n2*? The diagram doesn't tell us. The order of arrival of n1.2 and n2 depends entirely on the implementation. The order is causal if n1.2 reaches C before n2, because the event e1 occurred before event e2, which triggers n2.

Problems might occur if notifications arrive in noncausal order, because the receiver might not be in the proper state to accommodate the notifications. Much work has been done regarding the preservation of causal order in notification delivery. One approach is to add timestamps to each notification in a system. The timestamps are obtained from a centralized timeserver. During debugging, timestamps allow you to see the relative ordering of notifications captured using a diagnostic tool. At run time, however, timestamps don't help as much as you might think. Using the example in Figure 3-35, assume Object C receives a timestamped notification n2 before n1.2. In all likelihood, C has no way of knowing that n1.2 is on its way, unless it waits for a certain amount of time, postponing the handling of n2. Systems aren't usually designed to linger after an event occurs, so the fact that n1.2 arrives with a timestamp doesn't help the system process n1.2 and n2 in causal order.

Another approach for ensuring the preservation of causal order is to add a number, taken from a monotonically increasing number sequence, to each notification sent in the system. A centralized number server would have to generate the numbers, so all notifications in a given system would use numbers obtained from the same server. Assume the notifications in Figure 3-35 were numbered as in Table 3-1.

Table 3-1. *Using Sequence Numbers to Order Notifications*

Notification	Sequence Number
n1.1	1
n1.2	2
n2	3

Any numbering scheme is possible, as long as it identifies the relative order between two arbitrary values. The scheme makes missing notifications obvious, but you still have a problem. When C receives e2 with sequence number 2, how does it know that a notification with a smaller sequence number (e1.2) is in transit? Without adding something to your scheme, C can't know.

An entirely different approach uses formal methods to prove or deduce causal order.[32] Rather than trying to determine causal order *a posteriori*, when notifications arrive, it can be more advantageous to design the delivery mechanism so that notifications are sent in the right order to begin with, shifting the ordering emphasis from the receivers to the senders.

Partial Order

In a system implemented with multiple parts, many parts can exchange notifications. From the perspective of each part (be it an object or component), it usually isn't important to know the order of incoming and outgoing notifications with respect to the timing of events in the entire system. What counts is the *partial order* of the notifications, which considers only a subset of all the notifications in the system—typically, those associated with a given part or its immediate neighborhoods. The concept of partial ordering was first introduced by Lamport[33] and is described in Figure 3-36.

---

32. Masoud Mansouri-Samani and Morris Sloman, "GEM: A Generalized Event Monitoring Language for Distributed Systems," *IEE/IOP/BCS Distributed Systems Engineering Journal*, June 1997.
    Christian Toinard, Gerard Florin, and C. Carrez, "A Formal Method to Prove Ordering Properties of Multicast Systems," *ACM SIGOPS Operating Systems Review*, October 1999.

33. Leslie Lamport, "Time, Clocks, and the Ordering of Events in a Distributed System," *Communications of the ACM*, July 1978.

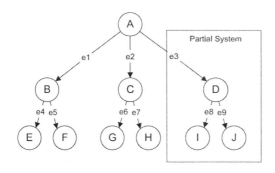

Figure 3-36. *Identifying a partial system on which a partial ordering of notifications can be applied*

From the point of view of D, the only ordering that matters regards notifications e3, e8, and e9. Using Lamport's notation, the partial order of two notifications p and q is described by an arrow, so p ➤ q indicates that p precedes q in the partial order. The notification p therefore has the potential to affect q. The partial order for notifications related to D might be e3 ➤ e8 ➤ e9.

Partial order is much easier to deal with in a distributed system, because each system can maintain its own internal clock and order events according to this clock. Using partial ordering, you adopt a centrist view of notifications: The only ones you care about are those in a given subset of the overall system. The typical subset includes one part, with its direct neighbors. There are two broad ways notifications can be partially ordered: depth-first and breadth-first. The following sections describe them in some detail.

Depth-First

With depth-first delivery, an event source must block when sending a notification and remain blocked until the recipient is through processing the notification. The recipient's processing might entail sending notifications to other components or even back to the original sender. Figure 3-37 shows an example.

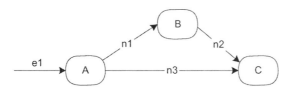

Figure 3-37. *A system using depth-first notification delivery order*

Following the detection of event *e1*, A sends a notification to B. While B is processing *n1*, A is blocked. When B gets the notification, it reacts by sending a notification *n2* to C. While C is processing n2, B is also blocked. Once C is through, B unblocks and returns control to A, which now can send the next notification *n3*. Figure 3-38 shows the system timing.

The delivery order might appear to be stable and predictable, but you must take care if event handlers can make reentrant calls back to the event source. If, after receiving n2, C sends a notification to A, A might not be prepared to handle it, since it is blocked waiting for B to finish handling n1. If A locks a resource before sending n1 and needs access to that resource to handle the callback from C, then the system deadlocks. A simple solution is to adopt the policy to never lock a resource while sending a notification.

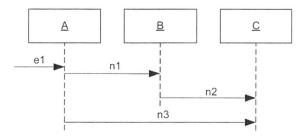

Figure 3-38. *The timing of depth-first delivery*

Depth-first delivery order is common in single-threaded systems where notification delivery is based on procedure calls, because procedure calls block naturally without requiring any extra work on the part of the system.

When dealing with multicast notifications, depth-first order can produce an ordering that isn't causal. This can happen both in single-threaded and multithreaded systems. For example, consider the diagram in Figure 3-39, in which an event e1 triggers notifications n1.1 and n1.2 that are sent to B and C, respectively.

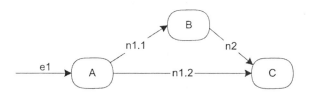

Figure 3-39. *A depth-first system using multicast notifications*

Figure 3-40 shows the timing sequence.

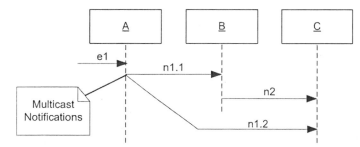

Figure 3-40. *The sequence of depth-first delivery with multicast notifications*

C receives the notification n2 before n1.2, because A blocks after sending n1.1. While A is blocked, B sends the notification n2 to C, making n1.2 and n2 reach C in noncausal order.

Even though depth-first delivery doesn't preserve causal order, it is used widely because it is easy to implement and reliable: The delivery order is fixed and guaranteed. The order is not a function of the delivery latency time. The only implementation requirement to support depth-first delivery is this: When sending a notification, the sender must block until the receiver has finished handling the notification.

Breadth-First

Breadth-first delivery is used primarily in concurrent systems. You can deliver notifications using either procedure calls or shared resources, but the delivery must be asynchronous. The event source must not block when sending a notification. Breadth-first delivery may provide causal ordering of notifications in some cases.

As an example, consider again the system in Figure 3-40. Assume that A multicasts n1.1 to B and then n1.2 to C in rapid succession. The idea here is that n1.1 and n1.2 are separated by a negligible amount of time. If this is true, n1.2 reaches C before B has a chance to handle n1.1 and send n2 to C. The notifications have the timing shown in Figure 3-41.

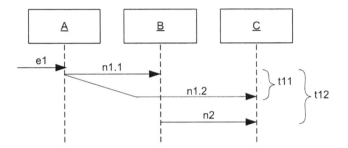

Figure 3-41. *Breadth-first delivery timing*

In order for A to be able to send n1.1 and n1.2 in a breadth-first manner, A must not block when sending n1.1. Right after sending n1.1, A sends n1.2. The underpinning assumption in breadth-first delivery is that t11 < t12, as shown in Figure 3-41. In some situations, due to uncontrollable delivery latencies, it might be possible to have t11 > t12. If this happens, n2 reaches C before n1.2, resulting in noncausal order.

Race Conditions

In the digital hardware world, the expression *race condition* is used to describe a situation in which signals in a synchronized (clock-driven) system reach their destinations in the wrong order, due to timing violations or asynchronous glitches. In event-based systems, the expression *race condition* denotes notifications that are delivered in an unpredictable order, based on variations in the latency of the delivery system, system load, and other imponderables.

Without explicit safeguards, breadth-first delivery can incur race conditions. To prevent a race condition in the system shown in Figure 3-41, B must not deliver n2 to C before A delivers n1.2 to C. If the values of t11 and t12 can vary, there could be situations in which C receives n2 before n1.2. The problem with race conditions is that they are hard to duplicate and therefore hard to detect and fix, but there are a number of workarounds.

One solution might be to rearrange the notification multicasting order. For example, if A sends n1.1 to C first and then n1.2 to B, you can be confident that C gets the notification from A before getting the one from B, regardless of B's timing, as shown in Figure 3-42.

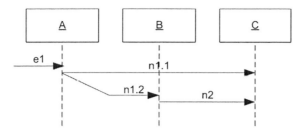

Figure 3-42. *Avoiding a race condition by reordering notifications*

A potential problem can occur if C sends a new notification n3 (not shown in the figure) to B while processing n1.1, because B might be expecting n1.2 before n3. The decision to rearrange the order in which A sends notifications to B and C solves one problem but creates potential others. A tempting idea might be to stamp notifications with a time or sequence number, as mentioned earlier. But this approach has at least two problems:

1. The burden of message ordering is put on receivers. This burden might be considered excessive in many systems.

2. To reorder out-of-order messages, the receiver often needs to buffer messages over a period of time.

With time and sequence stamps, the receiver can't always start processing a notification the moment it is received, because the receiver might not be able to instantaneously determine whether a message is in the expected order. For example, consider a notification system that numbers messages incrementally. Each time a receiver gets a message, it saves the message number. Say the number is 100. If the next message has the number 101, the receiver can process it immediately, because it is the next message created in the entire system. But what if the number is 102? The receiver might wait for a short while to see if 101 arrives late. This waiting period is called the *grace period* and is obviously related to the system's delivery latency. Once the grace period expires, the receiver can assume message 101 isn't going to arrive and can get to work on message 102. If message 101 arrives during the grace period, the receiver can immediately process messages 101 and 102 in succession. If message 101 arrives after the grace period expires, you have a problem.

Another solution to race conditions is to distribute the multicasting machinery throughout the system, as peer-to-peer architectures do. Instead of having A send two notifications, n1.1 and n1.2, it sends only the first one. In this notification, A adds extra information telling B to send n1.2 to C before doing anything else. The system is shown in Figure 3-43.

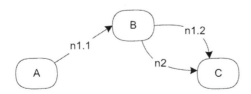

Figure 3-43. *Using a notification relay system to handle multicasting*

B acts as a relayer of notifications on behalf of A. The timing of this new arrangement is shown in Figure 3-44.

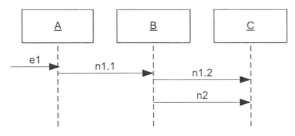

Figure 3-44. *The delivery timing of a notification relayer system*

The advantage of the relayer approach is that it is deterministically stable: C always gets n2 after n1.2, because B is in charge of sending both. Of course, B needs to wait for n1.2 to be delivered to C before sending n2, and can do so by using a synchronous delivery protocol.

Unfortunately, demons lurk in the shadows with the relayer approach. Not only does it require ad hoc coding in each component, but there is another problem: If n1.1 and n1.2 are sent in a *pull* mode to retrieve data from B and C, then A expects the response from n1.1 to contain both B's and C's data. B needs some extra intelligence regarding how to reconcile its own returned data with C's returned data. This extra intelligence is needed only because B is trying to solve a problem created by A (the requirement to use multicasting with n1).

Other solutions are possible for avoiding race conditions, but a completely generic solution that is easy to implement doesn't currently exist.

Total Order

When notifications cross process, machine, or network boundaries, you sometimes need to be extra careful with their ordering. Consider a system consisting of three concurrent processes, P1, P2, and P2, as shown in Figure 3-45.

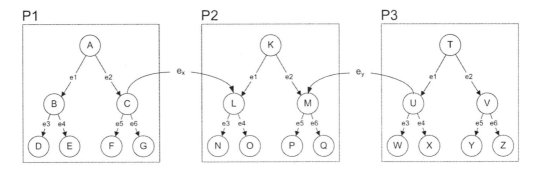

Figure 3-45. *A system consisting of three concurrent processes*

Inside each process, there are multitudes of partially ordered notifications. If a notification e_x goes from P1 to P2, and another e_y goes from P3 to P2, how do you determine the partial order of e_x and e_y from the point of view of P2? In other words, how do you know whether to deliver e_x or e_y first to P2? You need a way to map the timing of an item from one partial order space to another. The most common solution uses absolute timestamps. Somewhere in the system there must be a time server that maintains the global clock used for all timestamps. When an event occurs, it is recorded with a timestamp. When a notification is fired, it is tagged with the timestamp of the event that triggered it. There are problems with timestamps, as mentioned earlier, but those problems can be overcome.

Total order generally requires the presence of a centralized notification service that handles all notifications between processes. In large systems, multiple networked machines, arranged in some topology, can implement the service. When a notification arrives, it is delivered according to its global timestamp.

There are two important variants of total order, first identified by Wilhelm and Schiper:[34] strong and weak. Strong total order is used in systems with mobile nodes that can disconnect from the network and reconnect at a different physical network location. In these systems, strong total order guarantees that messages are delivered in the same order to all intended recipients, even in the presence of disconnections from the network and reconnections. Weak order applies to fixed systems, in which nodes aren't mobile and don't disconnect and reconnect to the network.

Summary

When designing an event-based system, choosing a delivery protocol is not necessarily a simple task. The protocol is a function of several things, including complexity, cost, and system architecture. People have a tendency to master one protocol, such as synchronous procedure call delivery, and then use it to death, applying it even in situations where better choices are available. In the real world, you'll find that one system parameter often outweighs others, narrowing your choices. For example, in real-time systems, speed usually trumps reliability. It would be out of the question to use a messaging service in such a system. In financial applications, reliability usually trumps speed. If the notification delivery system lost notifications, you'd have a hard time keeping customers. In some systems, security might trump both speed and reliability. To each his own. Hopefully this chapter has helped you choose the right protocol for each situation.

---

34. Uwe Wilhelm and Andre Schiper, "A Hierarchy of Totally Ordered Multicasts" (proceedings of the 14th IEEE Symposium on Reliable Distributed Systems, Bad Neuenahr, Germany, September 1995).

CHAPTER 4

■ ■ ■

Notification Payloads

Event notifications are used to indicate that something of interest to subscribers has occurred. As you saw in Chapter 3, you can deliver notifications in two basic ways: by using shared resources (SRs) and by using procedure calls (PCs). A notification should carry with it enough information to allow subscribers to use it with no further interaction with the sender. This information is what makes up the notification payload. If a notification doesn't provide the necessary information to the recipient, the latter might need to embark on a potentially expensive query back to the event source to get the missing information.

The Delivery Mechanism As a Constraint

In theory, any type of object can be passed in the payload of a notification, but the delivery mechanism (PC or SR) often introduces constraints on the payload content or handling. The most common restrictions are on payload type, size, and throughput, but there are others as well. With PC delivery, there is usually a marshaling process that can require a significant amount of processing to transfer payloads across process and machine boundaries.

In terms of payload types, the most commonly supported type is text. Virtually all notification and messaging systems in use today support text payloads. Many middleware systems support nontext types by encoding the payload contents as a base64-encoded string. Passing entire objects in the payload is allowed only with some delivery mechanisms. With byte-oriented delivery mechanisms that require the payload to be serialized, such as remote procedure calls, objects must be broken down into a stream of bytes on one end and rebuilt on the other.

The delivery mechanism often imposes constraints on the size of the payload. For example, if notifications are delivered by writing data to a shared memory area, the payload must fit in the available space. If it doesn't, the payload might have to be compressed or broken down into a series of smaller pieces sent separately.

Probably the most limiting constraint of all is throughput. You can't send information faster than the delivery channel can handle it. Large EBSs often use messaging middleware to manage and distribute the notifications sent between major subsystems. Such middleware uses network connections to send and receive notifications as messages. The network bandwidth is one bottleneck, but the messaging middleware itself also has its own limits on how fast it can handle, filter, and distribute incoming messages.

Delivery latency is another constraint. If the communication channel involves a satellite link, the latency might be hundreds of milliseconds. Even if the bandwidth is high, the round-trip time might be a serious problem. The round-trip time is the time it takes a message and its response to travel back and forth through a communication channel. Delivery mechanisms that rely on acknowledgments for each packet sent may be highly sensitive to the round-trip time. A system that runs fine during testing on a local area network might be completely unacceptable in the final production environment if it runs using a satellite link or in a wide-area network.

Another constraint is reliability. The delivery channel might not always be open, or it might have a fluctuating capacity dependent on other traffic through the channel. For example, an extreme case is represented by systems that operate at the bottom of the ocean. These systems sometimes use special modems to send signals through water, much like sonar pings. Water is an extremely uncooperative signal carrier, delivering sound through many different paths that are changing constantly. The various paths can have different lengths and transmission characteristics, so signals from one path might arrive out of sync with those of another path. Turbulence and water currents add additional problems, so a modem sending signals through water might have a bandwidth and latency that could change substantially from moment to moment. At times, the channel may be completely cut off.

Fortunately, most systems don't rely on submerged modems to deliver event notifications, but even computer networks can be flaky or unreliable. Anytime the sender and receiver run as separate processes (even if in the same box), some sort of communication mechanism is required, and no type of mechanism is infallible. Even if one were, there are no guarantees that the receiver will be available, willing, or able to receive what is sent.

Payload Size vs. Notification Frequency

Is it better to send lots of notifications with small payloads, or fewer notifications with larger payloads? There is no universal answer, of course. Each system has different requirements, in some cases favoring larger payloads and in other cases smaller ones. As a general rule, the higher the notification frequency, the smaller the payload should be, to avoid saturating the system's resources—be they memory, network bandwidth, or processor time.

Most EBSs consider notification frequency as a fundamental requirement. Starting from the notification frequency, the payload size is designed to avoid overloading the system. If the bandwidth of the notification delivery channel is insufficient to carry the load, something has got to give. Typical choices are

- The notification frequency
- The payload size
- The number of subscribers supported

If all these parameters are critical, then perhaps the system can use a different type of delivery mechanism that offers greater bandwidth. Some systems can reduce the notification frequency by filtering notifications. If subscriptions cover a very broad scope, many of the notifications sent to subscribers may be of little interest. By introducing filters on the event-source side, it is often possible to reduce notification traffic substantially and save precious resources on the sender and receiver ends. Another solution that might save bandwidth is to merge multiple notifications into a single one, as I'll discuss toward the end of this chapter in the section titled "Composite Payloads." A third solution might be to compress the notifications, but this adds a significant burden to the overall system.

Notifications Sent Using Shared Resources

Network connections are the most commonly used shared resources in notification delivery. With all network connections, the sender communicates with the receiver by sending messages. Software protocols like SOAP allow distributed systems to use network connections for remote procedure calls, making all the network communication details essentially transparent to application-level code on the sending and receiving ends.

In this chapter, network communication that uses RPCs will be considered a form of PC delivery, even though you know that a shared resource is involved at the lowest level. SR delivery is relegated to those cases in which only messages are sent over the wire, without any procedure call semantics on the sending or receiving ends. In those cases, messages need to provide all the information necessary in order for the recipient to know what to do with it.

Messages generally consist of a header and a body portion. The header provides information about the message, such as who the intended recipient is, what type of message is being sent, who the sender is, and so on. The header might contain information describing key aspects of the payload, such as the subject or an event identifier. The header might also contain properties related to QoS, such as delivery priority, timeout values, and what to do if a recipient is unavailable.

Message payloads are often strings, but a number of messaging middleware systems also support binary data in a variety of formats. To facilitate notification filtering, message headers sometimes use a *record* format, in which message properties appear at fixed offsets in the header. Chapter 5 describes the header and body formats of several popular commercial systems. Probably the most common form of header format involves the structure shown in Figure 4-1.

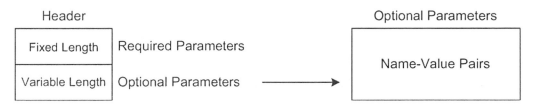

Figure 4-1. *The typical structure of message headers*

In many cases, the fixed-length header section consists of a series of values placed at specific offsets. The recipient and/or the notification delivery middleware must know the size, type, and location of the fields in this section, because the data is not self-describing. Because the sender and recipient must both know the structure and layout of the fixed header, the sender and recipient are logically coupled. Any changes to the record layout will affect both the sender and receiver.

The variable-length section usually contains a list of properties, as name-value pairs. Most systems allow only simple scalar data types, like numbers and characters, to be used. Header properties are a convenient place for storing event-classification data, used by the notification infrastructure for filtering purposes.

There are a number of variations to the message body, which is the true payload. In the simplest cases, the body contains one or more values. High-performance designs store predesignated values at specific offsets. Many systems use a name-value list for the message body, allowing properties to appear in arbitrary order. Some systems allow the body to contain binary information like images.

Systems supporting streaming data, such as audio or video, use a high-performance messaging design with very small headers and fixed-size message bodies that carry one or more frames of information. Frames are usually of fixed size. For audio, a frame might be a 100 ms slice of contiguous sound. For video, a frame may include one or more images in a sequence, compressed in various ways.

Most messaging systems allow objects to be passed from sender to receiver in serialized form, but many systems disallow binary data in the message body. The limitation might not be due to the middleware itself, but rather due to the use of specific Internet protocols to handle part of the delivery path. For example, the commonly used HTTP protocol doesn't support binary data directly. To render binary data suitable for transmission over HTTP and similar protocols, you must encode it somehow. The most common technique uses base64 encoding, which maps binary values into displayable characters. This type of encoding uses six bits of an eight-bit character to carry data, allowing each character to carry a base64 value. The encoding format is fairly efficient, using four eight-bit characters to carry three bytes of binary information.

When delivery is accomplished using lower-level protocols like TCP or UDP, binary data can be transferred directly, relieving the system of the need to encode and decode it during transmission.

Notifications Sent Using Procedure Calls

When a notification is delivered using a procedure call, the caller can supply any number of arguments to the receiver. These arguments represent the payload. In the simplest case, a notification might have no payload. Arguments should be included only if necessary to provide contextual information about the event that occurred. The sender should not try to guess what the recipient is going to do when handling the notification.

Several component platforms, including JavaBeans and the .NET Framework, use the convention of including in the parameter list a reference to the sender, of type Object, which is the root class of all classes. The idea is that the recipient may need to know something about the sender while processing the notification. While passing a sender reference in the parameter list is extremely common in notifications that travel between objects packaged in the same component, it may be problematic when firing events across component boundaries for these two reasons:

1. If the call goes over a network connection, the sender object will be serialized and sent over the wire. This is not only inefficient, but it has the side effect of requiring the sender class to be serializable. In most computing platforms, not all classes are serializable, because there is a certain amount of overhead in making a class serializable, requiring the implementation of specific interfaces.

2. To use the sender object passed in the notification, the recipient would need to know the type of the sender. The recipient would then need to perform a typecast in order to invoke properties and methods in the sender. The problem here is that the recipient component might have been developed with no knowledge of the sender. The addition of a typecast in the receiver's code would require the receiver to *know* the sender's type, thus introducing type coupling between the receiver and sender classes.

When looking at the way notifications are consumed in many systems with PC delivery, it appears that notification recipients usually don't care where a notification came from, often because the system is wired in such a way that a particular type of notification can arrive from only one place. The sender should include any information that the recipient is *likely* to need when handling a notification. What the recipient is *likely* to need should not depend on who the recipient is, but rather on the type and context of the event that occurred.

For example, if a user-interface Tree component fires an event when the user clicks on a node, the notification payload might provide information identifying the old node being deselected and the new node being selected. Event handlers are free to do what they want with this information, including nothing.

Payload data can also be used to specify event subtype information, allowing a centralized event-handling method to handle all incoming notifications. A good example of such a centralized handler is the WndProc handler of Windows applications. Windows sends all mouse, keyboard, and other events to an application by invoking the program's WndProc entry point. The call carries a number of parameters that allow the method to distinguish event types and process them correctly.

Should the Payload Be Immutable?

Some arguments might be passed by reference in a notification. For example, languages like C#, Java, and Delphi Object Pascal pass all objects by reference. Doing so opens the possibility of the notification handler modifying those objects, possibly causing undesirable side effects later in the caller.

There is no conceptual reason why the objects passed to event handlers should be immutable when dealing with unicast events. Such objects are merely the arguments of a procedure call. With multicast events, things are different. Why? Assume a notification carries a by-reference argument P and that the sender expects recipients to change the state of P while handling the notification. In a multicast situation, the first handler might set P to one state, but a subsequent handler might set P to a different state. After multicasting the notification to all subscribers, P would have the state set by the last event handler. The states saved by the previous handlers would be lost. Such a system would probably behave erratically, depending on the multicast order to subscribers.

As a practical example, consider a multicast notification used to allow subscribers to cancel a Closing operation that is about to take place. For the purposes of this discussion, it doesn't matter what the Closing operation is about to close. What counts is the fact that event subscribers are given the chance of vetoing an operation in progress by returning a certain value. The notification might have the following C# signature:

```
void OnClosing(ref bool doCancel);
```

An event handler would set doCancel to true to veto the Closing operation. If there were two handlers, one called after the other, the second handler would overwrite the first one's doCancel value.

When dealing with multicast events, you must take special precautions to safeguard any by-reference parameters set by notification handlers. Such parameters are passed by address, so the callee has the opportunity to replace the object being pointed at with a new one. Fortunately, the solution is simple and involves the use of *envelopes*, described at the end of this chapter. An envelope is nothing more than a holder of objects. Envelopes allow event handlers to put values into it, without disturbing values already in it. The envelope then can carry back to the sender all the values set by each event handler.

String-Based Payloads

It is very common to use payloads containing nothing but strings. After all, strings can be used to represent many different scalar values, like Booleans, numbers, and dates. When a payload uses only strings to encode scalar types, the notification recipient incurs no type coupling to custom types. For Internet-based distributed systems, UTF-8 character encoding is the most efficient for Western languages. UTF-16 is required for most Asian character sets.

As an example of a string-based payload, consider a component that might display book pages to the user. When the user changes the page, the component might fire an event. The payload could provide information about the selected page, such as the page title, page number, and document author, using the payload shown in Figure 4-2.

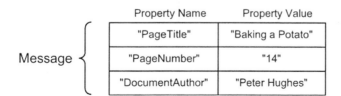

	Property Name	Property Value
	"PageTitle"	"Baking a Potato"
Message	"PageNumber"	"14"
	"DocumentAuthor"	"Peter Hughes"

Figure 4-2. *A message with a string payload*

If the payload contains variable-length property names and values, a header would need to describe the position of each payload element. There are several design variations that can improve performance. If the payload always contains the same properties and in the same order, which is a very common scenario, then the property names could be omitted. If the values have varying lengths, the payload might need a header to indicate where each property value begins. The header could help recipients access each value randomly.

If the property values have assigned a fixed size, a header isn't necessary. The receiver can access any property value randomly, because it knows the location of all the values. The drawback is that there may be some waste in the payload, because short values will have to be padded with filler characters to fill all the space allotted to the payload.

Another way to utilize string payloads is with structured content, such as XML documents. The notification payload will then contain a single string for each XML document carried. The receiver will have to parse the XML strings to extract the individual elements and attributes.

Record-Based Payloads

In a record-based payload, the payload carries fields at fixed positions in a record. The recipient must know the offset and semantics of each field. Figure 4-3 shows a simple record-based payload.

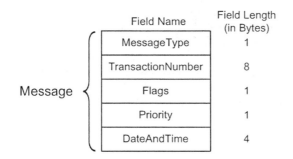

Figure 4-3. *Using a record layout for a notification payload*

A number of systems employ record-based payloads. Some allow variable-length records, where certain fields contain values that indicate the presence or absence of fields later in the record. Record-based payloads have two advantages over string-based payloads: speed and size. When processing a message, the handler doesn't have to search through a list of strings to find a given value. Recipients can access fixed-length records randomly, because the location of each field is known a priori.

Record-based payloads, because of their ease of processing, are well suited for filtering in large EBSs. In some Internet-scale implementations, the notification infrastructure maintains a list of subscriber filters that are based on easily accessible fields in the payload. Consider a payload that contains world news. The payload might use a record layout to facilitate content-based filtering. As an example, consider the payload in Figure 4-4.

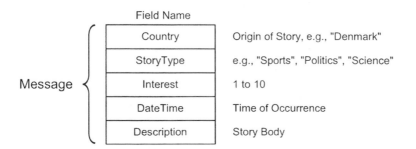

Figure 4-4. *Using a record layout to facilitate content-based filtering*

You could create a subscription filter to efficiently reject stories not conforming to some criteria. The filtering program would not have to scan record fields not included in the filter statement. Assume a filter statement were defined using a SQL-like syntax as follows:

```
(Country = 'France') and (StoryType = 'Science')
```

The filtering program would read the Country and StoryType fields to determine whether to reject a notification or not. The record fields basically define an n-dimensional space. A payload's coordinates in that space are determined by its field values. A problem with record-based payloads is that the space they define is generally domain-specific. If you want to use the previous record structure to handle notifications related to a different domain, such as weather conditions, you would either have to find a way to utilize the existing fields in a weather-compatible manner, or you would need to add additional fields, such as WindDirection, AirTemperature, and so on.

Object-Based Payloads

When delivering notifications with local procedure calls, it is common to pass objects in the payload. The objects provide information to the recipients about the nature of the event that occurred. In JavaBeans, the event-listener design pattern specifies that the event source pass an Event object as an argument to the listener. Types derived from the built-in class Event are typically used, such as ActionEvent or ItemEvent. In the .NET Framework, the built-in event model uses a different convention, borrowed from Delphi: The sender includes in the argument list a reference to itself. The reference is of type Object, which is the root of the .NET Common Type System class hierarchy. Some built-in .NET event-handler signatures have a number of objects, of various types, in the argument list.

Regardless of the component platform and language used, user-defined types should be avoided in notification payloads, because including them can introduce type coupling. Let's see how. Let T1 be the type of an event source class and T2 be the type of a class containing the event-handler code. Let MyType be a user-defined type passed as an argument in a PC notification from T1 to T2. Depending on how T1 and T2 are packaged, with respect to MyType, four different coupling scenarios can occur, as shown in the coupling diagrams in Figure 4-5, Figure 4-6, Figure 4-7, and Figure 4-8.

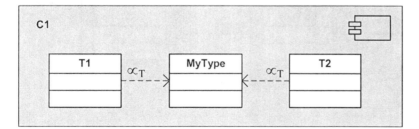

Figure 4-5. *Coupling to MyType, when T1 and T2 are in the same component*

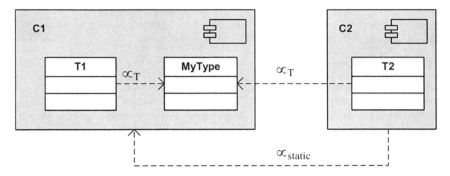

Figure 4-6. *Coupling to MyType, when T1 is packaged with MyType, but not with T2*

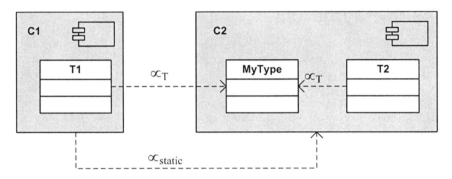

Figure 4-7. *Coupling to MyType, when T2 is packaged with MyType, but not with T1*

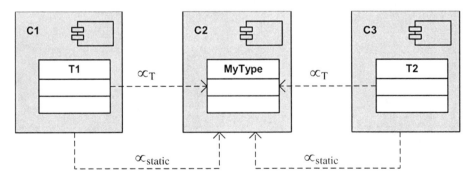

Figure 4-8. *Coupling to MyType when T1, T2, and MyType are all in different components*

In the first case, there is type coupling, but no intercomponent coupling. This case doesn't make the code more difficult to test, nor does it introduce compile-time problems, because all the types are in the same place.

In all but the first case, there is intercomponent coupling. This coupling is static in nature, so T1 and T2 invariably require MyType to be present at compile time. The only safe way to avoid type coupling is to avoid using user-defined types as arguments in notification payloads. The alternative is to use built-in platform types, such as integers, Booleans, and strings.

The .NET convention of including a sender reference in the payload doesn't automatically couple the recipient to the sender, because the recipient gets a generic reference to an `Object`. The recipient would become coupled to the sender if the recipient needed to access properties or methods of the sender. To do so, the recipient would typically contain code to typecast the `Object` argument into the sender's type, causing type coupling.

Obvents[1] are an example of a system using object-based payloads in a distributed environment. Obvents are the objects used as arguments in a PC-based notification delivery system, and are conceptually similar to the `Event` arguments used in the JavaBeans event-listener model. Using Obvents, subscribers subscribe to publishers by specifying the type of Obvent they're interested in, which functions as a sort of subscription filter.

Another way to use objects in the payload is to support what might be called *notification forwarding* or *relaying*, shown in Figure 4-9.

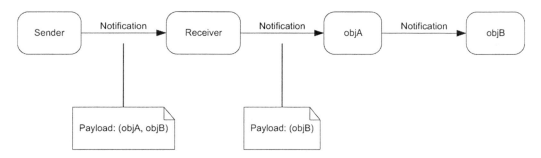

Figure 4-9. *Using the payload to affect delivery daisy-chaining*

Notification forwarding achieves the effect of a multicast, as described in Chapter 3. The idea is for the sender to delegate to receivers the task of forwarding the notification to other receivers. The payload contains the list of intended recipients of the notification, in addition to regular arguments. To support notification forwarding, the `Sender` object must know which destinations the `Receiver` object is able to forward notifications to.

In Figure 4-9, `Sender` sends a notification with a payload referencing two objects, `objA` and `objB`. When `Receiver` gets the notification, it discovers that the notification should be forwarded to `objA`. `Receiver` then removes `objA` from the payload and forwards the notification to `objA`, which repeats the process and forwards the notification to `objB`. Obviously, you can use this technique for any number of forwardees. Intermediate forwarding recipients can choose to handle the notification before or after forwarding it, resulting in the two timing diagrams shown in Figure 4-10.

In Figure 4-10, the assumption is that all notifications are delivered with blocking procedure calls. The dotted lines represent return of execution control from the callees. Each forwarding recipient has control over what other objects a notification is sent to. An intermediate recipient might add additional forwardees to the payload or remove some already present. Care must be taken to prevent infinite loops in the delivery path. In the previous example, such a case would occur if `objB` added itself to the forwarding list.

1. Patrick Th. Eugster, Rachid Guerraoui, and Christian Heide Damm, "On Objects and Events" (proceedings of the Conference on Object-Oriented Programming, Systems, Languages, and Applications (OOPSLA), Tampa Bay, FL, October 2001).

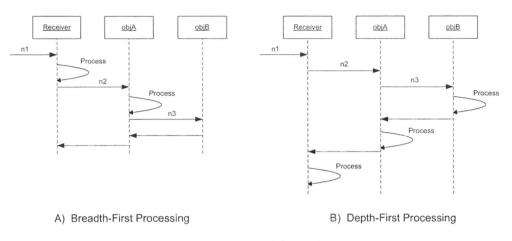

A) Breadth-First Processing   B) Depth-First Processing

Figure 4-10. *Achieving different processing orders with forwarding*

Payload Marshaling

Payload marshaling is required when the sender and receiver of a notification are in different process spaces. Marshaling entails organizing and converting the data types defined in one process space for use in another. Marshaling is a two-step affair: Data is packaged up on the sender's side and unpackaged on the receiver's side. (Regarding the spelling of the word *marshaling*, in this book I use the American version with one 'l'.)

Marshaling is sometimes confused with serialization. The two are related, but distinct. Serialization is the process of converting a data structure into a sequence of bytes. What those bytes are used for may have nothing to do with marshaling. Deserialization is the reverse process of reconstituting a data structure from a sequence of bytes. Data structures must be serialized before they can be written to a stream or sent over a network connection. Since marshaling frequently involves sending data over a serial connection as arguments of a procedure call, serialization is usually involved. A situation in which marshaling probably wouldn't use serialization is when sending arguments across a process boundary using shared memory.

Marshaling scalar data types, like integers, Booleans, and characters, is straightforward. For example, if a value is Boolean, marshaling in most cases will transfer the value packaged as a single byte. If the value is multibyte, such as a 32-bit integer or a 16-bit Unicode character, serialization will need to take place to produce a byte sequence. You can order the sequence in two ways: in *little-endian* or *big-endian* format. Little endian has bytes ordered from least to most significant. Big endian has bytes ordered from most to least significant. Which endian format is adopted depends typically on a machine's microprocessor. For example, Intel x86 and compatible processors use little-endian format, while Motorola 68xxx and IBM PowerPC processors use big-endian format.

Arrays of scalar data types are a bit more complicated to marshal. Things get a lot more complicated anytime pointers are involved, and most OO languages use pointers extensively. If you don't understand the nuances of marshaling when designing the payload of a notification, the system might incur a significant marshaling performance hit.

Marshaling By-Value Payloads

The simplest way to pass an argument in a procedure call is by value: The caller sends the value to the callee. What the callee does to the value isn't visible to the caller after the callee returns control. The following is a C# example:

```
int x = 5;
Callee callee = new Callee();
callee.DoSomething(x);
```

Assume the Callee object is in a different process space from the Caller object, so that marshaling is required. When the method Callee.DoSomething is invoked, the value of the integer x is marshaled across the process boundary into the callee's space, so there are two separate copies of the value 5: one in the caller's space and one in the callee's. The callee can only change the one in its own space. When the call returns, the caller will find the local x integer has the same value it had before invoking the callee.

Marshaling By-Reference Payloads

An argument is passed *by reference* in a procedure call if its address, rather than its value, is passed. When passing an argument by reference across a process boundary, the marshaling process can't simply pass a pointer to the callee, because pointers are address-space-dependent. Passing by reference requires a certain amount of work, because the marshaling process has to transfer copies of objects in the caller's address space over to the callee's address space. There are varying levels of complexity with by-reference arguments, depending on exactly what happens to the pointers involved. Let's look at a simple case, in which the caller passes a pointer to a simple object, using C# code:

```
Object obj = new Object();
Callee callee = new Callee();
callee.DoSomething(obj);
```

C# and many other OO languages pass objects by reference, so the calling statement doesn't need any special keywords. The marshaling process needs to transfer a copy of obj to the callee. On the callee side, a new Object instance is created with the same state as the original obj in the caller's space. In the callee's space, the marshaling process then creates a pointer that references the newly created object and then passes this pointer to the callee's DoSomething method. Figure 4-11 shows the memory layout of the caller and callee address spaces.

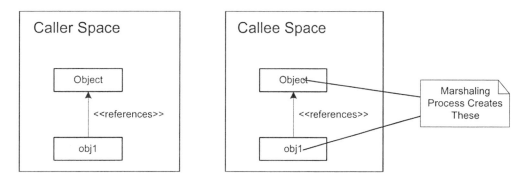

Figure 4-11. *Marshaling objects passed by reference*

Changes to obj on the callee's side are propagated back to the caller when the call completes. This marshaling process involves serializing the callee's object and sending it back to the caller, then updating the caller's object with the values of the deserialized callee object.

In OMG IDL, this kind of call uses an [in] modifier on the obj argument. Changes to the pointer are not allowed to propagate back to the caller. For example, if the callee changes its obj pointer to reference a new object, the caller's obj pointer will not be changed. When Callee.DoSomething ends, the marshaling process will realize that the callee changed its obj pointer, so the caller and callee will no longer reference the same object. The marshaling process will then leave the caller's object intact.

In order for the changes made to the obj pointer to be propagated back to the caller, the C# keyword ref is required in the call:

```
callee.DoSomething(ref obj);
```

In OMG IDL, this kind of call uses an [in, out] modifier on the obj argument. If the callee doesn't make any changes to its version of the obj pointer, the marshaling process will act the same way as before. If the pointer is changed to point to a new object in the callee's address space, when Callee.DoSomething returns, the marshaling process will create a new object in the caller's space, initialize it with the callee's deserialized object, and then adjust the caller's pointer to reference this new object.

Let's look at a C# example. Say you have an object of class A that needs to send a notification to a subscriber of class B, located in a different process space. The notification uses PC delivery, and the event handler has the following signature:

```
void GetEmployeeInfo(Employee theEmployee);
```

The signature is simple, not involving explicit use of pointers. Under the covers, you know that pointers are present, because objects are always passed by reference in C#, as well as in most other OO languages. Let the Employee class contain just two fields, as shown in Figure 4-12.

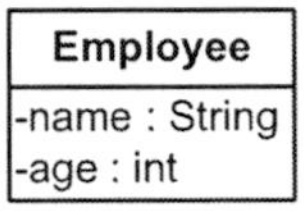

```
┌─────────────────┐
│    Employee     │
├─────────────────┤
│ -name : String  │
│ -age : int      │
└─────────────────┘
```

Figure 4-12. *A simple class containing a scalar field and a class field*

Don't worry about the methods defined in Employee. Marshaling involves the transfer of an object's data, never its methods. Listing 4-1 shows a simple implementation of an event source that sends an object in the notification payload.

Listing 4-1. *A C# Event Source That Uses an Object in the Notification Payload*

```csharp
public class A
{
  public void ProcessEmployee(Employee theEmployee)
  {
    FireGetEmployeeInfo(theEmployee);
  }

  public delegate void GetEmployeeInfoHandler(Employee theEmployee);
  public event GetEmployeeInfoHandler OnGetEmployeeInfo;
  public void FireGetEmployeeInfo(Employee theEmployee)
  {
    if (OnGetEmployeeInfo != null)
      OnGetEmployeeInfo(theEmployee);
  }
}
```

Class A uses a delegate called OnGetEmployeeInfo to fire events when it needs information about an employee. C# delegates are simply pointers to methods. Let's assume that OnGetEmployeeInfo is initialized at run time to point to the method GetEmployeeInfo in class B, shown in Listing 4-2.

Listing 4-2. *A C# Event Handler That Modifies an Object in the Notification Payload*

```csharp
public class B
{
  public void GetEmployeeInfo(Employee theEmployee)
  {
    if (theEmployee.name == "Mike")
      theEmployee.age = 32;
    else
      theEmployee.age = 21;
  }
}
```

Let `objA` and `objB` be instances of classes `A` and `B`, respectively. When `objA` fires the `OnGetEmployeeInfo` event, an `Employee` object already exists in `objA`'s space. The `Employee` object contains a reference to a `String` object, also located in `objA`'s space. The `Employee` age field is an `int` field, involving no objects. The marshaling process transfers the `Employee` object, along with the associated `String` object for the employee's name, into `objB`'s space. The process involves creating new `Employee` and `String` objects initialized to match the objects in `objA`'s space. Upon entry into `B.GetEmployeeInfo`, the `Employee` argument references the new `Employee` object created in `objB`'s space. While handling the event, `objB` changes the value of the `Employee` fields, then returns. At this point, the marshaling process transfers the new `Employee` and `String` objects from `objB`'s space back to `objA`'s space. The values contained in the returned objects are used to update the corresponding values of the `Employee` and `String` objects in `objA`'s space. When the call completes, `objA` finds it local `Employee` object updated.

When passing an argument by reference, the marshaler sometimes might transfer a large number of objects unexpectedly. The reason is that any objects referenced directly or indirectly by the original object also need to be reconstituted on the callee's side. In a worst-case scenario, passing a single argument by reference could result in all the objects in the caller's space being transferred into the callee's space. To minimize the marshaling overhead, it is important to avoid passing objects if they point to large numbers of objects directly or indirectly.

Payloads for Fetching Data: Envelopes

In the last section, you saw that objects are passed by reference when used as arguments in a procedure call. If the callee makes any changes to fields of such objects, the changes will be visible to the caller once the method returns. You can exploit this fact to allow notification senders to fetch data from notification receivers. For example, an instance of the `Employee` class, described in the previous section, allows an event source to retrieve `name` and `age` values from a subscriber. The problem with a class like `Employee` is that it isn't designed to carry multiple values for each property. An employee can have only one name and age.

What if you want to fire a multicast notification to retrieve a series of results from subscribers? You need some sort of collection to hold all the returned values. If you pass this collection as the payload of a notification, the subscribers could add values to the collection by calling an `Add` method. Each subscriber could add a new value. Once all subscribers were notified, the notification sender could inspect all the values in the collection. A problem with this simple approach is that a malicious notification handler might call the collection's `Clear` method to wipe out the results added by other subscribers. To overcome this drawback, you can use a data structure called an *envelope*. The envelope concept has been around for a while, albeit under different names, such as collector object.[2]

---

2. Clemens Szyperski, *Component Software: Beyond Object-Oriented Programming* (Boston: Addison-Wesley Professional, 2002).

An envelope manages an internal collection, allowing items to only be added, not removed. I'll use a class called Envelope for the implementation. A simple implementation is shown in Figure 4-13.

Figure 4-13. *An Envelope class*

The Contents property doesn't return the privately managed collection, but rather a copy. Changes to this copy do not affect the items in the Envelope's internal collection. Listing 4-3 shows a simple C# implementation of the Envelope class.

Listing 4-3. *A Simple Envelope Implemented in C#*

```
public class Envelope
{
  ArrayList contents = new ArrayList();

  public void Add(Object theObject)
  {
    contents.Add(theObject);
  }

  public Object[] Contents
  {
    get
    {
      // return a copy of the internal contents
      return contents.ToArray(typeof(Object)) as Object[];
    }
  }
}
```

When sending a notification, the sender uses the envelope as the payload. Listing 4-4 shows a simple implementation of the sender.

Listing 4-4. *A C# Event Source That Uses an Envelope in the Notification Payload*

```
public class Sender
{
  public void ProcessEmployees()
  {
    Object[] employees = FireGetEmployees();
    if (employees == null)
      return;

    foreach (Object obj in employees)
    {
      // process employee
    }
  }
```

```
public delegate void GetEmployeesHandler(Envelope theEnvelope);
public event GetEmployeesHandler OnGetEmployees;
public object[] FireGetEmployees()
{
  if (OnGetEmployees == null)
    return null;

  Envelope envelope = new Envelope();
  OnGetEmployees(envelope);
  return envelope.Contents;
}
}
```

In many situations, it may be convenient to strongly type the contents of an envelope. The Add and Contents fields would then be defined with a specific type, such as String or Employee. You can also use an envelope to carry information from the event source to the event handlers. You can make the envelope values read-only to prevent subscribers from inadvertently or maliciously changing the incoming envelope contents. You can set the values using arguments passed to the Envelope constructor. Listing 4-5 shows an Envelope with a read-only field called UserId. The field UserId is read-only, because it has a getter method but not a setter method.

Listing 4-5. *An Envelope Class That Exposes a Read-Only Property to Notification Handlers*

```
public class Envelope1
{

  // ...
  private string userId;
  public string UserId
  {
    get {return userId;}
  }

  public Envelope1(string theUserId)
  {
    userId = theUserId;
  }
}
```

The envelopes shown thus far allow subscribers to inspect the values added by other subscribers. Listing 4-6 shows an envelope variant that prevents this.

Listing 4-6. *An Envelope That Prevents Subscribers from Seeing Each Other's Returned Values*

```
public class SecureEnvelope
{
  private ArrayList contents;

  public void Add(Object theObject)
  {
    contents.Add(theObject);
  }
```

```
   public SecureEnvelope(ArrayList theArrayList)
   {
     contents = theArrayList;
   }
}
```

The SecureEnvelope class no longer exposes its internal collection to subscribers, or anyone else, for that matter. The event source is expected to create the collection and pass it to the SecureEnvelope constructor. After all subscribers are notified, the event source can then inspect the items in the ArrayList.

Composite Payloads

Until now, I have discussed what might be called *simple* payloads. For each event detected, the notification payload contains information about that event. An appealing idea is the use of *composite* payloads, which can hold the data related to multiple events. Composite payloads should not be confused with composite events, such as those available in the Cambridge Event Architecture.[3] Composite events trigger a notification when a certain sequence of simple events is detected. Composite payloads are a stratagem to increase the performance of a system whose notification traffic exceeds the available bandwidth. When events are detected faster than notifications can be sent, the sender will need to buffer notifications until the communication channel has processed the traffic in progress. Once the channel becomes available again, the sender can send multiple notifications obtained from the queue. Composite payloads can contain the following:

1. Sequences of a single type of notification payload
2. Sequences of any type of notification payload

In the first case, the sender searches the queue of pending notifications and groups together all those of a given kind. In the second case, all the pending notifications are grouped together.

A drawback of the first technique is that notifications might be delivered in noncausal order. For example, assume the sender's queue of pending notifications contains four notifications, related to the event sequence T1, T2, T1, T2. The first composite payload carries the payloads for the first and second T1 payloads. The second composite payload carries the payloads for the first and second T2 payloads. The arrival sequence of the payloads is T1, T1, T2, T2, which is obviously different from the original order.

The second technique does maintain causal ordering but is more expensive to implement, because each payload in the composite payload must be tagged with information defining the event it relates to. For example, using a type-based delivery model, each payload would be tagged with the event type.

A variation on the theme of composite payloads involves payload *coalescing*. This technique applies to notifications to which the notion of *composition* applies. Two notifications N1 and N2 can be composed if a notification N3 has the same effect as N1 and N2. Composition doesn't necessarily require the order of N1 and N2 to be maintained in N3. N3, in fact, may contain no trace of the original notifications N1 and N2.

---

3. Jean Bacon, Ken Moody, John Bates, Richard Hayton, Chaoying Ma, Andrew McNeil, Oliver Seidel, and Mark Spiteri, "Generic Support for Distributed Applications," *IEEE Computer*, March 2000.

As an example of notification composition, consider the way GUI operating systems use Paint notifications to tell application programs which areas of the screen need to be repainted. The Paint payload typically contains a `Rectangle` argument that encloses stale portions of the screen. If a client program, at some point, quickly requests the update of several different parts of the screen, the OS will need to send multiple Paint notifications to the application. To increase performance and reduce possible screen flicker caused by screen repainting, the OS can coalesce multiple Paint events together, combining the paint areas of each event into a larger area. As a result, the application might receive just a single Paint notification, indicating an area that encloses all the smaller areas that need updating.

Summary

Event notifications are the lifeblood of an event-based system, so it is very important to choose the right type of delivery mechanism and payload. When notifications cross process boundaries, you have to be really careful about what kind of information is in the payload, because expensive marshaling might be involved. A common solution is to make use of lightweight business objects in notification payloads. These lightweight objects are sculpted carefully to exclude references to unnecessary user-defined types. Such lightweight objects can be passed across process boundaries with a minimum of overhead.

CHAPTER 5

■■■

A Survey of Commercial Systems

During the 1990s, software companies geared to the enterprise jumped onto the EBS bandwagon, developing a myriad of messaging and notification systems. However, one problem when approaching these systems is how to determine which is best for a particular situation. Vendors don't always use a common terminology when describing their products, and the degrees of scalability, flexibility, and power of one system vs. another are difficult to ascertain in an objective context. Product literature is often deceiving and doesn't give a bird's-eye view of the design choices made, architectures adopted, and ensuing constraints.

In this chapter, I'll describe some of the most important commercial systems in use today. The material presented here focuses only on system architecture and is not intended to promote specific products. Moreover, due to space limitations, I won't survey every commercial product in existence or include systems developed only for research purposes.

For my survey, I'll divide commercial EBSs into two broad categories: direct- and indirect-delivery systems. In the former, event sources are connected directly with the event targets. In the latter, a middleware system handles the distribution of event notifications. Peer-to-peer systems, such as TIBCO Rendezvous, fall somewhere between direct and indirect and are included as indirect systems.

There is a further subdivision of indirect systems. The middleware systems used in indirect-delivery systems come in two basic varieties: those that support a publish-subscribe style, and those that support a point-to-point (PTP) style. With the former, the publisher is completely unaware of subscribers. It fires events to the middleware, which then dispatches notifications to the appropriate destinations. With the latter, the sender uses the middleware like a post office, which acts simply as a message relayer, forwarding messages to one or more recipients. In PTP systems, the sender is fully aware of the existence of the receivers. It is in fact the sender that specifies explicitly which receiver or receivers a message is directed to.

Direct-Delivery Systems

In a direct-delivery EBS, there are no middlemen involved in delivering notifications. The event publisher is linked directly with the event subscribers, according to the simple model shown in Figure 5-1.

Figure 5-1. *The direct-delivery model*

Direct-delivery systems are relatively simple to build, given the absence of a notification dispatching, filtering, and routing infrastructure. The publisher talks directly to each of its subscribers, handling notification dispatching itself. Direct delivery is commonly used to interconnect objects running in the same thread or process space. In publish-subscribe systems, it is common for the subscriber to call a method of the publisher to register a subscription, requiring the subscriber to be coupled to some degree to the publisher or one of its interfaces. There are ways to decouple the subscriber by relying on a separate *binder* component to register subscriptions on behalf of the subscriber, as shown in the coupling diagram in Figure 5-2.

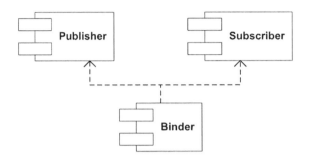

Figure 5-2. *Using a binder to avoid coupling between subscriber and publisher*

The binder takes no part in the handling of notifications from publisher to subscriber. It registers the subscriber at setup time and then steps out of the way. Direct-delivery systems are generally based on procedure call (PC) delivery, but only because PCs are the most natural way to connect objects running in the same process space. There is nothing that conceptually prevents a direct-delivery system from using shared resource (SR) notifications. In the following sections, I'll describe some of the direct-delivery systems supported by the most popular component models.

.NET

The Microsoft .NET Framework[1] is a managed environment, consisting of a large set of classes and frameworks that support a wide spectrum of programming scenarios. The Framework runs code in an interpreted mode inside a virtual machine sandbox, much like Java. The Framework defines a component model based on *assemblies*, which are deployable executable files containing a manifest and one or more classes. The manifest contains metadata, describing the contents of an assembly. Classes also contain metadata, supporting tool-based introspection and tool-assisted composition of .NET classes.

The .NET Framework supports two types of event-delivery models, both of which are based on procedure calls: untyped object calls and typed object calls. The models differ in the way procedure calls are made. Although the two models have the same goal (calling a method), they are philosophically quite different, as I'll show in the next few sections.

Untyped Object Calls, Using Delegates and Events

The Microsoft .NET Framework, or more precisely, the framework's *Common Type System*, supports untyped object calls using a native data type representing a reference to a method. This data type is called a *delegate*, and it allows calls to be made directly to a method, bypassing any interfaces of the

---

1. "Inside the .NET Framework," http://msdn.microsoft.com/library/default.asp?url=/library/en-us/cpguide/html/cpconinsidenetframework.asp.

class to which the method belongs. .NET delegates are similar to member function pointers used in C++, and allow the caller to call a method of an object whose type is completely unknown at compile time. While C++ function pointers can only point to a single function, .NET delegates support multicasting and internally hold an *invocation list* of method references. When a call is made through a delegate, the methods referenced are called in their order of appearance in the invocation list.

In the .NET literature, the originator of an event is called the event source. The method invoked is called the handler. The object to which the handler belongs is called the event target. Figure 5-3 shows an example of a .NET delegate at compile time and run time.

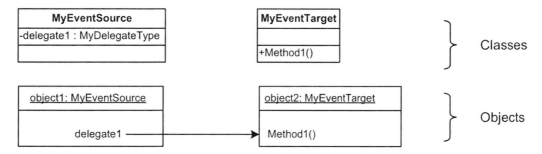

Figure 5-3. *Using a .NET delegate to reference a target method directly*

MyDelegateType is a delegate declared to reference a method having a given signature. At run time, object1 uses delegate1 to reference Method1 of object2. Listing 5-1 shows a C# implementation. Listing 5-2 shows a VB .NET implementation.

Listing 5-1. *A Simple C# Event Source and Target*

```
public class MyEventSource
{
  public delegate void MyDelegateType( );
  public MyDelegateType delegate1;

  public void FireDelegate1( )
  {
    if (delegate1 != null)
      delegate1();
  }
}

public class MyEventTarget
{
  public void MyMethod( ) { }
}
```

Listing 5-2. *A Simple VB .NET Event Source and Target*

```
Public Class MyEventSource
  Public Delegate Sub MyDelegateType( )
  Public delegate1 As MyDelegateType
```

```
  Public Sub FireDelegate1( )
    If Not delegate1 Is Nothing Then
      delegate1( )
    End If
  End Sub
End Class

Public Class MyEventTarget
  Public Sub MyMethod( )
  End Sub
End Class
```

In order to use the delegate, it must point at a method of some object. The method must have the same signature as the one expected by the delegate. The process of setting a delegate to point to a handler method is called *binding*. Binding is always a run-time affair. Listing 5-3 shows the binding process in C#. Listing 5-4 shows the process in VB .NET.

Listing 5-3. *Binding a Delegate to an Event Target, Using C#*

```
// create source and target
MyEventSource object1 = new MyEventSource( );
MyEventTarget object2 = new MyEventTarget( );

// bind event source to target
object1.delegate1 = new MyEventSource.MyDelegateType(object2.MyMethod);

// fire event to target
object1.FireDelegate1( );
```

Listing 5-4. *Binding a Delegate to an Event Target, Using VB .NET*

```
'create source and target
Dim object1 As New MyEventSource
Dim object2 As New MyEventTarget

'bind event source to target
object1.delegate1 = AddressOf object2.MyMethod

' fire event to target
object1.FireDelegate1( )
```

Once delegate1 is bound to a target, object1 can make calls through the delegate. C# delegates are initialized by using the = or += operators. The former sets the delegate to point exclusively at a given method. VB .NET delegates are bound using the = operator.

■**Note** Delegates support multicasting and can be defined for methods with any signature. In particular, you can use delegates with methods that have a return value. You can set the return value only with unicast delegates, which are delegates whose invocation list has only a single method reference.

In C#, you can use the += operator to bind a delegate to a new handler, without removing other handlers already in the delegate's invocation list. Similarly, you can use the -= operator to remove a method reference from a delegate. Here are a couple C# examples:

```
object1.delegate1 = new EventSourceDelegates.MyDelegateType(obj2.Method1);
object1.delegate1 += new EventSourceDelegates.MyDelegateType(obj3.Method2);
```

The first statement removes any previously bound methods from delegate1 and then adds a reference to obj2.Method1. The second statement adds an additional reference to obj3.Method2. If object1 then makes a call through delegate1, obj2.Method1 and obj3.Method2 will be called, in that order. To wipe out the entire invocation list of a C# delegate, just assign a null to it like this:

```
object1.delegate1 = null;
```

In VB .NET, delegates don't support += and -= operators. Instead, you must use one of the static methods exposed by the standard .NET Delegate class. The equivalent of the += operator is the Delegate.Combine method, which takes a list of delegates, concatenates them, and returns a new delegate encapsulating the concatenated delegates. Here's an example:

```
object1.delegate1 = [Delegate].Combine(object1.delegate1, object2.delegate2)
```

If a delegate contains a concatenated list of delegates, you can remove specific delegates from the list using the Delegate.Remove method like this:

```
object1.delegate1 = [Delegate].Remove(object1.delegate1, object2.delegate2)
```

You can completely wipe out the invocation list of a VB .NET delegate by setting it to Nothing, like this:

```
object1.delegate1 = Nothing;
```

Protecting the Invocation List with Events

Having a class expose a delegate field to the outside world can be risky, because a careless binder could accidentally add a handler using the = operator, thus wiping out previously registered handlers. To protect the delegate's invocation list, the .NET Framework defines an event keyword, which is used to declare a field that manages a list of delegates internally. .NET event fields only let you add or remove handlers. There is no direct way to clear the list of delegates managed by an event field. Events and delegates have similar semantics, in the sense that you can use both to make untyped object calls, but C# and VB .NET differ somewhat at the implementation level, so I'll discuss events separately for each language.

C# Events C# delegates expose the operators =, +=, and -= to assign, add, and remove handlers from a delegate field. C# events only support the operators += and -=. To declare a C# event, you must use a delegate type like this:

```
public delegate void MyEventHandler( );   // declare a delegate
public event MyEventHandler OnMyEvent;  // declare an event field
```

You can change the event source class in Listing 5-1 to expose an event field instead of a delegate field, as shown in Listing 5-5.

Listing 5-5. *A C# Event Source Using Events*

```
public class MyEventSource
{
  public MyEventSource ( ) { }

  public delegate void MyEventHandler( );
  public event MyEventHandler OnMyEvent;  // declare an event field
```

```
  public void FireMyEvent( )
  {
    if (OnMyEvent != null)        // use the event field
      OnMyEvent( );
  }
}
```

Apart from the fact that events preclude the use of the assignment operator, events and delegates are similar. Listing 5-6 shows how an event field is bound to an event handler.

Listing 5-6. *Binding an Event Field to an Event Target, Using C#*

```
// create source and target
MyEventSource object1 = new MyEventSource( );
MyEventTarget object2 = new MyEventTarget( );

// bind event source to target
object1.OnMyEvent += new MyEventSource.MyEventHandler(object2.MyMethod);

// fire event to handler
object1.FireMyEvent( );
```

VB .NET Events VB .NET has two ways to declare events: the hard way and the easy way. The hard way relies on declaring a delegate and then using that delegate to declare an Event field. C# uses this approach. In VB .NET, the code looks like this:

```
Public Delegate Sub MyDelegateType( )
Public Event Event1 As MyDelegateType
```

The easy way bypasses the declaration of the delegate, allowing you to shorten the code like this:

```
Public Event Event1( )
```

The easy way is possible because VB knows how to create internal delegates on the fly. From the Event declaration, VB can see the signature of the event-handler method. The method can define any number of parameters, but cannot have a return type.

Note While C# events can be used with delegates that define a return type, VB .NET events can't. A VB .NET Event field can only be declared with a delegate associated with a Sub. Delegates associated with a Function can't be used with Event fields.

VB .NET defines a special RaiseEvent keyword to make calls through an event. When using RaiseEvent, you specify the name of the Event field to use. You don't have to check if the event is bound, because RaiseEvent returns with no errors if there are no methods to call, as shown in Listing 5-7.

Listing 5-7. *A VB .NET Event Source Using Events*

```
Public Class MyEventSource2

  Public Delegate Sub MyDelegateType( )
  Public Event event1 As MyDelegateType
```

```
Public Sub FireEvent1( )
  RaiseEvent event1( )
End Sub

End Class
```

The VB .NET Event keyword doesn't support += and -= operators, as C# does. To add and remove handlers, you must use the VB AddHandler/RemoveHandler statements, as shown in Listing 5-8.

Listing 5-8. *Binding an Event Field to an Event Target, Using VB .NET*

```
'create source and target
Dim object1 As New MyEventSource2
Dim object2 As New MyEventTarget2

'bind event source to target
AddHandler object1.Event1, AddressOf object2.MyMethod

'unbind event source from target
RemoveHandler object1.Event1, AddressOf object2.MyMethod

'fire event to target
object1.FireEvent1()
```

If the binder needs to bind an event to a method contained in the Binder class, VB .NET supports an alternative binding technique based on the WithEvents keyword. If you declare an event source object with this keyword, VB .NET lets you designate a handler by adorning the method with a Handles <object.eventName> suffix, as shown in Listing 5-9.

Listing 5-9. *Using the WithEvent and Handles Keywords to Bind an Event Source to a Handler*

```
Public Class MyEventSource3

  Public Event Event1()

  Public Sub FireEvent1()
    RaiseEvent Event1()
  End Sub
End Class

Public Class Binder3

  Private WithEvents object1 As MyEventSource2

  Public Sub Binder3()
    object1 = New MyEventSource2
  End Sub

  'declare an event handler for MyEventSource3.Event1
  Public Sub MyHandler() Handles object1.Event1
    'do something...
  End Sub
End Class
```

The key thing to remember about the WithEvents technique is this: You can only use it to bind events to your own handler methods. In other words, the binder is also the event target.

Typed Object Calls, Using Interfaces

Typed object calls are method calls that go through classes or interfaces. The caller has a reference to a class or interface, and designates at compile time the method to call. Figure 5-4 shows the caller-callee relationship.

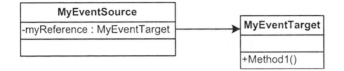

Figure 5-4. *A typed object call, using a class reference*

With a typed object call, the caller is type-coupled to the callee's class. To eliminate the direct type coupling between caller and callee, you can have the callee implement an interface and use the interface to make the call to Method1, as shown in Figure 5-5.

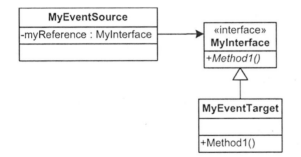

Figure 5-5. *A typed object call, using an interface*

The use of interfaces in typed object calls is often advantageous, compared to calling through a class, because interfaces can reduce the magnitude of intercomponent coupling. By packaging many interfaces together into a single component, event sources incur coupling only to the interface component, as shown in Figure 5-6.

In a large system, all the commonly used interfaces might be packaged together, and that package would tend to be at the center of the system's coupling diagram.

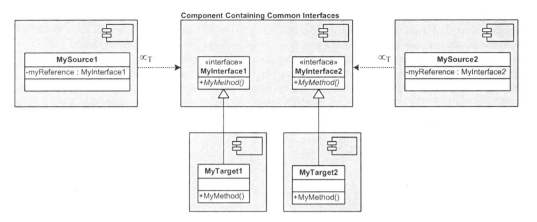

Figure 5-6. *Packaging interfaces separately, to reduce intercomponent coupling in a system*

JavaBeans

JavaBeans are essentially Java objects that support properties, methods, and events. JavaBeans also carry metadata, allowing tools to inspect their internal structure at run time to aid a tool-assisted composition of JavaBeans. The JavaBeans event model is largely based on the Observer design pattern.[2] The object that publishes events is called the *event source*. An object receiving event notifications from an event source is called a *listener*. Listeners are required to implement the EventListener interface directly or indirectly. Event notifications are sent using a typed object call from the source to the listener, as shown in Figure 5-7.

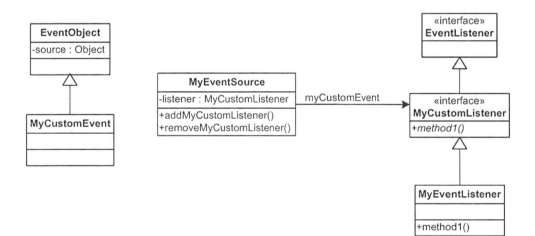

Figure 5-7. *JavaBeans event notifications sent from an event source to an event listener*

2. Erich Gamma, Richard Helm, Ralph Johnson, and John Vlissides, *Design Patterns: Elements of Reusable Object-Oriented Software* (Boston: Addison-Wesley Professional, 1995).

The notification procedure call can carry an arbitrary number of parameters. By convention, a single parameter is used, derived directly or indirectly from class EventObject, which has a field that references the event source. Figure 5-7 shows a custom event type called MyCustomEvent.

JavaBeans event sources publish events by using a special naming convention. For example, given an event of type MyCustomEvent, the source must have two public methods named addMyCustomListener and removeMyCustomListener to add and remove listeners, respectively. JavaBeans development tools use reflection on classes to find events, based on the naming convention. Listing 5-10 shows how you might implement class MyEventSource.

Listing 5-10. *A Simple JavaBeans Event Source*

```
public class MyEventSource{

  MyCustomListener listener;

  public synchronized void removeMyCustomListener(MyCustomListener l) {
    if (listener == l)
      listener = null;
  }

  public synchronized void addMyCustomListener(MyCustomListener l) {
    listener = l;
  }

  protected void fireMethod1(MyCustomEvent e) {
    if (listener != null)
      listener.method1(e);
  }

  public void testMyCustomEvent() {
    MyCustomEvent e = new MyCustomEvent(this);
    fireMethod1(e);
  }
}
```

In order to support multicasting, an event source must use a collection to store references to multiple listeners. When firing an event, the event source must iterate over the listeners in the collection. Listing 5-11 shows how MyEventSource might look when supporting multicast MyCustomEvents.

Listing 5-11. *A JavaBeans Event Source with a Multicast Event*

```
public class MyEventSource {

  private Vector myCustomListeners = new Vector( );

  public synchronized void removeMyCustomListener(MyCustomListener l) {
    if (myCustomListeners.contains(l))
      myCustomListeners.removeElement(l);
  }
```

```
  public synchronized void addMyCustomListener(MyCustomListener l) {
    if (!myCustomListeners.contains(l))
      myCustomListeners.addElement(l);
  }

  protected void fireMethod1(MyCustomEvent e) {
    int count = myCustomListeners.size();
    for (int i = 0; i < count; i++) {
      MyCustomListener l = (MyCustomListener) myCustomListeners.elementAt(i);
      l.method1(e);
    }
  }

  public void testMyCustomEvent( ) {
    MyCustomEvent e = new MyCustomEvent(this);
    fireMethod1(e);
  }
}
```

Although there is no requirement for listener classes to use a naming convention, most Java programs name listeners after the events they relate to, so a listener interface for MyCustomEvent would be named MyCustomListener. Listing 5-12 shows how the listener implementation might look.

Listing 5-12. *A JavaBeans Event Listener*

```
public class MyEventListener implements MyCustomListener {

  public void method1(MyCustomEvent e) {
    // handle event...
  }
}
```

When using the JavaBeans event model with listeners that only provide a single method, the work required to set up the event source and listener seems excessive. Although calls through interfaces allow you to use interface contracts between the caller and callee, interactions consisting of a single method call can sometimes be handled without all the interface overhead.

Untyped Object Calls

Although the standard JavaBeans event model delivers notifications by calling through a listener interface, Java also makes it possible to support untyped object calls, bypassing interfaces. The technique requires the use of reflection to obtain a java.reflect.Method object referencing the target method. The class java.reflect.Method encapsulates method references. Figure 5-8 shows how an event source would use a java.reflect.Method object to invoke a target method without using the target object's interface.

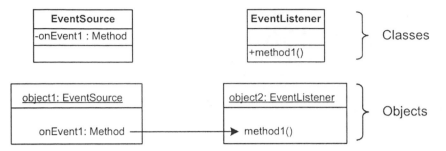

Figure 5-8. *Using java.lang.Method objects to invoke a target method directly*

Using untyped object calls with `java.reflect.Method`, the target object is no longer required to implement any special interfaces to satisfy the event model. The event source has a `java.reflect.Method` field that can hold a reference to any method of any class. At run time, the field is set to reference a specific method of a specific target. Listing 5-13 shows a simple implementation of an event source using a `java.reflect.Method`.

Listing 5-13. *A JavaBeans Event Source Supporting Untyped Object Calls*

```
public class EventSource {

  private Object onMyCustomEventTarget;
  private java.lang.reflect.Method onMyCustomEvent;

  public void setOnMyCustomEvent(Object theTarget,
                                  java.lang.reflect.Method theMethod) {
    onMyCustomEventTarget = theTarget;
    onMyCustomEvent = theMethod;
  }

  public void fireEvent1( ) {
    if (onMyCustomEvent == null)
      return;
    if (onMyCustomEventTarget == null)
      return;
    MyCustomEvent e = new MyCustomEvent(this);
    Object[ ] arguments = new Object[ ] {e};
    try {
      onMyCustomEvent.invoke(onMyCustomEventTarget, arguments);
    }
    catch (Exception ex) {  }
  }
}
```

The event source class contains an event called `OnMyCustomEvent`, which you can set via the method `setOnMyCustomEvent`. For each event, the class requires two fields: one to store the method to call, and one to store the target object to invoke the method on. You can improve the implementation by encapsulating the management of the target method and object in a separate class that I'll call `Delegate`. Listing 5-14 shows a possible implementation.

Listing 5-14. *A Delegate Class in Java, to Handle the Management of Method References*

```java
public class Delegate {
  private Object targetObject;
  private java.lang.reflect.Method targetMethod;
  private Class[ ] parameterTypes;

  public Delegate(Object theObject, java.lang.reflect.Method theMethod) {
    targetObject = theObject;
    targetMethod = theMethod;

    // get the parameter types expected by the method
    parameterTypes = theMethod.getParameterTypes();
  }

  public void invoke(Object[ ] parameters)
  {
    if (targetObject == null) return;
    if (targetMethod == null) return;

    // verify that the parameters match the signature
    // of the target method
    if (parameters.length != parameterTypes.length)
      throw new IllegalArgumentException("Wrong number of parameters");

    for (int i = 0; i < parameters.length; i++)
      if (parameters[i].getClass( ) != parameterTypes[i])
        throw new IllegalArgumentException("Wrong type of parameters");

    try {
      targetMethod.invoke(targetObject, parameters);
    }
    catch (Exception ex) { }
  }
}
```

When creating a Delegate, the caller provides a reference to the target object and method. The invoke method verifies the number and type of parameters to ensure that the method being called has the expected signature. Using the Delegate class, you can now simplify the previous EventSource implementation, as shown in Listing 5-15.

Listing 5-15. *An Improved EventSource Class, Based on the Delegate Class*

```java
public class EventSource {

  private Delegate onMyCustomEvent;

  public void setOnMyEvent1(Object theTarget, java.lang.reflect.Method theMethod) {
    onMyCustomEvent = new Delegate(theTarget, theMethod);
  }

  public void fireEvent1() {
    Object[ ] parameters = new Object[ ] {new MyCustomEvent(this) };
    onMyCustomEvent.invoke(parameters);
  }
}
```

A weakness in the use of `java.lang.reflect.Method` objects is that the compiler can no longer assist in determining whether you're assigning the right type of method in expressions of the kind:

```
source.setOnMyCustomEvent(target, targetMethod);
```

The system will, however, generate an exception at run time if an incorrect set of parameters is passed to the `Method.invoke`. Whether the lack of compile-time parameter checking is important depends on how a system is designed and how components are used. In the Espresso[3] system, for example, the lack of compile-time parameter checking is not a problem, because the development environment uses live components. Since components are running even at design time, the run-time parameter checking offered by Java is adequate. If compile-time checking is important, then it might be best to stick with the standard JavaBeans event model, based on interface calls.

Enterprise JavaBeans

Enterprise JavaBeans (EJBs) are essentially a variant of standard JavaBeans and are designed to run on a Java 2 Platform, Enterprise Edition (J2EE) server in a multithreaded environment. EJBs process requests from concurrent clients and are used in distributed systems. EJBs run inside the special environment produced by *EJB containers*, as shown in Figure 5-9.

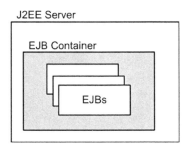

Figure 5-9. *EJBs running inside an EJB container*

EJB containers insulate EJBs from platform-specific services. It is the container's responsibility to manage things like threading, object pooling, transactions, and persistence. Containers control the life cycle of EJBs and shield them from direct access by clients. Clients can only access EJBs indirectly through a container. There are three kinds of EJBs: session beans, entity beans, and message-driven beans.

A session bean exposes methods that clients can invoke (through the container). A session is a period of time over which a client uses the session bean. Session beans come in two variations: stateful and stateless. Stateful beans have a one-to-one relationship with clients and cannot be shared across clients. Each client accesses a different instance of the session bean, which maintains its own internal state between client invocations. A stateful session bean is created when a client first requests its services, and is destroyed when the session terminates. Stateless beans don't contain any state information and are therefore shareable across clients.

An entity bean is a persistent object and is mapped to a persistent store, such as a database table. Each instance of an entity bean is mapped to a different row in the table. Entity beans are essentially OO facades to the persistent store and have features borrowed from the database world, such as primary keys and one-to-many relationships. There is even a query language to select and

---

3. Ted Faison, "Interactive Component-Based Software Development with Espresso" (proceedings of the International Conference on Automated Software Engineering, Lake Tahoe, NV, November 1997).

navigate through the rows to which an entity bean is associated. The language is called Enterprise JavaBeans Query Language (EJB QL) and is a subset of SQL-92. Clients can manipulate the data in the store through the properties and methods of entity beans. The state of entity beans (the values of the related database table row) has global scope, so entity beans can be shared across multiple clients. Entity and session beans use the same event model as ordinary JavaBeans, described earlier.

A message-driven bean (MDB) is somewhat different from the other two types of EJBs. The first two expose methods that clients can call (through the container). MDBs are different: Clients interact with them by sending messages. All MDBs expose the method OnMessage. When a client sends a message to an MDB, the EJB container intercepts the message and passes it to the MDB by calling the bean's OnMessage method, as shown in Figure 5-10.

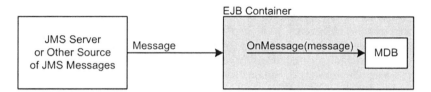

Figure 5-10. *How messages are delivered to a Java message-driven bean*

Messages sent to MDBs must be formatted according to the Java Message Service (JMS) specification. I'll describe JMS in more detail a bit later in this chapter. For the moment, suffice it to say that JMS messages come in several different flavors to handle common payload types such as strings, name-value pairs, binary data, and streams. All MDBs are required to implement two basic interfaces, as shown in the class diagram in Figure 5-11.

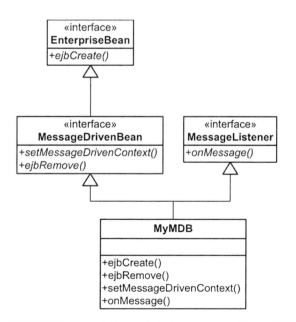

Figure 5-11. *The minimum interfaces required by an MDB*

MDBs are stateless, so they bear some structural resemblance to stateless session beans. An important difference between session beans and MDBs is that the former handle requests synchronously and can return data to the caller. On the other hand, MDBs always handle messages asynchronously. Moreover, messages are strictly one-way, so an MDB can't return data to the sender unless it either sends a new message back or calls back into the caller somehow.

Delphi

Delphi[4] is a rapid application development tool developed by Borland. The Delphi event model was loosely modeled after Visual Basic but uses Object Pascal as the development language. Interestingly, the Microsoft .NET event model is derived from the Delphi model. This shouldn't come as a big surprise, since the same person (Anders Hejlsberg) was the architect of both Delphi and C#, and played a crucial role in defining the .NET event architecture.

Delphi supports both untyped object calls, using method references, and typed object calls, using interfaces. The preferred event delivery technique is based on untyped object calls. Before going too far, let's look at the terminology used in Delphi regarding events. An *event* is a procedure call made to indicate an occurrence of some condition, like a button click or a buffer overflow. The procedure call can carry an arbitrary number of parameters with it and return a value. In Object Pascal, a method reference is a type that is declared according to the signature of the method to be called. It is common in Object Pascal events for the signature to include as the first parameter a reference to the caller. Listing 5-16 shows some method reference types.

Listing 5-16. *Examples of Method Reference Declarations in Object Pascal*

```
TEvent1 = procedure() of object;
TEvent2 = procedure(Sender: TObject) of object;
TEvent3 = procedure(Sender: TObject; Text: string) of object;
TEvent4 = function(Sender: TObject): Integer of object;
```

The types TEvent1, TEvent2, TEvent3, and TEvent4 are custom types. In Object Pascal, it is customary for type names to start with a T. TEvent1 references a method that takes and returns no parameters. Object Pascal has two types of methods: procedures and functions. Procedures don't have a return type, while functions do. TEvent2 references a method that takes a single TObject parameter and returns nothing. TEvent3 references a method that takes two parameters and returns nothing. TEvent4 is a reference to a method that takes one TObject parameter and returns an integer.

In Object Pascal, as in most object-oriented languages, objects are passed by reference, so the callee can modify fields and properties of objects passed to it, knowing that the caller will be able to observe these changes. Declaring a method reference requires the use of a method reference type, like this:

```
Event1: TEvent1;
```

At run time, you can set a method reference variable to reference a specific method of a specific object. To fire an event, the event source uses code that looks like the code in Listing 5-17.

---

4. Steve Teixeira and Xavier Pacheco, *Delphi 5 Developer's Guide* (Indianapolis, IN: Sams, 1999).

Listing 5-17. *Firing an Event in Object Pascal*

```
procedure TMyEventSource.FireEvent1;
begin
  if Assigned(Event1) then
    Event1();
end;
```

The method `Assigned` simply tests whether the method reference is initialized or not. Figure 5-12 shows the relationship between event sources and targets.

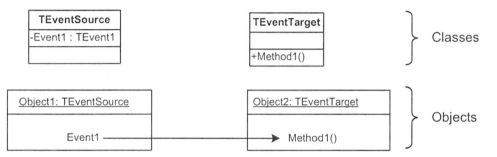

Figure 5-12. *The relationship between event sources and objects in Object Pascal*

The `Event1` field of `Object1` is set at run time to reference `Method1` of `Object2`. The type `TEvent1` offers type safety, ensuring that only methods with a given signature are used as references. Listing 5-18 shows how the event source might look. Listing 5-19 shows how the target classes might look.

Listing 5-18. *An Object Pascal Event Source*

```
unit EventSource;

interface

uses Classes;

type
  TEvent1 = procedure() of object;

  TEventSource = class
    public
      Event1: TEvent1;
      procedure FireEvent1;
  end;

implementation

procedure TEventSource.FireEvent1;
begin
  if Assigned(Event1) then
    Event1();
end;
end.
```

Listing 5-19. *An Object Pascal Event Target*

```
unit EventTarget;

interface

uses Classes;

type

  TEventTarget = class
    public
      procedure Method1;
  end;

implementation

procedure TEventTarget.Method1;
begin
  // handle the event...
end;
end.
```

To bind an event source to a handler method, use the := operator like this:

```
Object1.Event1 := Object2.Method1;
```

Listing 5-20 shows the process of binding an event source to a target.

Listing 5-20. *Binding an Event Source and Target in Object Pascal*

```
procedure MyClass.TestEvent;
var
  // declare variables
  Object1: TEventSource;
  Object2: TEventTarget;
begin
  // create source and target
  Object1 := TEventSource.Create;
  Object2 := TEventTarget.Create;

  // bind event source to target
  Object1.Event1 := Object2.Method1;

  // fire event to target
  object1.FireEvent1;
end;
```

Using an untyped object call to fire events allows the caller to call methods on a callee object whose type is unknown at compile time. All the caller knows is the signature of the method being called. By not having to know the type of the callee, no type coupling is introduced between the caller and callee.

As you've seen, Object Pascal untyped object calls use a simple pointer, so they don't support multicasting natively. For multicasting, the event source must implement a scheme to manage a list of method references.

You can also use Object Pascal to send event notifications using typed object calls through an interface. The caller is then responsible for identifying one of the interface's methods at compile time. Figure 5-13 shows the relationship between caller and callee.

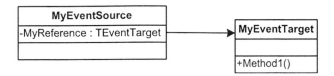

Figure 5-13. *Sending events by invoking a target method through an interface*

With this arrangement, the caller uses a field that can hold a reference to a class or interface. The field is initialized at run time to point to a specific object. The caller determines which callee method is invoked.

COM

The Microsoft Component Object Model (COM) was originally developed without support for events. Due to the recognized importance of events in many types of systems, Microsoft added an event model.[5] The model relies exclusively on the use of procedure calls to deliver notifications, and grew out of the use of callbacks allowing a server component to obtain information from a client. COM doesn't support untyped object calls, forcing notifications to propagate via calls through COM interfaces. Figure 5-14 shows the basic COM event model, where a client object receives event notifications from a server object.

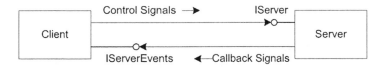

Figure 5-14. *The basic COM event model*

A bit of terminology is in order here. In COM, *clients* are generic users of other components, called *servers*. Client and server designations relate only to the roles objects play in relation to one another. Clients make requests to servers. Servers respond to requests from clients. An object may fulfill multiple roles, depending on how it interacts with its neighbors. An object may act as a server toward one object and as a client toward another.

In COM, an object capable of firing events is called an *event source*. An object receiving event notifications is called an *event sink*. The most common event architecture in COM is for event sinks to be clients of their event sources. In other words, there is usually a forward and return path for signals between clients and servers: The forward path is for the client to request services from the server, and the return path is for the server to notify the client of interesting events. Events can only flow from an event source to an event sink. Both event sources and event sinks must implement interfaces. Event sources receive client requests through an incoming interface, and they send responses back to clients using an outgoing interface.

Because COM supported only incoming interfaces originally, the requirement for outgoing interfaces made it necessary to add some additional plumbing to the COM specification. Microsoft

---

5. Don Box, *Essential COM* (Boston: Addison-Wesley Professional, 1997).

introduced *connection points* to handle outgoing interfaces; connection points are based on the interface IConnectionPoint. A connection point is necessary to bind an event source back to an event sink. To act as an event source, an object is required to implement an interface called IConnectionPointContainer. Clients query this interface to obtain an IConnectionPoint related to a particular type of outgoing interface for the callback signals to return on. An event source may provide any number of IConnectionPoints, as shown in Figure 5-15.

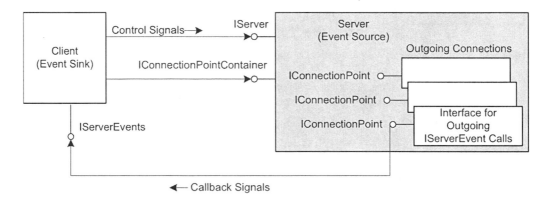

Figure 5-15. *Using IConnectionPoints to connect event sinks to sources*

Figure 5-15 shows a fictitious callback interface called IServerEvents on the client. In order for a client to bind itself to a server, the following things must occur:

1. The client must obtain a reference to one of the server's interfaces.

2. Using this interface, the client must query the server for the IConnectionPointContainer interface.

3. Using the IConnectionPointContainer interface, the client must call the FindConnectionPoint method, passing to the server the GUID of the client's callback interface (IServerEvents, in this example).

4. The server must return a reference to the appropriate IConnectionPoint, if one is available to handle the requested client interface.

5. Once an IConnectionPoint interface is found, the client must invoke the interface's Advise method to bind the event source to the client's callback interface.

COM event sources support multicasting: Any number of objects can sign up with an event source to receive notifications. Once a client has registered to receive events, the server will continue to send events to it until the client unregisters by calling the IConnectionPoint's method Unadvise. By default, COM restricts event callbacks to occur on the same thread on which the client registered when invoking IConnectionPoint.Advise, because COM doesn't allow interface references to be passed across thread boundaries. When a server implements its own internal threads, it must marshal any interfaces it passes in the callback. The marshaling is performed by a call to the COM method CoMarshalInterThreadInterfaceInStream.

Indirect-Delivery Systems

An indirect-delivery system decouples event senders from receivers by interposing one or more middleware components. Indirect delivery is particularly common in enterprise systems, in which the senders and receivers are on different machines. There are many technologies and products to choose from. The following sections discuss the ones that seem to be in greatest favor today.

CORBA

CORBA[6] is an architecture for distributed systems built on a series of standardized interfaces published by the Object Management Group (OMG). In CORBA, language independence is achieved through the use of OMG's Interface Definition Language (IDL) to describe all interfaces in a platform-independent way. All major programming language vendors that target distributed systems support IDL. CORBA includes specifications for three core platform technologies:

1. The object request broker
2. Common facilities
3. Common services

Support for events is provided through the *Common Services Specifications*. In terms of events, CORBA 2 originally included only a lightweight *Event Service*. In 2000, the OMG published a new service called *Notification Service*, whose purpose was to extend the features of the Event Service and provide support for QoS and notification filtering. The Notification Service is substantially more complicated than the Event Service, but both use procedure calls to deliver notifications. The Notification Service is backward-compatible with the Event Service.

The CORBA Event Service

First released in 1995, the CORBA Event Service[7] was designed as a relatively easy way to decouple distributed components using event notifications. The basic architecture is shown in Figure 5-16.

Figure 5-16. *The basic architecture of a system using the CORBA Event Service*

In the CORBA literature, the word *event* is used to denote an event notification. CORBA events are delivered using procedure calls. At the core of the architecture is an *event channel*, which is an object that mediates interactions between an *event supplier* and an *event consumer*. The supplier sends notifications by calling a method exposed by the event channel. The channel provides two ways to deliver the notifications to the consumer:

- *Push mode*: The event channel calls a method exposed by the consumer.
- *Pull mode*: The consumer calls an event channel method to poll for notifications. The channel, in turn, can call a method of the supplier to get notifications.

In pull mode, the polling calls can retrieve notifications using either blocking or nonblocking calls. One could argue that the pull mode is not really an event-based architecture at all and doesn't belong in an Event Service. In the typical event-based interaction, an event subscriber receives notifications at

---

6. Michi Henning and Steve Vinoski, *Advanced CORBA Programming with* C++ (Boston: Addison-Wesley Professional, 1999).
7. Object Management Group, "Event Service Specification" (technical report, www.omg.org/docs/formal/01-03-01.pdf, 2001).

a time determined by the publisher. Notifications are sent when the event publisher detects events of interest. The whole point of the event-based interaction model is to relieve subscribers from the necessity of polling an event source to see when a particular condition occurs. In event-based interactions, the event subscriber behaves reactively and is not responsible for deciding when notifications are received from the publisher.

The main function of the event channel is to act as a decoupler between suppliers and consumers. Any number of suppliers and consumers can use the same event channel. Events fired by any of the suppliers can be delivered to any of the consumers, as shown in Figure 5-17.

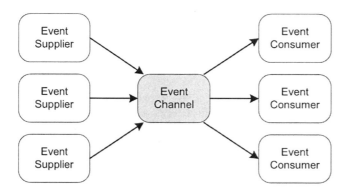

Figure 5-17. *Multiple suppliers and consumers sharing an event channel*

Event channels are typically instantiated by a separate administrative tool, before suppliers and consumers are created. At run time, suppliers and consumers typically use a directory service to locate an event channel and bind to it. Suppliers typically use the `EventChannel` interface to locate the channel's `SupplierAdmin` and `ProxyPushConsumer` interfaces, shown in Figure 5-18.

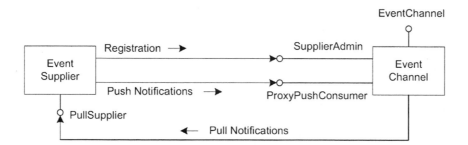

Figure 5-18. *Interactions between supplier and event channel*

The supplier, the consumer, or a separate object can establish a binding between supplier and consumer. When the supplier establishes the binding, the following three steps are necessary.

1. Use the `EventChannel` interface to get a `SupplierAdmin` reference.

2. Use the `SupplierAdmin` interface to get a `ProxyPushConsumer` or `ProxyPullConsumer` reference.

3. Use the proxy to register as a supplier with the event channel, providing a reference to the intended consumer. The consumer can be set up to operate in push or pull mode.

Consumers interact with the event channel is a way similar to suppliers, as shown in Figure 5-19.

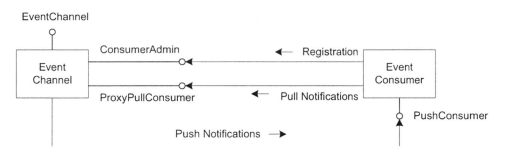

Figure 5-19. *Interactions between event channel and consumer*

When the consumer initiates the binding, the following three steps are necessary.

1. Use the `EventChannel` interface to get a `ConsumerAdmin` reference.

2. Use the `ConsumerAdmin` interface to get a `ProxyPushSupplier` or `ProxyPullSupplier` reference.

3. Use the proxy to register as a consumer with the event channel, providing a reference to the intended supplier. The supplier can be set up to operate in push or pull mode.

When using a push mode to deliver notifications to a consumer, the supplier controls the interaction. The supplier calls the event channel method `ProxyPushConsumer.push`. The event channel then calls the consumer's `PushConsumer.push` method.

When using a pull mode to get notifications from a supplier, the consumer controls the interaction. The consumer calls the event channel method `ProxyPullSupplier.pull`. The event channel then calls the supplier's `PullSupplier.pull` method. This pull method blocks if no notifications are available. To avoid blocking, you can use the alternative method `try_pull`.

A mixed push-pull model is also supported, whereby the supplier can push events to the event channel where they are stored locally. The consumer uses pull methods to retrieve notifications buffered by the event channel.

The CORBA Event Service specification leaves a number of features open to implementers. The spec is somewhat complex, and implementations are subject to vendor inconsistencies, due to lack of detailed information on how to handle error conditions. Issues such as delivery reliability, fault tolerance, and notification persistence are also left to implementers to define.

The CORBA Notification Service

Two features were deliberately left out of the CORBA Event Service specification: QoS and filtering. The authors felt that including these features would make the service too complicated and rigid. Organizations using the service were quick to clamor for an enterprise-quality Event Service that included the missing features and had better support for fault tolerance and scalability. Rather than expand the scope of CORBA Event Services, OMG preferred to publish a brand-new specification called Notification Services, geared toward large projects and support for large numbers of suppliers and consumers.

The Notification Service[8] is built using the same basic architecture (suppliers, event channels, and consumers) as the Event Service, so the former is a superset of the latter. To maintain backward-compatibility with the Event Service, the Notification Service uses interfaces derived from those used in the Event Service. As mentioned earlier, the primary features added to the Notification Service are filtering and QoS.

---

8. Object Management Group, "Notification Service Specification" (technical report, www.omg.org/cgi-bin/apps/doc?formal/02-08-04.pdf, 2002).

Structured Events

Both QoS and filtering rely on a new notification type introduced with Notification Services. The new type, called a *structured event*, largely replaces the older *typed events*, which were part of the Event Service specification. Typed events provided a mechanism through which a caller could call methods of an application-specific interface. Implementers and users alike had complained that typed events were confusing and difficult to implement. The newer structured events are essentially messages composed of a header and body, as shown in Figure 5-20.

Figure 5-20. *The layout of structured events*

The header is divided into two parts: a fixed portion and a variable portion. The fixed portion is very short and must be included in all structured event messages. It contains basic information, such as a domain name, a type name, and an event name. As an example, a stock-tracking application might create a structure event with the domain name "NYSE Stock Quotes", the type name "TickerAlarms", and the event name "IBM". The fixed portion of the header data makes it possible for an event channel to group notifications for storage in an *event repository*. The purpose of such a repository is to provide persistence in the case of hardware failures and to allow consumers to browse stored notifications by type, name, or name-value combination. The variable portion of the header is optional and can contain an arbitrary number of name-value pairs, which you can also use to set QoS settings on a per-message basis.

The message body is also divided into two parts, as the message header. The first part can contain an arbitrary number of name-value pairs that you can use for filtering purposes. The main body contains the real payload of the notification and can be arbitrarily long. The body is contained in a single variant field (of type `CORBA::Any`), so it can contain a string, a number, binary data, an array, or a custom type.

Filtering

Notification filtering is based on name-value pairs included in a payload header. The burden of filtering is not on the Event Service, but on the proxy objects that forward notifications from the supplier to the channel. To achieve filtering, special `Filter` objects are defined and attached to the proxy, as shown in Figure 5-21.

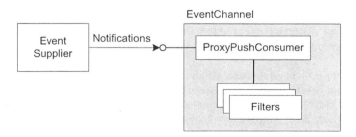

Figure 5-21. *Using filters on the supplier side*

When the proxy receives a notification, it calls the match method of each Filter. If any of the filters returns false, the notification is discarded; otherwise, it is forwarded to the event channel. The filters attached to a given proxy only affect that proxy. You create supplier proxies by calling a SupplierAdmin method. SupplierAdmin objects are the parents of supplier proxy objects. In order for all the proxies to use the same filters, the filters must be attached to the SupplierAdmin parent, as shown in Figure 5-22.

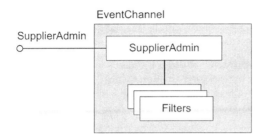

Figure 5-22. *Common filters that apply to all supplier proxies*

When a supply proxy is given a message to deliver, it first checks the parent SupplierAdmin filters, then its own filters. A notification must satisfy all the filters; otherwise, it is rejected.

You can also filter notifications on the consumer side of an event channel. Everything said thus far about filtering can be applied to the consumer side, so you can attach filters to ConsumerAdmin objects and consumer proxy objects. Filters can even be present simultaneously at both the supplier and consumer ends.

There are two kinds of filters available: those related to QoS properties defined in the notification header, and those related to properties defined in the notification body. Filters work with expressions defining constraints on notification name-value pairs contained both in the header and body. The syntax of the filtering expressions is defined in an extensible constraint language that all filters must support. Implementation-dependent extensions are allowed, as long as they don't break the core language.

QoS

As mentioned above, CORBA notifications have a header containing properties. Some of these properties have standard names and are used to support QoS options. Of all the Notification Services in current use, CORBA probably defines the greatest number of QoS features. It supports the following features:

- *Reliability*: This option determines the reliability of notification delivery. Two settings are possible: transient and persistent. If the event channel fails before delivering a notification with transient reliability, that notification will be lost. Notifications using persistent reliability are kept in a local store by the Notification Service and can be recovered after a failure and delivered.

- *Priority*: Notifications can be assigned a priority value. Priorities are significant only if notifications can't be delivered as fast as they are generated. For example, using push delivery, the event channel delivers notifications as soon as they are received, regardless of their priority. If notifications arrive faster than they can be delivered, the event channel uses the notification priority to determine the delivery order of buffered notifications.

- *Timing*: The supplier can constrain the timing of delivery by giving the earliest delivery time, the latest delivery time, or a timeout value. In the first case, the event channel will buffer the notification. When the specified time arrives, the channel will attempt to deliver the notification. When the latest time is specified, the channel will try to delivery the notification immediately, and discard the notification when the deadline occurs. Timeout constraints are similar, except they indicate the amount of time the channel has to complete delivery.

- *Queue sizes*: The event channel administrator can specify the size of queues used to store notifications in transit. Queue sizes affect two things: the total number of queued notifications in the channel, and the maximum number of queued notifications allowed for a particular consumer.

- *Delivery order*: When notifications get queued, the delivery order indicates in which order to deliver them. Standard options are `AnyOrder`, `FifoOrder` (first-in, first-out), `PriorityOrder`, and `DeadlineOrder`. The `DeadlineOrder` option indicates that notifications with the nearest deadline should be delivered first.

- *Discard policy*: When a queue becomes full, this option indicates which notifications to discard when new notifications arrive. Options are similar to those used in delivery order, but also include a `LiloOrder` (last-in, last-out). The `DeadlineOrder` option indicates that notifications with the nearest deadline should be discarded first.

- *Batch size*: Consumers can request to receive batches of notifications. A batch is just a sequence of notifications. The batch size specifies the longest sequence allowed.

- *Pacing interval*: When the consumer indicates that it wants to receive notifications in batches, the pacing interval determines the maximum amount of time the channel will wait before delivering the buffered sequences. When the pacing interval expires, the channel will send all buffered notifications as a series of batches. The maximum length of each batch is determined by the *batch size* option.

Due to the richness of QoS features defined and the fact that an event channel may not support them all, suppliers and consumers can interact with the event channel to negotiate a satisfactory level of QoS.

All CORBA Notification Services are required to understand all the QoS options but not necessarily to implement them. Any unrecognized or unimplemented options found in notification headers should be ignored. CORBA also allows additional name-value pairs to be added for custom features.

The CORBA Notification Service is a fairly complex specification, including more than 40 separate interfaces. The spec identifies a variety of participants, such as filters, typed events, factories, admin objects, and others. A detailed description of the service is beyond the scope of this book.

CORBA Messaging

While people were busy developing the CORBA Notification Service, a separate group of people was working on a somewhat overlapping specification known as CORBA Messaging[9] (CM). While the name would lead you to believe that CM relates to messages and messaging services, this isn't exactly the case. The typical CORBA interaction between objects is based on the synchronous request-response model. CM specifies a number of standard ways to support *asynchronous method invocation* (AMI) between CORBA objects. What makes CM interesting in an EBS context is that it supports a message-based interaction model based on intermediate *router* objects, as shown in Figure 5-23.

---

9. Object Management Group, "CORBA Messaging" (technical report, www.omg.org/docs/formal/02-12-09.pdf, 2002).

Figure 5-23. *CORBA objects interacting via a messaging router*

The purpose of messaging routers is to decouple the client from the server, not only in space, but also in time. In other words, routers allow a client to send requests to a server that may be temporarily unavailable. The router works as a store-and-forward system, storing requests until the server becomes available. The router uses an ad hoc protocol to poll servers and determine when they become available.

Rather than storing requests itself, a router can offload the task to another middleware system, such as a message queuing service. A new wire protocol called Interoperable Routing Protocol (IRP) is used to interact with middleware systems and to support routing between multiple CORBA messaging routers. This protocol is based on the standard OMG General Inter-ORB Protocol (GIOP), widely supported by vendors of CORBA systems. The use of routers becomes particularly useful when the path between a client and server includes the Internet. In this case, routers can act as Internet gateways at both ends of the client-server connection, as shown in Figure 5-24.

Figure 5-24. *Using routers to bridge the Internet*

Any number of intermediate routers may be involved in the client-to-server path. The router closest to the client is called a `ClientRouter`; the router closest to the server is called a `TargetRouter`. A `ClientRouter` exposes a custom interface to its client and acts as a proxy. Clients interact with the `ClientRouter` as if it were the actual server. On the other end, servers interact with the `TargetRouter` as if it were the actual client. Intermediate routers talk to other routers using a standard set of interfaces.

COM+

COM+[10] is a COM-based framework designed for enterprise systems. The event model in COM was designed using a direct-delivery model, making it ill versed for highly scalable systems. In COM+, the event model was changed to support an indirect-delivery model, based on a centralized *COM+ Event Service*. The Microsoft literature refers to COM+ events as *loosely coupled events (LCE)*. COM+ event publishers and subscribers never interact directly, but rather through the COM+ Event Service, which handles both subscriptions and notifications.

COM+ notifications are COM objects. You must register interfaces used by COM+ notifications with the COM+ Event Service. Subscribers wishing to receive notifications of a given type must implement the corresponding interface and register themselves with the Event Service. For example, to receive `IMyEventType` notifications, a subscriber would have to implement the `IMyEventType` interface, as shown in Figure 5-25.

---

10. David S. Platt, *Understanding COM+* (Redmond, WA: Microsoft Press, 1999).

Figure 5-25. *A simple event COM object exposing a user-defined interface*

The Event Service maintains a list of subscribers in an internal cache. Subscribers can specify which methods they support of a particular interface.

To fire an event, the publisher must create an object that implements an event interface, then call one of its methods. When the publisher creates an event object using standard COM functions like CreateObject, the COM+ Event Service handles the call, returning a COM+ object that routes all calls to its event interface methods to the Event Service.

For example, to fire an IMyEventType.Method1 event, a publisher might create an object called MyEvent. This object implements the interface IMyEventType, which is registered with the COM+ Event Service as an event interface. The publisher fires events by calling MyEvent.Method1, which is routed to the Event Service. At this point, the Event Service searches the subscriptions cache, looking for subscriptions that apply to IMyEventType. For each subscriber found, the designated interface method (e.g., IMyEventType.Method1) is called. Figure 5-26 shows the basic dynamics.

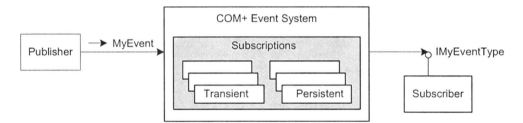

Figure 5-26. *How the COM+ Event Service handles event-notification delivery*

The way the COM+ Event Service delivers notifications to subscribers depends on the subscription type used, described in the next section.

Subscription Types

The COM+ Event Service supports two types of subscriptions: transient and persistent. Transient notifications are really just messages that are delivered using a point-to-point interaction. They are kept in a memory cache until they are delivered, so if the system crashes before delivery, they are lost. Transient notifications can be used only with point-to-point interactions, so the sender must always identify the recipient. The recipient must be running when the event is fired, because the Event Service doesn't support deferred delivery and has no control over the life cycle of the recipient.

With persistent subscriptions, the event publisher doesn't indicate a specific subscriber. No subscribers need to be running when an event is fired, because the Event Service is responsible for the subscriber's life cycle. When an event is fired and a persistent subscription is found for it, the COM+ Event Service creates the associated subscriber, delivers the notification to it, and then destroys the subscriber. Persistent subscriptions are kept on disk, so they survive system restarts. A persistent subscription can have any number of subscribers.

To improve performance when delivering a notification to many subscribers, publishers can tell the Event Service to deliver all notifications in parallel, using a separate thread for each one. This approach works well for small numbers of subscribers (e.g., less than 50). For larger numbers, the approach will adversely affect the machine on which the Event Service is running.

Filtering

COM+ supports two types of filters: subscription filters and publisher filters. The former allow a subscriber to specify a filtering expression consisting of predicates connected with Boolean operators such as AND, OR, and NOT. The variables used in the filtering expression are the parameters passed in method calls during event firing. For example, assume an event interface defines a method with this signature:

```
void Method1(float temperature);
```

The filter expression could be this string:

```
(temperature > 0) AND (temperature < 100)
```

At run time, the Event Service examines each subscription, looking for a subscription filter. If one is found, its expression is tested. A notification is sent to the subscriber only if the filter expression is satisfied.

Publisher filters don't use a filter expression to control whether a notification is sent to a particular subscriber or not, but instead use a custom filtering object. When registering an event interface, a publisher can specify a filter. When handling a notification, the Event Service calls the filter, which can accept or reject the notification. Publisher filters are commonly used to filter notifications based on which subscriber it is destined to. Publisher filters might be used in a fee-based subscription system, rejecting notifications to subscribers who haven't paid.

Queued Components

By default, the COM+ Event Service can only deliver notifications if a subscriber is available immediately or can be created on the fly. In many situations, subscribers might be programs running on other machines, and the life cycle of such subscribers is beyond the control of the Event Service. In these cases, COM+ supports *queued components*, which I'll describe in more detail in the next section, "Microsoft MSMQ." Queued components are used in distributed systems and have two parts: a client side and a server side. Between them sits MSMQ, Microsoft's message queuing middleware. Figure 5-27 shows the parties involved with queued components.

A queued component allows a publisher to send notifications to a remote subscriber, even if the subscriber is disconnected. MSMQ buffers notifications sent while the subscriber is offline. When the subscriber goes online, the server side of the queued component delivers the notifications stored in MSMQ. The whole process is essentially transparent to both the publisher and the subscriber. From the programmer's perspective, the only change necessary to support events with temporarily disconnected servers is to designate the event object (e.g., MyEvent, which implements IMyEventType) as a queued component. The COM+ infrastructure takes care of most of the plumbing details.

By default, COM+ events do not support any QoS options: Delivery is always attempted, but only once. To support QoS, you must use queued components, offloading the QoS management on MSMQ.

Implementing a system using COM+ events is fairly complicated from the programming perspective. The .NET Framework alleviates much of the pain by wrapping lower-level COM plumbing gunk in .NET classes. You can also handle many types of operations, such as managing subscribers, filters, and queued components, using a variety of administration tools.

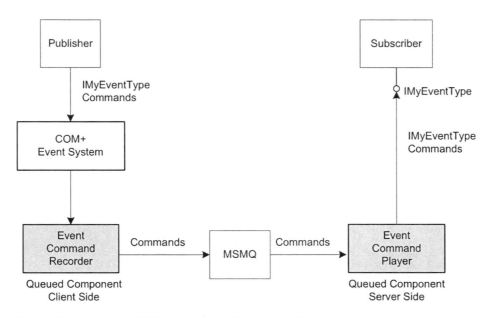

Figure 5-27. *Combining COM+ events with COM+ queued components*

Microsoft MSMQ

In the mid-1990s, enterprise systems and directory services were hot topics, and many companies were scrambling to announce enterprise-level products of various kinds. Enterprise systems are about distributed computing, scalability, and reliability. Messaging is a pivotal component in the overall picture. MSMQ[11] is Microsoft's enterprise-level message queuing service. Microsoft introduced MSMQ originally as part of a marketing effort that went by the unfortunate name *DNA* (Distributed interNet Applications). DNA included other technologies besides MSMQ, such as Distributed COM and Microsoft Transaction Server.

You can use MSMQ in both single-server or distributed-server systems. In a single-server system, clients running on the server machine or on separate machines use message queues stored on the server machine. The collection of an MSMQ server and its clients is called a *site*. Figure 5-28 shows a site with three clients.

All the machines of a site are typically in the same place, such as the same building or the same floor. The MSMQ server machine uses a local database to store site information such as configuration data, persistent messages, and administrative data. Machines in a site are presumed to have high-speed network connectivity with each other.

Clients whose queues are stored on the server are called *dependent* clients, because they depend on a connection to the server to access their message queues. Clients are called *independent* if they have their own local message queues and can work while disconnected temporarily from the site server. Independent clients use a local MSMQ Queue Manager service on each client machine, as shown in Figure 5-29.

---

11. "Microsoft Message Queuing" (technical report, www.microsoft.com/windowsserver2003/technologies/msmq/default.mspx).

MSMQ Site

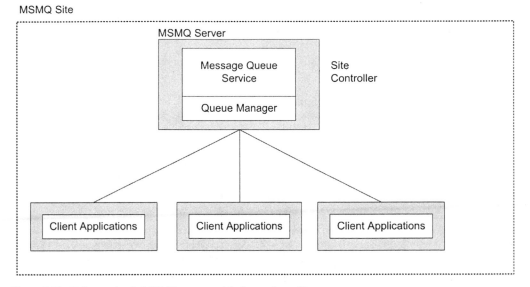

Figure 5-28. *Using a single MSMQ server with dependent clients*

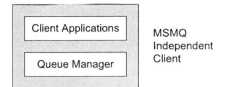

Figure 5-29. *An independent client*

The Queue Manager buffers outgoing requests to the site server if the client is disconnected temporarily. When the client reconnects, all messages are sent to their respective destinations. Incoming messages are retrieved from the local queue, regardless of whether the client is connected to the site or not. When the client is connected, the local queue can receive messages from the other clients in the site or from other sites via the MSMQ server. You can connect MSMQ sites together, using a two-level hierarchy of sites, as shown in Figure 5-30.

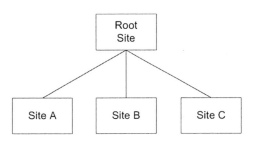

Figure 5-30. *A two-level hierarchy of MSMQ sites*

The MSMQ server in the root site is called the Enterprise Controller. The MSMQ servers in the other sites are called Site Controllers. The Enterprise Controller is also a Site Controller. The purpose of the Enterprise Controller is to maintain information on all the queues, sites, and clients in an enterprise.

When sending messages, the sender can provide the address of the destination queue in the following ways:

- *Using a URL*: The two schemes supported are http and https. Examples might be `http://www.mycompany.com/msmq/MyQueue` or `http://192.167.10.1/MyQueue`.

- *Using a UNC*: The *Universal Naming Convention* is a way to identify network paths using computer names with a double slash or double backslash notation. Contrary to its name, UNC is not a universally adopted naming convention and is not supported by the Internet Engineering Task Force (IETF) or the World Wide Web Consortium (W3C). A queue might be identified with the UNC path //MyComputer/msmq/MyQueue.

- *Using a GUID*: Destination queues can be identified by a *Globally Unique Identifier*—a unique 128-bit value that is assigned to either a queue or a computer running MSMQ. A queue is identified with names of the type `<queue GUID>` or `<computer GUID>\<queue number>`. A GUID is expressed textually as a 32-character hexadecimal string divided into sections with hyphens to facilitate readability. A GUID example is 518E75C0-6EB2-D4CA-C03B-58002A10757E.

Message Routing

The lines in Figure 5-30 depict relationships between site servers, not necessarily message paths. There are two ways MSMQ routes messages: point-to-point (PTP) or something called store-and-forward (SAF). Using PTP, the sender identifies the destination queue. The sender must have a direct (one-hop) connection to the destination, and MSMQ sends the message over that connection. When a message is sent from one site to another, MSMQ uses a special Routing Server component to get the message to the destination site. Figure 5-31 shows three sites with direct connections between them.

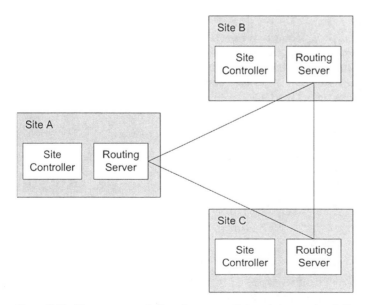

Figure 5-31. *Sites connected directly, supporting point-to-point delivery*

When the sender only provides the destination site name, MSMQ provides SAF delivery, and MSMQ determines the routing path itself. Just because two sites are linked directly doesn't ensure that messages between then will be delivered using PTP. All connections between sites are associated with a *cost* property. The connection cost is related to the bandwidth and type of connection, and has a numeric value set by the MSMQ administrator. MSMQ internally uses the connection costs to determine the *cheapest* SAF routing path, which is not necessarily the shortest one.

Interoperability

MSMQ sites can connect to *foreign* systems to interoperate with systems using non-Microsoft components, such as IBM WebSphere MQ, e-mail post offices, or fax servers. The connection is managed by a custom Connector Service, which translates incoming and outgoing messages to meet the requirements of the foreign system, as shown in Figure 5-32.

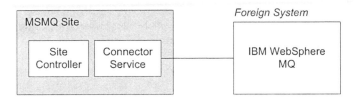

Figure 5-32. *Using a Connector Service to interoperate with a non-Microsoft system*

Once a Connector Service is installed on a site, MSMQ clients can send and receive messages to and from the foreign site using standard MSMQ commands. Transactions are supported with messages destined to foreign systems.

Interfaces

MSMQ servers can be accessed in four basic ways:

- *Using the MSMQ API*: The MSMQ API is a static C library representing the most basic interface.

- *Using the ActiveX interface*: MSMQ exposes a series of ActiveX interfaces that clients can call directly.

- *Using the .NET interface*: Access the servers via a set of wrapper classes in the System. Messaging namespace.

- *Using a network connection*: The network connection is based on HTTP messages formatted using the SOAP Reliable Messaging Protocol (SRMP), a proprietary Microsoft protocol built on top of WS-Routing.[12] Although Microsoft literature indicates that SRMP is a *published* specification, don't infer that it is a standard specification. The IETF and W3C have no information about it.

Message Structure

MSMQ messages have a completely flat structure, in the sense that they only carry properties. Everything is considered a property, including the message body. Figure 5-33 shows the basic message structure.

---

12. Henrik Frystyk Nielsen and Satish Thatte, "Web Services Routing Protocol (WS-Routing)" (technical report, http://msdn.microsoft.com/library/default.asp?url=/library/en-us/dnglobspec/html/ws-routing.asp, 2001).

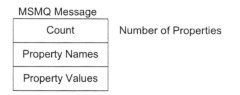

Figure 5-33. *The structure of MSMQ messages*

Rather than contain an array of name-value pairs, MSMQ messages contain separate arrays for names and values. Names are numeric identifiers published by MSMQ. There is no minimal set of properties that a message must define. At a limit, a message can be sent with no properties at all. Variable-length properties, such as those carrying strings, come in pairs. The first carries the value (e.g., the string), the second the length. Messages typically carry properties for a body and a message ID.

The body can contain any kind of data, including strings, binary arrays, and serialized binary data. A sender application can use MSMQ to transfer objects or graphs of objects to a receiver. Using .NET senders and receivers, objects can be passed by value with no programming overhead. The .NET Framework provides wrapper components that automatically serialize objects into XML on the sender side and reconstruct the objects from XML on the receiver side.

QoS

MSMQ supports QoS at two levels: the queue level and the message level. The options at each level are different. Options set at the queue level affect all the messages in that queue, as one might expect. At the queue level, the following QoS features are supported:

- *Transactions*: MSMQ supports two kinds of queues: transacted and nontransacted. Messages sent via a transacted queue are ensured *exactly-once-delivery* QoS. Distributed transactions are also supported.

- *Security*: A queue can authenticate incoming messages. Encrypted messages are also supported.

- *Quotas*: The size of a queue can be set. There is no QoS feature to indicate what MSMQ should do when messages arrive at a full queue. MSMQ simply ignores incoming messages.

- *Priorities*: Queues can be tagged with a priority value. When a queue receives messages from other queues, the priority of the sending queues is used to prioritize incoming messages.

At the message level, the following QoS features are available:

- *Return receipts*: The sender can request a response acknowledging receipt of a message.

- *Timing*: The sender can set two types of timing deadlines: the time for a message to reach the receiver's incoming queue, and the time for the receiver to actually retrieve the message. The first option is similar to the time-to-live option used in IP packets. When a message hits a deadline, there are no MSMQ options that tell the system what to do. MSMQ simply deletes the message.

Delivery Models

Recipients can get messages using either push or pull interactions. In pull mode, the recipient calls an MSMQ method to get the next message. The call blocks if no messages are available, or until a timeout occurs. A Peek method is supported to check for incoming messages without retrieving them. Clients can navigate up and down in the list of messages stored in a queue by using a *cursor*, with operations for visiting the first, last, previous, and next messages.

In push mode, MSMQ calls the client when a message arrives. In order to be called this way, clients must register a callback function. MSMQ doesn't allow conditions to be attached to callback functions, so the client has no way of filtering out messages of a particular kind from the message queue. The callback will be called any time a message arrives in the associated queue.

Filtering

Although MSMQ doesn't support filtering directly, an indirect form of filtering is possible using *triggers*. A trigger is a rule that can be attached to incoming queues. When a message arrives that satisfies a trigger condition, the trigger action is performed.

Trigger conditions consist of a true-false predicate. Multiple predicates can be chained together, but only with AND operators. Conditions can be associated with various message properties or the message body. As an example, a trigger might have this condition:

```
Message body contains "Toyota"
```

When a trigger fires, its action is performed. Actions can invoke a COM object method or a standalone executable program. Triggers can only be set using an administrative tool and not programmatically. Actions can include a set of predefined parameters, indicating the value of a message property, a queue property, or other.

Triggers add overhead to message queues. Every time a message arrives, MSMQ checks all the triggers attached to the queue. The overhead is proportional to the number of triggers defined. Since triggers can run essentially any program, there is the possibility that a trigger can take a fairly long time to execute. To improve performance, MSMQ supports two ways to run the triggers: sequentially or in parallel. In the first case, all the triggers are checked sequentially. In the second case, the triggers are run concurrently on separate threads.

Multicasting

When a message needs to be sent to multiple recipients, MSMQ supports the following two addressing schemes:

- *Distribution lists*: A distribution list contains a series of GUIDs identifying destination queues, and can only identify MSMQ destinations. Sending a message to a distribution list causes the message to be sent to all the queues in the list.

- *Multicast addresses*: A queue can be given a multicast address, which is a standard class D IP address. Class D IP addresses are between 224.0.0.0 and 239.255.255.255. Multicast addresses are more efficient than distribution lists, because the delivery is handled at the networking level rather than the application level.

Queued Components

MSMQ is designed to support distributed components in a disconnected mode. In the classic client-server architecture, clients invoke server methods using RPC, as shown in Figure 5-34.

Figure 5-34. *Invoking server methods in a classic client-server system*

The problem is that clients must be connected to the server to invoke its methods. You can use MSMQ to allow clients to invoke methods of servers that are temporarily disconnected, using what Microsoft calls a *queued component*, which sits between the client and server MSMQ components, as shown in Figure 5-35.

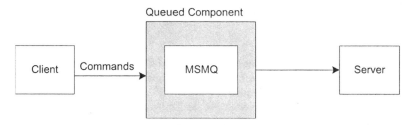

Figure 5-35. *Using MSMQ to create a queued component*

Queued components can be broken down into a client and server portion. On the client side, calls to the server are recorded into a *batch* and stored in a local MSMQ queue. Figure 5-36 shows the client portion of a queued component.

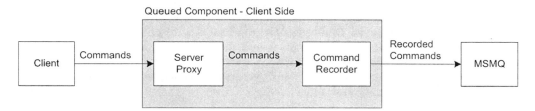

Figure 5-36. *The client side of a COM+ queued component*

When the server comes back online at some later time, the server side of the queued component interacts with the server, as shown in Figure 5-37.

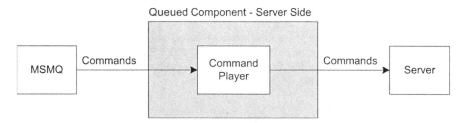

Figure 5-37. *The server side of a COM+ queued component*

The MSMQ server receives all the recorded commands together, in the order they were recorded. The commands can be sent either following a poll from the server or as soon as the messaging service discovers the availability of the server.

JMS

The Java Message Service[13] is a specification published by Sun Microsystems that describes a set of interfaces and practices to support a Java-based messaging system. JMS is not a product but a template for developing a messaging service. A number of vendors have developed messaging services based on JMS, and JMS is by far the most-supported messaging system in the world today. Figure 5-38 shows the basic architecture of a JMS system.

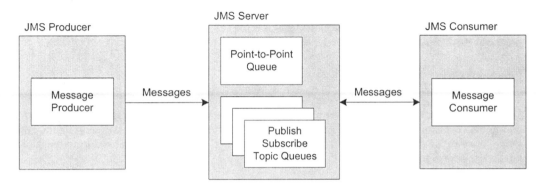

Figure 5-38. *The basic architecture of a JMS system*

All messages are delivered using procedure calls. The JMS server, often called the *provider* in the JMS literature, acts as a central distribution center for messages. Producers and consumers are often referred to generically as *clients*. Messages are posted to a queue by the sender and subsequently delivered by the JMS server to the recipient. Although clients can create queues, you typically create and manage queues using an administrative tool.

The JMS system architecture doesn't support distributed JMS servers. There is no predefined way for JMS servers to interoperate with each other. To support distributed servers, an implementation would need to create JMS servers that also acted as JMS producers and JMS consumers.

Message Routing

JMS supports two types of message-routing techniques: point-to-point (PTP) and publish-subscribe (PubSub). The two techniques are called *messaging domains* in the JMS literature. The former puts the burden of choosing recipients on the sender, and the latter puts the burden on the JMS server. In both messaging domains, the sender and recipient must be connected directly to the JMS server. Routing through a network or intermediate JMS servers is not contemplated by the JMS spec.

Using PTP, the sender specifies the destination queue of the message. The sender is therefore responsible for knowing which recipients are present in the system and deciding which recipients a message should be sent to. Clients wishing to receive messages from the server must register with the server, indicating which queue or queues they wish to use for incoming messages.

In the publish-subscribe domain, the server maintains a set of *topic-based* queues. Clients send messages to a specific topic queue. Topics may be related in a hierarchy or other manner. JMS poses no constraints and makes no assumptions regarding relationships among topics. Clients can subscribe to messages by topic and receive messages posted to the topic queue.

13. Mark Hapner, Rich Burridge, Rahul Sharma, Joseph Fialli, Kim Haase, *Java Message Service API Tutorial and Reference: Messaging for the J2EE Platform* (Boston: Addison-Wesley Professional, 2002).

JMS doesn't support a disconnected model for clients, because clients don't have their own local queues. The JMS server implements all queues, so if clients disconnect from the server, they lose access to all queues. Clients access their queues through a lightweight API, so JMS clients incur little overhead when incorporating messaging. Although generic disconnected clients aren't supported, there is support for a special kind of disconnected scenario based on something called *durable subscribers*. The idea is to allow producers to continue sending messages to consumers that are temporarily disconnected. Consumers register with the server as durable subscribers if they want the server to buffer their messages while they are temporarily disconnected. When the JMS server receives messages destined to disconnected durable subscribers, the server puts the messages in a persistent store. When the consumer reconnects, it is sent all the filtered topic-based messages posted to the recipient's queue while the consumer was disconnected.

Interoperability

The JMS specification doesn't define a way to support interoperability directly with non-Java systems. Since JMS delivers messages solely using procedure calls, only Java clients are supported. A bridging component is necessary at the provider level to allow JMS to interoperate with non-Java clients. The task of creating a bridge between JMS servers or between JMS and non-Java messaging systems is left for vendors to implement.

Interfaces

The only way to interact with a JMS system is via its Java interfaces, making JMS reachable only by Java components. Internet access, using protocols such as HTTP and SOAP, is not defined in the JMS specification. Vendors are left the task of implementing their own strategies for accessing JMS using Web or Internet protocols.

Message Structure

All JMS messages are serialized Java objects of type `javax.jms.Message`. The basic structure of a JMS message is shown in Figure 5-39.

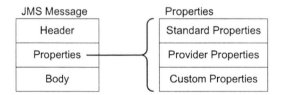

Figure 5-39. *The basic layout of JMS messages*

The `Message` class interface contains methods for accessing all three parts of the message. The message fields are defined as follows:

- *Header*: This field contains information regarding how to deliver the message, including QoS settings.

- *Properties*: This area contains a list of name-value properties. Standard properties are used to identify sender and recipient information, such as the sender's `UserID` and `GroupID`. Provider properties contain provider-specific properties. Custom properties hold name-pair values defined by the message sender.

- *Body*: This field contains the actual payload of the message and can contain text, byte arrays, or other entities, depending on the message type being used.

To support commonly used types, JMS defines the following specialized message classes:

- *TextMessage*: The message carries a string payload.
- *BytesMessage*: The message carries a byte-array payload.
- *MapMessage*: The message carries a list of name-value pairs.
- *StreamMessage*: The message contains a stream of values.
- *ObjectMessage*: The message contains a serialized Java object.

The message types are part of a standard message hierarchy shown in Figure 5-40.

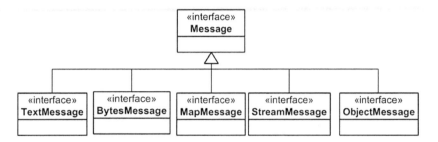

Figure 5-40. *The type space of JMS message payloads*

The sender creates a message that implements one of the interfaces and passes it to the JMS server in a method call. The message is serialized and sent over the wire to the server. The JMS spec doesn't define wire-specific protocols, so individual JMS providers can use any protocol they wish. Receivers can use run-time type identification (with the Java keyword `instanceof`) to determine the type of arriving messages.

QoS

Although JMS incorporates a number of CORBA Notification Service features, it is somewhat lighter than CORBA in its support for QoS. JMS QoS options can be set only at the message level, not at the queue level. There are no standard ways to set QoS options that apply to all messages associated with a given queue. At the message level, QoS options are specified using message properties. The following options are available:

- *Reliability*: Using the `JMSDeliveryMode` header field, the sender can specify whether a message should be handled persistently or not by the server. A persistent message must be kept in a safe store by the server, which promises to deliver it *once-and-only-once*. If a system failure occurs before the message is delivered, the server can recover it from the store and retry delivery until it succeeds. Nonpersistent messages are delivered *at-most-once*, so if a failure occurs before delivery, the message is lost.

- *Priority*: The sender can set the priority as a number in the range 0..9, with 9 being the highest priority. Priorities become important only when traffic starts backing up and messages can't be delivered as fast as they are sent. In these conditions, the server must try to deliver the higher priority messages first.

- *Expiration time*: The sender can specify timing constraints for message delivery using the JMSExpiration header field. If the server can't deliver a message before the expiration time, the message must be discarded. The JMS documentation doesn't specify whether the JMS server should notify the sender about discarded messages.

- *Transactions*: JMS supports transactions using the Java Transaction Service (JTS) or the Java Transaction API (JTA), allowing an arbitrary group of messages to be delivered completely or not delivered at all.

- *Acknowledgement*: Senders can request an acknowledgment of receipt of a message.

Delivery Models

Clients can receive messages using a push or pull mode. In the push mode, called *asynchronous mode* in the JMS literature, the recipient exposes the interface IMessageListener to the JMS server. When a message arrives, the server calls the recipient's IMessageListener.onMessage method, passing the Message object as a parameter. In the pull mode, the recipient calls the JMS server's MessageConsumer.receive method. Depending on the parameters supplied to it, the method can either block indefinitely until a message is found, or time out after a certain amount of time.

Filtering

Filtering is performed by the JMS server and is based on SQL-like filter expressions. Although filtering can conceivably apply to messages delivered using push or pull modes, the JMS spec doesn't describe the semantics of filtering in push mode.

Filters can only reference header fields and message properties. The body of the message can't be used. Filters are supported through a *message selector* string and can be used in both PTP and PubSub systems. In pull mode, consumers call the server and specify a filter expression. The server sequentially scans the messages in the queue, applying the filter to each message. Messages that don't satisfy the filter condition are skipped and left in the queue. When a message is found that satisfies the filter, it is removed from the queue and given to the consumer.

Consider an example in which a sender sends messages about cars. Messages might contain custom string properties named CarMake and CarModel to allow consumers to filter purchases by car make and model. To retrieve only messages related to Toyota Camry cars, the receiver could use the filter expression

```
(CarMake = 'Toyota') AND (CarModel = 'Camry')
```

Multicasting

The JMS specification doesn't define a mechanism for supporting multicasting, leaving it up to vendors or application programmers to implement their own scheme.

Commercial JMS Implementations

Like CORBA, JMS is published as a specification, not an implementation. Many details are left for vendors to interpret or provide, such as the level of JMS support they wish to include, which QoS features they support, how to interoperate with a JMS server from other vendors, and how to interoperate with non-JMS middleware systems.

A number of different vendors support JMS. Some of the most significant JMS products are described in the following sections.

IBM

IBM WebSphere MQ (WMQ),[14] formerly called MQSeries, is part of a large enterprise application integration (EAI) platform for building enterprise information systems. While WebSphere supports JMS and Java, you can also use it with several other programming languages, including C++ and Cobol. It also features a COM interface, usable by ActiveX clients. WMQ has two separate Java interfaces: one based on the internal WMQ interface, and one based on JMS. The former has classes such as `MQQueue` and `MQQueueManager`. The latter has standard JMS classes such as `MessageProducer` and `MessageConsumer`.

WMQ supports both PTP and PubSub messaging styles. You can achieve interoperability with foreign messaging systems and remote clients via network protocols such as TCP/IP and HTTP. Multicasting is handled using distribution lists. WMQ runs on several platforms, including AIX, Windows, and Linux.

BEA Systems

BEA WebLogic[15] is a multifaceted J2EE application infrastructure platform that comprises several services. One of them is called *WebLogic JMS* (WJMS), which is a complete implementation of the Java JMS specification. While IBM's WebSphere MQ can be accessed from many languages on multiple platforms, WJMS is targeted specifically at the Java platform. Interoperability with other systems and platforms is supported using *messaging bridge* components. These components support custom QoS options for messages sent/received across the bridge. Figure 5-41 shows the basic messaging bridge components.

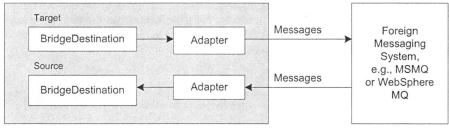

Figure 5-41. *Messaging bridges to connect WebLogic JMS to other systems*

Messaging bridges can connect with Java and non-Java systems. The connection details and message formatting are handled mostly by adapters. WJMS supports both PTP and PubSub messaging styles. Multicasting is handled using IP multicast addresses. WJMS runs on several platforms, including Solaris, Windows, and Linux.

TIBCO

TIBCO provides a number of EAI systems and was one of the early messaging pioneers. TIBCO has a JMS product called Enterprise for JMS (EJMS), which provides an implementation of the JMS API.

14. Mark Perry, Manesh Balachandran, Jorge Plata, Paul Solano, and Phillip Thomas, *MQSeries Programming Patterns* (White Plains, NY: IBM Redbooks, 2002, http://publib-b.boulder.ibm.com/Redbooks.nsf/RedbookAbstracts/sg246506.html?Open).

15. Jatinder Prem, Bernard Ciconte, Peter Go, Scott Dunbar, and Manish Devgan, *BEA WebLogic Platform 7* (Indianapolis, IN: Sams, 2003).

EJMS supports both PTP and PubSub messaging styles. EJMS provides APIs for Java, C, and C# clients. Interoperability with other systems and platforms is supported using *bridging* components. Multicasting is handled using IP multicast addresses. EJMS runs on several platforms, including Windows, Linux, and Solaris. Another TIBCO messaging product is SmartSockets, which I'll describe later. Curiously, SmartSockets is available in a JMS version, competing directly against EJMS.

Sun Microsystems

Although Sun Microsystems spearheaded the original JMS specification, the company didn't follow up immediately with an implementation. Sun now has a product called *Sun Java System Message Queue* (SJSMQ), formerly called *Sun ONE Message Queue*. Interoperability with other systems and platforms is supported via SOAP messaging. SJSMQ[16] is a full JMS implementation. The product also is accessible to C clients via a C API. Multicasting is handled using IP multicast addresses. SJSMQ runs on several platforms, including Solaris, Windows, and Linux. A variant called the *platform edition* of SJSMQ is free and can be downloaded from Sun's Web site at http://wwws.sun.com/software/download/index.html.

Oracle

Oracle Advanced Queuing[17] (OAQ) is a messaging system that is part of a large platform called Oracle Application Server (OAS), which is used to build enterprise information systems. OAQ uses an Oracle database to provide persistence to message queues. OAQ has two separate Java interfaces: a proprietary one and one based on JMS. Interoperability with non-Oracle systems is supported by a product suite called OracleAS Integration, which includes two bridging suites: InterConnect and ProcessConnect. Both come with a series of adapters that connect to popular non-Oracle systems.

OAQ supports both PTP and PubSub messaging styles. Using PubSub, notifications can be delivered in two different modes: multicast and broadcast. With the former, notifications are sent to all subscribers of a given topic. With the latter, notifications are sent to all subscribers. OAQ runs on several platforms, including Linux, Windows, and Solaris.

Others

Beside the vendors listed in the previous sections, there are several others, such as those listed in Table 5-1.

Table 5-1. *A Sample of Other Vendors with JMS Products*

Vendor	Product
Borland	VisiMessage
Sybase	EAServer
JBoss	JMS/JBoss
Sonic Software	SonicMQ

16. "Java Client Developer's Guide: Sun ONE Message Queue" (technical report, http://docs-pdf.sun.com/817-3728/817-3728.pdf, 2003).
17. "Advanced Oracle Queuing" (technical report, www.oracle.com/technology/products/aq/htdocs/9iaq_ds.html).

Sun maintains a list of JMS licensees on its Web site. JMS/JBoss is interesting because it is an open source implementation.

SmartSockets

TIBCO SmartSockets,[18] formerly Talarian SmartSockets, is a distributed notification service that supports a publish-subscribe architecture. Interactions between clients and server occur over *smart socket connections*, which provide features such as failover to an alternate connection in the event of a network failure. Each connection has its own queues that store messages in transit. Separate queues are managed for incoming and outgoing messages. Figure 5-42 shows the basic SmartSockets components.

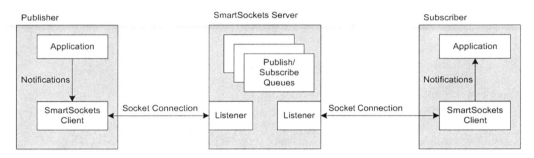

Figure 5-42. *The publish-subscribe interaction mode*

The publisher fires event notifications to a given queue in the SmartSockets server. Events are classified by subject, and all notifications for a given subject go to the same queue. Subscribers specify a subject of interest, which identifies the queue from which they will receive notifications. You can use SmartSockets servers in a distributed topology, as shown in Figure 5-43.

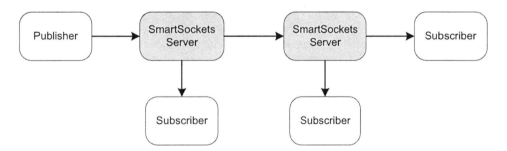

Figure 5-43. *Using a network of SmartSockets servers*

SmartSockets supports multicasting with IP multicasts and Pragmatic General Multicast (PGM),[19] a reliable multicasting transport protocol. SmartSockets runs on several platforms, including Unix, VMS, and Windows. It provides programming interfaces for C, Java, .NET, and ActiveX. A JMS interface is also available.

---

18. "TIBCO SmartSockets" (technical report, http://cf.tibco.com/eval/tibss.cfm).
19. Jim Gemmell, Todd Montgomery, Tony Speakman, Nidhi Bhaskar, and Jon Crowcroft, "The PGM Reliable Multicast Protocol," *IEEE Network*, January/February 2003.

SmartSockets can be considered to use a mixed delivery mode, using both shared resources and procedure calls to send messages: The publisher uses a socket connection to send notifications to the server. The connection acts as a shared resource between client and server. The server has a listener process that handles incoming messages. On the other side of the server, the subscriber runs a loop that checks periodically for incoming messages. When a message is found, the client calls a server method that tells the server to push the message to the client by calling a designated client method.

Message Structure

SmartSockets notification messages consist of two parts: a header and a body, as shown in Figure 5-44.

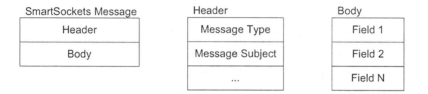

Figure 5-44. *The structure of a SmartSockets message*

The header contains a list of message properties, one of which is the message type. Several message types are supported to handle common data types such as strings, numbers, Booleans, and binary data. Types are also defined for JMS-compatible messages, used when interoperating with a JMS messaging service.

The message body can contain any number of *fields*, which contain the actual payload of a message. The structure of message fields depends on the message type. For example, with string message types, each field contains a (name, value) pair, both of which are strings. An example might be ("Title", "Alice in Wonderland"). With numeric message types, each field contains a (type, value) pair. An example might be (real4, 3.14). The type can be a numeric type, such as real4 or real8, but it can also be other types, such as Boolean, binary, or string. User-defined messages types are also supported.

QoS

SmartSockets supports QoS at two levels: the message level and the connection level. Message-level settings override connection-level settings. The following options are available:

- *Message priority*: The sender can indicate the priority of a message. The priority is significant only when messages are received by the server faster than they can be delivered. When multiple messages accumulate in a message queue, the message priority can be used to determine the next message delivered to receiver.

- *Reliable delivery*: Message queues can be set up as persistent, using a store such as a database or file system. If the SmartSockets system fails for any reason, persisted messages are not lost and will be delivered when the system restarts.

- *Timing*: Messages can have an expiration time. If a message can't be delivered before the expiration time, it is discarded. There are no QoS settings to indicate alternative ways of handling expired messages.

- *Burst delivery mode*: Multiple messages accumulated in a queue are delivered in a single burst as a composite message.

- *Failover recipients*: When recipients are sent messages in push mode and the SmartSockets service detects a failure in the recipient's callback method, the message is sent to an alternate recipient.

Filtering

Messages can be filtered based on their header properties. The subject property identifies which queue it will be sent to in the server. Subscribers can check the subject queue for messages, and also specify a particular message type. If a message is found, it is pushed to the subscriber by the server, using a callback method.

Rendezvous

TIBCO Rendezvous[20] (RV) is a distributed notification service that uses no centralized server. Each client machine has its own Rendezvous *daemon*, which runs as a background process. On one side, the daemon interacts with a client application, and on the other, with other RV clients. RV supports both PTP and PubSub interaction styles. Figure 5-45 shows what typical RV clients look like.

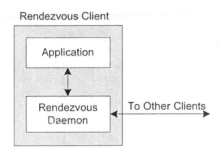

Figure 5-45. *A Rendezvous client*

The daemon is a gateway to other RV clients. There are no centralized message queues in RV, because each daemon has its own local buffers for outgoing and incoming messages, as shown in Figure 5-46.

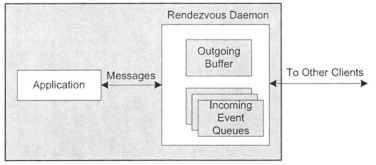

Figure 5-46. *Message buffers managed internally by Rendezvous daemons*

When a message arrives, it is put in an incoming event queue for subsequent delivery to the target application. A single RV client can contain multiple applications that communicate through a local shared daemon, as shown in Figure 5-47.

---

20. "TIBCO Rendezvous" (technical report, http://cf.tibco.com/eval/tibrv.cfm).

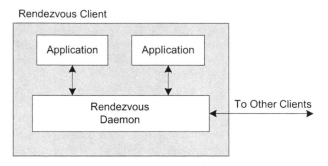

Figure 5-47. *Multiple applications sharing a local Rendezvous daemon*

Rendezvous clients are typically linked in a network, where clients talk directly to other clients, as shown in Figure 5-48.

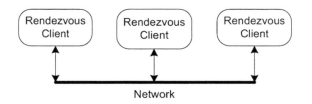

Figure 5-48. *A Rendezvous system, constituted by a network of Rendezvous clients*

Clients interact using a reliable protocol, such as PGM.[21] Networks of Rendezvous clients can be connected together using Rendezvous routers to form a network of networks. Each Rendezvous client that connects to another network uses a Rendezvous router instead of a simple daemon, as shown in Figure 5-49.

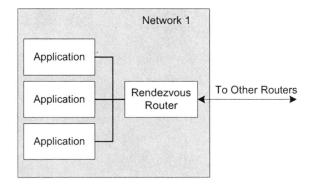

Figure 5-49. *A Rendezvous client using a router to connect to other networks*

---

21. Jim Gemmell, Todd Montgomery, Tony Speakman, Nidhi Bhaskar, and Jon Crowcroft, "The PGM Reliable Multicast Protocol," *IEEE Network*, January/February 2003.

The RV routers also act as daemons. When multiple networks are interconnected using routers, messages are passed through a series of client nodes until they reach their destination network and client, as shown in Figure 5-50.

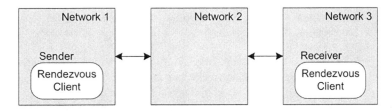

Figure 5-50. *Routing internetwork traffic through intermediate networks*

Each link between networks is associated with a *cost*. When there are different paths between networks, the routers use the cost to determine the least expensive path. When multiple paths have the same cost, traffic is split evenly across them to balance the load.

The distributed Rendezvous system architecture is peer-to-peer (P2P). When a client joins the system, a discovery process is launched automatically to locate nearby clients. Collectively, the RV routers and daemons implement an overlay network, called the *TIBCO information bus*. The bus hides lower-level networking details, such as TCP/IP or UDP properties.

Before sending a message in PTP mode, a client must know the identity of the intended recipient. When using the PubSub mode, subscribers must know which subjects are in use in the system. There is no central Rendezvous repository that stores client names or message subjects, but you can use a standard directory service for this purpose.

Message Structure

Rendezvous messages have a fairly simple structure and can carry a large variety of data types. Messages consist of a fixed-sized header and a variable-sized body, as shown in Figure 5-51.

Figure 5-51. *The structure of a Rendezvous message*

The header contains message properties, such as the field count, the message size, and the subject. The subject is used by Rendezvous daemons and routers, and essentially identifies the destination queue. The body contains a series of fields. Each field is a (name, value) pair containing data of several types, including strings, numbers, binary data, and arrays of data.

Message Routing and Delivery

In Rendezvous, the exchange of information between a sender and a receiver is based on a *rendezvous point*, of which there are two kinds. In PTP interactions, the rendezvous point is the destination client. The sender must know the name of the recipient client. The name may have nothing to do with the physical location or characteristics of the recipient. Names are arbitrary and established by the system architect. If the recipient is in the same network as the sender, the message is delivered directly to the recipient; otherwise, it is sent to a router, which then forwards the message toward the destination network. Once the message reaches the router of the destination network, the message is delivered to the recipient. There may be multiple routers in the delivery path. Multicasting is not supported in point-to-point, because the sender specifies a unique destination client.

All notification messages carry a subject property, and subscribers can listen for notifications with a given subject. In PubSub interactions, the rendezvous point is a message queue, which is identified by the message subject.

RV messages are delivered to the recipient application using a push model. The recipient registers with the local RV daemon, providing a queue name and a callback method. RV stores incoming messages in queues. There are queues for different kinds of messages, such as timer messages, diagnostic messages, and normal user messages. A subject can also be provided. When a message arrives, it is wrapped in an event object, and the object is placed in the appropriate event queue and subsequently dispatched to the recipient application by calling the registered callback method. When messages arrive faster than they can be processed, they are buffered up in the event queues. The RV daemon uses a separate dispatch thread for each event queue, so events in each queue are processed one at a time, in the order received.

Filtering

The basis for message filtering in RV is the message subject. Subject-based filtering is only available for PubSub messages. Subjects are specified using a dot notation, such as *Shipping.Air*. Subjects can define a hierarchical subject space. An example might be the three subjects *Shipping*, *Shipping.Air*, and *Shipping.Air.Priority*. Wildcard subjects are possible, so the subject *Shipping.** would indicate all types of Shipping messages.

RV doesn't have a centralized notification service, so the burden of filtering must be placed somewhere else. The RV architects opted for the receiving end. When an RV client publishes a message, a subject must be provided. The message is broadcast to all the other RV clients in the system. A multicast message only travels once through the network, regardless of the number of RV clients or subscribers. When an RV daemon receives a message, it checks the subject. If the subject was subscribed to by a client application, the message is grabbed, wrapped in an event object, and saved in an event queue for subsequent dispatching to the recipient application.

Multicasting

In RV, a sending client doesn't have direct control over whether a message is multicast or unicast: All PTP messages are sent to a single recipient, while all PubSub messages are multicast to the RV clients present in the system. Multicasting is based on reliable protocols, such as PGM or the proprietary TIBCO Reliable Data Protocol (TRDP), a UDP-based protocol.

QoS

RV supports a fairly short list of QoS options, compared to other middleware systems. The salient options are the following:

- *Reliable delivery*: This is the default delivery mechanism. Message delivery is reattempted until it succeeds or the message times out.

- *Certified delivery*: The sender is notified every time a message it sent is delivered to a recipient.

- *Timing*: The sender can specify an expiration time for certified delivery messages. Messages sent using the default reliable delivery QoS have a fixed time-out value. Messages not delivered in time are deleted.

Rendezvous doesn't support transactions directly. A separate product, called Rendezvous TX (RVTX), supports transactions using a centralized server architecture.

Interoperability

RV interoperates with other TIBCO messaging systems, such as SmartSockets and TIBCO Enterprise for JMS. Interoperability with non-TIBCO systems is accomplished using special adapters. A tool is available for building customized adapters.

Interfaces

Client applications interact with RV exclusively via the RV daemons and routers. Programming APIs are available for the following languages and component platforms:

- .NET
- C, C++
- Java
- ActiveX

TIBCO Rendezvous runs on all major platforms, including Windows, Unix, and VMS.

Summary

In this chapter, I've shown you some of the most common notification and messaging middleware systems in use today, but there are many more. The difference between a notification system and a messaging system is becoming increasingly blurred, and many commercial products provide support for both. While research systems tend to be more documented in the literature, commercial systems are on the front line and often push the envelope by using new techniques that can be of general interest.

CHAPTER 6

Diagrams for Event-Based Systems

When working on any kind of complicated task, it is useful to create a diagram showing the important aspects at some level of abstraction. The diagram is useful both to the person planning the project and to others wishing to understand it. The more complicated the project is, the more important diagrams are. Because diagrams are a representation of something from a certain perspective, they're often the best tools for conveying complex information to people quickly. Diagrams are invariably models of a system, so they don't contain every last detail.

When it comes to diagramming a software system in general, and an EBS in particular, there is no shortage of diagram choices. Each type focuses on certain aspects of the design, so no single diagram describes a system completely, and no single diagram suits everyone or every situation. Given the number of new types of diagrams created recently, it is clear that diagrams are a hot topic, and you can expect to see new types in the near future.

In this chapter, I'll take you on a brief tour of the most important types of diagrams in use today. In Chapter 7, I'll describe a new type of diagram developed specifically for event-based systems.

UML Diagrams

The Unified Modeling Language (UML) has been around for several years, and the version that most people are familiar with, as of this writing, is version 1.4. In this chapter, I'll show you the newer UML 2 diagrams, which extend 1.4 diagrams in many ways. All the diagrams shown will use UML 2 notation, but keep in mind that the UML 2 Final Adopted Specification was not available when this book went to press, so there may be small discrepancies with symbols and terminology used here with respect to the final published specification.

State Machine Diagrams

UML 2 State Machine diagrams are derived from UML 1.4 Statecharts, which in turn were derived from Harel Statecharts.[1] State Machine diagrams are a way to model systems that work in *modes* or states. In each state, the system responds to events in a certain way. Events, called *triggers* in the context of UML 2 State Machine diagrams, can be generated externally or internally, with respect to the system. Triggers produce transitions between states. You model a system by showing its states as boxes and its state transitions as arrows. Figure 6-1 shows a simple State Machine diagram for an elevator in a two-story building.

---

1. David Harel, "Statecharts: A Visual Formalism for Complex Systems," *Science of Computer Programming*, June 1987.

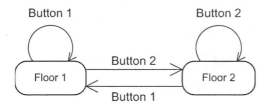

Figure 6-1. *A UML State Machine diagram showing states and transitions*

You label transitions to show their causes, which are called *triggers*. You can qualify triggers with a *guard condition* specifying the conditions that must apply in order for the trigger to be recognized. You show guard conditions on diagrams by adding the condition in square brackets after the trigger name. Figure 6-2 shows an example.

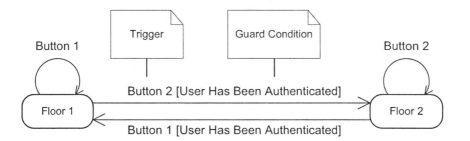

Figure 6-2. *A State Machine diagram showing trigger guard conditions*

You can also label transitions to show their effects, called *actions*. Actions represent behaviors of the system and are shown on transitions using the notation:

```
<trigger> / <action>
```

Figure 6-3 shows an example using transitions with actions.

In addition to actions produced by state transitions, there are actions that can be associated with each state. These actions can be performed when a state is entered or exited. You can also define actions to execute while the system is in a given state. State Machine diagrams also support *composite states*, in which a state can be decomposed into a number of substates.

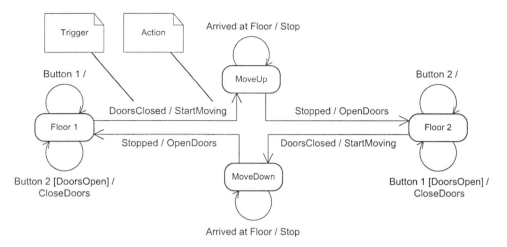

Figure 6-3. *A Statechart showing events, constraints, and actions*

Activity Diagrams

Activity diagrams are reminiscent of flowcharts and are useful for showing the process necessary to achieve a certain goal. Activity diagrams derive from concepts developed in Jim Odell's Event Diagrams.[2] Activity diagrams in UML 1.4 had a considerable amount of overlap with Statecharts, because they allowed diagrams to model both states and activities. UML 2 has eliminated the overlap, and activity diagrams no longer include state information.

Activities can be described as *work packages*, an expression borrowed from project cost accounting. Activities include a certain amount of work or logic, and can be at any level of abstraction. At the highest level, activities often correspond to a business process, such as *Ship Product* or *Bill Customer*. At the lowest level, activities might represent individual procedures to be implemented in a programming language. In this case, activity diagrams are essentially extended flowcharts. The flow of work from one activity to the next is called a *transition*. Transitions are denoted using arrows. Figure 6-4 shows the activity diagram for a simple mail-order processing system.

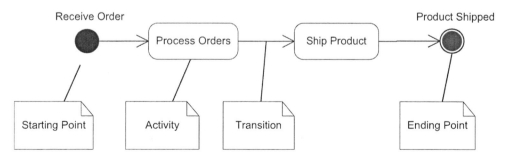

Figure 6-4. *A simple activity diagram showing the workflow of a mail-order system*

---

2. James Martin and James J. Odell, *Object-Oriented Methods: A Foundation–UML Edition* (Upper Saddle River, NJ: Prentice Hall, 1995).

Activities are shown as boxes with rounded corners. Starting and ending points are shown as black circles. You can break activities down into smaller parts, called *actions*, which are drawn inside an activity. The diagram in Figure 6-5 shows the actions that might be part of the Process Orders activity.

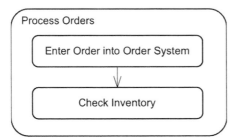

Figure 6-5. *Showing the actions inside an activity*

Data can be passed between actions. There are several ways to model this data on a diagram. The simplest involves a box with square corners, as shown in Figure 6-6.

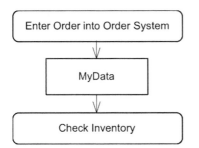

Figure 6-6. *Showing data passed between actions*

A more elaborate method to show data relies on the use of *pins*, which appear as small boxes attached to actions. Pins are either outputs or inputs. Pins are named after the data they handle. Figure 6-7 shows an example.

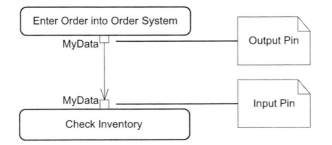

Figure 6-7. *Using pins to show data passed between actions*

There are a number of variations of pin symbols. Pins can contain small arrows that denote the direction of data flow, when this information is not clearly shown with a flow arrow between actions. You can also use pins with exception data and with streams. In the former case, you can add a small triangle near the pin. In the latter case, you can draw the pin using a solid black box or by attaching a solid arrowhead to it.

As with flowcharts, activity diagrams support branching on *decision points*, represented with a diamond symbol. A *merge point*, also represented with a diamond symbol, allows separate paths to come together. Figure 6-8 shows an example.

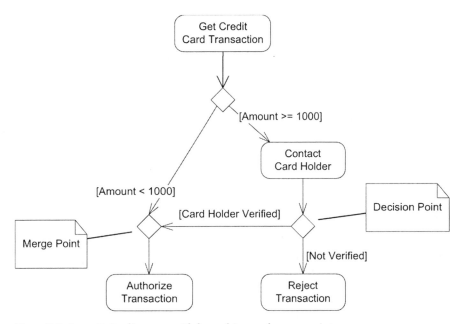

Figure 6-8. *An activity diagram with branching and merge points*

You can use activity diagrams to model concurrent workflows. A *fork node* is where a workflow branches off to concurrent flows. A *join node* is where multiple flows come back together in a synchronized way. A thick line acts both as a fork and join node, as shown in Figure 6-9.

Activity diagrams can be useful for modeling a system in different ways. You can use them to show the highest-level business processes or to show the specifics of individual use cases. At the lowest level, you can use activity diagrams to model individual procedures within classes.

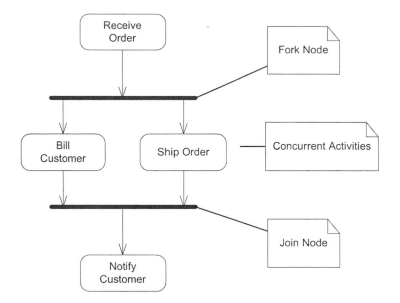

Figure 6-9. *Modeling concurrent activities*

Sequence Diagrams

When multiple objects collaborate to achieve a goal, there is interaction between them. UML 2 has two diagrams to model interactions: Sequence diagrams and Communication diagrams. I'll describe the latter in the next section. Sequence diagrams use vertical lines, called *lifelines*, that represent the participants of an interaction, with time increasing in the downward direction, as shown in Figure 6-10.

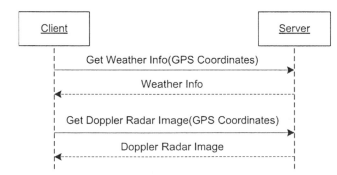

Figure 6-10. *A simple Sequence diagram*

Interactions are between objects, not classes. The object names appear at the top of the diagram in a rectangle called the *top box*. The messages exchanged use arrows, and the shape of the arrowhead indicates how the message is delivered. Messages can be synchronous or asynchronous. Return values are shown using dashed lines. A solid arrowhead indicates a synchronous message, typically delivered as a method call. The return values also use a solid arrowhead and dashed line.

Messages that create objects are connected to the object's top box instead of the vertical lifeline. You can put a gray box over certain sections of a lifeline to indicate which object is active at a given time. The box is called the *focus of control*. A large X at the end of the lifeline denotes the destruction of an object. Figure 6-11 shows a Sequence diagram in which an object is created, activated for a short operation, and then destroyed.

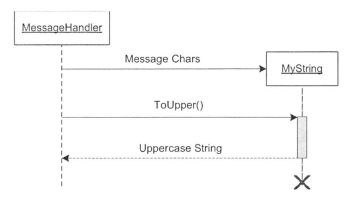

Figure 6-11. *A Sequence diagram showing object creation, activation, and destruction*

UML 2 Sequence diagrams have many features that weren't available in previous versions. *Frames* were introduced to represent fragments of an interaction that have given characteristics. Frames are represented by a box surrounding a Sequence diagram and have a pentagonal box in their upper-left corner with a heading that describes the type of fragment, as shown in Figure 6-12.

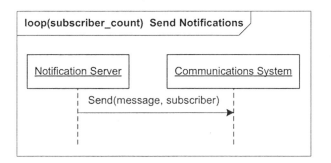

Figure 6-12. *A Sequence diagram frame showing a looped interaction*

Figure 6-12 shows an example of a frame containing a loop that is executed the number of times indicated by the variable subscriber_count. Table 6-1 describes the main headings used in Sequence diagram frames.

Sequence diagrams are great tools for modeling use cases, but are poor for modeling interactions with decision points. Each decision point requires an alt frame, which can lead to diagrams that are very difficult to understand. If you need to diagram interactions with lots of decision points, it is better to use Interaction Overview diagrams, described later, which use Activity diagrams and Sequence diagrams together to achieve more readable results.

Table 6-1. *Common Headings That Appear in Sequence Diagram Frames*

Heading	Description
Sd	Sequence diagram
alt	An alternative, used to model if/then/else
par	Indicates parallel execution of the contained lifelines
loop	A sequence that must be repeated a certain number of times
ref	A reference to another frame

Communication Diagrams

Communication diagrams, formerly called Collaboration diagrams in UML 1.4, are an alternative way to visualize interactions between objects. Communication diagrams carry the same information as Sequence diagrams, but have a structure and layout similar to a UML Object diagram. Communication diagrams emphasize the connections between objects, so interactions are shown in terms of connection paths that exist in the system. In contrast, Sequence diagrams make no assumptions about how messages are routed from one object to another. Figure 6-13 shows a simple Communication diagram.

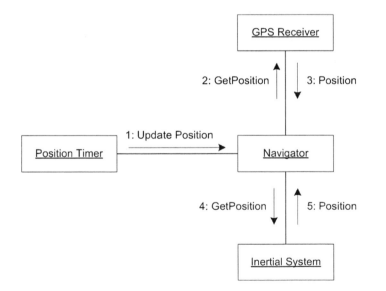

Figure 6-13. *A simple Communication diagram*

In the Sequence diagrams described in the previous section, the chronological order of messages is determined by the message position on the vertical lifelines. In Communication diagrams, there is no time axis, so messages are numbered. You can use a dotted notation to show nested procedure calls. For example, if an object calls two procedures as a result of message 1, then those calls could be labeled 1.1 and 1.2.

Interaction Overview Diagrams

This new diagram type was introduced with UML 2 and represents a specialization of Activity diagrams. An Interaction Overview is essentially an Activity diagram that also includes Sequence diagrams and Communication diagrams. The idea is to embed *interaction occurrences* in an Activity diagram, as shown in Figure 6-14.

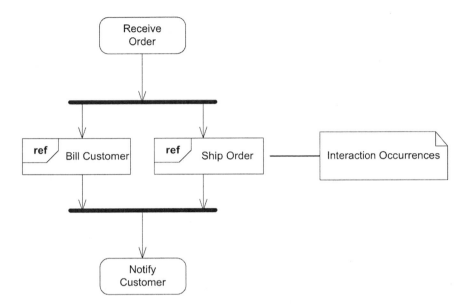

Figure 6-14. *An Interaction Overview diagram*

The diagram is similar to the one shown in Figure 6-9, with the Bill Customer and Ship Order activities replaced by two interaction occurrences that reference separate frames containing Sequence and Communication diagram fragments. The frame details are shown in Figure 6-15.

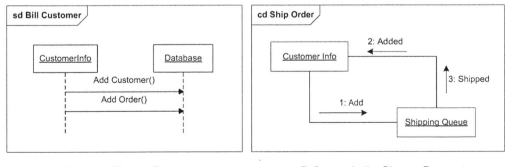

Figure 6-15. *Frames referenced in the previous Interaction Overview diagram*

Interaction Overviews can contain any mixture of symbols from Activity, Sequence, and Communication diagrams. While Activity diagrams are good at representing business processes, Sequence and Communication diagrams are better at showing the timing details of specific use cases.

Component Wiring Diagrams

Component Wiring diagrams are new to UML 2. They use the so-called *lollipop* symbol to represent interfaces exposed by a component. A lollipop symbol contains a small circle connected to a line. Component Wiring diagrams make the assumption that all outgoing calls are interface-based—in other words, made using the notation object.method, where object implements some interface. Outgoing calls connect to lollipops using a special connector symbol that wraps around one side of the lollipop circle, as shown in Figure 6-16.

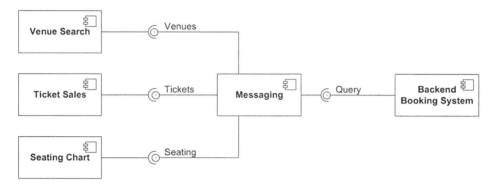

Figure 6-16. *A simple Component Wiring diagram showing assembly connectors*

There are two types of connectors: assembly connectors and delegation connectors. Assembly connectors appear between components and have an outgoing call connected to a lollipop symbol, as shown in Figure 6-16. Delegation connectors show how a component handles incoming interface-based calls internally. Figure 6-17 shows an example.

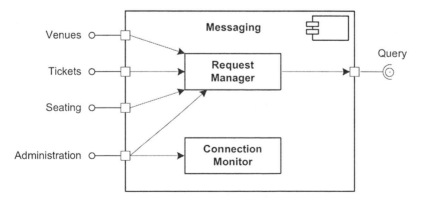

Figure 6-17. *A Component Wiring diagram showing delegation connectors*

The small square boxes on the border of the component are called *ports*. The ports that handle the incoming interfaces Venues, Tickets, Seating, and Administration are input ports. The Query port is an output port. UML 2 allows port symbols to contain an arrow in order to make explicit the direction of control flow through a port. Delegation connectors appear as arrows with dashed lines connecting ports to objects or vice versa. A single port may delegate to multiple objects, as shown in the case of the Administration interface in Figure 6-17. Delegation connectors can also redirect incoming calls to subcomponents, as shown in Figure 6-18.

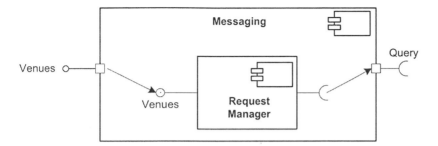

Figure 6-18. *Delegation connectors routed to a subordinate component*

The delegation connectors connect the incoming and outgoing interfaces of the subordinate component to input and output ports of the main component. Component Wiring diagrams make no assumptions about how calls from ports are physically delegated to internal objects or subordinate components.

Other Diagrams

Although UML is the most widely used methodology for modeling EBSs today, there are many others. Some had an influence on UML and were eventually incorporated into UML, such as Harel Statecharts and Jim Odell's Event Diagrams. Others were developed before the advent of OO or for vertical markets. For example, SDL (described later) was developed initially for telecom systems and has achieved more penetration in Europe than the United States. Here are some other techniques that are interesting but not in widespread use in EBS diagrams:

- Petri nets[3]
- Change propagation and response graphs[4]
- Architecture description languages,[5] such as Rapide[6]
- Workflow diagrams, available in many variations
- Event-driven Process Chains[7]

---

3. Tadao Murata, "Petri Nets: Properties, Analysis and Applications," *Proceedings of the IEEE*, April 1989.
4. John C. Grundy, John G. Hosking, and Warwick B. Mugridge, "Supporting Flexible Consistency Management via Discrete Change Description Propagation, Software," *Practice and Experience*, September 1996.
5. Nenad Medvidovic and Richard N. Taylor, "A Classification and Comparison Framework for Software Architecture Description Languages," *IEEE Transactions on Software Engineering*, January 2000.
6. David C. Luckham, John J. Kenney, Larry M. Augustin, James Vera, Doug Bryan, and Walter Mann, "Specification and Analysis of System Architecture Using Rapide," *IEEE Transactions on Software Engineering*, April 1995.
7. W.M.P. van der Aalst, "Formalization and Verification of Event-Driven Process Chains," *Information and Software Technology*, July 1999.

There are certainly many other proprietary diagrams that companies use but that never gained public recognition. In the following sections, I'll show you some of the better-known diagram types, as well as some lesser-known ones that have a great deal of relevance with EBSs.

Lollipop Diagrams

Lollipop diagrams use interfaces as the basis of component interconnection. I presented an example of lollipops used in UML 2 Component Wiring diagrams. On lollipop diagrams, components are represented by simple boxes, and incoming interfaces appear as *lollipops* with a circle at the end of a line. Figure 6-19 shows an example.

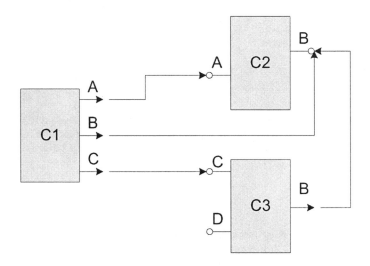

Figure 6-19. *A simple lollipop diagram*

Outgoing interface-based calls are shown with arrows emerging from a component. Lollipop diagrams were used extensively to model COM[8] component systems. They are similar to other diagrams, including Szyperski's connection-oriented diagrams.[9]

Lollipop diagrams only show connections at the interface level. They provide no information regarding which methods of an interface are called, or in which order. All inputs are in terms of interfaces. Outgoing calls are shown with a simple outbound arrow, with no explanation of where the outbound call originates inside the caller.

SDL Diagrams

The Specification and Description Language[10] (SDL) was developed several years ago, under the auspices of the CCITT international standards body (currently the ITU), to support the modeling of telecom systems. Such systems consist often of concurrent processes that communicate by sending signals to each other. SDL signals are essentially event notifications, so SDL diagrams are of interest

---

8. Don Box, *Essential COM* (Boston: Addison-Wesley Professional, 1997).
9. Clemens Szyperski, *Component Software: Beyond Object-Oriented Programming* (Boston: Addison-Wesley Professional, 2000).
10. Jan Ellsberger, Dieter Hogrefe, and Amardeo Sarma, *SDL: Formal Object-Oriented Language for Communicating Systems* (Upper Saddle River, NJ: Prentice Hall, 1997).

to EBS architects. SDL has evolved considerably with the advent of OO and component-based development (CBD).

SDL supports a number of different diagram types. Those relevant to this discussion are Process and Block diagrams. The former model processes finite State Machine diagrams with flowchart-like decision points, as shown in Figure 6-20.

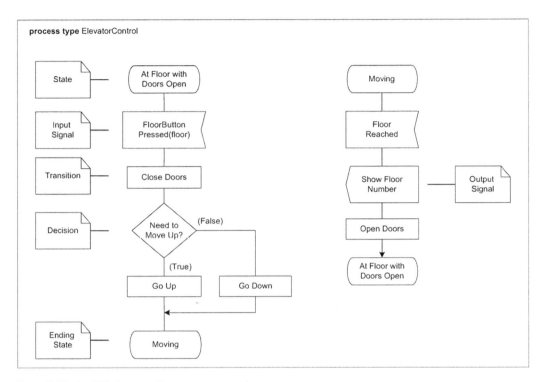

Figure 6-20. *An SDL Process diagram*

Boxes with rounded sides represent states. Tasks are executed as part of a state transition and are enclosed in a box with straight sides. Input signals, including user actions, are events detected by the environment. Output signals include messages displayed on the user interface.

Another way to picture a system in SDL is with Block diagrams, in which processes or other entities are shown exchanging signals. Figure 6-21 shows a Block diagram with processes.

The connections between processes are called *signalroutes*. The name of the signal that travels over a signalroute is shown in square brackets. Signals can carry any number of parameters. Blocks can be assembled together and the signals exchanged between blocks are sent over *channels*.

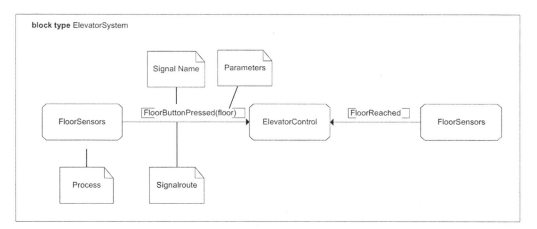

Figure 6-21. *An SDL Block diagram*

A process can also receive signals from another process, in which case the sending process identifies the destination process in an output signal symbol, as shown in Figure 6-22.

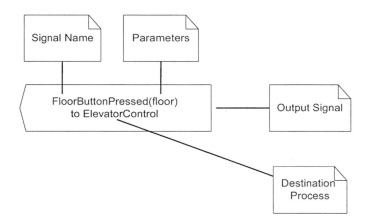

Figure 6-22. *An outgoing signal directed to another process*

Signals are assumed to be asynchronous in SDL. To avoid indeterminate behaviors, signal-routes and channels are required to preserve signal ordering. For example, if the three signals are sent in the order S1, S2 and S3, the receiver must get them in the same order, regardless of the delay involved in the transmission.

Espresso Diagrams

Espresso diagrams were developed in the context of the Espresso[11] component model. In Espresso, events are signals that represent the sole means of communication between components. Components

---

11. Ted Faison, "Interactive Component-Based Software Development with Espresso" (proceedings of the International Conference on Automated Software Engineering, Lake Tahoe, NV, November 1997).

are diagrammed as boxes, and signals enter and leave components through an entity called a *port*, represented using an arrow that connects to the border of a component box.

A port is a logical grouping of signals, and input ports are nothing more than exposed interfaces. An output port denotes outgoing calls. A port can contain both input and output signals, in which case the port is bidirectional. In Espresso, signals are delivered using method calls, and an arrow depicts the direction of control flow through the port. Figure 6-23 shows an example of a simple Espresso diagram.

Figure 6-23. *A simple Espresso diagram with a bidirectional port connection*

When it is useful to show the details of the signals involved with a port connection, you can use a special diagramming variation, as shown in Figure 6-24.

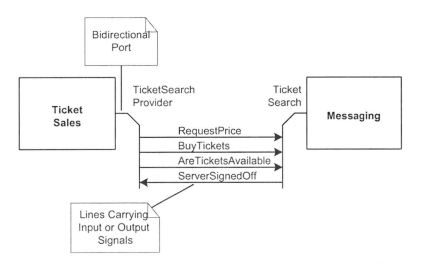

Figure 6-24. *An Espresso diagram, showing ports and lines*

The detailed connection is shown using a notation called *port-breakout*. The individual signals travel on entities called *lines*, which also show the direction of control flow for each method call.

Espresso components can have any number of ports, and a port can have any number of lines. While input lines have a one-to-one correspondence with methods, output lines have a one-to-one correspondence with method pointers exposed by the component. Although input ports are equivalent conceptually to interfaces, the individual calls made into an input line are made at the method level, using a method reference that bypasses interfaces.

Catalysis Diagrams

Catalysis[12] is a methodology for building component-based software developed by Wills and D'Souza. It defines a number of different types of diagrams, some of which had a great influence on UML 2 diagrams. One type of Catalysis diagram that is of particular interest for EBSs is the Connector diagram, in which components are denoted by boxes that have outgoing and incoming signals.

There are two kinds of outgoing signals: events and properties. Output events are notifications sent when a component changes state or senses that *something has happened*. A Button component might have a clicked output event that is fired when the button is pressed. Output properties are notifications sent when a given attribute changes value. Output events are depicted with open arrowheads; output properties are depicted with solid arrowheads, as shown in Figure 6-25.

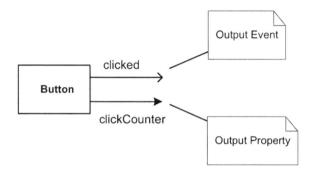

Figure 6-25. *A component with two kinds of outputs*

The arrows on outputs show the direction of control flow. Outputs are meant to be wired to inputs, which can also be of two types: input events and input properties. Both are depicted with a lollipop symbol. Input events use a hollow lollipop and input properties use a solid lollipop, as shown in Figure 6-26.

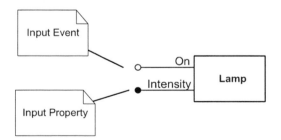

Figure 6-26. *A component with two kinds of inputs*

The point at which an input or output attaches to a component is called a *port*. A port can handle only a single input or output. Components are wired together on a Connector diagram by connecting output arrows to lollipops. Figure 6-27 shows a simple elevator-control system depicted using a Connector diagram.

---

12. Desmond Francis D'Souza and Alan Cameron Wills, *Objects, Components, and Frameworks with UML: The Catalysis Approach* (Boston: Addison-Wesley Professional, 1998).

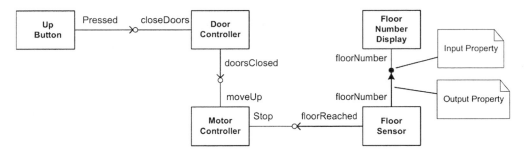

Figure 6-27. *A simple Connector diagram*

Figure 6-27 represents an early version of the Connector diagram. A later version evolved[13] in which ports are shown as small squares on the border of a component. Figure 6-28 shows the four variations of the port symbol.

Figure 6-28. *Port symbols used in later versions of Connector diagrams*

Given that outputs have a different symbol than inputs, Connection diagrams no longer need arrows to show the direction of control flow. The lollipop symbols were also dropped, so a connection is shown simply as a line connecting an output port to an input port. Figure 6-29 shows the elevator-control system with the later version of the Connector diagram.

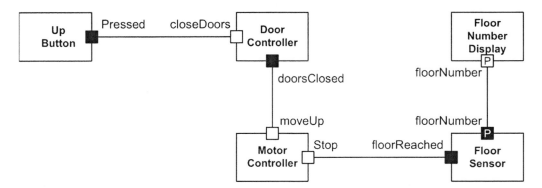

Figure 6-29. *The elevator-control system, shown with a later version of the Connector diagram*

---

13. George T. Heineman and William T. Councill, *Component-Based Software Engineering: Putting the Pieces Together* (Boston: Addison-Wesley Professional, 2001, p. 308).

Connector diagrams have a certain similarity with circuit diagrams, modeling components as software integrated circuits (ICs) sporting input and output connection points. OMG later used the early style of Connector diagrams, with output arrows attached to lollipops, as the basis for the UML 2 Component Wiring diagram.

Summary

With so many different types of diagrams out there, you might think there is no room for improvement. UML certainly dominates the landscape of software diagrams, but many people are starting to feel that UML has gotten too complex—that it is trying to solve too many problems at once. Is it a modeling language, a set of diagramming conventions, or a high-level programming language? Depending on how you use it, it can be all three. When dealing with event-based designs, a circuit-oriented diagram is often a good choice. Event notifications travel around the system like signals in an electrical circuit, so it makes sense to depict the system using the same kinds of concepts adopted in hardware diagrams. The next chapter is dedicated to a new kind of diagram developed specifically for event-based systems.

■ ■ ■

CHAPTER 7

Signal Wiring Diagrams

In this section, I'll show you a new type of software design diagram called *Signal Wiring diagram,* usually abbreviated as *wiring diagram.* This type of diagram depicts a system focusing not on the structure of its components and objects, but rather on the signals they exchange. Existing diagrams, such as UML Collaboration diagrams, Interaction diagrams, and Component Wiring diagrams, show how selected parts of the system are connected or interoperate, but sometimes those diagrams can be either too detailed or not detailed enough.

Wiring diagrams rely on a hardware metaphor, describing the connectivity of a system in ways similar to hardware-schematic diagrams. They also act like maps, showing the itineraries that signals follow to go from one place to another. In digital systems, most functionality usually comes from integrated circuits (ICs). Wiring diagrams show objects and components in a role very similar to the ICs on schematic diagrams.

Software ICs

The notion of objects as software ICs is not new. In the early days of the object-oriented programming tide, it was recognized that objects might be used in ways conceptually similar to the integrated circuits used in the hardware world.[1] The software IC idea was intuitive and widely publicized, but there were a number of problems at the time that were waiting for a solution. One problem was coupling between classes: Rarely were classes completely decoupled from others. If a class was coupled to others, then it represented an inseparable part of a larger system. To use a single class C1 that was coupled to others, say C2 and C3, you had to have C2 and C3. But C2 and C3 might have been coupled to other classes, which in turn might have been coupled to others. In the end, sometimes you were required to include an entire class framework into a design, even if you needed only one class in it.

Another problem was that the event concept hadn't taken hold yet. At the time, there were no languages that natively supported what we would call events. Also, it wasn't clear what the software equivalent of an output signal was. The software IC concept was simply ahead of its time, and software ICs became another idea that came and went.

Wiring diagrams resurrect Brad Cox's idea, showing objects as boxes with *pins* attached to *wires.* Obviously, the pins and wires are diagrammatic abstractions, but they are easy to understand conceptually, and the diagrams are easy to follow. The diagrams make no assumptions on exactly how pins are implemented.

---

1. Brad J.Cox, *Object-Oriented Programming: An Evolutionary Approach* (Boston: Addison-Wesley Professional, 1986).

There are certain inherent differences between objects and ICs, due to the fact that the former are abstractions, while the latter are real. In the real world of signals, you need to deal with the physical characteristics of conductors, transmission lines, and signals. Hardware pins are classified as input, output, or input/output. An I/O pin can support both input and output, but can only do one thing at a time. It can also do neither, acting as if the internal circuitry has been disconnected from the pin. This internal disconnection requires the pin to support something called *tri-state mode*, in which the pin is put into high impedance mode and disconnected from any internal input or output circuits. Tri-state mode is required on all output pins that can be connected to a wire that other output pins are connected to. Only one of the output pins connected to a wire can be active at a given time. All other pins connected to the wire must either be inputs or outputs in tri-state mode. If two output signals were active at the same time and connected to the same wire, they would fight each other for control over the signal's state (i.e., high or low). The *strength* of an output signal, which connotes the signal's ability to *win* in a fight, is measured by its impedance. The lower the impedance, the *stronger* the signal.

Impedances are related to a parameter known as *fanout*. The fanout of an output pin indicates how many inputs it can drive. In an ideal situation, the fanout should be infinite: An output pin should be able to drive any number of input pins. For the fanout to be infinite, inputs and pins in the tri-state mode would need to have infinite impedance. In practice, the fanout is not infinite, and dependent largely on the technology used to build the IC. In the old days of TTL,[2] the fanout was often below 10. With the advent of CMOS logic,[3] the fanout increased significantly.

Let's look at some of the characteristics of software outputs and inputs. For one thing, the concept of tri-state mode doesn't apply. Inputs correspond to callable procedures, or data arriving from somewhere. Outputs correspond to procedure calls, or data written somewhere. If multiple outputs are connected to the same input, the outputs don't conflict with each other—unless they are active concurrently in multithreaded or multiprocessing systems. Even though impedance fails to apply to software outputs, the concept of fanout continues to be valid. The fanout of an output signal is dependent on the implementation mechanism used to send the signal. Unicast senders have a fanout of one, while multicast senders can potentially be connected to any number of receivers, limited only by the constraints of the implementation.

Notwithstanding the differences between the hardware and software worlds, there is much to be learned from hardware diagrams, which have been around far longer than anything in the software realm. The wiring diagrams described in this chapter borrow many of the concepts and techniques that have matured over decades in the digital design world. Wiring diagrams might be described as hybrids—a cross between several diagram types. They are especially useful in showing the plumbing of a system, focusing on the signals exchanged by the players and the paths the signals take.

Objects

On a wiring diagram, signals travel between objects. Objects are represented by a box. The size of the box is dictated by aesthetic considerations, but also constrained by the number of signals entering and leaving the object. Figure 7-1 shows an object with no signals entering or leaving.

---

2. TTL stands for Transistor-Transistor Logic and was the standard semiconductor technology used in digital logic until the early 1980s.
3. CMOS stands for Complementary Metal Oxide Semiconductor and became the standard semiconductor technology for digital logic in the early 1980s. CMOS reigns supreme to this day, due to its low power consumption and high speed.

Figure 7-1. *The symbol for an object*

Every object must have a name and can also include an optional ID. The name is the name of the object as used in the source code. If the object is used as a singleton, the object's class name can be used. Whether the name is uppercase or lowercase depends on the conventions of the programming environment or component platform. You may include namespaces, if necessary, to distinguish between similarly named objects in different namespaces. When it is important to specify the class of an object, the name can be followed by a colon and the class name—e.g., `myName: MyClass`.

The ID is a numbered label of the form Cn, where C is an uppercase string and n is a decimal number, starting at 1. The string portion of the label designates the object's role in the system. I'll discuss roles later, in Chapter 10. Table 7-1 shows the role-based labels used in the diagrams of this book.

Table 7-1. *Role-Based Labels Used in Wiring Diagrams*

Label	Role
W	Worker
C	Coordinator
B	Builder, Binder, or both
R	Router
G	Generic
U	Utility
SW	Switch

Figure 7-2 shows a couple of objects as they might appear on a diagram.

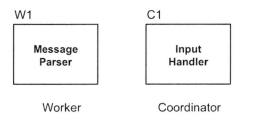

Figure 7-2. *An example of two objects, with name and ID*

IDs can be omitted on simple one-page diagrams, but in complex diagrams, IDs become very useful for cross-referencing objects that are on different pages.

Signals

Signals carry information from one object to another. Objects can send signals in two basic ways:

1. *Using procedure calls*: Execution control is passed from the sender to the receiver.

2. *Using a shared resource*: With shared resource interactions, signals transfer data, not execution control, from the sender to the receiver.

On a wiring diagram, the abstract path over which signals travel from sender to receiver is depicted with lines. The lines are also known as *wires*. A wire can only carry one type of signal. You must label every wire in a diagram to show the name of the signal associated with it and to indicate the direction of travel of the signal. Figure 7-3 shows how a signal is represented on diagrams.

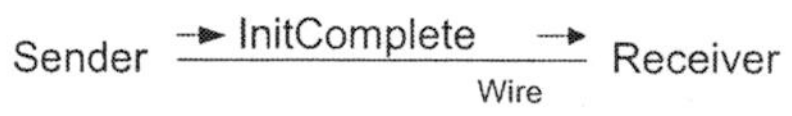

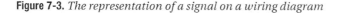

Figure 7-3. *The representation of a signal on a wiring diagram*

If a signal with a given name can originate from more than one place, the name of the sender can be included with a signal, using a dot notation. Figure 7-4 shows an example.

Figure 7-4. *Qualifying a signal name with the sender's name*

Alternatively, you can also label a signal with the sender's ID, as shown in Figure 7-5.

Figure 7-5. *Qualifying a signal name with the sender's ID*

PC Signals

When using procedure call (PC) signals, the sending component calls a procedure of the receiving component. Whether the call is local or remote is immaterial for diagramming purposes. The signal is the procedure call itself. The name of the signal is chosen by the designer purely for documentation purposes, but is usually related to an operation of the caller or callee. Often the name is derived from the name of the output pin where the signal originates. I'll describe pins a bit later in this chapter.

Procedure calls have the option of carrying data. The signal's arrow always denotes the direction in which execution control (and not data) is passed, and is therefore directed from caller to callee. With procedure calls, data can be returned not only by the return value of the called procedure, but also by modified fields of entities passed by reference. Signals sent to a notification server are classified as PC signals if clients interact with the server using procedure calls or use procedure call emulations (e.g., with RPC or SOAP).

As indicated earlier, PC signals involve a transfer of execution control from the sender to the receiver. If the receiver handles the call synchronously, the sender blocks until the receiver completes the call. If the receiver handles the call asynchronously, the call is processed on a separate thread. Execution control can then be returned immediately to the sender, perhaps with a code indicating whether the call was accepted or not.

When it is important to indicate that a signal is PC signal, the signal name can be followed by parentheses. The arguments of procedure calls are not shown inside the parentheses. Pin legend tables, described later, are used to describe the data passed to and from the receiver. Figure 7-6 shows a PC signal.

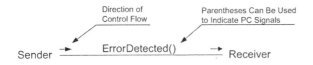

Figure 7-6. *A simple PC signal*

Returning Data to Sender

Because PC signals are delivered with procedure calls, it is possible for them to return data to the sender. Returned values are those identified by the called method's signature. For example, consider the method with the following C# signature:

```
bool DoSomething(Hashtable ht);
```

The method returns a Boolean value. What about the Hashtable? In most OO languages, objects are passed by reference. If the callee makes changes to an object passed by reference, the caller will be able to observe those changes. Changes made to objects passed by reference are considered *side effects* of a call, not returned values. Neither side effects nor returned values are shown on wires of wiring diagrams. Where it is important to document them, a pin legend table can be used, as described later.

SR Signals

When using shared resource (SR) signals, the sender writes data to a resource shared with the receiver. The receiver independently reads data from this resource, which can be a file, shared memory, a network connection, a pipe, or an interprocess control structure. With shared-resource delivery, only data (and not execution control) is transferred from the sender to the receiver. Although the sender can send any number of variables to the receiver, returned values are not possible. In a send interaction, the sender writes data to the resource. The receiver reads data from the resource. The signal's arrow on the diagram denotes the direction of data flow. When it is important to indicate that a signal is an SR signal, you can put the signal name in parentheses. Figure 7-7 shows an SR signal.

Figure 7-7. *A simple SR signal*

When it is important to indicate the provenance of an SR signal, the signal name can be qualified in the usual ways (using the sender's name or ID), but it can also be qualified with the sender's DNS name, network address, computer name, or process name, as shown in Figures 7-8 through 7-11.

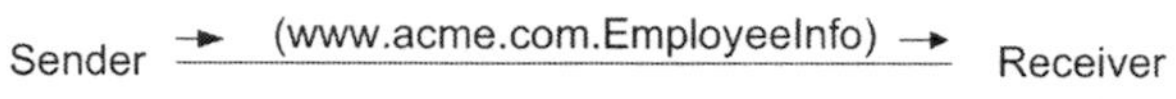

Sender ——→ (www.acme.com.EmployeeInfo) —→ Receiver

Figure 7-8. *Using the sender's DNS name*

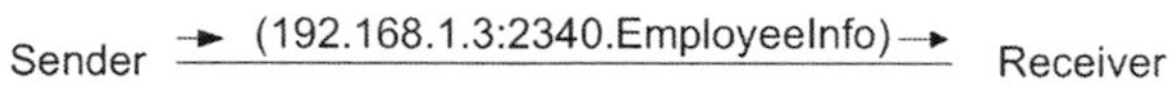

Sender ——→ (192.168.1.3:2340.EmployeeInfo) —→ Receiver

Figure 7-9. *Using the sender's IP address and port number*

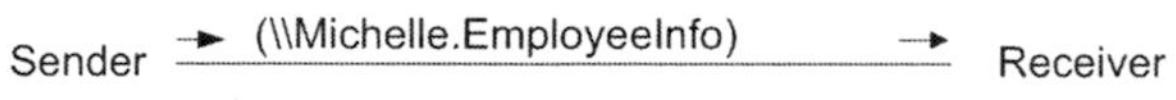

Sender ——→ (\\Michelle.EmployeeInfo) ——→ Receiver

Figure 7-10. *Using the sender's UNC computer name*

Sender ——→ (\\Michelle.Payroll.EmployeeInfo) —→ Receiver

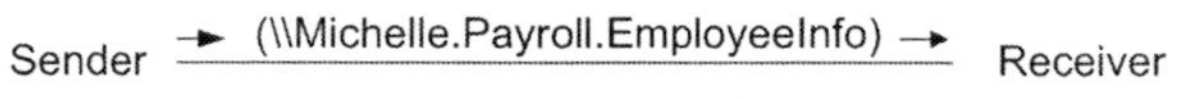

Figure 7-11. *Using the sender's UNC computer name and process name*

Although you can qualify signals in several ways, you should include only information that is significant, to avoid cluttering the diagram with useless details. For example, you might omit the sender's port number if the sender can only send from that port, or if the sender uses a TCP/IP *ephemeral port*, in which case the sender doesn't specify explicitly which port the outbound traffic is sent from.

Synchronicity

Signals delivered with procedure calls can be handled synchronously or asynchronously. Signals delivered as messages can also be synchronous or asynchronous, depending on the communication protocol used. For example, using low-level TCP socket operations, the sender can send data and continue without waiting for any confirmation from the receiver. If HTTP is used, the sender might use POST verbs to send data. When the POST is sent, the sender can block, waiting for data to be returned. Whether messages are sent synchronously or not depends on how the communication layer is designed.

You can use differently shaped arrowheads on wiring diagrams to show the synchronicity of signals. A similar convention is used in UML Interaction diagrams. If the arrowhead is complete, the signal is synchronous, as shown in Figure 7-12. If the arrowhead is missing the upper portion, the signal is asynchronous, as shown in Figure 7-13.

Sender ——→ ErrorDetected() —→ Receiver

Figure 7-12. *A synchronous signal*

Figure 7-13. *An asynchronous signal*

Pins

The idea of using a dedicated entity to represent signal entry/exit points of software components has been around for years. The *port* metaphor is used by several Architecture Description Languages (ADLs), including several ACME[4] and several Wright.[5] The Espresso component model[6] uses input/output *lines* that can be grouped into ports. C2[7] uses *messages* that all flow through a common port.

On wiring diagrams, the term *pin* refers to the signal entry/exit points of objects. Pins are obviously abstractions, but they are useful to reinforce the notion that objects send and receive signals, and that wiring is required to move those signals around in a system. On wiring diagrams, each pin handles one signal. Pins are represented by black squares on the border of an object, as shown in Figure 7-14.

Figure 7-14. *An object with pins*

The object W1 has a total of seven pins. The pin placing is arbitrary and is dictated only by the requirements of the diagram layout and/or the number of pins present. Some pins might be associated to inputs or outputs that aren't used. You can omit these pins, if doing so makes the diagram easier to understand.

Naming Pins

Pins should be labeled to indicate the nature of the signal entering or exiting. When present, the label must appear on the inside of the component, right next to the pin. Figure 7-15 shows a component with two labeled pins.

4. David Garlan, Robert Monroe, and Dave Wile, "Acme: An Architecture Description Interchange Language" (proceedings of IBM Centers for Advanced Studies Conference, Toronto, Ontario, Canada, November 1997).

5. Robert Allen and David Garlan, "A Formal Basis for Architectural Connection," *ACM Transactions on Software Engineering and Methodology,* July 1997.

6. Ted Faison, "Interactive Component-Based Software Development with Espresso" (proceedings of the International Conference on Automated Software Engineering, Lake Tahoe, NV, November 1997).

7. Nenad Medvidovic, David S. Rosenblum, and Richard N. Taylor, "A Language and Environment for Architecture-Based Software Development and Evolution" (proceedings of the 21st International Conference on Software Engineering, Los Angeles, CA, May 1999).

Figure 7-15. *A component with two named pins*

What name is used for a pin depends on the signal direction and type, as described in the following sections.

Input Pins

An input pin represents the point at which a signal enters an object. An arrow indicates the direction of signal flow. For PC signals, the arrow denotes the direction of control flow; for SR signals, the arrow denotes the direction of data flow.

Input pins are named differently, depending on whether they handle PC or SR signals. For PC signals, the name is that of the method that is invoked through the pin. If the method name is overloaded, the full method signature may be required. If the signature is very long, the pin can be numbered, and the pin's full description can be referenced in a pin legend table, as described in the later section, "Numbering Pins."

Figure 7-16 shows a Worker object with an input pin through which a method named Parse can be called.

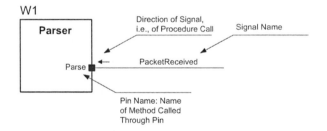

Figure 7-16. *A named input pin associated with a PC signal*

You can prefix the name with the name of the called method's interface to distinguish between methods of the same name belonging to different interfaces. You can also include the namespace, or a fragment of it, where useful to properly identify a method.

Wiring diagrams should strive to provide only as much information as necessary to clarify ambiguities. Putting complete namespace paths on every input pin would result in diagrams that are difficult to read. Figure 7-17 shows an input pin labeled with namespace and interface identifiers.

When multiple pins need to include the interface name in the pin name, showing the interface on every pin becomes tedious. A simple convention uses a shaded box to designate the interface, with all the related input pins on an edge of the box, as shown in Figure 7-18.

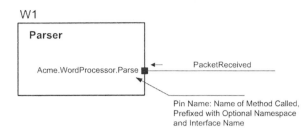

Figure 7-17. *An input pin whose name includes a namespace and interface*

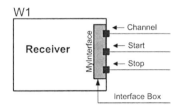

Figure 7-18. *Showing the interface to which a group of input pins belong*

Because the interface box leaves no room for the pin names, pin numbers can be used, as described later. When pin numbers are not used, the incoming signal names must match the name of the method called through the pin. The interface box can appear on any side of an object. The name of the interface is displayed along a border of the interface box.

For input pins handling an SR signal, the pin name is that of the variable that references the shared resource from which the signal is read. The variable may contain an IP address, a URI, a telephone number, a shared memory pointer, a filename, or other. Figure 7-19 shows an object with an input pin associated with an SR signal.

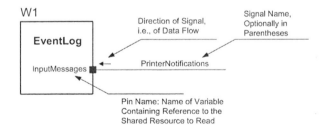
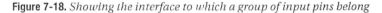

Figure 7-19. *A named input pin associated with an SR signal*

Wiring diagrams use the same symbol for PC and SR pins. When it is important to clarify which type of signal is entering a pin, the signal name can be followed by parentheses (for PC signals) or the signal name can be enclosed in parentheses (for SR signals).

Accessing Properties

Objects sometimes expose not just methods, but also properties. Properties are really nothing more than method calls in disguise, so wires bound to a property need little additional explanation.

One restriction is that properties cannot be used on output pins, because properties can only be called—to set or get values.

At the implementation level, some OO languages pose constraints regarding binding an output signal to a property. Consider C#, in which run-time binding is based on the use of *delegates*, which can only be associated to methods. Since C# properties are accessed through compiler-generated getter and setter methods, you would need to create a delegate referencing one of these methods. Currently, C# doesn't allow you to reference a property setter or getter method explicitly, so you can't bind an output signal to a property. The best you can do is bind the output signal to an ad hoc method, which in turn calls the property setter or getter. In Java, you can call property setters and getters like all other methods, so no special conditions apply to properties.

Output Pins

As with input pins, the naming of output pins depends on whether the pin handles PC or SR signals. With PC signals, outgoing calls are made indirectly, either through a reference to a method or a reference to an interface. In both cases, the reference must be held in a variable.

When calling through a method reference, the output pin's name is the name of the variable holding the reference. It is common to name this variable using the word *On* followed by the signal name. The type used to hold the method reference is implementation-dependent. Table 7-2 shows types used in a few popular OO languages.

Table 7-2. *Types and Names of Objects Used with Output Pins to Reference a Method*

Language	Method Reference Type	Example
C#	event	`event EventHandler OnMyEvent;`
VB .NET	Event	`Event Sub OnMyEvent()`
Java	`java.reflect.Method`	`java.reflect.Method OnMyEvent;`
Object Pascal	`procedure of object`	`TMyEvent = procedure() of object;` `OnMyEvent: TMyEvent;`

Figure 7-20 shows a `Worker` object with an output pin called `OnChannelChanged`.

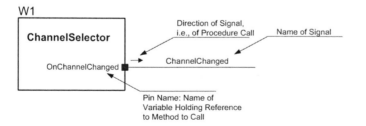

Figure 7-20. *A named output pin associated with a PC signal*

Don't name output pins that call through a dynamically initialized interface reference. Instead, draw the pins inside a gray interface box, as shown in Figure 7-21.

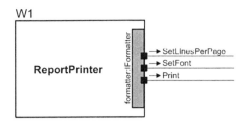

Figure 7-21. *Output pins calling through an interface reference*

The interface box is labeled formatter:IFormatter. The first word is the name of the variable exposed by ReportPrinter; the second word is the type of the variable. The names of the signals emerging from the output pins must be the names of the methods called through the given interface. Figure 7-22 shows the ReportPrinter object connected to an object implementing the IFormatter interface.

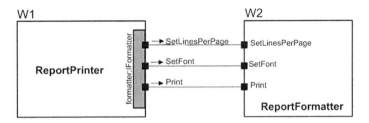

Figure 7-22. *Connecting signals from output pins calling through an interface reference*

When useful, you can show that the pins exposed by ReportFormatter belong to the IFormatter interface by adding a gray interface box to ReportFormatter, as shown in Figure 7-23.

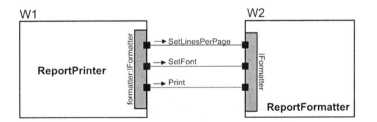

Figure 7-23. *Showing the interface on incoming signals on ReportFormatter*

By changing the value or the single interface reference ReportPrinter.formatter, all the signals emerging from W1 can be changed to go to a different object. I'll describe signal switching in more detail in the later section, "Switching at the Interface Level."

With SR signals, output pins don't invoke methods, but instead write messages to a shared resource. The pin is named after the variable holding a reference to the shared resource. The variable may be an IP address, a telephone number, a shared memory pointer, a filename, or other. For example, if an object sent messages to a shared resource referenced by the variable named OutputMessages, the output pin could be named OutputMessages, as shown in Figure 7-24.

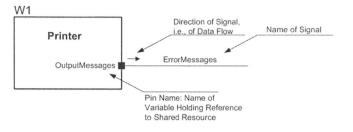

Figure 7-24. *A named output pin associated with an SR signal*

Wiring Pins Together

The lines denoting the path followed by a signal are called *wires*, for the obvious similarity with the hardware world. The process of connecting pins together is often called *wiring*. When wiring two pins together, one of them must be an output and the other an input. Figure 7-25 shows two pins wired together.

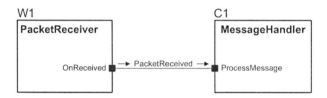

Figure 7-25. *Two pins wired together*

Arrows should appear at both the sender and receiver ends of the wire, unless the wire is very short. When showing PC signals, arguments passed to the callee and returned values are omitted. When showing SR signals, the contents of the data transferred are not shown. The purpose of wiring diagrams is to show what is connected to what. The nature of the connection should be indicated by a judicious choice of the signal name. The details regarding exactly what the signal carries to or from the sender are not shown directly on wires. When using numbered pins, you can use a pin legend to describe the signal details in more detail.

Numbering Pins

Hardware-circuit diagrams number the pins on ICs. The numbers correspond to the chip specifications published by the IC manufacturer. Although software components don't have an absolute requirement for numbered pins, numbers can be useful on busy diagrams. You can use a separate pin legend to describe each pin. Figure 7-26 shows two objects with numbered pins.

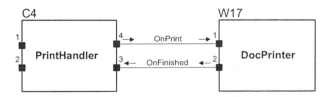

Figure 7-26. *A diagram with numbered pins*

Pin numbers appear on the outside of objects, right next to the related pins. If an object has many pins, it becomes tedious to locate a pin by its number, unless the numbers are in some sort of order. In Figure 7-26, the pins were ordered sequentially, following a counterclockwise direction. This happens to be the same convention used by ICs, when viewed from the topside.

Pin-Legend Tables

Pin numbers are especially useful when pin names are insufficient to describe a pin and you want to provide detailed information in a separate pin-legend table. For pins related to PC signals, it may be useful to show the signatures of the methods called. For pins related to SR signals, a description of the data messages may be necessary. Table 7-3 shows an example of a pin legend for the previous diagram.

Table 7-3. *A Pin-Legend Table, Describing Numbered Pins Associated with PC Signals*

Object	Pin	Direction	Name	Arguments	Returned Values
C4	1	In	Print	docName: string	status: Boolean
C4	2	Out	OnError	message: string	
C4	3	In	Done	pagesPrinted: int	
C4	4	Out	OnPrint	pageNumber: int header: string	canPrint: Boolean
W17	1	In	PrintPage	pageNumber: int header: string	canPrint: Boolean
W17	2	Out	OnFinished	pagesPrinted: int	

A single table can describe all the objects of a given component, page, or subsystem. Due to the physical size of these tables, they are often printed separately on their own page. In the legend, each pin carries a name and a list of the arguments passed in and out. Naming conventions, including capitalization, follow local conventions based on the programming language or component model being used.

When connecting inputs to outputs, it is only reasonable to connect inputs and outputs that have the same signal type (PC or SR). For PC signals, the signature of the inputs and outputs must match. For SR signals, the inputs and outputs must both understand the format of exchanged messages. Returned values are only possible with PC signals. The Returned Values column in Table 7-3 lists only values returned directly by the procedure call. Side effects of the procedure call are not listed. When describing output pins, it may be important to indicate whether a pin supports multicasting, allowing it to be bound to more than one input pin. The word Out, in the Direction column, indicates a multicast pin. Pins not marked with the plus sign may also be multicast, if the component platform provides this feature by default. For example, C# objects use the built-in delegate type to handle outputs, and this type supports multicasting implicitly. When describing SR signals in a pin-legend table, the Arguments column describes the fields in the messages sent. The Returned Values column is left blank.

The pins described up to this point were used in one-to-one connections. It is also possible for an output pin to be connected to multiple inputs, and for multiple output pins to be connected to a single input.

One-to-Many Connections

Multicast operations allow signals to be sent from one output pin to multiple input pins. All input pins must be compatible with the output pin's signal. The order in which the signal is delivered to each input pin is sometimes important and can be shown on the wiring diagram using numbers in front of the signal name. Figure 7-27 shows a multicast signal sent to two different receivers in a specific sequence.

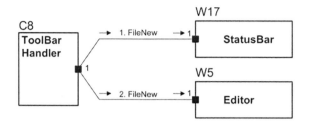

Figure 7-27. *An output pin connected to multiple input pins*

The diagram's pin-legend table was not shown, for brevity. When the delivery order of a signal is not important, you may omit the ordering numbers from the diagram.

Many-to-One Connections

Connecting multiple output pins to the same input pin is a situation that is not generally allowed in the hardware world. The outputs signals would clash, causing problems. With software components, the output signals may not interfere with each other in single-threaded systems. In multithreaded systems, care must be taken that a signal output from one thread doesn't interfere with a signal output from a different thread, if the two signals call the same method. Figure 7-28 shows a many-to-one connection scenario.

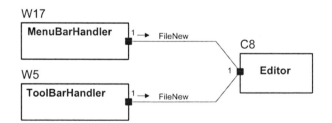

Figure 7-28. *Two output pins connected to the same input pin*

When space is tight, you can join the incoming signals at a distance from the input pin, as shown in Figure 7-29. When useful, the signals shown are labeled with the ID of the objects from which they emanate, as shown in the diagram.

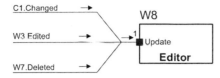

Figure 7-29. *Joining input signals away from an input pin*

Statically Bound Signals

A signal whose binding is determined at compile time is said to be *statically bound*. This type of signal can't be wired at run time, as described earlier, and must be diagrammed differently from the signals described up to this point. You can use statically bound signals in two ways: to invoke a target method directly, or to invoke a target method through an interface. I'll discuss each case separately.

Calling Methods Directly

Consider an object that loads a dynamic library called Graphics3D.dll, which contains methods for 3-D drawing and texturing. As a first example, let's assume the library exposes methods, as opposed to classes or interfaces. Let the methods be named Initialize, RenderTexture, and ShutDown. Listing 7-1 shows how a C# class called GraphicsSurface might invoke the Graphics3D methods.

Listing 7-1. *A C# Class Calling Methods Contained in a Library*

```
using System;
using System.Runtime.InteropServices;

namespace GraphicsRendering
{
  public class GraphicsSurface
  {
    [DllImport("Graphics3D.dll")]
    public static extern void Initialize();

    [DllImport("Graphics3D.dll")]
    public static extern void RenderTexture();

    [DllImport("Graphics3D.dll")]
    public static extern void ShutDown();

    public void AddTexture()
    {
      Initialize();
      RenderTexture();
      ShutDown();
    }
  }
}
```

Figure 7-30 shows the system's wiring diagram.

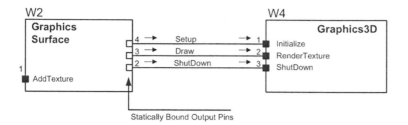

Figure 7-30. *Statically bound signals calling directly into methods*

Statically bound signals are indicated by special output pins. The pins are hollow and are drawn inside the border of the sender to reinforce the fact that the signals originate from inside the object, beyond the reach of would-be run-time binders. The name of the statically bound output pins should reflect the purpose of the signal being sent. Statically bound signals represent a constraint on the sender's side, not the receiver's. An input pin receiving a statically bound signal is not aware of the static nature of the incoming signal.

In Figure 7-30, the Graphics3D library is shown as an object. Its methods are called directly without using any classes or interfaces. In C# programs, the library is loaded into memory automatically the first time one of its methods is called. A separate output pin in W2 is used for each method called in the Graphics3D library.

The signals sent by GraphicsSurface to Graphics3D are all PC signals in this example, but SR signals can also be statically bound. If the sender uses an SR reference that is initialized at compile time, the signal is statically bound.

When the wires connecting the sender to the receiver are short, you can omit the signal names if the pins on the receiver are named. In this case, the arrows designating the signal directions can be put directly on the wires, attached to their respective destination pins, as shown in Figure 7-31.

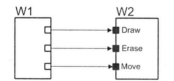

Figure 7-31. *Omitting signal names on short wires*

Calling Methods Through an Interface

Statically bound signals can also be used to invoke methods of typed objects, using an interface. As an example, assume GraphicsSurface uses an object-oriented version of the Graphics3D library, called OoGraphics3D.dll. This new library might expose a class called GraphicsDrawing containing the same methods used before: Initialize, RenderTexture, and ShutDown. Figure 7-32 is a class diagram showing how the GraphicsSurface class would use the GraphicsDrawing class in the OoGraphics3D library.

The presence of a link between classes on a class diagram is an immediate indication of statically bound signals. The link represents an interface—a conduit—over which calls can be made. The interface reference provides no indications of which methods are called. The assumption is that clients *know* which methods to call and when to call them.

Figure 7-32. *Calling into an object using a class interface*

Even if the renderingEngine link could be switched at run time to reference a different GraphicsDrawing object, the methods called though the interface are nonetheless considered statically bound: You can't change them at run time. Listing 7-2 shows how you might implement the GraphicsSurface class in C#.

Listing 7-2. *A C# Class Calling Statically Bound Methods Through an Interface*

```csharp
using System;
using OoGraphics3D;

namespace GraphicsRendering
{
  public class GraphicsSurface
  {
    GraphicsDrawing renderingEngine = new GraphicsDrawing();

    public void AddTexture()
    {
      renderingEngine.Initialize();
      renderingEngine.RenderTexture();
      renderingEngine.ShutDown();
    }
  }
}
```

GraphicsSurface invokes the OoGraphics3D methods through the GraphicsDrawing class. The fact that the calls go through an outgoing interface is sometimes significant and may need to be shown on wiring diagrams. Figure 7-33 shows statically bound signals associated with an outgoing interface.

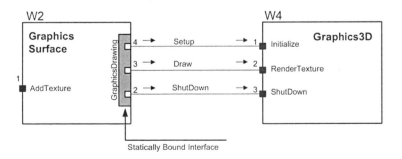

Figure 7-33. *Statically bound signals calling methods associated with an interface*

The outgoing pins for the statically bound signals are enclosed in a box labeled with the outgoing interface's name. You can include the interface's namespace where useful. The labeled box should be shown only when it is useful for readers to know that outgoing signals are called through an interface. To reinforce the presence of the interface, input pins receiving the signals can include the interface name. Going even further, you can enclose the input pins with a box denoting the input interface they belong to. Notice the absence of names for the output pins. Statically bound output pins have no name, since there is no variable associated with the pins. The signal names used on output pins are arbitrary, but commonly use the names of the interface methods being called.

Components

Although the protagonists of wiring diagrams are objects and signals, sometimes it is useful to show which component an object is contained in or came from. The object is simply drawn inside a component symbol, as shown in Figure 7-34.

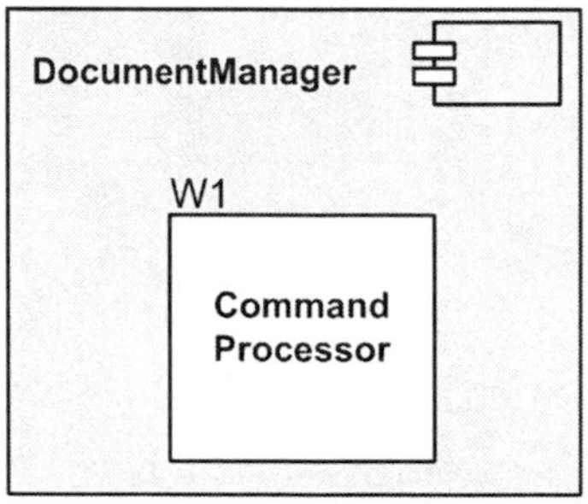

Figure 7-34. *Showing which component an object belongs to*

The component box is the symbol used also in UML 2. A component can contain any number of objects or classes. Showing components on diagrams can be useful to emphasize signal paths that cross component boundaries. Of note is the fact that components don't need to be numbered.

In top-level diagrams, it may be convenient to show the signals entering and leaving a component, without regard to which internal objects are involved. When showing signals entering and leaving a component, pins are not used, because pins are an indication of an internal mechanism that receives and sends signals. Instead, signals attach directly to the component box, as shown in Figure 7-35.

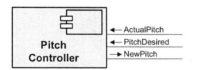

Figure 7-35. *Signals shown at the component level*

If a diagram shows signals at the component level, there should also be a diagram that reveals the inner objects of the component, showing exactly which objects send and receive the signals, as shown in Figure 7-36.

Signals that travel between objects in the same component may be shown, if useful. As mentioned earlier, the goal is to show only those signals that are appropriate for the level of detail depicted in the diagram. With describing a complex component, the full details of its inner workings might be shown at different levels, using different diagrams.

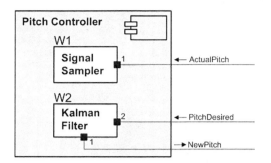

Figure 7-36. *A component with internal objects that handle signals*

When a group of signals enters or leaves a component, and it isn't important to describe each signal separately, you can use a bus, as described in the next section.

Buses

To simplify diagrams in which there are lots of wires going from one place to another, you can group wires together into something called a *bus*, borrowing the term from the hardware world. The term *bus* has been used extensively in the software world to connote an infrastructure for connecting objects and components in various ways. Examples of bus technologies are CORBA,[8] Ivy,[9] SWBus,[10] Java iBus,[11] Polylith,[12] the Eureka Software Factory,[13] and ToolBus.[14] Architecture Description Languages use abstractions that are logically equivalent to buses. These abstractions are called *connectors* by a number of ADLs, such as ACME,[15] Aesop,[16] C2,[17] UniCon,[18] and Wright.[19] The Darwin ADL calls the interconnection abstraction a *binding*.

8. Object Management Group, "Common Object Request Broker Architecture: Core Specification," www.omg.org/docs/formal/02-12-06.pdf, 2002.

9. Stephane Chatty, "The Ivy Software Bus" (white paper, www.tls.cena.fr/products/ivy/documentation/ivy.pdf, 2003).

10. "SWBus Technical Overview," www2.hrp.no/swbus/overview/overview.html, 2000.

11. Silvano Maffeis, "Components Need Software Bus Middleware" (proceedings of the CHOOSE Forum on Object-Oriented Software Architecture, University of Bern, Bern, Switzerland, March 1999, www.riehle.org/community-service/choose/1999-forum/maffeis.pdf).

12. James M. Purtilo, "The Polylith Software Bus," *ACM Transactions on Programming Languages and Systems*, January 1994.

13. Herbert Weber, *The Software Factory Challenge: Results of the Eureka Software Factory Project* (Amsterdam, The Netherlands: IOS Press, 1997).

14. J.A. Bergstra and Paul Klint, "The Discrete Time ToolBus: A Software Coordination Architecture," *Science of Computer Programming*, July 1998.

15. David Garlan, Robert Monroe, and Dave Wile, "Acme: An Architecture Description Interchange Language" (proceedings of IBM Centers for Advanced Studies Conference, Toronto, Ontario, Canada, November 1997). For a relevant excerpt, also see "An Overview of Acme," www-2.cs.cmu.edu/~acme/language_overview.html

16. "The Acme Architectural Description Language," www-2.cs.cmu.edu/~acme.

17. Nenad Medvidovic, David S. Rosenblum, and Richard N.Taylor, "A Language and Environment for Architecture-Based Software Development and Evolution" (proceedings of the 21st International Conference on Software Engineering, Los Angeles, CA, May 1999).

18. Mary Shaw, Robert DeLine, and Gregory Zelesnik, "Abstractions and Implementations for Architectural Connections" (proceedings of the Third International Conference on Configurable Distributed Systems, Annapolis, MD, May 1996).

19. Robert J. Allen and David Garlan, "A Formal Basis for Architectural Connection," *ACM Transactions on Software Engineering and Methodology*, July 1997.

Wiring diagram buses represent a logical or physical path containing a group of signals. Figure 7-37 shows a simple bus.

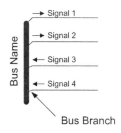

Figure 7-37. *A bus, with two signals entering and two leaving*

Where a wire joins a bus, draw a short *bus branch* at a 45-degree angle to the bus. On dense diagrams, the short line makes it easier to distinguish wires that cross over the bus from those that are connected to the bus.

Signals are identified both entering and leaving the bus, with an arrow drawn close to the bus to indicate the signal's direction. Signals may enter or leave from both sides of the bus. Whether a bus is drawn vertically or horizontally is dictated only by aesthetic demands of the diagram. Figure 7-38 shows a bus that has both vertical and horizontal segments.

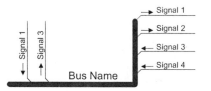

Figure 7-38. *A bus with vertical and horizontal segments*

Signals grouped on a bus usually have something in common. Perhaps the signals originate in the same subsystem or serve collectively to achieve a common objective. The bus name should reflect what the signals have in common. When a signal leaving a bus has a short wire and goes to an input pin that is named, the signal name can sometimes be omitted, as shown in Figure 7-39.

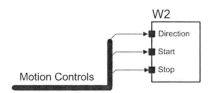

Figure 7-39. *Omitting signal names on short wires connected to a bus*

When the signal name is omitted, the assumption is that the signal has the same name as the input pin it goes to.

Showing One-to-Many Connections

A bus can simplify the depiction of a signal delivered to multiple recipients. A single wire enters the bus from the sender. The signal exits the bus in multiple places—once for each recipient. Figure 7-40 shows an example.

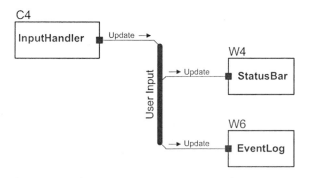

Figure 7-40. *A bus carrying a multicast signal to two receivers*

The names of signals exiting a bus must match the names of signals entering the bus. When showing a signal routed to multiple receivers, the bus doesn't contribute in any way to the physical delivery of the signal. The output pin must support multicasting.

In Figure 7-40, looking only at C4, you can't tell that the signal Update is sent to two receivers. When it is important to clarify on the sender side that a signal is connected to multiple receivers using a bus, you can show multiple signals entering the bus, as shown in Figure 7-41.

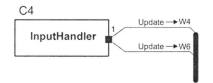

Figure 7-41. *Specifying the destination of outgoing signals as they enter a bus*

If the number of outgoing signals from a pin is large, you can use a separate bus to group the signals, as shown in Figure 7-42.

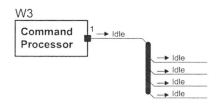

Figure 7-42. *Using a bus to group outgoing signals from the same pin*

A signal exiting a bus can also be renamed before it reaches its destination, as shown in Figure 7-43.

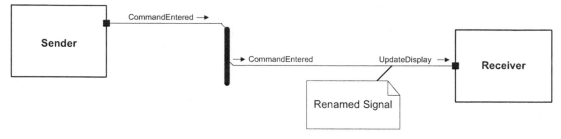

Figure 7-43. *Renaming a signal on exit from a bus*

Renamed signals are useful to more clearly indicate what a signal is being used for at the receiver end.

Showing Many-to-One Connections

A bus can also show multiple signals being routed to a common receiver. In Figure 7-44, two objects send signals that are delivered to the same input pin of a receiver.

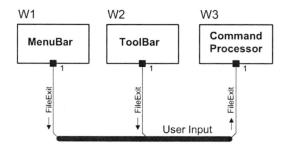

Figure 7-44. *A bus carrying two signals routed to the same input pin*

If you look only at W3 in Figure 7-44, you can't tell that the FileExit signal comes from multiple sources. To clarify that an incoming signal has multiple senders, you can draw multiple signals exiting the bus. At the bus exit point, each signal is labeled with the ID of the sender, as shown in Figure 7-45.

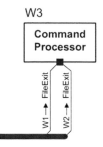

Figure 7-45. *Showing signals from different senders before they enter a common pin*

If the number of signals going into the pin is large, you can use a separate bus to group the signals, as shown in Figure 7-46.

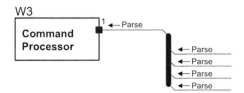

Figure 7-46. *Using a bus to group signals entering the same pin*

Depicting Distributed Systems

When depicting distributed systems, buses are useful to describe the connections between each system. Buses then represent physical entities present in the system and are not simply a diagramming convenience. Buses may represent a network connection, a pipe, a modem connection, or other. A number of commercial products use the bus abstraction to describe remote connections. For example, TIBCO Rendezvous uses an *information bus* for incoming and outgoing messages.

When used to model a remote connection, a bus is essentially an abstraction of a cable harness, carrying multiple signals. Figure 7-47 shows a bus connecting a client-server system.

Figure 7-47. *Using a bus to show a network connection between distributed components*

As the bus name indicates in the figure, the bus represents an HTTP connection, routed through a Virtual Private Network (VPN). The system is based on two top-level components, called Client and Server. The SOAP protocol tells you that signals sent over the bus are PC signals, because SOAP is a technology that uses XML documents to emulate remote procedure calls.

When depicting distributed system interconnections with a bus, you can show individual signals entering or leaving buses, if relevant. Figure 7-48 shows an example.

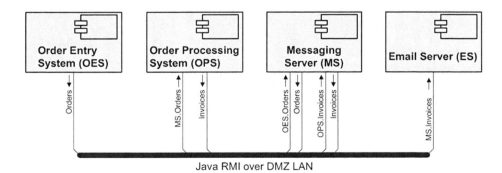

Figure 7-48. *A distributed system for an order-entry system*

In Figure 7-48, DMZ is a *demilitarized zone*, which is a section of enterprise infrastructure protected from the outside world by firewalls. Buses can carry both PC and SR signals. In Figure 7-48, the bus name tells you that PC signals are sent over the bus, because the Java RMI protocol is used. Two signals in the diagrams are qualified with the sender's name to distinguish between signals with the same name sent from different places.

When useful to readers, a bus name can include other details about a remote connection, such as the protocol, the transmission speed, the connection type (e.g., dial-up or leased line), or other.

Signals exiting a bus in a distributed system may need to be qualified with connection information, such as the protocol used, the network address, the network port, or other. Figure 7-49 shows a component accepting SR signals from a bus.

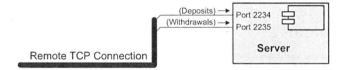

Figure 7-49. *Input pins labeled to indicate their TCP socket port*

The Server component handles Deposit messages on one port and Withdrawals on another. The signals attach directly to the component body, with no pins. The descriptions (the port numbers, in this case) of the attachment points are shown on the inside of the component, like pin names.

Switches

If the routing of a signal can be changed at run time, based on the mode of the system, it is sometimes important to show this on diagrams. The way to do so is by using a switch, shown in Figure 7-50.

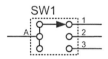

Figure 7-50. *A single-pole, 3-throw switch*

By convention, switches use the label "SW". The number of incoming signals a switch controls is called the number of *poles*. Signals enter a switch through a line labeled with an uppercase letter. A switch is called single-pole if it controls one signal. The number of positions a switch has is called the number of *throws*. The etymology of the word is from the common expression *throwing a switch*. In abbreviated form, a switch is described by the number of poles and throws. The single-pole, 3-throw switch shown in Figure 7-50 can be abbreviated as 1P3T.

Signals exit a switch through numbered lines corresponding to throw positions. The arrow inside the switch indicates the signal direction. As indicated earlier, for PC signals the direction indicates execution flow; for SR signals, the direction indicates data flow. The exit path selected at any given time depends on the switch's setting (in other words, its position).

A switch is enclosed in a box with a dashed border to denote the fact that the switch is not a real object, but an abstraction—a virtual object. The switch merely shows the possible receivers of the signal. Switching is accomplished by changing the signal's destination, which you do by assigning a new value to the variable that controls the output pin of the signal's sender.

In many situations, multiple signals need to be switched at the same time, which requires the use of a multi-pole switch. Figure 7-51 shows a 2-pole, 3-throw switch.

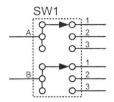

Figure 7-51. *A 2-pole, 3-throw switch*

When dealing with multi-pole switches, you can qualify the exit number for a signal with the letter of the input pole. For the 2P3T switch in Figure 7-51, the exits for signal A can be labeled A1, A2, and A3. All poles are switched as a group. For example, when A is switched to A2, B is also switched to B2.

Switch Controllers

Software switches are controlled by objects. The controllers are often *late* `Binder`s, as described in Chapter 10. To indicate the controller of a switch, a dashed line can connect the switch either to the controller or to a label indicating the name or ID of the controller. Figure 7-52 shows both cases.

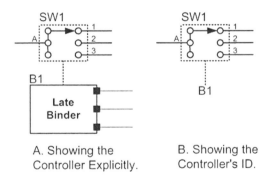

A. Showing the
Controller Explicitly.

B. Showing the
Controller's ID.

Figure 7-52. *A 1P3T switch with its controller*

The controlling `Binder` often has an input pin for each position of the switch it controls. A 3-throw switch would be controlled by a `Binder` with three input pins. When a switch has multiple poles, the same controller controls all poles at once. When the setting of a switch is changed, there are two strategies you can use when modifying signal paths:

- Remove the old path first, and then establish the new path.
- Establish the new path first, and then remove the old path.

The first strategy is often called *break before make* (BBM). The switch controller accesses the output pin where the signal originates, upstream from the switch itself. The controller then removes the reference to the old recipient and adds a reference to the new recipient. Care must be taken in concurrent systems to guard against lost signals. When a sender gets ready to send a signal, it checks the signal's output pin to see if any recipients are available. If, just before this check, the switch controller removes the reference to the old recipient (but hasn't yet installed the new recipient), the sender will think there are no recipients and send nothing.

The second strategy is often called *make before break* (MBB). The switch controller accesses the output pin where the signal originates, again upstream from the switch itself. The controller then adds a reference to the new recipient and removes the old recipient. Care must be taken in concurrent systems to guard against duplicate signals. When a sender gets ready to send a signal, it checks the signal's output pin to see if any recipients are available. If, just before this check, the switch controller adds the reference to the new recipient (but hasn't yet removed the old recipient), the sender will think there are two recipients and send the signal to each one.

Figure 7-53 shows a complete example of a signal being switched by a 1P2T switch.

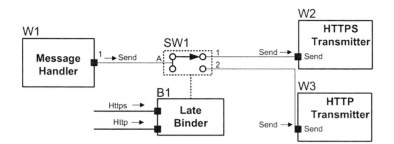

Figure 7-53. *A signal switched by a 1P2T switch*

The signal W1.Send is controlled by the late Binder object B1. The switch routes the signal to either W2 or W3, controlling whether a message is sent using the HTTPS protocol or regular HTTP. Listing 7-3 shows a possible C# implementation, where the late Binder is a class called Protocols. ProtocolController.

Listing 7-3. *A C# Implementation of a Simple System Using a Switch*

```
/* HTTPS Transmitter code */

using System;
namespace Https
{
  public class HttpsTransmitter
  {
    public void Send(string theMessage) {/*send message...*/}
  }
}


/* HTTP Transmitter code */

using System;
namespace Http
{
  public class HttpTransmitter
  {
    public void Send(string theMessage) {/*send message...*/}
  }
}
```

```csharp
/* MessageHandler code */

using System;
namespace Messaging
{
  public class MessageHandler
  {
    public void Send(string theMessage) {FireSend(theMessage);}

    public delegate void SendHandler(string theMessage);
    public SendHandler OnSend;
    void FireSend(string theMessage)
    {
      if (OnSend == null) return;
      OnSend(theMessage);
    }
  }
}


/* ProtocolController code */

using System;
using Http;
using Https;
using Messaging;
namespace Protocols
{
  public class ProtocolController
  {
    public MessageHandler messageHandler;
    HttpTransmitter httpTransmitter;
    HttpsTransmitter httpsTransmitter;

    // delegates to use with switch
    MessageHandler.SendHandler httpSender;
    MessageHandler.SendHandler httpsSender;

    public ProtocolController()
    {
      messageHandler = new MessageHandler();
      httpTransmitter = new HttpTransmitter();
      httpsTransmitter = new HttpsTransmitter();

      httpSender  = new MessageHandler.SendHandler(httpTransmitter.Send);
      httpsSender = new MessageHandler.SendHandler(httpsTransmitter.Send);
    }

    public void SelectHttps()
    {
      // use a break-before-make strategy
      messageHandler.OnSend -= httpSender;   // break old path
      messageHandler.OnSend += httpsSender;  // make new path
    }
```

```
    public void SelectHttp()
    {
      // use a break-before-make strategy
      messageHandler.OnSend -= httpsSender;  // break old path
      messageHandler.OnSend += httpSender;   // make new path
    }
  }
}


/* System initializer */

using System;
using Messaging;
using Protocols;
namespace Client
{
  public class Client
  {
    ProtocolController protocolController;
    MessageHandler messageHandler;

    public Client()
    {
      protocolController = new ProtocolController();
      protocolController.SelectHttps();
      messageHandler = protocolController.messageHandler;
    }

    public void SelectHttp()
    {
      protocolController.SelectHttp();
    }

    public void SelectHttps()
    {
      protocolController.SelectHttps();
    }

    public void Send(string theText)
    {
      messageHandler.Send(theText);
    }
  }
}
```

Showing Switching Information

The setting of switches depends on signals sent to the switch controller. For example, in the previous example, the controller had two input signals, Http and Https. The diagram in Figure 7-53 showed the presence of the switch, but didn't tell you how the control signals set the switch. When B1 receives an Https signal, which setting would the switch be set to? When this kind of information is useful, you can include it in the wiring diagram using a *switch table* next to the switch controller. The table shows the switch setting for each input signal of the switch controller. Figure 7-54 shows SW1 from Figure 7-53 with a switch table.

The Pin column in the table indicates which pin is connected to pin A. When a switch table is associated with a multi-pole switch, all poles switch together, so it is not necessary to describe each pole separately in the table. When a switch is initialized at start-up time in a certain position, you can use a signal named <default> in the switch table, as shown in Figure 7-55.

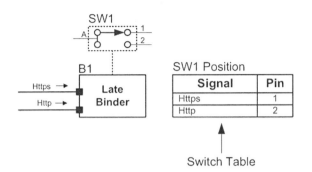

Figure 7-54. *Including a switch table to show how a switch is controlled*

SW1 Position

Signal	Pin
<default>	1
Http	2

Figure 7-55. *A switch table, showing the default setting*

The switch table tells you that in the absence of any signals to the switch's controlling Binder, pin 1 is selected. If the default setting can also be set using a signal, then the signal name should follow the word <default>, as shown in Figure 7-56.

SW1 Position

Signal	Pin
<default>, Https	1
Http	2

Figure 7-56. *A switch table in which the default setting is also set using a signal*

Switching at the Interface Level

PC signals are sent sometimes by calling methods through an interface. If the interface is referenced by a variable that is externally accessible, a switch controller can change it at run time. Doing so switches all calls through the interface to a new recipient. On wiring diagrams, you can show a switchable interface by connecting the outgoing interface box to a switch. In this scenario, the interface constitutes a virtual pole. Figure 7-57 shows an example.

The switch SW1 controls the path of C1's outgoing signals DrawText and DrawBox. The signals are shown going through the switch to W1 or W2. C1's switched interface is connected by a dotted line to the switch. The switch table tells you when the signals go to W1 and when they go to W2.

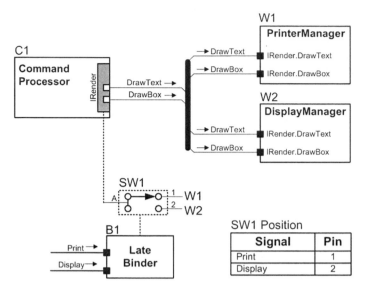

Figure 7-57. *Using a switch to reroute all the calls of an outgoing interface*

Pages

Diagrams are organized into pages. Simple diagrams fit on one page; complex ones usually require multiple pages. It is important that you label each page with information to clearly identify what is on it. When dealing with multipage diagrams, it is necessary to define conventions for routing signals from one page to another. In the following sections, I'll show you some of the most important issues related to diagram pages.

Labeling Pages

Pages should also carry some descriptive information about what the page represents, who created it, what revision it is, the name of the company, and other information that may be useful. On hardware diagrams, this information is traditionally carried in a small legend box in the lower-right corner of the page. You can use the same convention in wiring diagrams. Figure 7-58 shows an example.

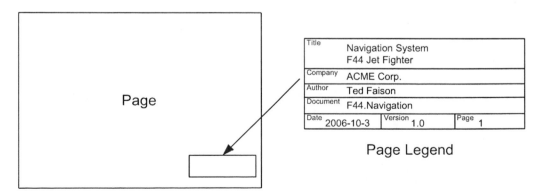

Figure 7-58. *Identifying pages with a page legend*

The fields in the page label are self-explanatory. You can add others where necessary. The Document field carries a unique name or number identifying the page. The name might be a file-name, a URI, a database key, of some sort or other.

Multipage Signals

When a signal from one page is used on another, there must be a way to reference signals entering and leaving a page. Borrowing from hardware-schematic diagrams, Signal Wiring diagrams use a hollow arrow, pointing in the direction of the signal flow. Figure 7-59 shows the details.

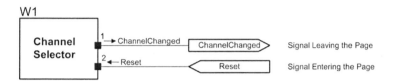

Figure 7-59. *Signals entering and leaving a page*

The hollow arrows are called *off-page signal references*, or sometimes just *signal references*. You should place the signal references near the left or right margin to make them easy to find on busy diagrams. Label the arrows with the name of the signal they refer to. If a signal leaves a page with a given name in the hollow arrow, all pages on which the signal enters must use the same name. When there are multiple signals with the same name, you can prepend the ID of the sender to the signal name to eliminate ambiguities. You might also include a signal's complete namespace. For example, the hollow arrow might contain the text `W1.ChannelChanged` or `Avionics.W1.ChannelChanged`. The text would have to appear verbatim on all pages referencing the signal.

Signals leaving a page can also identify the destination by specifying its ID or name. For PC signals, you can include the destination's handler method, as shown in Figure 7-60.

Figure 7-60. *Showing the destination's name and handler on a signal reference*

Buses contain multiple signals. Just as signals can cross page boundaries, so can buses. The one difference between buses and signals is that buses can contain signals traveling in different directions. Signal references for buses with bidirectional signals use a double-headed arrow. Figure 7-61 shows some examples.

You can also attach buses and wires to the top or bottom of signal references, if this helps simplify a diagram. Figure 7-62 shows some examples.

Signals entering a bus that leaves the page can show the destination of each signal, as shown in Figure 7-63.

The diagram shows signals being routed to a bus that leaves the page through an off-page signal reference called `StatusBar Commands`. The signal `Parser.Begin` is connected to the destination `StatusBar.ShowMessage`.

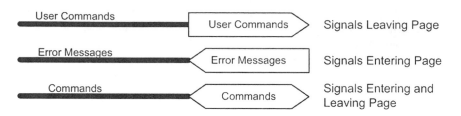

Figure 7-61. *Extending buses across page boundaries*

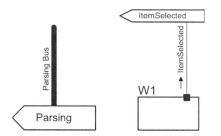

Figure 7-62. *Signals attached to the top and bottom of off-page signal references*

Figure 7-63. *Showing the destination of signals leaving the page through a bus reference*

When a signal leaving a page has multiple destinations, you can show all the destinations explicitly using a bus, as shown in Figure 7-64.

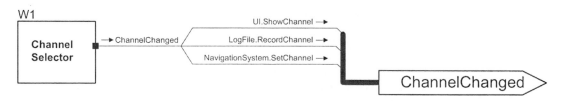

Figure 7-64. *Showing the multiple destinations of a signal*

This diagram tells you that the signal W1.ChannelChanged is wired to three separate off-page destinations. With synchronously delivered signals, you must list the destinations in the order of delivery. The diagram indicates that UI.ChannelChanged is delivered first to UI, then to LogFile, and last to NavigationSystem. You can also show the delivery order explicitly by numbering the signals, as shown in Figure 7-65.

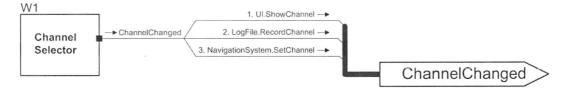

Figure 7-65. *Numbering the signals leaving the page*

Levels of Detail

When diagramming a small system, the entire wiring diagram might fit on a single page. With larger systems, there may be multiple subsystems. With even larger systems, there may be multiple systems and/or computers involved. To make it easier to understand large systems, it is necessary to diagram the system at different levels of detail. Each level may require multiple pages.

The top level shows the entire system. The boxes represent the main systems or computers involved. The boxes might represent processes, services, computers, or groups of computers. The boxes are interconnected with buses. Pins and individual signals are generally not shown on the top level, unless the system is fairly simple. Figure 7-66 shows an example.

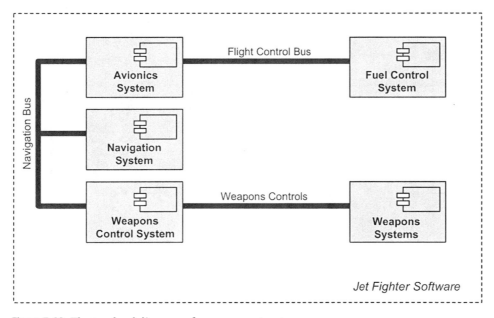

Figure 7-66. *The top-level diagram of a component system*

In the bottom-right corner, you would normally replace the descriptive text with a page legend. The next level of diagram shows the details when drilling down into one of the systems. Each system may be composed of multiple subsystems. Figure 7-67 shows the top-level view of one system.

The reader should be able to drill down into each subsystem shown. At some point, you'll define subsystems in terms of objects. This is the most detailed level of wiring diagrams, and is where the individual signals are shown. Figure 7-68 shows a detailed view of the Flight Controls Subsystem.

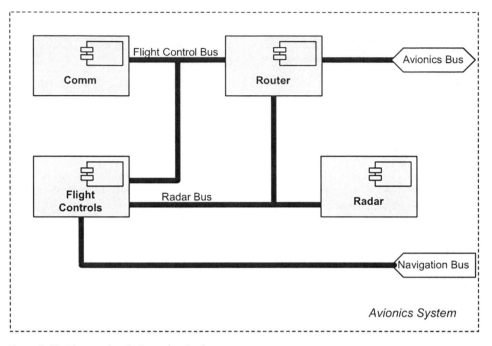

Figure 7-67. *The top-level view of a single system*

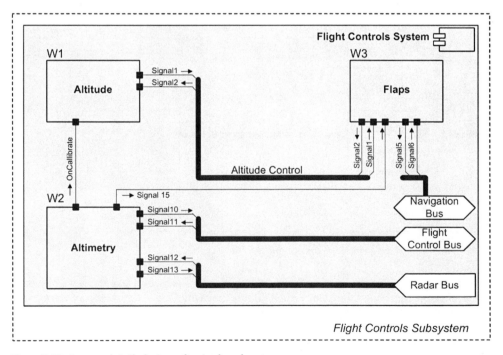

Figure 7-68. *A more detailed view of a single subsystem*

Labeling Items in Multipage Diagrams

When the wiring diagram of a system has different levels of detail, it is important to use a consistent schema for naming the various parts. In the hardware design world, parts are numbered using an incrementing series, starting with the value 1. Each type of part has its own series, so resistors are numbered R1, R2, etc., while capacitors are numbered C1, C2, etc. Each subsystem numbers its parts independently of other subsystems, so multiple subsystems might have a part called R1. To fully identify a part, you must indicate which subsystem and system it belongs to. To fully specify a resistor R1 in a complex hardware system, you might say something like *R1 of the Signal Conditioning module of the Altitude Control subsystem of the Avionics system of the F44 Jet Fighter*. Hardware engineers routinely use acronyms to avoid such long expressions, shortening the description of R1 to something like R1 of the SCM of the ACS, with the assumption that they are talking about the avionics system of the F44 fighter jet.

Wiring diagrams can use a similar numbering scheme, and you can use the namespace concept to label parts in wiring diagrams. The namespace should contain the complete logical path to reach an object's diagram, starting at the top level. For example, using the three-level system shown in the previous three figures, the unambiguous label for W1 in the Flight Controls Subsystem would be something like *F44.Avionics.FlightControls.W1*. For each level of abstraction, a wiring diagram should number its items starting at 1, so an object named W1 might appear on several pages.

Signal Timing

Wiring diagrams are conceptually similar to the blueprints used by the construction industry or the schematic diagrams used in hardware design. They show how the parts of a system fit together. It is important to try not to cram too much information on them; otherwise, they become difficult to read.

When it is important to show the order of signals, you can number the signals, following the same conventions used on UML Communication diagrams. Figure 7-69 shows an example.

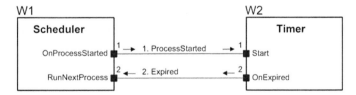

Figure 7-69. *Numbering signals to show their order*

When a diagram has a lot of signals and objects, numbered signals can be difficult to follow. In these cases, it might be better to show the signals using a separate UML sequence diagram.

Considerations on Wiring Diagrams

Once you start designing systems with classes that have little or no coupling to classes in other components, you discover that traditional class diagrams aren't very useful at the component level. The classes inside one component generally have no relationships with classes in other components, until a binding process takes place at run time. Consider, for example, the diagram in Figure 7-69. The Scheduler and Timer talk to each other, but their class diagram, shown in Figure 7-70, doesn't show this.

Figure 7-70. *The class diagram for two decoupled classes*

When the `Scheduler` fires a `ProcessStarted` event, the `Scheduler` doesn't know that the event causes a `Timer`'s `Start` method to be called. It doesn't know anything about the `Timer` class, and this is good. If a manufacturer decides to market the `Scheduler` as a component, the part can be sold and used not only by `Timer` components, but also with many others.

Summary

Wiring diagrams abstract away the structure of components to reveal the interconnection fabric of a system at run time: They focus on what signals are available in a system and what itineraries the signals take to travel from place to place. Showing the paths is more than an exercise in aesthetics. When a system is designed largely or solely with parts interconnected by event notification signals, signal paths become crucial for understanding the system-level logic, in terms of where signals originate, which components they affect, and in which order. When an event-driven system is found to work incorrectly, the problem often turns out to be related to signals and signal paths.

UML Communication diagrams have similarities with wiring diagrams, but are used mostly to show the set of signals used in specific scenarios. By numbering messages, Communication diagrams show very well the sequence of events when a relatively small number of entities collaborate.

UML Interaction diagrams focus on the messages exchanged by a small number of components. Due to the way the communicating entities are laid out horizontally, there is a limit to how many participants will fit on a piece of paper or a computer screen. Interaction diagrams are extremely useful when showing the small details of timing, but are not practical for describing the operation of entire subsystems or systems, especially when conditional logic is involved.

UML Component Wiring diagrams focus on what is connected to what, but only at the interface level. As such, they only show PC signals. SR signals are not included, because those signals are not sent using procedure calls. Component Wiring diagrams tell you the direction of calls over a connection (from the *requires* component to the *provides* component), but nothing about which methods are called or their order of invocation. Also, these diagrams have no clear semantics for multipage diagrams or buses. They work only at the subsystem detail level, where interfaces are defined, so you can't use them to show a top-level view of a complex system.

Wiring diagrams are not designed to replace other types of diagrams, but merely to complement them, providing a different look at the connectivity of the system from the point of view of signals and signal paths.

CHAPTER 8

■■■

The Mechanics of Event Firing

Firing an event is the process of sending an event notification from an event source (the publisher) to registered event targets (the subscribers). The expression *firing an event*, although not semantically correct, is engrained in the industry and is understood to be synonymous with the expressions *sending a signal* or *dispatching a notification*.

All event-based systems must incorporate logic of some kind to handle event firing. In direct-delivery systems, the event source manages the list of subscribers directly and must send notifications to each subscriber. In indirect-delivery systems, event sources are connected to middleware messaging or notification systems, which handle the list of subscribers. In such systems, the event source might have only one subscriber (the middleware system). The event source would then delegate to the middleware the task of firing events to each subscriber. From the perspective of subscribers, the middleware system *is* the event source. In many cases, the middleware buffers incoming notifications, handling delivery asynchronously with respect to the true event source. This way, the actual event source is not affected by the rate at which subscribers receive or handle notifications. Direct-delivery systems rarely deliver notifications asynchronously, because it's too complicated to have each event source deal with notification buffers, delivery threads, and the associated synchronization logic.

Firing an event is conceptually a fairly simple affair: The event source has a list of subscribers and their subscriptions. The subscriptions may identify events by type, channel, or other means, using one of the subscription models described in Chapter 2. When the event source detects an event, it checks to see if there are any subscribers to the event. If there aren't, no further action is taken. The absence of subscribers is not typically an error condition for an event source and may not even be an unusual situation.

Assuming there are subscribers, the event source creates a notification payload and sends it to each subscriber. Although the steps are straightforward, there are a number of details that you must consider, which is what the rest of this chapter is about. For example, consider notifications designed to fetch a value from subscribers. What should you do if there are no subscribers? Another problem might be this: What happens when an exception occurs while firing a multicast event? As always, the devil is in the details. Event firing entails the following two phases on the event source:

1. Determining whether the preconditions for firing the event are satisfied

2. Delivering the notification

Each phase may be broken down further. If you denote the event with E, step 1 entails the following conditions:

1. The conditions that define E are detected.

2. E has at least one subscriber.

3. The event source knows how to fire events.

Once these conditions are found, an event notification *N* can be sent. The following steps are required:

1. If N requires a payload, you must create and package the payload into a form suitable for transmission to subscribers.

2. You must protect the subscriber list from modifications while notifications are being sent.

3. N is sent to all subscribers. A path must exist to each subscriber.

4. The sender must deal with exceptions that occur during notification delivery.

The exceptions alluded to in step 4 include those related to the delivery process and those thrown by event subscribers. Some component models, such as JavaBeans, rely on exceptions, in certain situations, to return information from subscribers back to publishers. For example, JavaBeans constrained properties use *vetoable* events, in which the publisher sends a notification indicating that a change is about to take place. Subscribers wishing to block the change can fire a special exception, which acts as a signal back to the publisher to inhibit the change.

It is interesting to observe that the basic steps required to fire an event are not dependent on the delivery model chosen. It doesn't matter if notifications are sent between two objects in the same process using a local procedure call or sent around the world to another system over the Internet. Obviously, the implementation of each step will be application-dependent, but the overall process doesn't change conceptually.

Checking to See if Subscribers Exist

Notifications must not be sent unless there are subscribers. In systems that use PCs to send notifications, subscribers are often managed through references to interfaces or methods. If no subscribers are present, those references won't point to anything. Attempting to make an indirect call would cause a run-time error.

When firing events using shared resources, there will generally be a data structure that holds addresses or names of the resources. When no subscribers are available, the addresses or names should have easily testable values, such as blank strings or null values.

What to Do When No Subscribers Are Available

If the purpose of a notification is to send information to subscribers, and there are none, the publisher can simply do nothing: It doesn't send the notification. Things are different if a notification allows subscribers to return data to the publisher. For example, say an event source fires an event to retrieve an integer value from each event target. If there are no targets, what should the system do?

The primary purpose of events is to *push* information from the event source to the event target, so it might appear that using notifications to retrieve data is a design flaw. This may indeed be the case. On the other hand, event notifications are an excellent decoupling mechanism for objects that are part of the same local system, so you might use them in a *pull* mode, with the sole aim of reducing coupling between the event source and the event target. In pull mode, notifications simply replace direct procedure calls between source and target. The event source now relies on the presence of event targets to carry out its job. If no targets are available when the event needs to be fired, it means the system is probably not wired correctly and might have to be stopped. Alternatively, if a default value exists, the system might carry on using the default value.

Packaging the Notification Payload

The notification payload is the information carried by a notification to subscribers. When notifications are sent using PCs, the payload is represented by the parameters passed as arguments in the procedure call. The call itself is the notification, and the call might have no parameters, in which case the notification has no payload.

In a large percentage of cases, notifications do have a payload. When a payload is required, you need to package it in a manner suitable for transmission to subscribers. Packaging may entail serializing objects into a binary stream, converting an object into XML, or other. When transferring data in binary format, it is important to be clear about how multibyte numbers are represented. In the *little-endian* format, the least significant byte of a multibyte value is sent first. In the *big-endian* format, the most significant byte is sent first. Some middleware messaging systems can handle both formats. A message property would then be necessary to tell subscribers which *endian* format is used.

Protecting the Subscriber List

While an event is fired, it is important to prevent the list of subscribers from modifications until all subscribers have been notified. Some subscribers may try to respond to a notification by removing themselves from the list or adding other subscribers. This can cause race conditions in the system, and must be prevented. A simple solution is to take a snapshot of the subscriber list and store the copy in a private data structure. Only subscribers in this private list will be targeted. Any changes to the original subscriber list will take effect the next time the associated event is fired.

Listing 8-1 and Listing 8-2 show C# and VB .NET examples in which the subscriber list is a collection holding subscriber names or addresses.

Listing 8-1. *Copying the Subscriber List into a Local Collection During Event Firing, Using C#*

```
ArrayList subscribers = new ArrayList();

public void FireEvent()
{
  // protect the subscriber list by making a private copy
  ArrayList privateSubscriberList = subscribers.Clone() as ArrayList;

  foreach (string subscriber in privateSubscriberList)
    // send message to each subscriber
    SendMessage("Hello", subscriber);
}

void SendMessage(string theMessage, string theSubscriber)
{
  // ...
}
```

Listing 8-2. *Copying the Subscriber List into a Local Collection During Event Firing, Using VB .NET*

```
Private subscribers As New ArrayList

Public Sub FireEvent()
  ' protect the subscriber list by making a private copy
  Dim privateSubscriberList As ArrayList
  privateSubscriberList = CType(subscribers.Clone(), ArrayList)
```

```
  For Each subscriber As String In privateSubscriberList
    ' send message to each subscriber
    SendMessage("Hello", subscriber)
  Next
End Sub

Sub SendMessage(ByVal theMessage As String, ByVal theSubscriber As String)
  ' ...
End Sub
```

Before dispatching any notifications to subscribers, a snapshot is taken of the subscriber array using the Clone method and is stored in a local variable. The clone is then safe from changes that might occur to the main subscriber ArrayList during event firing.

Sending the Event Notification

You can send notifications using a variety of delivery protocols, such as with shared files, network connections, procedure calls, and others, as described earlier in Chapter 3. The two most common protocols use messages and procedure calls.

Using Messages

In EBSs, messages are packets of data sent from one place to another. The most common scenario is for messages to be sent over a network connection. The receiver must have a listener daemon running, to handle incoming messages. Because the sender and receiver are in different process spaces, messages usually entail an asynchronous interaction. Moreover, messages are strictly one-way payloads. The only way the recipient can return data to the sender is by sending it a separate response message.

When sending messages to another system, it is common to use a point-to-point (PTP) interaction, rather than a publish-subscribe one. Using PTP, the sender must know the name or address of the recipient. If the recipient is running on a different machine, it is common for the sender to use a directory service to look up the recipient's address. The name of the directory service is often hard-coded in the sender. The sender's code will then contain at least two hard-coded values:

1. The name of the recipient, to be passed to the directory service

2. The name of the directory service

Embedding names or addresses in the code makes it more difficult to test a component in a nonproduction environment, because it introduces logic coupling. If the name of a resource changes at some point, you'll need to update the source code. A better approach is for the sender to expose properties for the names or addresses, so they can be set at startup time by some Initializer object. The advantage to using an Initializer is that the same object might handle the initialization of multiple senders. Even though the Initializer winds up being logically coupled to all those objects it knows the names or addresses of, it is a simple object because it only provides other objects with the data they need to function. Figure 8-1 shows the operation of the Initializer.

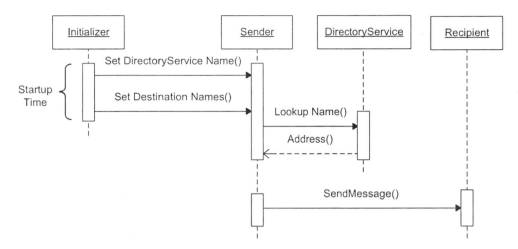

Figure 8-1. *Using an Initializer to initialize names of external systems at run time*

An even better approach is to remove directory lookup and message-sending code entirely from objects that need to send messages. But without that code, how would an object send its messages? By using event notifications! When an object needs to send a message, it fires an event whose payload contains two things:

1. The name of the recipient
2. The message to send

The recipient's name is obtained from a property initialized with the correct values at run time by an Initializer object, as shown in Figure 8-2.

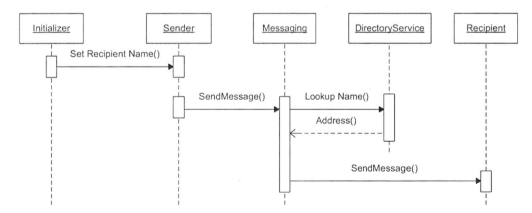

Figure 8-2. *Using a Messaging object to handle the communication details of sending messages*

When Sender needs to send a message to Recipient, it fires a SendMessage event. The recipient's name is the one set by the Initializer, so Sender doesn't know at compile time which object will get its messages. At startup time, the Initializer binds the Sender's SendMessage event to the Messaging object. The Messaging object manages an internal cache of name-address values. To determine the address for a given name, it accesses a directory service. Recipient names might be something like AccountingSystem; addresses might be something like accounting.mycompany.com or 192.168.10.2. Once the address is known, the Messaging object sends the message to the recipient. Listing 8-3 and Listing 8-4 show a simple example, in C# and VB .NET.

Listing 8-3. *Sending Messages Through a Messaging Object, in C#*

```csharp
public class Initializer
{
  public void InitializeSender(Sender theSender, Messaging theMessagingObject)
  {
    theSender.Recipient = "Accounting";
    theSender.OnSendMessage += new
      Sender.SendMessageHandler(theMessagingObject.SendMessage);
  }
}

public class Sender
{
  string recipient;
  public string Recipient
  {
    get {return recipient;}
    set {recipient = value;}
  }

  public void SendMessage()
  {
    // fire the OnSendMessage event
    FireSendMessage(Recipient, "Hello");
  }

  public delegate void SendMessageHandler(string theName, string theMessage);
  public event SendMessageHandler OnSendMessage;
  public void FireSendMessage(string theName, string theMessage)
  {
    if (OnSendMessage == null) return;
    OnSendMessage(theName, theMessage);
  }
}

public class Messaging
{
  Hashtable recipients = new Hashtable();  // key is name, value is address

  public string LookupAddress(string theRecipientName)
  {
    if (recipients.ContainsKey(theRecipientName))
      return recipients[theRecipientName] as string;
```

```
    else
    {
      // lookup recipient's address in Directory Service
      string address = DirectoryService.Lookup(theRecipientName);
      recipients.Add(theRecipientName, address);
      return address;
    }
  }

  public void SendMessage(string theRecipientName, string theMessage)
  {
    // get recipient's address
    string address = LookupAddress(theRecipientName);

    // send message ...
  }
}
```

Listing 8-4. *Sending Messages Through a Messaging Object, in VB .NET*

```
Public Class Initializer
  Public Sub InitializeSender(ByVal theSender As Sender, _
                              ByVal theMessagingObject As Messaging)
    theSender.Recipient = "Accounting"
    AddHandler theSender.OnSendMessage, AddressOf theMessagingObject.SendMessage
  End Sub
End Class

Public Class Sender
  Private _recipient As String
  Public Property Recipient() As String
    Get
      Return _recipient
    End Get
    Set(ByVal Value As String)
      _recipient = Value
    End Set
  End Property

  Public Sub SendMessage()
    ' fire the OnSendMessage event
    FireSendMessage(Recipient, "Hello")
  End Sub

  Public Event OnSendMessage(ByVal theName As String, ByVal theMessage As String)
  Public Sub FireSendMessage(ByVal theName As String, ByVal theMessage As String)
    RaiseEvent OnSendMessage(theName, theMessage)
  End Sub
End Class

Public Class Messaging
  Private recipients As New Hashtable    ' key is name, value is address
```

```vb.net
Public Function LookupAddress(ByVal theRecipientName As String) As String
  If (recipients.ContainsKey(theRecipientName)) Then
    Return CStr(recipients(theRecipientName))
  Else
    ' lookup recipient's address in Directory Service
    Dim address As String = DirectoryService.Lookup(theRecipientName)
    recipients.Add(theRecipientName, address)
    Return address
  End If
End Function

Public Sub SendMessage(ByVal theRecipientName As String, _
                       ByVal theMessage As String)
  ' get recipient's address
  Dim address As String = LookupAddress(theRecipientName)

  ' send message ...
  End Sub
End Class
```

The messages described so far use text payloads. Messages are often used to transfer other types of information, such as serialized objects, name-value pairs, and binary arrays. While text is pretty much platform-independent, other types of payloads may not be. For example, if a message contains a serialized Java object, the payload will only be useful to Java recipients. For binary payloads, the format of binary values (little- or big-endian) may be an issue.

Buffering Messages

Once you move all messaging details into a separate Messaging component, it becomes much easier to add certain features that middleware systems commonly support. For example, you can add internal queues that buffer incoming messages, in case the recipient is temporarily disconnected or the messages arrive faster than they can be delivered.

In the previous example, incoming messages arrived synchronously with the sender via procedure calls. Outgoing messages were delivered to recipients using a network connection or other shared resource. It is common to use separate threads to handle incoming and outgoing traffic, with the internal queues serving as the rendezvous point of the two threads. The incoming thread adds messages to the queue, and the outgoing thread removes messages, as shown in Figure 8-3.

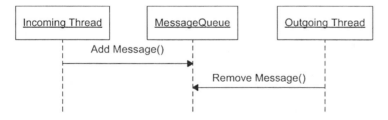

Figure 8-3. *Using a queue to buffer incoming messages*

Listing 8-5 and Listing 8-6 show possible implementations, in C# and VB .NET.

Listing 8-5. *Queuing Messages in the Messaging Component, in C#*

```csharp
using System.Threading;

public class MessageQueue
{
  // items of this type are put in the queue
  class QueuedItem
  {
    public string address;    // address of recipient
    public string message;   // message to deliver

    public QueuedItem(string theAddress, string theMessage)
    {
      address = theAddress;
      message = theMessage;
    }
  }

  Hashtable recipients = new Hashtable();      // key is name, value is address
  Queue incomingMessages = new Queue();       // the message queue
  Thread deliveryThread;                      // handles delivery to recipients

  private bool stopDeliveryRequested;
  public void StopDelivery()
  {
    stopDeliveryRequested = true;
  }

  public MessageQueue()
  {
    deliveryThread = new Thread(new ThreadStart(MessageProcessor) );
    deliveryThread.Start();
  }

  void MessageProcessor()
  {
    while (!stopDeliveryRequested)
    {
      ProcessNextMessage();
      Thread.Sleep(10);      // pause for 10 ms
    }
  }

  // this method executes on the outgoing thread
  void ProcessNextMessage()
  {
    QueuedItem item;
    if (incomingMessages.Count == 0) return;
    lock(incomingMessages)
    {
      item = incomingMessages.Dequeue() as QueuedItem;
    }
    DeliverMessage(item.address, item.message);
  }
```

```csharp
void DeliverMessage(string theAddress, string theMessage)
{
  // send message...
}

public string LookupAddress(string theRecipientName)
{
  if (recipients.ContainsKey(theRecipientName) )
    return recipients[theRecipientName] as string;
  else
  {
    // lookup recipient's address in Directory Service
    string address = DirectoryService.Lookup(theRecipientName);
    recipients.Add(theRecipientName, address);
    return address;
  }
}

// this method executes on the incoming thread. If the sender
// is in the same process, it will execute on the sender's thread
public void SendMessage(string theRecipientName, string theMessage)
{
  // get recipient's address
  string address = LookupAddress(theRecipientName);

  // add incoming message to queue
  QueuedItem item = new QueuedItem(address, theMessage);

  lock(incomingMessages)
  {
    incomingMessages.Enqueue(item);
  }
}
}
```

Listing 8-6. *Queuing Messages in the Messaging Component, in VB .NET*

```vbnet
Imports System.Threading

Public Class MessageQueue

  ' items of this type are put in the queue
  Class QueuedItem
    Public address As String     ' address of recipient
    Public message As String   ' message to deliver

    Public Sub New(ByVal theAddress As String, ByVal theMessage As String)
      address = theAddress
      message = theMessage
    End Sub
  End Class

  Private recipients As New Hashtable         ' key is name, value is address
  Private incomingMessages As New Queue       ' the message queue
  Private deliveryThread As Thread            ' handles delivery to recipients
```

```vbnet
Private _stopDeliveryRequested As Boolean
Public Sub StopDelivery()
  _stopDeliveryRequested = True
End Sub

Public Sub New()
  deliveryThread = New Thread(New ThreadStart(AddressOf MessageProcessor))
  deliveryThread.Start()
End Sub

Sub MessageProcessor()
  While Not _stopDeliveryRequested
    ProcessNextMessage()
    Thread.Sleep(10)    'pause for 10 ms
  End While
End Sub

' this method executes on the outgoing thread
Sub ProcessNextMessage()
  Dim item As QueuedItem
  If incomingMessages.Count = 0 Then Return
  SyncLock (incomingMessages)
    item = DirectCast(incomingMessages.Dequeue(), QueuedItem)
  End SyncLock
  DeliverMessage(item.address, item.message)
End Sub

Sub DeliverMessage(ByVal theAddress As String, ByVal theMessage As String)
  ' send message...
End Sub

Public Function LookupAddress(ByVal theRecipientName As String) As String
  If (recipients.ContainsKey(theRecipientName) ) Then
    Return CStr(recipients(theRecipientName) )
  Else
    ' lookup recipient's address in Directory Service
    Dim address As String = DirectoryService.Lookup(theRecipientName)
    recipients.Add(theRecipientName, address)
    Return address
  End If
End Function

' this method executes on the incoming thread. If the sender
' is in the same process, it will execute on the sender's thread
Public Sub SendMessage(ByVal theRecipientName As String, _
                                        ByVal theMessage As String)
  ' get recipient's address
  Dim address As String = LookupAddress(theRecipientName)

  ' add incoming message to queue
  Dim item As New QueuedItem(address, theMessage)
```

```
    SyncLock (incomingMessages)
      incomingMessages.Enqueue(item)
    End SyncLock
  End Sub
End Class
```

The code examples don't show the actual details of message transmission, since they are implementation-dependent and not terribly important for this discussion. MessageQueue keeps messages in an in-memory queue. To improve reliability of delivery, the MessageQueue could save queued messages in a persistent store, such as a file system or a database. This way, messages could be recovered if the system crashed or was shut down while messages were in the queue.

Using Procedure Calls

When delivering event notifications using PCs, four variations can occur, depending on the location of the sender with respect to the receiver, and on the timing of the call. A PC can be either local or remote, and either synchronous or asynchronous.

Remote Procedure Calls

Although LPCs and RPCs are semantically equivalent, they are quite different in terms of implementation and operation. While LPCs are supported directly by languages and microprocessors, RPCs aren't and must rely on a calling substrate that handles the plumbing. Although the RPC details are usually hidden from the application code layer, you should at least keep them in mind. The fundamental tasks of the RPC plumbing are

- To provide location transparency of remote calls
- To deal with the communication channel
- To provide a receiver-side daemon to accept incoming calls
- To marshal input parameters into the receiver's process space
- To marshal output parameters back to the sender's process space

The RPC substrate handles most of these tasks transparently, but one thing is important: Communication channels are not always reliable, so the sender may need to include exception handling for communication failures or timeouts.

All the various distributed component models use their own RPC implementation. For example, CORBA components use OMG RPC, JavaBeans components use Java RMI, and .NET components use .NET Remoting. The substrates are different at both the application interface and wire levels, so it isn't possible to use a .NET component to invoke a CORBA component using .NET Remoting, or to use a CORBA component to invoke a .NET component using OMG RPC. Although the RPCs are incompatible, it is possible to build *bridging* components, which allow cross-platform calls.

Calling Untyped Targets

Event targets are the recipients of event notifications. A target is said to be *untyped* (from the perspective of an event source) if the source knows nothing about the interface of the target. When dealing with untyped targets, event sources send notifications directly to a method of the target, bypassing the target's interfaces. To do so, the event source must have a direct reference to the method, as shown in Figure 8-4.

In Figure 8-4, MethodReference alludes to a platform-specific method reference type. The reference is initialized at run time to point to a method with a compatible signature, introducing signature coupling between the event source object and the event target object. The source and target are coupled at the object level, but are decoupled at the class level. At compile time, the source doesn't know what class the method referenced will belong to, which means the event source is entirely independent of the type of objects that might be chosen as targets. Any object that exposes methods with the required signature can be used as an event target.

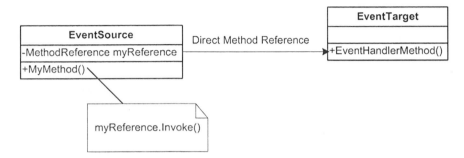

Figure 8-4. *Invoking methods of untyped event targets*

The use of calls to untyped targets make it possible for any public method of an object to be used potentially as an event handler, and the same method can be registered simultaneously as a handler for different events associated with different event source objects.

Relatively recent languages, such as C# and Delphi Object Pascal, support method references at the language level. The Ada language doesn't natively support method references, but Garlan[1] describes a technique to add support for untyped object calls to the language. Garlan uses the expression *implicit invocations* to refer to untyped object calls. C++ supports pointers to member functions, but restricts targets to be of a particular compile-time-defined class. Listing 8-7 shows an example:

Listing 8-7. *Untyped Object Calls in C++*

```
// declare supporting items
typedef void (MyClass::*EventXHandler)();
MyClass* eventXTarget;
EventXHandler onEventX;

// fire an event...
if (eventXTarget && onEventX)
  (*eventXTarget.*onEventX)();
```

Using this C++ syntax, methods assigned to the variable onEventX must belong to MyClass. Attempts have also been made to support events in C++ in a more coherent way. ECO[2] is one example, based on new language constructs and classes. A precompiler converts the language constructs into C++ code.

---

1. David Garlan and Curtis Scott, "Adding Implicit Invocation to Traditional Programming Languages" (proceedings of the 15th International Conference on Software Engineering, Baltimore, MD, May 1993).

2. Mads Haahr, Rene Meier, Paddy Nixon, Vinny Cahill, and Eric Jul, "Filtering and Scalability in the ECO Distributed Event Model" (proceedings of the 5th International Symposium on Software Engineering for Parallel and Distributed Systems, Limerick, Ireland, June 2000).

Universal Methods

Using untyped object calls, the caller only requires a method with a given signature to be present in the callee. The shorter the argument list of the method signature, the more likely it will be compatible with methods exposed by other objects. The most compatible signature of all is the one with no arguments and no return value; it looks like this:

```
void f();
```

The method can have any name. Methods having this signature are the lingua franca of the untyped call world, and for this reason I call them *universal methods*. Since they don't make references to any types, all programming languages can support them (in theory), if one ignores differences in calling conventions between languages. A calling convention specifies three language- and microprocessor-specific rules: how to pass parameters to a method, how to get returned values from the method, and who cleans up the stack when the called method returns.

The signature of a universal method is called, unsurprisingly, the *universal signature*. When developing classes in an EBS, it is often advantageous to expose methods with the shortest argument list possible, because this way you increase the potential for reuse. Ideally, all methods might be universal. This isn't usually possible, of course, but sometimes a little forethought can help. For example, assume you're creating an LED component that has two states: on and off. You might expose the method SetState(bool) to turn the LED on or off. While this method is useful, you might also want to expose a couple of universal methods that achieve the same goals:

```
void TurnOn();
void TurnOff();
```

Universal methods are not only more likely to be used as event targets, but they are also easier to use because you don't have to worry about parameters.

Reflection

Not all languages—even relatively recent ones—support method references directly. A notable case is Java. However, this language does support *reflection*, a run-time process to get class and object metadata. You can use reflection as a workaround to obtain a direct reference to a method, using the built-in class java.lang.reflect.Method to call an untyped target method directly. To fire an event using a Method object, its invoke method must be called, with a parameter identifying which object to call. The Java code fragment in Listing 8-8 shows the essentials.

Listing 8-8. *Using Reflection in Java to Fire Events to Untyped Targets*

```java
public class EventSource {

  private java.lang.reflect.Method onEventX;    // method to invoke
  private Object eventTarget;                    // object that owns method

  public void methodThatFiresAnEvent() {

    // do something...

    // fire an event
    if (onEventX == null) return;
    if (eventTarget == null) return;
    try {
      onEventX.invoke(eventTarget, null);
    }
```

```
        catch (Exception ex) {...}
        //...
    }
}
```

This example shows an event source that can handle only a single subscriber. To support multicasting, you would need to use collections to store the Method and Object references. The second parameter passed to Method.invoke is an optional array of parameters.

Calling Typed Targets

A typed object call uses this implementation pattern:

```
ICallee calleeInstance;
// initialize calleeInstance...

// invoke a method through the interface
calleeInstance.methodName();
```

To call a typed target is to invoke a method of a target object through an interface. The caller must obviously know the callee's type (either its class or one of its interfaces), so typed object calls introduce type coupling between caller and callee—even if the called method has a universal signature. The method invoked belongs to the callee's class, or one of the interfaces it implements. Depending on where the callee's class or interface is defined with respect to the caller, there are four coupling scenarios, as shown in Figure 8-5 through Figure 8-8.

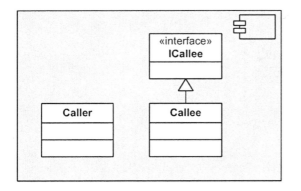

Figure 8-5. *The caller and callee are part of the same component.*

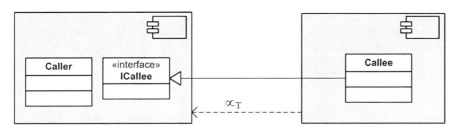

Figure 8-6. *The callee component is coupled to the caller component.*

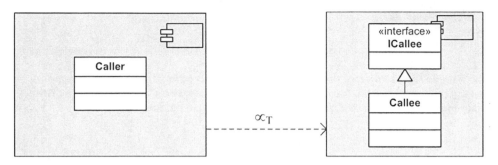

Figure 8-7. *The calling component is coupled to the callee component.*

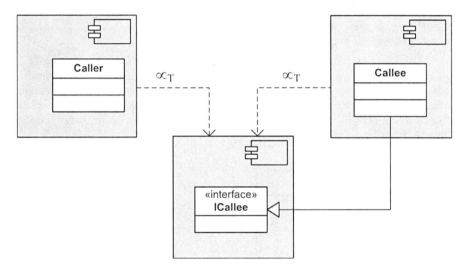

Figure 8-8. *The calling and callee components are coupled to a third component.*

The first situation introduces no component-level coupling, since the caller and callee are in the same component. The last three situations depicted have type coupling between components. Apart from the packaging dependency, typed object calls place an additional dependency on the caller, because the caller must decide which method of the callee to call. In most cases, this decision in made at compile time, by embedding the method's name in the caller's code. If, at some point in the future, the method's name is changed in ICallee, or the method is moved to another interface during a refactoring process of ICallee, the caller's code will break.

In spite of these dependencies, typed object calls are heavily engrained in the programming community. Typed object calls are in fact at the very core of the object-oriented programming paradigm. A large number of design patterns are based on it, and all OO programming languages support it.

Drawbacks of Typed Object Calls

Let's look at the implications of typed-object-call coupling a bit closer with an example. Assume you purchase two components A and B, developed by different vendors. Assume also that A fires events as typed object calls; in other words, A makes calls through an outgoing interface. You want to use A and B together in a system, wiring an event fired by A to B. Assume A uses an outgoing interface Interface1 to call a method M1. Component B implements a different interface Interface2, whose method M2 is to be used as the event handler.

Since A's outgoing interface doesn't match B's interface (because the two vendors for A and B didn't know anything about each other), there is no way to directly connect A to B. The solution is to create an *adapter* component that on one side exposes the proper interface for A to call, and on the other side calls the proper interface and method of B. The signal diagram in Figure 8-9 shows the adapter you would need to connect A to B.

If using typed object calls, the only way for A to be directly interoperable with B is for A to call through an outgoing interface that B implements. In other words, A must be tailor-built to suit B. Or you can turn the picture around and say that to use B with A, B must implement the interface that A calls. Either way, components A and B would have to be developed with knowledge of each other. While an adapter is generally a very simple class, it is nonetheless a new class, whose purpose is solely to act as a workaround for a problem caused by the mismatch between event source and target. In an EBS, you're going to need to wire lots of incompatible parts together, so you're going to wind up with countless adapters.

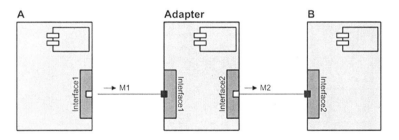

Figure 8-9. *Using a custom adapter to connect incompatible components together*

Apart from the clutter introduced by these added adapters, untyped object calls have a serious drawback. Assume you have two identical components A and B. You want A's M1 event notification to do one thing on C, and B's event notification to do something else on C. As an example, assume A and B are simple UI Button controls. The buttons fire the outgoing call Interface1.M1 when the button is clicked. Assume C exposes the interface Interface1 and that you need A and B to call different methods of C when the two buttons are clicked. You would need to wire the system as shown in Figure 8-10.

The problem is that you don't want B to call the same method as A. Component C would have to implement Interface1 twice, providing separate implementations, which is not allowed in any OO language (and for good reason!). The only solution is to route A or B's outgoing signal through an adapter, and to have C implement a separate interface I'll call InterfaceX that supports exactly the same features as Interface1, but with a different name, as shown in Figure 8-11.

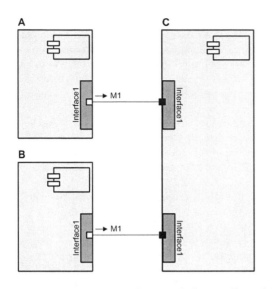

Figure 8-10. *A situation that typed object calls can't handle*

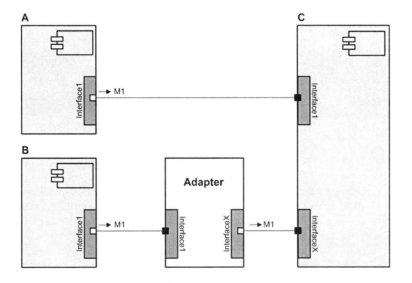

Figure 8-11. *Using an adapter to solve the problem shown in Figure 8-10*

If you had lots of buttons in the system, you might wind up with lots of adapters. Even with their drawbacks, typed object calls are sometimes a better approach than untyped object calls. The following list shows the pros of typed object calls:

- They support polymorphism.
- They define a clear contract between source and target.
- They are supported by all OO languages.

Here are the cons of typed object calls:

- They often require classes to be modified (typically by implementing interfaces) to function as event targets.
- They require event sources to be prefabricated with advance knowledge of the interfaces they will call.
- They introduce type coupling on the event source class.
- They are overkill for many situations.
- They prevent a target from handling the same type of event in different ways, because a target can only implement a given interface once.
- They require the event source to know which methods of the target interface to call.

As a result of the pros and cons, untyped object calls will often be preferable in the following situations:

- When the event source only calls one method of the target
- When an event target uses the same event type with more than one handler method
- When you don't want to type-couple the caller to the callee
- When you can't or don't want to change the target class to make it an event target

Typed object calls will often be preferable in the following situations:

- When the event source calls multiple methods of the target
- When you need the target to handle events polymorphically
- When you want to specify interaction constraints using contracts

When components interact through events based on a single untyped object call, the only contract regulating the interaction is the signature of the method being called. When an interaction is expected to be complex, an interface-based event notification model is often more appropriate.

Notifications Used to Retrieve Data

In most cases, notifications are used in a push model, somewhat like messages in a bottle tossed into the ocean. The sender doesn't rely on how receivers react to the notification and doesn't even care if there are any receivers. Receivers operate in a *reactive* mode, doing essentially nothing unless they receive an event notification. In this push model, it is generally the sender that passes data to the receiver, assuming data is transferred at all.

But it is also possible to use notifications in a pull model, to retrieve data from the subscriber. By using events both to push and pull data, you now have a means to replace virtually all procedure calls across component boundaries with notifications: Some calls will push data, others will pull, and still others may do both.

Keep in mind that using notifications to pull data from subscribers violates the basic event interaction pattern: The sender is not only broadcasting information to the world, but also wants an answer back from at least one subscriber. If there are no subscribers, the sender may need to take a special course of action. For example, if the sender uses a notification to request the value of a Boolean variable, the sender might use a default value if there are no receivers. Using default values is just one course of action. The sender might do any number of things, including logging the occurrence as an error, throwing an exception, firing an alternative event, and prompting the user.

Another problem when using notifications in a pull mode might occur when there are multiple receivers, because the receivers might overwrite each other's return values. If multiple receivers are expected, the notification payload should contain an Envelope (or an equivalent data structure), as described at the end of Chapter 4. It is the sender's job to reconcile and interpret the returned values. Rather than using event notifications to retrieve data from receivers, you can use an alternative design pattern that relies on two separate notifications, as described in the next section.

Regardless of the problems arising out of the presence of multiple subscribers, using notifications in a pull mode is useful because they decouple the sender from the receiver. Notifications can be advantageously used even between objects that are packaged together. Assume A and B are objects that will eventually be packaged together, and that A needs data from B. If you embed in A a direct method call to B, you would type-couple A to B. You would no longer be able to test A without B. Using events and notifications, you can develop and test A and B separately, each with their own test fixture.

A C# example of notifications used to retrieve information from receivers is the Closing notification, sent by Form objects. When the user clicks the Close box on a form's caption bar, the form fires a Closing event. The notification carries a payload object of type System.ComponentModel. CancelEventArgs. This object exposes a Cancel field that receivers can set if they wish to veto the event and prevent the form from closing. A Java example includes Vetoable notifications, which are sent to subscribers just before a constrained property is changed. Any of the subscribers can veto the change by throwing an exception, which is caught by the event source. The exception conceptually returns a value to the sender, indicating a veto.

Using notifications to fetch information from subscribers is only possible with notifications delivered using procedure calls. When using messages to deliver notifications, fetching data is impossible, because message data can only flow in one direction: from sender to receiver. To return data to the sender, a subscriber would have to resort to a secondary notification of its own.

As mentioned earlier, there is also a problem when the sender expects a value to return from subscribers: What if there are no subscribers? There are four common solutions that you can use on the sender's side:

- Continue using a safe default, if possible.

- Attempt an alternative action.

- Throw an exception.

- Stop the system.

Continuing with a safe default is the most common technique, but is only possible if such a value exists. Whether a *safe default* exists is strictly application-dependent. For example, consider an event notification used to fetch an integer value. A return value of 0 may be a safe default, but perhaps even this value is potentially unsafe, preventing the system from continuing.

If an event has no subscribers, and no safe defaults are available, the sender may be able to proceed by taking an alternative action. Popular choices are

- Fire a backup or alternative event.

- Call a method to compute a fallback value.

Listing 8-9 shows C# Fire methods that use the two techniques when no listeners are available.

Listing 8-9. *C# Fire Methods Taking Alternative Action If No Listeners Are Available*

```
public delegate string MyDelegate();
public event MyDelegate OnEventX;
public event MyDelegate OnEventY;
```

```csharp
// if no subscribers, try a different event
string FireEventX1()
{
  if (OnEventX != null)
    return OnEventX();
  return FireEventY();   // a backup or alternative event
}

// if no subscribers, return a default value
string FireEventX2()
{
  if (OnEventX != null)
    return OnEventX();
  return DoSomethingElse();
}

string FireEventY()
{
  if (OnEventY != null)
    return OnEventY();
}

// compute a default or fallback value
string DoSomethingElse()
{
  return "";
}
```

Listing 8-10 shows VB .NET Fire methods that use the two techniques when no listeners are available.

Listing 8-10. *VB .NET Fire Methods Taking Alternative Action If No Listeners Are Available*

```vbnet
Public Delegate Function MyDelegate() As String
Public OnEventX As MyDelegate
Public OnEventY As MyDelegate

' if no subscribers, try a different event
Function FireEventX1() As String
  If Not OnEventX Is Nothing Then
    Return OnEventX()
  Else
    Return FireEventY()  ' a backup or alternative event
  End If
End Function

' if no subscribers, return a default value
Function FireEventX2() As String
  If Not OnEventX Is Nothing Then
    Return OnEventX()
  Else
    Return DoSomethingElse()
  End If
End Function
```

```
Function FireEventY() As String
  If Not OnEventX Is Nothing Then
    Return OnEventX()
  End If
End Function

' compute a default or fallback value
Function DoSomethingElse() As String
  Return ""
End Function
```

VB .NET EVENTS CAN'T RETURN A VALUE

There is a small but significant difference between C# event and VB .NET Event keywords. In C#, an event can define a return value. In VB .NET, an Event is not allowed to define a return value. In VB .NET, to fire an event that defines a return value, you must use a delegate. Here's an example:

```
Public Delegate Function MyDelegate() As String
Public OnEventX As MyDelegate

Function FireEventX() As String
  If Not OnEventX Is Nothing Then
    Return OnEventX()    'fire the event using a delegate
  End If
End Function
```

When no listeners are available and no alternative courses of action are possible, it may be necessary for the sender to throw an exception. A special exception might be defined for this purpose, such as ExceptionNoSubscribersAvailable. The exception handler might react by notifying the end user, making an entry in a log journal, or even shutting the system down.

Two Notifications Might Be Better Than One

As you've seen, using a notification to retrieve data has drawbacks. Besides the problem of how to proceed in the absence of subscribers, another problem is that the notifications often must be sent using synchronous procedure calls. When the sender requests data, it generally must block and wait until the subscribers return control.

An alternative technique is based on the use of two notifications to achieve the original goal of sending a notification and getting data back. If A is the event source and B is the event target from which data is returned, the diagram in Figure 8-12 shows the two notifications.

When A sends the DataRequest notification, the sender blocks. Once B gets the data requested, it makes a reentrant DataReturned call back into A, which is still blocked on the original DataRequest call. Using synchronous calls this way can be cumbersome, and the call that B makes into A requires A to be reentrant. An alternative is to use asynchronous calls from A to B, as shown in Figure 8-13.

Using an asynchronous call, A can continue with its internal tasks while B processes the DataRequest notification. The technique is even more powerful when A needs information that comes from different subscribers. It can use separate asynchronous calls to fire events to all the necessary subscribers, so all the work in the receivers is carried out in parallel instead of sequentially.

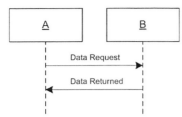

Figure 8-12. *Using two notifications to retrieve data*

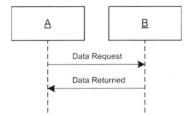

Figure 8-13. *Using an asynchronous call from A to B*

Avoiding Deadlocks

There is always the possibility of deadlocks in systems that have reentrant calls or concurrent code, unless you take precautions. Deadlocks are typically caused by the incorrect use of process synchronization primitives, such as monitors. When designing an object or component that fires events to the surrounding world, you have to be especially careful on where to use resource locks in relation to fired events. The first and foremost rule to avoid deadlocks in event-based code is this:

`Never fire events after locking a resource.`

The reason is obvious: You can't predict who is going to handle the notifications, and there is the possibility that the event handler may need the locked resource. In terms of lockable resources, there are two fundamental types: code and data. Listing 8-11 and Listing 8-12 show what *not* to do, because they lock a section of code before firing an event. The section of code protected by the lock is called a *critical section*, and only one thread can enter it at any given time.

Listing 8-11. *C# Example of Locking a Resource and Then Firing an Event*

```
// DON'T DO THIS!
public class EventSource
{
  public delegate void SomethingHappenedHandler();
  public event SomethingHappenedHandler OnSomethingHappened;

  public void M1()
  {
    lock (this)
    {
      if (OnSomethingHappened != null)
        OnSomethingHappened();
    }
  }
}
```

Listing 8-12. *VB .NET Example of Locking a Resource and Then Firing an Event*

```
' DON'T DO THIS!
Public Class BadEventSource

  Public Delegate Sub SomethingHappenedHandler()
  Public OnSomethingHappened As SomethingHappenedHandler

  Public Sub M1()
    SyncLock (Me)
      If Not OnSomethingHappened Is Nothing Then
        OnSomethingHappened()
      End If
    End SyncLock
  End Sub
End Class
```

The code lock could cause a deadlock if a SomethingHappened subscriber caused BadEventSource.M1 to be called directly or indirectly while processing the event notification.

Another type of deadlock can occur even in the absence of reentrant calls, when the event source locks a resource that is shared with other objects or components. For example, say S is a file, A is an event source, and B is an event subscriber. Assume A locks S for exclusive access and then fires an event to B using a synchronous call. When B gets the event notification, say it needs access to S before it can complete its job and return control to A. Obviously, the system will freeze, with B waiting forever for A to release the lock on S. Again, the solution is to design A so it doesn't need to lock S while it fires events.

Dealing with Exceptions from Targets

When an event is fired using a procedure call, there is the potential for event targets to throw exceptions while handling the event, disrupting the normal sequence of notifications. Event sources may need to be coded defensively and be prepared to handle exceptions thrown by event targets. You must consider two kinds of problems:

1. What to do if an exception occurs

2. How to proceed

For the former problem, you might need to fire a different event or call a fallback method. For the latter problem, options include doing nothing, letting the exception propagate up the stack, throwing an exception of a new type, notifying the operator, and logging the exception.

Using a Shared Resource

Instead of using messages or procedure calls to send notifications, you can also use a shared resource. As stated earlier, messages are actually a special case of shared resource delivery, because the sender and receiver share the communication channel through which messages are delivered. Let's look at how events are fired using other kinds of shared resources.

Shared Memory

Shared memory has long been used in distributed systems to allow different processes to exchange information. What is noteworthy is the fact that, from the perspective of an event-based programmer, information that passes through shared memory looks just like an event notification. Why? For the following reasons:

- The sender is like an event source, because it sends out information without knowing what potential receivers will do with it.

- Receivers look like subscribers, because they monitor the shared memory, waiting for information to appear.

Sender and receiver must agree on a designated *rendezvous area* in the shared memory. When the notification signal is written to the rendezvous area, the subscriber must somehow *clear it* after handling it; otherwise, the subscriber will go into an infinite loop and keep trying to handle the notification over and over again. If the rendezvous area is a single byte, the *clearing* operation might entail setting the byte to 0. If the area is a data structure, you could designate a separate byte to act as the signaling flag. You should protect the flag by a semaphore or other process synchronization mechanism to prevent concurrent writing by the sender and subscriber. Figure 8-14 shows a possible solution supporting unicast events.

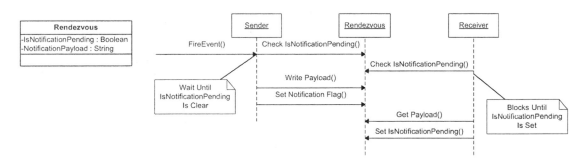

Figure 8-14. *Using a shared Rendezvous object to send notifications*

A class called Rendezvous is defined to coordinate the sender and receiver. An instance of Rendezvous is stored at a given location in the shared memory, known to both sender and receiver. A flag called IsNotificationPending coordinates access to the Rendezvous payload. When the sender wishes to send a notification, it must wait for the flag to be clear, indicating that the receiver has read the last notification sent. Once the flag is clear, the sender can write the notification payload to the Rendezvous object and then set the notification flag. The receiver monitors the notification flag. When the flag is found to be set, the receiver gets the notification payload and then clears the flag. Listing 8-13 shows a C# implementation.

Listing 8-13. *Using a Simple Shared C# Rendezvous Object to Deliver Notifications*

```csharp
public class Rendezvous
{
  bool isNotificationPending;
  public bool IsNotificationPending
  {
    get {return isNotificationPending;}
    set { lock(this)   { isNotificationPending = value; } }
  }

  string notificationPayload;
  public string NotificationPayload
  {
```

```csharp
      get {return notificationPayload;}
      set {notificationPayload = value;}
    }
  }

public class Sender
{
  Rendezvous sharedMemory;

  public Sender(Rendezvous theSharedMemory)
  {
    sharedMemory = theSharedMemory;
  }

  int notificationCount = 0;
  public void FireEvent()
  {
    while (sharedMemory.IsNotificationPending)
      Thread.Sleep(10);  // wait for receiver to read last notification

    // fire the event
    string payload = string.Format("Notification {0}", notificationCount++);
    sharedMemory.NotificationPayload = payload;
    sharedMemory.IsNotificationPending = true;
  }
}

public class Receiver
{
  Rendezvous sharedMemory;
  public bool terminationRequested;

  public Receiver(Rendezvous theSharedMemory)
  {
    sharedMemory = theSharedMemory;
  }

  public void Run()
  {
    while (!terminationRequested)
    {
      WaitForNotifications();
      Thread.Sleep(10);
    }
  }

  void WaitForNotifications()
  {
    if (sharedMemory.IsNotificationPending)
    {
      // notification found: get the payload
      string s = sharedMemory.NotificationPayload;
```

```
      // indicate that notification has been read
      sharedMemory.IsNotificationPending = false;
    }
  }
}
```

This implementation assumes that Sender and Receiver are running in different threads of the same process. The class uses a C# lock to protect concurrent writing of IsNotificationPending by different threads sharing the same instance of Rendezvous. The lock forms a critical section around the code that modifies the property. The lock isn't strictly necessary in this example, because the sender and receivers are guaranteed to set the flag's value at different times. Why? Because the sender can set the flag, but only if the flag's value is false. The receiver can clear the flag, but only if the flag's value is true.

A problem with this implementation is that the sender can't send a new notification if the receiver hasn't read the last one sent. The sender is essentially at the mercy of the receiver, in terms of timing. The situation is analogous to notifications sent using synchronous procedure calls: The sender blocks until the receiver's event handler method finishes.

To remove the timing constraint with shared memory notifications, you can change the Rendezvous object, adding an internal queue to store notifications. The sender can only add items to the queue, and the receiver can only remove them. The diagram in Figure 8-15 shows the interactions involved.

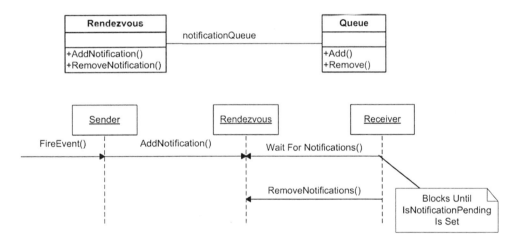

Figure 8-15. *Using a shared Rendezvous with a queue to send notifications*

Listing 8-14 and Listing 8-15 show C# and VB .NET implementations.

Listing 8-14. *C# Example with a Queued Rendezvous Object*

```
public class Rendezvous
{
  public bool IsNotificationPending
  {
    get {return notificationQueue.Count > 0;}
  }
```

```
  Queue notificationQueue = new Queue();

  public void AddNotification(string thePayoad)
  {
    lock(this)
    {
      notificationQueue.Enqueue(thePayoad);
    }
  }

  public string RemoveNotification()
  {
    lock(this)
    {
      return notificationQueue.Dequeue() as string;
    }
  }
}

public class Sender
{
  Rendezvous sharedMemory;

  public Sender(Rendezvous theSharedMemory)
  {
    sharedMemory = theSharedMemory;
  }

  int notificationCount = 0;
  public void FireEvent()
  {
    string payload = string.Format("Notification {0}", notificationCount);
    notificationCount += 1;
    sharedMemory.AddNotification(payload);
  }
}

public class Receiver
{
  Rendezvous sharedMemory;
  public bool terminationRequested;

  public Receiver(Rendezvous theSharedMemory)
  {
    sharedMemory = theSharedMemory;
  }

public void Run()
{
  while (!terminationRequested)
  {
    WaitForNotifications();
    System.Threading.Thread.Sleep(10);
  }
```

```csharp
}

void WaitForNotifications()
{
  if (!sharedMemory.IsNotificationPending) return;

  // notification found: get the payload
  string s = sharedMemory.RemoveNotification();
  ProcessNotification(s);
}

void ProcessNotification(string s) { }
}
```

Listing 8-15. *VB .NET Example with a Queued Rendezvous Object*

```vbnet
Public Class Rendezvous
  Public ReadOnly Property IsNotificationPending() As Boolean
    Get
      Return notificationQueue.Count > 0
    End Get
  End Property

  Dim notificationQueue As New Queue

  Public Sub AddNotification(ByVal thePayoad As String)
    SyncLock (Me)
      notificationQueue.Enqueue(thePayoad)
    End SyncLock
  End Sub

  Public Function RemoveNotification() As String
    SyncLock (Me)
      Return CStr(notificationQueue.Dequeue())
    End SyncLock
  End Function
End Class

Public Class Sender
  Dim sharedMemory As Rendezvous

  Public Sub New(ByVal theSharedMemory As Rendezvous)
      sharedMemory = theSharedMemory;
  End Sub

  Dim notificationCount As Integer = 0
  Public Sub FireEvent()
    Dim payload As String = String.Format("Notification {0}", notificationCount)
    notificationCount += 1
    sharedMemory.AddNotification(payload)
  End Sub
End Class
```

```
Public Class Receiver
  Private sharedMemory As Rendezvous
  Public terminationRequested As Boolean

  Public Sub New(ByVal theSharedMemory As Rendezvous)
    sharedMemory = theSharedMemory
  End Sub

  Public Sub Run()
    While Not terminationRequested
      WaitForNotifications()
      System.Threading.Thread.Sleep(10)
    End While
  End Sub

  Sub WaitForNotifications()
    If Not sharedMemory.IsNotificationPending Then Return

    ' notification found: get the payload
    Dim s As String = sharedMemory.RemoveNotification()
    ProcessNotification(s)
  End Sub

  Sub ProcessNotification(ByVal s As String)
  End Sub
End Class
```

The Rendezvous class uses C# locks to protect critical sections. Locks only work at the thread level, so if Sender and Receiver were in different processes, a semaphore or other process synchronization object would be required.

To handle multiple receivers, you could change the Rendezvous object to manage a subscription process. When a receiver subscribes, the Rendezvous object might add the new subscriber to an internal list and then create a queue to which the subscriber's notifications are written. Each time the sender calls AddNotification to add a notification, the Rendezvous object would add it to the queues of all subscribers. The Rendezvous object could also handle notification filtering.

Shared memory notifications are generally used only in a unicast mode, because they become cumbersome with multiple subscribers. The problem with multicast mode is due to the way subscribers typically wait for notifications, by monitoring a designated rendezvous area of shared memory. To support multiple subscribers, you would need to make sure that each subscriber had a different signaling flag. This entails that subscribers understand that they might not be alone in accessing the notification data, and must obey certain rules to prevent interfering with each other.

Shared Files

Using files as a shared resource is a fairly simple, if inefficient, way to send notifications. You can use files to send notifications between processes on the same machine or on different machines. In the first case, you can use a single file. The simplest technique is to have the sender save the notification payload in a shared file. The subscriber must obviously know the name of the file and directory. The subscriber watches the directory, waiting for the file to appear. When it appears, the subscriber reads the file contents and then deletes the file. The diagram in Figure 8-16 shows the timing.

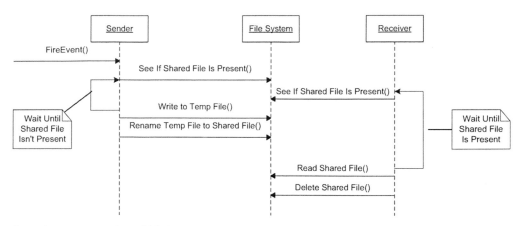

Figure 8-16. *Using a shared file between processes on the same machine*

The sender writes the notification payload to a temporary file in the shared folder. Once the file has been written, its name is changed into the shared file's designated name. The file system executes the `Rename` command as an uninterruptible command, so the receiver doesn't see the shared file appear until the temp file has been completely written, closed, renamed, and is ready to be read. The renaming stratagem spares the sender and receiver from having to deal with file locks.

A significant problem with this simplistic approach is that the sender can't send further notifications until the subscriber has read the previous one. There are two typical solutions. The simplest is to use multiple files, named according to a numbering scheme. The alternative is to use a single file, but with new rules, to allow the file to contain multiple notifications.

Using multiple files, the sender uses the same approach shown in the previous sequence diagram, but creates a new shared file for each notification sent, using a predefined naming sequence. It might create files named SharedFile000, SharedFile001, etc. The receiver would delete each file after reading it. Listing 8-16 and Listing 8-17 show implementations in C# and VB .NET.

Listing 8-16. *Using Numbered Files to Fire Events in C#*

```csharp
public class Sender
{
  string sharedDirectory;
  int fileNumber = 0;

  public Sender(string theSharedDirectory)
  {
    sharedDirectory = theSharedDirectory;
    if (!System.IO.Directory.Exists(theSharedDirectory))
      System.IO.Directory.CreateDirectory(theSharedDirectory);
  }

  public void FireEvent(string thePayload)
  {
    string tempFileName = sharedDirectory + @"\temp";

    // create the temp file
    System.IO.StreamWriter writer = new System.IO.StreamWriter(tempFileName);
    writer.WriteLine(thePayload);
    writer.Close();
```

```
        string fileName = string.Format(@"{0}\File{1:000}",
                                  sharedDirectory, fileNumber);

        // rename the file
        System.IO.File.Move(tempFileName, fileName);

        fileNumber++;
        if (fileNumber > 999)
          fileNumber = 0;
    }
}

public class Receiver
{
  public bool terminationRequested;
  private string sharedDirectory;
  private int fileNumber = 0;

  public Receiver(string theSharedDirectory)
  {
    sharedDirectory = theSharedDirectory;
  }

  public void Run()
  {
    while (!terminationRequested)
      WaitForNotifications();
  }

  void WaitForNotifications()
  {
    WaitForFile();
    System.Threading.Thread.Sleep(10);
  }

  void WaitForFile()
  {
    string fileName = string.Format(@"{0}\File{0:000}",
                                sharedDirectory, fileNumber);

    if (!System.IO.Directory.Exists(sharedDirectory)  ) return;
    if (!System.IO.File.Exists(fileName)  ) return;

    // read shared file
    System.IO.StreamReader reader = new System.IO.StreamReader(fileName);
    string payload = reader.ReadLine();
    reader.Close();

    // delete the file
    System.IO.File.Delete(fileName);
```

```csharp
    // update file number
    fileNumber++;
    if (fileNumber > 999)
      fileNumber = 0;

    FireNotificationReceived(payload);
  }

  public delegate void NoticationReceivedHandler(string thePayload);
  public event NoticationReceivedHandler OnNotificationReceived;
  void FireNotificationReceived(string thePayload)
  {
    if (OnNotificationReceived != null)
      OnNotificationReceived(thePayload);
  }
}

public class SharedFileSystem
{
    System.Threading.Thread receiverThread;

    string sharedDirectory = @"c:\MyDirectory";

    Sender sender;
    Receiver receiver;

    public SharedFileSystem()
    {
      sender = new Sender(sharedDirectory);
      receiver = new Receiver(sharedDirectory);

      receiverThread = new System.Threading.Thread(
              new System.Threading.ThreadStart(receiver.Run) );
      receiverThread.Start();
    }

    public void Stop()
    {
      // stop the subscriber thread
      receiver.terminationRequested = true;
    }

    public void FireEvent()
    {
      // send a notification from Sender to Receiver
      sender.FireEvent(DateTime.Now.ToString() );
    }
}
```

Listing 8-17. *Using Numbered Files to Fire Events in VB .NET*

```vbnet
Public Class Sender
  Private sharedDirectory As String
  Private fileNumber As Integer = 0

  Public Sub New(ByVal theSharedDirectory As String)
    sharedDirectory = theSharedDirectory
    If Not System.IO.Directory.Exists(theSharedDirectory) Then
      System.IO.Directory.CreateDirectory(theSharedDirectory)
    End If
  End Sub

  Public Sub FireEvent(ByVal thePayload As String)
    Dim tempFileName As String = sharedDirectory + "\temp"

    ' create the temp file
    Dim writer As New System.IO.StreamWriter(tempFileName)
    writer.WriteLine(thePayload)
    writer.Close()

    Dim fileName As String = String.Format("{0}\File{1:000}", _
                                      sharedDirectory, fileNumber)

    ' rename the file
    System.IO.File.Move(tempFileName, fileName)

    fileNumber += 1
    If fileNumber > 999 Then
      fileNumber = 0
    End If
  End Sub
End Class

Public Class Receiver
  Public terminationRequested As Boolean
  Private sharedDirectory As String
  Private fileNumber As Integer = 0

  Public Sub New(ByVal theSharedDirectory As String)
    sharedDirectory = theSharedDirectory
  End Sub

  Public Sub Run()
    While Not terminationRequested
      WaitForNotifications()
    End While
  End Sub

  Public Sub WaitForNotifications()
    WaitForFile()
    System.Threading.Thread.Sleep(10)
  End Sub
```

```vb
  Sub WaitForFile()
    Dim fileName As String = String.Format("{0}\File{1:000}", _
                                    sharedDirectory, fileNumber)

    If Not System.IO.Directory.Exists(sharedDirectory) Then Return
    If Not System.IO.File.Exists(fileName) Then Return

    ' read shared file
    Dim reader As New System.IO.StreamReader(fileName)
    Dim payload As String = reader.ReadLine()
    reader.Close()

    ' delete the file
    System.IO.File.Delete(fileName)

    ' update file number
    fileNumber += 1
    If (fileNumber > 999) Then
      fileNumber = 0
    End If

    FireNotificationReceived(payload)
  End Sub

  Public Event OnNotificationReceived(ByVal thePayload As String)
  Sub FireNotificationReceived(ByVal thePayload As String)
    RaiseEvent OnNotificationReceived(thePayload)
  End Sub
End Class

Public Class SharedFileSystem
  Dim receiverThread As System.Threading.Thread
  Dim sharedDirectory As String = "c:\MyDirectory"

  Dim sender As Sender
  Dim receiver As Receiver

  Public Sub New()
    sender = New sender(sharedDirectory)
    receiver = New receiver(sharedDirectory)

    Dim entryPoint As New System.Threading.ThreadStart(AddressOf receiver.Run)
    receiverThread = New System.Threading.Thread(entryPoint)
    receiverThread.Start()
  End Sub

  Public Sub [Stop]()
    ' stop the subscriber thread
    receiver.terminationRequested = True
  End Sub
```

```
Public Sub FireEvent()
  ' send a notification from Sender to Receiver
  sender.FireEvent(DateTime.Now.ToString())
End Sub
End Class
```

The `Receiver` class fires a `NotificationReceived` event when a new file is found. A problem with the numbered-file approach is that it requires the sender and receiver to remain in sync regarding the next file number to use. If the sender or receiver crashes and restarts, the file numbers will get out of sync. The sender could resynchronize by scanning the shared directory and getting the number of the most recent file it finds. If no files were present, it would mean that there were no pending notifications, so the sender could start the number sequence from the beginning, saving the next file with the name SharedFile000. The receiver would also have to be modified: If it doesn't find the file using the expected number, it would have to check for a restarted file number (i.e., SharedFile000).

Using the single shared file approach, the sender would need to acquire a lock on the file, append the notification payload to it, and then close the file. The receiver might detect new notifications by monitoring the size of the file. When the file size changed, the reader would acquire a lock on the file, remove notifications from it, and then close the file. The receiver could read any number of notifications at once, including all of those found.

If there are no receivers, files will continue to accumulate indefinitely in the notification directory, so there must be a mechanism for deleting files at an opportune time. Also, the shared-files approach described works only in a one-to-one relationship between sender and receiver. If there are multiple receivers, you must also devise a mechanism to prevent subscribers from interfering with one another, since they all have to share the same files.

Pipes

Pipes are another type of shared resource that you can use to send notifications across thread and process boundaries. A pipe essentially acts as a conduit for a byte stream that is written at one end and read at the other. Pipes are communication channels, much like network connections. Pipes are synchronized internally and support concurrent reading and writing. The sender formats data in a pre-agreed fashion and writes it to the pipe. The reader can check the pipe on the other end to see if there is any data in it. If so, it can read the data, which will emerge as a sequence of bytes ordered the way they were written. Figure 8-17 shows a pipe used to exchange information between two processes.

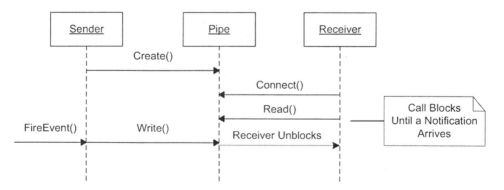

Figure 8-17. *Using pipes to send data between processes*

The diagram shows the receiver blocking on the pipe read. Pipes also support a nonblocking *peek* method, so readers can check for incoming data periodically. Most pipe implementations support bidirectional traffic, so a receiver can send information back to the sender over the same pipe it reads from.

Listing 8-18 shows an Object Pascal implementation of the sender. Object Pascal makes direct Win32 calls to create and manipulate pipes. A C++ program would make exactly the same calls. I didn't use C# for this example, because the .NET Framework doesn't support traditional pipes. In their place, there is an entire infrastructure called the *Remoting Framework* that provides much more functionality, and in an object-oriented way.

Listing 8-18. *Using Object Pascal to Fire Events Using a Pipe*

```
type
  TSender = class
  private
    NotificationPipe: THandle;
  public
    constructor Create;
    destructor Destroy; override;
    procedure FireEvent;
  end;

implementation

constructor TSender.Create;
const
  PipeName = '\\.\pipe\mynamedpipe';
  AccessMode = PIPE_TYPE_MESSAGE or PIPE_READMODE_MESSAGE or PIPE_WAIT;
  MaxPipeInstances = 2;
  InBufferSize = 4096;
  OutBufferSize = 0;
  ClientTimeout = NMPWAIT_USE_DEFAULT_WAIT;
  NoSecurityAttributes = nil;
begin
  NotificationPipe := CreateNamedPipe(PipeName, PIPE_ACCESS_OUTBOUND,
                                      AccessMode, MaxPipeInstances,
                                      OutBufferSize, InBufferSize,
                                      ClientTimeout, NoSecurityAttributes);
end;

destructor TSender.Destroy;
begin
  CloseHandle(NotificationPipe);
end;

procedure TSender.FireEvent;
var
  BytesWritten: Cardinal;
  Payload, ErrorMessage: String;
  Success: Boolean;
begin
  if NotificationPipe = INVALID_HANDLE_VALUE then
    Exit;
```

```
    Payload := 'Notification Payload';
    Success := WriteFile(NotificationPipe, PChar(Payload)^,
                         Length(Payload), BytesWritten, nil);
    if not Success then
      ErrorMessage := SysErrorMessage(GetLastError);
  end;
end.
```

The sender opens a write-only pipe using the Windows API method CreateNamedPipe. To fire an event, the sender writes to the pipe as if it were a file, using the Windows API method WriteFile. The Object Pascal receiver implementation is shown in Listing 8-19.

Listing 8-19. *Using Object Pascal to Receive Notifications over a Pipe*

```
type
  TReceiver = class
  private
   NotificationPipe: THandle;
  public
    constructor Create;
    destructor Destroy; override;
    procedure Run;
    procedure DoRun;
    function WaitForNotifications: String;
    procedure HandleEvent(ThePayload: String);
  end;

implementation

constructor TReceiver.Create;
const
  PipeName = '\\.\pipe\mynamedpipe';
  PipeAccess = GENERIC_READ;
  NoPipeSharing = 0;
  NoSecurityAttributes = nil;
  DefaultPipeAttributes = 0;
  NoTemplateFile = 0;
begin
  NotificationPipe := CreateFile(PipeName, PipeAccess, NoPipeSharing,
                                 NoSecurityAttributes, OPEN_EXISTING,
                                 DefaultPipeAttributes, NoTemplateFile);
end;

destructor TReceiver.Destroy;
begin
  CloseHandle(NotificationPipe);
end;

procedure TReceiver.Run;
begin
  while NotificationPipe <> INVALID_HANDLE_VALUE do
    DoRun;
end;
```

```
procedure TReceiver.DoRun;
var
  Payload: String;
begin
  Payload := WaitForNotifications;
  if (Payload <> '') then
    HandleEvent(Payload);
  Sleep(10);
end;

function TReceiver.WaitForNotifications : String;
var
  Buffer: Pointer;
  BufferSize, BytesRead: Cardinal;
begin
  Result := '';

  if not PeekNamedPipe(NotificationPipe, nil, 0, nil, @BufferSize, nil) then
    Exit;

  if (BufferSize = 0) then
    Exit;

  GetMem(Buffer, BufferSize);
  ReadFile(NotificationPipe, Buffer^, BufferSize, BytesRead, nil);
  Result := String(Buffer);
  FreeMem(Buffer, BufferSize);

end;

procedure TReceiver.HandleEvent(ThePayload: String);
begin
  // process the notification
end;
end.
```

The receiver connects to an existing pipe using the Windows API method CreateFile. The Windows API method PeekNamedPipe is a nonblocking method to check the pipe for data. The method ReadFile reads data from the pipe as if it were a file. You can configure the pipe to cause read operations to block if no data is available.

If multiple subscribers are present, the simple design described previously won't work. One solution is to use a separate pipe for each subscriber. The details of such an implementation are beyond the scope of this book.

Semaphores

You can use semaphores to send notifications between processes or threads running on the same machine. Semaphores are operating system kernel objects that should be used sparingly to send notifications, and only in the following circumstances:

- When speed is important
- When shared memory is not an option
- When pipes are not an option

- When the number of notification types is small
- When the number of senders and receivers is small
- When notifications carry no payload

You can combine semaphores with out-of-band data to support notifications carrying a payload.

Note For a discussion of semaphores and out-of-band data, see the "Semaphores" section in Chapter 3.

Each major platform has its own flavor of semaphore implementations. For example, the .NET Framework has a binary semaphore class named AutoResetEvent. The class exposes the two methods Set and WaitOne, to respectively signal and test the semaphore. The diagram in Figure 8-18 shows how you might use an AutoResetEvent semaphore to send notifications with no payload. Listing 8-20 shows a C# implementation.

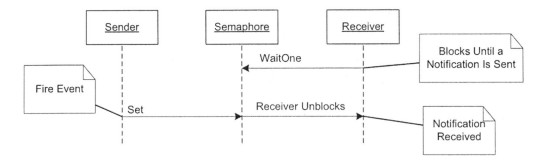

Figure 8-18. *Using a binary semaphore to deliver notifications*

Listing 8-20. *Using C# Binary Semaphores to Fire Events Between Threads*

```
public class Sender
{
  AutoResetEvent semaphore;

  public Sender(AutoResetEvent theSemaphore)
  {
    semaphore = theSemaphore;
  }

  void FireEvent()
  {
    semaphore.Set();
  }
}
```

```
public class Receiver
{
  AutoResetEvent semaphore;

  public Receiver(AutoResetEvent theSemaphore)
  {
    semaphore = theSemaphore;
  }

  public void WaitForEvents()
  {
    while (true)
    {
      semaphore.WaitOne();  // this call blocks until semaphore is signaled

      // notification received...
    }
  }
}
```

The sender and receiver are assumed to run in different threads of the same process. The Sender and Receiver objects are given a reference to the shared semaphore. When Sender wishes to fire an event, it signals the semaphore by calling the Set method. The Receiver object calls the semaphore's WaitOne method to block and wait for incoming notifications.

A problem with the example shown is that AutoResetEvent is a *binary* semaphore, so it only supports two states. If the semaphore is set before sender fires the event, it means there is a pending notification that the receiver hasn't read yet. The sender would need to wait until the receiver cleared the semaphore before firing a new event; otherwise, the receiver would miss the first notification. What you need is a regular semaphore that manages an internal counter that stores the number of pending notifications. The diagram in Figure 8-19 shows how the semaphore would be used.

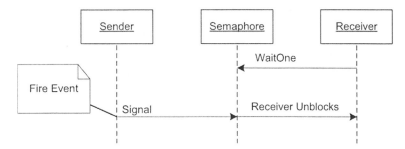

Figure 8-19. *Using a regular semaphore to deliver notifications*

The difference between this diagram and the one using a binary semaphore is the semaphore method called when an event is fired. With a regular semaphore, you call the Signal operation to increment the semaphore's internal counter. Now the sender doesn't have to wait for the receiver to read notifications, and can fire events at will. Listing 8-21 and Listing 8-22 show an Object Pascal implementation.

Listing 8-21. *Using Object Pascal Semaphores to Fire Events*

```pascal
unit Publisher;

interface

uses
  Windows, SysUtils, Classes;

type
  TSender = class
  private
    NotificationSemaphore: THandle;
  public
    constructor Create;
    destructor Destroy;
    procedure FireEvent;
  end;

implementation

constructor TSender.Create;
var
  InitialCount: LongInt;
  MaximumCount: LongInt;
begin
  InitialCount := 0;
  MaximumCount := 1000;
  NotificationSemaphore :=
            CreateSemaphore(nil, InitialCount,
                            MaximumCount,
                            'MyNotificationSemaphore');
end;

destructor TSender.Destroy;
begin
  CloseHandle(NotificationSemaphore);
end;

procedure TSender.FireEvent;
begin
  ReleaseSemaphore(NotificationSemaphore, 1, nil);
end;
end.
```

Listing 8-22. *Using Object Pascal Semaphores to Receive Notifications*

```pascal
unit Subscriber;

interface

uses
  Windows, SysUtils, Classes;
```

```
type
  TReceiver = class
  private
   NotificationSemaphore: THandle;
  public
    constructor Create;
    procedure Run;
    procedure HandleEvent;
  end;

implementation

constructor TReceiver.Create;
var
  InitialCount: LongInt;
  MaximumCount: LongInt;
begin
  InitialCount := 0;
  MaximumCount := 1000;

  NotificationSemaphore := CreateSemaphore(nil, InitialCount,
                                           MaximumCount,
                                           'MyNotificationSemaphore');
end;

procedure TReceiver.Run;
begin
  while True
  do begin
    WaitForSingleObject(NotificationSemaphore, INFINITE);  // wait forever
    HandleEvent;
  end;
end;

procedure TReceiver.HandleEvent;
begin
  // process the notification
end;
end.
```

The sender calls the Windows API method ReleaseSemaphore to signal the semaphore. The method name is rather unfortunate, as it seems to imply that it releases the resources used by a semaphore. On the contrary, it increments the internal counter associated with the given semaphore, releasing the next waiting thread waiting on the semaphore. Threads wait for a semaphore to become signaled by calling the Windows API method WaitForSingleObject. The call tests the semaphore and blocks if no notifications are pending.

Reaching All Subscribers

The relationship between event sources and event handlers may be one-to-one, one-to-many, many-to-one, or many-to-many. In all cases, it is important that event notifications reach the intended subscribers. The one-to-one relationship is the simplest arrangement, so I'll start my discussion with that one.

Unicast Notifications

The notifications sent in a one-to-one relationship are called *unicast* notifications. The signal diagram in Figure 8-20 shows a unicast notification wired from A to B.

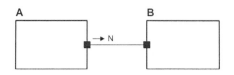

Figure 8-20. *A unicast notification*

When firing a synchronous unicast event using procedure calls, the event handler in B is run on A's calling thread. If the handler throws an exception, A may be adversely affected. If A is expected to fire events to other event targets, those targets may not get notified, causing the system to behave incorrectly. The obvious solution is for event sources to be prepared to catch exceptions thrown by event handlers.

Multicast Notifications

The diagram in Figure 8-21 shows a simple multicast notification.

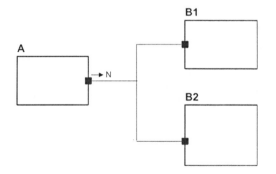

Figure 8-21. *A multicast notification*

Any number of subscribers may be present. When using procedure calls to deliver notifications, the sender maintains a list of subscribers and calls them in some order. In peer-to-peer (P2P) systems, one peer can subscribe to the events of another peer. An event fired by one peer may be multicast to others recursively, resulting in a cascaded multicast, as shown in Figure 8-22.

In P2P systems, events are typically fired asynchronously using messages, so P1 would not block while the notification rippled through the rest of the system. When sending notifications as messages, multicasting can also be handled independently at the communication substrate level, again saving the event source from having to block while subscribers are notified. Multicasts are handled this way in an IP network, where IP routers assume the task of multicasting. The original sender in this case is oblivious to the fact that multiple subscribers are receiving its notifications.

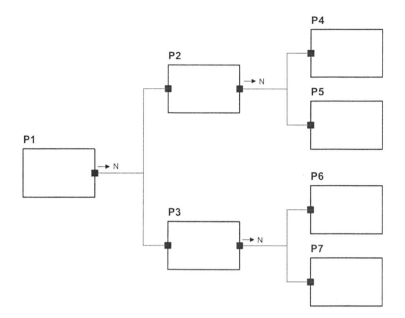

Figure 8-22. *A cascaded multicast notification in a peer-to-peer system*

Delivery Order

If an event has multiple subscribers, what order should be used to notify subscribers? One approach is to allow subscribers to provide a notification priority when they subscribe. Subscribers can then be notified in order of priority. But what happens if two subscribers have the same priority (or no priority)? The most natural order is *first-come, first-serve*. Ensuring this order is not as easy as one might think. If you chose to manage the list of subscribers using a collection like a C# ArrayList or a Java Vector, you could use the Add method to add a reference to each new subscriber. Subscribers would then be ordered in the collection according to their subscription order. Say there are three subscribers: S1, S2, and S3. Let's see what would happen if S1 later unsubscribed and a new subscriber S4 showed up. When adding S4 to the collection, the collection's Add method might put S4 in S1's old slot, which is available. If this happened, the subscribers would subsequently be notified in the order S4, S2, S3, which isn't the order you wanted. To prevent this, the collection would have to be *normalized* each time a subscriber is removed. The normalization process would remove all the empty slots—created by Remove operations—from the collection.

Sending Notifications Concurrently

If you use synchronous procedure calls to deliver notifications, the sender delivers the notification in succession to each subscriber, blocking during each delivery. The time it takes to deliver the notification completely to all subscribers is the sum of the processing times of all subscribers. Figure 8-23 shows the notification delivery sequence of A sending notifications to B and then to C.

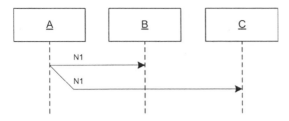

Figure 8-23. *Delivering notifications synchronously*

It may be inefficient for the sender to wait all this time. To reduce the processing time, the sender could notify all the subscribers concurrently, using separate threads. While the immediate effect of concurrent delivery is a reduced delivery time, a side effect is the loss of predictability in the delivery order. If B and C send notifications to a subscriber D, the notifications may arrive at D in a different order with respect to the nonconcurrent delivery case, as shown in Figure 8-24.

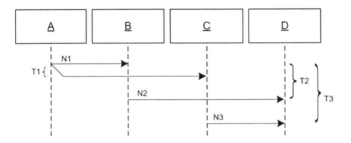

Figure 8-24. *Concurrent delivery may affect the notification delivery order.*

The time T1 is the difference in time between the two firings of N1. T2 measures the time from the arrival of N1 at B to the arrival of N2 at D. T3 measures the time from the arrival of N1 at B to the arrival of N3 at D.

The timing corresponds essentially to what you already saw in the discussion of breadth-first delivery order, back in Chapter 3. Note that T2 is independent of T1. Normally, T1 is much smaller than T2, guaranteeing that N1 is sent to C before N2 is sent to D. But T2 depends on how long it takes B to process N1. If there is a trivial amount of processing involved, it's possible for T2 to be smaller than T1, making it possible for N3 to be sent before N2. The bottom line is that while nonconcurrent delivery is slower, it yields a predictable delivery order. Concurrent delivery provides no such guarantees.

Dealing with Errors

Errors can occur in a system at any time, including while an event is being fired. What should the event source do if one of the subscribers throws an exception while processing a notification, or if the firing process itself causes an exception? To avoid erratic system behavior, the event source should catch the exception and have a strategy for determining what to do next. In general, two courses of action are possible: The sender can either continue firing the event to the remaining subscribers or stop firing the event.

The errors that can occur while firing events are obviously application-dependent, but most systems should be prepared to deal with the following special conditions:

• An event target is unreachable.

• An event target throws an exception.

- An event target returns an unexpected response.
- A timeout occurs while waiting for target to process a notification.

Once an error occurs, the event source may need to log the error. Alternatively, the event source may collect all the errors that occur in a multicast and then log them together.

Dealing with Returned Values

Some notifications are designed to retrieve values from subscribers. Such notifications must necessarily be delivered using procedure calls, because shared resource delivery supports a strictly one-way data flow. With multicast events, you can't use methods that simply return a value, because the method is called on multiple subscribers. You need to reconcile all the return values from each subscriber into a single master return value presented back to the event source.

A simple technique to retrieve return values from multicast notifications is to use *envelopes*, described at the end of Chapter 4. An envelope is just an object that can hold other objects. If the envelope contains a collection, subscribers could return a value by adding it to the envelope's collection with an ad hoc AddValue method. When useful, the envelope could hide its contents from subscribers, allowing subscribers only to add (and not remove or browse) its contents. Upon return, the event sender would check the contents of the envelope, reconciling the returned values found.

The Fire Method

The process of firing an event requires a number of recurring steps to check for the presence of subscribers, to ensure that notifications are sent to all intended subscribers, and to handle other issues. To avoid duplicating this code each time an event needs to be fired, you should designate a method to handle the firing. I'll call this method the Fire method. There are two strategies for creating Fire methods:

- Creating one method to handle each type of event that can be fired
- Creating a single method to handle all the types of events that can be fired

When events are fired, they typically carry a payload. Using a separate Fire method for each event type avoids complexity, because the method only deals with a specific type of payload. Using a common Fire method for all events, on the other hand, yields a more complex Fire method. A common method might make sense if you need to have a simple way to monitor all the events fired by an event source. The method would be a convenient place to put breakpoints or event logging code.

Using Fire methods to handle notification dispatching is important, because these methods insulate the rest of the code in the event source from the details of how notifications are sent. Only the Fire method needs to know how to use the event subscription data structures to fire events, how to handle multiple subscribers, what to do if exceptions occur during event firing, and so on.

Naming Conventions

If you decide to create a Fire method for each type of event, the obvious consequence is that there are going to be a number of Fire methods in the code. To simplify keeping track of which Fire method handles which events, you should use a naming convention, relating Fire methods to events and other data structures.

Let's start with the naming of event properties. These properties are exposed by event sources that support subscriptions by type. Subscribers access these properties to subscribe or unsubscribe to a given event. One convention, first introduced with Visual Basic in the early 1990s, is to prefix event property names with the word "On", to make it easy to distinguish event properties from ordinary properties. Using this convention, events like ButtonClicked and DocumentDownloaded would be exposed through event properties called OnButtonClicked and OnDocumentLoaded. The related Fire methods would be named FireButtonClicked and FireDocumentLoaded, respectively. Once you adopt a naming convention, it allows you to make certain inferences from a wiring diagram. Consider the simple diagram in Figure 8-25.

Figure 8-25. *A wiring diagram with only one signal*

The diagram shows a single notification signal, called DownloadComplete, being sent from A to B. If you implement the system using your naming convention, you could infer that object A would have two things: an event property called OnDownloadComplete and a fire method called FireDownloadComplete. To bind a handler to the event, subscribers would access A's OnDownloadComplete property.

While the "On" naming pattern originated with Visual Basic, it was adopted by other systems, such as Microsoft Foundation Classes (MFC), COM, and Delphi. The use of a naming convention is good, because it simplifies the task of locating artifacts in the source code that aren't documented explicitly.

The JavaBeans world uses a different naming convention that relates events, notification payload types, and listener interfaces. If an object supports an event named Action, then it can fire notifications that carry a payload of type ActionEvent. Listeners must expose an interface named ActionListener. The event source advertises the presence of its Action event by exposing the methods addActionListener and removeActionListener, which subscribers can call to subscribe and unsubscribe. As an example, consider the wiring diagram for a Java system, shown in Figure 8-26.

Figure 8-26. *Signals based on the JavaBeans naming pattern*

A and B exchange only one signal, called actionPerformed. Since the notification is delivered by a call through the ActionListener interface, you can infer that the signal is related to the Action event, and that a payload object of type ActionEvent is passed in the notification to B. In the source code for A, the actionPerformed notification might be sent by a Fire method named FireAction.

The problem with the JavaBeans event naming convention is that it ties event names to internal plumbing details, such as interface and method names. When used on a wiring diagram, these names often don't provide enough information about what event was detected and what the event notification is telling the subscriber. In the previous diagram, you could use an Action event to notify object B of almost anything. The diagram provides no clues that might help you understand why the connection is made between A and B, and what the signal does. The situation is akin to an electrical diagram labeling a wire only by its color or its gauge, neither of which help understand what the wire is for.

Using Procedure Calls

Events fired using procedure calls use a reference to the subscriber. Before firing a PC event, the sender must always check to see if the subscriber reference points to something; otherwise, a run-time error will occur. Since PC events are fired as indirect procedure calls, the subscriber reference will contain a reference either to a typed object or to a method. In both cases, the reference is usually initialized to zero or null, indicating no subscribers. When an object subscribes, a reference to it is saved in the event source. Firing events using procedure calls is conceptually similar across most languages, but each language imposes its own details at the implementation level.

C#

In C#, the preferred model for event firing is based on untyped-object calls. Special constructs were added to the language to make the process simple. The *delegate* keyword supports the definition of a reference-to-method type. For example, to declare a reference to a universal method (which takes no parameters and returns no values), you would declare a delegate like this:

```
delegate void UniversalMethod();
```

The word `UniversalMethod` is an arbitrarily chosen name for the new reference-to-universal-method type. The simplest `Fire` method for an untyped method call for an event named X would look something like the one shown in Listing 8-23.

Listing 8-23. *The C# Fire Method for Event X, Using Delegates*

```
public delegate void UniversalMethod();
public UniversalMethod OnX;

void FireX()
{
  if (OnX != null)
    OnX();
}
```

The example uses a delegate variable called `OnX` to store a list of subscribers and invoke them. Assume the variable `OnX` is part of an object named `myObject`, of type `MyClass`. A subscriber containing a universal method called `DoSomething` might be subscribed to `myObject` using this notation:

```
myObject.OnX = new MyClass.UniversalMethod(DoSomething);
```

The code instantiates a new `UniversalMethod` variable, pointing at the subscriber's `DoSomething` method. The variable is then assigned to `myObject.OnX`, using a plain assignment operator. While the assignment operator can be used to register subscriptions, it is rarely used in the context of events. Why? The reason is simple. C# delegates support multicasting, and the assignment operator does exactly what you would expect: It assigns a value to a delegate variable. In doing so, it wipes out any other references being held by the delegate. To avoid this problem, subscribers must subscribe using the += operator, to add a subscription to those already present. To hide the assignment operator from subscribers, C# allows access to delegate variables to be restricted through the use of special *event properties*, which support only the += and -= operators on the underlying delegate, allowing a subscriber to add or remove itself without disturbing previous subscriptions.

A ménage-a-trois pattern emerges here: For every C# event, there is a `delegate` type, an event property, and a `Fire` method. The `delegate` defines the signature of the method to call. The (Fire, delegate, event) triad for event X is shown in Listing 8-24.

Listing 8-24. *The C# Naming Conventions for a Universal Event X*

```
public delegate void UniversalMethod();
public event UniversalMethod OnX;

void FireX()
{
  if (OnX != null)
    OnX();
}
```

Notice the event keyword in the declaration of property OnX. For method signatures other than the universal one, it is common for the delegate type to include the name of the event it is associated with. The delegate name might include the word Delegate or Handler, e.g., DelegateX or HandlerX. For example, if the delegate specified a method signature accepting an int and string parameter, the delegate-event-Fire triad would be named, as in Listing 8-25.

Listing 8-25. *The C# Fire Method for Event X, Using Delegates and Events*

```
public delegate void XHandler (int theLength, string theName);
public event XHandler OnX;

void FireX(int theLength, string theName)
{
  if (OnX != null)
    OnX(theLength, theName);
}
```

When dealing with events that return values, the Fire method will have a return value. Listing 8-26 shows an event called GetName that fetches a string from a subscriber and returns it.

Listing 8-26. *A C# Fire Method That Returns a Value*

```
public delegate string GetNameHandler();
public event GetNameHandler OnGetName;

string FireGetName()
{
  if (OnGetName!= null)
    return null;
  return OnGetName();
}
```

The Fire method in the example returns a default value (in this case, a null) when no subscribers are available. It is up to the invoker of the Fire method to determine what to do if a default is returned. With multicast notifications, the Fire method will return the value returned by the last subscriber invoked, so you shouldn't use return values with multicast events. When using notifications to fetch values from subscribers, envelopes are a good solution, as described previously in the section "Dealing with Returned Values."

VB .NET

Since VB .NET supports the same types as C#, the naming conventions for Fire methods, delegates, and events are similar, but there are enough differences to justify a separate discussion of VB .NET. When dealing with universal events—in other words, those whose handlers take no arguments and return nothing—VB .NET allows you to declare an Event without having to explicitly declare a corresponding Delegate, as shown in Listing 8-27.

Listing 8-27. *VB .NET Events Declared Without an Explicit Delegate*

```
Public Class EventWithoutExplicitDelegate
  Public Event OnX()

  Sub FireX()
    RaiseEvent OnX()
  End Sub
End Class
```

Declaring an event directly, using syntax like Public Event OnX(), VB .NET automatically creates an internal Delegate and associates it with the Event. You can also declare the Delegate explicitly, as shown in Listing 8-28.

Listing 8-28. *VB .NET Events Declared with a Delegate*

```
Public Class EventWithDelegate
  Public Delegate Sub UniversalMethod()
  Public Event OnX As UniversalMethod

  Sub FireX()
    RaiseEvent OnX()
  End Sub
End Class
```

VB .NET doesn't allow you to declare an Event that returns a value. For example, the following code will produce a compiler error:

```
'you can't do this in VB .NET
Public Delegate Function MyHandler() As Integer
Public Event OnX As MyHandler
```

To declare an event that returns a value, you have to work with Delegates. Listing 8-29 shows how to declare an event and related Fire method to return a value.

Listing 8-29. *VB .NET Events Declared with a Delegate*

```
Public Class EventWithReturnValue
  Public Delegate Function MyHandler() As Integer
  Public OnX As MyHandler

  Function FireX() As Integer
    If Not OnX Is Nothing Then
      Return OnX()
    Else
      Throw New Exception("No subscribers.")
    End If
  End Function
End Class
```

Since the Fire method is declared to return a value, you must define a strategy to deal with situations where there is no subscriber. You might returned a reserved or default value. In the example, the Fire method throws an exception.

Object Pascal

Delphi Object Pascal supports the declaration of pointer-to-method types, which are conceptually similar to C# delegates. Pointer-to-method variables in Object Pascal don't support multicasting, because they are simple pointers and can only hold one reference at a time. Subscriptions are made by assigning the address of a method to a pointer-to-method variable exposed by an event source. Listing 8-30 shows a simple Object Pascal class that declares a single event called Event1.

Listing 8-30. *A Simple Object Pascal Event Source Class*

```
type
  TEvent1 = procedure() of object;

  TMyEventSource = class
    public
      OnEvent1: TEvent1;
      procedure FireEvent1;
  end;

implementation

procedure TMyEventSource.FireEvent1;
begin
  if Assigned(OnEvent1) then
    OnEvent1();
end;
```

The OnEvent1 event property is of type TEvent1, which is declared as a pointer to a method of a class. In this example, the method referenced has a universal signature: no parameters and no return values, but Object Pascal places no restrictions of the signature of the method pointed at. Event1's Fire method is called FireEvent1. The method tests to see if the OnEvent1 pointer was initialized. If so, the function pointed at is called. The built-in Object Pascal function Assigned returns true if a pointer contains a non-null value.

Subscribers only need to expose a method whose signature matches the one used by the event source. Listing 8-31 shows a simple class exposing a method compatible with the signature used by TEvent1.

Listing 8-31. *An Object Pascal Class Exposing a Method That Can Handle TEvent1 Events*

```
type

  TMyEventTarget = class
    public
      procedure Method1;
  end;

implementation

procedure TMyEventTarget.Method1;
begin
  // ...
end;
```

If a system has instances of the source and target—named MySource and MyTarget, respectively—you could use the following notation to register MyTarget as a subscriber to MySource:

```
MySource.OnEvent1 := MyTarget.Method;
```

Java

Java defines no special constructs or types at the language level to deal with events. To expose an event, a JavaBean must expose two methods to add and remove subscribers of that event. For an event named Timeout, you must name the methods addTimeoutListener and removeTimeoutListener. You might use a Fire method called FireTimeout to handle the details of firing Timeout events. Following the Java event-naming conventions, a Timeout event notification will carry a payload object of type TimeoutEvent. The class must be derived from the built-in EventObject class, and Listing 8-32 shows how it might look.

Listing 8-32. *A JavaBean Event Notification Payload*

```
public class TimeoutEvent extends EventObject {

  public TimeoutEvent(Object source) {
    super(source);
  }
}
```

Subscribers of Timeout events will need to implement the interface TimeoutListener. This interface can have an arbitrary number of methods. Listing 8-33 shows an example.

Listing 8-33. *A Simple JavaBean Interface for Timeout Event Subscribers*

```
public interface TimeoutListener extends EventListener {
  void timeoutOccurred(TimeoutEvent e);
}
```

You might implement a subscriber as shown in Listing 8-34.

Listing 8-34. *A Simple JavaBean Subscriber to Timeout Events*

```
public class TimeoutSubscriber implements TimeoutListener {
  public TimeoutSubscriber() { … }
  public void timeoutOccurred(TimeoutEvent e) {  … }
}
```

The event source class can store subscribers in two ways: with a simple reference-to-TimeoutListener variable, or with a collection. The latter case allows you to handle multiple listeners, and is shown in Listing 8-35.

Listing 8-35. *A Java Event Source Supporting Multicast Timeout Events*

```
public class TimeoutSource{
  public TimeoutSource() {
  }

  private Vector timeoutListeners = new Vector();
```

```java
public synchronized void removeMyCustomListener(TimeoutListener l) {
  if (timeoutListeners.contains(l))
    timeoutListeners.removeElement(l);
}

public synchronized void addMyCustomListener(TimeoutListener l) {
  if (!timeoutListeners.contains(l))
    timeoutListeners.addElement(l);
}

protected void fireMethod1(TimeoutEvent e) {
  int count = timeoutListeners.size();
  for (int i = 0; i < count; i++) {
    TimeoutListener l = (TimeoutListener) timeoutListeners.elementAt(i);
    l.timeoutOccurred(e);
  }
}
}
```

The class uses a collection of type Vector to store subscribers. The Fire method iterates over the items in the Vector, calling the timeoutOccurred method of each subscriber found. The Fire method should use a clone of the original Vector while firing events, to avoid race conditions or errors in case a subscriber adds or removes subscriptions while processing a notification.

Using Messages

While Fire methods can be used to send notifications using procedure calls, they can also be used to send notifications using messages. Any type of shared resource can be used to send the messages, but the most common one is a network connection. No special language constructs or types are required, so messages are easy to send. The sender usually makes calls into a communication system, which then takes responsibility for delivering the messages.

Asynchronous Firing

When using PCs to deliver notifications, the most natural type of call is the synchronous one, but using synchronous calls to deliver notifications forces the event source to depend on the timing of the event subscriber. When the subscriber is expected to take a long time, or when the subscriber's processing time is completely unpredictable, asynchronous calls are sometimes indicated. With asynchronous calls, the subscriber executes the event handler method on a separate thread from the event source. Who spawns this separate thread? In theory, either the event source or the event target could handle the task. If you have access to the source code of both objects, the most common scenario is to have the event source create the thread to run the event handler method on, as shown in Figure 8-27.

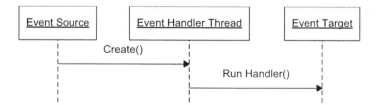

Figure 8-27. *Invoking the event handler method on a thread created by the event source*

Figure 8-28 shows a case in which the event target creates a separate event handler thread.

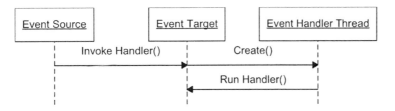

Figure 8-28. *Creating an event handler thread on the event target side*

Although both techniques achieve the same goal, it sometimes makes more sense to use the first technique. Why? Because other objects might call the target event handler method, and those objects may not require an asynchronous behavior. By putting the threading burden on the event source, the event target doesn't have to undergo modifications just because you happen to be using it with an event source desiring asynchronous execution. If the target were already designed to use background threads, then obviously you would want to leverage that fact and avoid adding additional threading logic to the event source.

If you don't have access to the event source's source code, but you don't want to have the event target manage the threading logic, you can use an adapter between the event source and the target, as shown in Figure 8-29.

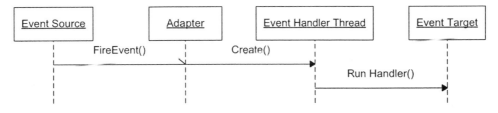

Figure 8-29. *Using an adapter to fire an event asynchronously*

With the adapter, both the event source and target remain unchanged. Note the asynchronous call between the event source and the adapter. The event source immediately gets control back from the adapter after firing an event. The adapter internally spawns a secondary thread and runs the event target call on it with a synchronous call. If the event target makes calls back to the event source, either directly or indirectly, there may be problems if the event source isn't prepared to handle reentrant calls. While adapters make it possible to fire events without blocking the event source, they can potentially introduce problems related to reentrancy or concurrency, which aren't always easy to troubleshoot.

Optimization

When using notifications to make calls between objects, there is a certain penalty incurred due to the indirect nature of the interactions. The overhead of making a single indirect call is generally minimal in a system, often accounting for a very small fraction of the system load. But the overhead may need to include other activities that add up quickly to big numbers.

As stated earlier, there are two main categories of `Fire` methods: those dedicated to a single event type and those that handle arbitrary event types. The latter case has the potential to perform poorly, because the Fire method must parse a parameter list or use other means to create the notification payload for an event whose type is determined on the fly at run time. Some studies have shown that in extreme cases, this overhead can represent a significant fraction of a system's activity.[3] In such cases, optimizations might become necessary.

While optimization of event-based systems is currently at the experimental level, a number of techniques have been studied and shown to be useful. In traditional systems, static analysis of call graphs can identify heavily used sections of code, providing a way to determine which methods should be optimized to give the greatest benefit. In an event-based system, a large number of bindings between objects is established at run time, so static tools are of little help. Optimization techniques with event-based systems must necessarily be dynamic and be based on the observation of the system while it is running.

There is an irony in the performance analysis of component-based systems: The analysis may pinpoint problems that you can do little to correct, because the majority of optimizations often require modification of source code. When using third-party components, you often don't have access to the source code.

Before any optimizations are done, you need to know what the *event profile* of the system is. An event profiler is a tool that essentially single-steps a system, much like a traditional debugger. Each time an event is fired, an entry is made in a profile log. The system is then run for a long enough time to build a statistically significant profile log. The log will then show the firing order of events in the system. You can then use tools to organize and visualize the event firing statistics, creating a top-level profile of the system and identifying which events are most often fired, which event handlers are called, and other details. Profiling may identify not only high-frequency events, but also common event sequences that you might need to coalesce into shorter sequences. You may need to build different profiles if a system has different modes of operation.

Once the profile of the system is known, you can apply static optimization techniques. Handlers called with the highest frequency can be recoded carefully to improve their speed. You can also apply compiler optimizations to inline code or store variables in CPU registers.

Using a more dynamic technique, you can instrument the system with code that monitors the event firing patterns. When high-frequency events are detected, the associated code can be optimized on the fly through event-coalescing and other source code changes. The changes can then be compiled just-in-time and subsequently used.[4] A number of experimental dynamic optimization systems have been proposed, including Tempo,[5] Dynamo,[6] and DynamoRIO.[7]

---

3. Mohan Rajagopalan, Saumya K. Debray, Matti A. Hiltunen, and Richard D. Schlichting, "Profile-Directed Optimization of Event-Based Programs" (proceedings of the ACM Special Interest Group on Programming Languages [SIGPLAN], Berlin, Germany, June 2002).

4. Andreas Krall, "Efficient JavaVM Just-in-Time Compilation" (proceedings of the International Conference on Parallel Architectures and Compilation Techniques, Paris, France, October 1998).
Matthew Arnold, Michael Hind, and Barbara Ryder, "An Empirical Study of Adaptive Optimization" (proceedings of the 13th International Workshop on Languages and Compilers for Parallel Computing, Yorktown Heights, New York, August 2000).

5. Charles Consel, Luke Hornof, Julia L. Lawall, Renaud Marlet, Gilles Muller, Jacques Noye, Scott Thibault, and Eugen-Nicolae Volanschi, "Tempo: Specializing Systems Applications and Beyond," *ACM Computing Surveys, Symposium on Partial Evaluation*, September 1998.

6. Vasanth Bala, Evelyn Duesterwald, and Sanjeev Banerjia, "Dynamo: A Transparent Dynamic Optimization System" (proceedings of the SIGPLAN 2000 Conference on Programming Language Design and Implementation, Vancouver, British Columbia, Canada, June 2000).

7. Derek Bruening, Timothy Garnett, and Saman Amarasinghe, "An Infrastructure for Adaptive Dynamic Optimization" (proceedings of the 1st International Symposium on Code Generation and Optimization, San Francisco, CA, March 2003).

Summary

The simplest way to fire an event is with a procedure call. All OO programming languages have built-in support for firing events this way, but languages vary in the details. All languages support typed object calls, using interfaces, but not all support untyped object calls. Typed object calls are the traditional technique used by people with an object-oriented programming background. People with component-based development and event-based programming experience often favor untyped object calls, to minimize coupling between the event source and event handler.

CHAPTER 9

■ ■ ■

Event-Based Interaction Patterns

In an EBS, notifications represent the bulk of intercomponent and interobject communication traffic. As you've seen, you can deliver notifications using any number of delivery models, such as messages or procedure calls, but the delivery model is really only a low-level detail. Looking at a system from a higher level, you can abstract away the details of how communication occurs and focus on what an interaction is trying to accomplish and how. Software systems can be considered societies of communicating and cooperating processes. Process interactions are similar to conversations between people. The expression *interaction dynamics* is used to describe the ways software processes interact with each other over time, with particular interest in the following areas:

- *Roles*: Which process is giving information to the other? The word *information* is used here to denote both commands and data. One process might assume the role of caller or data provider with respect to the other.

- *Control*: Which process is in charge of the interaction? Which one is responsible for initiating it? Can the interaction be aborted? If so, by which process? Is one of the processes responsible for monitoring the progress of the interaction? Which process decides when the interaction terminates?

- *Timing*: When sending messages, can the sender wait forever for a response? Can the sender continue with other work while waiting for a response? Does the sender require a response within a certain time frame? Can the receiver accept other messages while processing a prior one?

- *Flow*: Is information sent in a single exchange, or it is broken down into an iteration of smaller ones? If an iterative flow is used, how is the end of the iteration signaled?

Looking at different kinds of software systems, it becomes apparent that there are recurring ways that processes interact in terms of communication mechanics, assumptions made by the communicating parties, goals of the sender, overall timing, and so on. I'll call these recurrences *interaction patterns*, and I'll show that they describe situations that are extremely common, not just in software systems but in everyday life.

The patterns presented in this chapter are based on a paper I presented at a patterns workshop in the summer of 1998.[1] I've renamed some patterns to give them a broader characterization. In keeping with the conventions adopted by popular patterns handbooks, I'll begin each pattern with a synopsis box, describing the context in which the pattern applies. A list of forces follows, describing the system constraints that the pattern must deal with. Each pattern has at least two examples, depicting an occurrence in everyday life and in a software system.

---

1. Ted Faison, "Interaction Patterns for Communicating Processes" (proceedings of PLoP98, Pattern Languages of Programs, Monticello, IL, August 1998, `http://citeseer.ist.psu.edu/faison98interaction.html`).

A Natural Language Perspective

Much of the work on software patterns centers on the structure, relationship, and organization of objects and classes. The emphasis is on characterizing what objects do and what structure they have, especially in relationship to one another. This inclination toward function and structure is due to the influence of Alexander's work 20 years ago,[2] regarding the patterns adopted in the architecture of buildings and cities.

But software systems are more than collections of objects with a purpose. They are rather like a group of people that accomplish a task by conversing or exchanging messages with one another. Studying the dynamics of conversations can be useful, because it reveals that there are patterns in the way we communicate. Implied assumptions, expectations, understandings, and goals drive entities to communicate. In terms of dynamics, what is important is how the entities carry out a conversation or transaction: who starts it, who ends it, who gives information to the other, whether both parties can talk at the same time, what the goals are, and so on.

When analyzing communication and looking for communication patterns, a good place to look for analogies is natural language: the language we use every day to talk to each other. After all, natural languages have evolved over thousands of years and have developed ways to support every conceivable type of communication situation. There are hundreds of natural languages in use today, and probably even more that have died out. Some, like Latin and Sanskrit, have disappeared from speech but continue to survive in writing.

Linguistics is the field that studies the structure and dynamics of language, so one would expect to learn a great deal about communication patterns from linguistics. When considering linguistics, what is most interesting for the current discussion is sentence morphology. The shortest complete sequence of words that has meaning by itself is a sentence. There are different types of sentences, depending on what needs to be said and how. The three most important types are imperative, declarative, and interrogative. Table 9-1 provides a brief description.

Table 9-1. *Important Sentence Types in Natural Language*

Sentence Type	Purpose	Example
Imperative	To issue orders	Finish your homework!
Declarative	To describe something	The cat is black.
Interrogative	To obtain information	What time is it?

Punctuation symbols are used to emphasize sentence types. Imperative sentences often end with an exclamation mark. Declarative sentences end with a period. Interrogative sentences end with a question mark. The punctuation marks guide readers, indicating how to *inflect* the sentence—in other words, where to put the emphasis and with what tone. How a sentence is inflected contributes to the way a listener interprets it.

There are other sentence types, such as vocative and performative, but the ones that are of interest in a software context are primarily the three listed. When applied to communication between software entities, imperative sentences represent commands, such as method calls that return no data. Declarative sentences represent statements of fact, such as notifications in a publish-subscribe

---

2. Christopher Alexander, Sara Ishikawa, and Murray Silverstein, *A Pattern Language: Towns, Buildings, Construction* (New York: Oxford University Press, 1977); Christopher Alexander, *The Timeless Way of Building* (New York: Oxford University Press, 1979).

system, alerting subscribers of potentially interesting occurrences. An interrogative sentence is a request for information, such as a method that returns data. When applied to software interactions, I'll call sentence types *interaction types*. Table 9-2 shows software examples for each interaction type.

Table 9-2. *Examples of Interaction Types*

Interaction Type	C# Example
Imperative	`a.DoSomething();`
Declarative	`FireDownloadComplete();`
Interrogative	`int i = a.GetValue();`

The imperative example invokes a method to make an object do something. The declarative example fires an event, telling any subscribers that a download operation has completed. The interrogative example calls a method to obtain the value of a variable.

Interactions are often more complex than a single method call, requiring several exchanges between the parties involved. I'll use the word *conversation* to include all the exchanges that are part of a larger interaction. When characterizing conversations, there are other things to consider besides interaction types, such as who starts the conversation, who controls it, who finishes it, what the purpose of it is, what assumptions govern it, and so on. Different interaction patterns emerge, depending on which variables you focus on.

The Push-Pull Model

One of the simplest ways of classifying an interaction is based on which way information flows in relationship to the party starting the interaction. If one party gives information to another party, the information is said to be *pushed*. If one party requests information from another party, the information is said to be *pulled*. In push-pull models, don't worry about lower-level interaction details, such as whether exchanges are synchronous or asynchronous. What matters the most is the overall direction of information flow relative to the party starting the conversation. Let's look at push and pull interactions more in detail.

Push Interactions

■**Context** A process P_1 needs to send commands to P_2. The frequency of commands is unknown or extremely variable. The system is sensitive to the processing load of P_2, and it is crucial for P_2 to never miss a command.

■**Forces** If commands are expected to be infrequent, it is inefficient for P_2 to continually poll P_1 to see if commands are available. Since P_1 *knows* when commands need to be sent, and you want P_2 to get commands as soon as possible, it is more efficient to let P_1 control the interaction.

The purpose of a push interaction is for one party to deliver information and/or execution control to another. I'll use the word *talker* to designate the party starting the interaction, and the word *listener* for the party with whom the talker interacts. In a push interaction, the talker sends a command to the listener, as shown in Figure 9-1.

Figure 9-1. *The push-interaction pattern*

A command can include data. A push interaction is an imperative interaction. Push interactions are effective when the following two things apply:

1. The talker acts as a controller of the listener.

2. The talker decides when to issue commands to the listener.

Push interactions form the basis of event-driven systems. Publishers are talkers, and subscribers are listeners. When something occurs to the publisher, notifications are sent to available subscribers to inform them of the event. Using push interactions to propagate changes through a system is particularly efficient when the talker needs to send the same command to a large number of listeners.

If you have to implement the system without using push interactions, the alternative would require each listener to poll the talker periodically, waiting for changes to occur. A significant amount of processing time would be wasted in polling loops. Using a push interaction pattern frees the listeners from devoting resources to monitor the talker. While the talker has no new data, the listener can use its own resources to do more useful things than sitting in a polling loop. Due to their efficiency, push interactions are a good solution in real-time systems. When changes occur at very high speed, you might use a single notification to describe multiple changes at once.

There are numerous examples of the push pattern in everyday life and in computing.

Example 1 Consider the process of getting up one morning at a given time, using a clock. One option is to stay awake all night, monitor the clock, and get up at the given time. The problem with this polling approach is that it wastes resources when the desired information (the time to get up) isn't available frequently (once every 24 hours). If you want to get up on time by means of a polled interaction with the clock, you would have to stay awake the entire night to watch the time. The polling process itself would impede the implementation of an important goal (getting some sleep). The push interaction centralizes the decision of when to consume processing time to send a notification. If no information is available, no notifications are ever pushed. An alarm clock is just the ticket. You tell it what data you are interested in (the time to go off), and you get your full night's sleep. The alarm clock notifies you when it's time to get up.

Example 2 In a system that must react to the depressing of a button, it isn't efficient for the system to poll the button's status constantly because the button is only used occasionally. Using a push interaction, the button notifies the system when it is depressed.

Example 3 The classic Model View Controller paradigm, or more specifically, the way the model interacts with the viewers, illustrates a push interaction. When the controller makes changes to the model, the latter *pushes* notifications to the viewers. The model acts as an event publisher, the viewers as event subscribers. The model can support any number of viewers. When changes occur in the model, a *change notification* is broadcast to all viewers. In response, the latter usually refresh all or part of a window. Viewers have no knowledge of each other and are controlled by the model's notifications.

Pull Interactions

■**Context** A process P_1 needs to monitor the status of a process P_2. P_1 only needs to know the status of P_2 at specific times, and it gets the status by issuing a request to P_2. P_2 does not provide any information unless requested by P_1.

■**Forces** If P_1 doesn't need status information except at specific times, it is time-consuming and wasteful for P_2 to send notifications every time a status change occurs. P_1 might ignore many of the notifications. If only P_1 knows when status information is necessary or useful, it is natural for P_1 to control when status information is exchanged.

The purpose of a pull interaction is for one party to obtain information from another. I'll use the word *interrogator* to designate the party starting the interaction, and the word *respondent* for the party that answers with the data. In a pull interaction, the interrogator sends a request to the respondent, which replies with a response, as shown in Figure 9-2.

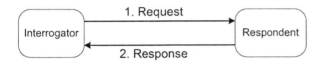

Figure 9-2. *The pull interaction pattern*

Linguistically, a pull interaction is associated with an interrogative sentence type. Pull interactions are effective when the following two things apply:

1. The interrogator needs to control when information is retrieved.

2. The interrogator only needs information at a given time.

The interrogator's request can convey the type of information needed. The respondent's response supplies the information. If the interrogator uses a method call to query for information, the method can define parameters to hold the response information. If the interrogator uses a message for the query, a separate interaction is required for the response. The response is not considered a push interaction, because the interrogator determined its timing.

Pull interactions are particularly effective when the interrogator only needs information at specific and infrequent times. It would be wasteful for the respondent to push the information using change notifications, especially if changes occurred frequently. Pull interactions are very common for two reasons:

1. They are simple to implement, because both the interrogator and the respondent can be synchronous. A simple method call is sufficient.

2. They apply to the common situation in which status changes in the respondent don't require the interrogator to react immediately: The interrogator will discover the change the next time it requests status.

There are numerous examples of the pull pattern in everyday life and in computing.

Example 4 When you want to know the outdoor temperature, you might look out the window at an outdoor thermometer hanging on a wall and see the temperature. You are the interrogator, and the thermometer is the respondent. You control when to read the outdoor temperature. Unless you take the action of requesting the temperature by looking at the thermometer, you'll never know what the thermometer reading is. The thermometer can't, by itself, give you its temperature reading.

Example 5 A software system needs to monitor the state of keys on a keyboard. Consider a simple system in which a keyboard device contains an initially empty FIFO buffer that stores the keys typed by the user. A separate process issues Read commands to the keyboard device to get the keys typed. Each Read command returns one key. The reader process is the interrogator, the keyboard device the respondent. The reader will never receive typed keys unless it asks the keyboard device explicitly.

The Round-Robin Polling Pattern

■**Context** A process P_1 needs to continuously monitor the status of a number of other processes P_i. Status changes can only be handled at a certain rate, decided by P_1. The status requests can be fulfilled by the P_i processes *very quickly*—e.g., by returning the value of an internal state variable or performing a simple computation.

■**Forces** If a single process P_1 is monitoring multiple processes P_i, it is possible for more than one of the *i* processes to have new status information at the same time. Allowing each of the P_i processes to send the information immediately would create the requirement for P_1 to handle multiple status updates simultaneously. This would require P_1 to use multiple threads or other computational resources, which could result in a significant amount of complexity. If P_1 controls the timing of the status exchanges, a specific order can be imposed on status retrieval from each of the P_i processes, using simple synchronous requests.

In general, polling is a pull type of interaction and is especially efficient when new data is frequently available or if changes occur with some predictability. If changes occur rarely, many requests by the interrogator will result in a *no-new-information* response, which usually equates to a wasted or useless interaction.

You can use a pull interaction pattern to poll multiple respondents in sequence. A respondent can be anything from a hardware mechanism to a variable to a remote process. After one respondent is polled, the next one is polled, and so on. After polling the last respondent in the sequence, the entire process repeats. This interaction arrangement is known as *round-robin polling*, and is shown in Figure 9-3.

Round-robin polling applies to situations in which respondents are reliable and respond quickly. In many cases, the interrogator makes a polling pass over all the respondents and then goes on to do other things. The interrogator only polls again when some condition applies, such as the passage of a certain amount of time or the detection of an event. Polling requires a certain amount of faith in the respondents. If a respondent hangs for any reason, by crashing or waiting for results from another process, it might hang the entire polling loop.

In the simplest round-robin polling scheme, the polling sequence is fixed. Consider a scenario in which multiple respondents have new data simultaneously. If one respondent has a greater chance of having new information, or if its information is more important than that of other respondents, the interrogator might need to poll that respondent more frequently than the others or poll the respondents in a certain order. Because the interrogator is in control, it can decide when and how often to check respondents and in what order. A complication may arise if the respondents have dynamically changing priorities or highly variable traffic patterns, in which cases push interactions are often more suitable.

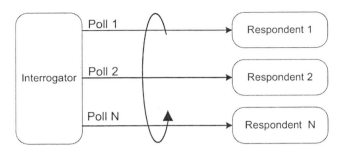

Figure 9-3. *Using pull interactions in round-robin polling*

Example 6 A cook is cooking items in three pots on the stove. To determine which items are done, the cook checks the contents of each pot. The cook is essentially *polling* the three pots to monitor their status. The poll operation is represented by the cook's glance at each pot. The polling result is the image of each pot's contents, indicating whether the contents are ready or not. This polling operation is very quick and doesn't appreciably affect the overall system's performance—in other words, the cooking time.

Example 7 A software system displays weather conditions, showing temperature, humidity, and pressure. The system uses a thermometer, a hygrometer, and a barometer. Once a minute, the system polls the three devices, updating the display. After obtaining the latest values, the system is free to do other things. Polling works well in this situation because the weather variables are needed only occasionally, and the time required to obtain each measurement is very small.

Blind Interactions

▪**Context** A process P_1 wishes to send a message to a process P_2. The message may be a command or a request for information. While the message is being processed, P_1 does not need to obtain progress feedback from P_2.

▪**Forces** When the execution time of a command is expected to be short, there may be little justification for progress feedback. Even if the execution time is long, it may not be feasible for P_2 to report partial completion feedback results, because it might be too complicated to do, unwarranted, impractical, or even impossible.

Blind interactions apply to both push and pull interactions. Let P_1 be the talker or interrogator, and let P_2 be the listener or respondent. An interaction is called *blind* when P_1 can't obtain status updates from P_2 while P_2 is busy processing the command or request. P_1 basically issues a command and waits for P_2 to execute it. While execution is underway, P_1 might go off and do other things. What's important about blind interactions is that P_1 can't ask P_2 how long the command will take to complete or how far along P_2 is in the execution of a command. Both synchronous and asynchronous interactions can be blind.

Synchronous Blind Interactions

■**Context** A process P_1 wishes to send a command to a process P_2, and P_1 must wait until P_2 has finished with the command before proceeding. P_2 is trusted to return control within a timeframe that is acceptable to P_1.

■**Forces** P_1 can't continue until P_2 is finished processing the command. If P_1 knows that P_2 will finish quickly, or if P_1 has a good estimate of how long execution will take, then progress updates may not be required.

Synchronous blind interactions are the simplest interaction to implement and indeed the most common type used in software systems. They are typically accomplished using a simple method call. The caller makes a call to a function contained in the callee, and the caller blocks until the callee finishes. The call executes on the caller's thread and the callee returns control to the caller only when the command has been completely executed. If the command cannot be completed due to errors, the premature completion will still be regarded as a completion. When errors are expected, the interaction should arrange a way for the callee to notify the caller, perhaps by returning an error status code or throwing an exception. Figure 9-4 depicts a blind synchronous interaction.

Figure 9-4. *A synchronous blind interaction*

The notion of trust is important in this type of interaction. If the callee dies while executing the command, control may never return to the caller, and the whole system will appear to have died. A software system built exclusively using synchronous interactions will only be as reliable as the least reliable component. Components calling other components synchronously place a great deal of faith in the callees. For this reason, synchronous blind interactions are used most commonly with simple commands and when the probability of success is extremely high.

Example 8 Two persons, A and B, are talking on the phone. Person A asks, "What time is it?" Person B replies, "2:30 p.m." When asking the question, person A expects a response to be returned very quickly. Because the interaction is expected to be brief, he puts his other activities and thoughts on hold momentarily until the response is returned. Person B also knows the request will only take a few seconds to handle, and also decides to put everything else on hold while looking at his watch. The interaction is therefore synchronous. Person A can't watch person B as the latter determines the time because person A has no idea exactly what is going on at the other end of the line. The interaction is therefore blind.

Example 9 A navigation system in an avionics package uses a Global Positioning System (GPS) receiver to get the current position. The GPS receiver always maintains the current position internally, so it can honor requests almost immediately at all times. The navigation system uses a synchronous blind interaction to interrogate the receiver for the current position. Assume the specifications for the GPS receiver indicate that data is generally returned in less than 50 microseconds. A synchronous blind transaction works well here, because the current position is obtained quickly and with little strain on the GPS receiver, allowing the navigation system to decide when and how often to request new data. While the receiver is fetching the data to return, the navigation system has no idea how much time the response will actually take, although it has expectations derived from the receiver's spec sheet. If the GPS receiver loses contact with a satellite and needs to resynchronize, there may occasionally be a delay before a response can be returned.

Asynchronous Blind Interactions

▪**Context**   A process P_1 wishes to send a command to a process P_2. While P_2 is handling the command, P_1 needs to be able to continue with other tasks.

▪**Forces**   When a command is expected to take a significant time to be processed, or execution time is highly variable, it may be inefficient for the caller to block. An asynchronous interaction also makes sense when the caller needs to make concurrent requests to multiple processes.

Asynchronous blind interactions are more complicated than their synchronous cousins, because asynchrony requires multiple threads, multiple processes, or both. When using method calls as the interaction delivery vehicle, asynchrony can be supported on the caller's end or the callee's end. Asynchronous blind interactions are useful when the caller can continue with other operations while a call is in progress. In this case, the caller can run the call on a secondary thread and continue with the main thread. In UML, an asynchronous interaction is shown using an arrow with half the arrowhead missing, as shown in Figure 9-5.

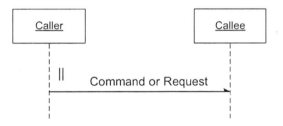

Figure 9-5. *An asynchronous interaction*

I use two vertical parallel bars (which aren't standard UML) to indicate which side the asynchronous (i.e., parallel) behavior is implemented on. The bars can appear on the caller side or the callee side—or on both sides.

In the simplest of cases, the caller may not need any feedback from the callee regarding execution progress of completion status. Calls made without the expectation of a completion response are a special case of asynchronous blind interactions known as *fire-and-forget*. Asynchronous interactions often require completion status from the callee. You can consider the returned status to be a form of feedback. As you shall see a bit later, interactions with completion feedback are a subset of *transparent* interactions, in which the caller can receive progress feedback from the callee while a command is being carried out.

Feedback

In the field of hardware control systems, feedback denotes any output signal that is routed back as an input. For example, given a system that provides analog signal amplification, feedback is a portion of the output signal that is taken and fed back into an input, as shown in Figure 9-6.

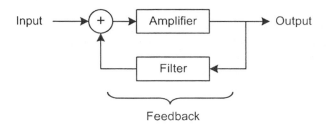

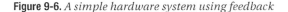

Figure 9-6. *A simple hardware system using feedback*

Hardware feedback is generally used to improve a system's linearity, bandwidth, and stability. Digital signal filters, known as *infinite impulse response* filters, use a digital form of feedback to achieve impressive filtering characteristics with relatively simple algorithms.

Feedback has also been used in software systems for quite some time. Given a system in which one object calls another, I'll use the word *feedback* to denote any information returned from the callee back to the caller, during or at the end of an asynchronous operation. When feedback is used only to signal the end of an asynchronous operation, it is sometimes referred to as a *completion token*.[3] While feedback can conceptually be used in purely synchronous systems, it is much more common in asynchronous ones. In asynchronous interactions, the caller might be interested in something about the progress or outcome of commands sent to the callee, such as the following:

- How far along the command is

- How much more time the command will take

- When the command has been completed

- The outcome of the command

When the caller requires feedback, there must exist a separate communication channel to get it from the callee. There are two ways for a caller to get feedback from the callee:

1. The callee pushes feedback to the caller.

2. The caller pulls feedback from the callee.

I'll describe each case in more detail.

---

3. Douglas C. Schmidt, Timothy H. Harrison, and Irfan Pyarali, "Asynchronous Completion Token - An Object Behavioral Pattern for Efficient Asynchronous Event Handling" (proceedings of the 3rd Annual Pattern Languages of Programs Conference, Allerton Park, IL, September 1996).

Pushed Feedback

This technique, which is a very common way to obtain completion feedback for asynchronous blind commands, is shown in Figure 9-7.

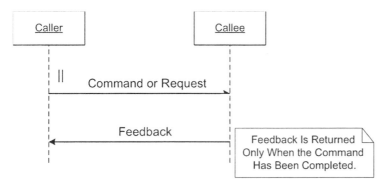

Figure 9-7. *An asynchronous blind interaction, with feedback pushed to caller*

When the callee finishes executing the command, it invokes a caller method, providing the appropriate completion feedback information. In the context of blind interactions, feedback only returns completion information. Progress updates, which report how far along a command is, are a form of feedback classified under "transparent interactions," described a bit later in the chapter.

Example 10 A person looking for work is sent to a company's personnel department. The clerk asks her to fill out an employment history form. While the applicant works, the clerk resumes with her own work. When the applicant finishes, she walks over to the clerk's desk and hands her the completed form. In this example, the clerk is the caller, the applicant the callee. While the callee is busy filling out the form, the caller works on something else, so the caller and callee operate asynchronously with respect to each other. When the callee is finished, she uses a push interaction to return completion feedback (the completed employment form) to the caller.

Example 11 A satellite system, during the course of initialization, needs to start up three subsystems to become operational. Each subsystem requires a variable amount of time to start up, and the satellite system can't begin operation until all subsystems have been started up. The Startup Controller (StartCon) issues asynchronous Start commands to all the subsystems, and resumes other tasks until the subsystems report they are all up. Figure 9-8 shows the system.

As each system starts, it fires an event notification to the Startup Controller. Completion feedback is therefore pushed from the callees to the caller. The order of arrival of completion feedback is not predictable by StartCon, which must wait until all systems report *done* before continuing.

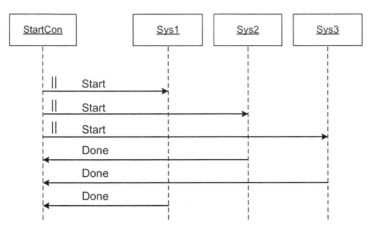

Figure 9-8. *An asynchronous interaction, with feedback pulled from callee*

Polled Feedback

Using this technique, the caller uses polling operations to obtain feedback information. Figure 9-9 shows an example.

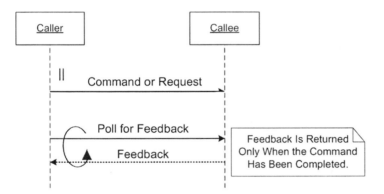

Figure 9-9. *An asynchronous interaction, with feedback pulled from the callee*

After the caller invokes the callee on a secondary thread, the caller's main thread checks periodically for completion feedback. The caller might run a timer to protect itself in case the callee doesn't finish in the expected time frame. The completion feedback requests can be made on the caller's main thread or a dedicated thread. To support polled feedback, the callee should be reentrant and thread-safe, because the feedback requests will occur while the original command is in progress. As mentioned earlier, in the context of blind interactions, feedback only returns completion information, not progress updates. I'll deal with the latter in the next section.

Example 12 A person wishes to rewind a videocassette in a videocassette recorder (VCR). She pushes the Rewind button on the VCR. The person doesn't know how long the operation will take, but decides there will be enough time to get something from the kitchen. While the Rewind command is in progress, the person is therefore busy doing something other than staring at the VCR. When a characteristic *click* sound emanates from the VCR, the person knows the Rewind command has completed. The VCR pushes completion feedback to the person, in the form of a *click* sound.

Example 13 A temperature-controlled industrial vat is used to mix three chemicals. After the first two chemicals are loaded at room temperature, the vat contents must be raised to a temperature of at least 95 degrees Celsius before loading a third chemical. The vat has a heater that a system controller (SysCon) can turn on and off. The vat status is reported by a sensor that returns the value 0 if the temperature is below 95; otherwise, it returns the value 1. SysCon turns on the vat heater and then continues on with other chores. Periodically, SysCon reads the vat status. Once the vat reaches 95 degrees, SysCon starts adding the third chemical. The diagram in Figure 9-10 shows the interactions.

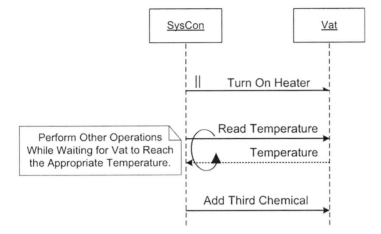

Figure 9-10. *An industrial system using asynchronous interactions with polled feedback*

In this example, SysCon is the caller and the vat is the callee. The vat is expected to take a long time to heat up, once the heater is turned on. SysCon is therefore designed to use an asynchronous call to turn the heater on. While the vat warms up, SysCon continues with its internal chores, checking the vat temperature occasionally. SysCon uses a polling loop to read the temperature sensor. The temperature sensor is purely reactive, so it isn't capable of sending signals to SysCon by itself. The sensor makes progress unavailable to SysCon, reporting a 1 only when the temperature exceeds 95 degrees Celsius. Once SysCon reads the appropriate temperature, the asynchronous interaction ends and SysCon starts loading the third chemical.

Transparent Interactions

■**Context** A process P_1 sends a command to a process P_2. P_1 needs to monitor the execution progress of P_2.

■**Forces** When an operation can result in widely varying processing times or intermediate steps, the caller may wish to monitor the callee's progress. This allows the caller to alter or adjust its course of action, based on intermediate results.

With blind interactions, the caller has no way to monitor the execution progress of the callee. At most, the caller can determine whether a command completes. During command execution, the caller has no idea about what is going on at the callee side. When an interaction is considerably variable in duration or is expected to take a long time, a transparent interaction is often appropriate.

Transparent interactions allow the caller to *see inside* the callee, as it were, in the sense that progress feedback can be obtained from the callee regarding the command execution.

From a linguistic perspective, transparent interactions are usually associated with imperative sentences, such as "Download this file." Transparent interactions are usually more complex than blind ones, because both the caller and callee must have certain capabilities:

1. The callee must be able to measure progress in a meaningful way.

2. The callee must be able to report feedback while executing a command.

3. The caller must be able to handle feedback while a previously issued command is being executed.

Although transparent interactions can be implemented strictly with synchronous calls, as described in the following "Pushed Feedback" section, it is far more common to use asynchronous interactions. Whether the asynchronous behavior is on the caller side, the callee side, or both is a design decision.

Pushed Feedback

■**Context** A process P_1 wishes to send a command to a process P_2. P_1 needs progress feedback as soon as P_2 has any status information available.

■**Forces** When intermediate status information is needed during the processing of a command, the caller may not know how often to request status, possibly because the command entails a widely varying number of steps or amount of processing time by the callee. It is wasteful for the caller to poll the callee continuously, because this taxes the callee while the callee is already busy. Moreover, the caller might miss a status update, if feedback isn't polled fast enough. A safe approach is to put the burden of status reporting on the callee, with a push model.

Using a pushed feedback model, the callee can send feedback notifications to the caller only when there is a change in progress. If changes occur at unpredictable times or are expensive to calculate, it would be wasteful for the caller to poll for feedback continually. Using a push model, the caller is notified only when the callee detects progress changes. The diagram in Figure 9-11 shows a transparent interaction with pushed feedback.

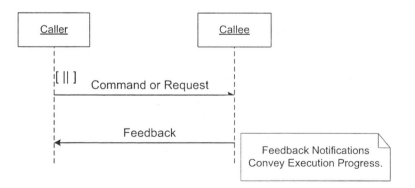

Figure 9-11. *A transparent interaction with push feedback*

The square brackets around the vertical bars indicate that the caller may or may not make calls asynchronously. If the caller and callee both execute synchronously, the callee's feedback notifications will provoke reentrant execution on the caller side. Although synchronous transparent interactions are relatively simple, asynchronous interactions are often a better solution. The reason is this: If a command is expected to take a long time, the caller may want to do other things while the callee is busy. By running the call on a secondary thread, the caller is free to do what it likes during the command execution.

Example 14 A person gets in an elevator and pushes the button for the desired floor. While traveling, the person checks some papers for an upcoming meeting. As the elevator travels, it notifies the passenger of progress using a numeric readout display in the elevator and issuing a beep. The interaction between the passenger (the caller) and the elevator (the callee) is transparent and uses pushed feedback in the form of beeps sent from the callee to the caller.

Example 15 A laser printer uses heat to fix toner ink to paper. Before loading paper into the paper path, SysCon must turn on the heater in the toner Fuser unit and wait for a certain temperature to be reached. The Fuser measures the temperature using a sensor, and fires temperature notifications for each five-degree Celsius change detected. It sends the notifications to SysCon. When the correct temperature is reached, SysCon starts the print process. Figure 9-12 shows the system.

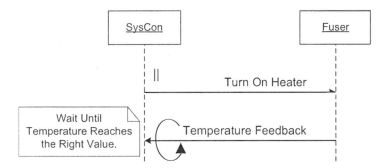

Figure 9-12. *A laser printer using transparent interactions with push feedback*

In this system, the Fuser doesn't know what SysCon will do with the temperature notifications, and in fact knows nothing about SysCon. After issuing the command to turn on the Fuser heater, SysCon begins receiving temperature notifications. SysCon might run a timer while waiting for the Fuser to reach its operating temperature. If the temperature notifications show the temperature is not changing, SysCon will time out and conclude that the Fuser heater is broken.

Polled Feedback

▪**Context** A process P_1 wishes to send a command to a process P_2. P_1 needs execution feedback at specific times, designated by P_1. Feedback is not necessary except at those specific times. P_2 is able to provide the feedback quickly and reliably.

▪**Forces** When the caller doesn't care about or can't handle changes in status of the callee except at given moments, it is inefficient for the callee to issue unsolicited status-change notifications. By having the caller ask for status, it can control the frequency of status requests during the various intermediate steps taken by the callee.

In a transparent interaction with polled feedback, the caller polls the callee for progress updates, while a previously issued asynchronous command is being executed. After sending the main command on a secondary thread, the caller enters a polling loop, as shown in Figure 9-13.

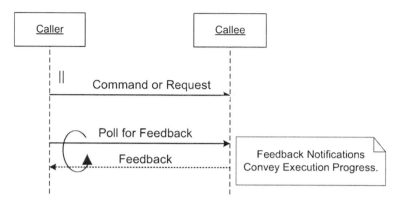

Figure 9-13. *A transparent interaction with polled feedback*

Because the callee must be able to support polling requests while it is executing a command on a different thread, the callee must use thread-safe operations to return the progress feedback.

Example 16 A person needs to catch a plane and is running late. She stops a taxicab and says, "Take me to the airport." Along the way, traffic conditions change considerably. In fear of missing her flight, the passenger asks the driver, "How much more time do you think the ride will take?" The cab driver answers, "Probably another 20 minutes." The passenger acts as the caller, the driver as the callee. The trip to the airport represents the asynchronous execution of a command. The passenger uses a polling technique to get progress reports back from the cab driver during the trip.

Example 17 A person surfs the Internet with a Web browser. He clicks the hyperlink on one HTML document to go to another document. Inside the browser, the HTML rendering component (HtmlCom) issues a GetDocument command to the HTTP communication component (HttpCom), as shown in Figure 9-14.
    While HttpCom loads the requested page, HtmlCom issues a series of GetProgress queries to HttpCom. HtmlCom uses the information to display a progress bar on the user's screen to give an indication of how long the load process will take.

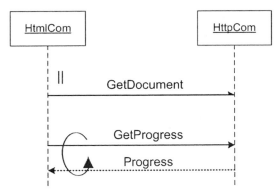

Figure 9-14. *Loading an HTML page using a transparent interaction with polled feedback*

Interruptible Interactions

■**Context** A process P_1 wishes to send a command to a process P_2. While the command is being executed, certain conditions can arise that require P_1 to cancel the command before it is completed.

■**Forces** Many systems require the ability to adapt to unusual or unreliable situations. If P_1 detects certain conditions during the execution of a previously issued command, it may need to cancel the command and resort to an alternative course of action.

Assume P_1 calls P_2 to execute a command. During execution, it may be necessary for P_1 to abort execution for any number of reasons, such as excessive time to complete, errors detected in other parts of the system, or unexpected partial results. An interaction is interruptible if the caller can interrupt it before the command has been completed. In theory, either the caller or the callee could interrupt command execution; however, you only consider an interaction to be an *interruptible interaction pattern* if the caller has control over command termination. If the callee terminates the command prematurely, you consider this to be an ordinary error condition, because no special interactions between caller and callee are necessary in this case. Figure 9-15 shows the basic steps in an interruptible interaction.

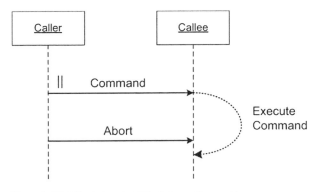

Figure 9-15. *The interruptible interaction pattern*

In order for an interaction to be interruptible, the caller must be asynchronous, because the caller must have the ability to send the abort command during the execution of a previously issued command. The callee is not required to be asynchronous, but must have the ability to execute the abort command using thread-safe operations, since the original command and the abort command will arrive on different threads.

Both blind and transparent interactions can be made interruptible. The hallmark of an interruptible interaction is the presence of a dedicated channel to carry abort commands from the caller to the callee. While the concept of interruptible interactions is simple, aborting a command may require extensive processing to clean up intermediate results or other side effects of the partially completed command. This cleanup work is not considered part of the interruptible interaction pattern itself.

Interruptible Blind Interactions

■Context A process P_1 sends a command to a process P_2. P_1 gets no progress reports while P_2 executes the command. Before P_2 completes the command, P_1 may decide to abort the operation.

■Forces When a blind interaction is underway, the caller has no way of knowing how far along the callee is or how soon the callee will finish. The caller can only monitor the amount of time the callee is taking to respond, or other side effects of the interaction. Certain conditions may require the caller to abort a command in progress.

Blind interactions have the drawback that the caller has no way to determine how long a command will take, or even *if* the command will succeed, except perhaps for previous experience with that command. Even so, a system whose computing resources vary at run time may be difficult to predict in terms of how quickly a command will be executed. There are many situations in which a system may need to attempt a command. Should the command fail to complete within a certain time limit, the system may opt to abort the command and change the course of action.

In another scenario, a caller may initiate concurrent commands in multiple callees through asynchronous blind interactions. The caller might want to execute the commands as a single transaction. Should any of the commands fail, all other commands would have to be cancelled. A subsequent *rollback* operation might be necessary to restore the system to its original state before the failure. The rollback operation itself is not part of the interruptible interaction pattern. Figure 9-16 shows an interruptible blind interaction.

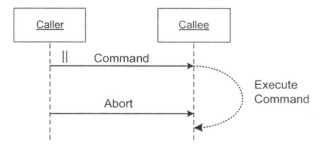

Figure 9-16. *An interruptible blind interaction*

abort commands only make sense if issued *during* the execution of a previously issued command. An abort command may abort a single command or a whole series of concurrent commands. The interruptible interaction pattern doesn't characterize how the abort command works inside the callee, what it affects, or how long it takes. If a callee receives an abort command after a command has already been terminated or before a command was received, the callee may choose to return an error code to the caller or take some other action.

Example 18 A person wishes to buy a drink from a vending machine. He inserts some coins, selects a product, and waits for it to drop to the bottom tray. While waiting for the product, the customer glances at his watch. After a second, he grows impatient and bangs on the side of the machine. Nothing happens, so he presses the *return coins* button to cancel the purchase. In this example, the person represents the caller; the vending machine is the callee. The asynchronous command is *buy product*. The command is blind because the person can't see the inside of the vending machine. The command is asynchronous, because the customer can do other things (such as look at his watch) while the command is being executed. The *return coins* command is the abort command to the machine.

Example 19 A person desires to test a TCP/IP local area network connection between computers by using a ping command. The person types in the IP address of the computer and waits for the ping response. When the command doesn't complete within a certain amount of time, the person gives up and closes the console window in which the ping command was running. Because the command was blind, the person had no idea why the command was taking so long. Some part of the networking software may have failed, or perhaps the pinged machined was off. How long a person waits will depend on how long the person can or is willing to wait. At any point during execution of the command, the person may decide to abort and do something else.

Interruptible Transparent Interactions

■**Context** A process P_1 sends a command to a process P_2. While P_2 is busy executing the command, P_1 needs to obtain execution progress information from P_2. At any time during command execution, P_1 may need to interrupt the transaction.

■**Forces** Transparent interactions utilize feedback to keep the caller informed of progress the callee makes in processing a command. The caller may utilize the feedback information to decide to abort the operation in progress.

When the execution of a command is expected to be lengthy or to involve several intermediate steps, a transparent interaction may be useful, because it allows the caller to monitor progress of the callee. If the progress feedback indicates that the callee is not following the expected course of action, the caller may choose to interrupt the command. Any number of reasons might be valid for aborting a command, including incorrect intermediate results or excessive time to complete the command. Figure 9-17 shows the basics of the interruptible transparent interaction pattern.

Figure 9-17 shows a system using push feedback. As stated earlier, transparent interactions can use push or pull operations to get progress feedback to the caller. The basic interruptible transparent interaction pattern is not concerned with how feedback is returned to the caller, as long as feedback is provided in some way.

If the caller uses pull interactions to get the progress updates, it is possible for the caller to include a flag in the requests to signal an abort request. A separate abort channel is desirable because it makes a clear distinction between the ordinary and extraordinary processing. For example, if the caller sends an abort command to the callee, the command may need to be executed in a thread that has higher priority than the original message. Using a separate abort message also makes it clear who has the power to interrupt the interaction.

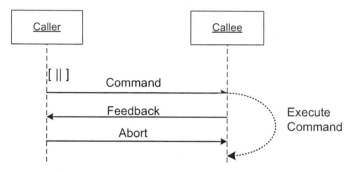

Figure 9-17. *An interruptible transparent interaction*

Example 20 An office worker wishes to have lunch. She goes to the company cafeteria, finds a short waiting line, and gets in line. The line progresses along nicely until the drink dispenser machine breaks. The line stops moving. After waiting a few minutes to see if the problem gets resolved, she decides to get in a different line. In this situation, the woman is monitoring the progress of the waiting line. She can see that a problem developed before reaching the head of the line. Being in a position to monitor the situation, the person is able to make an informed decision to stop waiting and choose a different course of action.

Example 21 A machine is designed to measure a person's blood pressure automatically. It works by having patients insert their left arm into a circular strap and pressing a Start button. The machine internally uses a control component (SysCom) to monitor the Start button. When the button is pressed, SysCom issues a start command to the strap control component (StrapCom), which begins pressurizing the strap to tighten it around the patient's arm. Figure 9-18 shows the interactions between SysCom and StrapCom.

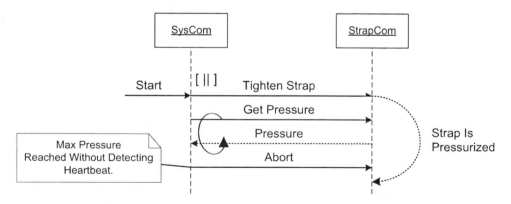

Figure 9-18. *A blood-pressure-measurement machine using an interruptible transparent interaction*

As pressurization is in progress, SysCom makes frequent status requests to obtain the instantaneous blood-pressure reading. The strap pressure needs to be increased until StrapCom can read a heartbeat. If the pressure reaches a limit value before a heartbeat is detected, SysCom concludes that the strap wasn't placed around the arm correctly and issues an abort command to release the strap.

Handshaking

■**Context** A process P_1 wishes to transfer a large amount of information to a process P_2. The information can be broken down into a series of messages. It may be necessary to stop the message flow before all the intended information is sent. P_1, P_2, or both may have control over when messages should stop being sent.

■**Forces** Perhaps the P_1 caller gains access to this information one piece at a time, from a third party, or perhaps the communication channel between P_1 and P_2 can only handle messages of a certain size.

When lengthy or complex operations can be carried out by the repeated application of simpler ones, the interaction consists of an iteration: The caller issues a command, and the callee acknowledges it. The caller continues to repeat the command (possibly with different data) until the overall operation is complete, or until one of the two parties stops the process. I'll call this type of interaction a *handshaking interaction*, because of its similarity with hardware handshaking, used frequently in data communications, where the receiver tells the sender when it is ready for the next command or message. Figure 9-19 shows the pattern.

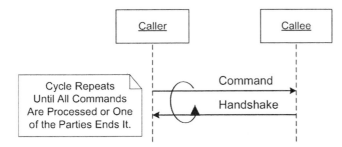

Figure 9-19. *The basic handshaking interaction pattern*

Each handshake tells the caller to send more information, if available. The callee can return a handshake immediately upon receipt of each command, or after each command has been processed.

An important decision to make when using a handshaking interaction is this: Who has control over termination of the iteration—the caller or the callee? The answer depends on which party knows when *enough is enough*. If the caller knows there are no further commands available, the caller will control termination. If the callee can arbitrarily decide when to bail out of the interaction, the callee will control termination. It's also possible for both parties to control termination. When the callee controls termination, the handshake might contain a reserved field or value to indicate a termination request to make the caller stop issuing commands or sending data.

Example 22 A person is eating a plate of spaghetti for dinner. He decides to add some salt. He picks up the saltshaker and shakes it over the pasta repeatedly until the desired amount of salt has been added. In this example, the command is *add salt to spaghetti*. The caller is the person; the callee is the saltshaker. The handshake is the image of the salt falling on the spaghetti. The interaction is a caller-controlled handshake, because it is the person who decides when to stop adding salt.

Example 23 A system is designed to transmit satellite images over a network. The transmission channel uses packets to carry information, and each packet can hold 2 KB. Typical images are more than 50 MB in size, so you must break them down into blocks that fit into channel packets. Figure 9-20 shows the interactions between the transmitter and receiver components.

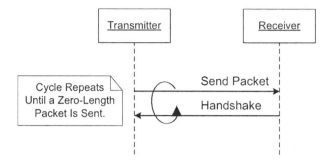

Figure 9-20. *Handshaking in an image transmission system*

The transmitter acts as the caller, the receiver as the callee. To signal the end of an image, a last packet is sent with zero bytes. During the interaction, the receiver doesn't know how much data will arrive. Only the caller does, and it uses a special signal to tell the receiver when the interaction is complete.

Summary

Many of the interaction patterns that occur between software processes are similar to those that occur in the hardware world. When deciding which type of pattern to use, you should first determine whether you need a push or pull interaction. This decision usually depends on who has control of the interaction—the caller or the callee. The timing of the interaction (synchronous or asynchronous) is probably the second-most important decision. When creating asynchronous interactions, remember that it is usually better to handle the asynchrony on the caller side than the callee side.

CHAPTER 10

■■■

Functional Roles

If you look at lots of different types of software systems, you soon realize that they have certain things in common. On the surface, a financial-planning system might not seem to have anything in common with an elevator-control system; a washing-machine program might not seem to have anything in common with a data-decryption system. However, if you step back a bit and look at the broader picture, similarities start to emerge. For example, all software systems need an initialization process before they can perform their main task. Many software systems have a shutdown process when they are terminated. All useful software systems must implement some level of business logic. The expression *business logic* is used in the broadest sense and includes the rules of whatever domain the software system is designed for. For example, in a temperature-control system, the business rules relate to heating and cooling laws. In a flight-control system, the rules relate to controlling the attitude[1] and heading of an aircraft according to the laws of aerodynamics. In an accounting system, the rules might describe how to calculate a person's withholdings from his gross salary.

Among the many similarities across software systems, *functional roles* are important. A functional role, often called simply a *role*, denotes what function a part has in relationship to the rest of the system. A part might be an object or a component. It is interesting to note that decoupled parts can often operate in a functional role without knowing how the rest of the system works. For example, an accounting system part that computes a person's withholdings could do so without knowing why its calculations were needed or where. The part would be able to function normally without knowing which other parts existed in the system, how the system worked, or how the various parts in the system were interconnected.

When it comes to functional roles, probably the easiest one to understand is what I call the *worker* role, to use a business metaphor. In a software system, workers are the specialized parts that produce tangible results, as it were. Workers are the ones that implement the business logic of the system. Workers are the most valuable parts of a system, because they contain the rules for solving problems in a specific domain. Those rules are often nontrivial and often take the author a lot of time to learn and understand.

A business organization is more than just a collection of workers, and so is a software system. When complex business rules need to be implemented, a common strategy is to divide the overall work into smaller increments and distribute the workload across groups of workers. Since the workers must interact and collaborate to be successful, it becomes important for the workers to be managed somehow. Those software parts that fulfill management roles are called *coordinators* in this book. Coordinators manage workers. Large business organizations often have several layers of management, with higher-level managers managing groups of lower-level managers. In an EBS, the management layers become a hierarchy of coordinators, with groups of lower-level coordinators managed by higher-level ones.

---

1. For readers unfamiliar with aviation terms, a plane's attitude includes the aircraft's pitch, roll, and yaw. Essentially, the attitude measures the orientation of the plane relative to the direction of motion, in three dimensions. Don't confuse *attitude* with *altitude*!

The most important and complex parts of an EBS are the coordinators and workers. Because they are complex, relative to other types of parts, workers and coordinators should be as decoupled as possible from the rest of the system to make them easier to build, test, and deploy. While office workers and managers in an office can talk to each other easily, decoupled parts have no built-in connections to other parts, so they can't communicate with others until a communication path is established. In an EBS, the dominant form of communication between the salient parts is through event notifications, so you must establish notification paths at run time in a process called *binding* or *wiring*. The *wires* of an EBS act in much the same way as the old pneumatic tube message-delivery systems used in the 1800s in large businesses. Each tube could carry messages from one specific office to another.

The wiring in an EBS establishes paths for event notifications. The part designated to wire a system can do so without needing to know how the parts being wired actually work. I'll call the wiring part a *binder*. Like a contractor installing a pneumatic tube delivery system, a binder only needs a list of items to hook together. The binder doesn't need to know why the items need to be connected, what type of traffic will be sent over the connections, or how the overall business works.

Binders connect outputs to inputs. Outputs are outgoing calls, and inputs are methods to call, exposed by objects. Outputs and inputs come into existence only after objects are created at run time (if you ignore the case of *class methods*, which can be called without having to create any objects). Before a binder can do any binding, there must be objects to bind. It is possible to centralize the instantiation of the main objects (the coordinators and workers), giving the responsibility to a dedicated component I'll call a *builder*.

In one form or another, functional roles are present in all software systems. In a messy system, the roles are scattered across groups of parts, and the parts are generally heavily coupled to each other. In a well-designed EBS, the roles are much more recognizable, with each part playing a clear role. Once you've worked with EBSs and roles long enough, you'll start to think of software systems as a network of parts with specific roles. But don't underestimate the importance of wiring, because wiring is what is responsible for making the whole greater than the sum of the parts. Biological systems, while infinitely more complex that any software system today, are a reminder of this. For example, the cortex of the human brain is a large network of neurons, but looking at a neuron doesn't even begin to describe how the brain works at a higher level. You'd be hard-pressed to find a person's aspirations or beliefs by looking at their brain under a microscope. But before I go too far off track, let's come back to reality and look at the most important roles in more depth.

Workers

Workers are the objects or components that implement the business logic of a system. To use a human metaphor, workers represent the *skilled labor* of a system. If software systems were implemented in hardware, workers would be the custom chips that do all the business-specific or application-specific work, delivering the most valuable services. Virtually no useful software system can be built without workers, because such a system would contain no business logic. Workers are also known in the literature as *business components*.[2]

What Workers Should Do

Workers implement business logic and are often highly specialized and complex, compared to parts with other roles. Any code not related to business logic, such as notification routing, thread management, and exception handling, should be removed from workers and put elsewhere. Workers should

---

2. George T. Heineman and William T. Councill, *Component-Based Software Engineering: Putting the Pieces Together* (Boston: Addison-Wesley Professional, 2001).

be designed with a very narrow focus. It is usually better to design many small workers rather than a single large one. Smaller workers are easier to develop, to test, and to reuse.

If workers are the most complex parts in a system, then, according to Axiom 1 in Chapter 1, they should also be the least coupled parts. Ideally, a Worker should be completely decoupled from the rest of the system. If coupling occurs, it should be related only to the use of user-defined types, generally kept in well-known components. These well-known components should appear in the center of a star-shaped or concentric coupling diagram, as discussed at the end of Chapter 1.

From a notification-wiring perspective, you can consider workers as event sources and targets. Internally, workers fulfill their mission by implementing all sorts of business logic. Externally, from the system perspective, workers do this only by handling and firing events.

Once you decouple workers from the rest of the system, you can design, implement, and test them individually, or at most with the presence of the well-known components containing the user-defined types referenced by the Worker. Each Worker, in effect, becomes a separate project with its own test fixture. While developing and testing workers, what really matters are the classes inside the Worker and how the classes relate to one another. But once you've fully tested and added the Worker to a larger system, the Worker is little more than a black box that solves business problems. It's a software IC with pins. At this stage, attention shifts away from a Worker's internal structure and operation, focusing more on how the Worker interacts with the outside world.

Workers fire events to let the rest of the system know what it's doing or to request other parts to do something. A Coordinator is often given the task of handling worker notifications, using the Observer design pattern.[3] In this scenario, the Coordinator is the observer and the Worker is the subject. Coordinators provide methods that handle Worker notifications.

Composite Workers

Some situations require workers to be very complex. Perhaps a simple command requires scores of operations belonging to several different classes. Rather than designing a single super-worker part, it is advisable to subdivide the workload among multiple workers, arranged in some fashion. When parts are arranged in a hierarchy, an important issue is how parts on different layers communicate. The event-based approach uses event notifications, not just between different layers, but also between any two components, as shown in Figure 10-1.

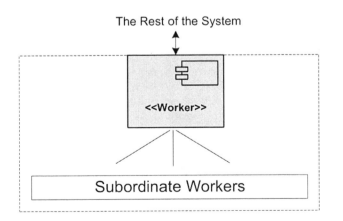

Figure 10-1. *A composite Worker with internal subordinate workers*

3. Erich Gamma, Richard Helm, Ralph Johnson, and John Vlissides, *Design Patterns: Elements of Reusable Object-Oriented Software* (Boston: Addison-Wesley Professional, 1995).

UML stereotypes are used to denote the role of a component in diagrams. In Figure 10-1, the top-level Worker acts as a façade for the others and is the only Worker that interacts with the rest of the system. The top-level Worker leverages the results of the lower-level workers, but should not deal with threading or thread-synchronization issues. If the lower-level workers must run on separate threads, you should place a Coordinator in charge of threading, and the top-level Worker should interact with the Coordinator, as shown in Figure 10-2.

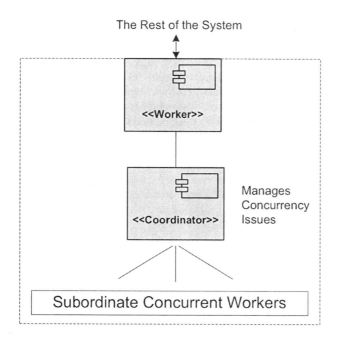

Figure 10-2. *A composite Worker with concurrent subordinate workers*

If subordinate workers fire events, the Coordinator can handle any thread synchronization necessary before sending the notifications to other concurrent workers or to the top-level Worker.

What Workers Shouldn't Do

Workers should be focused on solving problems related to business logic, without knowledge of how end users initiate a particular task, whether an operation should be carried out synchronously or asynchronously, or what effect a result has on the rest of the system. Within these guidelines, there are a few types of things a worker probably *shouldn't* get involved with, except under special application-specific conditions:

- *Exposed Worker methods shouldn't be asynchronous*: Public Worker methods are simpler to develop and test if they are synchronous. If client objects calling a specific method need an asynchronous behavior, the burden of asynchrony should be placed on the client. In practice, the client might use a Coordinator to handle the Worker threading logic.

- *Workers shouldn't deal with thread issues*: Workers should not contain logic that interacts with other threads. Workers should not create threads for internal purposes, and they should not contain thread-synchronization logic. Thread-related code belongs in a Coordinator. When firing events, workers should not try to send notifications across thread boundaries. The less a worker knows about threads, the better.

- *Workers shouldn't manage transactions*: A transaction is a group of tasks that all must succeed or fail collectively. If they succeed, a *commit* operation is performed, making all the transaction results available at once. If any of the tasks fail, a *rollback* operation is performed, restoring the system to the state it was in before the transaction started. Normally, you should assign transaction management to a Coordinator, even if the same Worker handles all the tasks. The Coordinator is put in charge of a list of tasks that are part of a transaction. Workers carry out the individual tasks. If all the tasks succeed, the Coordinator commits the changes; otherwise, it rolls the changes back. The commit and rollback operations might be considered tasks themselves and therefore be performed by workers, especially if the details of committing or rolling back changes are business-rule-dependent.

- *Workers shouldn't handle notification routing*: Workers should communicate with the rest of the system using notifications exclusively. When using method calls to deliver notifications, workers should use untyped object calls, where possible, to introduce the least amount of run-time coupling possible. To avoid the introduction of extraneous coupling, workers should not be responsible for binding their notifications to event handler methods. A separate Coordinator or a dedicated Binder component should handle binding.

How Complex Should a Worker Be?

There is obviously no universal answer regarding complexity, but here is a useful guideline:

> *A worker should be as simple as possible, but complex enough to justify the construction of a dedicated test fixture.*

You can measure complexity in two ways: internally and externally. The internal complexity is related to the amount of logic required to achieve the worker's mission. You might measure this complexity using any number of metrics, including the number of internal classes, the number of lines of code, or function points. The external complexity is related to the footprint of the worker's interface. The interface is represented by methods, properties, and events. A worker might expose only one method externally, but have hundreds of internal ones distributed across dozens of internal classes. This worker part would be internally complex but externally simple. Another worker might expose 50 methods, but have only one class with a total of 50 lines of code. This part would be internally simple but externally complex.

The internal complexity affects the level of difficulty to design, implement, and maintain a part. The external complexity affects the level of difficulty to test and integrate a component. How externally complex should a component be? The simpler, the better. In the absence of a perfect answer, heuristics are useful. A reasonable one might be what I call the *10-10-10 guideline*:[4]

> *A worker should not expose more than 10 properties, 10 methods, and 10 events.*

Most workers don't expose the same number of properties, methods, and events, but the interface footprint should contain 30 items or less. If a worker exposed only methods, it should expose no more than 30. There is nothing magical about the number 30, but workers exposing more than 30 interface items are probably trying to do too much and will be difficult to test and maintain.

---

4. Ted Faison, *Component-Based Development with Visual C#* (Indianapolis, IN: John Wiley & Sons, 2002), p. 40.

Worker Examples

Let's take a look at some interesting scenarios in which you might use workers. The first example shows how you can use a worker to implement user-interface elements. What is most significant about this example is what the Worker *doesn't* do, using a Coordinator to handle certain kinds of things. The second example shows how a composite Worker might manage concurrent subordinate workers, using an internal Coordinator to manage concurrency issues.

User-Interface Elements As Workers

When implementing user interfaces as workers, first answer this question: "What business rules should the Worker implement?" UI elements have two main tasks:

- To render data

- To capture user actions

You can partially accomplish the first task using a visual designer to lay out UI controls in a design environment. For screen-oriented interfaces, place the controls on a form, dialog, or window element. For printer-oriented interfaces, you often place the controls on a report element, which handles printer layout details at run time. A visual designer allows you to lay out the UI controls in a way that satisfies the business requirements. The requirements might be simply "The screen needs to look like so and so . . ." or "The screen must allow the end user to do this and this . . ." More in-depth requirements would spell out the exact appearance and behavior of each control.

The second task is to capture user actions. The Worker should handle actions that require simple cosmetic changes to the interface, such as showing or hiding something. Actions that require the fetching of new data should generally be handled by firing events that are handled by a Coordinator. Once you bring a Coordinator into the picture, you need to be clear about who handles what. The division of labor between the Coordinator and Worker is straightforward: The Coordinator is in charge of *what* to display—in other words, fetching the data—while the Worker decides *how* to display it, which includes laying controls out on the UI and formatting data for presentation.

As a practical example, consider a simple UI that might be used in a real-estate search program, allowing people to search for a home. The system must let users search for different types of properties in a number of cities. Assume the system has a search form that looks like Figure 10-3 at design time.

The business requires that the UI allow a user to choose between renting and buying. The user then enters a price, a city, and a state and then runs a search that returns a list of properties. The UI Worker might be implemented using a single class, consisting of a form with embedded UI controls. The Payment Model group box displays two panels, shown with dashed borders. At run time, only one of these panels will be visible, based on the radio button selected. The middle group box displays two drop-down lists that show the states and cities supported by the real-estate system. The bottom group box contains a list of properties found after the user clicks the Search button.

Let's see how the nonvisual part of the system is handled. When the user clicks either the Rent or Buy radio button, the only action required is to show or hide panels. This action doesn't require retrieving any new data, so the Worker can handle it directly.

When the search form is first displayed, it must contain a list of states and cities. The retrieval of the lists is not a data-presentation problem, so you should delegate it to another object. In this example, you can use a Coordinator to obtain the lists, which will be string arrays. The Coordinator *gives* the state list to the Worker, who then puts the states in the appropriate drop-down list and selects an initial state. The Worker then needs to get a list of cities for the selected state. The Worker fires an event to the Coordinator, specifying which state is currently selected. The Coordinator then retrieves the city list and gives it to the Worker, as before.

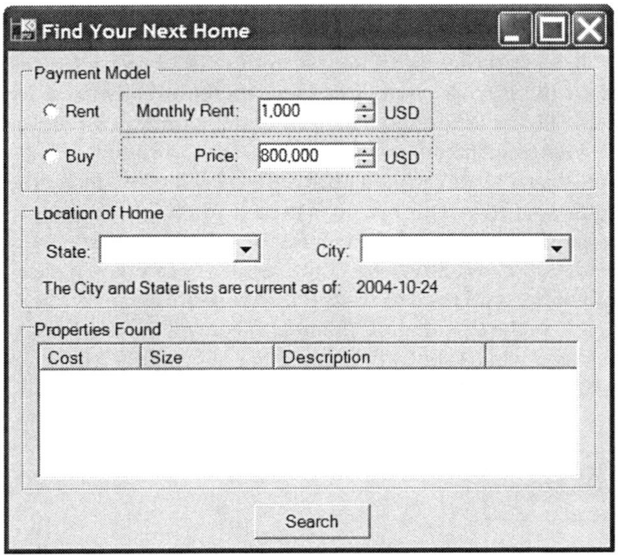

Figure 10-3. *The design-time appearance of a simple UI implemented as a Worker*

Just below the two drop-down lists in the UI is a text field that displays a date. Assign to the Coordinator the task of figuring out what date to display. The Worker then shows the date, formatted according to the business requirements.

The bottom group box contains the list of properties that satisfy the search criteria. When the user clicks the Search button, the Worker fires an event to the Coordinator, which retrieves the appropriate properties. It gives the properties to the Worker, which formats the data and displays it in the list at the bottom of the screen. Figure 10-4 shows how the system might look after running a search.

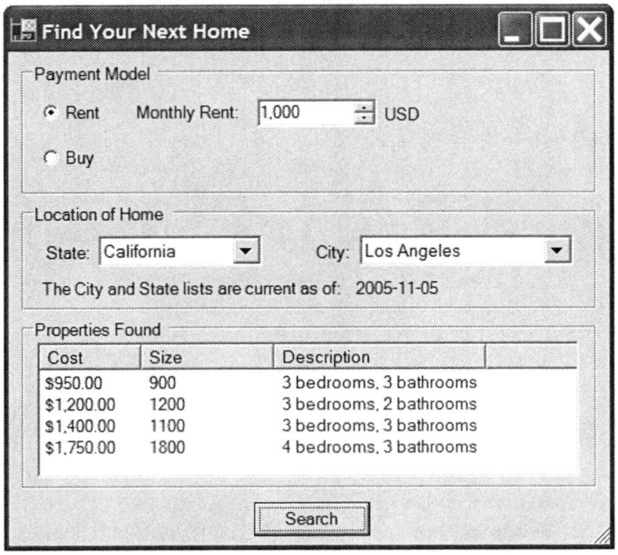

Figure 10-4. *The run-time appearance of the UI component*

Figure 10-4 shows that the Cost column includes some data formatting, such as the dollar sign, the thousands-grouping comma, the decimal point, and two decimals. The Worker handles this data formatting. The business requirements indicate that users must be able to sort the list by clicking on a column header. The Worker should handle the sort operation, since no data retrieval is necessary.

One last design note regards the mouse cursor. Who should control it? It is common for the mouse cursor to show an hourglass when a lengthy operation is under way. The Coordinator is responsible for retrieving data. The Worker doesn't know whether the retrieval will take a long time or not, so it doesn't know when to display busy cursors. One option is to have the Worker display a busy cursor just before firing any event, restoring the normal cursor when the event completes. Alternatively, the Coordinator could control the cursor. Since the Coordinator doesn't have a user interface and the Worker does, the Coordinator would need to control the Worker's cursor during lengthy retrieval operations. By the same token, the Coordinator might also control the Worker status bar, if one is present, to display messages while lengthy operations are in progress. The interaction diagrams in Figures 10-5 through 10-7 show the basic use cases for the system.

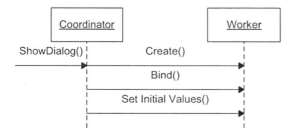

Figure 10-5. *The Coordinator that instantiates and wires the Worker*

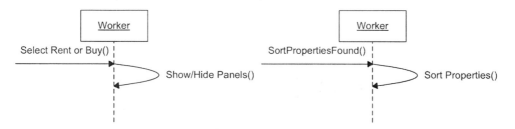

Figure 10-6. *User actions that the Worker can handle by itself*

Figure 10-7. *Handling user actions that involve the Coordinator*

Note that Figure 10-7 shows reentrant calls into the Worker. The Update Cities and Update Properties Found notifications are reentrant. While the Worker is blocked after sending an Update Cities notification, the Coordinator gets the list of cities and calls back into the Worker. If reentrancy is undesirable, a slightly different interaction can be used: When the Worker fires the StateChanged event, it might supply an envelope into which the Coordinator can put the list of cities. Listing 10-1 and Listing 10-2 show C# and VB .NET implementations of the Coordinator and Worker.

Listing 10-1. *The C# Implementation of the UI Example*

```csharp
// Coordinator.cs
using System;
using System.Windows.Forms;
using System.Threading;

namespace UserInterfaceExample
{
  public class Coordinator
  {
    FormWorker worker;

    public void ShowDialog()
    {
      if (worker == null)
      {
        worker = new FormWorker();
        worker.OnStateChanged +=
            new FormWorker.StateChangedHandler(worker_OnStateChanged);
        worker.OnSearchToBuy +=
            new FormWorker.SearchToBuyHandler(worker_OnSearchToBuy);
        worker.OnSearchToRent +=
            new FormWorker.SearchToRentHandler(worker_OnSearchToRent);

        worker.States = new string[ ] {"California", "Texas", "New York"};
        worker.DateOfLastUpdate = DateTime.Now;
      }
      worker.ShowDialog();
    }

    private void worker_OnStateChanged(string theState)
    {
      worker.Cursor = Cursors.WaitCursor;

      switch (theState)
      {
        case "California":
          worker.Cities = new string[ ] {"Los Angeles", "San Francisco"};
          break;
        case "Texas":
          worker.Cities = new string[ ] {"Dallas", "Austin"};
          break;
        case "New York":
          worker.Cities = new string[ ] {"New York City", "Albany"};
          break;
        default:
          worker.Cities = null;
          break;
      }
```

```
        Thread.Sleep(500);  //  simulate a lengthy operation
        worker.Cursor = Cursors.Default;
    }

    private void worker_OnSearchToBuy(string theState, string theCity,
                      float theMonthlyRent)
    {
      worker.Cursor = Cursors.WaitCursor;

      worker.PropertiesFound = new PropertyFound[ ]
      {
        new PropertyFound(600000, 2200, "3 bedrooms, 4 bathrooms"),
        new PropertyFound(850000, 2100, "3 bedrooms, 3 bathrooms"),
        new PropertyFound(1000000, 3300, "4 bedrooms, 4 bathrooms"),
        new PropertyFound(1200000, 4000, "5 bedrooms, 5 bathrooms")
      };

      Thread.Sleep(500);  //  simulate a lengthy operation
      worker.Cursor = Cursors.Default;
    }

    private void worker_OnSearchToRent(string theState, string theCity,
                      float theMonthlyRent)
    {
      worker.Cursor = Cursors.WaitCursor;

      worker.PropertiesFound = new PropertyFound[ ]
      {
        new PropertyFound(950, 900, "3 bedrooms, 3 bathrooms"),
        new PropertyFound(1200, 1200, "3 bedrooms, 2 bathrooms"),
        new PropertyFound(1400, 1100, "3 bedrooms, 3 bathrooms"),
        new PropertyFound(1750, 1800, "4 bedrooms, 3 bathrooms")
      };

      Thread.Sleep(500);  //  simulate a lengthy operation
      worker.Cursor = Cursors.Default;
    }
  }
}


// FormWorker.cs

using System;
using System.Drawing;
using System.Collections;
using System.ComponentModel;
using System.Windows.Forms;
```

```csharp
namespace UserInterfaceExample
{
  public class FormWorker : System.Windows.Forms.Form
  {
    // declare all the controls
    private System.Windows.Forms.RadioButton radioButtonRent;
    private System.Windows.Forms.RadioButton radioButtonBuy;
    // …

    public FormWorker()
    {
        InitializeComponent();
        radioButtonRent.Checked = true;
    }

    #region Windows Form Designer generated code
      // …
    #endregion

    public string[ ] States
    {
      set
      {
        comboBoxState.Items.Clear();
        comboBoxState.Items.AddRange(value);
        comboBoxState.SelectedIndex = 0;
      }
    }

    public string[ ] Cities
    {
      set
      {
        comboBoxCity.Items.Clear();
        if (value == null) return;
        comboBoxCity.Items.AddRange(value);
        comboBoxCity.SelectedIndex = 0;
      }
    }

    public DateTime DateOfLastUpdate
    {
      // date only, e.g. "2006-12-19"
      set {labelDate.Text = value.Date.ToString("d");}
    }

    public PropertyFound[ ] PropertiesFound
    {
      set
      {
        listViewPropertiesFound.Items.Clear();
        if (value == null) return;
```

```csharp
      foreach (PropertyFound property in value)
      {
        // display cost as a currency
        ListViewItem item = new ListViewItem(property.Cost.ToString("C"));
        item.SubItems.Add(property.Size.ToString());
        item.SubItems.Add(property.Description);
        listViewPropertiesFound.Items.Add(item);
      }
    }
}

private void comboBoxState_SelectedIndexChanged(object sender,
                   System.EventArgs e)
{
  if (comboBoxState.SelectedIndex >= 0)
    FireStateChanged(comboBoxState.Text);
}

private void radioButtonRent_CheckedChanged(object sender, System.EventArgs e)
{
  panelRent.Visible = radioButtonRent.Checked;
  panelBuy.Visible = !radioButtonRent.Checked;
}

private void radioButtonBuy_CheckedChanged(object sender, System.EventArgs e)
{
  panelRent.Visible = !radioButtonBuy.Checked;
  panelBuy.Visible = radioButtonBuy.Checked;
}

private void buttonSearch_Click(object sender, System.EventArgs e)
{
  if (radioButtonRent.Checked)
    FireSearchToRent(comboBoxState.Text, comboBoxCity.Text,
                            (float) numericUpDownMontlyRent.Value);
  else
    FireSearchToBuy(comboBoxState.Text, comboBoxCity.Text,
                           (float) numericUpDownPrice.Value);
}

private void listViewPropertiesFound_ColumnClick(object sender,
                   System.Windows.Forms.ColumnClickEventArgs e)
{
  // set sorter and resort listview
  listViewPropertiesFound.ListViewItemSorter = new PropertyComparer(e.Column);
}

public delegate void StateChangedHandler(string theState);
public event StateChangedHandler OnStateChanged;
void FireStateChanged(string theState)
{
  if (OnStateChanged == null) return;
  OnStateChanged(theState);
}
```

```csharp
      public delegate void SearchToRentHandler(string theState,
                                   string theCity,
                                   float theMonthlyRent);
      public event SearchToRentHandler OnSearchToRent;
      void FireSearchToRent(string theState, string theCity, float theMonthlyRent)
      {
        if (OnSearchToRent == null) return;
        OnSearchToRent(theState, theCity, theMonthlyRent);
      }

      public delegate void SearchToBuyHandler(string theState,
                                  string theCity,
                                  float thePrice);
      public event SearchToBuyHandler OnSearchToBuy;
      void FireSearchToBuy(string theState, string theCity, float thePrice)
      {
        if (OnSearchToBuy == null) return;
        OnSearchToBuy(theState, theCity, thePrice);
      }
  }

// PropertyFound.cs

using System;
using System.Collections;
using System.Windows.Forms;
using System.Globalization;

namespace UserInterfaceExample
{
  public class PropertyFound
  {
    public float Cost;
    public float Size;
    public string Description;

    public PropertyFound(float theCost, float theSize, string theDescription)
    {
      Cost = theCost;
      Size = theSize;
      Description = theDescription;
    }
  }

  // used in the Properties Found ListView to sort by column
  class PropertyComparer : IComparer
  {
    private int column;

    public PropertyComparer(int theColumn)
    {
      column = theColumn;
    }
```

```
  public int Compare(object x, object y)
  {
    string s1 = ((ListViewItem) x).SubItems[column].Text;
    string s2 = ((ListViewItem) y).SubItems[column].Text;

    if (column == 2)
      // column 2 has strings
      return string.Compare(s1, s2);
    else
    {
      // columns 0 and 1 have floats
      NumberStyles currencyStyle =
        NumberStyles.AllowCurrencySymbol |
        NumberStyles.AllowThousands |
        NumberStyles.AllowDecimalPoint;
      float a = float.Parse(s1, currencyStyle);
      float b = float.Parse(s2, currencyStyle);
      return a.CompareTo(b);
    }
  }
 }
}
}
```

Listing 10-2. *The VB .NET Implementation of the UI Example*

```
'Coordinator.vb

Imports System.Threading

Public Class Coordinator
  Private worker As FormWorker

  Public Sub ShowDialog()
    If worker Is Nothing Then
      worker = New FormWorker
      AddHandler worker.OnStateChanged, AddressOf worker_OnStateChanged
      AddHandler worker.OnSearchToBuy, AddressOf worker_OnSearchToBuy
      AddHandler worker.OnSearchToRent, AddressOf worker_OnSearchToRent
      worker.States = New String() {"California", "Texas", "New York"}
      worker.DateOfLastUpdate = DateTime.Now
    End If
    worker.ShowDialog()
  End Sub

  Private Sub worker_OnStateChanged(ByVal theState As String)
    worker.Cursor = Cursors.WaitCursor

    Select Case theState
      Case "California"
        worker.Cities = New String() {"Los Angeles", "San Francisco"}
      Case "Texas"
        worker.Cities = New String() {"Dallas", "Austin"}
      Case "New York"
        worker.Cities = New String() {"New York City", "Albany"}
```

```vb
        Case Else
          worker.Cities = Nothing
      End Select

      Thread.Sleep(500)  '  simulate a lengthy operation
      worker.Cursor = Cursors.Default
    End Sub

    Private Sub worker_OnSearchToBuy(ByVal theState As String, _
                      ByVal theCity As String, _
                      ByVal theMonthlyRent As Single)
      worker.Cursor = Cursors.WaitCursor

      Dim properties() As PropertyFound = New PropertyFound() { _
          New PropertyFound(600000, 2200, "3 bedrooms, 4 bathrooms"), _
          New PropertyFound(850000, 2100, "3 bedrooms, 3 bathrooms"), _
          New PropertyFound(1000000, 3300, "4 bedrooms, 4 bathrooms"), _
          New PropertyFound(1200000, 4000, "5 bedrooms, 5 bathrooms") _
        }
      worker.PropertiesFound = properties

      Thread.Sleep(500)  '  simulate a lengthy operation
      worker.Cursor = Cursors.Default
    End Sub

    Private Sub worker_OnSearchToRent(ByVal theState As String, _
                      ByVal theCity As String, _
                      ByVal theMonthlyRent As Single)
      worker.Cursor = Cursors.WaitCursor

      Dim properties() As PropertyFound = New PropertyFound() { _
          New PropertyFound(950, 900, "3 bedrooms, 3 bathrooms"), _
          New PropertyFound(1200, 1200, "3 bedrooms, 2 bathrooms"), _
          New PropertyFound(1400, 1100, "3 bedrooms, 3 bathrooms"), _
          New PropertyFound(1750, 1800, "4 bedrooms, 3 bathrooms") _
        }
      worker.PropertiesFound = properties

      Thread.Sleep(500)  '  simulate a lengthy operation
      worker.Cursor = Cursors.Default
    End Sub

End Class


'FormWorker.vb

Public Class FormWorker
    Inherits System.Windows.Forms.Form

#Region " Windows Form Designer generated code "

    Public Sub New()
        MyBase.New()
```

```vbnet
        'This call is required by the Windows Form Designer.
        InitializeComponent()

        RadioButtonRent.Checked = True
    End Sub


    'declare all controls
    Friend WithEvents RadioButtonBuy As RadioButton
    Friend WithEvents RadioButtonRent As RadioButton
    ' ...

    #region "Windows Form Designer generated code"
        ' ...
    #end region

Public WriteOnly Property States() As String()
  Set(ByVal Value As String() )
    ComboBoxState.Items.Clear()
    ComboBoxState.Items.AddRange(Value)
    ComboBoxState.SelectedIndex = 0
  End Set
End Property

Public WriteOnly Property Cities() As String()
  Set(ByVal Value As String() )
    comboBoxCity.Items.Clear()
    If value Is Nothing Then Return
    comboBoxCity.Items.AddRange(value)
    comboBoxCity.SelectedIndex = 0
  End Set
End Property

Public WriteOnly Property DateOfLastUpdate() As DateTime
  Set(ByVal Value As DateTime)
    ' date only, e.g. "2006-12-19"
    LabelDate.Text = Value.Date.ToString("d")
  End Set
End Property

Public WriteOnly Property PropertiesFound() As PropertyFound()
  Set(ByVal Value As PropertyFound() )
    ListViewPropertiesFound.Items.Clear()
    If Value Is Nothing Then Return

    For Each p As PropertyFound In Value
      ' display cost as a currency
      Dim item As New ListViewItem(p.Cost.ToString("C") )
      item.SubItems.Add(p.Size.ToString() )
      item.SubItems.Add(p.Description)
      ListViewPropertiesFound.Items.Add(item)
    Next
  End Set
End Property
```

```vbnet
Private Sub ComboBoxState_SelectedValueChanged(ByVal sender As Object, _
            ByVal e As System.EventArgs) _
            Handles ComboBoxState.SelectedValueChanged
  If ComboBoxState.SelectedIndex >= 0 Then
    FireStateChanged(ComboBoxState.Text)
  End If
End Sub

Private Sub RadioButtonRent_CheckedChanged(ByVal sender As System.Object, _
            ByVal e As System.EventArgs) Handles RadioButtonRent.CheckedChanged
  PanelRent.Visible = RadioButtonRent.Checked
  PanelBuy.Visible = Not RadioButtonRent.Checked
End Sub

Private Sub RadioButtonBuy_CheckedChanged(ByVal sender As System.Object, _
            ByVal e As System.EventArgs) _
            Handles RadioButtonBuy.CheckedChanged
  PanelRent.Visible = Not RadioButtonBuy.Checked
  PanelBuy.Visible = RadioButtonBuy.Checked
End Sub

Private Sub ButtonSearch_Click(ByVal sender As System.Object, _
            ByVal e As System.EventArgs) _
            Handles ButtonSearch.Click
  If (RadioButtonRent.Checked) Then
    FireSearchToRent(ComboBoxState.Text, ComboBoxCity.Text, _
                              CType(NumericUpDownMontlyRent.Value, Single))
  Else
    FireSearchToBuy(ComboBoxState.Text, ComboBoxCity.Text, _
                              CType(NumericUpDownPrice.Value, Single))
  End If
End Sub

Private Sub ListViewPropertiesFound_ColumnClick(ByVal sender As Object, _
            ByVal e As System.Windows.Forms.ColumnClickEventArgs) _
            Handles ListViewPropertiesFound.ColumnClick
  ' set sorter and resort listview
  ListViewPropertiesFound.ListViewItemSorter = New PropertyComparer(e.Column)
End Sub

Public Event OnStateChanged(ByVal theState As String)
Sub FireStateChanged(ByVal theState As String)
  RaiseEvent OnStateChanged(theState)
End Sub

Public Event OnSearchToRent(ByVal theState As String, ByVal theCity As String, _
                        ByVal theMonthlyRent As Single)
Sub FireSearchToRent(ByVal theState As String, ByVal theCity As String, _
                    ByVal theMonthlyRent As Single)
  RaiseEvent OnSearchToRent(theState, theCity, theMonthlyRent)
End Sub

Public Event OnSearchToBuy(ByVal theState As String, ByVal theCity As String, _
                        ByVal theMonthlyRent As Single)
```

```vb
    Sub FireSearchToBuy(ByVal theState As String, ByVal theCity As String, _
                    ByVal theMonthlyRent As Single)
      RaiseEvent OnSearchToBuy(theState, theCity, theMonthlyRent)
    End Sub

End Class

' PropertyFound.vb

Imports System.Globalization

Public Class PropertyFound
  Public Cost As Single
  Public Size As Single
  Public Description As String

  Public Sub New(ByVal theCost As Single, ByVal theSize As Single, _
              ByVal theDescription As String)
    Cost = theCost
    Size = theSize
    Description = theDescription
  End Sub
End Class

' used in the Properties Found ListView to sort by column
Class PropertyComparer
  Implements IComparer

  Private column As Integer

  Public Sub New(ByVal theColumn As Integer)
    column = theColumn
  End Sub

  Public Function Compare(ByVal x As Object, ByVal y As Object) As Integer _
            Implements IComparer.Compare

    Dim s1 As String = CType(x, ListViewItem).SubItems(column).Text
    Dim s2 As String = CType(y, ListViewItem).SubItems(column).Text

    If (column = 2) Then
      ' column 2 has strings
      Return String.Compare(s1, s2)
    Else
      ' columns 0 and 1 have floats
      Dim currencyStyle As NumberStyles = _
          NumberStyles.AllowCurrencySymbol Or _
          NumberStyles.AllowThousands Or _
          NumberStyles.AllowDecimalPoint
      Dim a As Single = Single.Parse(s1, currencyStyle)
      Dim b As Single = Single.Parse(s2, currencyStyle)
      Return a.CompareTo(b)
    End If
  End Function
End Class
```

To keep the example simple, I didn't make use of a separate Binder object to wire the Coordinator and Worker together. The Coordinator instantiates the Worker and does the wiring itself, so the Coordinator is type-coupled to the Worker. The coupling poses no special problems in this example. The Worker communicates with the Coordinator exclusively via untyped object call notifications, so the Worker is in no way coupled to the Coordinator. Therefore, you can develop and test the Worker separately from the Coordinator.

Data-Bound User Interfaces

Many UIs contain *data-bound* controls, which are controls tied to a database result set. Data-bound controls display values contained in the result set. There are two basic kinds of data-bound controls: simple and complex. The former show only one field of the currently selected row in the result set. The latter show multiple fields from multiple rows of the result set. How should you split the workload between the Coordinator and the Worker when dealing with data-bound controls? The basic guidelines are the same as before, but can rephrased like this:

- Coordinators are responsible for retrieving data.

- Workers are responsible for presenting data to the user.

The guideline doesn't imply that coordinators always retrieve data directly by themselves. In many cases, coordinators need to fire events to other coordinators to get the data they need, sometimes putting in motion a whole slew of activity. Once the coordinators have the requested information, they give it to the Worker. In the case of data-bound controls, the information is in the form of a result set.

User interfaces often provide a way for users to change the *current row* in the result set. All those UI controls that are bound to the given result set should be able to update their displayed values without calling into action a coordinator. Sometimes, changing the current row of a result set requires the retrieval of other data. For example, if the result set is the master in a master-detail relationship, changing the master row selected requires new child rows to be retrieved. In such cases, you should use a coordinator directly or indirectly to fetch the new child rows.

Concurrent Workers

In many situations, a worker may need to handle requests asynchronously, perhaps to service different clients or to do multiple things at once. Rather than using a single-worker design, it is advantageous to break the system into multiple parts, as shown back in Figure 10-2. The top-level Worker handles the incoming requests, dispatching them to subordinate workers that run on separate threads. The task of managing threading issues is assigned to a coordinator, so that the workers can concentrate just on getting their job done without worrying about timing problems.

As an example, assume you have a requirement to build a service that handles concurrent requests from client applications. All the clients interact with the same service, which exposes a single ProcessRequest method. The service must be able to handle any number of requests simultaneously. You can design the system using three classes, as shown in Figure 10-8.

The class named WorkerRequestDispatcher handles incoming client requests. When a request arrives, the dispatcher calls Coordinator.Run, which creates a WorkerRequestHandler and runs it on a separate thread, as shown in Figure 10-9.

The design entails an asynchronous blind interaction between the top-level Worker (WorkerRequestDispatcher) and the Coordinator. The interaction is blind because the top-level Worker doesn't receive completion feedback from the subordinates. To add feedback, the simplest solution is to have the WorkerRequestHandler fire a completion event that is wired back to WorkerRequestDispatcher.

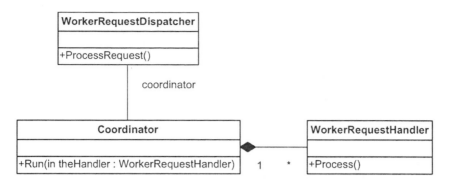

Figure 10-8. *The class diagram for a concurrent Worker system*

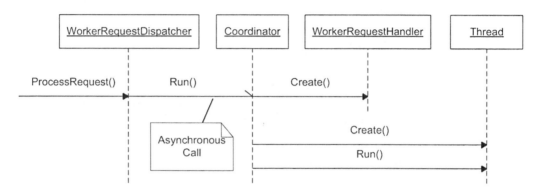

Figure 10-9. *How the top-level Worker uses the Coordinator to run subordinate workers concurrently*

While there is nothing inherently wrong with this approach, it is important to point out that the event handler in the top-level Worker would execute on the subordinate Worker's thread. This will cause problems if the top-level Worker is not thread-safe—a situation that is more common than one might expect. In many software systems that have a UI, a significant part of the code is often executed on the UI thread. If the dispatcher is running on the UI thread and, in response to a subordinate notification, tries to update the UI when the Worker completion event fires, problems might occur. Why? Because GUI operating systems typically expect the UI to be updated only by code running on the UI thread. Updates performed from other threads might cause strange behaviors or race conditions.

What this all means is that you shouldn't have subordinate workers fire events to the dispatcher on their own background threads. Any notifications reaching the dispatcher must be running on the UI thread, which the dispatcher is running on. Since none of the workers should have any thread-related code in them, you must use a separate object for the thread-switching management during notification delivery. The design shown back in Figure 10-9 uses a Coordinator to create threads to run the subordinate workers on. It is reasonable to also use the Coordinator to handle the thread-switching logic for the completion notifications. The Coordinator acts as a mediator between the subordinate workers and the top-level one. Synchronization with the UI thread is an OS-dependent operation. In the .NET Framework, it is accomplished by the method Control.Invoke. Class Control is a base class for all UI controls. The method accepts two arguments: a reference to a method and an array of objects. Control.Invoke calls the referenced method on the UI thread, passing the method the array of objects as parameters. The diagram in Figure 10-10 shows the event notification sequence.

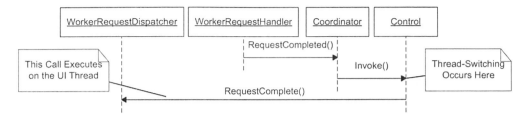

Figure 10-10. *Using a Coordinator to switch subordinate Worker completion feedback notifications to the UI thread*

The Control class shown in the diagram can be any UI control in the system, because all UI elements for a given program are run on the same UI thread. What Control.Invoke does internally is to inject a call to the referenced method into the message queue of the application. Control.Invoke blocks until the referenced method returns.

Listing 10-3 and Listing 10-4 show C# and VB .NET implementations of the dispatcher class.

Listing 10-3. *A C# Implementation of the Top-Level Dispatcher Worker*

```
using System;
using System.Windows.Forms;

namespace ConcurrentWorkers
{
  public class WorkerRequestDispatcher
  {
    Coordinator coordinator;

    public WorkerRequestDispatcher(Control theUiControl)
    {
      coordinator = new Coordinator(theUiControl);
      coordinator.OnRequestCompleted +=
            new Coordinator.RequestCompletedHandler(RequestCompletedHandler);
    }

    public void ProcessRequest()
    {
      coordinator.Run();
    }

    public void Stop()
    {
      coordinator.Stop();
    }

    private void RequestCompletedHandler()
    {
      FireRequestCompleted();
    }
```

```csharp
    public delegate void EventRequestCompleted();
    public event EventRequestCompleted OnRequestCompleted;
    public void FireRequestCompleted()
    {
      if (OnRequestCompleted == null) return;
      OnRequestCompleted();
    }
  }
}
```

Listing 10-4. *A VB .NET Implementation of the Top-Level Dispatcher Worker*

```vbnet
Public Class WorkerRequestDispatcher
  Private _coordinator As Coordinator

  Public Sub New(ByVal theUiControl As Control)
    _coordinator = New Coordinator(theUiControl)

    'we can't use AddHandler here, because
    'OnRequestCompleted is a Delegate, not an Event
    _coordinator.OnRequestCompleted = AddressOf RequestCompletedHandler
  End Sub

  Public Sub ProcessRequest()
    _coordinator.Run()
  End Sub

  Public Sub [Stop]()
    _coordinator.Stop()
  End Sub

  Private Sub RequestCompletedHandler()
    FireRequestCompleted()
  End Sub

  Public Event OnRequestCompleted()
  Public Sub FireRequestCompleted()
    RaiseEvent OnRequestCompleted()
  End Sub
End Class
```

The constructor of the top-level Worker expects a Control object as a parameter. This is the object that will be used later in the Coordinator to switch to the UI thread, when firing subordinate feedback completion events to the dispatcher. Listing 10-5 and Listing 10-6 show C# and VB .NET implementations of the subordinate Worker class.

Listing 10-5. *A C# Implementation of the Subordinate Worker*

```csharp
using System;
using System.Threading;

namespace ConcurrentWorkers
{
  public class WorkerRequestHandler
  {
```

```csharp
    // used to generate a variable execution time
    static Random random = new Random();

    public void Process()
    {
      DoProcess();
      FireRequestCompleted();
    }

    void DoProcess()
    {
      // determine a random execution time (< 5 seconds)
      int delay = random.Next(50);
      if (delay < 1)
        delay = 1;

      // pretend we're doing something...
      while (delay > 0)
      {
        Thread.Sleep(100);
        delay--;
      }
    }

    public delegate void EventRequestCompleted(WorkerRequestHandler theHandler);
    public event EventRequestCompleted OnRequestCompleted;
    public void FireRequestCompleted()
    {
      if (OnRequestCompleted == null) return;
      OnRequestCompleted(this);
    }
  }
}
```

Listing 10-6. *A VB .NET Implementation of the Subordinate Worker*

```vbnet
Imports System.Threading

Public Class WorkerRequestHandler
  ' used to generate a variable execution time
  Shared _random As New Random

  Public Sub Process()
    DoProcess()
    FireRequestCompleted()
  End Sub

  Private Sub DoProcess()
    ' determine a random execution time (< 5 seconds)
    Dim delay As Integer = _random.Next(50)
    If delay < 1 Then
      delay = 1
    End If
```

```
    ' pretend we're doing something...
    While (delay > 0)
      Thread.Sleep(100)
      delay -= 1
    End While
  End Sub

  Public Event OnRequestCompleted(ByVal theHandler As WorkerRequestHandler)
  Public Sub FireRequestCompleted()
    RaiseEvent OnRequestCompleted(Me)
  End Sub
End Class
```

The method DoProcess is where the subordinate would accomplish the bulk of its processing. The example just sleeps for a random amount of time. When the subordinate finishes processing a request, it fires a RequestCompleted event to the Coordinator. Listing 10-7 and Listing 10-8 show C# and VB .NET implementations of the Coordinator.

Listing 10-7. *A C# Implementation of the Coordinator*

```csharp
using System;
using System.Collections;
using System.Windows.Forms;
using System.Threading;

namespace ConcurrentWorkers
{
  public class Coordinator
  {
    Control uiControl;

    // key is WorkerRequestHandler, value is Thread
    Hashtable threads = new Hashtable();

    public Coordinator(Control theUiControl)
    {
      uiControl = theUiControl;
    }

    public void Run()
    {
      lock(this)
      {
        WorkerRequestHandler handler = new WorkerRequestHandler();
        Thread thread = new Thread(new ThreadStart(handler.Process));
        handler.OnRequestCompleted +=
            new WorkerRequestHandler.EventRequestCompleted(HandlerCompleted);
        threads.Add(handler, thread);
        thread.Start();
      }
    }
```

```csharp
    public void Stop()
    {
      lock(this)
      {
        foreach (Thread thread in threads.Values)
          thread.Abort();
        threads.Clear();
      }
    }

    public void HandlerCompleted(WorkerRequestHandler theHandler)
    {
      lock(this)
      {
        threads.Remove(theHandler);
      }
      FireRequestCompleted();
    }

    public delegate void RequestCompletedHandler();
    public event RequestCompletedHandler OnRequestCompleted;
    public void FireRequestCompleted()
    {
      if (OnRequestCompleted == null) return;

      // fire event on the UI thread
      lock(this)
      {
        uiControl.Invoke(OnRequestCompleted);
      }
    }
  }
}
```

Listing 10-8. *A VB .NET Implementation of the Coordinator*

```vbnet
Imports System.Threading

Public Class Coordinator
  Private uiControl As Control

  ' key is WorkerRequestHandler, value is Thread
  Dim threads As New Hashtable

  Public Sub New(ByVal theUiControl As Control)
    uiControl = theUiControl
  End Sub

  Public Sub Run()
    SyncLock (Me)
      Dim handler As New WorkerRequestHandler
      Dim thread As New Thread(AddressOf handler.Process)
      AddHandler handler.OnRequestCompleted, AddressOf HandlerCompleted
      threads.Add(handler, thread)
```

```
      thread.Start()
    End SyncLock
  End Sub

  Public Sub [Stop]()
    SyncLock (Me)
      For Each t As Thread In threads.Values
        t.Abort()
      Next
      threads.Clear()
    End SyncLock
  End Sub

  Public Sub HandlerCompleted(ByVal theHandler As WorkerRequestHandler)
    SyncLock (Me)
      threads.Remove(theHandler)
    End SyncLock
    FireRequestCompleted()
  End Sub

  Public Delegate Sub RequestCompletedHandler()
  Public OnRequestCompleted As RequestCompletedHandler
  Public Sub FireRequestCompleted()
    ' fire event on the UI thread
    SyncLock (Me)
      uiControl.Invoke(OnRequestCompleted)
    End SyncLock
  End Sub
End Class
```

Coordinator is the only class in the system with thread synchronization logic. In this example, there is type coupling between the various classes, as shown in Figure 10-11.

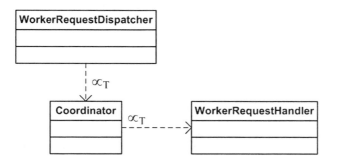

Figure 10-11. *The coupling between the classes in the sample implementation*

All the classes are in the same component, so the coupling wouldn't create any deployment problems. The coupling would, however, prevent you from testing WorkerRequestHandler and Coordinator separately. In the "Binders" section later in this chapter, I'll show you how to use binders to eliminate the type coupling.

Coordinators

The idea behind coordinators is not new in software systems. In the design pattern literature, there are various names for classes that act in ways similar to coordinators: handlers, relayers, mediators, adapters, dispatchers, façades, liaisons, and others. How a coordinator is implemented internally, in terms of classes and design patterns, is not important for the purposes of this chapter. Coordinators have a specific purpose in life: to *coordinate* the actions of one or more workers assigned to them. They do so in two ways: by handling the events fired by workers, and by calling workers to carry out detailed operations as part of a broader task.

What Is a Coordinator?

Coordinators are like managers in a small company department. They handle many of the infrastructure details, such as scheduling, resource allocation, and resource coordination. By having coordinators assume these tasks, workers can focus better on the business logic they must implement. The coordination task itself might be considered a sort of business rule or metarule.

In a distributed system, coordinators fulfill tasks similar to Dispatching Servers (DSs) in JEDI,[5] but they also contain coordination logic specific to the workers they manage, and are therefore application-specific. There is a difference in scope between coordinators and JEDI DSs. The latter are designed to control the events over a node in a distributed system. Coordinators are used to control a narrow group of workers, which may or may not be in the same address space as the coordinator.

The purpose of a coordinator is to reduce the complexity of workers by offloading tasks that are not strictly part of the workers' main mission. A coordinator controls one or more workers assigned to it. It does so by interacting with the workers, using events or direct method calls. Figure 10-12 shows two typical coordinator usages.

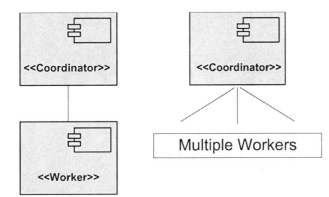

Figure 10-12. *Coordinators can control one or more workers.*

The lines connecting the coordinators and workers aren't meant to imply a relationship or an association, in the UML sense. The fact that a coordinator can be assigned to handle just one worker is significant for reasons that may not be immediately obvious. After all, if the outside system needs to interact with a single worker, why introduce a middleman? Besides being useful for managing

---

5. Gianpaolo Cugola, Elisabetta Di Nitto, and Alfonso Fuggetta, "The JEDI Event-Based Infrastructure and Its Application to the Development of the OPSS WFMS," *IEEE Transactions of Software Engineering*, September 2001.

threading details, as seen in the previous sections, an additional reason is that a worker may expose a set of low-level operations that are only useful to the system when combined together. The Coordinator could then be given the responsibility of invoking the low-level operations at the right time and in the right order to achieve the desired result. The outside system would then be able to call a high-level method in the Coordinator, without needing to deal with all the low-level details related to the underlying Worker.

Coordinators are often used to control multiple workers. Under the Coordinator's supervision, the workers can collaborate to carry out a nontrivial task. The Coordinator handles all thread-related logic, necessary in those cases in which the managed workers need to be run concurrently. The workers are implemented using synchronous methods, making them easy to test individually. It is the Coordinator that puts the ensemble together, like an orchestra conductor, making the magic happen.

Coordinator Teams

When using coordinators as front ends or façades for groups of workers, you might view each coordinator-worker group as a functional *team* of the system, much like a project team in a business. Each Coordinator is responsible for its own workers, and each team implements a nontrivial subset of the system's requirements. You then might view the complete system as a collection of teams, each headed by a Coordinator, as shown in Figure 10-13.

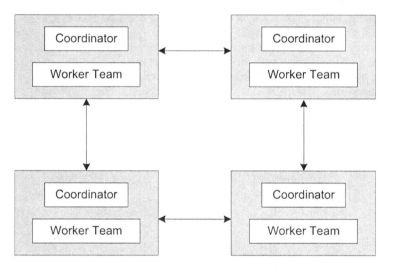

Figure 10-13. *Envisioning a system as a network of Coordinator teams*

In Figure 10-13, the dotted gray boxes are team boundaries, not packaging boundaries. Coordinators are typically deployed in the same component as their subordinate workers. The arrows between the teams represent event-notification traffic. The workers in one team are allowed to talk only to co-workers in the same team or to the local Coordinator. Workers communicate solely using event notifications, so workers are not coupled to other team members. Workers can't talk to other teams directly. Only coordinators are allowed to communicate with other teams, and they do so with event notifications. The use of notifications to tie everything together keeps the teams decoupled from each other. A separate Binder object, described later in the chapter, can handle the task of wiring the teams together.

Using the Coordinator-team approach, you can develop and test each team separately, using a dedicated test fixture that emulates the features of the other teams. You can take the team approach further, building super-teams out of simple teams. Using the business metaphor, a super-team would be roughly equivalent to a division in a large company. Each super-team would again be testable using a dedicated test fixture. You can design some software systems as a hierarchy of teams, in which the highest-level team includes all the teams in the system.

Key Coordination Tasks

Coordinating software workers is, in some ways, a problem similar to coordinating people. Everyone is different from everyone else in this world, so how you manage subordinate employees depends on several factors, including their expertise, their willingness to cooperate with others, their communication skills, their ability to work independently, and so on. Software coordinators face similar management issues, and coordinators typically handle tasks that fall into the following categories:

- Managing threading issues
- Managing a Worker team
- Mediating communication between workers
- Mediating communication between Coordinator teams
- Managing state across a group of workers

I've already provided some description on the first two categories in the Worker examples shown previously, but I'll reiterate and deepen the discussion a bit in the following sections.

Managing Threading Issues

When workers are required to execute operations concurrently, the threading logic can introduce a substantial amount of complexity. In many cases, you can remove the threading code from the Worker and migrate it into a coordinator. By doing so, you can implement all the worker methods as synchronous, making it much easier to design and test the Worker. A coordinator that controls worker threading can also synchronize workers together, when necessary for specific operations. Each worker can then focus on its own mission, without regard to how and when its results will be used with results of other workers in the same team.

Coordinators generally use two types of asynchronous interactions with their subordinates: blind and transparent. In both cases, the workers involved are oblivious to threading issues. In both cases, the Coordinator creates a thread for each worker to run on. In a blind interaction, no further action is required, since workers provide no feedback. In transparent interactions, workers do provide feedback. Notifications delivered using method calls are received on worker threads. While handling these notifications, the Coordinator might need to fire events to other parts of the system or to other workers in the same team. The Coordinator often needs logic to synchronize with other threads before sending notifications. The most common case is the requirement to synchronize with the UI thread. Figure 10-10, back in the example on concurrent workers, showed a way to accomplish this.

Synchronizing concurrent workers is another fairly common requirement. Assume a coordinator needs to manage two workers as a team. Figure 10-14 shows the class diagram of the system.

A BuilderBinder class is used to instantiate the classes and bind them together. The Coordinator and workers interact solely through event notifications, delivered as untyped object calls. As a result, the Coordinator and Worker classes are completely decoupled from each other, and can therefore be developed, tested, and deployed independently.

Let's assume the team exposes a single DoSomething method at the Coordinator level. To implement this method, the Coordinator must run Worker1.Method1 and Worker2.Method1 concurrently. Once both methods complete, Worker2.Method2 must run synchronously. The diagram in Figure 10-15 shows the interactions.

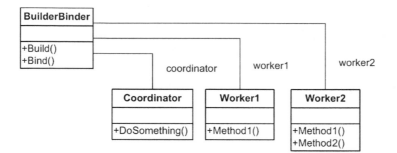

Figure 10-14. *A coordinator that synchronizes two workers*

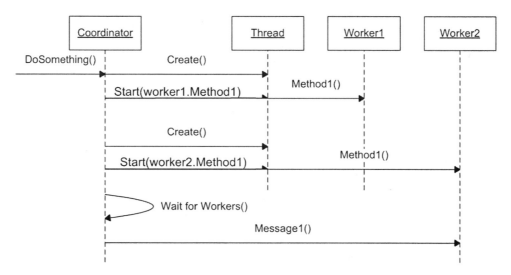

Figure 10-15. *Using a coordinator to run workers concurrently*

The Coordinator manages the workers using event notifications, so the Coordinator class is not coupled to the Worker classes in any way. At run time, the Binder gives the Coordinator references to the Worker methods that need to be run. The Coordinator then calls these methods directly or indirectly, with a Thread.Start call. The Coordinator doesn't know what objects or methods are being invoked. Listing 10-9 and Listing 10-10 show C# and VB .NET implementations of the complete system.

Listing 10-9. *A C# Implementation of the Coordinator Team*

```csharp
public class BuilderBinder
{
  public Coordinator coordinator;
  public Worker1 worker1;
  public Worker2 worker2;

  public void Build()
  {
    coordinator = new Coordinator();
    worker1 = new Worker1();
    worker2 = new Worker2();
  }
```

```csharp
  public void Bind()
  {
    coordinator.OnWorker1Method1 =
                    new Coordinator.Method1Handler(worker1.Method1);
    coordinator.OnWorker2Method1 =
                    new Coordinator.Method1Handler(worker2.Method1);
    coordinator.OnWorker2Method2 +=
                    new Coordinator.Method2Handler(worker2.Method2);
  }
}

public class Coordinator
{
  Thread threadWorker1, threadWorker2;

  public void DoSomething()
  {
    threadWorker1 = new Thread(new ThreadStart(OnWorker1Method1) );
    threadWorker2 = new Thread(new ThreadStart(OnWorker2Method1) );

    threadWorker1.Start();
    threadWorker2.Start();

    threadWorker1.Join();
    threadWorker2.Join();

    FireWorker2Method2();
  }

  public delegate void Method1Handler();
  public Method1Handler OnWorker1Method1;
  public Method1Handler OnWorker2Method1;

  public delegate void Method2Handler();
  public event Method2Handler OnWorker2Method2;
  void FireWorker2Method2()
  {
    if (OnWorker2Method2 != null)
      OnWorker2Method2();
  }
}

public class Worker1
{
  public void Method1() {/*...*/}
}

public class Worker2
{
  public void Method1() {/*...*/}
  public void Method2() {/*...*/}
}
```

Listing 10-10. *A VB .NET Implementation of the Coordinator Team*

```vb
Public Class BuilderBinder
  Public _coordinator As Coordinator
  Public _worker1 As Worker1
  Public _worker2 As Worker2

  Public Sub Build()
    _coordinator = New Coordinator
    _worker1 = New Worker1
    _worker2 = New Worker2
  End Sub

  Public Sub Bind()
    _coordinator.OnWorker1Method1 = AddressOf _worker1.Method1
    _coordinator.OnWorker2Method1 = AddressOf _worker2.Method1
    AddHandler _coordinator.OnWorker2Method2, AddressOf _worker2.Method2
  End Sub
End Class

Public Class Coordinator
  Private threadWorker1, threadWorker2 As Thread

  Public Sub DoSomething()
    threadWorker1 = New Thread(OnWorker1Method1)
    threadWorker2 = New Thread(OnWorker2Method1)

    threadWorker1.Start()
    threadWorker2.Start()

    threadWorker1.Join()
    threadWorker2.Join()

    FireWorker2Method2()
  End Sub

  Public OnWorker1Method1 As ThreadStart
  Public OnWorker2Method1 As ThreadStart

  Public Event OnWorker2Method2()
  Sub FireWorker2Method2()
    RaiseEvent OnWorker2Method2()
  End Sub
End Class

Public Class Worker1
  Public Sub Method1()
    '...
  End Sub
End Class
```

```
Public Class Worker2
  Public Sub Method1()
    '...
  End Sub

  Public Sub Method2()
    '...
  End Sub
End Class
```

By relegating all the worker-synchronization logic in the Coordinator, the workers are simple, with a very high degree of coherence. The design introduces no coupling between the Coordinator and Worker classes. At run time, there is signature coupling between the Coordinator instance and the two Worker instances. You could use the Coordinator, without changes, to control entirely different kinds of workers. Figure 10-16 shows the coupling diagram of the system.

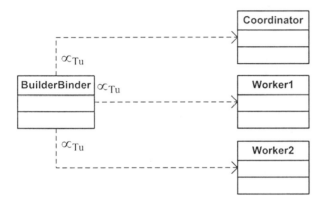

Figure 10-16. *The coupling diagram of the system*

Leveraging Multiple Workers to Achieve an Objective

Using a coordinator to manage the various workers makes it possible to achieve a collaborative effort by workers without the individual workers knowing anything about each other. Splitting a task into subtasks, handled by different workers, is often an effective design strategy, because each worker is simpler and easier to develop and test.

When a Coordinator uses multiple workers as a team, a high-level command to the Coordinator generally results in a series of lower-level commands to the workers, as shown in Figure 10-17.

Any number of workers can make up a team. The Coordinator is responsible for calling the right Worker method at the right time. The Coordinator also has full control over which thread a Worker call is made on.

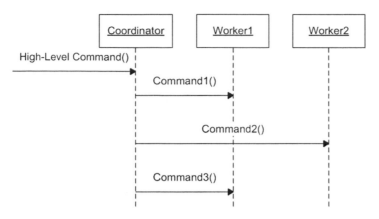

Figure 10-17. *Workers collaborating to support a complex task*

Mediating Communication Between Workers

When workers collaborate to achieve an objective, some workers may need to fire events to other workers directly. For example, assume a system has two workers, A and B, and that A needs a service provided by B. A problem arises when B provides the service not as a single operation, but rather with a series of smaller-grained operations M1, M2, and M3. To achieve the desired result, A would have to call those three methods, and in a specific order. Assuming Worker A uses a signal N1 to request B's service, you have a problem: You can't bind N1 to B directly, because B doesn't expose a single method that provides the entire service needed, as shown in Figure 10-18.

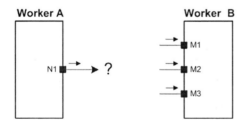

Figure 10-18. *Incompatible workers*

Your first inclination might be to modify A to fire three separate events, which you could then route to the individual methods of B. The problem here is that you're changing one worker to adapt to the structure of another. If later you change B, it might be necessary to change A as well. You should *try* to design workers to perform a specific task or set of business rules, without worrying about how the rest of the system is structured. The idea is that workers are the experts in a certain area of the business logic.

One approach in solving the Worker interaction problem could use event multicasting. If N1 supports multicasting, you could wire N1 to the three separate B methods: M1, M2, and M3. Although interesting, this approach has its drawbacks. First, you're relying on N1 being a multicast signal. Not all components or signals provide support for multicasting. Moreover, notifications that expect a result (such as the outcome of the service provided by B) generally don't use multicasting, because it could be difficult to reconcile multiple results. Another problem is that, in order to fulfill A's request, B must execute three methods in a very specific order. Not all languages or component models support built-in multicasting that guarantees the order of notification delivery. A solution that works with all languages, without relying on multicasting, uses a coordinator as a mediator, as shown in Figure 10-19.

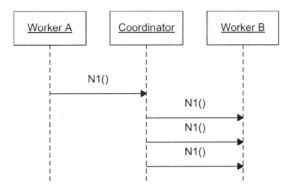

Figure 10-19. *Using a coordinator as a mediator between workers*

Worker A sends the single notification N1 to the Coordinator, which assumes the responsibility of making three separate requests to Worker B. The presence of the Coordinator not only simplifies Worker A, but also protects Worker A from changes to Worker B. For example, if later the method M1 were broken into two smaller methods M1A and M1B, the Coordinator would need to be changed, but not Worker A. Is changing a coordinator better than changing a worker? Possibly, because coordinators are usually simpler than workers, making it easier to identify the code to change and reducing the probability of inadvertently changing business logic, which is mostly contained in workers.

Managing State Across a Group of Workers

Many systems are designed as state machines: How the system responds to an event depends on what state the system is in. When a system has multiple workers, an important issue is this: Who manages the state? One solution is to use a coordinator, which contains a state machine. The Coordinator might wire the subordinate workers in a state-dependent manner or call the workers in a state-dependent way. The Coordinator might add or remove subordinate workers from its team, based on the system's state. Using a coordinator to manage state allows workers to be oblivious to the state-driven design of the system, so they can better focus on supporting their business functions.

An Example: Managing the Life-Cycle State of an Application

As a concrete example of state management, consider the life cycle of a typical application. When a user runs the application, a number of states are generally involved. These states can be managed by a coordinator that I'll call LifecycleCoordinator. The life-cycle states are the following:

- *Starting up*: The application loads, initializes, and brings up its main user interface.
- *Running*: The application performs its main functions.
- *Shutting down*: The application closes and exits.

Each state has substates. Depending on how complex the substates are, you might decide to implement each major state using a dedicated state coordinator, such as a StartupCoordinator, a RunCoordinator, and a ShutdownCoordinator. The main LifecycleCoordinator would then switch states by instantiating one of the state coordinators.

Example 1: Using a Single LifecycleCoordinator

A single LifecycleCoordinator can manage applications that aren't too complicated. For this first example, I'll assume a system has a simple startup process with no user interface. Once the startup is complete, the user interface is made visible. When the user closes the application, the system switches to the shutdown state, during which user commands are ignored and the user interface is torn down. Figure 10-20 shows the state machine diagram of the system.

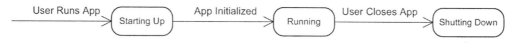

Figure 10-20. *The LifecycleCoordinator state machine diagram*

Figure 10-21 shows the system's class diagram.

LifecycleCoordinator	-builderBinder	BuilderBinder	-formMain	FormMain
+Main() +Run()		+Build() +Bind()		

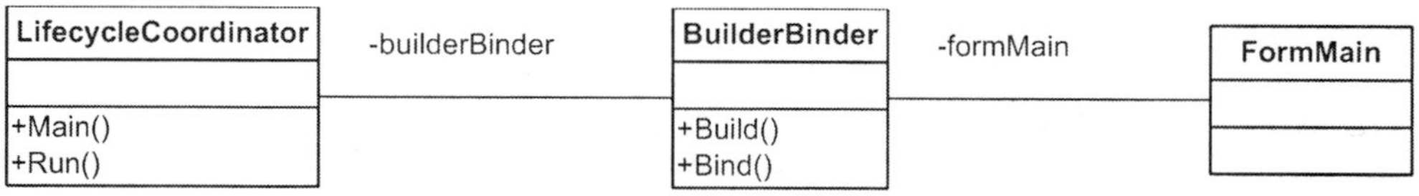

Figure 10-21. *The system's class diagram*

Listing 10-11 and Listing 10-12 show C# and VB .NET implementations. I omitted the code for FormMain, since the class is an arbitrary form with the application's user interface.

Listing 10-11. *A C# Implementation of a Simple LifecycleCoordinator System*

```csharp
public class LifecycleCoordinator
{
    // The main entry point for the application
    [STAThread]
    static void Main()
    {
        LifecycleCoordinator coordinator = new LifecycleCoordinator();
        coordinator.Run(); // the app exits when this call completes
    }

    enum LifecycleState {StartingUp, Running, ShuttingDown};
    LifecycleState state;

    BuilderBinder builderBinder = BuilderBinder.Singleton;

    public void Run()
    {
        state = LifecycleState.StartingUp;

        // build and bind all the top-level objects
        builderBinder.Build();
        builderBinder.Bind();
```

```csharp
      // listen for app closing events
      builderBinder.formMain.Closing += new CancelEventHandler(formMain_Closing);

      // run the system
      state = LifecycleState.Running;
      Application.Run(builderBinder.formMain);
    }

    private void formMain_Closing(object sender,
                                 System.ComponentModel.CancelEventArgs e)
    {
      // user is closing the app's main form
      state = LifecycleState.ShuttingDown;

      // disable the user interface during shutdown
      builderBinder.formMain.Visible = false;
    }

    public void HandleWorkerEvent()
    {
      // ignore worker events unless in the Running state
      if (state == LifecycleState.StartingUp) return;
      if (state == LifecycleState.ShuttingDown) return;

      // handle the event...
    }
}


public class BuilderBinder
{
    static BuilderBinder singleton;
    static public BuilderBinder Singleton
    {
      get
      {
        if (singleton == null)
          singleton = new BuilderBinder();
        return singleton;
      }
    }

    public FormMain formMain;

    // private constructor, to force access through Singleton property
    private BuilderBinder()  { }

    public void Build()
    {
      // create all the top-level objects
      formMain = new FormMain();
    }
```

```csharp
    public void Bind()
    {
      // wire all the top-level objects
    }
}
```

Listing 10-12. *A VB .NET Implementation of a Simple LifecycleCoordinator System*

```vbnet
Public Class LifecycleCoordinator

  ' the application's main entry point
  Shared Sub Main()
    Dim coordinator As New LifecycleCoordinator
    coordinator.Run() ' the app exits when this call completes
  End Sub

  Enum LifecycleState
    StartingUp
    Running
    ShuttingDown
  End Enum

  Private state As LifecycleState
  Private builderBinder As BuilderBinder = BuilderBinder.Singleton

  Public Sub Run()
    state = LifecycleState.StartingUp

    ' build and bind all the top-level objects
    builderBinder.Build()
    builderBinder.Bind()

    ' listen for app closing events
    AddHandler builderBinder._formMain.Closing, AddressOf formMain_Closing

    ' run the system
    state = LifecycleState.Running
    Application.Run(builderBinder._formMain)
  End Sub

  Private Sub formMain_Closing(ByVal sender As Object, _
          ByVal e As System.ComponentModel.CancelEventArgs)
    ' user is closing the app's main form
    state = LifecycleState.ShuttingDown

    ' disable the user interface during shutdown
    builderBinder._formMain.Visible = False
  End Sub

  Public Sub HandleWorkerEvent()
    ' ignore worker events unless in the Running state
    If state = LifecycleState.StartingUp Then Return
    If state = LifecycleState.ShuttingDown Then Return
```

```vb
        ' handle the event...
    End Sub

End Class


Public Class BuilderBinder

    Private Shared _singleton As BuilderBinder
    Public Shared ReadOnly Property Singleton() As BuilderBinder
      Get
        If _singleton Is Nothing Then
          _singleton = New BuilderBinder
        End If
        Return _singleton
      End Get
    End Property

    Public _formMain As FormMain

    ' private constructor, to force access through Singleton property
    Private Sub New()
    End Sub

    Public Sub Build()
      ' create all the top-level objects
      _formMain = New FormMain
    End Sub

    Public Sub Bind()
      ' wire all the top-level objects
    End Sub

End Class
```

The main entry point of the application is the method LifecyleCoordinator.Main. When this method returns, the operating system unloads the application. The Main method just creates an instance of the Coordinator and calls the Run method. The Coordinator uses a BuilderBinder, which is implemented as a singleton class, to create and bind all the system's important parts. More details on builders and binders appear in later sections of this chapter.

The LifecycleCoordinator class doesn't really do much except set the life-cycle state and ensure that the system doesn't attempt to do things that are disallowed in the current state. For example, when the user tries to close the app's main form, the Coordinator hides the form immediately, effectively barring the user from further interactions with the UI. Shutting the application down might take a long time, and you don't want the user to enter any more commands once the shutdown phase has begun.

Example 2: Using a LifecycleCoordinator with Separate State Coordinators

Many applications are substantially more complicated than the one described in the previous section. In the next example, I'll show how a fairly complex application might benefit from the state management of a LifecycleCoordinator. Each life-cycle state is associated with a separate dedicated coordinator. The application displays a splash screen while the main form is loading. The splash screen contains a message area and a progress bar to provide initial feedback to the user about the load process. The splash screen looks like Figure 10-22.

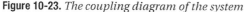

Figure 10-22. *The splash screen used in the example*

The design uses a main LifecycleCoordinator, which in turn uses three separate coordinators to manage the details of the Startup, Running, and Shutdown states. The system's coupling diagram is shown in Figure 10-23.

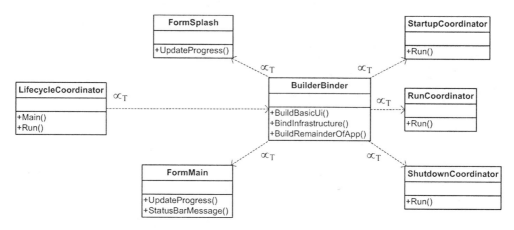

Figure 10-23. *The coupling diagram of the system*

The Startup state has three substates: NoUi, Splash, and NormalUi. When the system first starts, no UI is available, so no user feedback can be given to the user. The splash screen is a very simple form, so its setup time is negligible and the screen appears almost immediately. You use the screen to show feedback during the rest of the initialization phase. A skeletal UI is then loaded, consisting of a plain form with a status bar for text and progress feedback. This form is the main form of the application but may not yet contain all the final UI elements, such as menus, toolbars, and other content. Those elements might be loaded later if they take a long time to set up. As soon as the skeletal UI loads, the splash screen is removed and feedback messages are sent to the new UI. The coordinators for the Running and ShutDown states don't have any substates in this example, to keep the code simple. Listing 10-13 and Listing 10-14 show C# and VB .NET implementations.

Listing 10-13. *A C# Implementation Using Separate Lifecycle State Coordinators*

```
public class LifecycleCoordinator
{
    // The main entry point for the application
    [STAThread]
    static void Main()
```

```
  {
    LifecycleCoordinator coordinator = new LifecycleCoordinator();
    coordinator.Start(); // app exits when this call completes
  }

  enum LifecycleState {StartingUp, Running, ShuttingDown};
  LifecycleState state;

  // shortcut property
  BuilderBinder BuilderBinder
  {
    get {return BuilderBinder.Singleton;}
  }

  public void Start()
  {
    StartupSystem();
    RunSystem(); // app exits when this call completes
  }

  void StartupSystem()
  {
    state = LifecycleState.StartingUp;
    BuilderBinder.startup.Run();
  }

  void RunSystem()
  {
    state = LifecycleState.Running;
    BuilderBinder.running.OnExiting +=
        new RunCoordinator.ExitingHandler(ShutDownSystem);
    BuilderBinder.running.Run(); // app exits when this call completes
  }

  void ShutDownSystem()
  {
    state = LifecycleState.ShuttingDown;
    BuilderBinder.shutdown.Run();
  }

  public void HandleWorkerEvent()
  {
    // ignore worker events unless in the Running state
    if (state == LifecycleState.StartingUp) return;
    if (state == LifecycleState.ShuttingDown) return;

    // handle the event...
  }
}
```

```csharp
public class BuilderBinder
{
    static BuilderBinder singleton;
    static public BuilderBinder Singleton
    {
      get
      {
        if (singleton == null)
          singleton = new BuilderBinder();
        return singleton;
      }
    }

    public FormSplash formSplash = new FormSplash();

    // lifecycle state coordinators
    public StartupCoordinator startup = new StartupCoordinator();
    public RunCoordinator running = new RunCoordinator();
    public ShutdownCoordinator shutdown = new ShutdownCoordinator();

    // the app's main form
    public FormMain formMain;

    // private constructor, to force access through Singleton property
    private BuilderBinder()  { }

    public void BuildBasicUi()
    {
      // create all the top-level objects
      formMain = new FormMain();
    }

    public void BuildInfrastructure()
    {
      int progress = 20;
      for (int i = 0; i < 5; i++)
      {  // simulate a lengthy load process...
        System.Threading.Thread.Sleep(1000);

        // provide completion feedback
        FireProgressChangedHandler(progress);
        progress+= 20;
      }
    }

    public void BuildRemainderOfApp()
    {
      for (int i = 1; i <= 10; i++)
      {
        // simulate a lengthy operation
        System.Threading.Thread.Sleep(500);
```

```csharp
        // provide progress feedback
        FireProgressChangedHandler(i * 10);
        string message = string.Format("Loading component {0}", i);
        FireProgressChangedHandler(message);
      }
    }

    public void BindInfrastructure()
    {
      // wire all the infrastructure objects
    }

    public void BindUi()
    {
      // wire all the top-level objects
    }

    public delegate void ProgressChangedHandler(int theValue);
    public event ProgressChangedHandler OnProgressChanged;
    void FireProgressChangedHandler(int theValue)
    {
      if (OnProgressChanged == null) return;
      OnProgressChanged(theValue);
    }

    public delegate void ProgressChangedTextHandler(string theText);
    public event ProgressChangedTextHandler OnProgressTextChanged;
    void FireProgressChangedHandler(string theText)
    {
      if (OnProgressTextChanged == null) return;
      OnProgressTextChanged(theText);
    }
}


public class StartupCoordinator
{
    enum StartupState {NoUi, Splash, NormalUi};
    StartupState state;

    // shortcut property
    BuilderBinder BuilderBinder
    {
      get {return BuilderBinder.Singleton;}
    }

    // shortcut property
    FormSplash FormSplash
    {
      get {return BuilderBinder.Singleton.formSplash;}
    }
```

```csharp
// shortcut property
FormMain FormMain
{
  get {return BuilderBinder.Singleton.formMain;}
}

public StartupCoordinator()
{
  state = StartupState.NoUi;
}

public void Run()
{
  FormSplash.Show();
  FormSplash.Update(); // otherwise it appears one piece at time

  state = StartupState.Splash;

  LoadInfrastructure();
  LoadBasicUi();
  LoadRemainderOfApp();

  // we're done
  FormMain.StatusBarMessage("Ready");
}

void LoadInfrastructure()
{
  BuilderBinder.OnProgressChanged +=
  new BuilderBinder.ProgressChangedHandler(builderBinder_OnProgressChanged);
  BuilderBinder.OnProgressTextChanged +=
  new BuilderBinder.ProgressChangedTextHandler(
                            builderBinder_OnProgressTextChanged);
  BuilderBinder.BuildInfrastructure();
}

// get a skeletal UI up on the screen
void LoadBasicUi()
{
  BuilderBinder.BuildBasicUi();
  FormMain.Show();
  FormMain.Update();

  // now the main UI is up: hide the splash screen
  state = StartupState.NormalUi;
  FormSplash.Hide();
}

void LoadRemainderOfApp()
{
  BuilderBinder.BuildRemainderOfApp();
}
```

```csharp
    delegate void ValueHandler(int theValue);
    delegate void TextHandler(string theText);

    // event handler can be called on a background thread
    private void builderBinder_OnProgressChanged(int theValue)
    {
      ValueHandler handler = null;

      if (state == StartupState.Splash)
        // update formSplash
        handler = new ValueHandler(FormSplash.UpdateProgress);

      else if (state == StartupState.NormalUi)
        // update formMain
        handler = new ValueHandler(FormMain.UpdateProgress);

      else return;

      // update screen on UI thread
      FormSplash.Invoke(handler, new object[] {theValue});
    }

    // event handler can be called on a background thread
    private void builderBinder_OnProgressTextChanged(string theText)
    {
      // we only handle textual progress when
      // the main UI is already on the screen

      if (state != StartupState.NormalUi) return;

      // update formMain on UI thread
      TextHandler handler = new TextHandler(FormMain.StatusBarMessage);
      FormMain.Invoke(handler, new object[] {theText});
    }
  }


public class RunCoordinator
{
    // shortcut property
    BuilderBinder BuilderBinder
    {
      get {return BuilderBinder.Singleton;}
    }

    public void Run()
    {
      BuilderBinder.formMain.Closing +=
          new CancelEventHandler(formMain_Closing);
     // app exits when this call completes
      Application.Run(BuilderBinder.formMain);
    }
```

```csharp
    private void formMain_Closing(object sender,
                    System.ComponentModel.CancelEventArgs e)
    {
      // to prevent the app from closing, do this
      // e.Cancel = true;
      // return;

      // let the app shut the app down
      FireExiting();
    }

    public void HandleTopLevelEvents()
    {
      // handle the top-level events than occur during
      // the normal operation of the system...
    }

    public delegate void ExitingHandler();
    public event ExitingHandler OnExiting;
    void FireExiting()
    {
      if (OnExiting == null) return;
      OnExiting();
    }
}


public class ShutdownCoordinator
{
    public void Run()
    {
      // disable the user interface during shutdown
      if (BuilderBinder.Singleton.formMain != null)
        BuilderBinder.Singleton.formMain.Visible = false;
    }
}
```

Listing 10-14. *A VB .NET Implementation Using Separate Lifecycle State Coordinators*

```vbnet
Public Class LifecycleCoordinator

  'the application's main entry point
  Shared Sub Main()
    Dim coordinator As New LifecycleCoordinator
    coordinator.Start() ' app exits when this call completes
  End Sub

  Enum LifecycleState
    StartingUp
    Running
    ShuttingDown
  End Enum
```

```vbnet
    Private state As LifecycleState

    ' shortcut property
    ReadOnly Property BuilderBinder() As BuilderBinder
      Get
        Return BuilderBinder.Singleton
      End Get
    End Property

    Public Sub Start()
      StartupSystem()
      RunSystem() ' app exits when this call completes
    End Sub

    Sub StartupSystem()
      state = LifecycleState.StartingUp
      BuilderBinder._startup.Run()
    End Sub

    Sub RunSystem()
      state = LifecycleState.Running
      AddHandler BuilderBinder._running.OnExiting, AddressOf ShutDownSystem
      BuilderBinder._running.Run()   ' app exits when this call completes
    End Sub

    Sub ShutDownSystem()
      state = LifecycleState.ShuttingDown
      BuilderBinder._shutdown.Run()
    End Sub

    Public Sub HandleWorkerEvent()
        ' ignore worker events unless in the Running state
      If state = LifecycleState.StartingUp Then Return
      If state = LifecycleState.ShuttingDown Then Return

        ' handle the event...
    End Sub

End Class


Public Class BuilderBinder

    Private Shared _singleton As BuilderBinder
    Public Shared ReadOnly Property Singleton() As BuilderBinder
      Get
        If _singleton Is Nothing Then
          _singleton = New BuilderBinder
        End If
        Return _singleton
      End Get
    End Property
```

```vbnet
Public _formSplash As New FormSplash

' lifecycle state coordinators
Public _startup As New StartupCoordinator
Public _running As New RunCoordinator
Public _shutdown As New ShutdownCoordinator

' the app's main form
Public _formMain As FormMain

' private constructor, to force access through Singleton property
Private Sub New()
End Sub

Public Sub BuildBasicUi()
  ' create all the top-level objects
  _formMain = New FormMain
End Sub


Public Sub BuildInfrastructure()
  Dim progress As Integer = 20
  For i As Integer = 0 To 4
    ' simulate a lengthy load process...
    System.Threading.Thread.Sleep(1000)

    ' provide completion feedback
    FireProgressChangedHandler(progress)
    progress += 20
  Next
End Sub

Public Sub BuildRemainderOfApp()
  For i As Integer = 1 To 10
    ' simulate a lengthy operation
    System.Threading.Thread.Sleep(500)

    ' provide progress feedback
    FireProgressChangedHandler(i * 10)
    Dim message As String = String.Format("Loading component {0}", i)
    FireProgressChangedHandler(Message)
  Next
End Sub

Public Sub BindInfrastructure()
  ' wire all the infrastructure objects
End Sub

Public Sub BindUi()
  ' wire all the top-level objects
End Sub
```

```vbnet
   Public Event OnProgressChanged(ByVal theValue As Integer)
   Private Sub FireProgressChangedHandler(ByVal theValue As Integer)
     RaiseEvent OnProgressChanged(theValue)
   End Sub

   Public Event OnProgressTextChanged(ByVal theText As String)
   Private Sub FireProgressChangedHandler(ByVal theText As String)
     RaiseEvent OnProgressTextChanged(theText)
   End Sub

End Class


Public Class StartupCoordinator

   Enum StartupState
     NoUi
     Splash
     NormalUi
   End Enum

   Private state As StartupState

   ' shortcut property
   ReadOnly Property BuilderBinder() As BuilderBinder
     Get
       Return BuilderBinder.Singleton
     End Get
   End Property

   ' shortcut property
   ReadOnly Property FormSplash() As FormSplash
     Get
       Return BuilderBinder.Singleton._formSplash
     End Get
   End Property

   ' shortcut property
   ReadOnly Property FormMain() As FormMain
     Get
       Return BuilderBinder.Singleton._formMain
     End Get
   End Property

   Public Sub New()
     state = StartupState.NoUi
   End Sub

   Public Sub Run()
     FormSplash.Show()
     FormSplash.Update() ' otherwise it appears one piece at time

     state = StartupState.Splash
```

```vb
    LoadInfrastructure()
    LoadBasicUi()
    LoadRemainderOfApp()

    ' we're done
    FormMain.StatusBarMessage("Ready")
End Sub

Sub LoadInfrastructure()
    AddHandler BuilderBinder.OnProgressChanged, _
        AddressOf builderBinder_OnProgressChanged
    AddHandler BuilderBinder.OnProgressTextChanged, _
        AddressOf builderBinder_OnProgressTextChanged
    BuilderBinder.BuildInfrastructure()
End Sub

' get a skeletal UI up on the screen
Sub LoadBasicUi()
    BuilderBinder.BuildBasicUi()
    FormMain.Show()
    FormMain.Update()

    ' now the main UI is up: hide the splash screen
    state = StartupState.NormalUi
    FormSplash.Hide()
End Sub

Sub LoadRemainderOfApp()
    BuilderBinder.BuildRemainderOfApp()
End Sub

Delegate Sub ValueHandler(ByVal theValue As Integer)
Delegate Sub TextHandler(ByVal theText As String)

' event handler can be called on a background thread
Private Sub builderBinder_OnProgressChanged(ByVal theValue As Integer)

    Dim handler As ValueHandler = Nothing

    If state = StartupState.Splash Then
        ' update formSplash
        handler = AddressOf FormSplash.UpdateProgress

    ElseIf state = StartupState.NormalUi Then
        ' update formMain
        handler = AddressOf FormMain.UpdateProgress

    Else
        Return
    End If
```

```vbnet
      ' update screen on UI thread
      FormSplash.Invoke(handler, New Object() {theValue})
   End Sub


   ' event handler can be called on a background thread
   Private Sub builderBinder_OnProgressTextChanged(ByVal theText As String)
      ' we only handle textual progress when
      ' the main UI is already on the screen

      If state <> StartupState.NormalUi Then Return

      ' update formMain on UI thread
      Dim handler As TextHandler = AddressOf FormMain.StatusBarMessage
      FormMain.Invoke(handler, New Object() {theText})
   End Sub

End Class


Public Class RunCoordinator

   ' shortcut property
   ReadOnly Property BuilderBinder() As BuilderBinder
      Get
         Return BuilderBinder.Singleton
      End Get
   End Property

   Public Sub Run()
      AddHandler BuilderBinder._formMain.Closing, AddressOf formMain_Closing
      Application.Run(BuilderBinder._formMain)  ' app exits when this call completes
   End Sub

   Private Sub formMain_Closing(ByVal sender As Object, _
            ByVal e As System.ComponentModel.CancelEventArgs)
      ' to prevent the app from closing, do this
      ' e.Cancel = true;
      ' return

      ' let the app shut the app down
      FireExiting()
   End Sub

   Public Sub HandleTopLevelEvents()
      ' handle the top-level events than occur during
      ' the normal operation of the system...
   End Sub

   Public Event OnExiting()
   Sub FireExiting()
      RaiseEvent OnExiting()
   End Sub

End Class
```

```
Public Class ShutdownCoordinator
  Public Sub Run()
    ' disable the user interface during shutdown
    If Not BuilderBinder.Singleton._formMain Is Nothing Then
      BuilderBinder.Singleton._formMain.Visible = False
    End If
  End Sub
End Class
```

The wiring diagram of the system is shown in Figure 10-24.

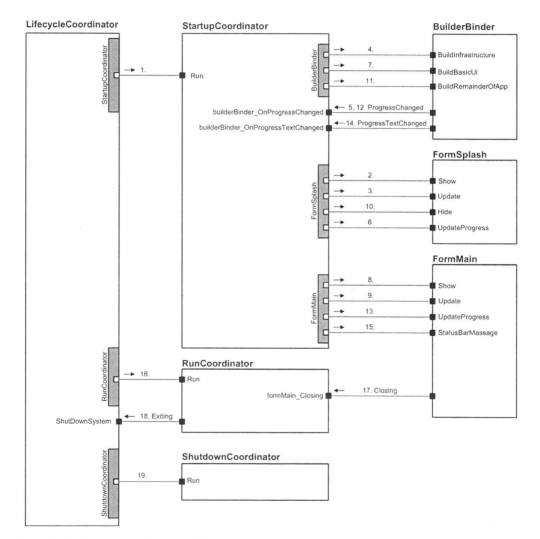

Figure 10-24. *The wiring diagram of the system*

The wiring diagram shows numbered signals, but given the number of signals involved, a sequence diagram is more suited for describing the signal chronology, as shown in Figure 10-25.

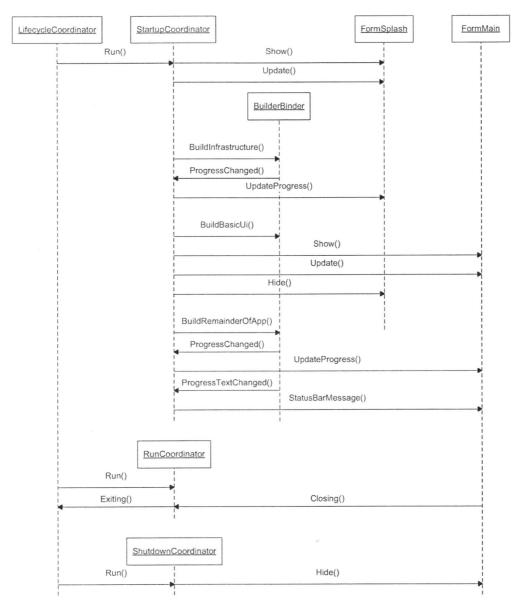

Figure 10-25. *The system's sequence diagram*

StartupCoordinator controls the BuilderBinder using transparent interactions with pushed feedback. The call to BuilderBinder.BuildInfrastructure results in one or more ProgressChanged feedback notifications. The call to BuilderBinder.BuildRemainderOfApp is similar, but results in two kinds of feedback notifications: one with a completion percentage value (ProgressChanged) and one with an update message (ProgressTextChanged).

The two forms—FormMain and FormSplash—can be considered workers, whose mission during the initialization phase is to display text and progress feedback. FormMain has the additional task of hosting the main UI elements, such as a menu, a toolbar, and a content area. The example uses a BuilderBinder to create instances of all the top-level objects. The purpose of a builder is to centralize the instantiation of important objects, keeping references to all the objects they build in order to prevent them from being garbage-collected. I cover builders and binders in more detail in the next sections.

In many systems, you can load the infrastructure in a background thread. The infrastructure includes the non-UI-related plumbing. When threading is involved, it is StartupCoordinator's job to spawn the background thread and call BuilderBinder.BuildInfrastructure on it. When the Builder fires progress updates, it is again StartupCoordinator's job to switch to the UI thread before sending the updates to the splash or main forms. In my sample code, StartupCoordinator uses Control. Invoke in builderBinder_OnProgressChanged and builderBinder_OnProgressTextChanged to achieve the proper thread switching before invoking methods of FormSplash and FormMain.

The RunCoordinator class shown doesn't do much, but in a real application it might contain a significant amount of code to handle events from Worker objects. In my code, RunCoordinator just handles FormMain's Closing event by notifying the LifecycleCoordinator to initiate the shutdown sequence. I kept this sequence to a minimum, but in many systems you might need to clean up and dispose of resources or update persistent settings for the next run.

Builders

Before introducing builders, let me digress slightly and look again at the life cycle of an EBS. No matter what the system's size and domain are, you must perform the following tasks at run time.

- Create a series of objects.
- Wire the objects together.
- Use the objects.
- Destroy the objects.

You generally can't use an EBS until you've instantiated and wired together at least some of its objects in some fashion. These first two steps are problematic from the coupling perspective, because an object containing the creation and wiring logic is coupled to the classes it instantiates and wires. If the instantiation relies on constructor calls (e.g., the new keyword in languages such as C# and Java), type coupling will occur, which is static in nature. If the instantiation and wiring rely on reflection, logic coupling will occur, which is dynamic in nature. As an example, assume a system has two components C1 and C2, and that C1 contains a Worker class T1 that instantiates, using a constructor call, a Worker class T2 contained in C2. The system will have the coupling diagram shown in Figure 10-26.

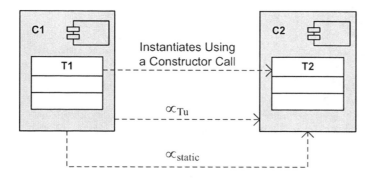

Figure 10-26. *Instantiation through constructor calls introduces type coupling.*

As shown in the diagram, C1 has unambiguous type coupling to C2. You can't compile, link, test, or deploy C1 without C2. To remove the coupling between C1 and C2, you need to remove the requirement for T1 to call the constructor of T2. If a separate object instantiates T2 on behalf of T1, there would be no coupling between them. I'll call this separate object a Builder, and the system's coupling diagram would look like Figure 10-27.

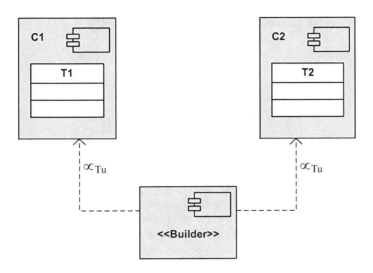

Figure 10-27. *Using a Builder to centralize coupling*

In the figure, T1 isn't shown calling any methods of T2. If T1 makes direct calls into T2 or calls T2 methods through an interface, C1 will still be ambiguously type-coupled to C2. You can remove this residual type coupling by having T1 use untyped object calls to T2—in other words, by making T1 call T2 methods through method pointers. If a separate object (a Binder) initializes these pointers, all type coupling between C1 and C2 would disappear.

With the introduction of the Builder in the design, you eliminate the coupling between C1 and C2, but now the Builder is coupled to both C1 and C2. Is the new coupling situation better than the old one? Definitely, according to Axiom 1, back in Chapter 1: *The more complex a class or component is, the more decoupled it should be.* It is reasonable to believe that C1 and C2 are not trivial components, since they contain business logic in the two Worker classes. The Builder, on the other hand, can be an extremely simple part, because all it does is create instances to be used somewhere else. The Builder in the diagram might have only the code shown in Listing 10-15, if implemented in a language such as C# or Java.

Listing 10-15. *A Simple Builder*

```
public class Builder
{
  public T1 t1;
  public T2 t2;

  public void Build()
  {
    t1 = new T1();
    t2 = new T2();
  }
}
```

In many OO languages, there are other ways to create objects besides using the new operator. You might use reflection to instantiate objects whose class name is provided at run time, or you might build an object by deserializing the bytes obtained from a stream.

The Builder in Listing 10-15 exposes the created objects as public fields or properties. The Builder has no interest in using the objects it creates, so the objects must be accessible to the rest of the system. The purpose of a Builder might be summarized in a single sentence:

Builders assume the burden of coupling, removing it from complex parts.

Builders essentially shift coupling around in a system so that it impacts simple objects (the builders) more than complex ones (the workers and coordinators).

Smart Builders

Not all systems are designed to be initialized in a fixed way. In many situations, the objects to create might depend on the state of the system at a particular point in time. A builder is called *smart* when it is capable of deciding which objects to build. In smart builders, the decision logic should be simple, because builders are often used to create many types of objects and therefore incur a substantial amount of coupling. Remember Axiom 1 from Chapter 1 again: *The more complex a class or component is, the more decoupled it should be.* If a smart builder needs a substantial amount of logic to decide which objects to create, it would be both complex and heavily coupled, defeating the purpose of a builder. If the logic were complex, it would need to be packaged in a separate object. This new object would be a worker or a coordinator, depending on the details of the implementation.

As a practical example of a smart builder, consider a two-tier distributed system in which the client is connected to the server tier via the Internet. The system has two modes of operation. If a fast connection is available, a rich user interface is used. If a fast connection is not available, the system falls back on a slower connection and uses a much simpler user interface. The Builder's decision is based on a single Boolean variable, which I'll call IsFastConnectionAvailable. There are three common ways the Builder could get the value of the Boolean:

- As a parameter in a Builder method called at startup time
- By firing an event to retrieve the value
- By calling a method in one of the objects created by the Builder

Listing 10-16 and Listing 10-17 show simple C# and VB .NET implementations of the Builder.

Listing 10-16. *A C# Example of a Smart Builder*

```csharp
public class SmartBuilder
{
  public WorkerUiRich workerUiRich;
  public WorkerUiPlain workerUiPlain;

  public void Build(bool isFastConnectionAvailable)
  {
    if (isFastConnectionAvailable)
      workerUiRich = new WorkerUiRich();
    else
      workerUiPlain = new WorkerUiPlain();
  }
}
```

Listing 10-17. *A VB .NET Example of a Smart Builder*

```
Public Class SmartBuilder
  Public _workerUiRich As WorkerUiRich
  Public _workerUiPlain As WorkerUiPlain

  Public Sub Build(ByVal isFastConnectionAvailable As Boolean)
    If isFastConnectionAvailable Then
      _workerUiRich = New WorkerUiRich
    Else
      _workerUiPlain = New WorkerUiPlain
    End If
  End Sub
End Class
```

It's very important to keep builders as simple as possible, because they can become coupled to a large number of classes in the system. The primary task of builders is to *build*, not to make difficult decisions on what to build, when to build it, and why.

Background Builders

Large systems can take a considerable amount of time to load all the executable modules and create the initial set of objects. While this loading is taking place, programs with a UI should display feedback to the user, using a splash screen as described in Example 2 at the end of the "Coordinators" section. If no feedback is given to the users quickly, they might be inclined to try to start the program again, resulting eventually in multiple running instances. One way to design the initialization of complex systems is by using a two-stage process, as shown in Figure 10-28.

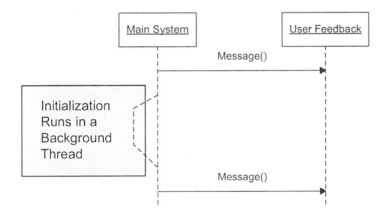

Figure 10-28. *Using a background thread to initialize a slow-starting system*

This approach uses an asynchronous blind interaction to start the background build process. When the system first starts, initialization feedback is shown immediately, typically using a splash screen. While the background process proceeds, the user interface is built and put up on the screen. When the background initialization is complete, a completion message of some kind is displayed.

You can use a builder in this type of system. The startup module of the system displays user feedback on the screen. A LifecycleCoordinator, described in the "Coordinators" section, runs the Builder on a background thread, as shown in Figure 10-29.

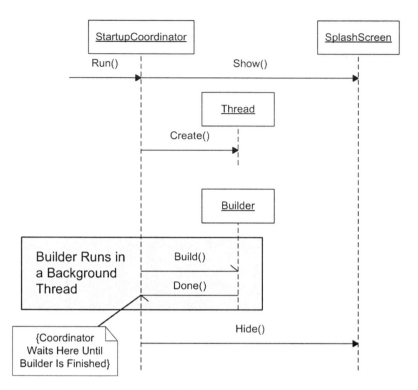

Figure 10-29. *Using a background Builder to start complex systems*

The interaction between the Starter and the Builder is asynchronous and blind. Figure 10-29 shows an interaction that provides only completion feedback, but the Builder might also provide progress feedback. Listing 10-18 and Listing 10-19 show C# and VB .NET implementations.

Listing 10-18. *A C# System with a Background Builder*

```
public class StartupCoordinator
{
    // The main entry point for the application.
    [STAThread]
    static void Main()
    {
        StartupCoordinator starter = new StartupCoordinator();
        starter.Run();
    }

    void Run()
    {
        Builder builder = Builder.Singleton;
        builder.formSplash.Show();
        builder.formSplash.Update(); // otherwise form shows up slowly
```

```csharp
    Thread background = BackgroundBuild();
    builder.BuildUi();
    background.Join(); // wait for background build to finish
    builder.formSplash.Hide();
    builder.formMain.Show();
    builder.formMain.Update(); // otherwise form shows up slowly
    RunSystem();
  }

  Thread BackgroundBuild()
  {
    ThreadStart entryPoint = new ThreadStart(DoBackgroundBuild);
    Thread thread = new Thread(entryPoint);
    thread.IsBackground = true;
    thread.Start();
    return thread;
  }

  void DoBackgroundBuild()
  {
    Builder.Singleton.BuildInfrastructure();
  }

  public void RunSystem()
  {
    System.Windows.Forms.Application.Run(Builder.Singleton.formMain);
  }
}

public class Builder
{
  static Builder singleton;
  static public Builder Singleton
  {
    get
    {
      if (singleton == null)
        singleton = new Builder();
      return singleton;
    }
  }

  public FormSplash formSplash;
  public FormMain formMain;

  // some arbitrary objects to build
  public Worker1 worker1;
  public Worker2 worker2;

  // private constructor, to force access through Singleton property
  private Builder()
  {
    formSplash = new FormSplash();
  }
```

```
    public void BuildInfrastructure()
    {
      worker1 = new Worker1();
      worker2 = new Worker2();

      // simulate a lengthy process
      System.Threading.Thread.Sleep(5000);
    }

    public void BuildUi()
    {
      formMain = new FormMain();
    }
}
```

Listing 10-19. *A VB .NET System with a Background Builder*

```vb
Public Class StartupCoordinator

  Public Shared Sub Main()
    Dim starter As New StartupCoordinator
    starter.Run()
  End Sub

  Sub Run()
    Dim myBuilder As Builder = Builder.Singleton
    myBuilder._formSplash.Show()
    myBuilder._formSplash.Update() ' otherwise form shows up slowly

    Dim background As Thread = BackgroundBuild()
    myBuilder.BuildUi()
    background.Join() ' wait for background build to finish
    myBuilder._formSplash.Hide()
    myBuilder._formMain.Show()
    myBuilder._formMain.Update() ' otherwise form shows up slowly
    RunSystem()
  End Sub

  Function BackgroundBuild() As Thread
    Dim bgndThread As New Thread(AddressOf DoBackgroundBuild)
    bgndThread.IsBackground = True
    bgndThread.Start()
    Return bgndThread
  End Function

  Sub DoBackgroundBuild()
    Builder.Singleton.BuildInfrastructure()
  End Sub

  Sub RunSystem()
    System.Windows.Forms.Application.Run(Builder.Singleton._formMain)
  End Sub
End Class
```

```
Public Class Builder

  Private Shared _singleton As Builder
  Shared ReadOnly Property Singleton() As Builder
    Get
      If _singleton Is Nothing Then
        _singleton = New Builder
      End If
      Return _singleton
    End Get
  End Property

  Public _formSplash As FormSplash
  Public _formMain As FormMain

  ' some arbitrary objects to build
  Public _worker1 As Worker1
  Public _worker2 As Worker2

  ' private constructor, to force access through Singleton property
  Private Sub New()
    _formSplash = New FormSplash
  End Sub

  Public Sub BuildInfrastructure()
    _worker1 = New Worker1
    _worker2 = New Worker2

    ' simulate a lengthy process
    System.Threading.Thread.Sleep(5000)
  End Sub

  Public Sub BuildUi()
    _formMain = New FormMain
  End Sub
End Class
```

The splash screen just contains static text. To detect the end of the background initialization, the Coordinator waits for the Builder thread to finish, using Thread.Join. An event notification could also have been used to signal the Builder's completion, as described in the example at the end of the "Coordinators" section.

While the background Builder is busy, the Coordinator gets the main UI built on the main thread. Once the background Builder completes, the splash screen is removed and the main UI is shown. Note that the Builder is unaware that its BuildInfrastructure method runs on a background thread. The Builder knows nothing about threads. You could easily modify the design to run the Builder on the main thread, without needing to modify the Builder. The only class in the system that knows anything about the background thread is the Coordinator.

Some systems may need to include progress feedback during the background build process, perhaps to show the name of each component being loaded, the amount of memory used, the amount of time remaining, and so on. To support progress feedback, the Coordinator can invoke the Builder using a transparent asynchronous interaction with pushed feedback. It's important to remember that the event handler in the Coordinator doesn't execute on the UI thread, but rather on a background thread. The event handler therefore needs to synchronize with the UI thread before updating the user feedback window. In the .NET world, you accomplish the synchronization using the method System.Windows.Forms.Control.Invoke, as shown in the second example at the end of the "Coordinators" section.

JIT Builders

Just In Time (JIT) building, also known as *lazy loading* or late loading, is used in systems when a complete system initialization would take too long. Rather than build all the run-time objects at once, the idea is to build only those objects that are absolutely necessary to get the system up. All other objects are built *just in time*, when they are needed.

You need to treat JIT Builders somewhat differently from ordinary builders. Unless you're careful, JIT Builders can introduce a lot of unnecessary coupling into the system. To see how coupling might creep in, assume you have a very simple system consisting of a Coordinator team with one coordinator and two subordinate workers. Since the workers are expected to take a long time to build and aren't needed immediately on startup, the system JIT-builds them. Figure 10-30 shows the Coordinator team.

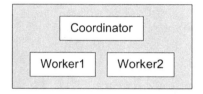

Figure 10-30. *A Coordinator team that uses a JIT Builder*

Ideally, you want no coupling to occur between the Coordinator and workers. At initialization time, assume that only the Coordinator need be present, perhaps because it handles certain simple tasks without needing any workers. Say the Coordinator only needs the workers if you call the Coordinator.DoSomething method. To create the workers, the Coordinator needs to invoke the services of a JIT Builder. Since this Builder instantiates the two workers, it is also type-coupled to the Worker classes, as shown in the coupling diagram in Figure 10-31.

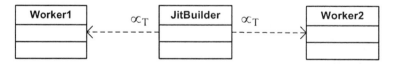

Figure 10-31. *JIT Builders are statically coupled to the classes they instantiate.*

If the Coordinator calls the JIT Builder directly to get the workers built, the Coordinator would incur type coupling to the Builder. Since the Builder is type-coupled to the workers, and the Coordinator is type-coupled to the Builder, the Coordinator would be indirectly type-coupled to the workers. To avoid adding this extra coupling to the Coordinator, the Coordinator must interact with the JIT Builder indirectly, using event notifications. The wiring diagram in Figure 10-32 shows the system.

When the Coordinator's DoSomething method is invoked for the first time, the Coordinator fires a JitSetup event to the JIT Builder, which builds the two workers on the fly and binds them to the Coordinator. Subsequent invocations of DoSomething bypass the JIT Builder, since the system is set up already. A regular Builder creates the Coordinator and the JIT Builder at initialization time. Listing 10-20 and Listing 10-21 show how the regular Builder might be implemented in C# and VB .NET.

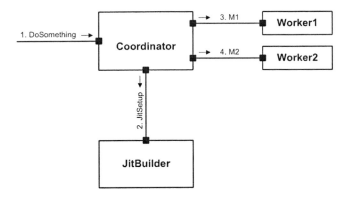

Figure 10-32. *Interaction with a JIT Builder using event notifications*

Listing 10-20. *A C# Implementation of the System's Normal Builder*

```csharp
public class Builder
{
  public JitBuilder jitBuilder;
  public Coordinator coordinator;

  public void Build()
  {
    jitBuilder = new JitBuilder();
    coordinator = new Coordinator();
  }

  public void Bind()
  {
    coordinator.OnJitSetup +=
      new Coordinator.EventJitSetup(jitBuilder.BuildBind);
  }
}
```

Listing 10-21. *A VB .NET Implementation of the System's Normal Builder*

```vbnet
Public Class Builder
  Public _jitBuilder As JitBuilder
  Public _coordinator As Coordinator

  Public Sub Build()
    _jitBuilder = New JitBuilder
    _coordinator = New Coordinator
  End Sub

  Public Sub Bind()
    AddHandler _coordinator.OnJitSetup, AddressOf _jitBuilder.BuildBind
  End Sub
End Class
```

The Coordinator has an event called `OnJitSetup` that is wired to the JIT Builder's `BuildBind` method. The `OnJitSetup` event is fired when the Coordinator needs to get the two workers instantiated. Listing 10-22 and Listing 10-23 show C# and VB .NET implementations of the Coordinator.

Listing 10-22. *A C# Implementation of the Coordinator*

```csharp
public class Coordinator
{
  bool workersInitialized;

  public void DoSomething()
  {
    if (!workersInitialized)
    {
      // build and bind workers
      FireJitSetup();
      workersInitialized = true;
    }

    // call workers
    FireM1();
    FireM2();
  }

  public delegate void EventJitSetup(Coordinator c);
  public event EventJitSetup OnJitSetup;
  public void FireJitSetup()
  {
    if (OnJitSetup != null)
      OnJitSetup(this);
  }

  public delegate void UniversalHandler();
  public event UniversalHandler OnM1;
  public void FireM1()
  {
    if (OnM1 != null)
      OnM1();
  }

  public event UniversalHandler OnM2;
  public void FireM2()
  {
    if (OnM2 != null)
      OnM2();
  }
}
```

Listing 10-23. *A VB .NET Implementation of the Coordinator*

```vbnet
Public Class Coordinator
  Private _workersInitialized As Boolean

  Public Sub DoSomething()
    If Not _workersInitialized Then
      ' build and bind workers
      FireJitSetup()
      _workersInitialized = True
    End If
```

```
    ' call workers
    FireM1()
    FireM2()
  End Sub

  Public Event OnJitSetup(ByVal c As Coordinator)
  Public Sub FireJitSetup()
    RaiseEvent OnJitSetup(Me)
  End Sub

  Public Event OnM1()
  Public Sub FireM1()
    RaiseEvent OnM1()
  End Sub

  Public Event OnM2()
  Public Sub FireM2()
    RaiseEvent OnM2()
  End Sub

End Class
```

The JIT Builder is also very simple. It handles the binding of the Coordinator to the two workers. Listing 10-24 and Listing 10-25 show C# and VB .NET implementations.

Listing 10-24. *A C# Implementation of the JIT Builder*

```csharp
public class JitBuilder
{
  Worker1 worker1;
  Worker2 worker2;

  public void BuildBind(Coordinator theCoordinator)
  {
    // build
    worker1 = new Worker1();
    worker2 = new Worker2();

    // bind
    theCoordinator.OnM1 += new Coordinator.UniversalHandler(worker1.M1);
    theCoordinator.OnM2 += new Coordinator.UniversalHandler(worker2.M2);
  }
}
```

Listing 10-25. *A VB .NET Implementation of the JIT Builder*

```vb
Public Class JitBuilder
  Dim _worker1 As Worker1
  Dim _worker2 As Worker2

  Public Sub BuildBind(ByVal theCoordinator As Coordinator)
    ' build
    _worker1 = New Worker1
    _worker2 = New Worker2
```

```
      ' bind
      AddHandler theCoordinator.OnM1, AddressOf _worker1.M1
      AddHandler theCoordinator.OnM2, AddressOf _worker2.M2
    End Sub

End Class
```

By using events to tie the system together, you avoid adding coupling to the most complex classes (the Coordinator and the workers), as shown in the coupling diagram in Figure 10-33.

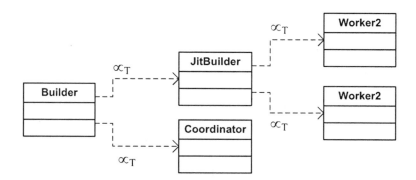

Figure 10-33. *The coupling diagram of the sample system*

Binders

I've used simple binders in several examples in the previous sections. Builders and binders are typically used together, but binders can be considerably more complicated than builders. Both builders and binders are considered part of the infrastructure of a system: They help set up the coordinators and workers that implement a system's requirements. They create the environment in which coordinators and workers subsequently work.

Builders are responsible for creating instances of all the top-level objects and holding onto them to prevent the objects from being garbage-collected until the program no longer needs them. The purpose of a Binder is also simple, at least on the surface: to wire parts together. Binding can get more complicated when a system needs to change its wiring at a later time, as I'll discuss a bit later. Binders connect outputs (event sources) to inputs (event handlers). Binders can work at two levels:

1. At the method level

2. At the interface level

The first case is an untyped object call: An outgoing call is wired to a specific method, whose type may be unknown to the caller. On a signal diagram, this type of binding is indicated by a wire connecting two pins, as shown in the wiring diagram in Figure 10-34.

Figure 10-34. *A wiring diagram showing binding at the method level*

The second case is a typed object call: An interface pointer in the event source is wired to a specific event handler object, effectively wiring all the methods that are part of the interface. On a signal diagram, interface-level binding is shown by a gray box enclosing a series of pins, as shown in Figure 10-35.

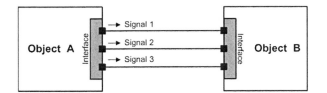

Figure 10-35. *A wiring diagram showing binding at the interface level*

Wiring two objects at the interface level requires setting a single pointer in the event source. The caller may not actually call all the methods of the wired interface. The methods that are called must appear in the diagram; the others are generally not shown.

Why use a dedicated object to handle binding? The simple reason is to reduce the coupling load on more complex classes, such as workers and coordinators. Consider the two objects back in Figure 10-34. If A wired itself to B, then A would have had to obtain a reference to a method in B. Assume B had the method M1, whose signature was universal (no arguments and no return value). Listing 10-26 and Listing 10-27 show what C# and VB .NET code would be needed in class A.

Listing 10-26. *A C# Class That Binds Itself to Another Class*

```csharp
public class A
{
  B b = new B();

  public void BindToB()
  {
    OnSignal += new EventUniversal(b.M1);
  }

  public delegate void EventUniversal();
  public event EventUniversal OnSignal;
  public void FireSignal()
  {
    if (OnSignal != null)
      OnSignal();
  }
}
```

Listing 10-27. *A VB .NET Class That Binds Itself to Another Class*

```vbnet
Public Class A
  Private _b As New B

  Public Sub BindToB()
    AddHandler OnSignal, AddressOf _b.M1
  End Sub
```

```
  Public Event OnSignal()
  Public Sub FireSignal()
    RaiseEvent OnSignal()
  End Sub

End Class
```

The coupling problem with this self-binding approach is evident: Class A is type-coupled to class B, because the method A.BindToB must identify a specific method of B. It doesn't matter whether the instance of B that is being wired was created inside class A or somewhere else. To keep A decoupled from B, the solution is to use a separate Binder object to bind them together, as shown in Figure 10-36.

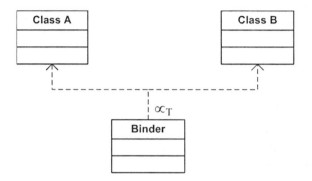

Figure 10-36. *Using a Binder to keep classes decoupled*

By putting the binding logic in the Binder, you can simplify class A. Listing 10-28 shows C# and VB .NET implementations of class A.

Listing 10-28. *Class A, After Removing the Binding Logic*

```
C#
public class A
{
  public delegate void UniversalHandler();
  public event UniversalHandler OnSignal;
  public void FireSignal()
  {
    if (OnSignal)
      OnSignal();
  }
}


VB .NET

Public Class A

  Public Event OnSignal()
  Public Sub FireSignal()
    RaiseEvent OnSignal()
  End Sub
End Class
```

Class A is no longer type-coupled to B. Without the binding logic, A has no idea what object or method will be called when it fires the Signal event. By having no coupling to class B, you can fully develop, implement, and test class A without the presence of class B. A separate Binder class is now required to wire A to B. The Binder might look something like Listing 10-29.

Listing 10-29. *Using a Separate Binder to Wire A to B*

C#

```
public class Binder
{
  public void Bind(A a, B b)
  {
    a.OnSignal += new A.EventUniversal(b.M1);
  }
}
```

VB .NET

```
Public Class Binder

  Public Sub Bind(ByVal theA As A, ByVal theB As B)
    AddHandler theA.OnSignal, AddressOf theB.M1
  End Sub

End Class
```

The addition of the Binder to the design hasn't eliminated coupling from the system, but the Binder allows you to shift the coupling away from complex classes (A and B). Since binders generally contain no business logic, they are very simple and can afford to be more heavily coupled than parts containing serious business logic.

Note that binding doesn't include building. Any objects a Binder wires together must have been created somewhere, typically in a Binder. For simple systems, the Builder and Binder functions are often combined into a single BuilderBinder class.

Late Binding

It isn't always practical to bind a system completely at startup time. Objects that can't be wired up at startup time have to be bound later. You may have to postpone binding for any number of reasons, including the following:

- Not all objects are created immediately at startup.

- The system doesn't know yet how to bind the objects.

- Binding is time-consuming or expensive, and should only be done if really necessary.

The binding process adds new wiring to the system. When binders are called into action at startup time, they typically wire up objects that had no prior wiring. With late binding, binders might have to change existing wiring between objects. If a new connection replaces an old one, then notifications that previously went to one object will now go to another, as shown in the two diagrams in Figure 10-37.

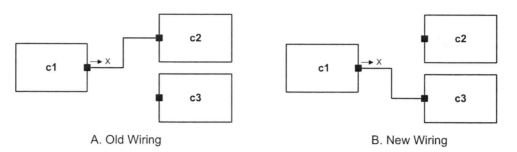

A. Old Wiring   B. New Wiring

Figure 10-37. *Late Binders can change the existing wiring of a system.*

In the diagram, c1, c2, and c3 are instances of arbitrary classes C1, C2, and C3. Diagram A shows the wiring established at startup time, from c1 to c2. At a subsequent point in time, a late Binder changes the wiring of c1.X, making the signal go to c3. The late binding produces the effect of a hardware switch, changing the path of notification signals on the fly. When a signal has a switchable path, you can show the various paths using a Switch symbol on wiring diagrams.

Figure 10-38 shows how you can merge the previous two figures together by adding a switch.

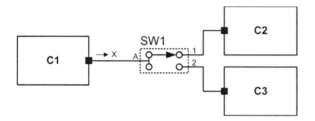

Figure 10-38. *Using a switch symbol to indicate signal paths that are late-bound*

The Switch symbol has a dashed border because it is a virtual part: It serves to show how signals are routed in the system, but there is no Switch object, per se. A switch is merely an abstraction of what a late Binder does.

A late Binder doesn't necessarily have to change an existing connection. If there is no previous connection, the Binder simply creates one. On a signal diagram, you can show the late binding of a previously nonexistent connection again with a switch, one of whose positions has no wiring. In Figure 10-39, position 1 of the switch might represent the initial, unwired system. Position 2 of the switch shows the path established by a late Binder.

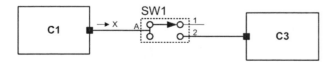

Figure 10-39. *Using a switch to show a late-bound signal path*

The diagram doesn't show the conditions that control the late-binding process. When this information is important to show, you can augment the diagram by showing the Binder that operates the switch, as shown in Figure 10-40.

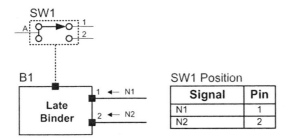

Figure 10-40. *Showing the Binder that operates a switch*

The signals that control the switch can come from any objects in the system. The switch table in Figure 10-40 shows that when the Binder receives the signal N1, the switch position is set to pin 1, so the signal entering the switch through pin A exits through pin 1. When the Binder receives signal N2, the switch position is set to pin 2. Figure 10-41 shows a diagram that includes two objects (C4 and C5) that fire events that control the late Binder.

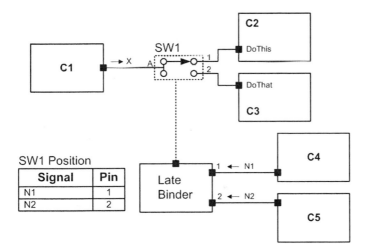

Figure 10-41. *A complete diagram, showing a switch, a late Binder, and its control signals*

The notification signals N1 and N2 control the late-binding process. The Binder would use the following statements to initially wire C1 to C2:

```
C#
c1.OnX += new C1.EventX(c2.DoThis);
```

```
VB .NET
AddHandler c1.OnX, AddressOf c2.DoThis
```

In order for a late Binder to remove old wiring, the Binder sometimes must *know* about that wiring. How wiring is represented at the implementation level is language-specific. In C# and VB .NET, wires are just references to methods and are implemented using .NET delegates. In Java, wires are Method objects that reference a method.

Note that .NET delegates support multicasting. To remove an old binding, you can't simply use the = operator to overwrite the old delegate with a new one, because doing so would remove *all* the handlers installed for that event, while the intention was only to remove one of the handlers. To remove a specific handler, you must know which delegate you want to remove and use the -= operator to remove it, like this:

```
C#
c1.OnX -= delegateToRemove
```

```
VB .NET
RemoveHandler c1.OnX, delegateToRemove
```

Getting back to the example in Figure 10-41, to switch signal X from C2 to C3, the Binder must first remove the wiring between C1 and C2, and then add new wiring between C1 and C3. Listing 10-30 and Listing 10-31 show how the Binder might be implemented in C# and VB .NET.

Listing 10-30. *A C# Implementation of the Late Binder*

```
public class LateBinder
{
  Builder builder;
  C1.UniversalHandler c2Wiring, c3Wiring;

  public LateBinder(Builder theBuilder)
  {
    builder = theBuilder;
  }

  private void RemoveOldWiring()
  {
    if (c2Wiring != null)
      builder.c1.OnX -= c2Wiring;

    if (c3Wiring != null)
      builder.c1.OnX -= c3Wiring;
  }

  public void SwitchXToC2()
  {
    RemoveOldWiring();

    // add new path
    if (c2Wiring == null)
      c2Wiring = new C1.UniversalHandler(builder.c2.DoThis);
    builder.c1.OnX += c2Wiring;
  }

  public void SwitchXToC3()
  {
    RemoveOldWiring();

    // add new path
    if (c3Wiring == null)
      c3Wiring = new C1.UniversalHandler(builder.c3.DoThat);
    builder.c1.OnX += c3Wiring;
  }
}
```

Listing 10-31. *A VB .NET Implementation of the Late Binder*

```
Public Class LateBinder
  Private _builder As Builder
  Private c2Wiring, c3Wiring As C1.UniversalHandler

  Public Sub New(ByVal theBuilder As Builder)
    _builder = theBuilder
  End Sub

  Private Sub RemoveOldWiring()
    If Not c2Wiring Is Nothing Then
      RemoveHandler _builder._c1.OnX, c2Wiring
    End If

    If Not c3Wiring Is Nothing Then
      RemoveHandler _builder._c1.OnX, c3Wiring
    End If
  End Sub

  Public Sub SwitchXToC2()
    RemoveOldWiring()

    ' add new path
    If c2Wiring Is Nothing Then
      c2Wiring = AddressOf _builder._c2.DoThis
    End If

    AddHandler _builder._c1.OnX, c2Wiring
  End Sub

  Public Sub SwitchXToC3()
    RemoveOldWiring()

    ' add new path
    If c3Wiring Is Nothing Then
      c3Wiring = AddressOf _builder._c3.DoThat
    End If
    AddHandler _builder._c1.OnX, c3Wiring
  End Sub

End Class
```

The code assumes that C1.UniversalHandler is a delegate defined in C1 like this:

```
C#
public delegate void UniversalHandler();
```

```
VB .NET
Public Delegate Sub UniversalHandler()
```

This Binder example uses a *break before make* (BBM) algorithm to switch the X signal: It breaks the old connection between c1 and c2 before making a new one from c1 to c3. The alternative to BBM is *make before break* (MBB), in which the new connection is made before removing the old one.

The difference between BBM and MBB may seem academic, but it can be very important in asynchronous systems, if C1 can fire event X *while* the Binder is in the process of changing the binding.

With a BBM switch in an asynchronous system, it is possible for a notification to fall between the cracks and not get sent to C2 or C3. With an MBB switch, again in an asynchronous system, it is possible for a notification to be delivered to both C2 and C3. In a synchronous system, in which the event source, the event handler, and the Binder all run on the same thread, these types of problems can't occur: C1 can't fire events while a switch is taking place, because the system can only be doing one thing at a given time.

State Machines with Late Binders

State machines are systems whose behavior depends on their history. State machines start out in some initial state and change state in response to events that occur. How the system reacts to an event depends on which state it is in when the event is detected. You diagram state machines using UML 2 State Machine diagrams, in which states are depicted using rounded boxes and the events that provoke state transitions are depicted with arrows, as described Chapter 6. For those of you who skipped that chapter, I'll give a 15-second tour of state machines. Figure 10-42 shows a simple diagram for an elevator in a two-story building.

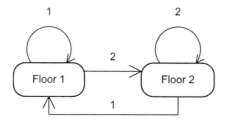

Figure 10-42. *A simple UML 2 State Machine diagram*

The elevator has only two buttons, for floors 1 and 2. When a floor button is pressed, a state transition takes place. Pressing button 1 on floor 1 causes a null transition that leaves the elevator in the same state (floor 1). Button 2 also produces a similar result when on floor 2.

A state machine may react differently to an event, based on some condition. For example, given a state S1 and an event E1, a system might go to a state S2 if a condition C is true and go to a state S3 if condition C is false. Figure 10-43 shows the state machine diagram of a system using one conditional transition and two unconditional ones.

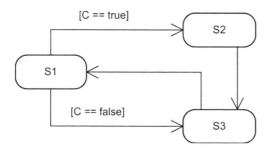

Figure 10-43. *The UML State Machine diagram for a system using conditional state transitions*

It is possible to implement a state machine in an object-oriented manner, using classes for each state.[6] Figure 10-44 shows an implementation with three classes: S1, S2, and S3.

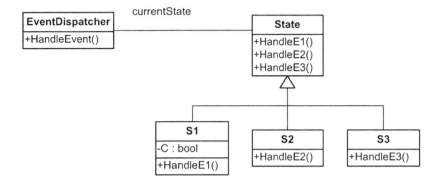

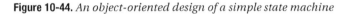

Figure 10-44. *An object-oriented design of a simple state machine*

The class EventDispatcher is the central class that detects all events. The class holds a reference to an object representing the current state. When an event is detected, EventDispatcher delegates processing to the currentState object, calling the handler method corresponding to the event detected. Listing 10-32 and Listing 10-33 show simple C# and VB .NET implementations.

Listing 10-32. *An Object-Oriented Way to Implement the State Machine Example in C#*

```csharp
public class EventDispatcher
{
  public enum Event {E1, E2, E3};
  State currentState =  new S1();  // initial state

  public void HandleEvent(Event theEvent)
  {
    switch (theEvent)
    {
      case Event.E1:
        currentState = currentState.HandleE1();
        break;
      case Event.E2:
        currentState = currentState.HandleE2();
        break;
      case Event.E3:
        currentState = currentState.HandleE3();
        break;
    }
  }
}
```

---

6. Ted Faison, "Object-Oriented State Machines," *Software Development Magazine*, September 1993.

```csharp
public class State
{
  public virtual State HandleE1() {return this;}  // do nothing
  public virtual State HandleE2() {return this;}  // do nothing
  public virtual State HandleE3() {return this;}  // do nothing
}

public class S1 : State
{
  bool C = true;  // a condition affecting the E1 transition

  public override State HandleE1()
  {
    // handle event...

    // go to next state
    if (C)
      return new S2();
    else
      return new S3();
  }
}

public class S2 : State
{
  public override State HandleE2()
  {
    // handle event...

    // go to next state
    return new S3();
  }
}

public class S3 : State
{
  public override State HandleE3()
  {
    // handle event...

    // go to next state
    return new S1();
  }
}
```

Listing 10-33. *An Object-Oriented Way to Implement the State Machine Example in VB .NET*

```vbnet
Public Class EventDispatcher
  Public Enum [Event]
    E1
    E2
    E3
  End Enum
```

```vb
    Private currentState As State = New S1    ' initial state

    Public Sub HandleEvent(ByVal theEvent As [Event])
      Select Case theEvent
        Case [Event].E1
          currentState = currentState.HandleE1()
        Case [Event].E2
          currentState = currentState.HandleE2()
        Case [Event].E3
          currentState = currentState.HandleE3()
      End Select
    End Sub

End Class

Public Class State
  Public Overridable Function HandleE1() As State
    Return Me ' do nothing
  End Function

  Public Overridable Function HandleE2() As State
    Return Me ' do nothing
  End Function

  Public Overridable Function HandleE3() As State
    Return Me ' do nothing
  End Function
End Class

Public Class S1
  Inherits State
  Private C As Boolean = True ' a condition affecting the E1 transition

  Public Overrides Function HandleE1() As State
    ' handle event...

    ' go to next state
    If C Then
      Return New S2
    Else
      Return New S3
    End If
  End Function
End Class

Public Class S2
  Inherits State
  Public Overrides Function HandleE2() As State
    ' handle event...

    ' go to next state
    Return New S3
  End Function
End Class
```

```
Public Class S3
  Inherits State
  Public Overrides Function HandleE3() As State
    ' handle event...

    ' go to next state
    Return New S1
  End Function

End Class
```

The classes derived from State only need to override methods for the events that can occur in each state. The base class State handles missing methods by doing nothing, alerting the operator, or taking some other default action.

This first design of the state machine is simple, but it has the drawback of relying on a class hierarchy of state classes: All the states are derived from a common base class. When relying on separate components to handle events for each state, it is unlikely the classes for each state will derive from a common base class, especially if the components come from different vendors. A different approach is required that doesn't rely on class hierarchies. One solution is to use an event-based design, using event notifications to deliver signals between the state-handler classes using a switch, as shown in the wiring diagram in Figure 10-45.

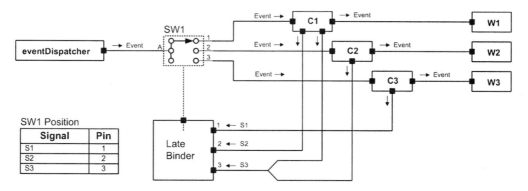

Figure 10-45. *An event-based design of a simple state machine*

The Event signal coming out of EventDispatcher is routed through a switch that sends it to objects W1, W2, or W3. Although these objects are part of a state machine, they have no state-related logic in them. They are the workers that contain the logic that applies to each state. The system uses three coordinators, labeled C1, C2, and C3, to handle state switching. Each coordinator fires events to the late Binder to control the event dispatcher's switch. Coordinator C1 fires two events: S2 if condition C is true; otherwise, S3. As the switch state table indicates, the Binder signal S2 causes SW1 to switch to its second position. The Binder signal S1 causes SW1 to switch to its first position. Listing 10-34 and Listing 10-35 show C# and VB .NET implementations of the system's Builder and Binder.

Listing 10-34. *The C# Builder and Binder for the System*

```
public class BuilderBinder
{
  public EventDispatcher eventDispatcher;
  public LateBinder lateBinder;
  public C1 c1;
```

```
    public C2 c2;
    public C3 c3;

    public void Build()
    {
      eventDispatcher = new EventDispatcher();
      lateBinder = new LateBinder(this);
      c1 = new C1();
      c2 = new C2();
      c3 = new C3();
    }

    public void Bind()
    {
      c1.OnS2 += new C1.EventNextState(lateBinder.SwitchToPin2);
      c1.OnS3 += new C1.EventNextState(lateBinder.SwitchToPin3);
      c2.OnS3 += new C2.EventNextState(lateBinder.SwitchToPin3);
      c3.OnS1 += new C3.EventNextState(lateBinder.SwitchToPin1);

      lateBinder.SwitchInitialize();
    }
}

public class LateBinder
{
  BuilderBinder builderBinder;

  EventDispatcher.MyEventHandler pin1, pin2, pin3;

  public LateBinder(BuilderBinder theBuilderBinder)
  {
    builderBinder = theBuilderBinder;
  }

  public void SwitchInitialize()
  {
    pin1 = new EventDispatcher.MyEventHandler(builderBinder.c1.HandleEvent);
    pin2 = new EventDispatcher.MyEventHandler(builderBinder.c2.HandleEvent);
    pin3 = new EventDispatcher.MyEventHandler(builderBinder.c3.HandleEvent);

    SwitchToPin1();
  }

  public void SwitchToPin1()
  {
    builderBinder.eventDispatcher.OnEvent = pin1;
  }

  public void SwitchToPin2()
  {
    builderBinder.eventDispatcher.OnEvent = pin2;
  }
```

```
  public void SwitchToPin3()
  {
    builderBinder.eventDispatcher.OnEvent = pin3;
  }
}
```

Listing 10-35. *The VB .NET Builder and Binder for the System*

```
Public Class BuilderBinder
  Public _eventDispatcher As EventDispatcher
  Public _lateBinder As LateBinder
  Public _c1 As C1
  Public _c2 As C2
  Public _c3 As C3

  Public Sub Build()
    _eventDispatcher = New EventDispatcher
    _lateBinder = New LateBinder(Me)
    _c1 = New C1
    _c2 = New C2
    _c3 = New C3
  End Sub

  Public Sub Bind()
    AddHandler _c1.OnS2, AddressOf _lateBinder.SwitchToPin2
    AddHandler _c1.OnS3, AddressOf _lateBinder.SwitchToPin3
    AddHandler _c2.OnS3, AddressOf _lateBinder.SwitchToPin3
    AddHandler _c3.OnS1, AddressOf _lateBinder.SwitchToPin1

    _lateBinder.SwitchInitialize()
  End Sub
End Class

Public Class LateBinder
  Private _builderBinder As BuilderBinder

  Private pin1, pin2, pin3 As EventDispatcher.MyEventHandler

  Public Sub New(ByVal theBuilderBinder As BuilderBinder)
    _builderBinder = theBuilderBinder
  End Sub

  Public Sub SwitchInitialize()
    pin1 = AddressOf _builderBinder._c1.HandleEvent
    pin2 = AddressOf _builderBinder._c2.HandleEvent
    pin3 = AddressOf _builderBinder._c3.HandleEvent

    SwitchToPin1()
  End Sub

  Public Sub SwitchToPin1()
    _builderBinder._eventDispatcher.OnEvent = pin1
  End Sub
```

```
    Public Sub SwitchToPin2()
      _builderBinder._eventDispatcher.OnEvent = pin2
    End Sub

    Public Sub SwitchToPin3()
      _builderBinder._eventDispatcher.OnEvent = pin3
    End Sub
End Class
```

The BuilderBinder class handles the startup binding, wiring the coordinators to the late Binder. The method LateBinder.SwitchInitialize creates the wiring for all three pins of the switch and sets the switch's initial position to pin 1.

Events enter the system through EventDispatcher, which then fires events that are routed through the switch to reach the Coordinator for the current state. The combination of BuilderBinder, LateBinder, and the coordinators represents a generic infrastructure for state-driven systems. Listing 10-36 and Listing 10-37 show C# and VB .NET implementations for EventDispatcher and the coordinators. The workers are not shown because they contain a single HandleEvent method whose implementation is dependent on the system requirements.

Listing 10-36. *The EventDispatcher and Coordinators for the System (C#)*

```
public class EventDispatcher
{
  // events the system can handle
  public enum Event {E1, E2, E3};

  public void HandleEvent(Event theEvent)
  {
    FireEvent(theEvent);
  }

  public delegate void MyEventHandler(Event theEvent);
  public MyEventHandler OnEvent;
  void FireEvent(Event theEvent)
  {
    if (OnEvent == null) return;

    // use a clone to fire the event,
    // because the wiring of OnEvent will
    // change during event handling
    MyEventHandler localEvent = OnEvent.Clone() as MyEventHandler;
    localEvent(theEvent);
  }
}
}

public class C1
{
  bool C = true; // condition that controls next state
  W1 w1 = new W1();
```

```
  public void HandleEvent(EventDispatcher.Event theEvent)
  {
    w1.HandleEvent(theEvent);

    if (C)
      FireS2();
    else
      FireS3();
  }

  public delegate void EventNextState();
  public event EventNextState OnS2;
  void FireS2()
  {
    if (OnS2 != null)
      OnS2();
  }

  public event EventNextState OnS3;
  void FireS3()
  {
    if (OnS3 != null)
      OnS3();
  }
}

public class C2
{
  W2 w2 = new W2();

  public void HandleEvent(EventDispatcher.Event theEvent)
  {
    w2.HandleEvent(theEvent);
    FireS3();
  }

  public delegate void EventNextState();
  public event EventNextState OnS3;
  void FireS3()
  {
    if (OnS3 != null)
      OnS3();
  }
}

public class C3
{
  W3 w3 = new W3();

  public void HandleEvent(EventDispatcher.Event theEvent)
  {
    w3.HandleEvent(theEvent);
    FireS1();
  }
```

```
   public delegate void EventNextState();
   public event EventNextState OnS1;
   void FireS1()
   {
     if (OnS1 != null)
       OnS1();
   }
}
```

Listing 10-37. *The EventDispatcher and Coordinators for the System (VB .NET)*

```
Public Class EventDispatcher
  ' events the system can handle
  Public Enum [Event]
    E1
    E2
    E3
  End Enum

  Public Sub HandleEvent(ByVal theEvent As [Event])
    FireEvent(theEvent)
  End Sub

  Public Delegate Sub MyEventHandler(ByVal theEvent As [Event])
  Public OnEvent As MyEventHandler
  Sub FireEvent(ByVal theEvent As [Event])
    If OnEvent Is Nothing Then Return

    ' use a clone to fire the event, because the wiring
    ' of OnEvent will change during event handling
    Dim localEvent As MyEventHandler
    localEvent = DirectCast(OnEvent.Clone(), MyEventHandler)
    localEvent(theEvent)
  End Sub
End Class

Public Class C1
  Private C As Boolean = True   ' condition that controls next state
  Private _w1 As New W1

  Public Sub HandleEvent(ByVal theEvent As EventDispatcher.Event)
    _w1.HandleEvent(theEvent)

    If (C) Then
      FireS2()
    Else
      FireS3()
    End If
  End Sub

  Public Event OnS2()
  Sub FireS2()
    RaiseEvent OnS2()
  End Sub
```

```
    Public Event OnS3()
    Sub FireS3()
      RaiseEvent OnS3()
    End Sub
End Class

Public Class C2
  Private _w2 As New W2

    Public Sub HandleEvent(ByVal theEvent As EventDispatcher.Event)
      _w2.HandleEvent(theEvent)
      FireS3()
    End Sub

    Public Event OnS3()
    Sub FireS3()
      RaiseEvent OnS3()
    End Sub
End Class

Public Class C3
  Private _w3 As New W3

    Public Sub HandleEvent(ByVal theEvent As EventDispatcher.Event)
      _w3.HandleEvent(theEvent)
      FireS1()
    End Sub

    Public Event OnS1()
    Sub FireS1()
      RaiseEvent OnS1()
    End Sub
End Class
```

Note that the Fire method in EventHandler uses a local copy of the delegate variable to fire events. The copy protects the subscriber list during event firing, because the coordinators change the subscriber list while handling notifications. The coordinators first call W1, W2, or W3 to handle the event, and then the coordinators fire events to the late Binder to change the switch position, putting the system into the proper next state.

The three coordinators create the worker instances directly, introducing static coupling between the coordinators and the workers. To create a completely decoupled state machine infrastructure, the coordinators could be changed to interact with the workers by firing events instead of making direct method calls.

Smart Binders

Just as builders can be smart, so can binders, because there are situations in which a binder may need to bind objects depending on run-time conditions. Take the example given when discussing smart builders: a two-tier distributed system, in which the client is connected to the server tier via the Internet. The system has two different UIs:

- A rich UI, used when a fast connection to the server is available

- A plain UI, used when only the slower backup connection is available

If a fast connection is available, you'll need to build and bind the constituents of a rich UI; otherwise, you'll fall back on the plain UI. Listing 10-38 and Listing 10-39 show how a smart Binder might be implemented in C# and VB .NET.

Listing 10-38. *A Simple C# Smart Binder*

```csharp
public class SmartBinder
{
  Builder builder;

  public SmartBinder(Builder theBuilder)
  {
    builder = theBuilder;
  }

  public void Bind(bool isFastConnectionAvailable)
  {
    if (isFastConnectionAvailable)
      builder.w1.OnE1 += new W1.UniversalHandler(builder.w2.DoThis);
    else
      builder.w1.OnE1 += new W1.UniversalHandler(builder. w2.DoThat);
  }
}
```

Listing 10-39. *A Simple VB .NET Smart Binder*

```vbnet
Public Class SmartBinder
  Private _builder As Builder

  Public Sub New(ByVal theBuilder As Builder)
    _builder = theBuilder
  End Sub

  Public Sub Bind(ByVal isFastConnectionAvailable As Boolean)
    If isFastConnectionAvailable Then
      AddHandler _builder._w1.OnE1, AddressOf _builder._w2.DoThis
    Else
      AddHandler _builder._w1.OnE1, AddressOf _builder._w2.DoThat
    End If
  End Sub
End Class
```

In the example, binding is controlled through a Boolean parameter passed to the Bind method. The Binder wires an event E1 of a class W1 to one of two possible destinations. The logic controlling binding should be as simple as possible, because the purpose of a Binder is to bind. If there is a substantial amount of logic required to control the binding, you should put that logic elsewhere: in a worker or coordinator.

JIT Binders

JIT Binders are used with objects created by a JIT Builder. As with JIT Builders, JIT Binders are called into action by notifications. The typical use of JIT building and binding is with coordinators that use JIT workers, created on the fly when certain operations are requested, as shown in Figure 10-46.

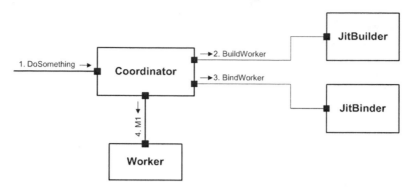

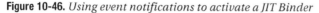

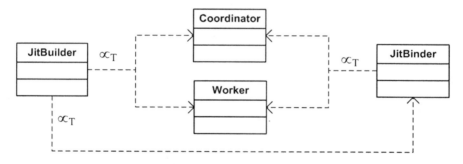

Figure 10-46. *Using event notifications to activate a JIT Binder*

In this example, the Coordinator uses a Worker that is created on the fly, when the DoSomething signal is received. The Coordinator fires an event first to the JIT Builder to create the Worker, then to a JIT Binder to wire the Worker to the Coordinator. Once the two are connected, the Coordinator can fire the M1 signal to the Worker. Figure 10-47 shows the coupling diagram for the system.

Figure 10-47. *The coupling diagram of a system with JIT Builders and Binders*

Using this design, the Coordinator and Worker classes are totally decoupled from each other, while the Builder and Binder are coupled to both the Coordinator and the Worker classes.

A JIT Binding Example

As a practical example of JIT Binding, I'll reimplement the *concurrent Worker* example given earlier in this chapter in the "Concurrent Workers" section, but this time I'll use JIT Builders and JIT Binders. To recall the concurrent Worker example briefly, you have a system in which a Worker uses a Coordinator to manage a team of subordinate concurrent Workers, as shown in Figure 10-48. When the system receives a ProcessRequest signal, it handles it asynchronously using a Worker created on the fly.

The goal is to implement the system without introducing coupling between any of the three classes shown in the diagram. A JIT Builder and Binder allow you to achieve this goal, resulting in the coupling shown in Figure 10-49.

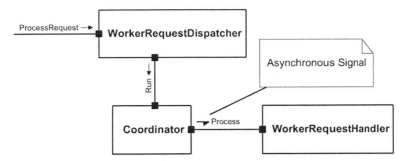

Figure 10-48. *A system using concurrent subordinate workers to process requests*

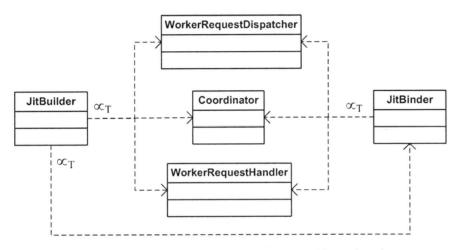

Figure 10-49. *The coupling diagram of the system, using a Builder and Binder*

The system also employs a regular Builder and Binder, not shown in the diagram, to create the parts that aren't added just in time, such as the Coordinator and the WorkerRequestHandler. With a Builder and Binder in the system, you can remove from WorkerRequestDispatcher the logic that instantiates the Coordinator. When the Coordinator receives a Run signal, it fires two events: the first to the JIT Builder, which instantiates a new subordinate Worker; the second to the JIT Binder, which binds the Worker to the Coordinator. Listing 10-40 and Listing 10-41 show C# and VB .NET implementations of the dispatcher Worker.

Listing 10-40. *A C# Implementation of the Top-Level Dispatching Worker*

```
public class WorkerRequestDispatcher
{
  public void ProcessRequest()
  {
    FireProcessRequest();
  }

  public void Stop()
  {
    FireStop();
  }
```

```csharp
public void RequestCompletedHandler()
{
  FireRequestCompleted();
}

public delegate void EventProcessRequest();
public event EventProcessRequest OnProcessRequest;
void FireProcessRequest()
{
  if (OnProcessRequest != null)
    OnProcessRequest();
}

public delegate void EventRequestCompleted();
public event EventRequestCompleted OnRequestCompleted;
public void FireRequestCompleted()
{
  if (OnRequestCompleted == null) return;
  OnRequestCompleted();
}

public delegate void EventStop();
public event EventStop OnStop;
public void FireStop()
{
  if (OnStop == null) return;
  OnStop();
}
}
```

Listing 10-41. *A VB .NET Implementation of the Top-Level Dispatching Worker*

```vbnet
Public Class WorkerRequestDispatcher
  Public Sub ProcessRequest()
    FireProcessRequest()
  End Sub

  Public Sub [Stop]()
    FireStop()
  End Sub

  Public Sub RequestCompletedHandler()
    FireRequestCompleted()
  End Sub

  Public Event OnProcessRequest()
  Sub FireProcessRequest()
    RaiseEvent OnProcessRequest()
  End Sub

  Public Event OnRequestCompleted()
  Sub FireRequestCompleted()
    RaiseEvent OnRequestCompleted()
  End Sub
```

```vbnet
    Public Event OnStop()
    Sub FireStop()
      RaiseEvent OnStop()
    End Sub
End Class
```

This Worker hasn't changed very much compared to the previous implementation. What is missing is a reference to the Coordinator, which the old Worker used to call the Run and Stop methods. The new implementation of the Worker achieves the same result by firing two events that are wired to the Coordinator, whose C# and VB .NET implementations are shown in Listing 10-42 and Listing 10-43.

Listing 10-42. *A C# Implementation of the Coordinator*

```csharp
public class Coordinator
{
  Control uiControl;

  // key is WorkerRequestHandler, value is Thread
  Hashtable threads = new Hashtable();

  public Coordinator(Control theUiControl)
  {
    uiControl = theUiControl;
  }

  public void Run()
  {
    lock(this)
    {
      // create a subordinate Worker
      object handler = FireBuildHandler();
      if (handler == null) return;

      // bind Worker to Coordinator
      FireBindHandler(handler);

      // get Worker's entry point
      ThreadStart entryPoint = FireGetHandlerEntryPoint(handler);
      if (entryPoint == null) return;

      // run Worker
      Thread thread = new Thread(entryPoint);
      thread.Start();
      threads.Add(handler, thread);
    }
  }

  public void Stop()
  {
    lock(this)
    {
      foreach (Thread thread in threads.Values)
        thread.Abort();
      threads.Clear();
```

```csharp
      }
    }

    public void HandlerCompleted(object theHandler)
    {
      lock(this)
      {
        threads.Remove(theHandler);
      }
        FireRequestCompleted();
    }

    public delegate object EventBuildHandler();
    public event EventBuildHandler OnBuildHandler;
    object FireBuildHandler()
    {
      if (OnBuildHandler != null)
        return OnBuildHandler();
      else
        return null;
    }

    public delegate void EventBindHandler(object theHandler);
    public event EventBindHandler OnBindHandler;
    void FireBindHandler(object theHandler)
    {
      if (OnBindHandler != null)
        OnBindHandler(theHandler);
    }

    public delegate ThreadStart EventGetHandlerEntryPoint(object theHandler);
    public event EventGetHandlerEntryPoint OnGetHandlerEntryPoint;
    ThreadStart FireGetHandlerEntryPoint(object theHandler)
    {
      if (OnGetHandlerEntryPoint != null)
        return OnGetHandlerEntryPoint(theHandler);
      else
        return null;
    }

    public delegate void EventRequestCompleted();
    public event EventRequestCompleted OnRequestCompleted;
    public void FireRequestCompleted()
    {
      if (OnRequestCompleted == null) return;

      // fire event on the UI thread
      uiControl.Invoke(OnRequestCompleted);
    }
}
```

Listing 10-43. *A VB .NET Implementation of the Coordinator*

```
Public Class Coordinator
  Private _uiControl As Control

  ' key is WorkerRequestHandler, value is Thread
  Private _threads As New Hashtable

  Public Sub New(ByVal theUiControl As Control)
    _uiControl = theUiControl
  End Sub

  Public Sub Run()
    SyncLock (Me)
      ' create a subordinate Worker
      Dim handler As Object = FireBuildHandler()
      If handler Is Nothing Then Return

      ' bind Worker to Coordinator
      FireBindHandler(handler)

      ' get Worker's entry point
      Dim entryPoint As ThreadStart = FireGetHandlerEntryPoint(handler)
      If entryPoint Is Nothing Then Return

      ' run Worker
      Dim _thread As New Thread(entryPoint)
      _thread.Start()
      _threads.Add(handler, _thread)
    End SyncLock
  End Sub

  Public Sub [Stop]()
    SyncLock (Me)
      For Each _thread As Thread In _threads.Values
        _thread.Abort()
      Next
      _threads.Clear()
    End SyncLock
  End Sub

  Public Sub HandlerCompleted(ByVal theHandler As Object)
    SyncLock (Me)
      _threads.Remove(theHandler)
    End SyncLock
    FireRequestCompleted()
  End Sub

  Public Delegate Function EventBuildHandler() As Object
  Public OnBuildHandler As EventBuildHandler
  Function FireBuildHandler() As Object
    If Not OnBuildHandler Is Nothing Then
      Return OnBuildHandler()
```

```
      Else
        Return Nothing
      End If
   End Function

   Public Event OnBindHandler(ByVal theHandler As Object)
   Sub FireBindHandler(ByVal theHandler As Object)
     RaiseEvent OnBindHandler(theHandler)
   End Sub

   Public Delegate Function EventGetHandlerEntryPoint( _
            ByVal theHandler As Object) As ThreadStart
   Public OnGetHandlerEntryPoint As EventGetHandlerEntryPoint
   Function FireGetHandlerEntryPoint(ByVal theHandler As Object) As ThreadStart
     If Not OnGetHandlerEntryPoint Is Nothing Then
       Return OnGetHandlerEntryPoint(theHandler)
     Else
       Return Nothing
     End If
   End Function

   Public Delegate Sub UniversalHandler()
   Public OnRequestCompleted As UniversalHandler
   Sub FireRequestCompleted()
     If OnRequestCompleted Is Nothing Then Return
     ' swith to the UI thread
     _uiControl.Invoke(New UniversalHandler(AddressOf DoFireRequestCompleted))
   End Sub
   Sub DoFireRequestCompleted()
     ' we're on the UI thread
     OnRequestCompleted() 'fire event on the UI thread
   End Sub

End Class
```

The only significant change in the Coordinator, compared to the earlier version, is in the Run method. The new Coordinator is decoupled from WorkerRequestHandler, and all direct calls to the Worker have been replaced by event notifications. The implementation of WorkerRequestHandler requires no changes with the new design, because in the old design the Worker wasn't coupled to other classes.

The Coordinator builds and binds WorkerRequestHandler objects on the fly, so a JIT Builder and a JIT Binder are used to handle the Coordinator events pertaining to WorkerRequestHandler initialization. The JIT Builder is trivial; see how it is implemented in Listing 10-44.

Listing 10-44. *The Implementation of the JIT Builder*

```C#
C#
public class JitBuilder
{
  public object BuildHandler()
  {
    return new WorkerRequestHandler();
  }
}
```

```
VB .NET
Public Class JitBuilder
  Public Function BuildHandler() As Object
    Return New WorkerRequestHandler
  End Function
End Class
```

The JIT Binder is a little more complicated. Listing 10-45 and Listing 10-46 show the C# and VB .NET implementations.

Listing 10-45. *The C# Implementation of the JIT Binder*

```csharp
public class JitBinder
{
  Builder builder;

  public JitBinder(Builder theBuilder)
  {
    builder = theBuilder;
  }

  public void BindHandler(object theHandler)
  {
    WorkerRequestHandler handler = theHandler as WorkerRequestHandler;
    if (handler == null) return;

    handler.OnRequestCompleted += new
        WorkerRequestHandler.EventRequestCompleted(
          builder.coordinator.HandlerCompleted);
  }

  public ThreadStart GetEntryPoint(object theHandler)
  {
    WorkerRequestHandler handler = theHandler as WorkerRequestHandler;
    if (handler == null) return null;

    return new ThreadStart(handler.Process);
  }
}
```

Listing 10-46. *The VB .NET Implementation of the JIT Binder*

```vbnet
Public Class JitBinder
  Private _builder As Builder

  Public Sub New(ByVal theBuilder As Builder)
    _builder = theBuilder
  End Sub

  Public Sub BindHandler(ByVal theHandler As Object)
    If theHandler Is Nothing Then Return
    Dim handler As WorkerRequestHandler = _
            DirectCast(theHandler, WorkerRequestHandler)
    If handler Is Nothing Then Return
```

```
    AddHandler handler.OnRequestCompleted, _
        AddressOf _builder._coordinator.HandlerCompleted
    End Sub

    Public Function GetEntryPoint(ByVal theHandler As Object) As ThreadStart
        If theHandler Is Nothing Then Return Nothing
        Dim handler As WorkerRequestHandler = _
            DirectCast(theHandler, WorkerRequestHandler)
        If handler Is Nothing Then Return Nothing

        Return New ThreadStart(AddressOf handler.Process)
    End Function
End Class
```

The last pieces missing are the builders and binders that initialize the static part of the system, as shown in Listing 10-47 and Listing 10-48.

Listing 10-47. *The C# Implementation of the Static Builder and Binder*

```csharp
public class Builder
{
    public WorkerRequestDispatcher dispatcher;
    public Coordinator coordinator;
    public Binder binder;

    public JitBuilder jitBuilder;
    public JitBinder jitBinder;

    public void Build(Control theUiControl)
    {
        jitBuilder = new JitBuilder();

        dispatcher = new WorkerRequestDispatcher();
        coordinator = new Coordinator(theUiControl);

        binder = new Binder(this);
        jitBinder = new JitBinder(this);
    }
}

public class Binder
{
    Builder builder;

    public Binder(Builder theBuilder)
    {
        builder = theBuilder;
    }

    public void Bind(FormMain theFormMain)
    {
        builder.coordinator.OnBuildHandler +=
            new Coordinator.EventBuildHandler(builder.jitBuilder.BuildHandler);
        builder.coordinator.OnBindHandler +=
            new Coordinator.EventBindHandler(builder.jitBinder.BindHandler);
```

```
    builder.coordinator.OnGetHandlerEntryPoint +=
        new Coordinator.EventGetHandlerEntryPoint(builder.jitBinder.GetEntryPoint);
    builder.coordinator.OnRequestCompleted +=
        new Coordinator.EventRequestCompleted(
        builder.dispatcher.RequestCompletedHandler);

    builder.dispatcher.OnProcessRequest +=
        new WorkerRequestDispatcher.EventProcessRequest(builder.coordinator.Run);
    builder.dispatcher.OnRequestCompleted +=
        new WorkerRequestDispatcher.EventRequestCompleted(
        theFormMain.RequestCompletedHandler);
    builder.dispatcher.OnStop +=
        new WorkerRequestDispatcher.EventStop(builder.coordinator.Stop);
  }
}
```

Listing 10-48. *The VB .NET Implementation of the Static Builder and Binder*

```
Public Class Builder
  Public _dispatcher As WorkerRequestDispatcher
  Public _coordinator As Coordinator
  Public _binder As Binder

  Public _jitBuilder As JitBuilder
  Public _jitBinder As JitBinder

  Public Sub Build(ByVal theUiControl As Control)
    _jitBuilder = New JitBuilder

    _dispatcher = New WorkerRequestDispatcher
    _coordinator = New Coordinator(theUiControl)

    _binder = New Binder(Me)
    _jitBinder = New JitBinder(Me)
  End Sub
End Class

Public Class Binder
  Private _builder As Builder

  Public Sub New(ByVal theBuilder As Builder)
    _builder = theBuilder
  End Sub

  Public Sub Bind(ByVal theFormMain As FormMain)
    _builder._coordinator.OnBuildHandler = _
                        AddressOf _builder._jitBuilder.BuildHandler
    AddHandler _builder._coordinator.OnBindHandler, _
                        AddressOf _builder._jitBinder.BindHandler
    _builder._coordinator.OnGetHandlerEntryPoint = _
                        AddressOf _builder._jitBinder.GetEntryPoint
    _builder._coordinator.OnRequestCompleted = _
                        AddressOf _builder._dispatcher.RequestCompletedHandler
```

```
        AddHandler _builder._dispatcher.OnProcessRequest,
                        AddressOf _builder._coordinator.Run
        AddHandler _builder._dispatcher.OnRequestCompleted,
                        AddressOf theFormMain.RequestCompletedHandler
        AddHandler _builder._dispatcher.OnStop,
                        AddressOf _builder._coordinator.Stop
    End Sub
End Class
```

By wiring all the complex objects together with event notifications, the important classes remain completely decoupled from all others. Thus, you can implement and fully test the Coordinator and the two Worker classes independently.

A side effect of the introduction of events to replace all interclass calls is a fragmentation of the system. Looking at the implementation of the Coordinator, for example, one can't understand how the class functions with other parts of the system, because the code shows events being fired, with no evidence of where the resulting notifications go. The event handlers are not determined until run time. But this is exactly the situation you wanted to create in the first place: You wanted each class to be fully decoupled from all others. The only way to achieve this is by wiring objects together at run time, so the only way to determine how all the classes work together is by looking at a system's wiring diagram.

In the hardware world, things are similar. Integrated circuits are conceptually equivalent to objects. Each IC is completely detached from all other ICs, before being added to the system. By looking solely at a circuit diagram of the internal design of an IC, you can't tell how the IC functions in relationship to other parts of the system. ICs come with pins, because they are *designed* to be wired to other components, so the only way to determine how everything works together is by looking at the wiring diagram of the system.

Dynamic Binding

The binders described so far have all had one thing in common: The connections they wired were all described statically. The source code specifies exactly which inputs and outputs to wire together. There is another type of Binder that can wire inputs to outputs *dynamically*, in the sense that the list of inputs and outputs to wire is determined at run time. The source code no longer contains a static list of connections to be established. Dynamic binding can be nondeterministic, because before running a system you might not be able to predict which connections will be made. It is the system, and not the programmer, that ultimately decides what bindings are made in the system.

Dynamic binders are driven by notifications from the system, and from a certain perspective behave like a living organism. When specific stimuli are sensed, the system reacts by creating new objects and connections. Systems that are capable of growing and adapting to input from the environment are known as *evolvable systems*, and dynamic binding is a fundamental part of any such system.

Describing a dynamic system is challenging, because the system changes over time. A common approach is to diagram snapshots of the system at important times in its lifetime, much the way you might draw a picture of a person. If a system's evolution pattern is predictable, then you know what objects and connections might appear at some point. The wiring diagram in Figure 10-50 shows a simple evolvable system whose growth is predictable.

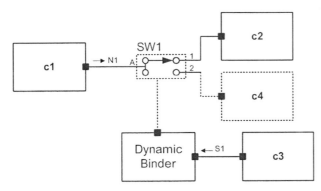

Figure 10-50. *Predictable objects and connections can be shown with dotted outlines.*

The system can evolve by creating new objects and connections. A DynamicBinder controls the connections in the system. Figure 10-50 tells you that at startup time, c2 is created and wired to c1, because pin 1 is the default position of SW1. At some point after startup, the object c4 is created and the signal S1 is sent to the DynamicBinder to connect c1 to c4. The lines associated with c4 are dotted to indicate parts that aren't created when the system first starts up but are expected to be created if the right conditions occur. Although the diagram doesn't show when c4 is created, you should infer that c4 will exist when the switch routes N1 to pin 2. You could implement the system with two pair of builders and binders: a static pair for the startup configuration, and a dynamic pair to handle the system changes at run time. Listing 10-49 and Listing 10-50 show how you might implement the static Builder and Binder in C# and VB .NET for such a system.

Listing 10-49. *The C# Implementation of Static Builder and Binder*

```
public class Builder
{
  public C1 c1;
  public C2 c2;
  public C3 c3;

  public Binder binder;
  public DynamicBuilder dynamicBuilder;
  public DynamicBinder dynamicBinder;

  public void Build()
  {
    c1 = new C1();
    c2 = new C2();
    c3 = new C3();

    binder = new Binder(this);
    dynamicBuilder = new DynamicBuilder(this);
    dynamicBinder = new DynamicBinder(this);
  }
}
```

```csharp
public class Binder
{
  Builder builder;
  public C1.UniversalHandler c1N1Connection;

  public Binder(Builder theBuilder)
  {
    builder = theBuilder;
  }

  public void Bind()
  {
    c1N1Connection = new C1.UniversalHandler(builder.c2.M1);
    builder.c1.OnN1 += c1N1Connection;

    builder.c3.OnS1 += new C3.EventS1(builder.dynamicBuilder.EvolveSystem);
  }
}
```

Listing 10-50. *The VB .NET Implementation of Static Builder and Binder*

```vbnet
Public Class Builder
  Public _c1 As C1
  Public _c2 As C2
  Public _c3 As C3

  Public _binder As Binder
  Public _dynamicBuilder As DynamicBuilder
  Public _dynamicBinder As DynamicBinder

  Public Sub Build()
    _c1 = New C1
    _c2 = New C2
    _c3 = New C3

    _binder = New Binder(Me)
    _dynamicBuilder = New DynamicBuilder(Me)
    _dynamicBinder = New DynamicBinder(Me)
  End Sub
End Class

Public Class Binder
  Private _builder As Builder
  Public _c1N1Connection As C1.UniversalHandler

  Public Sub New(ByVal theBuilder As Builder)
    _builder = theBuilder
  End Sub

  Public Sub Bind()
    _c1N1Connection = AddressOf _builder._c2.M1
    AddHandler _builder._c1.OnN1, AddressOf _builder._c2.M1
    AddHandler _builder._c3.OnS1, AddressOf _builder._dynamicBuilder.EvolveSystem
  End Sub
End Class
```

Listing 10-51 and Listing 10-52 show how you might implement the dynamic Builder and Binder in C# and VB .NET.

Listing 10-51. *The C# Implementation of DynamicBuilder and Binder*

```csharp
public class DynamicBuilder
{
  Builder builder;
  public object c4;

  public DynamicBuilder(Builder theBuilder)
  {
    builder = theBuilder;
  }

  public void EvolveSystem()
  {
    // use reflection to create a C4 instance
    c4 = Assembly.GetExecutingAssembly().CreateInstance("Dynamic_Binders.C4");

    // use reflection to find a reference to C4.MyMethod
    Delegate delObj = Delegate.CreateDelegate(
                              typeof(C1.UniversalHandler), c4, "MyMethod");
    C1.UniversalHandler newHandler = delObj as C1.UniversalHandler;

    // replace the c1->c2 connection with c1->c4 connection
    C1.UniversalHandler oldHandler = builder.binder.c1N1Connection;
    EventInfo ei = builder.c1.GetType().GetEvent("OnN1");
    builder.dynamicBinder.DynamicallyRebind(ei, builder.c1, oldHandler, newHandler);
  }
}
public class DynamicBinder
{
  Builder builder;

  public DynamicBinder(Builder theBuilder)
  {
    builder = theBuilder;
  }

  public void DynamicallyRebind(EventInfo theEvent,
    object theEventSource,
    Delegate theOldHandler,
    Delegate theNewHandler)
  {
    theEvent.RemoveEventHandler(theEventSource, theOldHandler);
    theEvent.AddEventHandler(theEventSource, theNewHandler);
  }
}
```

Listing 10-52. *The VB .NET Implementation of DynamicBuilder and DynamicBinder*

```vbnet
Public Class DynamicBuilder
  Private _builder As Builder
  Public _c4 As Object

  Public Sub New(ByVal theBuilder As Builder)
    _builder = theBuilder
  End Sub

  Public Sub EvolveSystem()
    ' use reflection to create a C4 instance
    _c4 = [Assembly].GetExecutingAssembly().CreateInstance("Dynamic_Binders.C4")

    ' use reflection to find a reference to C4.MyMethod
    Dim delObj As Object = [Delegate].CreateDelegate( _
            GetType(C1.UniversalHandler), _c4, "MyMethod")
    Dim newHandler As C1.UniversalHandler = DirectCast(delObj, C1.UniversalHandler)

    ' replace the c1->c2 connection with c1->c4 connection
    Dim oldHandler As C1.UniversalHandler = _builder._binder._c1N1Connection
    Dim ei As EventInfo = _builder._c1.GetType().GetEvent("OnN1")
    _builder._dynamicBinder.DynamicallyRebind(ei, _builder._c1, _
                oldHandler, newHandler)
  End Sub
End Class

Public Class DynamicBinder
  Private _builder As Builder

  Public Sub New(ByVal theBuilder As Builder)
    _builder = theBuilder
  End Sub

  Public Sub DynamicallyRebind(ByVal theEvent As EventInfo, _
    ByVal theEventSource As Object, _
    ByVal theOldHandler As [Delegate], _
    ByVal theNewHandler As [Delegate])
    theEvent.RemoveEventHandler(theEventSource, theOldHandler)
    theEvent.AddEventHandler(theEventSource, theNewHandler)
  End Sub
End Class
```

The static Binder initially wires c1.N1 to c2.M1. When c3 fires the S1 event, the DynamicBuilder handles it by removing the old wiring between c1 and c2, creating c4, and dynamically wiring c1 to c4. The method DynamicBuilder.EvolveSystem uses hard-coded strings to designate the class to instantiate and the connections to make, so the source code tells you what objects are created and wired. But the strings could easily have been read from a file or arrived as parameters in a method call, leaving no trace in DynamicBuilder of what objects to create and wire up. The Builder can instantiate any class in the executing assembly and wire any two objects. The Binder tries to bind c1.OnN1 to any method specified. Something missing from Binder.DynamicallyRebind is a run-time check to verify that the method being bound to c1.OnN1 has the expected signature. In a production system, the test might throw an exception if an incompatible method signature were encountered.

Routers

The purpose of a Router component is to forward event notifications from one area of the system to another. When building large software systems, the number of signals can become so high that just keeping track of how signals are directed through the system becomes a substantial chore. Routers then become useful, because they concentrate on themselves a large number of signals, allowing you to think of them almost as a cable harness in a hardware system. Depending on the system architecture, routers can appear in different places.

Routers in Layered Architectures

As you've seen in the "Coordinators" section, coordinators and workers can be organized into teams, and teams can be wired together to implement a complete system. You can break some systems down into a hierarchy of teams organized into layers, as shown in Figure 10-51.

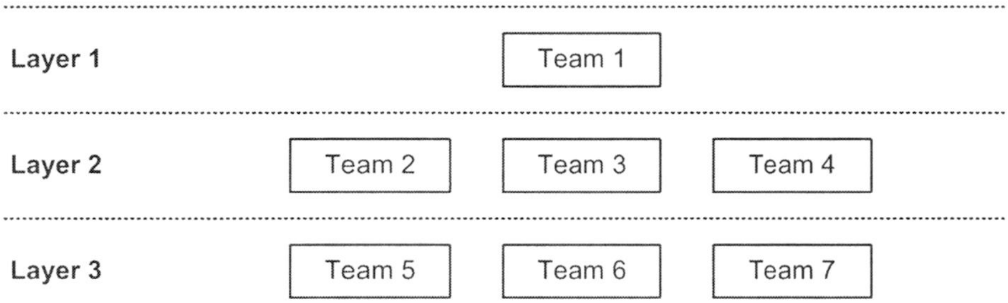

Layer 1
Team 1
Layer 2
Team 2
Team 3
Team 4
Layer 3
Team 5
Team 6
Team 7

Figure 10-51. *A system design organized by layer*

While in theory any team can talk to any other team, in a layered design you'll often impose constraints on how communication between layers is handled. The following are common constraints:

- A team on one layer can only talk to one team on adjacent layers.
- A team on one layer can talk to any team on adjacent layers.
- Each layer has a dedicated component that handles interlayer communication.

In the first case, there are multiple communication paths between layers, as shown in the diagram in Figure 10-52.

Layer 2
Team 2
Team 3
Team 4
Layer 3
Team 5
Team 6
Team 7

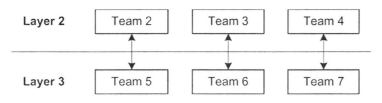

Figure 10-52. *A system with a vertical pattern of interlayer communication*

This type of interlayer interaction pattern is called *vertical*, for obvious reasons. Given any team on any layer, there is a single vertical path to adjacent layers.

In the second case, interlayer communication is fairly chaotic, as shown in Figure 10-53.

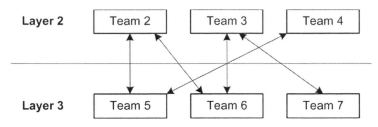

Figure 10-53. *A system with a chaotic pattern of interlayer communication*

In the third case, all interlayer communication is based on notifications that are funneled through dedicated `Router` components, resulting in the interlayer communication pattern shown in Figure 10-54.

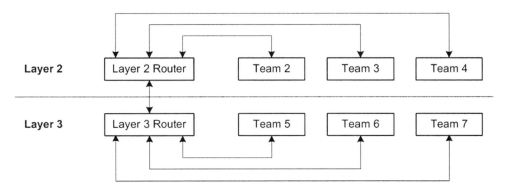

Figure 10-54. *Using routers to control interlayer communication*

The routers in the diagram act as gateways between layers. All signals crossing a layer boundary are channeled through a specific Router, which acts much like a hardware connector. If you disconnect the Router, all traffic with the adjoining layer is cut off. Using a Router like this makes it very convenient for debugging and system monitoring, because all signals between layers travel through a single object.

Routers As Notification Forwarders

You can also use routers as intermediate forwarders of notifications, as shown in Figure 10-55.

Routers may support message filters or rules to constrain notification delivery. Routers have been appearing in component systems for some time. For example, they're used in the EBI framework.[7] Routers are also somewhat similar to the *connectors* used in C2[8] to interconnect layers in a GUI system.

---

7. Daniel J. Barrett, Lori A. Clarke, Peri L. Tarr, and Alexander E. Wise, "A Framework for Event-Based Software Integration," *ACM Transactions on Software Engineering and Methodology*, October 1996.

8. Richard N. Taylor, Nenad Medvidovic, Kenneth M. Anderson, E. James Whitehead Jr., and Jason E. Robbins, "A Component- and Message-Based Architectural Style for GUI Software" (proceedings of the 17th International Conference on Software Engineering, Seattle, WA, April 1995).

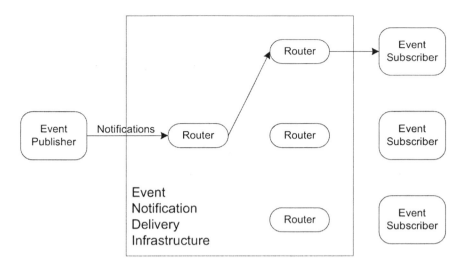

Figure 10-55. *Using routers to handle notification forwarding in complex publish-subscribe systems*

Routers As Bridges

Routers can also be employed in distributed system to connect the various systems together. In this capacity, you usually deploy routers at both ends of a connection, as shown in Figure 10-56.

Figure 10-56. *A Router used to bridge a remote connection between systems*

The bridging routers would encapsulate the communication logic. The routers would act essentially as proxies for the remote system.

An Example: Interconnecting Coordinators

Routers don't generally contain much logic, so they're very straightforward to implement. As a practical example, let's create a small system in which a router sits between two coordinators, as shown in the wiring diagram in Figure 10-57.

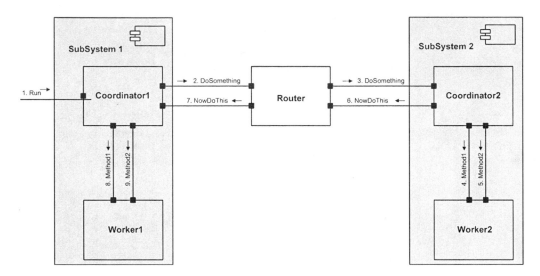

Figure 10-57. *An example of a system using a router*

The system consists of two major components, SubSystem1 and SubSystem2, with a router sitting between them. The Run command on SubSystem1 causes a flurry of activity, as shown in the diagram. Note that some of the objects, like C1, must be reentrant. When C1 fires the DoSomething event, the calls blocks until the event notification is processed. To process it, the Router forwards the notification to C2, which calls back through the Router into C1. To remove the reentrancy requirement, some of the events would have to be fired asynchronously. Listing 10-53 and Listing 10-54 show a C# and VB .NET implementation of the system.

Listing 10-53. *A C# Implementation of a System Using a Router*

```csharp
public delegate void UniversalHandler();

public class Router
{
  public void DoSomething()
  {
    FireDoSomething();
  }

  public void NowDoThis()
  {
    FireNowDoThis();
  }

  public event UniversalHandler OnDoSomething;
  void FireDoSomething()
  {
    if (OnDoSomething != null)
      OnDoSomething();
  }
```

```csharp
  public event UniversalHandler OnNowDoThis;
  void FireNowDoThis()
  {
    if (OnNowDoThis != null)
      OnNowDoThis();
  }

  public event UniversalHandler OnMethod1;
  void FireMethod1()
  {
    if (OnMethod1 != null)
      OnMethod1();
  }

  public event UniversalHandler OnMethod2;
  void FireMethod2()
  {
    if (OnMethod2 != null)
      OnMethod2();
  }
}

public class Coordinator1
{
  public void Run()
  {
    FireDoSomething();
  }

  public void NowDoThis()
  {
    FireMethod1();
    FireMethod2();
  }

  public event UniversalHandler OnDoSomething;
  void FireDoSomething()
  {
    if (OnDoSomething != null)
      OnDoSomething();
  }

  public event UniversalHandler OnMethod1;
  void FireMethod1()
  {
    if (OnMethod1 != null)
      OnMethod1();
  }
```

```
    public event UniversalHandler OnMethod2;
    void FireMethod2()
    {
      if (OnMethod2 != null)
        OnMethod2();
    }
  }
public class Coordinator2
{
  public void DoSomething()
  {
    FireMethod1();
    FireMethod2();
    FireNowDoThis();
  }

  public event UniversalHandler OnNowDoThis;
  void FireNowDoThis()
  {
    if (OnNowDoThis != null)
      OnNowDoThis();
  }

  public event UniversalHandler OnMethod1;
  void FireMethod1()
  {
    if (OnMethod1 != null)
      OnMethod1();
  }

  public event UniversalHandler OnMethod2;
  void FireMethod2()
  {
    if (OnMethod2 != null)
      OnMethod2();
  }
}
public class BuilderBinder
{
  public Coordinator1 coordinator1;
  public Worker1 worker1;
  public Router router;
  public Coordinator2 coordinator2;
  public Worker2 worker2;

  public void Build()
  {
    coordinator1 = new Coordinator1();
    worker1 = new Worker1();
    router = new Router();
    coordinator2 = new Coordinator2();
    worker2 = new Worker2();
  }
```

```csharp
  public void Bind()
  {
    coordinator1.OnDoSomething += new UniversalHandler(router.DoSomething);
    coordinator1.OnMethod1 += new UniversalHandler(worker1.Method1);
    coordinator1.OnMethod2 += new UniversalHandler(worker1.Method2);

    router.OnDoSomething += new UniversalHandler(coordinator2.DoSomething);
    router.OnNowDoThis += new UniversalHandler(coordinator1.NowDoThis);

    coordinator2.OnNowDoThis += new UniversalHandler(router.NowDoThis);
    coordinator2.OnMethod1 += new UniversalHandler(worker2.Method1);
    coordinator2.OnMethod2 += new UniversalHandler(worker2.Method2);
  }
}

public class Worker1
{
  public void Method1() {/*..*/}
  public void Method2() {/*..*/}
}

public class Worker2
{
  public void Method1() {/*..*/}
  public void Method2() {/*..*/}
}
```

Listing 10-54. *A VB .NET Implementation of a System Using a Router*

```vbnet
Public Delegate Sub UniversalHandler()

Public Class Router
  Public Sub DoSomething()
    FireDoSomething()
  End Sub

  Public Sub NowDoThis()
    FireNowDoThis()
  End Sub

  Public Event OnDoSomething As UniversalHandler
  Sub FireDoSomething()
    RaiseEvent OnDoSomething()
  End Sub

  Public Event OnNowDoThis As UniversalHandler
  Sub FireNowDoThis()
    RaiseEvent OnNowDoThis()
  End Sub

  Public Event OnMethod1 As UniversalHandler
  Sub FireMethod1()
    RaiseEvent OnMethod1()
  End Sub
```

```vbnet
    Public Event OnMethod2 As UniversalHandler
    Sub FireMethod2()
      RaiseEvent OnMethod2()
    End Sub
End Class
Public Class Coordinator1
  Public Sub Run()
    FireDoSomething()
  End Sub

  Public Sub NowDoThis()
    FireMethod1()
    FireMethod2()
  End Sub

  Public Event OnDoSomething As UniversalHandler
  Sub FireDoSomething()
    RaiseEvent OnDoSomething()
  End Sub

  Public Event OnMethod1 As UniversalHandler
  Sub FireMethod1()
    RaiseEvent OnMethod1()
  End Sub

  Public Event OnMethod2 As UniversalHandler
  Sub FireMethod2()
    RaiseEvent OnMethod2()
  End Sub
End Class

Public Class Coordinator2
  Public Sub DoSomething()
    FireMethod1()
    FireMethod2()
    FireNowDoThis()
  End Sub

  Public Event OnNowDoThis As UniversalHandler
  Sub FireNowDoThis()
    RaiseEvent OnNowDoThis()
  End Sub

  Public Event OnMethod1 As UniversalHandler
  Sub FireMethod1()
    RaiseEvent OnMethod1()
  End Sub

  Public Event OnMethod2 As UniversalHandler
  Sub FireMethod2()
    RaiseEvent OnMethod2()
  End Sub
End Class
```

```vb
Public Class BuilderBinder
  Public _coordinator1 As Coordinator1
  Public _worker1 As Worker1
  Public _router As Router
  Public _coordinator2 As Coordinator2
  Public _worker2 As Worker2

  Public Sub Build()
    _coordinator1 = New Coordinator1
    _worker1 = New Worker1
    _router = New Router
    _coordinator2 = New Coordinator2
    _worker2 = New Worker2
  End Sub

  Public Sub Bind()
    AddHandler _coordinator1.OnDoSomething, AddressOf _router.DoSomething
    AddHandler _coordinator1.OnMethod1, AddressOf _worker1.Method1
    AddHandler _coordinator1.OnMethod2, AddressOf _worker1.Method2

    AddHandler _router.OnDoSomething, AddressOf _coordinator2.DoSomething
    AddHandler _router.OnNowDoThis, AddressOf _coordinator1.NowDoThis

    AddHandler _coordinator2.OnNowDoThis, AddressOf _router.NowDoThis
    AddHandler _coordinator2.OnMethod1, AddressOf _worker2.Method1
    AddHandler _coordinator2.OnMethod2, AddressOf _worker2.Method2
  End Sub
End Class

Public Class Worker1
  Public Sub Method1()
  End Sub
  Public Sub Method2()
  End Sub
End Class

Public Class Worker2
  Public Sub Method1()
  End Sub
  Public Sub Method2()
  End Sub
End Class
```

The Router implementation contains only inputs that are wired directly to outputs. Routers often have no other logic. If you opt to add logic to a Router, the logic should only be related to notification routing. For example, a Router serving as a bridge across a remote connection may use a high-speed connection by default, but fall back on an alternate and slower connection if problems arise with the fast connection.

Summary

Software systems are used in the most disparate applications, making it difficult to imagine that their internal structures could have much in common. What could the real-time temperature-control system in your kitchen refrigerator have in common with a graphics weather program simulating the development of tornados? What could a word-processing program have in common with a credit-card-processing service? The answer to both is *functional roles*. You can envision event-based programs as a collection of parts that communicate using notification signals. These parts are not arbitrary in function: They tend to fall into well-defined categories, depending on their overall role in the system. Whether the parts are components, objects, or modules is not important: They can all be considered black boxes that provide a certain type of service to the surrounding system. By identifying roles explicitly in your designs, you make clear the separation of responsibilities across parts. Workers handle the bulk of the business logic. Coordinators manage workers and threading issues. Builders and binders create and hook the parts together. Routers ensure that signals get to their intended destinations. In the next three chapters, I'll present complete case studies that illustrate real-world applications designed with parts fulfilling the functional roles described in this chapter.

CHAPTER 11

Case Study 1: A System Browser

Starting with this chapter, I'll switch gears and look at some complete case studies of event-based systems designed with decoupled parts. If you're like me and enjoy looking at code, you should find these case studies interesting, because they bring together many of the ideas and concepts introduced earlier.

The first example is a small desktop system browser, conceptually similar to Microsoft Windows Explorer. The program, called SystemBrowser, consists of only one component and allows users to browse the file system and search for files. The main purpose of the example is to show how you might use decoupled classes to build a program with a user interface. The program demonstrates the following tasks:

- Using workers and coordinators to build a GUI program
- Managing the startup and shutdown phases using `LifecycleCoordinators`
- Saving and retrieving persistent user settings
- Updating a splash screen during initialization
- Using a coordinator to manage multithreading
- Unit-testing workers with dedicated test fixtures

While you can develop all the system's design and concepts in any programming language that supports events, the implementation details will vary somewhat across operating systems and component platforms. I'll provide the complete source code in both C# and VB .NET.

System Requirements

The program needs to support a two pane-window with a navigation pane on the left side and a content pane on the right. The navigation pane must have two different navigator controls: a Folders navigator and a Search navigator. Only one must be visible at a time. The Folders navigator shows a hierarchical list of folders on the C: drive. The Search navigator contains controls to search for files. The right pane must display information related to the selection in the left pane. Figure 11-1 shows what the program should look like when the Folders navigator is selected.

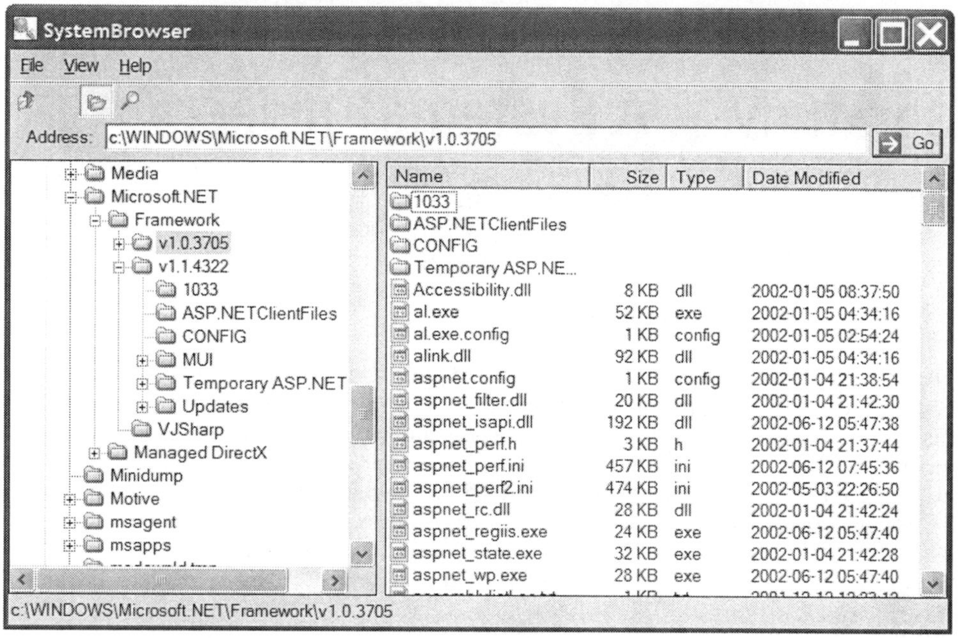

Figure 11-1. *A screenshot of SystemBrowser with the Folders navigator selected*

The navigator and content panes must be mutually synchronized, in the sense that selecting an item in one updates the other. When you select a folder in the Folders navigator, the content pane must show the folders and files in the selected folder. The status bar must display the complete path of the folder. When you select a file in the content pane, the status bar must show the file's size and its complete file path. Double-clicking a folder in the content pane should make two things happen: The Folders navigator should select the folder, and the content pane should show the contents of the folder.

The other navigator is a Search control that allows you to recursively search all subdirectories of a given directory for a file. SystemBrowser supports regular expressions for filenames, so you can do a search with names like m?.exe or *.doc. You must be able to interrupt the search at any time by clicking a button. While the search runs, the status bar must show the number of files found. The content pane must display a list of the files found. Selecting a file in the content pane must make the file's size and path appear in the status bar. Figure 11-2 shows the system after running a search.

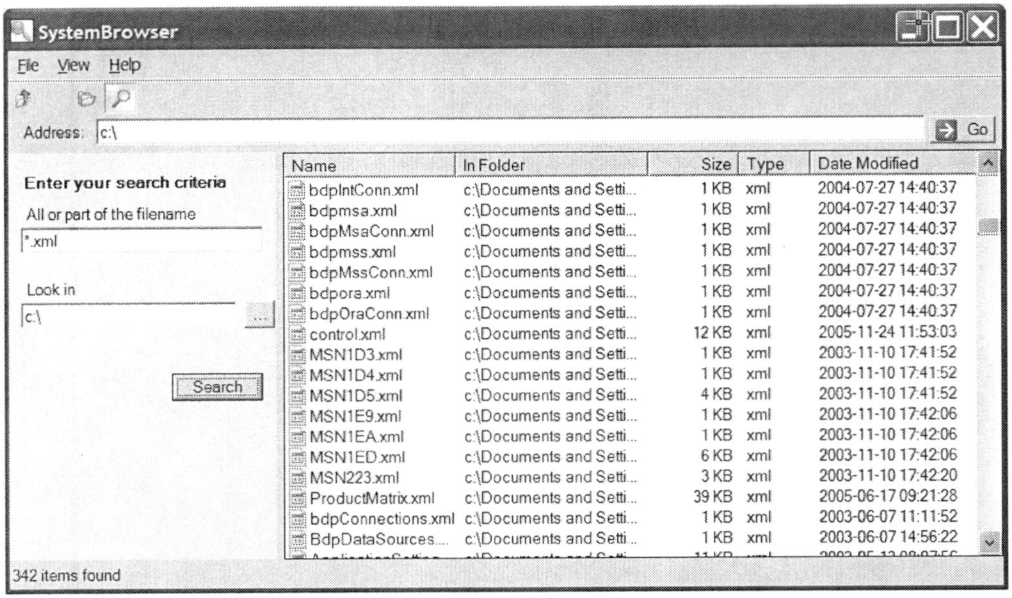

Figure 11-2. *A screenshot of SystemBrowser with the Search pane selected*

The program must have a menu bar. The File menu has only an Exit command. The View menu has two groups of menu items, as shown in Figure 11-3.

Figure 11-3. *The commands on the View menu*

The first two commands select the mode of the system: folder browsing or file searching. The second two commands affect the way the content panes appear. The Icons command should make the content panes display a single-column list of items, as shown in Figure 11-4.

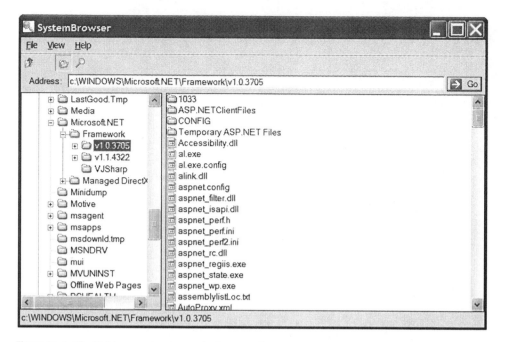

Figure 11-4. *The Folders content pane in Icon mode*

The Details command should produce a multicolumn display. The content pane must show the filename, size, type, and timestamp of each file, as shown back in Figure 11-1. The Search Results content pane must show the filename, directory, size, type, and date modified of each file, as shown back in Figure 11-2.

SystemBrowser also must have a toolbar with three buttons. The leftmost button must select the parent folder of the currently selected folder. The second and third buttons are shortcuts for the View ➤ Folders and View ➤ Search menu commands, respectively.

From the perspective of event-based programming, what is most important about the example is not how the individual functions are implemented, but how the various parts are interconnected. In many UI programs, the amount of logic contained in the main window is often disproportionately large, because it handles the menu commands, the toolbar commands, and the status bar, and it also coordinates interactions between top-level elements. In this case study, note how little code is contained in the main window (class FormMain).

System Design

The system is simple enough to be packaged in a single component. I've designed it using workers and coordinators, with the goal of having no coupling between them, so they can each be tested independently. I've used the following worker classes:

- NavigatorFolders: Occupies the left pane when the Folders mode is selected. It displays a hierarchical list of folders on the C: hard drive.

- NavigatorSearch: Occupies the left pane when the Search mode is selected. It displays a group of controls for running file searches.

- ContentFileList: Occupies the right pane and shows a list of folders and files.

- ContentSearchResults: Occupies the right file pane and shows a list of files that satisfy the search criteria.

- FormMenuToolBar: Hosts the main menu and the toolbar at design time. At run time, the menu and toolbar move over to FormMain.

- StatusBar: Consists of a gray strip that can display text messages.

The UI of SystemBrowser is hosted in a form called FormMain, which is used as a simple container to host the rest of the UI elements. FormMain controls the layout of the screen elements using a series of panels. The panels control the position and size of the various screen areas. Each panel hosts an object that contains the required UI elements for that area. Figure 11-5 shows how various panels are layered on the main form.

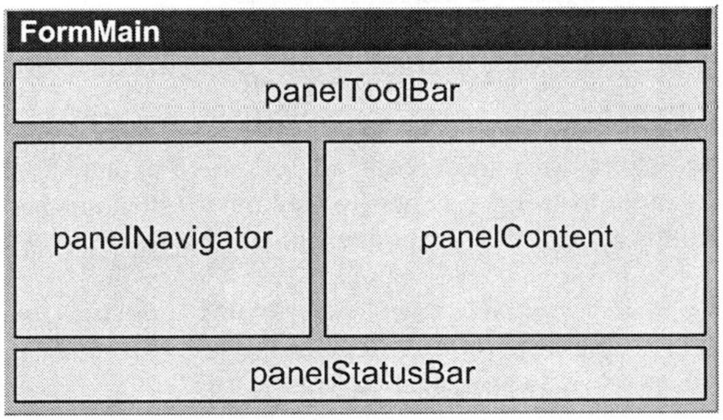

Figure 11-5. *The layered panels used to create SystemBrowser's UI layout*

The Folders and Search navigators are both hosted by panelNavigator. Only one navigator is visible at any given time. The Folders and Search content panes are hosted by panelContent. Again, only one content pane is visible at any given time. FormMain has only two public methods: ShowFolders and ShowSearch. These methods control which set of navigator-content controls are shown at a given time. FormMain has no idea what the hosted controls actually do. FormMain doesn't interact with those controls in any way. Figure 11-6 shows the class diagram of top-level classes.

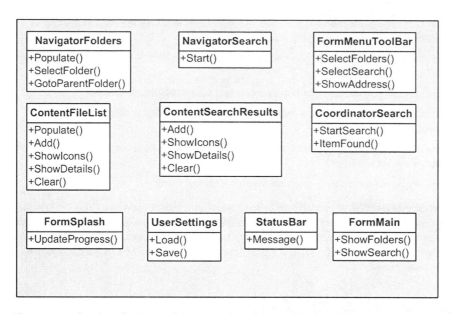

Figure 11-6. *The class diagram of the system's top-level classes*

The class diagram looks incomplete, because there are no relationships between any of the classes. I didn't forget the relationships: There simply are none. I designed the system so that all its top-level classes are decoupled from each other. The only classes missing from the diagram are those related to the infrastructure: the LifecycleCoordinators, the builder, and the binder, which I'll discuss shortly.

The classes are all pretty simple, but the class diagram tells you almost nothing about how the system is really structured, because you can't see how the parts interact when the system is running. A more useful way to show the system is with a wiring diagram, as shown in Figure 11-7.

The diagram depicts the system in the cruising state, which is the normal running state entered after system startup. There's a lot going on in the diagram, so later I'll describe important parts of it with separate use cases and partial-wiring diagrams. The shaded area enclosing the signals between NavigatorSearch and CoordinatorSearch represents a background operation. NavigatorSearch runs searches in a background thread, because you don't want the UI to freeze up while a search is in progress. The system requirements also specify that a search in progress must be interruptible using the Stop button. Using a separate thread to run the search on makes it easy to stop the search at any time, without the need to constantly poll the user interface for stop commands. CoordinatorSearch controls the threading, and there is no thread-related code anywhere in the system except in CoordinatorSearch. When the user clicks the Search button, NavigatorSearch fires a SearchRequested event to CoordinatorSearch, which spawns a background thread to run the search on. By keeping all the threading logic in the Coordinator, you can keep the NavigatorSearch Worker relatively simple.

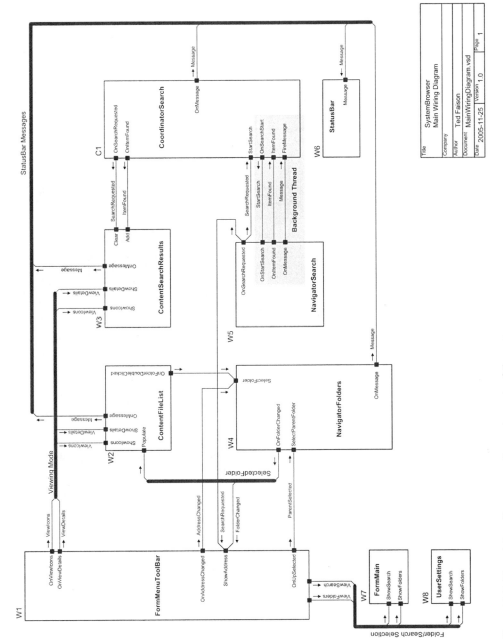

Figure 11-7. *The wiring diagram on the main parts of the system*

Although the system uses a `Builder` and `Binder`, those two classes don't appear in the wiring diagram, because they don't participate in the ordinary operation of the system. They set up the various parts, wire them together, and then step out of the picture. Since the `Builder` and `Binder` work directly with all the top-level classes in the system, they are also at the center of the system's coupling diagram, shown in Figure 11-8.

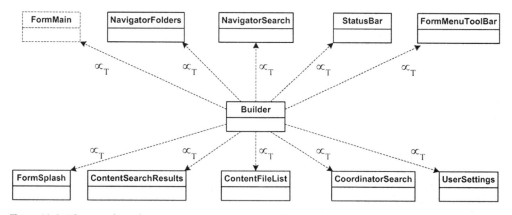

Figure 11-8. *The coupling diagram on the main parts of the system*

The star pattern tells you that the system coupling is ideal: One class is coupled to all the others, and the classes in the periphery are decoupled from each other. The diagram only shows the `Builder` at the center. The `Binder` is also at the center, but I omitted it to keep the diagram easier to read.

Life-Cycle Management

From the life-cycle perspective, SystemBrowser is like many systems because it has three modes of operation: startup, cruise, and shutdown. In the startup state, it displays a splash screen with a progress bar while the system is initialized. The splash screen is shown in Figure 11-9.

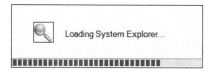

Figure 11-9. *The splash screen displayed by SystemBrowser*

During startup, the user's settings are read from a local file. In the cruise state, the main user interface is shown. The system spends most of its time in the cruise state. In the shutdown state, the UI is hidden to prevent further user interaction with the system. During shutdown, the user's settings are persisted to disk.

SystemBrowser uses a dedicated LifecycleCoordinator to manage its life-cycle states. Each state has its own Coordinator, as shown in the wiring diagram in Figure 11-10.

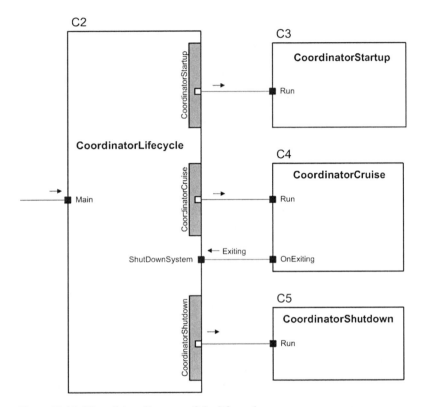

Figure 11-10. *The wiring diagram of the life-cycle-management system*

The main entry point of SystemBrowser is the static method LifecycleCoordinator.Main. This method is called by the operating system to start the program. The method creates an instance of LifecycleCoordinator, which in turn creates CoordinatorStartup. The latter class is responsible for getting the system loaded and ready to run. Once the system is ready, control is passed to CoordinatorCruise, which runs the system. The system is under control of CoordinatorCruise until it is ready to be shut down. When CoordinatorCruise requests that the system be shut down, LifecycleCoordinator gives control to CoordinatorShutdown, which handles the shutdown operation. The sequence diagram in Figure 11-11 shows the details.

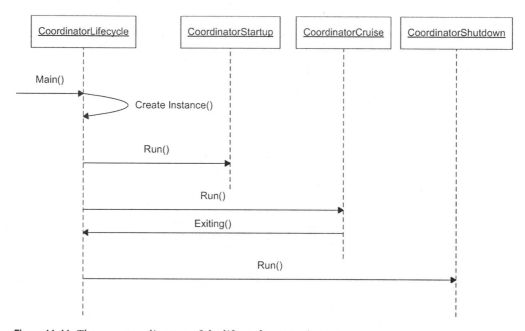

Figure 11-11. *The sequence diagram of the life-cycle-management system*

The wiring diagram in Figure 11-12 shows how CoordinatorStartup connects to the rest of the system.

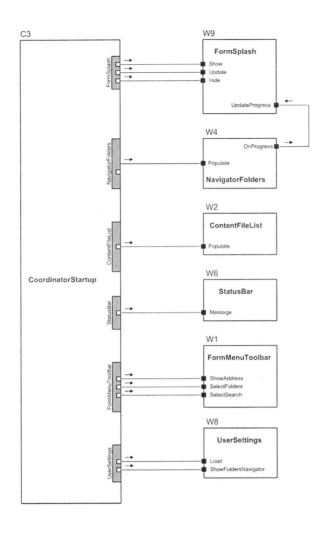

Title	SystemBrower Startup Wiring		
Company			
Author	Ted Faison		
Document	StartupWiring.vsd		
Date 2005-11-25	Version 1.0		Page 1

Figure 11-12. *The wiring diagram of the startup system*

Listing 11-1 and Listing 11-2 show C# and VB .NET implementations of the LifecycleCoordinators.

Listing 11-1. *The C# Implementation of the LifecycleCoordinators*

```
public class LifecycleCoordinator
{
  // The main entry point for the application
  [STAThread]
  static void Main()
  {
    LifecycleCoordinator coordinator = new LifecycleCoordinator();
    coordinator.Start(); // app exits when this call completes
  }
```

```csharp
enum LifecycleState {StartingUp, Running, ShuttingDown};
LifecycleState state;

// Gets a singleton instance of the main Builder.
Builder Builder
{
  get {return Builder.Singleton;}
}

public void Start()
{
  StartupSystem();
  RunSystem(); // app exits when this call completes
}

void StartupSystem()
{
  state = LifecycleState.StartingUp;
  Builder.startup.Run();
}

void RunSystem()
{
  if (state != LifecycleState.StartingUp)
    throw new Exception("Invalid lifecycle state");

  state = LifecycleState.Running;
  Builder.cruise.OnExiting +=
      new CoordinatorCruise.ExitingHandler(ShutDownSystem);
  Builder.cruise.Run(); // app exits when this call completes
}

void ShutDownSystem()
{
  if (state != LifecycleState.Running)
    throw new Exception("Invalid lifecycle state");

  state = LifecycleState.ShuttingDown;
  Builder.shutdown.Run();
}
}

public class CoordinatorStartup
{
  // Gets a singleton version of the Builder class.
  Builder Builder
  {
    get {return Builder.Singleton;}
  }

  public void Run()
  {
    // name the UI thread, so we can distinguish it
    // from other threads in the debugger window
```

```
      System.Threading.Thread.CurrentThread.Name = "User Interface";

      Builder.formSplash.Show();
      Builder.formSplash.Update(); // otherwise it appears in fragments

      Builder.Build();  // instantiate all the top-level classes
      Builder.binder.Bind();  // wire all the top-level objects

      // temporarily wire form splash to handle startup progress updates
      Builder.binder.BindFormSplash();

      InitializeSystem();

      // unwire form splash, since progress updates are no longer required
      Builder.binder.UnbindFormSplash();

      Builder.formMain.Show();
      Builder.formMain.Update();

      Builder.formSplash.Hide();
    }

    void InitializeSystem()
    {
      Builder.userSettings.Load();

      // show initial folders and files
      const string initialFolder = @"c:\";
      Builder.navigatorFolders.Populate(initialFolder);
      Builder.contentFolders.Populate(initialFolder);
      Builder.statusBar.Message(initialFolder);
      Builder.formMenuToolBar.ShowAddress(initialFolder);

      if (Builder.userSettings.ShowFoldersNavigator)
        Builder.formMenuToolBar.SelectFolders();
      else
        Builder.formMenuToolBar.SelectSearch();
    }
  }

  public class CoordinatorCruise
  {
    // Gets a singleton instance of the Builder class.
    Builder Builder
    {
      get {return Builder.Singleton;}
    }

    public void Run()
    {
      Builder.formMain.Closing += new CancelEventHandler(formMain_Closing);
      Application.Run(Builder.formMain);  // app exits when this call completes
    }
```

```csharp
    private void formMain_Closing(object sender,
                        System.ComponentModel.CancelEventArgs e)
    {
      // to prevent the app from closing, do this
      // e.Cancel = true;
      // return;

      // let the app shut the app down
      FireExiting();
    }

    public void HandleTopLevelEvents()
    {
      // handle the top-level events that occur during
      // the normal operation of the system...
    }

    public delegate void ExitingHandler();
    public event ExitingHandler OnExiting;
    void FireExiting()
    {
      if (OnExiting == null) return;
      OnExiting();
    }
}

public class CoordinatorShutdown
{
  // shortcut property
  Builder Builder
  {
    get {return Builder.Singleton;}
  }

  public void Run()
  {
    // disable the user interface during shutdown
    if (Builder.formMain != null)
      Builder.formMain.Visible = false;

    Builder.userSettings.Save();
  }
}
```

Listing 11-2. *The VB .NET Implementation of the LifecycleCoordinators*

```vbnet
Public Class LifecycleCoordinator

  ' The main entry point for the application
  Shared Sub Main()
    Dim coordinator As New LifecycleCoordinator
    coordinator.Start() ' app exits when this call completes
  End Sub
```

```vbnet
    Enum LifecycleState
      StartingUp
      Running
      ShuttingDown
    End Enum

    Private state As LifecycleState

    ' Gets a singleton instance of the Builder class.
    ReadOnly Property Builder() As Builder
      Get
        Return Builder.Singleton
      End Get
    End Property

    Public Sub Start()
      StartupSystem()
      RunSystem() ' app exits when this call completes
    End Sub

    Sub StartupSystem()
      state = LifecycleState.StartingUp
      Builder._startup.Run()
    End Sub

    Sub RunSystem()
      If state <> LifecycleState.StartingUp Then
        Throw New Exception("Invalid lifecycle state")
      End If

      state = LifecycleState.Running
      AddHandler Builder._cruise.OnExiting, AddressOf ShutDownSystem
      Builder._cruise.Run() ' app exits when this call completes
    End Sub

    Sub ShutDownSystem()
      If state <> LifecycleState.Running Then
        Throw New Exception("Invalid lifecycle state")
      End If

      state = LifecycleState.ShuttingDown
      Builder._shutdown.Run()
    End Sub

End Class
Public Class CoordinatorStartup
  ' Gets a singleton instance of the Builder class.
  ReadOnly Property Builder() As Builder
    Get
      Return Builder.Singleton
    End Get
  End Property
```

```vb
    Public Sub Run()
      ' name the UI thread, so we can distinguish it
      ' from other threads in the debugger window
      System.Threading.Thread.CurrentThread.Name = "User Interface"

      Builder._formSplash.Show()
      Builder._formSplash.Update() ' otherwise it appears in fragments

      Builder.Build()  ' instantiate all the top-level classes
      Builder._binder.Bind()  ' wire all the top-level objects

      ' temporarily wire form splash to handle startup progress updates
      Builder._binder.BindFormSplash()

      InitializeSystem()

      ' unwire form splash, since progress updates are no longer required
      Builder._binder.UnbindFormSplash()

      Builder._formMain.Show()
      Builder._formMain.Update()

      Builder._formSplash.Hide()
    End Sub

    Sub InitializeSystem()
      Builder._userSettings.Load()

      ' show initial folders and files
      Const initialFolder As String = "c:\"
      Builder._navigatorFolders.Populate(initialFolder)
      Builder._contentFolders.Populate(initialFolder)
      Builder._statusBar.Message(initialFolder)
      Builder._formMenuToolBar.ShowAddress(initialFolder)

      If (Builder._userSettings.ShowFoldersNavigator) Then
        Builder._formMenuToolBar.SelectFolders()
      Else
        Builder._formMenuToolBar.SelectSearch()
      End If
    End Sub
  End Class

Public Class CoordinatorCruise

  '  Gets a singleton instance of the Builder class.
  ReadOnly Property Builder() As Builder
    Get
      Return Builder.Singleton
    End Get
  End Property
```

```vbnet
  Public Sub Run()
    AddHandler Builder._formMain.Closing, AddressOf formMain_Closing
    Application.Run(Builder._formMain)  ' app exits when this call completes
  End Sub

  Private Sub formMain_Closing(ByVal sender As Object, _
              ByVal e As System.ComponentModel.CancelEventArgs)
    'to prevent the app from closing, do this
    'e.Cancel = true;
    'return;

    ' let the app shut the app down
    FireExiting()
  End Sub

  Public Sub HandleTopLevelEvents()
    ' handle the top-level events that occur during
    ' the normal operation of the system...
  End Sub

  Public Event OnExiting()
  Sub FireExiting()
    RaiseEvent OnExiting()
  End Sub

End Class
Public Class CoordinatorShutdown
  ' shortcut property
  ReadOnly Property Builder() As Builder
    Get
      Return Builder.Singleton
    End Get
  End Property

  Public Sub Run()
    ' disable the user interface during shutdown
    If Not Builder._formMain Is Nothing Then
      Builder._formMain.Visible = False
    End If

    Builder._userSettings.Save()
  End Sub
End Class
```

In the method CoordinatorStartup.Run, the call FormSplash.builder.Update is necessary after calling FormSplash.builder. Why? Because calling Form.Show simply schedules a repaint of invalidated areas of a Form. Since the system is busy loading the system when the splash screen is shown, the individual areas of the splash screen get painted one at a time, causing an annoying UI effect. By calling Form.Update, the whole form is painted at once.

Note that the LifecycleCoordinators are coupled to the Builder, so they are indirectly coupled to all the top-level classes in the system. This coupling is not usually a problem, because the LifecycleCoordinators are very simple compared to the top-level Workers and CoordinatorSearch.

Builder

Builder has only one task: to instantiate all the top-level classes in the system. Since the Builder holds references to the objects it creates, and only one instance of each top-level object is allowed, Builder is designed as a singleton. Using a Builder, you never have any doubts about which object is holding a top-level object alive, preventing it from being garbage-collected. Builder keeps all those top-level class instances in a single place, so they are easy to find and keep track of. Listing 11-3 and Listing 11-4 show C# and VB .NET implementations of the Builder.

Listing 11-3. *The C# Implementation of the Builder*

```
public class Builder
{
  // there can only be one instance of the Builder
  static Builder singleton;
  static public Builder Singleton
  {
    get
    {
      if (singleton == null)
        singleton = new Builder();
      return singleton;
    }
  }

  public Binder binder;
  public UserSettings userSettings;

  // UI elements
  public FormSplash formSplash;
  public FormMain formMain;
  public FormMenuToolBar formMenuToolBar;
  public StatusBar statusBar;

  // Workers
  public NavigatorFolders navigatorFolders;
  public NavigatorSearch navigatorSearch;
  public ContentFileList contentFolders;
  public ContentSearchResults contentSearch;

  // Coordinators
  public CoordinatorStartup startup;    // lifecycle: starting up state
  public CoordinatorShutdown shutdown;  // lifecycle: shutting down state
  public CoordinatorCruise cruise;      // lifecycle: cruising state
  public CoordinatorSearch coordinatorSearch;

  public Builder()
  {
    formSplash = new FormSplash();
    binder = new Binder(this);
    startup = new CoordinatorStartup();
    userSettings = new UserSettings();
  }
```

```
  public void Build()
  {
    // create the navigators for the left pane
    navigatorFolders = new NavigatorFolders();
    navigatorSearch = new NavigatorSearch();

    // create the content managers for the right pane
    contentFolders = new ContentFileList();
    contentSearch = new ContentSearchResults();

    // UI elements
    formMenuToolBar = new FormMenuToolBar();
    statusBar = new StatusBar();
    formMain = new FormMain();

    // Coordinators
    cruise = new CoordinatorCruise();
    shutdown = new CoordinatorShutdown();
    coordinatorSearch = new CoordinatorSearch(formMain);

    // move the navigators and content viewers into FormMain
    formMain.NavigatorFolders = navigatorFolders;
    formMain.NavigatorSearch = navigatorSearch;
    formMain.ContentFolders = contentFolders;
    formMain.ContentSearch = contentSearch;

    // move the menu, toolbar and statusbar into FormMain
    formMain.Menu = formMenuToolBar.mainMenu;
    formMain.Toolbar = formMenuToolBar.panelToolBar;
    formMain.Statusbar = statusBar;
  }
}
```

Listing 11-4. *The VB .NET Implementation of the Builder*

```
Public Class Builder
  ' there can only be one instance of the Builder
  Private Shared _singleton As Builder
  Public Shared ReadOnly Property Singleton() As Builder
    Get
      If _singleton Is Nothing Then
        _singleton = New Builder
      End If
      Return _singleton
    End Get
  End Property

  Public _binder As Binder
  Public _userSettings As UserSettings

  ' UI elements
  Public _formSplash As FormSplash
  Public _formMain As FormMain
  Public _formMenuToolBar As FormMenuToolBar
```

```
    Public _statusBar As StatusBar

    ' Workers
    Public _navigatorFolders As NavigatorFolders
    Public _navigatorSearch As NavigatorSearch
    Public _contentFolders As ContentFileList
    Public _contentSearch As ContentSearchResults

    ' Coordinators
    Public _startup As CoordinatorStartup 'lifecycle: starting up state
    Public _shutdown As CoordinatorShutdown 'lifecycle: shutting down state
    Public _cruise As CoordinatorCruise 'lifecycle: cruising state
    Public _coordinatorSearch As CoordinatorSearch '

    Public Sub New()
      _formSplash = New FormSplash
      _binder = New Binder(Me)
      _startup = New CoordinatorStartup
      _userSettings = New UserSettings
    End Sub

    Public Sub Build()
      ' create the navigators for the left pane
      _navigatorFolders = New NavigatorFolders
      _navigatorSearch = New NavigatorSearch

      ' create the content managers for the right pane
      _contentFolders = New ContentFileList
      _contentSearch = New ContentSearchResults

      ' UI elements
      _formMenuToolBar = New FormMenuToolBar
      _statusBar = New StatusBar
      _formMain = New FormMain

      ' Coordinators
      _cruise = New CoordinatorCruise
      _shutdown = New CoordinatorShutdown
      _coordinatorSearch = New CoordinatorSearch(_formMain)

      ' move the navigators and content viewers into FormMain
      _formMain.NavigatorFolders = _navigatorFolders
      _formMain.NavigatorSearch = _navigatorSearch
      _formMain.ContentFolders = _contentFolders
      _formMain.ContentSearch = _contentSearch

      ' move the menu, toolbar and statusbar into FormMain
      _formMain.Menu = _formMenuToolBar.mainMenu
      _formMain.Toolbar = _formMenuToolBar.panelToolBar
      _formMain.Statusbar = _statusBar
    End Sub
End Class
```

Binder

Binder wires the top-level objects together. All the wiring in SystemBrowser is fixed, except in one case: the signal Progress, emitted by NavigatorFolders to update the progress bar on the splash screen. After initialization, this signal is no longer used, so the Binder removes its wiring. All the other wiring is kept in place for the entire life cycle of the system. Listing 11-5 and Listing 11-6 show C# and VB .NET implementations of the Binder.

Listing 11-5. *The C# Implementation of the Binder*

```
public class Binder
{
  private Builder builder;

  // a handler will be used only during startup
  // to show progress on the splash screen
  NavigatorFolders.ProgressHandler progressUpdater;

  public Binder(Builder theBuilder)
  {
    builder = theBuilder;
    progressUpdater =
        new NavigatorFolders.ProgressHandler(builder.formSplash.UpdateProgress);
  }

  public void Bind()
  {
    builder.formMenuToolBar.OnViewFolders +=
        new FormMenuToolBar.UniversalHandler(builder.formMain.ShowFolders);
    builder.formMenuToolBar.OnViewFolders +=
        new FormMenuToolBar.UniversalHandler(builder.userSettings.ShowFolders);

    builder.formMenuToolBar.OnViewSearch +=
        new FormMenuToolBar.UniversalHandler(builder.formMain.ShowSearch);
    builder.formMenuToolBar.OnViewSearch +=
        new FormMenuToolBar.UniversalHandler(builder.userSettings.ShowSearch);

    builder.formMenuToolBar.OnViewIcons +=
        new FormMenuToolBar.UniversalHandler(builder.contentFolders.ShowIcons);
    builder.formMenuToolBar.OnViewIcons +=
        new FormMenuToolBar.UniversalHandler(builder.contentSearch.ShowIcons);

    builder.formMenuToolBar.OnViewDetails +=
        new FormMenuToolBar.UniversalHandler(builder.contentFolders.ShowDetails);
    builder.formMenuToolBar.OnViewDetails +=
        new FormMenuToolBar.UniversalHandler(builder.contentSearch.ShowDetails);

    builder.formMenuToolBar.OnUpSelected +=
        new FormMenuToolBar.UniversalHandler(
                builder.navigatorFolders.SelectParentFolder);
    builder.formMenuToolBar.OnAddressChanged +=
        new FormMenuToolBar.AddressChangedHandler(
                builder.navigatorFolders.SelectFolder);
```

```
        builder.navigatorFolders.OnFolderChanged +=
            new NavigatorFolders.FolderChangedHandler(builder.contentFolders.Populate);
        builder.navigatorFolders.OnFolderChanged +=
            new NavigatorFolders.FolderChangedHandler(
                    builder.formMenuToolBar.ShowAddress);
        builder.navigatorFolders.OnMessage +=
            new NavigatorFolders.MessageHandler(builder.statusBar.Message);

        builder.contentFolders.OnMessage +=
            new ContentFileList.MessageHandler(builder.statusBar.Message);
        builder.contentFolders.OnFolderDoubleClicked +=
            new ContentFileList.FolderDoubleClickedHandler(
                    builder.navigatorFolders.SelectFolder);

        builder.coordinatorSearch.OnSearchRequested +=
            new CoordinatorSearch.SearchRequestedHandler(
                    builder.contentSearch.Clear);
        builder.coordinatorSearch.OnSearchStart +=
            new ThreadStart(builder.navigatorSearch.Start);
        builder.coordinatorSearch.OnItemFound +=
            new CoordinatorSearch.ItemFoundHandler(builder.contentSearch.Add);
        builder.coordinatorSearch.OnMessage +=
            new  CoordinatorSearch.MessageHandler(builder.statusBar.Message);

        builder.navigatorSearch.OnSearchRequested +=
            new NavigatorSearch.SearchRequestedHandler(
                    builder.formMenuToolBar.ShowAddress);
        builder.navigatorSearch.OnSearchRequested +=
            new NavigatorSearch.SearchRequestedHandler(
                    builder.coordinatorSearch.StartSearch);
        builder.navigatorSearch.OnItemFound +=
            new NavigatorSearch.ItemFoundHandler(builder.coordinatorSearch.ItemFound);
        builder.navigatorSearch.OnMessage +=
            new NavigatorSearch.MessageHandler(builder.coordinatorSearch.FireMessage);

        builder.contentSearch.OnMessage +=
            new ContentSearchResults.MessageHandler(builder.statusBar.Message);
    }

    public void BindFormSplash()
    {
      builder.navigatorFolders.OnProgress += progressUpdater;
    }

    public void UnbindFormSplash()
    {
      builder.navigatorFolders.OnProgress -= progressUpdater;
    }
}
```

Listing 11-6. *The VB .NET Implementation of the Binder*

```vb
Public Class Binder

  Private _builder As Builder

  ' a handler will be used only during startup,
  ' to show progress on the splash screen
  Private _progressUpdater As NavigatorFolders.ProgressHandler

  Public Sub New(ByVal theBuilder As Builder)
    _builder = theBuilder
    _progressUpdater = AddressOf _builder._formSplash.UpdateProgress
  End Sub

  Public Sub Bind()
    AddHandler _builder._formMenuToolBar.OnViewFolders, _
                  AddressOf _builder._formMain.ShowFolders
    AddHandler _builder._formMenuToolBar.OnViewFolders, _
                  AddressOf _builder._userSettings.ShowFolders

    AddHandler _builder._formMenuToolBar.OnViewSearch, _
                  AddressOf _builder._formMain.ShowSearch
    AddHandler _builder._formMenuToolBar.OnViewSearch, _
                  AddressOf _builder._userSettings.ShowSearch

    AddHandler _builder._formMenuToolBar.OnViewIcons, _
                  AddressOf _builder._contentFolders.ShowIcons
    AddHandler _builder._formMenuToolBar.OnViewIcons, _
                  AddressOf _builder._contentSearch.ShowIcons

    AddHandler _builder._formMenuToolBar.OnViewDetails, _
                  AddressOf _builder._contentFolders.ShowDetails
    AddHandler _builder._formMenuToolBar.OnViewDetails, _
                  AddressOf _builder._contentSearch.ShowDetails

    AddHandler _builder._formMenuToolBar.OnUpSelected, _
                  AddressOf _builder._navigatorFolders.SelectParentFolder
    AddHandler _builder._formMenuToolBar.OnAddressChanged, _
                  AddressOf _builder._navigatorFolders.SelectFolder

    AddHandler _builder._navigatorFolders.OnFolderChanged, _
                  AddressOf _builder._contentFolders.Populate
    AddHandler _builder._navigatorFolders.OnFolderChanged, _
                  AddressOf _builder._formMenuToolBar.ShowAddress
    AddHandler _builder._navigatorFolders.OnMessage, _
                  AddressOf _builder._statusBar.Message

    AddHandler _builder._contentFolders.OnMessage, _
                  AddressOf _builder._statusBar.Message
    AddHandler _builder._contentFolders.OnFolderDoubleClicked, _
                  AddressOf _builder._navigatorFolders.SelectFolder
```

```vb
        AddHandler _builder._coordinatorSearch.OnSearchRequested, _
                        AddressOf _builder._contentSearch.Clear
        'the following is a delegate, not an event
        _builder._coordinatorSearch.OnSearchStart = _
                        AddressOf _builder._navigatorSearch.Start
        AddHandler _builder._coordinatorSearch.OnItemFound, _
                        AddressOf _builder._contentSearch.Add
        AddHandler _builder._coordinatorSearch.OnMessage, _
                        AddressOf _builder._statusBar.Message

        AddHandler _builder._navigatorSearch.OnSearchRequested, _
                        AddressOf _builder._formMenuToolBar.ShowAddress
        AddHandler _builder._navigatorSearch.OnSearchRequested, _
                        AddressOf _builder._coordinatorSearch.StartSearch
        AddHandler _builder._navigatorSearch.OnItemFound, _
                        AddressOf _builder._coordinatorSearch.ItemFound
        AddHandler _builder._navigatorSearch.OnMessage, _
                        AddressOf _builder._coordinatorSearch.FireMessage

        AddHandler _builder._contentSearch.OnMessage, _
                        AddressOf _builder._statusBar.Message
    End Sub

    Public Sub BindFormSplash()
      AddHandler _builder._navigatorFolders.OnProgress, _progressUpdater
    End Sub

    Public Sub UnbindFormSplash()
      RemoveHandler _builder._navigatorFolders.OnProgress, _progressUpdater
    End Sub

End Class
```

The Menu and Toolbar

In many desktop applications, the toolbar contains shortcuts to menu commands, so it makes sense to put the menu and toolbar handling code in the same place. SystemBrowser uses a form called FormMenuToolBar to host the menu and toolbar at design time. This form also contains the event-handling code for the menus and toolbar. At run time, the Builder moves the menu and toolbar to FormMain. Listing 11-7 and Listing 11-8 show C# and VB .NET implementations of FormMenuToolBar.

Listing 11-7. *The C# Implementation of FormMenuToolBar*

```csharp
public class FormMenuToolBar : System.Windows.Forms.Form
{
  public FormMenuToolBar()
  {
    // Required for Windows Form Designer support
    InitializeComponent();
  }
```

```csharp
public void SelectFolders()
{
  toolBarButtonFolders.Pushed = true;
  toolBarButtonSearch.Pushed = false;

  menuItemViewFolders.Checked = true;
  menuItemViewSearch.Checked = false;

  FireViewFolders();
}

public void SelectSearch()
{
  toolBarButtonFolders.Pushed = false;
  toolBarButtonSearch.Pushed = true;

  menuItemViewFolders.Checked = false;
  menuItemViewSearch.Checked = true;

  FireViewSearch();
}

public void ShowAddress(string theAddress)
{
  if (theAddress == null) theAddress = string.Empty;
  textBoxAddress.Text = theAddress;
  textBoxAddress.SelectionStart = textBoxAddress.Text.Length;
}

protected override void Dispose( bool disposing )
{
  //...
}

#region Windows Form Designer generated code
  // ...
#endregion

#region Event Handlers
private void menuItemFileExit_Click(object sender, System.EventArgs e)
{
  Application.Exit();
}

private void menuItemViewFolders_Click(object sender, System.EventArgs e)
{
  SelectFolders();
}

private void menuItemViewSearch_Click(object sender, System.EventArgs e)
{
  SelectSearch();
}
```

```csharp
private void menuItemViewIcons_Click(object sender, System.EventArgs e)
{
  menuItemViewIcons.Checked = true;
  menuItemViewDetails.Checked = false;
  FireViewIcons();
}

private void menuItemViewDetails_Click(object sender, System.EventArgs e)
{
  menuItemViewIcons.Checked = false;
  menuItemViewDetails.Checked = true;
  FireViewDetails();
}

private void menuItemHelpAbout_Click(object sender, System.EventArgs e)
{
  FormAbout formAbout = new FormAbout();
  formAbout.ShowDialog();
}

private void toolBar1_ButtonClick(object sender, ToolBarButtonClickEventArgs e)
{
  if (e.Button == toolBarButtonUp)
  {
    SelectFolders();
    FireUpSelected();
  }
  else if (e.Button == toolBarButtonFolders)
  {
    SelectFolders();
  }
  else if (e.Button == toolBarButtonSearch)
  {
    SelectSearch();
  }
}

private void buttonGo_Click(object sender, System.EventArgs e)
{
  FireAddressChanged(textBoxAddress.Text);
}

private void textBoxAddress_KeyPress(object sender, KeyPressEventArgs e)
{
  if (e.KeyChar == '\r')
  {
    e.Handled = true; // to prevent Windows from beeping
    FireAddressChanged(textBoxAddress.Text);
  }
}
#endregion
```

```csharp
#region Events
public delegate void UniversalHandler();

public event UniversalHandler OnViewFolders;
void FireViewFolders()
{
  if (OnViewFolders != null)
    OnViewFolders();
}

public event UniversalHandler OnViewSearch;
void FireViewSearch()
{
  if (OnViewSearch != null)
    OnViewSearch();
}

public event UniversalHandler OnViewIcons;
void FireViewIcons()
{
  if (OnViewIcons != null)
    OnViewIcons();
}

public event UniversalHandler OnViewDetails;
void FireViewDetails()
{
  if (OnViewDetails != null)
    OnViewDetails();
}

public event UniversalHandler OnUpSelected;
void FireUpSelected()
{
  if (OnUpSelected != null)
    OnUpSelected();
}

public delegate void AddressChangedHandler(string theNewAddress);
public event AddressChangedHandler OnAddressChanged;
void FireAddressChanged(string theNewAddress)
{
  if (OnAddressChanged != null)
    OnAddressChanged(theNewAddress);
}
#endregion
}
```

Listing 11-8. *The VB .NET Implementation of FormMenuToolBar*

```vb
Public Class FormMenuToolBar
    Inherits System.Windows.Forms.Form

  Public Sub SelectFolders()
    toolBarButtonFolders.Pushed = True
    toolBarButtonSearch.Pushed = False

    menuItemViewFolders.Checked = True
    menuItemViewSearch.Checked = False

    FireViewFolders()
  End Sub

  Public Sub SelectSearch()
    toolBarButtonFolders.Pushed = False
    toolBarButtonSearch.Pushed = True

    menuItemViewFolders.Checked = False
    menuItemViewSearch.Checked = True

    FireViewSearch()
  End Sub

  Public Sub ShowAddress(ByVal theAddress As String)
    If theAddress Is Nothing Then theAddress = String.Empty
    textBoxAddress.Text = theAddress
    textBoxAddress.SelectionStart = textBoxAddress.Text.Length
  End Sub

#Region " Windows Form Designer generated code "

  Public Sub New()
    MyBase.New()

    'This call is required by the Windows Form Designer.
    InitializeComponent()

    'Add any initialization after the InitializeComponent() call

  End Sub

    'other initialization…

#End Region

#Region "Event Handlers"

  Private Sub menuItemFileExit_Click(ByVal sender As System.Object, _
            ByVal e As System.EventArgs) Handles menuItemFileExit.Click
    Application.Exit()
  End Sub
```

```vbnet
Private Sub menuItemViewFolders_Click(ByVal sender As System.Object, _
            ByVal e As System.EventArgs) Handles menuItemViewFolders.Click
  SelectFolders()
End Sub

Private Sub menuItemViewSearch_Click(ByVal sender As System.Object, _
            ByVal e As System.EventArgs) Handles menuItemViewSearch.Click
  SelectSearch()
End Sub

Private Sub menuItemViewIcons_Click(ByVal sender As System.Object, _
            ByVal e As System.EventArgs) Handles menuItemViewIcons.Click
  menuItemViewIcons.Checked = True
  menuItemViewDetails.Checked = False
  FireViewIcons()
End Sub

Private Sub menuItemViewDetails_Click(ByVal sender As System.Object, _
            ByVal e As System.EventArgs) Handles menuItemViewDetails.Click
  menuItemViewIcons.Checked = False
  menuItemViewDetails.Checked = True
  FireViewDetails()
End Sub

Private Sub menuItemHelpAbout_Click(ByVal sender As System.Object, _
            ByVal e As System.EventArgs) Handles menuItemHelpAbout.Click
  Dim formAbout As New FormAbout
  formAbout.ShowDialog()
End Sub

Private Sub toolBar_ButtonClick(ByVal sender As Object, _
            ByVal e As System.Windows.Forms.ToolBarButtonClickEventArgs) _
            Handles toolBar.ButtonClick
  If e.Button Is toolBarButtonUp Then
    SelectFolders()
    FireUpSelected()
  ElseIf e.Button Is toolBarButtonFolders Then
    SelectFolders()
  ElseIf e.Button Is toolBarButtonSearch Then
    SelectSearch()
  End If
End Sub

Private Sub buttonGo_Click(ByVal sender As System.Object, _
            ByVal e As System.EventArgs) Handles buttonGo.Click
  FireAddressChanged(textBoxAddress.Text)
End Sub

Private Sub textBoxAddress_KeyPress(ByVal sender As Object, _
            ByVal e As System.Windows.Forms.KeyPressEventArgs) _
            Handles textBoxAddress.KeyPress
```

```
      If e.KeyChar = vbCr Then
        e.Handled = True   ' to prevent Windows from beeping
        FireAddressChanged(textBoxAddress.Text)
      End If
    End Sub

#End Region

#Region "Events"
  Public Event OnViewFolders()
  Sub FireViewFolders()
    RaiseEvent OnViewFolders()
  End Sub

  Public Event OnViewSearch()
  Sub FireViewSearch()
    RaiseEvent OnViewSearch()
  End Sub

  Public Event OnViewIcons()
  Sub FireViewIcons()
    RaiseEvent OnViewIcons()
  End Sub

  Public Event OnViewDetails()
  Sub FireViewDetails()
    RaiseEvent OnViewDetails()
  End Sub

  Public Event OnUpSelected()
  Sub FireUpSelected()
    RaiseEvent OnUpSelected()
  End Sub

  Public Event OnAddressChanged(ByVal theNewAddress As String)
  Sub FireAddressChanged(ByVal theNewAddress As String)
    RaiseEvent OnAddressChanged(theNewAddress)
  End Sub
#End Region

End Class
```

Persistent User Settings

User settings track selections and preferences made by the user. SystemBrowser has only a single
setting, but it nevertheless is useful in showing the infrastructure for user setting management. The
class UserSettings has two methods: Load and Save, which read and write its data to a persistent
store, which is just an XML file in this example. UserSettings exposes each of the settings as a typed
field, so the rest of the system can be unaware of the XML format of the persisted data. While you can
consider UserSettings part of the infrastructure, like Builder and Binder, you can also consider it a
worker: Its mission is to persist the selected settings and make them available to the rest of the system.
Listing 11-9 and Listing 11-10 show C# and VB .NET implementations of UserSettings.

Listing 11-9. *The C# Implementation of UserSettings*

```csharp
public class UserSettings
{
  private string persistentFilePath;

  private bool showFoldersNavigator; // ShowFolders if true, ShowSearch if false
  public bool ShowFoldersNavigator
  {
    get {return showFoldersNavigator;}
    set {showFoldersNavigator = value;}
  }

  public void ShowFolders()
  {
    ShowFoldersNavigator = true;
  }

  public void ShowSearch()
  {
    ShowFoldersNavigator = false;
  }

  public UserSettings()
  {
    persistentFilePath = string.Format(@"{0}\settings.xml",
                                Application.StartupPath);

    // set default values for all settings (we only have one!)
    ShowFoldersNavigator = true;
  }

  public void Save()
  {
    try
    {
      StreamWriter writer = new StreamWriter(persistentFilePath);
      writer.WriteLine("<?xml version='1.0' encoding='UTF-8'?>");
      writer.WriteLine("<settings>");
      writer.WriteLine(string.Format("<ShowFolders>{0}</ShowFolders>",
                                          showFoldersNavigator));
      writer.WriteLine("</settings>");
      writer.Close();
    }
    catch (Exception ex)
    {
      MessageBox.Show(ex.ToString(), "Couldn't save settings");
    }
  }
}
```

```
public void Load()
{
  try
  {
    if (!File.Exists(persistentFilePath)) return;
    XmlDocument xmlDoc = new XmlDocument();
    xmlDoc.Load(persistentFilePath);
    XmlNode node = xmlDoc.SelectSingleNode("//ShowFolders");
    if (node == null) return;
    showFoldersNavigator = Boolean.Parse(node.InnerText.ToString());
  }
  catch (Exception ex)
  {
    MessageBox.Show(ex.ToString(), "Couldn't load settings");
  }
}
}
```

Listing 11-10. *The VB .NET Implementation of UserSettings*

```
Public Class UserSettings
  Private _persistentFilePath As String

  ' ShowFolders if true, ShowSearch if false
  Private _showFoldersNavigator As Boolean
  Public Property ShowFoldersNavigator() As Boolean
    Get
      Return _showFoldersNavigator
    End Get
    Set(ByVal Value As Boolean)
      _showFoldersNavigator = Value
    End Set
  End Property

  Public Sub ShowFolders()
    ShowFoldersNavigator = True
  End Sub

  Public Sub ShowSearch()
    ShowFoldersNavigator = False
  End Sub

  Public Sub New()
    _persistentFilePath = String.Format("{0}\settings.xml", Application.StartupPath)

    ' set default values for all settings (we only have one!)
    ShowFoldersNavigator = True
  End Sub

  Public Sub Save()
    Try
      Dim writer As New StreamWriter(_persistentFilePath)
      writer.WriteLine("<?xml version='1.0' encoding='UTF-8'?>")
      writer.WriteLine("<settings>")
```

```
        writer.WriteLine(String.Format("<ShowFolders>{0}</ShowFolders>", _
                                            ShowFoldersNavigator))
        writer.WriteLine("</settings>")
        writer.Close()
      Catch ex As Exception
        MessageBox.Show(ex.ToString(), "Couldn't save settings")
      End Try
    End Sub

    Public Sub Load()
      Try
        If Not File.Exists(_persistentFilePath) Then Return
        Dim xmlDoc As New XmlDocument
        xmlDoc.Load(_persistentFilePath)
        Dim node As XmlNode = xmlDoc.SelectSingleNode("//ShowFolders")
        If node Is Nothing Then Return
        ShowFoldersNavigator = Boolean.Parse(node.InnerText.ToString())
      Catch ex As Exception
        MessageBox.Show(ex.ToString(), "Couldn't load settings")
      End Try
    End Sub
  End Class
```

The Folders Navigator

The Folders navigator is a UI control that shows the folders (directories) of the local C: hard drive. The navigator, implemented in a class called NavigatorFolders, exposes two methods: Populate and SelectFolder. The former displays the top-level directories on the C: drive and is called at startup time. The latter populates the selected folder with subfolders.

When a folder is displayed, the system must already know if it has subfolders, so the Populate method searches for root-level folders and for their immediate subfolders. Why? Because folders that have subfolders must show a "+" sign, which users can click to see the subfolders. CoordinatorStartup calls the Populate method, using a transparent interaction with pushed feedback, described in the sequence diagram in Figure 11-13.

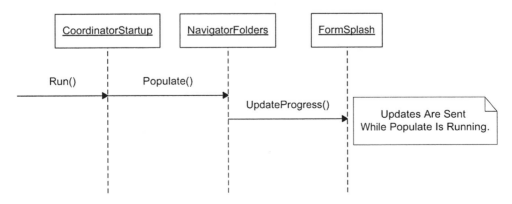

Figure 11-13. *Finding the root-level folders of the C: drive at startup time*

The feedback path is a bit unusual, because instead of going to the Coordinator, it goes to a different object (the splash screen). The feedback would need to go to the Coordinator if the feedback originated on a background thread, or if multiple objects needed to be managed on each progress update. If the feedback originated on a background thread, the Coordinator would be responsible for switching to the UI thread before forwarding the feedback to the rest of the system. Since System-Browser runs the Populate method on the UI thread, and no other objects besides the splash screen are involved in the progress-update processing, the feedback can go directly to the splash screen.

When the startup process is complete, SystemBrowser comes up showing the populated Folders navigator. Listing 11-11 and Listing 11-12 show C# and VB .NET implementations of NavigatorFolders.

Listing 11-11. *The C# Implementation of NavigatorFolders*

```csharp
public class NavigatorFolders : System.Windows.Forms.UserControl
{
  string folderSelected;

  // ImageList indexes
  const int ImageFolder = 0;
  const int ImageFolderOpened = 1;
  const int ImageHardDrive = 2;

  public NavigatorFolders()
  {
      // This call is required by the Windows.Forms Form Designer.
      InitializeComponent();
  }

  public void Populate(string theFolder)
  {
    Cursor = Cursors.WaitCursor;
    treeViewFolders.BeginUpdate();
    treeViewFolders.Nodes.Clear();

    int percentComplete = 0;

    // strip off trailing backslash
    string name = theFolder;
    if (name.EndsWith(@"\"))
      name = name.Substring(0, name.Length-1);

    TreeNode rootNode = new TreeNode(name, ImageHardDrive, ImageHardDrive);
    rootNode.Tag = theFolder;  // save the directory's full path
    treeViewFolders.Nodes.Add(rootNode);

    int i = 0;
    string[] directories = Directory.GetDirectories(theFolder);
    int totalFiles = directories.Length;
    foreach (string directory in directories)
    {
      AddNode(rootNode.Nodes, directory);
      percentComplete = (i * 100 ) / totalFiles;
      FireProgress(percentComplete);
      i++;
    }
```

```csharp
    treeViewFolders.EndUpdate();
    rootNode.Expand();
    FireProgress(100);
    Cursor = Cursors.Default;
}

public void SelectFolder(string thePath)
{
    if (thePath == null) return;
    if (treeViewFolders.Nodes.Count == 0) return;

    if (thePath.EndsWith("\\"))
    {
        // root folder
        treeViewFolders.SelectedNode = treeViewFolders.Nodes[0];
        return;
    }

    string[] directories = thePath.Split(new char[] {'\\'});
    TreeNode node = treeViewFolders.Nodes[0];
    foreach (string directory in directories)
    {
        node = FindNodeFor(node, directory);
        if (node == null) return;
    }

    AddChildren(node);
    treeViewFolders.SelectedNode = node;
}

public void SelectParentFolder()
{
    TreeNode currentNode = treeViewFolders.SelectedNode;
    if (currentNode == null) return;

    string currentDirectory = currentNode.Tag as string;
    DirectoryInfo parentDirectory = Directory.GetParent(currentDirectory);
    if (parentDirectory == null) return;
    SelectFolder(parentDirectory.FullName);
}

#region Component Designer generated code
// …
#endregion

void AddNode(TreeNodeCollection theParentCollection, string theDirectory)
{
    string name = Path.GetFileName(theDirectory);
    TreeNode node = new TreeNode(name, ImageFolder, ImageFolderOpened);
    node.Tag = theDirectory;  // save the directory's full path
    theParentCollection.Add(node);
```

```csharp
      string[] subdirectories = null;
      try
      {
        subdirectories = Directory.GetDirectories(theDirectory);
      }
      catch
      {
        return;  // ignore restricted directories
      }

      if (subdirectories == null) return;
      if (subdirectories.Length == 0) return;

      // if directory has subdirectories, add just 1 subdirectory, to
      // make a '+' sign appear next to the node
      name = Path.GetFileName(subdirectories[0]);
      TreeNode subNode = new TreeNode(name, ImageFolder, ImageFolder);
      subNode.Tag = string.Format(@"{0}\{1}", theDirectory, name);
      node.Nodes.Add(subNode);
    }

    void AddChildren(TreeNode theNode)
    {
      treeViewFolders.BeginUpdate();
      theNode.Nodes.Clear();  // remove the single subdirectory added
      string directory = theNode.Tag as string;
      foreach (string subdirectory in Directory.GetDirectories(directory))
        AddNode(theNode.Nodes, subdirectory);
      treeViewFolders.EndUpdate();
    }

    void UpdateStatusBar()
    {
      FireMessage(folderSelected);
    }

    TreeNode FindNodeFor(TreeNode theStartingNode, string theDirectory)
    {
      if (theStartingNode.Text.ToLower() == theDirectory.ToLower())
        return theStartingNode;

      // search the direct children
      foreach (TreeNode node in theStartingNode.Nodes)
        if (node.Text.ToLower() == theDirectory.ToLower())
          return node;
      return null;
    }

    #region Event Handlers
    private void treeViewFolders_BeforeExpand(object sender,
                    TreeViewCancelEventArgs e)
    {
      AddChildren(e.Node);
    }
```

```csharp
private void treeViewFolders_AfterSelect(object sender, TreeViewEventArgs e)
{
  if (e.Node == null) return;
  folderSelected = e.Node.Tag as string;
  FireFolderChanged(folderSelected);
  UpdateStatusBar();
}

private void treeViewFolders_Enter(object sender, System.EventArgs e)
{
  UpdateStatusBar();
}
#endregion

#region Events
public delegate void FolderChangedHandler(string theFolderPath);
public event FolderChangedHandler OnFolderChanged;
void FireFolderChanged(string theFolderPath)
{
  if (OnFolderChanged != null)
    OnFolderChanged(theFolderPath);
}

public delegate void MessageHandler(string theMessage);
public event MessageHandler OnMessage;
void FireMessage(string theMessage)
{
  if (OnMessage != null)
    OnMessage(theMessage);
}

public delegate void ProgressHandler(int percentComplete);
public event ProgressHandler OnProgress;
void FireProgress(int percentComplete)
{
  if (OnProgress != null)
    OnProgress(percentComplete);
}
#endregion
}
```

Listing 11-12. *The VB .NET Implementation of NavigatorFolders*

```vb
Public Class NavigatorFolders
  Inherits System.Windows.Forms.UserControl

  Private _folderSelected As String

  ' ImageList indexes
  Const ImageFolder As Integer = 0
  Const ImageFolderOpened As Integer = 1
  Const ImageHardDrive As Integer = 2
```

```vbnet
Public Sub Populate(ByVal theFolder As String)
  Cursor = Cursors.WaitCursor
  treeViewFolders.BeginUpdate()
  treeViewFolders.Nodes.Clear()

  Dim percentComplete As Integer = 0

  ' strip off trailing backslash
  Dim name As String = theFolder
  If name.EndsWith("\") Then
    name = name.Substring(0, name.Length - 1)
  End If

  Dim rootNode As New TreeNode(name, ImageHardDrive, ImageHardDrive)
  rootNode.Tag = theFolder  ' save the directory's full path
  treeViewFolders.Nodes.Add(rootNode)

  Dim i As Integer = 0
  Dim directories As String() = Directory.GetDirectories(theFolder)
  Dim totalFiles As Integer = directories.Length
  For Each directory As String In directories
    AddNode(rootNode.Nodes, directory)
    percentComplete = CInt((i * 100) / totalFiles)
    FireProgress(percentComplete)
    i += 1
  Next

  treeViewFolders.EndUpdate()
  rootNode.Expand()
  FireProgress(100)
  Cursor = Cursors.Default
End Sub

Public Sub SelectFolder(ByVal thePath As String)
  If thePath Is Nothing Then Return
  If treeViewFolders.Nodes.Count = 0 Then Return

  If thePath.EndsWith("\") Then
    ' root folder
    treeViewFolders.SelectedNode = treeViewFolders.Nodes(0)
    Return
  End If

  Dim directories As String() = thePath.Split(New Char() {"\"c})
  Dim node As TreeNode = treeViewFolders.Nodes(0)
  For Each directory As String In directories
    node = FindNodeFor(node, directory)
    If node Is Nothing Then Return
  Next

  AddChildren(node)
  treeViewFolders.SelectedNode = node
End Sub
```

```vbnet
    Public Sub SelectParentFolder()
      Dim currentNode As TreeNode = treeViewFolders.SelectedNode
      If currentNode Is Nothing Then Return

      Dim currentDirectory As String = CStr(currentNode.Tag)
      Dim parentDirectory As DirectoryInfo = Directory.GetParent(currentDirectory)
      If parentDirectory Is Nothing Then Return
      SelectFolder(parentDirectory.FullName)
    End Sub

#Region " Windows Form Designer generated code "

    Public Sub New()
      MyBase.New()

      'This call is required by the Windows Form Designer.
      InitializeComponent()

      'Add any initialization after the InitializeComponent() call

    End Sub

    ' other initialization …

#End Region

    Sub AddNode(ByVal theParentCollection As TreeNodeCollection, _
                        ByVal theDirectory As String)
      Dim name As String = Path.GetFileName(theDirectory)
      Dim node As New TreeNode(name, ImageFolder, ImageFolderOpened)
      node.Tag = theDirectory   ' save the directory's full path
      theParentCollection.Add(node)

      Dim subdirectories As String() = Nothing
      Try
        subdirectories = Directory.GetDirectories(theDirectory)
      Catch
        Return  ' ignore restricted directories
      End Try

      If subdirectories Is Nothing Then Return
      If subdirectories.Length = 0 Then Return

      ' if directory has subdirectories, add just 1 subdirectory, to
      ' make a '+' sign appear next to the node
      name = Path.GetFileName(subdirectories(0))
      Dim subNode As New TreeNode(name, ImageFolder, ImageFolder)
      subNode.Tag = String.Format("{0}\{1}", theDirectory, name)
      node.Nodes.Add(subNode)
    End Sub
```

```vb
  Sub AddChildren(ByVal theNode As TreeNode)
    treeViewFolders.BeginUpdate()
    theNode.Nodes.Clear()   ' remove the single subdirectory added
    Dim dir As String = CStr(theNode.Tag)
    For Each subdirectory As String In Directory.GetDirectories(dir)
      AddNode(theNode.Nodes, subdirectory)
      treeViewFolders.EndUpdate()
    Next
  End Sub


  Sub UpdateStatusBar()
    FireMessage(_folderSelected)
  End Sub


  Function FindNodeFor(ByVal theStartingNode As TreeNode, _
                                 ByVal theDirectory As String) As TreeNode
    If theStartingNode.Text.ToLower() = theDirectory.ToLower() Then
      Return theStartingNode
    End If

    ' search the direct children
    For Each node As TreeNode In theStartingNode.Nodes
      If node.Text.ToLower() = theDirectory.ToLower() Then Return node
    Next
    Return Nothing
  End Function

#Region "Event Handlers"
  Private Sub treeViewFolders_BeforeExpand(ByVal sender As Object, _
            ByVal e As System.Windows.Forms.TreeViewCancelEventArgs) _
            Handles treeViewFolders.BeforeExpand
    AddChildren(e.Node)
  End Sub


  Private Sub treeViewFolders_AfterSelect(ByVal sender As Object, _
            ByVal e As System.Windows.Forms.TreeViewEventArgs) _
            Handles treeViewFolders.AfterSelect
    If e.Node Is Nothing Then Return
    _folderSelected = CStr(e.Node.Tag)
    FireFolderChanged(_folderSelected)
    UpdateStatusBar()
  End Sub
```

```
    Private Sub treeViewFolders_Enter(ByVal sender As Object, _
            ByVal e As System.EventArgs) _
            Handles treeViewFolders.Enter
      UpdateStatusBar()
    End Sub

#End Region

#Region "Events"
  Public Event OnFolderChanged(ByVal theFolderPath As String)
  Sub FireFolderChanged(ByVal theFolderPath As String)
    RaiseEvent OnFolderChanged(theFolderPath)
  End Sub

  Public Event OnMessage(ByVal theMessage As String)
  Sub FireMessage(ByVal theMessage As String)
    RaiseEvent OnMessage(theMessage)
  End Sub

  Public Delegate Sub ProgressHandler(ByVal percentComplete As Integer)
  Public Event OnProgress As ProgressHandler
  Sub FireProgress(ByVal percentComplete As Integer)
    RaiseEvent OnProgress(percentComplete)
  End Sub
#End Region

End Class
```

The Search Navigator

The Search navigator handles searching for files and folders and is implemented with a class named NavigatorSearch. The navigator is functionally a worker and must run searches in a background thread. The worker is controlled by a coordinator, which handles all the threading details, as shown in the wiring diagram in Figure 11-14.

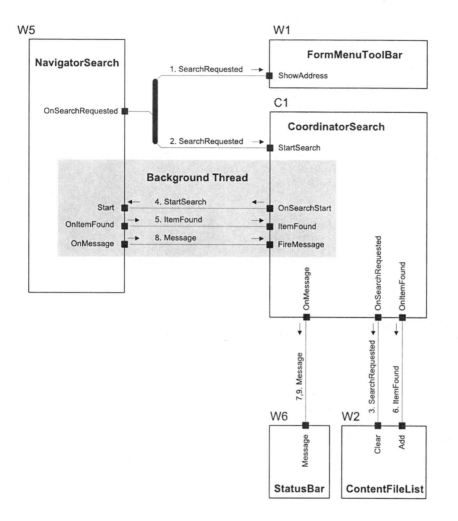

Figure 11-14. *The wiring diagram of the Search system*

The signals in the shaded area run on a background thread, as mentioned earlier. Although searches are run by code inside NavigatorSearch, the class contains no threading logic. Let's take a look at some of the details of the background threading management. When Binder wires CoordinatorSearch.OnSearchStart to NavigatorSearch.Start, Binder passes to CoordinatorSearch the entry point of a thread, using the code shown in Listing 11-13.

Listing 11-13. *The Code Used by Binder to Pass a Thread Entry Point to CoordinatorSearch*

C#

```
public class Binder
{
  public void Bind()
  {
    //..
    coordinatorSearch.OnSearchStart +=  new ThreadStart(navigatorSearch.Start);
  }
    //..
}
```

VB .NET

```
Public Class Binder
  Public Sub Bind()
    '  ...
    _builder._coordinatorSearch.OnSearchStart =
       AddressOf _builder._navigatorSearch.Start     'a delegate, not an event
    '  ...
  End Sub
End Class
```

When the user clicks the Search button on the UI, NavigatorSearch requests CoordinatorSearch to start the search and fires a SearchRequested event that is wired to CoordinatorSearch.StartSearch. The Coordinator checks to see if a prior search is in progress. If so, that search is aborted. The FireSearchStart method checks to see if a handler is available for the OnSearchStart event. If so, the Coordinator creates a background thread and runs the search on it. Listing 11-14 shows C# and VB .NET implementations.

Listing 11-14. *The Code Used by CoordinatorSearch to Run Searches on a Background Thread*

C#

```
public class CoordinatorSearch
  {
  Thread searchThread;

  public void StartSearch(string theFolderPath)
  {
    if (searchThread != null)
      if (searchThread.IsAlive)
        searchThread.Abort();
```

```csharp
      FireMessage("Searching...");
      FireSearchRequested();
      StartBackgroundSearch();
    }

    // a reference to the search entry point.
    // We call this method on a background thread
    public ThreadStart OnSearchStart;

    // start the search on a background thread
    void StartBackgroundSearch()
    {
      if (OnSearchStart == null) return;
      searchThread = new Thread(OnSearchStart);
      searchThread.Start();
    }

    //…
}
```

VB .NET

```vbnet
Public Class CoordinatorSearch
  Private _searchThread As Thread

  Public Sub StartSearch(ByVal theFolderPath As String)
    If Not _searchThread Is Nothing Then
      If _searchThread.IsAlive Then
        _searchThread.Abort()
      End If
    End If

    FireMessage("Searching...")
    FireSearchRequested()
    StartBackgroundSearch()
  End Sub

  ' a reference to the search entry point.
  ' We call this method on a background thread
  Public OnSearchStart As ThreadStart

  ' start the search on a background thread
  Sub StartBackgroundSearch()
    If OnSearchStart Is Nothing Then Return
    _searchThread = New Thread(OnSearchStart)
    _searchThread.Start()
  End Sub

  ' …
End Class
```

The Coordinator.OnSearchStart event is wired to NavigatorSearch.Start, which runs the actual search. Listing 11-15 and Listing 11-16 show a summary of the C# and VB .NET implementations of NavigatorSearch.

Listing 11-15. *The C# Implementation of NavigatorSearch*

```csharp
public class NavigatorSearch : System.Windows.Forms.UserControl
{
  int itemsFound;
  bool searching;
  bool stopRequested;

  public NavigatorSearch()
  {
    // This call is required by the Windows.Forms Form Designer.
    InitializeComponent();
  }

  public void Start()
  {
    Cursor = Cursors.WaitCursor;
    itemsFound = 0;
    buttonSearch.Text = "Stop";
    stopRequested = false;
    searching = true;
    DoSearch(textBoxLookIn.Text);
    searching = false;
    SearchFinished();
    Cursor = Cursors.Default;
  }

  // recursive method
  void DoSearch(string theFolder)
  {
    if (!Directory.Exists(theFolder)) return;

    // search this folder
    string pattern = textBoxFilename.Text;
    foreach (string filePath in Directory.GetFiles(theFolder, pattern))
    {
      itemsFound++;
      FireItemFound(filePath, itemsFound);
    }

    // search all subdirectories
    foreach (string directory in Directory.GetDirectories(theFolder))
    {
      DoSearch(directory);
      if (stopRequested)
      {
        FireMessage(string.Format("{0} items found", itemsFound));
        return;
      }
    }
  }
```

```csharp
void SearchFinished()
{
  buttonSearch.Text = "Search";
  Cursor = Cursors.Default;
}

void StartSearch(string theFolderPath)
{
  FireSearchRequested(theFolderPath);
  Cursor = Cursors.WaitCursor;
}

void StopSearch()
{
  stopRequested = true;
  Cursor = Cursors.Default;
}

#region Event Handlers
private void buttonSearch_Click(object sender, System.EventArgs e)
{
  if (!searching)
    StartSearch(textBoxLookIn.Text);
  else
    StopSearch();
}

private void buttonBrowse_Click(object sender, System.EventArgs e)
{
  if (folderBrowserDialog1.ShowDialog() == DialogResult.OK)
    textBoxLookIn.Text = folderBrowserDialog1.SelectedPath;
}
#endregion

#region Events
public delegate void SearchRequestedHandler(string theFolderPath);
public event SearchRequestedHandler OnSearchRequested;
void FireSearchRequested(string theFolderPath)
{
  if (OnSearchRequested != null)
    OnSearchRequested(theFolderPath);
}

public delegate void ItemFoundHandler(string thePath, int theCurrentCount);
public event ItemFoundHandler OnItemFound;
void FireItemFound(string thePath, int theCurrentCount)
{
  if (OnItemFound != null)
    OnItemFound(thePath, theCurrentCount);
}
```

```csharp
  public delegate void MessageHandler(string theMessage);
  public event MessageHandler OnMessage;
  void FireMessage(string theMessage)
  {
    if (OnMessage != null)
      OnMessage(theMessage);
  }
  #endregion
}
```

Listing 11-16. *The VB .NET Implementation of NavigatorSearch*

```vbnet
Public Class NavigatorSearch
  Inherits System.Windows.Forms.UserControl

  Private _itemsFound As Integer
  Private _searching As Boolean
  Private _stopRequested As Boolean

  Public Sub Start()
    Cursor = Cursors.WaitCursor
    _itemsFound = 0
    buttonSearch.Text = "Stop"
    _stopRequested = False
    _searching = True
    DoSearch(textBoxLookIn.Text)
    _searching = False
    SearchFinished()
    Cursor = Cursors.Default
  End Sub

#Region " Windows Form Designer generated code "

  Public Sub New()
    MyBase.New()

    'This call is required by the Windows Form Designer.
    InitializeComponent()

  End Sub

  ' ...

#End Region

  ' recursive method
  Sub DoSearch(ByVal theFolder As String)
    If Not Directory.Exists(theFolder) Then Return
```

```vbnet
    ' search this folder
    Dim pattern As String = textBoxFilename.Text
    For Each filePath As String In Directory.GetFiles(theFolder, pattern)
      _itemsFound += 1
      FireItemFound(filePath, _itemsFound)
    Next

    ' search all subdirectories
    For Each dir As String In Directory.GetDirectories(theFolder)
      DoSearch(dir)
      If _stopRequested Then
        FireMessage(String.Format("{0} items found", _itemsFound))
        Return
      End If
    Next
  End Sub

  Sub SearchFinished()
    buttonSearch.Text = "Search"
    Cursor = Cursors.Default
  End Sub

  Sub StartSearch(ByVal theFolderPath As String)
    FireSearchRequested(theFolderPath)
    Cursor = Cursors.WaitCursor
  End Sub

  Sub StopSearch()
    _stopRequested = True
    Cursor = Cursors.Default
  End Sub

#Region "Event Handlers"
  Private Sub buttonSearch_Click(ByVal sender As System.Object, _
              ByVal e As System.EventArgs) _
              Handles buttonSearch.Click
    If Not _searching Then
      StartSearch(textBoxLookIn.Text)
    Else
      StopSearch()
    End If
  End Sub

  Private Sub buttonBrowse_Click(ByVal sender As System.Object, _
              ByVal e As System.EventArgs) _
              Handles buttonBrowse.Click
    If folderBrowserDialog1.ShowDialog() = DialogResult.OK Then
      textBoxLookIn.Text = folderBrowserDialog1.SelectedPath
    End If
  End Sub

#End Region
```

```
#Region "Events"
  Public Event OnSearchRequested(ByVal theFolderPath As String)
  Sub FireSearchRequested(ByVal theFolderPath As String)
    RaiseEvent OnSearchRequested(theFolderPath)
  End Sub

  Public Event OnItemFound(ByVal thePath As String, _
            ByVal theCurrentCount As Integer)
  Sub FireItemFound(ByVal thePath As String, ByVal theCurrentCount As Integer)
    RaiseEvent OnItemFound(thePath, theCurrentCount)
  End Sub

  Public Event OnMessage(ByVal theMessage As String)
  Sub FireMessage(ByVal theMessage As String)
    RaiseEvent OnMessage(theMessage)
  End Sub
#End Region
End Class
```

Each time NavigatorSearch finds a file matching the search expression, it fires an OnItemFound event. The ItemFound signal is wired to CoordinatorSearch.ItemFound. The purpose of the notification is to show the filename and the number of files found, requiring the UI to be updated. Since the NavigatorSearch.ItemFound signal is sent on a background thread, CoordinatorSearch must switch to the UI thread before forwarding ItemFound to ContentSearchResults. Listing 11-17 and Listing 11-18 show the details.

Listing 11-17. *How CoordinatorSearch Switches to the UI Thread Before Forwarding Notifications to UI Elements (C# Code)*

```
public class CoordinatorSearch
{
  Control uiControl;

  public CoordinatorSearch(Control theUiControl)
  {
    uiControl = theUiControl;
  }

  public void ItemFound(string thePath, int theCurrentCount)
  {
    FireItemFound(thePath, theCurrentCount);

    if (theCurrentCount == 1)
      FireMessage("1 item found");
    else
      FireMessage(string.Format("{0} items found", theCurrentCount));
  }

  public delegate void ItemFoundHandler(string thePath, int theCurrentCount);
  public event ItemFoundHandler OnItemFound;
  void FireItemFound(string thePath, int theCurrentCount)
  {
    if (OnItemFound != null)
      uiControl.Invoke(OnItemFound, new object[] {thePath, theCurrentCount});
  }
```

```
  public delegate void MessageHandler(string theMessage);
  public event MessageHandler OnMessage;
  private void FireMessage(string theMessage)
  {
    if (OnMessage != null)
      uiControl.Invoke(OnMessage, new object[] {theMessage});
  }
}
```

Listing 11-18. *How CoordinatorSearch Switches to the UI Thread Before Forwarding Notifications to UI Elements (VB .NET Code)*

```
Public Class CoordinatorSearch
  Private _uiControl As Control

  Public Sub New(ByVal theUiControl As Control)
    _uiControl = theUiControl
  End Sub

  Public Sub ItemFound(ByVal thePath As String, ByVal theCurrentCount As Integer)
    FireItemFound(thePath, theCurrentCount)

    If (theCurrentCount = 1) Then
      FireMessage("1 item found")
    Else
      FireMessage(String.Format("{0} items found", theCurrentCount))
    End If
  End Sub

  Public Delegate Sub ItemFoundHandler(ByVal thePath As String, _
          ByVal theCurrentCount As Integer)
  Public Event OnItemFound As ItemFoundHandler

  Sub FireItemFound(ByVal thePath As String, ByVal theCurrentCount As Integer)
    _uiControl.Invoke(New ItemFoundHandler(AddressOf DoFireItemFound), _
                          New Object() {thePath, theCurrentCount})
  End Sub
  Sub DoFireItemFound(ByVal thePath As String, ByVal theCurrentCount As Integer)
    RaiseEvent OnItemFound(thePath, theCurrentCount)
  End Sub


  Public Delegate Sub MessageHandler(ByVal theMessage As String)
  Public Event OnMessage As MessageHandler

Public Sub FireMessage(ByVal theMessage As String)
    _uiControl.Invoke(New MessageHandler(AddressOf DoFireMessage), _
                          New Object() {theMessage})
  End Sub
  Sub DoFireMessage(ByVal theMessage As String)
    RaiseEvent OnMessage(theMessage)
  End Sub
#End Region

End Class
```

In the listings, the lines in bold show where the thread switching occurs. In .NET Windows Forms, all UI controls are derived from the class System.Windows.Forms.Control, which contains the method Control.Invoke. This method expects a delegate as a parameter. The uiControl variable is a reference to any UI control created on the UI thread. In SystemBrowser, FormMain is used, but you could use any other form or UI element. After switching to the UI thread, Control.Invoke calls the method referenced by the delegate. Systems developed for other component platforms, such as JavaBeans or Delphi, have their own ways to run methods on the user interface thread. The implementation details are different, but the concept is the same.

Use Cases

The remaining details of SystemBrowser are best described with use cases. I'll model each use case using wiring diagrams with numbered signals. See Figures 11-15 through 11-23.

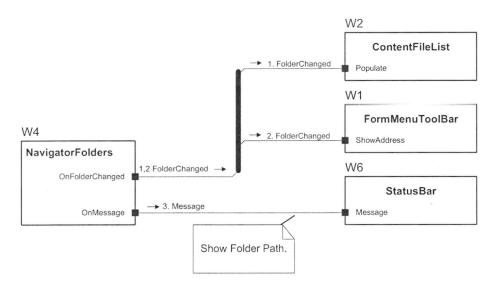

Figure 11-15. *Use case: The user changes the folder selected in the Folders navigator.*

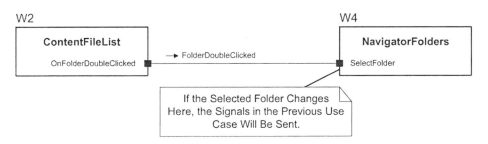

Figure 11-16. *Use case: The user double-clicks a folder in the Folders content pane.*

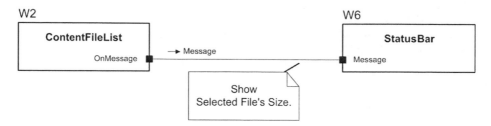

Figure 11-17. *Use case: The user clicks a file in the Folders content pane.*

Figure 11-18. *Use case: The user selects a file in the Search Results pane.*

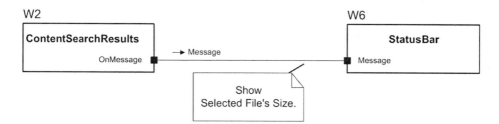

Figure 11-19. *Use case: The user clicks the Folders button on the toolbar.*

Figure 11-20. *Use case: The user clicks the Search button on the toolbar.*

Figure 11-21. *Use case: The user clicks the Up button on the toolbar.*

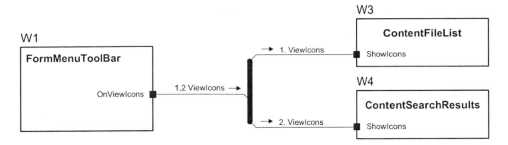

Figure 11-22. *Use case: The user selects the View ➤ Icons menu command.*

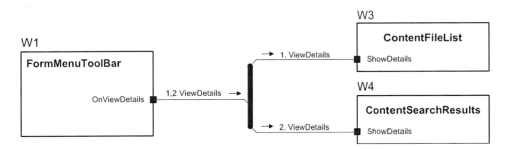

Figure 11-23. *Use case: The user selects the View ➤ Details menu command.*

Testing the System

Four parts of SystemBrowser are complex enough to justify their own test fixture: NavigatorFolders, ContentFileList, NavigatorSearch, and ContentSearchResults. Since ContentFileList is very similar to ContentSearchResults, I won't show a test fixture for the latter.

Although I'm presenting the test fixtures after showing most of the implementation of System-Browser, it is important to use test fixtures *during* development. As features are added to a class or component, you'll most likely think about special situations that might need testing, such as boundary conditions on parameters, timing issues, and threading issues. Each time you recognize a situation that might need special handling, you should extend the test fixture to test for that situation. You should develop the test fixture and the classes you want to test in parallel, so when you deliver the final code to the source-code control system, it includes the final test-fixture code.

The NavigatorFolders Test Fixture

Let's start with the NavigatorFolders test fixture. You need to test the object's inputs and outputs. The inputs are the public methods, and the outputs are the events. NavigatorFolders has three public methods: Populate, SelectFolder, and SelectParentFolder. The class also has three events: OnFolderChanged, OnMessage, and OnProgress. I'll create the test fixture as a simple Windows application that hosts NavigatorFolders, calling its inputs and handling its events. Figure 11-24 shows the user interface of the test fixture.

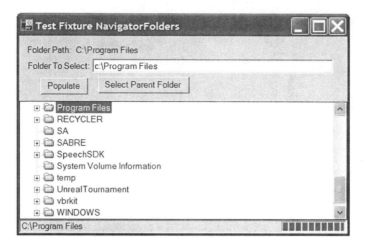

Figure 11-24. *The NavigatorFolders test fixture UI*

The center part of the UI contains the NavigatorFolders control. The wiring diagram in Figure 11-25 shows how the test fixture's main form is wired to NavigatorFolders.

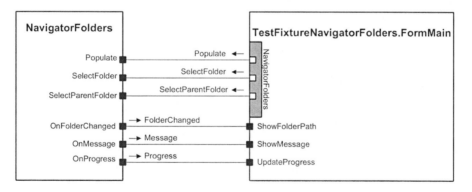

Figure 11-25. *The wiring diagram of the NavigatorFolders test fixture*

The test fixture's main form calls the NavigatorFolders inputs through the interface NavigatorFolders, so the diagram shows statically bound pins. The three events fired by NavigatorFolders are wired to methods that display the notification payloads on the screen. The FolderChanged payload is displayed at the top of FormMain. The Message payload is displayed at the bottom. The Progress payload is a percent-complete value, displayed in the progress bar on the right side of the status bar. Listing 11-19 shows the salient code of the test fixture in C# and VB .NET.

Listing 11-19. *The Salient Code of the Test Fixture*

```csharp
C#
public class FormMain : System.Windows.Forms.Form
{
  NavigatorFolders navigatorFolders;
```

```csharp
    public FormMain()
    {
      InitializeComponent();

      navigatorFolders = new NavigatorFolders();
      panelFolders.Controls.Add(navigatorFolders);
      navigatorFolders.Dock = DockStyle.Fill;

      navigatorFolders.OnFolderChanged +=
          new SystemBrowser.NavigatorFolders.FolderChangedHandler(ShowFolderPath);
      navigatorFolders.OnMessage +=
          new SystemBrowser.NavigatorFolders.MessageHandler(ShowMessage);
      navigatorFolders.OnProgress +=
          new SystemBrowser.NavigatorFolders.ProgressHandler(UpdateProgress);
    }

    private void ShowFolderPath(string theFolderPath)
    {
      labelFolderPath.Text = theFolderPath;
    }

    private void ShowMessage(string theMessage)
    {
      labelMessages.Text = theMessage;
    }

    private void UpdateProgress(int thePercentComplete)
    {
      progressBar1.Value = thePercentComplete;
      progressBar1.Update();
    }

   private void textBoxFolderToSelect_KeyPress(object sender, KeyPressEventArgs e)
    {
      if (e.KeyChar != '\r') return;
      e.Handled = true;  // to prevent the TextBox from beeping
      navigatorFolders.SelectFolder(textBoxFolderToSelect.Text);
    }

    private void buttonPopulate_Click(object sender, System.EventArgs e)
    {
      navigatorFolders.Populate(@"C:\");
    }

    private void buttonSelectParentFolder_Click(object sender , System.EventArgs e)
    {
      navigatorFolders.SelectParentFolder();
    }
}
```

```vbnet
VB .NET
Public Class FormMain
  Inherits System.Windows.Forms.Form

  Private _navigatorFolders As NavigatorFolders

  Private Sub ShowFolderPath(ByVal theFolderPath As String)
    labelFolderPath.Text = theFolderPath
  End Sub

  Private Sub ShowMessage(ByVal theMessage As String)
    labelMessages.Text = theMessage
  End Sub

  Private Sub UpdateProgress(ByVal thePercentComplete As Integer)
    progressBar1.Value = thePercentComplete
    progressBar1.Update()
  End Sub

  Private Sub textBoxFolderToSelect_KeyPress(ByVal sender As Object, _
            ByVal e As System.Windows.Forms.KeyPressEventArgs) _
            Handles textBoxFolderToSelect.KeyPress
    If e.KeyChar <> vbCr Then Return
    e.Handled = True   ' to prevent the TextBox from beeping
    _navigatorFolders.SelectFolder(textBoxFolderToSelect.Text)
  End Sub

  Private Sub buttonPopulate_Click(ByVal sender As System.Object, _
            ByVal e As System.EventArgs) _
            Handles buttonPopulate.Click
    _navigatorFolders.Populate("C:\")
  End Sub

  Private Sub buttonSelectParentFolder_Click(ByVal sender As System.Object, _
            ByVal e As System.EventArgs) _
            Handles buttonSelectParentFolder.Click
    _navigatorFolders.SelectParentFolder()
  End Sub

  Public Sub New()
    MyBase.New()

    'This call is required by the Windows Form Designer.
    InitializeComponent()

    _navigatorFolders = New NavigatorFolders
    panelFolders.Controls.Add(_navigatorFolders)
    _navigatorFolders.Dock = DockStyle.Fill

    AddHandler _navigatorFolders.OnFolderChanged, AddressOf ShowFolderPath
    AddHandler _navigatorFolders.OnMessage, AddressOf ShowMessage
    AddHandler _navigatorFolders.OnProgress, AddressOf UpdateProgress
  End Sub

End Class
```

The ContentFileList Test Fixture

ContentFileList shows the contents of a folder as a list of folders and files. Figure 11-26 shows the user interface of the test fixture.

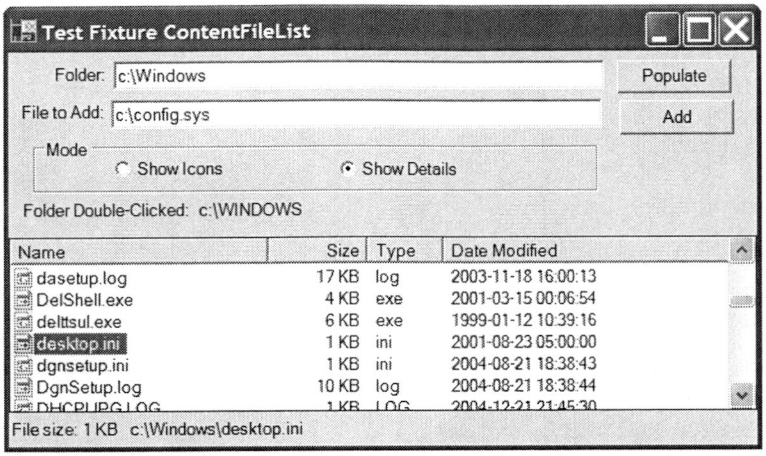

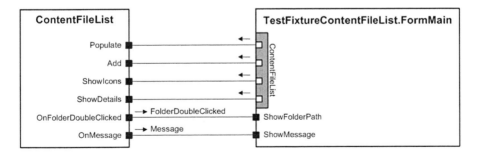

Figure 11-26. *The user interface of the ContentFileList test fixture*

ContentFileList has four inputs and two outputs. The inputs are the public methods Populate, Add, ShowIcons, and ShowDetails. The outputs are the events OnFolderDoubleClicked and OnMessage. The two buttons on the test fixture are wired to ContentFileList.Populate and ContentFileList.Add. When the user double-clicks a folder, an OnFolderDoubleClicked event is fired and handled by the test fixture. The name of the double-clicked folder is displayed in the middle of the form. The test fixture also handles the OnMessage event. The payload is a message, which is displayed at the bottom of the form. Figure 11-27 shows the test fixture's wiring diagram.

Figure 11-27. *The wiring diagram of the ContentFileList test fixture*

Listing 11-20 shows the salient code of the test fixture in C# and VB .NET.

Listing 11-20. *The Salient Code of the Test Fixture*

C#

```csharp
public class FormMain : System.Windows.Forms.Form
{

  ContentFileList contentFileList;

  public FormMain()
  {
    InitializeComponent();

    contentFileList = new ContentFileList();

    contentFileList.OnFolderDoubleClicked +=
        new ContentFileList.FolderDoubleClickedHandler(ShowFolderPath);
    contentFileList.OnMessage +=
        new ContentFileList.MessageHandler(ShowMessage);

    panelContent.Controls.Add(contentFileList);
    contentFileList.Dock = DockStyle.Fill;

    contentFileList.Populate(textBoxFolder.Text);
  }

  void ShowFolderPath(string thePath)
  {
    labelFolderDoubleClicked.Text = thePath;
  }

  private void ShowMessage(string theMessage)
  {
    labelMessages.Text = theMessage;
  }

  private void textBoxFolder_KeyPress(object sender,
              System.Windows.Forms.KeyPressEventArgs e)
  {
    if (e.KeyChar == '\r')  // the Enter key
    {
      contentFileList.Populate(textBoxFolder.Text);
      e.Handled = true; // to prevent TextBox from beeping
    }
  }

  private void buttonPopulate_Click(object sender, System.EventArgs e)
  {
    contentFileList.Populate(textBoxFolder.Text);
  }

  private void buttonAdd_Click(object sender, System.EventArgs e)
  {
    contentFileList.Add(textBoxFileToAdd.Text);
  }
```

```csharp
    private void radioButtonShowIcons_CheckedChanged(object sender,
                        System.EventArgs e)
    {
      SetMode();
    }

    private void radioButtonShowDetails_CheckedChanged(object sender,
                        System.EventArgs e)
    {
      SetMode();
    }

    void SetMode()
    {
      if (radioButtonShowIcons.Checked)
        contentFileList.ShowIcons();
      else
        contentFileList.ShowDetails();
    }
}
```

VB .NET

```vbnet
Public Class FormMain
  Inherits System.Windows.Forms.Form

  Private _contentFileList As ContentFileList

  Public Sub New()
    MyBase.New()

    _contentFileList = New ContentFileList

    'This call is required by the Windows Form Designer.
    InitializeComponent()

    AddHandler _contentFileList.OnFolderDoubleClicked, AddressOf ShowFolderPath
    AddHandler _contentFileList.OnMessage, AddressOf ShowMessage
    panelContent.Controls.Add(_contentFileList)
    _contentFileList.Dock = DockStyle.Fill
  End Sub

  Sub ShowFolderPath(ByVal thePath As String)
    labelFolderDoubleClicked.Text = thePath
  End Sub

  Private Sub ShowMessage(ByVal theMessage As String)
    labelMessages.Text = theMessage
  End Sub
```

```
  Private Sub textBoxFolder_KeyPress(ByVal sender As Object, _
           ByVal e As System.Windows.Forms.KeyPressEventArgs) _
           Handles textBoxFolder.KeyPress
    If e.KeyChar = vbCr Then   ' the Enter key
      _contentFileList.Populate(textBoxFolder.Text)
      e.Handled = True ' to prevent TextBox from beeping
    End If
  End Sub

  Private Sub buttonPopulate_Click(ByVal sender As System.Object, _
           ByVal e As System.EventArgs) _
           Handles buttonPopulate.Click
    _contentFileList.Populate(textBoxFolder.Text)
  End Sub

  Private Sub buttonAdd_Click(ByVal sender As System.Object, _
           ByVal e As System.EventArgs) _
           Handles buttonAdd.Click
    _contentFileList.Add(textBoxFileToAdd.Text)
  End Sub

  Private Sub radioButtonShowIcons_CheckedChanged(ByVal sender As System.Object, _
           ByVal e As System.EventArgs) _
           Handles radioButtonShowIcons.CheckedChanged
    SetMode()
  End Sub

  Private Sub radioButtonShowDetails_CheckedChanged(ByVal sender As System.Object, _
           ByVal e As System.EventArgs) _
           Handles radioButtonShowDetails.CheckedChanged
    SetMode()
  End Sub

  Sub SetMode()
    If radioButtonShowIcons.Checked Then
      _contentFileList.ShowIcons()
    Else
      _contentFileList.ShowDetails()
    End If
  End Sub
End Class
```

The NavigatorSearch Test Fixture

The NavigatorSearch test fixture is the most complicated one, which is why I'm presenting it last. Since the search functionality is spread over two classes (NavigatorSearch and CoordinatorSearch), this test fixture tests the two classes together. Figure 11-28 shows the UI of the test fixture.

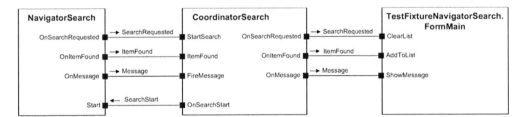

Figure 11-28. *The user interface of the NavigatorSearch test fixture, after running a search*

Figure 11-29 shows the test fixture's wiring diagram.

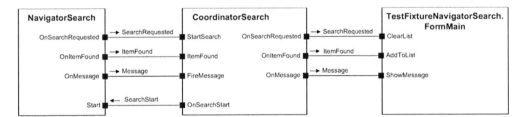

Figure 11-29. *The wiring diagram of the NavigatorSearch test fixture*

When the user clicks the Search button, NavigatorSearch fires an OnSearchRequested event, which is handled by CoordinatorSearch.StartSearch. The latter method creates a background thread and fires an OnSearchStart event that is wired to NavigatorSearch.Start. FormMain handles three CoordinatorSearch events: OnSearchRequested, OnItemFound, and OnMessage. The first clears the listbox at the top of the form. The second adds an item to the listbox. The third adds a message to a label at the bottom of the form. Listing 11-21 shows the salient code of the test fixture in C# and VB .NET.

Listing 11-21. *The Salient Test Fixture Code for NavigatorSearch*

C#

```
public class FormMain : System.Windows.Forms.Form
{
  CoordinatorSearch coordinatorSearch;
  NavigatorSearch navigatorSearch;
```

```csharp
    public FormMain()
    {
      InitializeComponent();

      navigatorSearch = new NavigatorSearch();
      coordinatorSearch = new CoordinatorSearch(navigatorSearch);

      coordinatorSearch.OnSearchRequested +=
          new CoordinatorSearch.SearchRequestedHandler(ClearList);
      coordinatorSearch.OnSearchStart += new ThreadStart(navigatorSearch.Start);
      coordinatorSearch.OnItemFound +=
          new CoordinatorSearch.ItemFoundHandler(AddToList);
      coordinatorSearch.OnMessage +=
          new CoordinatorSearch.MessageHandler(ShowMessage);

      navigatorSearch.OnSearchRequested +=
          new NavigatorSearch.SearchRequestedHandler(coordinatorSearch.StartSearch);
      navigatorSearch.OnItemFound +=
          new NavigatorSearch.ItemFoundHandler(coordinatorSearch.ItemFound);
      navigatorSearch.OnMessage +=
          new NavigatorSearch.MessageHandler(coordinatorSearch.FireMessage);

      panelSearch.Controls.Add(navigatorSearch);
      navigatorSearch.Dock = DockStyle.Fill;
    }

    private void ShowItemFound(string thePath, int theCurrentCount)
    {
      listBoxItemsFound.Items.Add(thePath);
    }

    private void ShowMessage(string theMessage)
    {
      labelMessages.Text = theMessage;
    }

    private void ClearList()
    {
      listBoxItemsFound.Items.Clear();
    }

    private void AddToList(string theText, int theCount)
    {
      listBoxItemsFound.Items.Add(theText);
    }
}
```

VB .NET

```vbnet
Public Class FormMain
  Inherits System.Windows.Forms.Form
```

```vbnet
Private _coordinatorSearch As CoordinatorSearch
Private _navigatorSearch As NavigatorSearch

Private Sub ShowItemFound(ByVal thePath As String, _
                          ByVal theCurrentCount As Integer)
    listBoxItemsFound.Items.Add(thePath)
End Sub

Private Sub ShowMessage(ByVal theMessage As String)
    labelMessages.Text = theMessage
End Sub

Private Sub ClearList()
    listBoxItemsFound.Items.Clear()
End Sub

Private Sub AddToList(ByVal theText As String, ByVal theCount As Integer)
    listBoxItemsFound.Items.Add(theText)
End Sub

Public Sub New()
    MyBase.New()

    'This call is required by the Windows Form Designer.
    InitializeComponent()

    _navigatorSearch = New NavigatorSearch
    _coordinatorSearch = New CoordinatorSearch(Me)

    AddHandler _coordinatorSearch.OnSearchRequested, _
                    AddressOf ClearList
    _coordinatorSearch.OnSearchStart = _
                    AddressOf _navigatorSearch.Start
    AddHandler _coordinatorSearch.OnItemFound, _
                    AddressOf AddToList
    AddHandler _coordinatorSearch.OnMessage, _
                    AddressOf ShowMessage

    AddHandler _navigatorSearch.OnSearchRequested, _
                    AddressOf _coordinatorSearch.StartSearch
    AddHandler _navigatorSearch.OnItemFound, _
                    AddressOf _coordinatorSearch.ItemFound
    AddHandler _navigatorSearch.OnMessage, _
                    AddressOf _coordinatorSearch.FireMessage

    panelSearch.Controls.Add(_navigatorSearch)
    _navigatorSearch.Dock = DockStyle.Fill

End Sub

End Class
```

Summary

When testing UI controls, automated unit testing is usually not practical. Why? Because to verify if a UI control is working correctly, you generally have to look at the screen and see if it looks right. Looking at the screen often entails more than just checking that the various fields have the right data. Often there are interactions between the controls, focus issues, or painting artifacts that a human can detect more easily than a mindless unit-testing program. Don't get me wrong: Automated unit testing with systems like NUnit and JUnit is definitely advisable for code that *doesn't* have a user interface.

You can download SystemBrowser's complete source code from the Source Code area of the Apress Web site (www.apress.com).

CHAPTER 12

■ ■ ■

Case Study 2: A Pipelined HTTP Service

In this case study, I'll describe a component that supports pipelined HTTP operations. The purpose of this study is to show how you can use an event-based approach to implement high-performance, multithreaded components that have no user interface. Before looking at the details, a short digression on HTTP is in order.

What is HTTP? If you haven't heard of it, you've either just come out of a 15-year coma, or you've been in solitary confinement for an extended period of time. In both cases, this chapter and the rest of the book are probably over your head. Getting back to the question, the short answer is this: HTTP is the main application-level protocol in current use on the Internet. An overwhelming proportion of Internet traffic is due to HTTP. Tim Berners-Lee submitted RFC 1945[1] to the Internet Engineering Task Force (IETF) in 1996. The RFC defined HTTP 1.0, a simple text-based protocol for client-server interactions. Version 1.0 was derived from version 0.9, which had been in use since 1990. HTTP is an application-level protocol built on top of TCP/IP; it supports a stateless client-server interaction model. In the standard HTTP interaction model, clients initiate interactions with servers. Servers are always passive and are designed to respond to client requests. An HTTP server has a listener service that waits for incoming requests. When a client needs to obtain information from a server, the client must establish a socket connection with the server. Once a connection is made, the client sends a request to the server and gets the information back as a response, assuming no errors occurred.

Most HTTP traffic is related to HTML documents, and most HTML-related client applications are Web browsers. With versions of HTTP prior to 1.1, a client could make only a single request after connecting to the host. Upon returning the response, the host closed the connection. Opening and closing a host connection with each request was a simple technique, but one that didn't work well with a complex HTML document. Why? Because when an HTTP 1.0-compliant Web browser was told to retrieve an HTML document, it first downloaded the HTML text of the document, then it scanned the HTML code and compiled a list of all the images embedded in the document. For each image, the browser established a new socket connection to the server hosting the image, downloaded the image, and then closed the connection. The connect-disconnect overhead quickly became a bottleneck for network traffic, because the establishment of a TCP socket connection requires a three-way handshake, which is fairly expensive in terms of networking usage. It is also fairly slow, taking more than 200 ms in normal Internet traffic conditions. When the images embedded in an HTML document reside on the same server as the document, it is wasteful to close and reopen connections for each image to fetch.

---

1. Tim Berners-Lee, Roy Fielding, and Henrik Frystyk Nielsen, "Hypertext Transfer Protocol -- HTTP/1.0" (technical report, www.w3.org/Protocols/rfc1945/rfc1945, 1996).

To reduce Internet congestion due to the HTTP reconnection overhead, HTTP was revised to version 1.1. The new version, which is the standard today, supports *persistent* connections. When a client establishes a connection, it has the option of requesting the server to keep the connection open after a response is returned. If a client needs to download additional resources from the same server, it can do so using the same connection, greatly reducing the total time required to display a complete HTML page containing embedded images or other resources.

HTTP 1.1 also introduced an additional feature to improve performance: pipelined requests, which become useful when a client knows in advance that it will need to send multiple requests to the server. Without using pipelined requests, the client would have to send a request, wait for the response, send the next request, wait for the response, and so on. The host would receive one request at a time and return one response at a time. Everything happens in strict sequential order. If the connection is persistent, a client that needs to send multiple requests can use the connection more efficiently by sending all the requests in a row, one after the other, without waiting for any responses. The server might then process the requests in parallel, using separate threads, and greatly reduce the overall response time.

The problem with HTTP 1.1 pipelined requests is that the protocol specifies that responses must be returned in the same order as the requests received. Using this approach is not as efficient as it could be. Ideally, a client should be able to submit a group of requests and have the server process them in parallel. The server should return responses as soon as they are available, without having to worry about their order in relationship to the requests. But how would the client know how to match up requests with responses? HTTP doesn't define a standard way to do this, but there is a simple solution.

HTTP uses header fields to convey information about requests and responses. The HTTP specification defines several standard header fields, but also allows you to define nonstandard header fields. HTTP proxy servers are required to forward all headers in a request and response—even the nonstandard ones—ensuring that they will travel correctly through the WWW infrastructure from client to server and back. To solve the request-response matching problem, all you need to do is add a custom header field that contains a sequence number. Both requests and responses use this header. Each time the client submits a new request, the sequence number is incremented, so all requests have a different sequence number. When the server sends a response back to the client, the response contains the sequence number of its request. On the client side, matching responses to requests is a simple matter of matching sequence numbers. Any pipelining implementation, regardless of whether it uses sequence numbers or not, must be multithreaded, because requests must wait for their respective responses, and those responses can return in arbitrary order. The threading details aren't too complicated, especially using an event-based design that uses coordinators to handle the threading.

System Requirements

Your mission is to build a component, which I'll call HttpService, that accepts requests from local client applications and forwards them to remote HTTP servers. The traffic between HttpService and the remote servers must consist of HTTP 1.1 requests and responses, using persistent connections. When a client sends multiple requests concurrently to the same remote server, HttpService must pipeline the requests and use a custom Sequence-Number HTTP header to match responses with requests. HttpService must support concurrent requests from multiple clients, as shown in Figure 12-1.

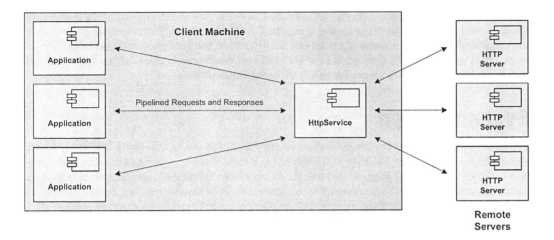

Figure 12-1. *HttpService supports multiple clients, each sending pipelined requests.*

Each client must be able to send requests to any arbitrary remote server. Those sent concurrently to the same server must be pipelined. The custom Sequence-Number HTTP header field must carry a value that is different for each request. A request using this header must look something like Listing 12-1.

Listing 12-1. *A Simple HTTP Request Using the Sequence-Number Header*

```
POST /MyPath/MyResource HTTP/1.1
Host: 192.168.0.2:8020
Sequence-Number: 1
Connection: Keep-Alive
Content-Length: 9

MyMessage
```

The HTTP request must use the verb POST, followed by a resource path. The code in this case study will ignore the path, but typically you would use the path to indicate what type of request to execute. The last word of the path might be a command code. Per the HTTP spec, all header lines are terminated with a carriage-return/line-feed (CR/LF) combination. The HTTP header ends with a blank line, terminated again with a CR/LF pair, so the header is actually terminated by two CR/LF pairs. The rest of the HTTP request is the message body. The HTTP Content-Length header refers only to the length (in bytes) of the message body.

The server returns a response with the same sequence number as the request. Listing 12-2 shows a simple response.

Listing 12-2. *A Simple HTTP Response Containing the Sequence-Number Header*

```
HTTP/1.1 200 OK
Sequence-Number: 1
Content-Length: 10

MyResponse
```

HttpService must expose a single method called Send that forwards a request to the designated remote server and blocks until a response is returned. A Send operation must time out if a response isn't returned within 20 seconds. If a time-out doesn't occur, the Send method must return the response. A multithreaded client must be able to call Send concurrently from different threads, and HttpService must be able to support multiple clients at the same time.

System Design

The requirements are simple enough to allow you to package all the functionality of HttpService in a single component. When a client sends a request to a remote server, you need to create a connection to the server, send the request, and wait for the response. When the response comes back, you keep the connection open in case further requests need to go to the same server. To manage the connections left open, keep them in a pool. If you don't use a connection for a certain amount of time, close it and remove it from the pool. You can design HttpService using three basic blocks, as shown in Figure 12-2.

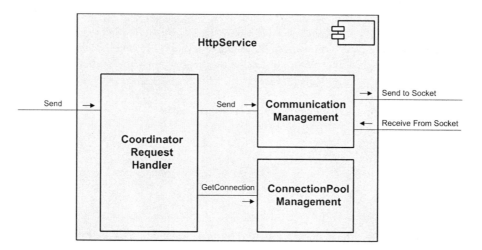

Figure 12-2. *The block diagram of HttpService*

CoordinatorRequestHandler is a singleton object that receives incoming requests and passes them to the communication management block. This block manages all the details of transmitting/receiving data to/from the remote server. Most of the functionality of the system is inside the Communication Management block, designed as a Coordinator team. The team consists of a top-level coordinator with six workers. The coordinator handles the interactions between the workers and is coupled to most of them, as shown in Figure 12-3.

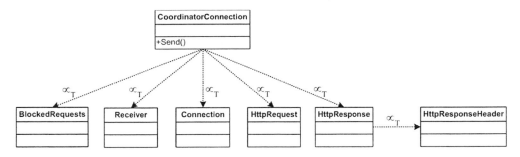

Figure 12-3. *The coupling diagram of the Coordinator team that represents the Communication Management block*

All the workers except HttpResponse are completely decoupled from each other and from the rest of the system. On the other hand, the Coordinator is coupled to five of the six workers. While it is perfectly possible to design the system so that the Coordinator is decoupled from the workers, I chose to leave the Coordinator coupled to avoid distracting you with separate builders and binders, which would have been necessary. In this case study, the Coordinator builds and binds the workers directly to avoid introducing unnecessary complexity.

The Coordinator exposes a single public method called Send. When CoordinatorRequestHandler calls this method, the Coordinator uses the workers to carry out the task. Noteworthy is the fact that HttpService supports concurrent operations, but none of the workers contains any threading logic. The workers are completely unaware of which thread they run in. The Coordinator handles all threading details, allowing the workers to focus only on specific tasks, without regard to the timing of those tasks in relationship to the rest of the system.

When the Coordinator team establishes a connection to a remote server, the connection is kept open and saved in a pool. Connections remain in the pool unless they're idle for a certain amount of time. The task of managing the pool and monitoring for idle connections is assigned to a coordinator called CoordinatorConnectionPool that has no workers. The Coordinator uses an internal Hashtable to hold the collection of active connections. Now you're in a position to see the entire signal diagram of the system, shown in Figure 12-4.

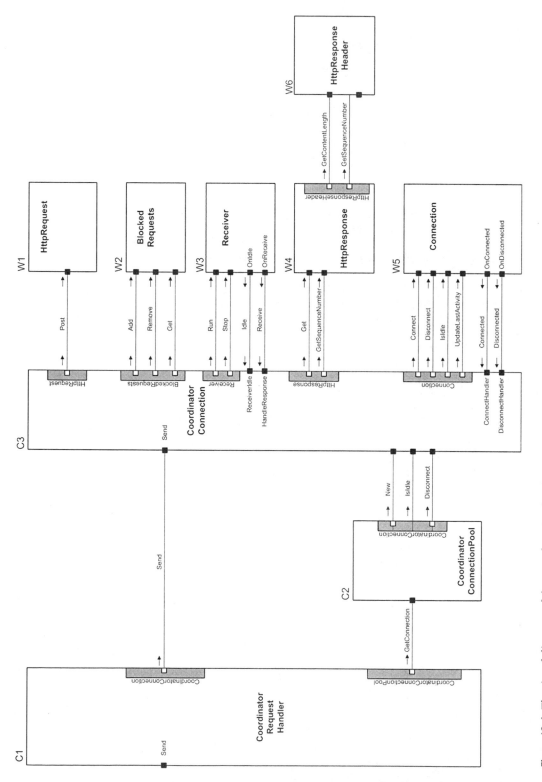

Figure 12-4. *The signal diagram of the complete HttpService*

Sequence diagrams are useful to see how the system processes a client request. Figure 12-5 shows the top-level sequence.

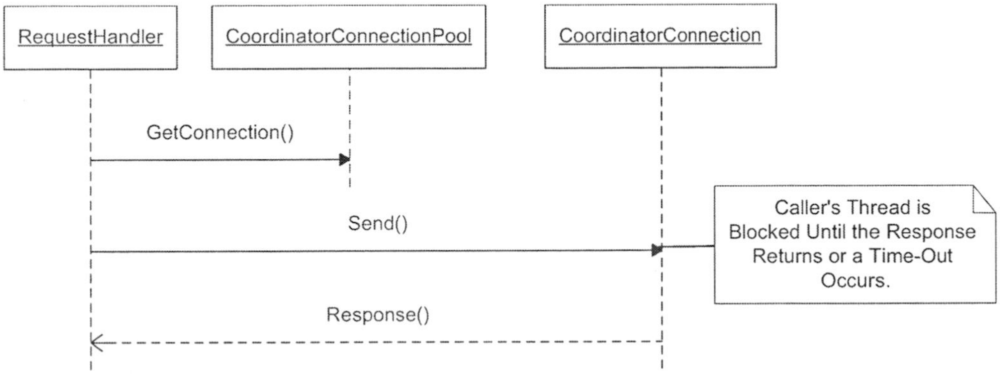

Figure 12-5. *The top-level sequence diagram of the system*

The diagram doesn't show how CoordinatorConnection uses the other objects in the system to actually send requests and handle responses. The sequence diagram in Figure 12-6 shows this lower level of detail.

The low-level diagram reveals a fair amount of activity. Perhaps surprisingly, the individual objects are rather simple. The signals going from right to left are sent as event notifications. All the workers have a very narrow focus.

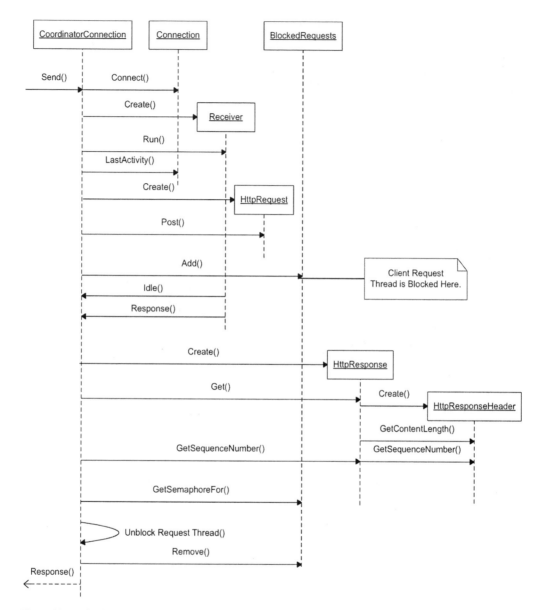

Figure 12-6. *The low-level sequence diagram of the system*

Managing the Connection Pool

When a connection is made to a remote server, the connection is kept in a pool. Subsequent requests directed to the same host reuse the connection. Once a connection is used, it may not be needed again. Since you don't want to keep idle connections open indefinitely, keep track of when a connection was last used. If the connection isn't used for a certain amount of time, close it and remove it from the pool. Use a background thread to check the pool periodically for idle connections. The activity diagram in Figure 12-7 shows the basic operations of the connection pool system.

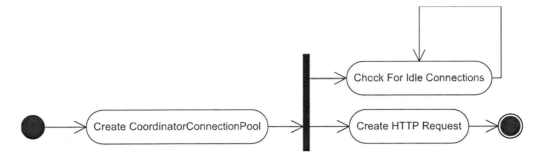

Figure 12-7. *Managing the connection pool*

When you create CoordinatorConnectionPool, you instantiate a ConnectionPool and create a separate thread to check for idle connections. This thread runs for the whole life of the system. Figure 12-8 shows the class diagram of the connection pool system.

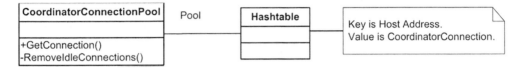

Figure 12-8. *The class diagram of the ConnectionPool team*

Calls to CoordinatorConnectionPool.GetConnection specify the address of the host to which a connection is desired. If the pool doesn't have a connection to that host, you can create a new connection Coordinator team by instantiating CoordinatorConnection. This class internally sets up and controls the connection Coordinator team. The connection pool is implemented as a Hashtable, whose key is a host address and whose value is a reference to the CoordinatorConnection managing connections to that host. The host address can be either an IP address such as "127.0.0.1" or a DNS address such as "www.myhost.com".

Listing 12-3 and Listing 12-4 show C# and VB .NET implementations of CoordinatorConnectionPool.

Listing 12-3. *The C# Implementation of CoordinatorConnectionPool*

```csharp
public class CoordinatorConnectionPool
{
  Thread idleConnectionMonitorThread;
  Hashtable pool = new Hashtable(); // key is host address,
                                    // value is ConnectionCoordinator

  public CoordinatorConnectionPool()
  {
    idleConnectionMonitorThread =
      new Thread(new ThreadStart(RemoveIdleConnections));
    idleConnectionMonitorThread.IsBackground = true;
    idleConnectionMonitorThread.Start();
  }
```

```
void RemoveIdleConnections()
{
  while (true)
  {
    lock(this)
    {
      DoRemoveIdleConnections();
    }

    Thread.Sleep(10000); // wait for 10 seconds
  }
}

private void DoRemoveIdleConnections()
{
  // Removing items from a collection during iteration
  // is not allowed, so we create a clone of the original
  // collection. We then iterate over the clone, but
  // remove items from the original collection
  Hashtable clonedHashtable = pool.Clone() as Hashtable;

  foreach (string hostAddress in clonedHashtable.Keys)
  {
    CoordinatorConnection coordinator =
            clonedHashtable[hostAddress] as CoordinatorConnection;
    if (coordinator.IsIdle)
    {
      pool.Remove(hostAddress);
      coordinator.Disconnect();
    }
  }
}

TimeSpan rxTimeout = new TimeSpan(0, 0, 20); // twenty seconds

public CoordinatorConnection GetConnection(string theHostAddress)
{
    CoordinatorConnection coordinator;
    lock(this) // don't let other threads get in
    {
      if (pool.Contains(theHostAddress))
        coordinator = pool[theHostAddress] as CoordinatorConnection;
      else
      {
        coordinator = new CoordinatorConnection(theHostAddress,
                                                rxTimeout);
        pool.Add(theHostAddress, coordinator);
      }
    } // let other threads in
    return coordinator;
}
}
```

Listing 12-4. *The VB .NET Implementation of CoordinatorConnectionPool*

```vb
Public Class CoordinatorConnectionPool

  Private _idleConnectionMonitorThread As Thread
  Private _pool As New Hashtable ' key is host address,
                                 ' value is ConnectionCoordinator

  Public Sub New()
    _idleConnectionMonitorThread = New Thread(AddressOf RemoveIdleConnections)
    _idleConnectionMonitorThread.IsBackground = True
    _idleConnectionMonitorThread.Start()
  End Sub

  Sub RemoveIdleConnections()
    While True
      SyncLock(Me)
        DoRemoveIdleConnections()
      End SyncLock
      Thread.Sleep(10000) ' wait for 10 seconds
    End While
  End Sub

  Private Sub DoRemoveIdleConnections()
    ' Removing items from a collection during iteration
    ' is not allowed, so we create a clone of the original
    ' collection. We then iterate over the clone, but
    ' remove items from the original collection
    Dim clonedHashtable As Hashtable = DirectCast(_pool.Clone(), Hashtable)

    For Each hostAddress As String In clonedHashtable.Keys
      Dim coordinator As CoordinatorConnection =
            DirectCast(clonedHashtable(hostAddress), CoordinatorConnection)
      If coordinator.IsIdle Then
        _pool.Remove(hostAddress)
        coordinator.Disconnect()
      End If
    Next
  End Sub

  Private _rxTimeout As New TimeSpan(0, 0, 20) ' twenty seconds

  'get an existing connection or create a new one
  Public Function GetConnection(ByVal theHostAddress As String) _
                      As CoordinatorConnection
    Dim coordinator As CoordinatorConnection
    SyncLock(Me) 'don't let other threads in
    If _pool.Contains(theHostAddress) Then
      coordinator = DirectCast(_pool(theHostAddress), CoordinatorConnection)
    Else
      coordinator = New CoordinatorConnection(theHostAddress, _rxTimeout)
      _pool.Add(theHostAddress, coordinator)
    End If
```

```
      End SyncLock 'let other threads in
      Return coordinator
    End Function
End Class
```

The Coordinator has two important jobs, both related to threading:

1. To create a thread to run RemoveIdleConnections on

2. To protect the connection pool from concurrent changes

Concurrent changes to the pool might occur if two clients call GetConnection at the same time, or if ConnectionPool.GetConnection and ConnectionPool.RemoveIdleConnections are called at the same time. To ensure that concurrent calls are handled correctly (i.e., one at a time), protect the calls to ConnectionPool with a Monitor.

The Connection Team

The connection Coordinator team handles the main tasks of establishing a connection to a remote server, sending requests, and getting responses. When requests are sent in a pipelined mode, meaning that multiple requests are sent before any responses come back, the connection Coordinator team also handles the process of matching responses with requests. Figure 12-9 shows the basic activity diagram of the team.

The connection Coordinator team is led by CoordinatorConnection, which handles all the threading logic. The team operates as follows: CoordinatorRequestHandler gets a CoordinatorConnection from the connection pool and calls the Coordinator with a sequence number to use. The Coordinator creates an HttpRequest object and uses it to send the request to the server. The request thread is then blocked, and a semaphore referencing the thread is stored in the blockedRequests collection, using the sequence number as a key. The semaphore is actually an object of class ThreadSemaphore. Figure 12-10 shows the class diagram.

When a response arrives, it contains a sequence number. The blockedRequests collection is then checked for a ThreadSemaphore with that sequence number. The response thread then stores the response in the ThreadSemaphore object and unblocks the request thread.

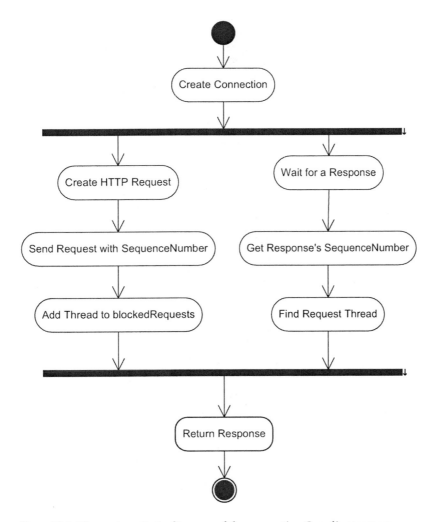

Figure 12-9. *The main activity diagram of the connection Coordinator team*

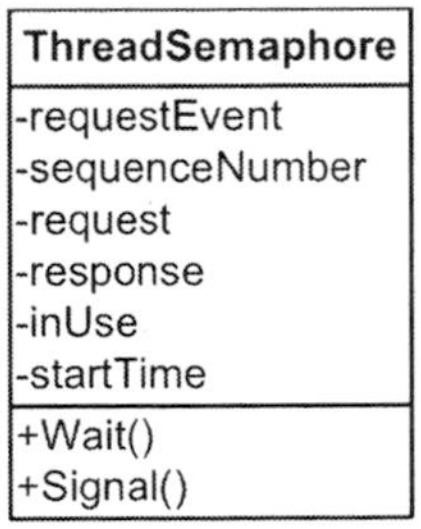

ThreadSemaphore
-requestEvent -sequenceNumber -request -response -inUse -startTime
+Wait() +Signal()

Figure 12-10. *The class used to synchronize the request and response threads*

Two fields of ThreadSemaphore are particularly important in the interaction between the request and response threads: requestEvent and response. The former is of type ManualResetEvent, which is a process synchronization class used to block and resume the request thread. The latter is of type string and is used by the response thread to store the response message. When the request thread is resumed, the Send method that was woken up fetches the response from ThreadSemaphore and returns it to the caller. Figure 12-11 shows the class diagram of the connection Coordinator team.

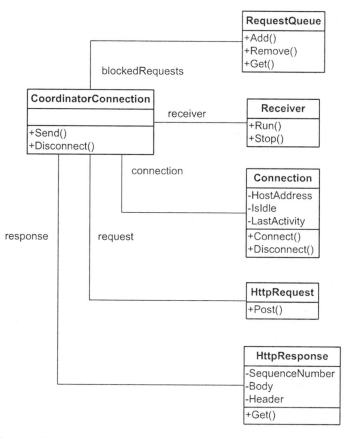

Figure 12-11. *The class diagram of the connection Coordinator team*

The five Worker classes on the right side are all independent of each other. When a worker needs to send information back to the Coordinator, events are used. Listing 12-5 and Listing 12-6 show C# and VB .NET implementations of the Coordinator.

Listing 12-5. *The C# Implementation of CoordinatorConnection*

```
public class CoordinatorConnection
{
    RequestQueue blockedRequests;   // a queue of blocked send threads
    Receiver receiver;              // listens for incoming traffic
    Connection connection;          // sends requests and handles responses
    TimeSpan rxTimeout;             // time to wait for a response
    Thread receiverThread;          // background receiver thread
```

```csharp
public bool IsIdle
{
  get {return connection.IsIdle;}
}

public CoordinatorConnection(string theHostAddress, TimeSpan theRxTimeout)
{
  rxTimeout = theRxTimeout;
  blockedRequests = new RequestQueue();

  connection = new Connection(theHostAddress);
  connection.OnConnected +=
      new HttpService.Connection.ConnectedHandler(ConnectHandler);
  connection.OnDisconnected +=
      new HttpService.Connection.DisconnectedHandler(DisconnectHandler);
}

// returns the response
public string Send(string theLocalPath, int theSequenceNumber, string theMessage)
{
  ThreadSemaphore semaphore = null;

  lock(this)
  {
    // we use a lock here, to prevent concurrent requests
    // from getting mixed together on their way out
    connection.Connect();
    connection.LastActivity = DateTime.Now;
    HttpRequest request = new HttpRequest(connection.Socket);
    request.Post(theLocalPath, theSequenceNumber, theMessage);
    semaphore = blockedRequests.Add(theSequenceNumber, theMessage);
  }

  // block until the response arrives, or a timeout occurs
  if (!semaphore.Wait(rxTimeout))
    throw new Exception("No response received");

  // get the response from the semaphore
  byte[] response = semaphore.response;
  blockedRequests.Remove(theSequenceNumber);
  return Encoding.UTF8.GetString(response);
}

public void Disconnect()
{
  connection.Disconnect();
}

void HandleResponse(Socket theSocket)
{
  // read the response
  HttpResponse response = new HttpResponse(theSocket);
  response.Get();
```

```csharp
      // get the semaphore for the blocked request thread
      ThreadSemaphore semaphore =
                      blockedRequests.Get(response.SequenceNumber);
      if (semaphore == null)
        throw new Exception("No pending request found for response");

      // save the response in the semaphore
      semaphore.response = response.Body;

      // unblock the request thread waiting for this response
      semaphore.Signal();
    }

    private void ConnectHandler(Socket theSocket)
    {
      receiver = new Receiver(theSocket);
      receiver.OnIdle += new HttpService.Receiver.IdleHandler(ReceiverIdle);
      receiver.OnResponse += new HttpService.Receiver.ResponseHandler(HandleResponse);
      receiverThread = new Thread(new ThreadStart(receiver.Run));
      receiverThread.Name = "Receiver";
      receiverThread.IsBackground = true;
      receiverThread.Start();
    }

    private void DisconnectHandler()
    {
      receiver.Stop();
      receiverThread.Join();   // wait for thread to stop
      receiver = null;
    }

    void ReceiverIdle()
    {
      Thread.Sleep(10);
    }
}
```

Listing 12-6. *The VB .NET Implementation of CoordinatorConnection*

```vbnet
Public Class CoordinatorConnection
  Private blockedRequests As RequestQueue ' blocked request threads
  Private receiver As Receiver   ' listens for incoming traffic
  Private connection As Connection  ' handles requests and responses
  Private rxTimeout As TimeSpan   ' time to wait for a response
  Private receiverThread As Thread   ' background receiver thread

  Public ReadOnly Property IsIdle() As Boolean
    Get
      Return _connection.IsIdle
    End Get
  End Property
```

```vbnet
Public Sub New(ByVal theHostAddress As String,  ByVal theRxTimeout As TimeSpan)
  _rxTimeout = theRxTimeout
  _blockedRequests = New RequestQueue

  _connection = New Connection(theHostAddress)
  AddHandler _connection.OnConnected, AddressOf ConnectHandler
  AddHandler _connection.OnDisconnected, AddressOf DisconnectHandler
End Sub

' returns the response
Public Function Send(ByVal theLocalPath As String, _
                     ByVal theSequenceNumber As Integer, _
                     ByVal theMessage As String) As String
  Dim semaphore As ThreadSemaphore = Nothing

  SyncLock (Me)
    ' we use a lock here, to prevent concurrent requests
    ' from getting mixed together on their way out
    _connection.Connect()
    _connection.LastActivity = DateTime.Now
    Dim request As New HttpRequest(_connection.Socket)
    request.Post(theLocalPath, theSequenceNumber, theMessage)
    semaphore = _blockedRequests.Add(theSequenceNumber, theMessage)
  End SyncLock

  ' block until the response arrives, or a timeout occurs
  If Not semaphore.Wait(_rxTimeout) Then
    Throw New Exception("No response received")
  End If

  ' get the response from the semaphore
  Dim response As Byte() = semaphore.response
  _blockedRequests.Remove(theSequenceNumber)
  Return Encoding.UTF8.GetString(response)
End Function

Public Sub Disconnect()
  _connection.Disconnect()
End Sub

Sub HandleResponse(ByVal theSocket As Socket)
  ' read the response
  Dim response As New HttpResponse(theSocket)
  response.Get()

  ' get the semaphore for the blocked request thread
  Dim semaphore As ThreadSemaphore =
     _blockedRequests.Get(response.SequenceNumber)
  If semaphore Is Nothing Then
    Throw New Exception("No pending request found for response")
  End If

  ' save the response in the semaphore
  semaphore.response = response.Body
```

```vbnet
    ' unblock the request thread waiting for this response
    semaphore.Signal()
  End Sub

  Private Sub ConnectHandler(ByVal theSocket As Socket)
    _receiver = New Receiver(theSocket)
    AddHandler _receiver.OnIdle, AddressOf ReceiverIdle
    AddHandler _receiver.OnResponse, AddressOf HandleResponse
    _receiverThread = New Thread(AddressOf _receiver.Run)
    _receiverThread.Name = "Receiver"
    _receiverThread.IsBackground = True
    _receiverThread.Start()
  End Sub

  Private Sub DisconnectHandler()
    _receiver.Stop()
    _receiverThread.Join()   ' wait for thread to stop
    _receiver = Nothing
  End Sub

  Sub ReceiverIdle()
    Thread.Sleep(10)
  End Sub

End Class
```

Let's look at the salient `Worker` objects in the connection `Coordinator` team, starting with `Connection`. This class just handles the opening and closing of TCP socket connections. It fires an event when a connection is opened or closed. Listing 12-7 and Listing 12-8 show C# and VB .NET implementations.

Listing 12-7. *The C# Implementation of the Connection Class*

```csharp
public class Connection
{
  Socket socket;
  public Socket Socket
  {
    get {return socket;}
  }

  string hostAddress;
  public string HostAddress
  {
    get {return hostAddress;}
    set {hostAddress = value;}
  }

  public bool Connected
  {
    get {return socket != null;}
  }
```

```csharp
DateTime lastActivity = DateTime.Now;
public DateTime LastActivity
{
  get {return lastActivity;}
  set {lastActivity = value;}
}

// theHostAddress can be an IP or a DNS Address
public Connection(string theHostAddress)
{
  hostAddress = theHostAddress;
}

TimeSpan TwentyMinutes = new TimeSpan(0, 20, 0);
public bool IsIdle
{
  get {return (DateTime.Now - LastActivity) > TwentyMinutes;}
}

public void Connect()
{
  if (Connected) return;

  socket = new Socket(AddressFamily.InterNetwork,
                      SocketType.Stream, ProtocolType.Tcp);
  IPHostEntry hostEntry = Dns.GetHostByName(hostAddress);
  IPEndPoint endPoint =
          new IPEndPoint(hostEntry.AddressList[0], 8020);
  socket.Connect(endPoint);

  FireConnected(socket);
}

public void Disconnect()
{
  if (socket == null) return;

  socket.Close();
  socket = null;

  FireDisconnected();
}

public delegate void ConnectedHandler(Socket theSocket);
public event ConnectedHandler OnConnected;
void FireConnected(Socket theSocket)
{
  if (OnConnected != null)
    OnConnected(theSocket);
}
```

```csharp
public delegate void DisconnectedHandler();
public event DisconnectedHandler OnDisconnected;
void FireDisconnected()
{
  if (OnDisconnected != null)
    OnDisconnected();
}
}
```

Listing 12-8. *The VB .NET Implementation of the Connection Class*

```vbnet
Public Class Connection
  Private _socket As Socket
  Public ReadOnly Property Socket() As Socket
    Get
      Return _socket
    End Get
  End Property

  Private _hostAddress As String
  Public Property HostAddress() As String
    Get
      Return _hostAddress
    End Get
    Set(ByVal Value As String)
      _hostAddress = Value
    End Set
  End Property

  Public ReadOnly Property Connected() As Boolean
    Get
      Return Not Socket Is Nothing
    End Get
  End Property

  Private _lastActivity As DateTime = DateTime.Now
  Public Property LastActivity() As DateTime
    Get
      Return _lastActivity
    End Get
    Set(ByVal Value As DateTime)
      _lastActivity = Value
    End Set
  End Property

  ' theHostAddress can be an IP or a DNS Address
  Public Sub New(ByVal theHostAddress As String)
    _hostAddress = theHostAddress
  End Sub
```

```
  Private TwentyMinutes As TimeSpan = New TimeSpan(0, 20, 0)
  Public ReadOnly Property IsIdle() As Boolean
    Get
      Return TimeSpan.op_GreaterThan(
             DateTime.Now.Subtract(LastActivity), TwentyMinutes)
    End Get
  End Property

  Public Sub Connect()
    If Connected Then Return

    _socket = New Socket(AddressFamily.InterNetwork,
                         SocketType.Stream, ProtocolType.Tcp)
    Dim hostEntry As IPHostEntry = Dns.GetHostByName(HostAddress)
    Dim endPoint As New IPEndPoint(hostEntry.AddressList(0), 8020)
    Socket.Connect(EndPoint)

    FireConnected(Socket)
  End Sub

  Public Sub Disconnect()
    If _socket Is Nothing Then Return

    _socket.Close()
    _socket = Nothing

    FireDisconnected()
  End Sub

  Public Event OnConnected(ByVal theSocket As Socket)
  Sub FireConnected(ByVal theSocket As Socket)
    RaiseEvent OnConnected(theSocket)
  End Sub

  Public Event OnDisconnected()
  Sub FireDisconnected()
    RaiseEvent OnDisconnected()
  End Sub
End Class
```

Once you open a connection, the Coordinator sends a request and starts a listener thread that waits for incoming messages from the server. Listing 12-9 and Listing 12-10 show C# and VB .NET implementations of HttpRequest.

Listing 12-9. *The C# Implementation of the HttpRequest Class*

```
public class HttpRequest
{
  Socket socket;

  public HttpRequest(Socket theSocket)
  {
    socket = theSocket;
  }
```

```
    public void Post(string theLocalPath, int theSequenceNumber,
                     string theMessage)
    {
      IPEndPoint endPoint = socket.RemoteEndPoint as IPEndPoint;
      string header = string.Format("POST {0} HTTP/1.1\r\n" +
                                    "Host: {1}:{2}\r\n" +
                                    "Sequence-Number: {3}\r\n" +
                                    "Connection: Keep-Alive\r\n" +
                                    "Content-Length: {4}\r\n",
                                    theLocalPath, endPoint.Address,
                                    endPoint.Port, theSequenceNumber,
                                    theMessage.Length);

      string message = string.Format("{0}\r\n{1}", header, theMessage);
      byte[] bytes = Encoding.UTF8.GetBytes(message);
      NetworkStream stream = new NetworkStream(socket);
      stream.Write(bytes, 0, bytes.Length);
    }
}
```

Listing 12-10. *The VB .NET Implementation of the HttpRequest Class*

```
Public Class HttpRequest
  Private _socket As Socket

  Public Sub New(ByVal theSocket As Socket)
    _socket = theSocket
  End Sub

  Public Sub Post(ByVal theLocalPath As String, _
                  ByVal theSequenceNumber As Integer, _
                  ByVal theMessage As String)
    Dim endPoint As IPEndPoint =
        DirectCast(socket.RemoteEndPoint, IPEndPoint)
    Dim header As String = String.Format("POST {0} HTTP/1.1" +
                                  ControlChars.NewLine + _
                                  "Host: {1}:{2}" +
                                  ControlChars.NewLine + _
                                  "Sequence-Number: {3}" +
                                  ControlChars.NewLine + _
                                  "Connection: Keep-Alive" +
                                  ControlChars.NewLine + _
                                  "Content-Length: {4}" +
                                  ControlChars.NewLine, _
                                  theLocalPath, endPoint.Address, _
                                  endPoint.Port, theSequenceNumber, _
                                  theMessage.Length)

    Dim message As String = String.Format("{0}{1}{2}", header, _
                              ControlChars.NewLine, theMessage)
    Dim bytes As Byte() = Encoding.UTF8.GetBytes(message)
    Dim stream As New NetworkStream(socket)
    stream.Write(bytes, 0, bytes.Length)
  End Sub
End Class
```

HttpRequest creates an HTTP message by appending an HTTP header to the request to send.
Note the SequenceNumber field in the header. I'll show you how to use this field later, when a response
is detected, to match the response with the right request. HttpService uses a listener thread to handle
responses. The code is contained in class Receiver, whose C# and VB .NET implementations are
shown in Listing 12-11 and Listing 12-12.

Listing 12-11. *The C# Implementation of the Receiver Class*

```csharp
public class Receiver
{
  bool stopRequested;
  Socket socket;

  public Receiver(Socket theSocket)
  {
    socket = theSocket;
  }

  public void Stop()
  {
    stopRequested = true;
  }

  public void Run()
  {
    stopRequested = false;
    while (!stopRequested)
      CheckForIncomingTraffic();
  }

  void CheckForIncomingTraffic()
  {
    if (socket.Available == 0)
      FireIdle();
    else
      FireResponse(socket);
  }

  public delegate void ResponseHandler(Socket theSocket);
  public event ResponseHandler OnResponse;
  void FireResponse(Socket theSocket)
  {
    if (OnResponse != null)
      OnResponse(theSocket);
  }

  public delegate void IdleHandler();
  public event IdleHandler OnIdle;
  void FireIdle()
  {
    if (OnIdle != null)
      OnIdle();
  }
}
```

Listing 12-12. *The VB .NET Implementation of the Receiver Class*

```
Public Class Receiver
  Private _stopRequested As Boolean
  Private _socket As Socket

  Public Sub New(ByVal theSocket As Socket)
    _socket = theSocket
  End Sub

  Public Sub [Stop]()
    _stopRequested = True
  End Sub

  Public Sub Run()
    _stopRequested = False
    While Not _stopRequested
      CheckForIncomingTraffic()
    End While
  End Sub

  Sub CheckForIncomingTraffic()
    If _socket.Available = 0 Then
      FireIdle()
    Else
      FireResponse(_socket)
    End If
  End Sub

  Public Event OnResponse(ByVal theSocket As Socket)
  Sub FireResponse(ByVal theSocket As Socket)
    RaiseEvent OnResponse(theSocket)
  End Sub

  Public Event OnIdle()
  Sub FireIdle()
    RaiseEvent OnIdle()
  End Sub
End Class
```

Receiver runs a loop in its Run method. To avoid using too much CPU time, the class idles after each iteration through the loop. The idle is accomplished by firing an event, which the Coordinator handles by putting the thread to sleep for a while. As soon as incoming data is detected on the receiver's socket, an event is fired. The Coordinator handles the event with the method HandleResponse. To read the response, the Coordinator creates an HttpResponse object and calls its Get method. Listing 12-13 and Listing 12-14 show C# and VB .NET implementations of HttpResponse.

Listing 12-13. *The C# Implementation of the HttpResponse Class*

```csharp
public class HttpResponse
{
  Socket socket;

  HttpResponseHeader header;
  public HttpResponseHeader Header
  {
    get {return header;}
  }

  byte[] body;
  public byte[] Body
  {
    get {return body;}
  }

  public int SequenceNumber
  {
    get {return header.SequenceNumber;}
  }

  public HttpResponse(Socket theSocket)
  {
    socket = theSocket;
  }

  public void Get()
  {
    NetworkStream networkStream = new NetworkStream(socket);

    // read the response header
    header = new HttpResponseHeader(networkStream);

    // read the response body (if any)
    if (header.ContentLength == 0)
      return;

    byte[] buffer = new byte[header.ContentLength];
    networkStream.Read(buffer, 0, buffer.Length);
    body = buffer;
  }
}
```

Listing 12-14. *The VB .NET Implementation of the HttpResponse Class*

```
Public Class HttpResponse
  Private _socket As Socket

  Private _header As HttpResponseHeader
  Public ReadOnly Property Header() As HttpResponseHeader
    Get
      Return _header
    End Get
  End Property

  Private _body As Byte()
  Public ReadOnly Property Body() As Byte()
    Get
      Return _body
    End Get
  End Property

  Public ReadOnly Property SequenceNumber() As Integer
    Get
      Return _header.SequenceNumber
    End Get
  End Property

  Public Sub New(ByVal theSocket As Socket)
    _socket = theSocket
  End Sub

  Public Sub [Get]()
    Dim networkStream As New NetworkStream(_socket)

    ' read the response header
    _header = New HttpResponseHeader(networkStream)

    ' read the response body (if any)
    If _header.ContentLength = 0 Then Return

    Dim buffer(_header.ContentLength - 1) As Byte
    networkStream.Read(buffer, 0, buffer.Length)
    _body = buffer
  End Sub
End Class
```

Class HttpResponse uses a helper class called HttpResponseHeader to handle the details of parsing the various fields of received HTTP messages. Listing 12-15 and Listing 12-16 show C# and VB .NET implementations of HttpResponseHeader.

Listing 12-15. *The C# Implementation of the HttpResponseHeader Class*

```csharp
public class HttpResponseHeader
{
  // key is name, value is value
  Hashtable headers = new Hashtable();

  HttpStatusCode statusCode;

  public int ContentLength
  {
    get
    {
      if (!headers.Contains("Content-Length"))
        return 0;
      string s = headers["Content-Length"] as string;
      return int.Parse(s);
    }
  }

  public int SequenceNumber
  {
    get
    {
      if (!headers.Contains("Sequence-Number"))
        throw new Exception("Sequence-Number not found");
      string s = headers["Sequence-Number"] as string;
      return int.Parse(s);
    }
  }

  public HttpResponseHeader(NetworkStream theNetworkStream)
  {
    StreamReader reader = GetStreamReader(theNetworkStream);
    Parse(reader);
  }

  StreamReader GetStreamReader(NetworkStream theNetworkStream)
  {
    const byte Cr = 0x0d;   // UTF8 CarriageReturn

    // read the incoming data and return it as a StreamReader
    MemoryStream memoryStream = new MemoryStream();

    byte b = (byte) theNetworkStream.ReadByte();

    // the header ends with "\r\n\r\n"
    while (true)
    {
      while (b != Cr)
      {
        memoryStream.WriteByte(b);
        b = (byte) theNetworkStream.ReadByte();
      }
```

```
      memoryStream.WriteByte(b); // Cr
      b = (byte) theNetworkStream.ReadByte();
      memoryStream.WriteByte(b); // Lf

      b = (byte) theNetworkStream.ReadByte();
      if (b == Cr)
      {
        memoryStream.WriteByte(b); // Cr
        b = (byte) theNetworkStream.ReadByte();
        memoryStream.WriteByte(b); // Lf
        memoryStream.Position = 0;
        StreamReader reader =
                    new StreamReader(memoryStream, Encoding.UTF8);
        return reader;
      }
    }
}

public void Parse(StreamReader theReader)
{
  headers.Clear();
  ParseStatusCode(theReader);
  ParseOtherLines(theReader);
}

// the response must start with a string like this:
// HTTP/1.1 200 OK\r\n
void ParseStatusCode(StreamReader theReader)
{
  string line = theReader.ReadLine();
  if (!line.StartsWith("HTTP"))
    throw new Exception("Invalid response header");

  string[] words = line.Split(' ');
  if (words.Length < 3)
    throw new Exception("Invalid response header");

  int i = int.Parse(words[1]);
  statusCode = (HttpStatusCode) i;
}

void ParseOtherLines(StreamReader theReader)
{
  string line = theReader.ReadLine();
  while (line != null)
  {
    if (line == "") return;
    ParseLine(line);
    line = theReader.ReadLine();
  }
}
```

```
  void ParseLine(string theLine)
  {
    string[] words = theLine.Split(':');
    if (words.Length == 0)
      throw new Exception("Invalid response header");

    headers.Add(words[0], words[1]);
  }
}
```

Listing 12-16. *The VB .NET Implementation of the HttpResponseHeader Class*

```
Public Class HttpResponseHeader
  ' key is name, value is value
  Private _headers As New Hashtable

  Private _statusCode As HttpStatusCode

  Public ReadOnly Property ContentLength() As Integer
    Get
      If Not _headers.Contains("Content-Length") Then Return 0
      Dim s As String = DirectCast(_headers("Content-Length"), String)
      Return Integer.Parse(s)
    End Get
  End Property

  Public ReadOnly Property SequenceNumber() As Integer
    Get
      If Not _headers.Contains("Sequence-Number") Then
        Throw New Exception("Sequence-Number not found")
      End If
      Dim s As String =
          DirectCast(_headers("Sequence-Number"), String)
      Return Integer.Parse(s)
    End Get
  End Property

  Public Sub New(ByVal theNetworkStream As NetworkStream)
    Dim reader As StreamReader = GetStreamReader(theNetworkStream)
    Parse(reader)
  End Sub

    Function GetStreamReader(ByVal theNetworkStream as NetworkStream)
            as StreamReader
    Const Cr As Byte = &HD        ' UTF8 CarriageReturn

    ' read the incoming data and return it as a StreamReader
    Dim memoryStream As New MemoryStream

    Dim b As Byte = CByte(theNetworkStream.ReadByte())
```

```vbnet
      ' the header ends with "\r\n\r\n"
      While True
        While (b <> Cr)
          memoryStream.WriteByte(b)
          b = CByte(theNetworkStream.ReadByte())
        End While

        memoryStream.WriteByte(b) ' Cr
        b = CByte(theNetworkStream.ReadByte())
        memoryStream.WriteByte(b) ' Lf

        b = CByte(theNetworkStream.ReadByte())
        If (b = Cr) Then
          memoryStream.WriteByte(b) ' Cr
          b = CByte(theNetworkStream.ReadByte())
          memoryStream.WriteByte(b) ' Lf
          memoryStream.Position = 0
          Dim reader As New StreamReader(memoryStream, Encoding.UTF8)
          Return reader
        End If
      End While
    End Function

    Public Sub Parse(ByVal theReader As StreamReader)
      _headers.Clear()
      ParseStatusCode(theReader)
      ParseOtherLines(theReader)
    End Sub

    ' the response must start with a string like this:
    ' HTTP/1.1 200 OK\r\n
    Sub ParseStatusCode(ByVal theReader As StreamReader)
      Dim line As String = theReader.ReadLine()
      If Not line.StartsWith("HTTP") Then
        Throw New Exception("Invalid response header")
      End If

      Dim words As String() = line.Split(" "c)
      If words.Length < 3 Then
        Throw New Exception("Invalid response header")
      End If

      Dim i As Integer = Integer.Parse(words(1))
      _statusCode = CType(i, HttpStatusCode)
    End Sub

    Sub ParseOtherLines(ByVal theReader As StreamReader)
      Dim line As String = theReader.ReadLine()
      While Not line Is Nothing
        If line = String.Empty Then Return
        ParseLine(line)
        line = theReader.ReadLine()
      End While
    End Sub
```

```
  Sub ParseLine(ByVal theLine As String)
    Dim words As String() = theLine.Split(":"c)
    If words.Length = 0 Then
      Throw New Exception("Invalid response header")
    End If
    _headers.Add(words(0), words(1))
  End Sub
End Class
```

While requests are waiting for responses, their threads are blocked. HttpService uses two classes called ThreadSemaphore and RequestQueue to manage blocked threads. Listing 12-17 and Listing 12-18 show C# and VB .NET implementations of the two classes.

Listing 12-17. *The C# Implementation of ThreadSemaphore and RequestQueue*

```csharp
public class ThreadSemaphore
{
  public ManualResetEvent requestEvent = new ManualResetEvent(false);
  public int sequenceNumber;
  public string request;
  public byte[] response;
  public bool inUse;
  public DateTime startTime;

  public bool Wait(TimeSpan theDuration)
  {
    return requestEvent.WaitOne(theDuration, true);
  }

  public void Signal()
  {
    requestEvent.Set();
  }
}
public class RequestQueue
{
  static RequestQueue singleton;
  public static RequestQueue Singleton
  {
    get
    {
      if (singleton == null)
        singleton = new RequestQueue();
      return singleton;
    }
  }

  // a pool of prebuilt semaphores used with blocked requests
  ThreadSemaphore[] semaphores;

  // key is SequenceNumber, value is RequestSemaphore
  Hashtable blockedRequests = new Hashtable();
```

```csharp
public RequestQueue()
{
  // we support up to 500 concurrent requests.
  // The value is arbitrary
  semaphores = new ThreadSemaphore[500];
  for (int i = 0; i < semaphores.Length; i++)
  {
    ThreadSemaphore semaphore = new ThreadSemaphore();
    semaphore.requestEvent = new ManualResetEvent(false);
    semaphores[i] = semaphore;
  }
}

public ThreadSemaphore Add(int theSequenceNumber, string theRequest)
{
  lock(this)
  {
    ThreadSemaphore semaphore = GetFirstAvailableSemaphore();
    blockedRequests.Add(theSequenceNumber, semaphore);
    semaphore.requestEvent.Reset();
    semaphore.sequenceNumber = theSequenceNumber;
    semaphore.request = theRequest;
    semaphore.response = null;
    semaphore.startTime = DateTime.Now;
    return semaphore;
  }
}

ThreadSemaphore GetFirstAvailableSemaphore()
{
  lock(this)
  {
    foreach (ThreadSemaphore semaphore in semaphores)
    {
      if (semaphore.inUse) continue;
      semaphore.inUse = true;
      return semaphore;
    }
  }
  throw new Exception("RequestQueue: No semaphores available");
}

public void Remove(int theSequenceNumber)
{
  lock(this)
  {
    ThreadSemaphore semaphore =
          blockedRequests[theSequenceNumber] as ThreadSemaphore;
    blockedRequests.Remove(theSequenceNumber);
    semaphore.inUse = false;
  }
}
```

```
  public ThreadSemaphore Get(int theSequenceNumber)
  {
    return blockedRequests[theSequenceNumber] as ThreadSemaphore;
  }
}
```

Listing 12-18. *The VB .NET Implementation of ThreadSemaphore and RequestQueue*

```vbnet
Public Class ThreadSemaphore
  Public requestEvent As New ManualResetEvent(False)
  Public sequenceNumber As Integer
  Public request As String
  Public response As Byte()
  Public inUse As Boolean
  Public startTime As DateTime

  Public Function Wait(ByVal theDuration As TimeSpan) As Boolean
    Return requestEvent.WaitOne(theDuration, True)
  End Function

  Public Sub Signal()
    requestEvent.Set()
  End Sub
End Class
Public Class RequestQueue

  Private Shared _singleton As RequestQueue
  Public Shared ReadOnly Property Singleton() As RequestQueue
    Get
      If singleton Is Nothing Then
        _singleton = New RequestQueue
      End If
      Return _singleton
    End Get
  End Property

  ' a pool of prebuilt semaphores used with blocked requests.
  ' We support up to 500 concurrent requests. The value is arbitrary
  Private _semaphores(500) As ThreadSemaphore

  ' key is SequenceNumber, value is RequestSemaphore
  Private _blockedRequests As New Hashtable

  Public Sub New()
    For i As Integer = 0 To _semaphores.Length - 1
      Dim semaphore As New ThreadSemaphore
      semaphore.requestEvent = New ManualResetEvent(False)
      _semaphores(i) = semaphore
    Next
  End Sub
```

```
   Public Function Add(ByVal theSequenceNumber As Integer,
                       ByVal theRequest As String) _
                       As ThreadSemaphore
     SyncLock (Me)
       Dim semaphore As ThreadSemaphore = GetFirstAvailableSemaphore()
       _blockedRequests.Add(theSequenceNumber, semaphore)
       semaphore.requestEvent.Reset()
       semaphore.sequenceNumber = theSequenceNumber
       semaphore.request = theRequest
       semaphore.response = Nothing
       semaphore.startTime = DateTime.Now
       Return semaphore
     End SyncLock
   End Function

   Function GetFirstAvailableSemaphore() As ThreadSemaphore
     SyncLock (Me)
       For Each semaphore As ThreadSemaphore In _semaphores
         If Not semaphore.inUse Then
           semaphore.inUse = True
           Return semaphore
         End If
       Next
     End SyncLock
     Throw New Exception("RequestQueue: No semaphores available")
   End Function

   Public Sub Remove(ByVal theSequenceNumber As Integer)
     SyncLock (Me)
       Dim semaphore As ThreadSemaphore = _
                       DirectCast(_blockedRequests(theSequenceNumber), _
                                       ThreadSemaphore)
       _blockedRequests.Remove(theSequenceNumber)
       semaphore.inUse = False
     End SyncLock
   End Sub

   Public Function [Get](ByVal theSequenceNumber As Integer) As ThreadSemaphore
     Return DirectCast(_blockedRequests(theSequenceNumber), ThreadSemaphore)
   End Function
End Class
```

When a response is detected, class Receiver fires a Receive event to CoordinatorConnection, which then uses code to get the sleeping request thread, give it the response, and wake the thread up. Listing 12-19 shows in bold line where the request thread's semaphore is signaled.

Listing 12-19. *Using the BlockedRequests Class to Match Responses with Requests*

C#

```csharp
void HandleResponse(Socket theSocket)
{
  // read the response
  HttpResponse response = new HttpResponse(theSocket);
  response.Get();

  // get the semaphore for the blocked request thread
  ThreadSemaphore
        semaphore = blockedRequests.Get(response.SequenceNumber);
  if (semaphore == null)
    throw new Exception("No pending request found for response");

  // save the response in the semaphore
  semaphore.response = response.Body;

  // unblock the request thread waiting for this response
  semaphore.Signal();
}
```

VB .NET

```vbnet
  Sub HandleResponse(ByVal theSocket As Socket)
    ' read the response
    Dim response As New HttpResponse(theSocket)
    response.Get()

    ' get the semaphore for the blocked request thread
    Dim semaphore As ThreadSemaphore =
      _blockedRequests.Get(response.SequenceNumber)
    If semaphore Is Nothing Then
      Throw New Exception("No pending request found for response")
    End If

    ' save the response in the semaphore
    semaphore.response = response.Body

    ' unblock the request thread waiting for this response
    semaphore.Signal()
  End Sub
```

The request thread was blocked in the Send method on the bold line shown in Listing 12-20. When the thread resumes (assuming a time-out doesn't occur), the response is available as a field in the ThreadSemaphore object. The code retrieves the response from ThreadSemaphore and returns it as the result of the Send method. When the method returns, the code is running on the original thread that the caller was on.

Listing 12-20. *Where the Send Method Blocks While Waiting for a Response*
C#

```csharp
public string Send(string theLocalPath, int theSequenceNumber,
                   string theMessage)
{
  ThreadSemaphore semaphore = null;

  lock(this)
  {
    // …
    semaphore = blockedRequests.Add(theSequenceNumber, theMessage);
  }

  // block until the response arrives, or a timeout occurs
  if (!semaphore.Wait(rxTimeout))
    throw new Exception("No response received");

  // get the response from the semaphore
  byte[] response = semaphore.response;
  blockedRequests.Remove(theSequenceNumber);
  return Encoding.UTF8.GetString(response);
}
```

VB .NET

```vbnet
Public Function Send(ByVal theLocalPath As String, _
                     ByVal theSequenceNumber As Integer, _
                     ByVal theMessage As String) As String
  Dim semaphore As ThreadSemaphore = Nothing

  SyncLock (Me)
    ' …
    semaphore = _blockedRequests.Add(theSequenceNumber, theMessage)
  End SyncLock

  ' block until the response arrives, or a timeout occurs
  If Not semaphore.Wait(_rxTimeout) Then
    Throw New Exception("No response received")
  End If

  ' get the response from the semaphore
  Dim response As Byte() = semaphore.response
  _blockedRequests.Remove(theSequenceNumber)
  Return Encoding.UTF8.GetString(response)
End Function
```

From the client's perspective, the call to CoordinatorRequestHandler.Send blocked until a response came back or until a time-out occurred. The caller has no knowledge that other requests might be going out on the very same connection to the same host.

Testing the System

When in operation, HttpService sits between clients and remote servers, as shown back in Figure 12-1. In order to test HttpService, you need to build a client and a remote server.

The Client Test Fixture

While building a multithreaded remote server to test HttpService sounds like a fairly complicated task, it really isn't. Figure 12-12 shows the client test fixture's UI.

Timestamp	Response Time	Sequence Number	Response Message
15:23:05.3113	1890 ms	9	Response 295750
15:23:05.3270	1906 ms	10	Response 327000
15:23:05.7488	2343 ms	5	Response 748875
15:23:05.7957	2390 ms	3	Response 795750
15:23:05.9363	2546 ms	4	Response 936375
15:23:06.0770	2656 ms	7	Response 077000
15:23:06.2332	2828 ms	6	Response 217625
15:23:06.3582	2968 ms	2	Response 358250
15:23:06.3895	2968 ms	8	Response 389500

Client Test Fixture for Pipelined HTTP Service

Number of pipelined requests to send: 10 — Send

Requests in progress: 0

Clear List

Responses:

Figure 12-12. *The client test fixture's user interface*

The client needs to support pipelined requests, so you know the client has to be multithreaded. When the user clicks the Send button, the client program must send as many concurrent requests as indicated by the user. Each request contains a simple string, indicating the current time. HttpService tags each request with a sequence number, which is displayed in the UI. The remote server's address is hard-coded to localhost, indicating the machine on which the client is running.

Two classes implement the client: a Worker and a Coordinator. The former is a Form class that hosts the user interface. The latter is a class that handles all the threading logic. Figure 12-13 shows the coupling diagram of the program.

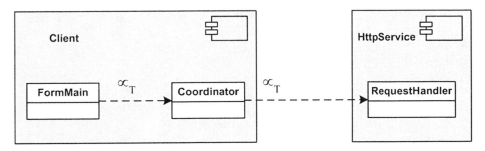

Figure 12-13. *The coupling diagram of the test fixture*

Figure 12-14 shows the sequence diagram of the client.

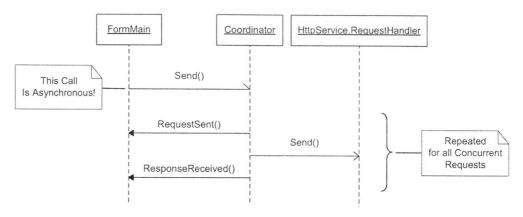

Figure 12-14. *The sequence diagram of the client program*

Listing 12-21 and Listing 12-22 show salient portions of the FormMain implementations in C# and VB .NET.

Listing 12-21. *The Most Significant Code of the Client's Main Form (C#)*

```csharp
public class FormMain : System.Windows.Forms.Form
{

  Coordinator coordinator;
  int numberOfRequestsInProgress;

  public FormMain()
  {
    // ...
    coordinator = new Coordinator(this);

    coordinator.OnRequestSent +=
      new Coordinator.RequestSentHandler(RequestSent);

    coordinator.OnResponseReceived +=
      new Coordinator.ResponseReceivedHandler(ResponseReceived);
  }

  private void buttonSend_Click(object sender, System.EventArgs e)
  {
    coordinator.Send(
      (int) numericUpDownNumberOfPipelinedRequests.Value);
  }

  private void RequestSent()
  {
    numberOfRequestsInProgress++;
    labelRequestsInProgress.Text =
      numberOfRequestsInProgress.ToString();
    labelRequestsInProgress.Update();
    Cursor = Cursors.WaitCursor;
  }
```

```csharp
  private void ResponseReceived(int theSequenceNumber,
                               string theResponse,
                               TimeSpan theProcessingTime)
{
  string s = DateTime.Now.ToString("HH:mm:ss.ffff");
  ListViewItem item = new ListViewItem(s);
  s = ( (int) theProcessingTime.TotalMilliseconds).ToString();
  item.SubItems.Add(s + " ms");
  item.SubItems.Add(theSequenceNumber.ToString() );
  item.SubItems.Add(theResponse);

  listViewResponses.Items.Add(item);

  numberOfRequestsInProgress--;
  labelRequestsInProgress.Text =
    numberOfRequestsInProgress.ToString();

  if (numberOfRequestsInProgress == 0)
    Cursor = Cursors.Default;
  }
}
```

Listing 12-22. *The Most Significant Code of the Client's Main Form (VB .NET)*

```vbnet
Public Class FormMain
  Inherits System.Windows.Forms.Form

  Private _coordinator As Coordinator
  Private _numberOfRequestsInProgress As Integer

  Public Sub New()
    MyBase.New()

    ' ...
    _coordinator = New Coordinator(Me)
    AddHandler coordinator.OnRequestSent,
             AddressOf RequestSent
    AddHandler coordinator.OnResponseReceived,
             AddressOf ResponseReceived
  End Sub

  Private Sub ButtonSend_Click(ByVal sender As System.Object, _
                               ByVal e As System.EventArgs) _
                               Handles ButtonSend.Click
    coordinator.Send(
        CInt(NumericUpDownNumberOfPipelinedRequests.Value))
  End Sub

  Private Sub RequestSent()
    _numberOfRequestsInProgress += 1
    LabelRequestsInProgress.Text =
     _numberOfRequestsInProgress.ToString()
    LabelRequestsInProgress.Update()
    Cursor = Cursors.WaitCursor
  End Sub
```

```vbnet
    Private Sub ResponseReceived(ByVal theSequenceNumber As Integer, _
                                 ByVal theResponse As String, _
                                 ByVal theProcessingTime As TimeSpan)
      Dim s As String = DateTime.Now.ToString("HH:mm:ss.ffff")
      Dim item As New ListViewItem(s)
      s = CInt(theProcessingTime.TotalMilliseconds).ToString()
      item.SubItems.Add(s + " ms")
      item.SubItems.Add(theSequenceNumber.ToString())
      item.SubItems.Add(theResponse)

      listViewResponses.Items.Add(item)

      _numberOfRequestsInProgress -= 1
      LabelRequestsInProgress.Text =
      _numberOfRequestsInProgress.ToString()
      If _numberOfRequestsInProgress = 0 Then
        Cursor = Cursors.Default
      End If
    End Sub
End Class
```

FormMain only handles logic related to the UI. Although the program uses multithreading to send pipelined requests, FormMain contains no threading logic whatsoever. Management of threading issues is relegated to the Coordinator, which is fairly simple. For each request, the Coordinator creates a new thread. Listing 12-23 and Listing 12-24 show C# and VB .NET implementations of the Coordinator.

Listing 12-23. *The C# Implementation of the Coordinator Used in the Client Program*

```csharp
public class Coordinator
{
  // object used to synchronize events with UI thread
  Control uiControl;

  // the component to test
  HttpService.CoordinatorRequestHandler requestHandler;

  public Coordinator(Control theUiControl)
  {
    uiControl = theUiControl;
    requestHandler = HttpService.CoordinatorRequestHandler.Singleton;
  }

  public void Send(int theNumberOfPipelinedRequests)
  {
    for (int i = 0; i < theNumberOfPipelinedRequests; i++)
    {
      Thread thread = new Thread(new ThreadStart(SendRequest));
      thread.Name = string.Format("Request{0}", i);
      thread.IsBackground = true;
      thread.Start();
    }
  }
}
```

```
// this method runs on a background thread
void SendRequest()
{
  DateTime startTime = DateTime.Now;
  FireRequestSent();

  // RequestHandlcr.Send blocks until a response comes back
  int sequenceNumber;
  string response = requestHandler.Send(
                    "http://localhost",
                    startTime.ToString("HH:mm:ss.ffffff"),
                    out sequenceNumber);

  TimeSpan responseTime = DateTime.Now.Subtract(startTime);
  FireResponseReceived(sequenceNumber, response, responseTime);
}

#region Events

// the following events are fired on the UI thread

public delegate void RequestSentHandler();
public event RequestSentHandler OnRequestSent;
void FireRequestSent()
{
  if (OnRequestSent != null)
    uiControl.Invoke(OnRequestSent);
}

public delegate void ResponseReceivedHandler(
                     int theSequenceNumber,
                     string theResponse,
                     TimeSpan theProcessingTime);
public event ResponseReceivedHandler OnResponseReceived;
void FireResponseReceived(int theSequenceNumber,
                          string theResponse,
                          TimeSpan theProcessingTime)
{
  if (OnResponseReceived != null)
    uiControl.Invoke(OnResponseReceived, new object[]
            {theSequenceNumber, theResponse, theProcessingTime});
}
  #endregion
}
```

Listing 12-24. *The VB .NET Implementation of the Coordinator Used in the Client Program*

```
Public Class Coordinator
  ' object used to synchronize events with UI thread
  Private _uiControl As Control

  ' the component to test
  Private _requestHandler As HttpService.CoordinatorRequestHandler
```

```vbnet
    Public Sub New(ByVal theUiControl As Control)
      _uiControl = theUiControl
      _requestHandler = HttpService.CoordinatorRequestHandler.Singleton
    End Sub

    Public Sub Send(ByVal theNumberOfPipelinedRequests As Integer)
      For i As Integer = 0 To theNumberOfPipelinedRequests - 1
        Dim thread As New Thread(AddressOf SendRequest)
        thread.Name = String.Format("Request{0}", i)
        thread.IsBackground = True
        thread.Start()
      Next
    End Sub

    ' this method runs on a background thread
    Sub SendRequest()
      Dim startTime As DateTime = DateTime.Now
      FireRequestSent()

      ' RequestHandler.Send blocks until a response comes back
      Dim sequenceNumber As Integer
      Dim response As String = requestHandler.Send(
                          "http://localhost",
                          startTime.ToString("HH:mm:ss.ffffff"),
                          sequenceNumber)

      Dim responseTime As TimeSpan = DateTime.Now.Subtract(startTime)
      FireResponseReceived(sequenceNumber, response, responseTime)
    End Sub

#Region "Events"

    ' the following events are fired on the UI thread

    Public Delegate Sub RequestSentHandler()
    Public Event OnRequestSent As RequestSentHandler
    Sub FireRequestSent()
      _uiControl.Invoke(New RequestSentHandler(AddressOf DoFireRequestSent))
    End Sub
    Sub DoFireRequestSent()
      RaiseEvent OnRequestSent()
    End Sub

    Public Delegate Sub ResponseReceivedHandler(
                      ByVal theSequenceNumber As Integer,
                      ByVal theResponse As String,
                      ByVal theProcessingTime As TimeSpan)
    Public Event OnResponseReceived As ResponseReceivedHandler
    Sub FireResponseReceived(ByVal theSequenceNumber As Integer, _
                          ByVal theResponse As String, _
                          ByVal theProcessingTime As TimeSpan)
```

```
    _uiControl.Invoke(
      New ResponseReceivedHandler(AddressOf DoFireResponseReceived), _
        New Object()
         {theSequenceNumber, theResponse, theProcessingTime})
  End Sub
  Sub DoFireResponseReceived(
        ByVal theSequenceNumber As Integer, _
        ByVal theResponse As String, _
        ByVal theProcessingTime As TimeSpan)
    RaiseEvent OnResponseReceived(theSequenceNumber, theResponse,
                                  theProcessingTime)
  End Sub
#End Region
End Class
```

When a response arrives back to the Coordinator, it comes in on the request thread. The Coordinator uses events to notify `FormMain` about requests sent and responses received. Since the Coordinator is in charge of all the threading in the system, events are fired on the UI thread, so `FormMain` can process the events without the need for any thread synchronization logic. To fire events on the UI thread, the Coordinator uses a field called `uiControl`, which references an arbitrary control created on the UI thread. Using this control, the Coordinator calls `Control.Invoke`, which the .NET Framework uses to deliver method calls on the UI thread. In the VB .NET code, the `Fire` method is in two parts, because VB doesn't allow you to call `RaiseEvent` and `Control.Invoke` together. In Listing 12-24, the `Fire` method uses `Control.Invoke` to call a `DoFire` method, which then calls `RaiseEvent`. The `DoFire` method is called on the UI thread from the `Fire` method.

The HostEmulator Test Fixture

The last piece of the HttpService test environment is a program to act as a remote server. This program needs to run a socket listener and handle requests on a secondary thread, allowing the listener to accept new requests while others are being processed. I'll call the program HostEmulator. Figure 12-15 shows its user interface.

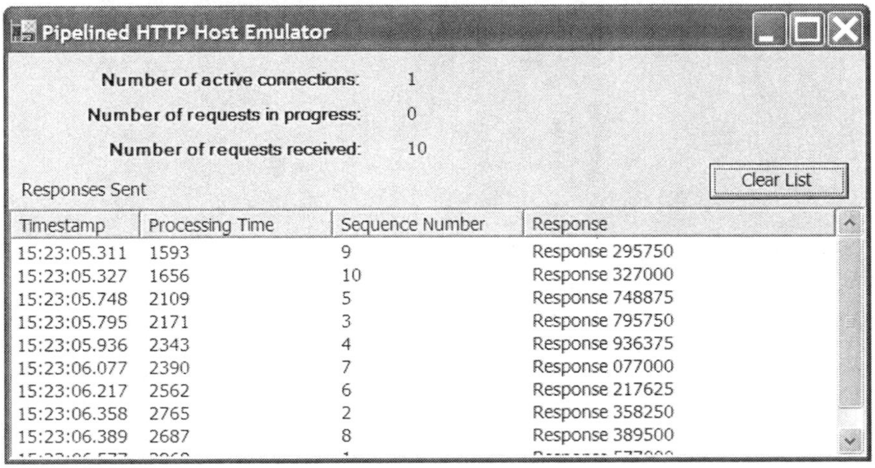
Pipelined HTTP Host Emulator
Number of active connections: 1
Number of requests in progress: 0
Number of requests received: 10
Clear List
Responses Sent
Timestamp
Processing Time
Sequence Number
Response
15:23:05.311 1593 9 Response 295750
15:23:05.327 1656 10 Response 327000
15:23:05.748 2109 5 Response 748875
15:23:05.795 2171 3 Response 795750
15:23:05.936 2343 4 Response 936375
15:23:06.077 2390 7 Response 077000
15:23:06.217 2562 6 Response 217625
15:23:06.358 2765 2 Response 358250
15:23:06.389 2687 8 Response 389500

Figure 12-15. *The user interface of the HostEmulator program*

A class called FormMain handles the user interface. A Coordinator team handles all incoming traffic, processing requests on separate threads. Figure 12-16 shows the basic class diagram of HostEmulator.

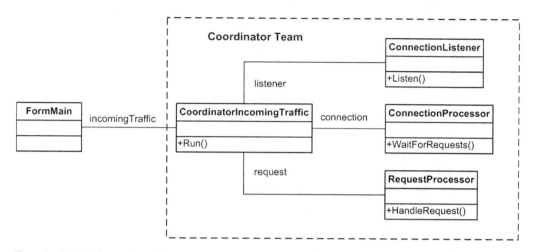

Figure 12-16. *The basic class diagram of HostEmulator*

The three classes on the right side of the Coordinator team are workers. ConnectionListener is the class that waits for client connections. When a connection arrives, ConnectionListener fires an event to the Coordinator. The Coordinator reacts by creating a new ConnectionProcessor and running it on a separate thread. ConnectionProcessor then waits for incoming data on the given connection. When data arrives, ConnectionProcessor fires an event to the Coordinator, which reacts by creating a RequestProcessor object, which is run on yet another thread. Using a separate thread for each RequestProcessor allows the same connection to continue receiving additional requests while an outstanding request is being processed. RequestProcessor has the task of processing a single request and returning a response. The response must have the same sequence number as the request. The task of parsing the request to extract the sequence number from the HTTP header is given to a small class named HttpRequest, not shown in the class diagram. Figure 12-17 shows the signal diagram of HostEmulator.

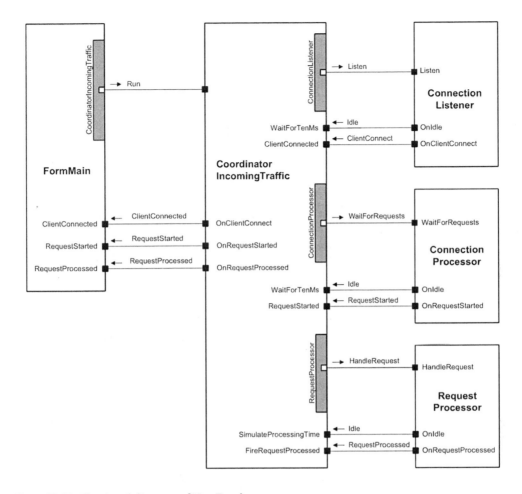

Figure 12-17. *The signal diagram of HostEmulator*

The Coordinator is shown making statically bound calls to the three `Worker` objects on the right, entailing type coupling between the Coordinator and the workers. To eliminate the coupling, you could have made the Coordinator talk to the workers using event notifications. This approach would have been a bit more complicated, because you would have needed a JIT `BuilderBinder`, since `ConnectionProcessor` and `RequestProcessor` are created on the fly when a client connects and sends a request. Listing 12-25 and Listing 12-26 show the salient portions of `FormMain`'s implementation in C# and VB .NET.

Listing 12-25. *The Salient Part of the FormMain Implementation (C#)*

```
public class FormMain : System.Windows.Forms.Form
{
  int numberOfActiveConnections;
  int numberOfRequestsReceived;
  int numberOfRequestsInProgress;

  CoordinatorIncomingTraffic incomingTraffic;
```

```csharp
public FormMain()
{
  //...
  ListenForRequests();
}

void ListenForRequests()
{
  incomingTraffic = new CoordinatorIncomingTraffic(this);

  incomingTraffic.OnClientConnected +=
    new CoordinatorIncomingTraffic.ClientConnectedHandler(ClientConnected);

  incomingTraffic.OnRequestStarted +=
    new CoordinatorIncomingTraffic.RequestStartedHandler(RequestStarted);

  incomingTraffic.OnRequestProcessed +=
    new CoordinatorIncomingTraffic.RequestProcessedHandler(RequestProcessed);

  incomingTraffic.Run();
}

private void ClientConnected()
{
  numberOfActiveConnections++;
  labelActiveConnections.Text =
    numberOfActiveConnections.ToString();
}

public void RequestStarted()
{
  numberOfRequestsReceived++;
  labelRequestsReceived.Text = numberOfRequestsReceived.ToString();

  numberOfRequestsInProgress++;
  labelRequestsInProgress.Text =
    numberOfRequestsInProgress.ToString();
}

public void RequestProcessed(string theRequest,
                             theSequenceNumber,
                             int theDuration, string theResponse)
{
  numberOfRequestsInProgress--;
  labelRequestsInProgress.Text =
    numberOfRequestsInProgress.ToString();

  ListViewItem item =
    new ListViewItem(DateTime.Now.ToString("HH:mm:ss.fff"));
```

```
    item.SubItems.Add(theDuration.ToString());
    item.SubItems.Add(theSequenceNumber.ToString());
    item.SubItems.Add(theResponse);
    listViewResponses.Items.Add(item);
  }

  private void buttonClearList_Click(object sender,
                                     System.EventArgs e)
  {
    numberOfRequestsReceived = 0;
    labelRequestsReceived.Text = numberOfRequestsReceived.ToString();
    listViewResponses.Items.Clear();
  }
}
```

Listing 12-26. *The Salient Part of the FormMain Implementation (VB .NET)*

```
Public Class FormMain
  Inherits System.Windows.Forms.Form

  Private _numberOfActiveConnections As Integer
  Private _numberOfRequestsReceived As Integer
  Private _numberOfRequestsInProgress As Integer

  Private _incomingTraffic As CoordinatorIncomingTraffic

    Public Sub New()
    MyBase.New()

    ' ...
    ListenForRequests()
  End Sub

Sub ListenForRequests()
    _incomingTraffic = New CoordinatorIncomingTraffic(Me)

    AddHandler _incomingTraffic.OnClientConnected,
               AddressOf ClientConnected
    AddHandler _incomingTraffic.OnRequestStarted,
               AddressOf RequestStarted
    AddHandler _incomingTraffic.OnRequestProcessed,
               AddressOf RequestProcessed

    _incomingTraffic.Run()
  End Sub

  Private Sub ClientConnected()
    _numberOfActiveConnections += 1
    LabelActiveConnections.Text = _numberOfActiveConnections.ToString()
  End Sub
```

```
  Public Sub RequestStarted()
    _numberOfRequestsReceived += 1
    LabelRequestsReceived.Text = _numberOfRequestsReceived.ToString()

    _numberOfRequestsInProgress += 1
    LabelRequestsInProgress.Text = _numberOfRequestsInProgress.ToString()
  End Sub

  Public Sub RequestProcessed(ByVal theRequest As String, _
                              ByVal theSequenceNumber As Integer, _
                              ByVal theDuration As Integer, _
                              ByVal theResponse As String)
    _numberOfRequestsInProgress -= 1
    LabelRequestsInProgress.Text =
      _numberOfRequestsInProgress.ToString()

    Dim item As
      New ListViewItem(DateTime.Now.ToString("HH:mm:ss.fff"))
    item.SubItems.Add(theDuration.ToString())
    item.SubItems.Add(theSequenceNumber.ToString())
    item.SubItems.Add(theResponse)
    ListViewResponses.Items.Add(item)
  End Sub

  Private Sub ButtonClearList_Click(ByVal sender As System.Object, _
                                    ByVal e As System.EventArgs) _
                                    Handles ButtonClearList.Click
    _numberOfRequestsReceived = 0
    LabelRequestsReceived.Text = numberOfRequestsReceived.ToString()
    ListViewResponses.Items.Clear()
  End Sub
End Class
```

Listing 12-27 and Listing 12-28 show C# and VB .NET implementations of CoordinatorIncomingTraffic, which is the key class in the system. It ties everything together and handles all the threading logic.

Listing 12-27. *The Implementation of CoordinatorIncomingTraffic (C#)*

```
public class CoordinatorIncomingTraffic
{
  Control uiControl;  // used for thread synchronization with events
  ConnectionListener listener;
  int basicProcessingTime;  // in ms
  int processingTime;  // in ms
  Random random = new Random();  // used to change the processing time

  public CoordinatorIncomingTraffic(Control theUiControl)
  {
    uiControl = theUiControl;
    basicProcessingTime = 2000;  // 2 secs
```

```
    listener = new ConnectionListener();
    listener.OnClientConnect += new
        ConnectionListener.ClientConnectHandler(ClientConnected);
    listener.OnIdle += new
        HostEmulator.ConnectionListener.IdleHandler(WaitForTenMs);
}

public void Run()
{
  Thread listenerThread =
        new Thread(new ThreadStart(listener.Listen) );
  listenerThread.IsBackground = true;
  listenerThread.Name = "ConnectionListener";
  listenerThread.Start();
}

void ClientConnected(Socket theSocket)
{
  // dispatch a thread to handle all the requests
  // on the connected socket

  ConnectionProcessor connection =
          new ConnectionProcessor(theSocket);
  connection.OnRequestStarted +- new
  ConnectionProcessor.RequestStartedHandler(RequestStarted);
  connection.OnRequestProcessed += new
  ConnectionProcessor.RequestProcessedHandler(FireRequestProcessed);
  connection.OnIdle += new
  ConnectionProcessor.IdleHandler(WaitForTenMs);
  Thread thread =
        new Thread(new ThreadStart(connection.WaitForRequests) );
  thread.IsBackground = true;
  thread.Name = "ConnectionProcessor";
  thread.Start();

  FireClientConnected();
}

void RequestStarted(Socket theSocket)
{
  FireRequestStarted();

  HttpRequest httpRequest = new HttpRequest(theSocket);
  httpRequest.Get();   // get the entire incoming request

  RequestProcessor request =
     new RequestProcessor(theSocket, httpRequest);
  request.OnRequestProcessed += new
     RequestProcessor.RequestProcessedHandler(FireRequestProcessed);
  request.OnIdle += new
     RequestProcessor.IdleHandler(SimulateProcessingTime);
```

```csharp
        // process request on a separate thread, to
        // allowing incoming requests to be pipelined
        Thread thread =
                new Thread(new ThreadStart(request.HandleRequest) );
        thread.IsBackground = true;
        thread.Name = "RequestProcessor";
        thread.Start();
    }

    int GetNextProcessingTime()
    {
      lock(this)
      {
          processingTime =
            random.Next(basicProcessingTime-1000,
                        basicProcessingTime+1000);
          return processingTime;
      }
    }

    private void WaitForTenMs()
    {
      Thread.Sleep(10);
    }

    private void SimulateProcessingTime()
    {
      int duration = GetNextProcessingTime();
      Thread.Sleep(duration);
    }

#region Events
    // ************************************************************
    // the following Fire methods switch to the UI thread
    // before firing events
    // ************************************************************

    public delegate void ClientConnectedHandler();
    public event ClientConnectedHandler OnClientConnected;
    public void FireClientConnected()
    {
      if (OnClientConnected != null)
        uiControl.Invoke(OnClientConnected, null);
    }

    public delegate void RequestStartedHandler();
    public event RequestStartedHandler OnRequestStarted;
    public void FireRequestStarted()
    {
      if (OnRequestStarted != null)
        uiControl.Invoke(OnRequestStarted);
    }
```

```csharp
public delegate void RequestProcessedHandler(string theRequest,
                                             int theSequenceNumber,
                                             int theDuration,
                                             string theResponse);
public event RequestProcessedHandler OnRequestProcessed;
public void FireRequestProcessed(string theRequest,
                                 int theSequenceNumber,
                                 int theDuration,
                                 string theResponse)
{
  if (OnRequestProcessed != null)
    uiControl.Invoke(OnRequestProcessed, new object[]
                  {theRequest, theSequenceNumber,
                   theDuration, theResponse});
}
#endregion
}
```

Listing 12-28. *The Implementation of CoordinatorIncomingTraffic (VB .NET)*

```vbnet
Public Class CoordinatorIncomingTraffic
  Private _uiControl As Control  ' used for thread synchronization
                                 ' with events
  Private _listener As ConnectionListener
  Private _basicProcessingTime As Integer  ' in ms
  Private _processingTime As Integer  ' in ms
  Private _random As New Random  ' used to change the processing time

  Public Sub New(ByVal theUiControl As Control)
    _uiControl = theUiControl
    _basicProcessingTime = 2000  ' 2 secs

    _listener = New ConnectionListener
    AddHandler _listener.OnClientConnect, AddressOf ClientConnected
    AddHandler _listener.OnIdle, AddressOf WaitForTenMs
  End Sub

  Public Sub Run()
    Dim listenerThread As New Thread(AddressOf _listener.Listen)
    listenerThread.IsBackground = True
    listenerThread.Name = "ConnectionListener"
    listenerThread.Start()
  End Sub

  Sub ClientConnected(ByVal theSocket As Socket)
    ' dispatch a thread to handle all the requests
    ' on the connected socket

    Dim connection As New ConnectionProcessor(theSocket)
    AddHandler connection.OnRequestStarted, AddressOf RequestStarted
    AddHandler connection.OnRequestProcessed,
                         AddressOf FireRequestProcessed
    AddHandler connection.OnIdle, AddressOf WaitForTenMs
```

```vbnet
    Dim thread As New Thread(AddressOf connection.WaitForRequests)
    thread.IsBackground = True
    thread.Name = "ConnectionProcessor"
    thread.Start()

    FireClientConnected()
  End Sub

  Sub RequestStarted(ByVal theSocket As Socket)
    FireRequestStarted()

    Dim httpRequest As New HttpRequest(theSocket)
    HttpRequest.Get()  ' get the entire incoming request

    Dim request As New RequestProcessor(theSocket, httpRequest)
    AddHandler request.OnRequestProcessed,
                    AddressOf FireRequestProcessed
    AddHandler request.OnIdle, AddressOf SimulateProcessingTime

    ' process request on a separate thread, to
    ' allowing incoming requests to be pipelined
    Dim thread As New Thread(AddressOf request.HandleRequest)
    Thread.IsBackground = True
    Thread.Name = "RequestProcessor"
    Thread.Start()
  End Sub

  Function GetNextProcessingTime() As Integer
    SyncLock (Me)
      processingTime = random.Next(
              basicProcessingTime - 1000,
              basicProcessingTime + 1000)
      Return processingTime
    End SyncLock
  End Function

  Private Sub WaitForTenMs()
    Thread.Sleep(10)
  End Sub

  Private Sub SimulateProcessingTime()
    Dim duration As Integer = GetNextProcessingTime()
    Thread.Sleep(duration)
  End Sub

#Region "Events"
  ' ***********************************************************
  ' the following Fire methods switch to the UI thread
  ' before firing events
  ' ***********************************************************
```

```
Public Delegate Sub ClientConnectedHandler()
Public Event OnClientConnected As ClientConnectedHandler
Public Sub FireClientConnected()
  _uiControl.Invoke(New ClientConnectedHandler(
                    AddressOf DoFireClientConnected))
End Sub
Public Sub DoFireClientConnected()
  RaiseEvent OnClientConnected()
End Sub

Public Delegate Sub RequestStartedHandler()
Public Event OnRequestStarted As RequestStartedHandler
Public Sub FireRequestStarted()
  _uiControl.Invoke(
      New RequestStartedHandler(AddressOf DoFireRequestStarted))
End Sub
Public Sub DoFireRequestStarted()
  RaiseEvent OnRequestStarted()
End Sub

Public Delegate Sub RequestProcessedHandler(
                    ByVal theRequest As String, _
                    ByVal theSequenceNumber As Integer, _
                    ByVal theDuration As Integer, _
                    ByVal theResponse As String)
Public Event OnRequestProcessed As RequestProcessedHandler
Public Sub FireRequestProcessed(ByVal theRequest As String, _
                    ByVal theSequenceNumber As Integer,_
                    ByVal theDuration As Integer, _
                    ByVal theResponse As String)
  _uiControl.Invoke(New RequestProcessedHandler(
      AddressOf DoFireRequestProcessed), _
      New Object()
       {theRequest, theSequenceNumber, theDuration, theResponse})
End Sub
Public Sub DoFireRequestProcessed(
          ByVal theRequest As String, _
          ByVal theSequenceNumber As Integer, _
          ByVal theDuration As Integer, _
          ByVal theResponse As String)
  RaiseEvent OnRequestProcessed(theRequest, theSequenceNumber,
                    theDuration, theResponse)
End Sub
#End Region
End Class
```

Listing 12-29 and Listing 12-30 show the C# and VB .NET implementations of
ConnectionListener.

Listing 12-29. *The C# Implementation of ConnectionListener*

```csharp
public class ConnectionListener
{
  TcpListener listener;

  public void Listen()
  {
    IPAddress ipAddress = Dns.Resolve("localhost").AddressList[0];
    listener = new TcpListener(ipAddress, 8020); // listen on port 8020
    listener.Start();

    while (true)
    {
      // wait until a client connects
      if (!listener.Pending() )
      {
        FireIdle();
        continue;
      }

      // process the client
      Socket socket = listener.AcceptSocket();

      FireClientConnected(socket);
    }
  }

  public delegate void ClientConnectHandler(Socket theSocket);
  public event ClientConnectHandler OnClientConnect;
  public void FireClientConnected(Socket theSocket)
  {
    if (OnClientConnect != null)
      OnClientConnect(theSocket);
  }

  public delegate void IdleHandler();
  public event IdleHandler OnIdle;
  public void FireIdle()
  {
    if (OnIdle != null)
      OnIdle();
  }
}
```

Listing 12-30. *The VB .NET Implementation of ConnectionListener*

```vbnet
Public Class ConnectionListener
  Dim _listener As TcpListener

  Public Sub Listen()
    Dim ipAddress As IPAddress =
        Dns.Resolve("localhost").AddressList(0)
    _listener = New TcpListener(ipAddress, 8020) ' listen on port 8020
    _listener.Start()
```

```
    While True
      ' wait until a client connects
      If Not _listener.Pending() Then
        FireIdle()
      Else
        ' process the client
        Dim socket As Socket = _listener.AcceptSocket()
        FireClientConnected(socket)
      End If
    End While
  End Sub

  Public Event OnClientConnect(ByVal theSocket As Socket)
  Public Sub FireClientConnected(ByVal theSocket As Socket)
    RaiseEvent OnClientConnect(theSocket)
  End Sub

  Public Event OnIdle()
  Public Sub FireIdle()
    RaiseEvent OnIdle()
  End Sub
End Class
```

Listing 12-31 and Listing 12-32 show C# and VB .NET implementations of ConnectionProcessor.

Listing 12-31. *The C# Implementation of ConnectionProcessor*

```csharp
public class ConnectionProcessor
{
  Socket socket;

  public ConnectionProcessor(Socket theSocket)
  {
    socket = theSocket;
  }

  public void WaitForRequests()
  {
    while (true)
    {
      if (socket.Available > 0)
        FireRequestStarted(socket);

      FireIdle();
    }
  }

  public delegate void RequestStartedHandler(Socket theSocket);
  public event RequestStartedHandler OnRequestStarted;
  public void FireRequestStarted(Socket theSocket)
  {
    if (OnRequestStarted != null)
      OnRequestStarted(theSocket);
  }
```

```
public delegate void RequestProcessedHandler(
                    string theRequest,
                    int theSequenceNumber,
                    int theDuration,
                    string theResponse);
public event RequestProcessedHandler OnRequestProcessed;
public void FireRequestProcessed(string theRequest,
                                 int theSequenceNumber,
                                 int theDuration,
                                 string theResponse)
{
  if (OnRequestProcessed != null)
    OnRequestProcessed(theRequest, theSequenceNumber,
                       theDuration, theResponse);
}

public delegate void IdleHandler();
public event IdleHandler OnIdle;
public void FireIdle()
{
  if (OnIdle != null)
    OnIdle();
}
}
```

Listing 12-32. *The VB .NET Implementation of ConnectionProcessor*

```
Public Class ConnectionProcessor
  Private _socket As Socket

  Public Sub New(ByVal theSocket As Socket)
    _socket = theSocket
  End Sub

  Public Sub WaitForRequests()
    While True
      If _socket.Available > 0 Then
        FireRequestStarted(socket)
      End If

      FireIdle()
    End While
  End Sub

  Public Event OnRequestStarted(ByVal theSocket As Socket)
  Public Sub FireRequestStarted(ByVal theSocket As Socket)
    RaiseEvent OnRequestStarted(theSocket)
  End Sub

  Public Event OnRequestProcessed(ByVal theRequest As String, _
                                  ByVal theSequenceNumber As Integer, _
                                  ByVal theDuration As Integer, _
                                  ByVal theResponse As String)
```

```
   Public Sub FireRequestProcessed(ByVal theRequest As String, _
                                   ByVal theSequenceNumber As Integer, _
                                   ByVal theDuration As Integer, _
                                   ByVal theResponse As String)
     RaiseEvent OnRequestProcessed(theRequest, theSequenceNumber, _
                                   theDuration, theResponse)
   End Sub

   Public Event OnIdle()
   Public Sub FireIdle()
     RaiseEvent OnIdle()
   End Sub
End Class
```

Listing 12-33 and Listing 12-34 show C# and VB .NET implementations of RequestProcessor.

Listing 12-33. *The C# Implementation of RequestProcessor*

```csharp
public class RequestProcessor
{
  Socket socket;
  HttpRequest httpRequest;

  public RequestProcessor(Socket theSocket,
                          HttpRequest theHttpRequest)
  {
    socket = theSocket;
    httpRequest = theHttpRequest;
  }

  public void HandleRequest()
  {
    DateTime startTime = DateTime.Now;
    FireIdle();  // simulate processing time
    TimeSpan duration = DateTime.Now.Subtract(startTime);
    SendResponse((int) duration.TotalMilliseconds);
  }

  private void SendResponse(int theProcessingTime)
  {
    IPEndPoint endPoint = socket.RemoteEndPoint as IPEndPoint;

    string body = string.Format("Response {0}",
                                DateTime.Now.ToString("ffffff"));
    string header = string.Format("HTTP/1.1 200 OK\r\n" +
                                  "Sequence-Number: {0}\r\n" +
                                  "Content-Length: {1}\r\n",
                                  httpRequest.SequenceNumber,
                                  body.Length);

    string message = string.Format("{0}\r\n{1}", header, body);

    byte[] bytes = Encoding.UTF8.GetBytes(message);
    NetworkStream stream = new NetworkStream(socket);
    stream.Write(bytes, 0, bytes.Length);
```

```
    string requestBody = Encoding.UTF8.GetString(httpRequest.Body);
    FireRequestProcessed(requestBody, httpRequest.SequenceNumber,
                      theProcessingTime, body);
  }

  public delegate void RequestProcessedHandler(
                      string theRequest,
                      int theSequenceNumber,
                      int theDuration,
                      string theResponse);
  public event RequestProcessedHandler OnRequestProcessed;
  public void FireRequestProcessed(string theRequest,
                                  int theSequenceNumber,
                                  int theDuration,
                                  string theResponse)
  {
    if (OnRequestProcessed == null) return;
    OnRequestProcessed(theRequest, theSequenceNumber,
                    theDuration, theResponse);
  }

  public delegate void IdleHandler();
  public event IdleHandler OnIdle;
  public void FireIdle()
  {
    if (OnIdle != null)
      OnIdle();
  }
}
```

Listing 12-34. *The VB .NET Implementation of RequestProcessor*

```
Public Class RequestProcessor
  Private _socket As Socket
  Private _httpRequest As HttpRequest

  Public Sub New(ByVal theSocket As Socket,
                 ByVal theHttpRequest As HttpRequest)
    _socket = theSocket
    _httpRequest = theHttpRequest
  End Sub

  Public Sub HandleRequest()
    Dim startTime As DateTime = DateTime.Now
    FireIdle()  ' simulate processing time
    Dim duration As TimeSpan = DateTime.Now.Subtract(startTime)
    SendResponse(CInt(duration.TotalMilliseconds))
  End Sub

  Private Sub SendResponse(ByVal theProcessingTime As Integer)
    Dim endPoint As IPEndPoint = DirectCast(_socket.RemoteEndPoint, IPEndPoint)
```

```
        Dim body As String =
            String.Format("Response {0}", DateTime.Now.ToString("ffffff"))
        Dim header As String =
            String.Format("HTTP/1.1 200 OK" +
                            ControlChars.NewLine + _ _
                            "Sequence-Number: {0}" + _
                            ControlChars.NewLine + _
                            "Content-Length: {1}" + _
                            ControlChars.NewLine, _
                            httpRequest.SequenceNumber, _
                            body.Length)

        Dim message As String = String.Format("{0}{1}{2}",
            header, ControlChars.NewLine, body)

        Dim bytes As Byte() = Encoding.UTF8.GetBytes(message)
        Dim stream As New NetworkStream(_socket)
        stream.Write(bytes, 0, bytes.Length)

        Dim requestBody As String =
            Encoding.UTF8.GetString(_httpRequest.Body)
        FireRequestProcessed(requestBody, _httpRequest.SequenceNumber, _
                            theProcessingTime, body)
    End Sub

    Public Event OnRequestProcessed(ByVal theRequest As String, _
                            ByVal theSequenceNumber As Integer,
                            ByVal theDuration As Integer, _
                            ByVal theResponse As String)
    Public Sub FireRequestProcessed(ByVal theRequest As String, _
                            ByVal theSequenceNumber As Integer,
                            ByVal theDuration As Integer, _
                            ByVal theResponse As String)
        RaiseEvent OnRequestProcessed(theRequest, theSequenceNumber, _
                            theDuration, theResponse)
    End Sub

    Public Event OnIdle()
    Public Sub FireIdle()
        RaiseEvent OnIdle()
    End Sub
End Class
```

When RequestProcessor gets a request to handle, it fires an OnIdle event to let the Coordinator simulate the processing time. The Coordinator uses a random number generator to pause the request thread for an amount of time between one and three seconds. I could have easily put the thread-pausing code in RequestProcessor, but since this class is a worker, I opted to keep the thread-related code out of it and put it in the Coordinator where it belongs.

The client program allows the user to run up to 200 requests at the same time. The upper limit is not determined as much by the software as it is by the hardware. HttpService uses an internal array of 500 ThreadSemaphores and therefore supports up to 500 concurrent requests, but the size of the array is arbitrary.

Summary

With this case study, you've seen how to use events and Coordinator teams to implement a multi-threaded service component. I also showed you how to use events and Coordinator teams to create the supporting test programs. By developing HttpService as a component with no coupling to other components, HttpService is independently deployable. Moreover, because its worker classes are also completely decoupled from other classes, the workers are relatively simple to test and easy to reuse.

■ ■ ■

CHAPTER 13

Case Study 3: A Distributed Workflow System

This case study shows how a distributed system might use a messaging service to implement a workflow system in an event-based manner. The system is a hypothetical order system for a car manufacturer I'll call ASAP Cars, which builds vehicles Just In Time (JIT). Instead of using forecasts to determine which models of cars to build, ASAP Cars builds a JIT car when an order is received. In a true JIT manufacturing system, all the main subassemblies reach the manufacturing floor just in time, arriving at the assembly line exactly when they are needed. The JIT approach allows the manufacturer to dispense with large warehouses containing inventories of parts or subassemblies, cutting costs dramatically. JIT manufacturers no longer need huge parking lots to hold cars waiting to be sold. On the other hand, the planning logistics to keep a JIT manufacturing system flowing smoothly are daunting, requiring the coordination of every step in the process. A distributed information system guides the workflow of all the processes.

What is most interesting about this case study is not the business logic implemented by the server components, but how those components are connected together and how they communicate using event notifications, channeled through a centralized messaging service. All the code in this chapter is available in the Source Code area of the Apress Web site (www.apress.com). To actually run the code, you'll need to have Microsoft Message Queuing (MSMQ) running somewhere in your environment. For instructions on setting up MSMQ, see the "Testing the Complete System" section at the end of the chapter.

Functional Requirements

ASAP Cars needs a system that connects to each of its business and operations centers to manage incoming orders and produce tailor-made cars. To keep this case study straightforward, I'll abstract away many of the low-level details of car manufacturing, concentrating instead on the coordination of the higher-level workflow that runs the system. ASAP Cars' simplified business model uses the following steps:

1. Accept an incoming order.
2. Create a work order.
3. Schedule JIT delivery of all parts.
4. Assembly vehicle.
5. Generate customer invoice.

The system consists of a client side and a server side. The client side implements an order-entry system used by dealers. The server side receives dealer orders and handles them using a workflow process, which is not visible to the client. From the client's perspective, the system appears as shown in Figure 13-1.

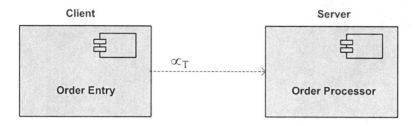

Figure 13-1. *The client-server structure of the system, from the perspective of the client*

The connection between client and server is based on RPCs, implemented using .NET remoting. Because the client calls the server through an interface, the client is type-coupled to the server component. As far as the client is concerned, the server consists of a single component—Order Processor. In reality, several components on the server side work together to handle an order. Figure 13-2 shows the top-level UML activity diagram of the overall system.

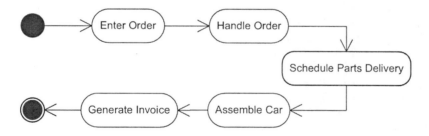

Figure 13-2. *The activity diagram of the system*

Each box in the figure represents an activity. The server portion of the system includes all the activities from Handle Order to Generate Invoice. The transition between the server activities is controlled through MSMQ message queues. MSMQ is a Microsoft messaging service discussed briefly in Chapter 5. Looking again at the diagram in Figure 13-2, when an activity is complete, it fires an event in the form of a message sent to MSMQ. The system uses a separate message queue for each activity. When a queue receives a message, it notifies the next activity.

The architecture of the system is such that you can implement all components, including MSMQ, on separate computers. When each server component starts up, it connects to MSMQ. Once the system has initialized, the arrival of messages in MSMQ message queues determines how the system runs. Figure 13-3 shows the coupling diagram of the main server-side components of the system and emphasizes the central role of the messaging component as a notification service.

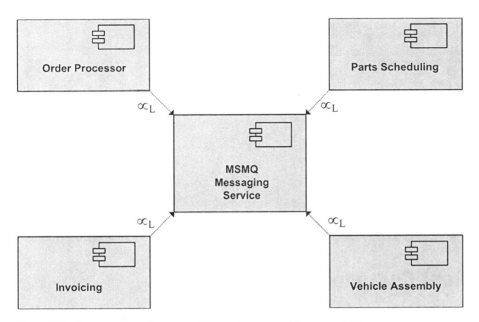

Figure 13-3. *The coupling diagram of the main server-side components*

The familiar star pattern in the diagram shows that although the server-side components are coupled to the messaging service, they are decoupled from each other. You can fully develop and test all the major components in isolation from the others. The flavor of coupling to the messaging service is logic coupling—literal logic coupling, to be precise—because each component contains a hard-coded literal defining the path of each message queue it accesses in the messaging service.

Project Configuration

ASAP Cars contains several components, some of which are in the client space and some in the server space. The client space includes components that run in the car dealer offices. The server space includes all the other components. Although this case study is relatively simple, it consists of nine components. To keep the implementation easy to follow, I'll use Visual Studio Enterprise Template Projects (ETPs) to organize the various projects. ETPs are really just containers of regular projects. ETPs show up in the Solution Explorer as nodes under the Solution node, with Project nodes inside them, as shown in Figure 13-4.

In Figure 13-4, the Enterprise Template Project nodes are highlighted. Visual Studio allows you to nest these nodes recursively, and in the figure you can see that the Order Processor System template is nested inside the Server Side template. In the following sections, I'll discuss the design and implementation of each component.

Figure 13-4. *The Visual Studio Solution Explorer, showing the use of Enterprise Template Projects*

The Client Component

The client side of the system consists of a simple UI allowing dealers to enter new car orders. Figure 13-5 shows the order-entry UI.

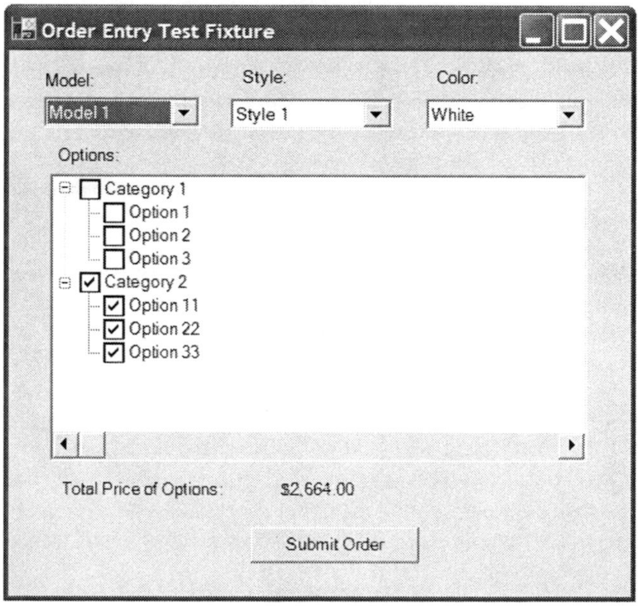

Figure 13-5. *The user interface of the order-entry component*

Anytime the user changes the model in the drop-down list, the Style drop-down is populated based on the model. The list of styles is obtained by making a remote call to the Order Processor component. Anytime the style is changed in the drop-down list, the Color drop-down and the Options tree are repopulated, based on the style. Again, the list of colors and options is obtained via a call to the Order Processor component. Each option is associated with a cost. When the user puts a checkmark next to an option, the Total Price of Options field is updated to reflect all the options checked.

I'll design the client UI by utilizing two classes called FormMain and WorkerOrderEntry, as shown in Figure 13-6.

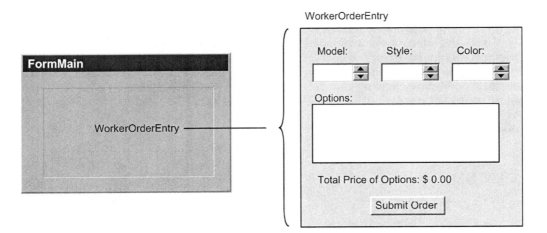

Figure 13-6. *The two user-interface classes of the client*

Class FormMain hosts WorkerOrderEntry, which contains all the UI controls. The purpose of FormMain is to act as the entry point and builder for the client application. When the user acts on a control in WorkerOrderEntry, this class fires events to a Coordinator class called CoordinatorOrderEntry. The Coordinator handles some of the worker notifications, but in most cases forwards the notifications to a Router class that is responsible for interacting with the server-side component. Figure 13-7 shows the coupling diagram of the client system.

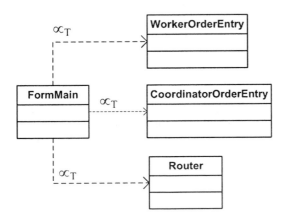

Figure 13-7. *The coupling diagram of the client system*

The classes that do the most work are the Coordinator and the Worker. The Worker is responsible for the layout of the UI controls. The Worker also has the following two responsibilities:

- Presenting the Total Price of Options as a currency value
- Managing checkmarks in the Options tree

The first option requires the currency amount to be displayed with a dollar symbol and two decimals. The second option is a bit more complicated. The Options tree displays a list of categories. Each category contains a list of options. If the user adds/removes a checkmark to a category, all the options in that category must be checked/unchecked.

For all user actions, the Worker fires events to the Coordinator. The Coordinator is responsible only for one task: computing the Total Price of Options when the user clicks on an option in the Options tree. For all other worker notifications, the Coordinator reacts by forwarding them to the Router. Only the Router contains logic that interacts with the remote Order Processor component.

Since the most important client classes are completely decoupled from each other, looking at a class diagram tells you almost nothing about how the client works. What you need to see is how the various client objects are wired together, as shown in Figure 13-8.

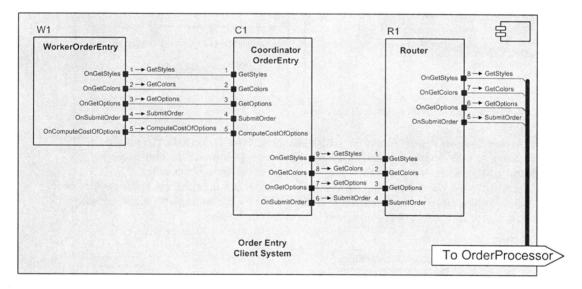

Figure 13-8. *The wiring diagram of the client component*

The client logic is contained in a component called Order Entry. Each of the five output signals of WorkerOrderEntry represents a different use case. The diagram is laid out so that WorkerOrderEntry notifications all flow from left to right, from worker to coordinator to router to server. For example, when the user changes the selected car style, a GetColors signal is passed through the coordinator to the router to the server. The signal retrieves a list of colors, which the worker then puts in the Colors drop-down list. Tables 13-1 through 13-3 show the pin legends for each of the main objects in Figure 13-8.

Table 13-1. *The Pin Legend for WorkerOrderEntry*

Object	Pin	Direction	Name	Arguments	Returned Values
W1	1	Output	GetStyles	String model	String[] styles
W1	2	Output	GetColors	String model	Color[] colors
				String style	
W1	3	Output	GetOptions	String model	ArrayList options
				String style	
W1	4	Output	SubmitOrder	String model	
				String style	
				ArrayList options	
W1	5	Output	ComputeCostOfOptions	PricedItem[] options	Decimal cost

Table 13-2. *The Pin Legend for CoordinatorOrderEntry*

Object	Pin	Direction	Name	Arguments	Returned Values
C1	1	Input	GetStyles	String model	String[] styles
C1	2	Input	GetColors	String model	Color[] colors
				String style	
C1	3	Input	GetOptions	String model	ArrayList options
				String style	
C1	4	Input	SubmitOrder	String model	
				String style	
				PricedItem[] options	
C1	5	Input	ComputeCostOfOptions	PricedItem[] options	Decimal cost
C1	6	Output	GetStyles	String model	String [] styles
C1	7	Output	GetColors	String model	Color[] colors
				String style	
C1	8	Output	GetOptions	String model	ArrayList options
				String style	
C1	9	Output	SubmitOrder	String model	
				String style	
				PricedItem[] options	

Table 13-3. *The Pin Legend for Router*

Object	Pin	Direction	Name	Arguments	Returned Values
R1	1	Input	GetStyles	String model	String [] styles
R1	2	Input	GetColors	String model	Color[] colors
				String style	
R1	3	Input	GetOptions	String model	ArrayList options
				String style	
R1	4	Input	SubmitOrder	String model	
				String style	
				PricedItem[] options	
R1	5	Output	GetStyles	String model	String [] styles
R1	6	Output	GetColors	String model	Color[] colors
				String style	
R1	7	Output	GetOptions	String model	ArrayList options
				String style	
R1	8	Output	SubmitOrder	String model	
				String style	
				PricedItem[] options	

To test the Order Entry system, create a simple test fixture consisting of a main form that hosts WorkerOrderEntry. The test fixture tests WorkerOrderEntry and CoordinatorOrderEntry together, but in a standalone configuration without the server components. The text fixture's main form class provides handlers for all the Coordinator events, simulating the presence of the Router. The test fixture's main form is very similar to the Order Entry main form, except for the extra handler methods.

■**Implementation Note** The test fixture resides in a separate directory from Order Entry and uses file links to reference the WorkerOrderEntry and CoordinatorOrderEntry classes. A file link is a Microsoft Visual Studio .NET way of including in one project a class contained in a different directory. With Visual Studio .NET, you create file links when adding a file to a project. On the Add Existing Item dialog box, select a file, then click the drop-down arrow on the Open button and select the Link File option from the list.

The client system makes use of only one user-defined type in method calls. The class is called PricedItem and is defined in a component called CommonTypes. Most of the classes in the OrderEntry client component are type coupled to CommonTypes. Figure 13-9 shows the details.

The following sections show the salient C# and VB .NET code for the client component. This case study dispenses with builders and binders to avoid introducing additional complexity and classes. The FormMain class in each project acts as both a builder and binder.

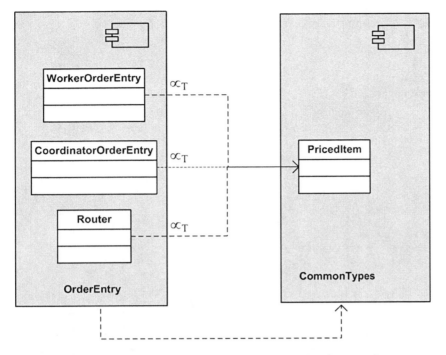

Figure 13-9. *The coupling related to the component containing the system's common user-defined types*

C# Code

The OrderEntry Component

```
// App.config
```

```xml
<configuration>
    <system.runtime.remoting>
        <application>
            <service>
                <wellknown
                    type="OrderProcessor.OrderSystem, OrderProcessor"
                    mode="Singleton"
                    url="tcp://localhost:8011/AsapOrders"/>
            </service>
        </application>
    </system.runtime.remoting>
</configuration>
```

```
// class FormMain
```

```csharp
public class FormMain : System.Windows.Forms.Form
{
```

```csharp
    WorkerOrderEntry workerOrderEntry;
    CoordinatorOrderEntry coordinatorOrderEntry;
    Router router;

    public FormMain()
    {
      InitializeComponent();

      Build();
      Bind();

      SetupUi();
    }

    void Build()
    {
      workerOrderEntry = new WorkerOrderEntry();
      coordinatorOrderEntry = new CoordinatorOrderEntry();
      router = new Router();
    }

    void Bind()
    {
      workerOrderEntry.OnGetColors +=
          new WorkerOrderEntry.GetColorsHandler(coordinatorOrderEntry.GetColors);
      workerOrderEntry.OnGetOptions +=
          new WorkerOrderEntry.GetOptionsHandler(coordinatorOrderEntry.GetOptions);
      workerOrderEntry.OnGetStyles +=
        new WorkerOrderEntry.GetStylesHandler(coordinatorOrderEntry.GetStyles);
      workerOrderEntry.OnSubmitOrder +=
          new WorkerOrderEntry.SubmitOrderHandler(coordinatorOrderEntry.SubmitOrder);
      workerOrderEntry.OnComputeCostOfOptions +=
          new WorkerOrderEntry.ComputeCostOfOptionsHandler(
                            coordinatorOrderEntry.ComputeCostOfOptions);

      coordinatorOrderEntry.OnGetColors +=
          new CoordinatorOrderEntry.GetColorsHandler(router.GetColors);
      coordinatorOrderEntry.OnGetOptions +=
          new  CoordinatorOrderEntry.GetOptionsHandler(router.GetOptions);
      coordinatorOrderEntry.OnGetStyles +=
          new CoordinatorOrderEntry.GetStylesHandler(router.GetStyles);
      coordinatorOrderEntry.OnSubmit +=
          new CoordinatorOrderEntry.SubmitHandler(router.SubmitOrder);
    }

    void SetupUi()
    {
      Controls.Add(workerOrderEntry.panelMain);
      PopulateModels();
    }
```

```csharp
    void PopulateModels()
    {
      try
      {
        string[] models = router.GetModels();
        workerOrderEntry.PopulateModels(models);
      }
      catch (Exception ex)
      {
        string msg = string.Format(
              "The server must be running before starting the Order Entry program. " +
              "To run the server, start OrderProcessingHostProgram.exe.\n" +
              "Exception Details: [{0}]", ex.Message);
        MessageBox.Show(msg, "An exception occurred while connecting to server");
        throw ex;
      }
    }

    // …

#endregion

    [STAThread]
    static void Main()
    {
      FormMain formMain = null;
      try
      {
        formMain = new FormMain();
      }
      catch (Exception ex)
      {
        // exceptions typically occur if the client can't connect to the server
        MessageBox.Show(ex.Message, "An exception occurred");
        return;
      }

      Application.Run(formMain);
    }
}


// class WorkerOrderEntry

public class WorkerOrderEntry : System.Windows.Forms.UserControl
{
  // …
  public WorkerOrderEntry()
  {
    // This call is required by the Windows.Forms Form Designer.
    InitializeComponent();
  }
```

```csharp
// …

private void comboBoxModel_SelectedIndexChanged(object sender,
                                                System.EventArgs e)
{
  comboBoxStyle.Items.Clear();
  string model = comboBoxModel.Text;
  string[] styles = FireGetStyles(model);
  if (styles == null) return;
  if (styles.Length == 0) return;
  comboBoxStyle.Items.AddRange(styles);
  comboBoxStyle.SelectedIndex = 0;
}

private void comboBoxStyle_SelectedIndexChanged(object sender,
                                                System.EventArgs e)
{
  treeViewOptions.Nodes.Clear();
  string model = comboBoxModel.Text;
  string style = comboBoxStyle.Text;
  ArrayList options = FireGetOptions(model, style);
  if (options != null)
    PopulateOptions(options);

  Color[] colors = FireGetColors(model, style);
  comboBoxColor.Items.Clear();
  if (colors == null) return;
  if (colors.Length == 0) return;
  foreach (Color color in colors)
    comboBoxColor.Items.Add(color.ToKnownColor().ToString());
  comboBoxColor.SelectedIndex = 0;
}

// each entry in the Options is a PricedItem array. In each array, the
// first element is the option category, the remaining elements
// are the options for the given category
void PopulateOptions(ArrayList theOptions)
{
  if (theOptions == null) return;

  foreach (PricedItem[] options in theOptions)
    PopulateOption(options);

  treeViewOptions.ExpandAll();
}

// first item is category, remainders are options
void PopulateOption(PricedItem[] theOptions)
{
  if (theOptions.Length == 0) return;
```

```csharp
  PricedItem category = theOptions[0];
  TreeNode categoryNode = new TreeNode(category.Name);
  categoryNode.Tag = category;
  treeViewOptions.Nodes.Add(categoryNode);

  for (int i = 1; i < theOptions.Length; i++)
  {
    PricedItem option = theOptions[i];
    TreeNode node = new TreeNode(option.Name);
    node.Tag = option;
    categoryNode.Nodes.Add(node);
  }
}

void PopulateOption(TreeNode theNode, PricedItem[] theOptions)
{
  foreach (PricedItem option in theOptions)
  {
    TreeNode node = new TreeNode(option.Name);
    theNode.Nodes.Add(node);
  }
}

public void PopulateModels(string[] theModels)
{
  comboBoxModel.Items.Clear();
  if (theModels == null) return;
  if (theModels.Length == 0) return;
  comboBoxModel.Items.AddRange(theModels);
  comboBoxModel.SelectedIndex = 0;
}

private void treeViewOptions_AfterCheck(object sender,
                               System.Windows.Forms.TreeViewEventArgs e)
{
  TreeNode node = e.Node;
  if (node == null) return;

  if (IsCategoryNode(node))
  {
    // check or uncheck all the child options
    foreach (TreeNode childNode in node.Nodes)
      childNode.Checked = node.Checked;
  }

  else
    // must be an Options node
    UpdateOptionsCost();
}
```

```csharp
bool IsCategoryNode(TreeNode theNode)
{
  // category nodes are at the root level
  return theNode.Parent == null;
}

void UpdateOptionsCost()
{
  ArrayList optionsSelected = new ArrayList();

  // get a list of all the selected options
  foreach (TreeNode categoryNode in treeViewOptions.Nodes)
    foreach (TreeNode optionNode in categoryNode.Nodes)
      if (optionNode.Checked)
        optionsSelected.Add(optionNode.Tag);

  // get total cost of options and show result
  PricedItem[] options =
        optionsSelected.ToArray(typeof(PricedItem)) as PricedItem[];
  decimal totalPrice = FireComputeCostOfOptions(options);
  labelTotalPrice.Text = totalPrice.ToString("C");  // display as a currency
}

private void buttonSubmit_Click(object sender, System.EventArgs e)
{
  ArrayList options = new ArrayList();
  foreach (TreeNode categoryNode in treeViewOptions.Nodes)
    foreach (TreeNode optionNode in categoryNode.Nodes)
      if (optionNode.Checked)
        options.Add(optionNode.Tag);

  PricedItem[] items = options.ToArray(typeof(PricedItem)) as PricedItem[];
  Color color = Color.FromName(comboBoxColor.Text);
  FireSubmitOrder(comboBoxModel.Text, comboBoxStyle.Text, color, items);
}

public delegate string[] GetStylesHandler(string theModel);
public event GetStylesHandler OnGetStyles;
string[] FireGetStyles(string theModel)
{
  if (OnGetStyles == null)
    return null;
  return OnGetStyles(theModel);
}

public delegate Color[] GetColorsHandler(string theModel, string theStyle);
public event GetColorsHandler OnGetColors;
Color[] FireGetColors(string theModel, string theStyle)
{
  if (OnGetColors == null)
    return null;
  return OnGetColors(theModel, theStyle);
}
```

```
  public delegate ArrayList GetOptionsHandler(string theModel, string theStyle);
  public event GetOptionsHandler OnGetOptions;
  ArrayList FireGetOptions(string theModel, string theStyle)
  {
    if (OnGetOptions == null)
      return null;
    return OnGetOptions(theModel, theStyle);
  }

  public delegate void SubmitOrderHandler(string theModel, string theStyle,
                                   Color theColor, PricedItem[] theOptions);
  public event SubmitOrderHandler OnSubmitOrder;
  void FireSubmitOrder(string theModel, string theStyle,
                   Color theColor, PricedItem[] theOptions)
  {
    if (OnSubmitOrder != null)
      OnSubmitOrder(theModel, theStyle, theColor, theOptions);
  }

  public delegate decimal
    ComputeCostOfOptionsHandler(PricedItem[] theOptionsSelected);
  public event ComputeCostOfOptionsHandler OnComputeCostOfOptions;
  decimal FireComputeCostOfOptions(PricedItem[] theOptionsSelected)
  {
    if (OnComputeCostOfOptions == null)
      return 0;
    return OnComputeCostOfOptions(theOptionsSelected);
  }
}

// class CoordinatorOrderEntry

public class CoordinatorOrderEntry
{
  public Color[] GetColors(string theModel, string theStyle)
  {
    return FireGetColors(theModel, theStyle);
  }

  // each entry in the returned ArrayList is a PriceItem[]
  public ArrayList GetOptions(string theModel, string theStyle)
  {
    return FireGetOptions(theModel, theStyle);
  }

  public string[] GetStyles(string theModel)
  {
    return FireGetStyles(theModel);
  }
```

```csharp
    public void SubmitOrder(string theModel, string theStyle, Color theColor,
                           PricedItem[] theOptions)
    {
      FireSubmit(theModel, theStyle, theColor, theOptions);
    }

    public decimal ComputeCostOfOptions(PricedItem[] theOptions)
    {
      decimal totalPrice = 0;

      foreach (PricedItem option in theOptions)
        totalPrice += option.Cost;

      return totalPrice;
    }

    public delegate string[] GetStylesHandler(string theModel);
    public event GetStylesHandler OnGetStyles;
    string[] FireGetStyles(string theModel)
    {
      if (OnGetStyles == null)
        return null;
      return OnGetStyles(theModel);
    }

    public delegate Color[] GetColorsHandler(string theModel, string theStyle);
    public event GetColorsHandler OnGetColors;
    Color[] FireGetColors(string theModel, string theStyle)
    {
      if (OnGetColors == null)
        return null;
      return OnGetColors(theModel, theStyle);
    }

    // each entry in the returned ArrayList is a PriceItem[]
    public delegate ArrayList GetOptionsHandler(string theModel, string theStyle);
    public event GetOptionsHandler OnGetOptions;
    ArrayList FireGetOptions(string theModel, string theStyle)
    {
      if (OnGetOptions == null)
        return null;
      return OnGetOptions(theModel, theStyle);
    }

    public delegate void SubmitHandler(string theModel, string theStyle,
                                      Color theColor, PricedItem[] theOptions);
    public event SubmitHandler OnSubmit;
    void FireSubmit(string theModel, string theStyle, Color theColor,
                   PricedItem[] theOptions)
    {
      if (OnSubmit != null)
        OnSubmit(theModel, theStyle, theColor, theOptions);
    }
  }
```

```csharp
// class Router

public class Router
{
  OrderProcessor.OrderSystem orderSystem;

  public Router()
  {
    EstablishConnectionToServer();
  }

  void EstablishConnectionToServer()
  {
    try
    {
      string configFile = System.Windows.Forms.Application.ExecutablePath +
                          ".config";
      RemotingConfiguration.Configure(configFile);

      orderSystem = (OrderProcessor.OrderSystem)Activator.GetObject(
                          typeof(OrderProcessor.OrderSystem),
                          "tcp://localhost:8011/AsapOrders");
    }
    catch (Exception ex)
    {
      throw new Exception("Couldn't connect to Order Processing server. " +
                                      "Details:\n\n" + ex.Message);
    }
  }

  public void SubmitOrder(string theModel, string theStyle,
                      Color theColor, PricedItem[] theOptions)
  {
    orderSystem.SubmitOrder(theModel, theStyle, theColor, theOptions);
  }

  public string[] GetModels()
  {
    return orderSystem.GetModels();
  }

  public string[] GetStyles(string theModel)
  {
    return orderSystem.GetStyles(theModel);
  }

  public Color[] GetColors(string theModel, string theStyle)
  {
    return orderSystem.GetColors(theModel, theStyle);
  }
```

```csharp
    // each entry in the returned array is a PricedItem[]
    public ArrayList GetOptions(string theModel, string theStyle)
    {
      return orderSystem.GetOptions(theModel, theStyle);
    }
}
```

The OrderEntry Test Fixture Component

```csharp
public class FormMain : System.Windows.Forms.Form
{
  Asap.Cars.OrderEntry.WorkerOrderEntry workerOrderEntry;
  Asap.Cars.OrderEntry.CoordinatorOrderEntry coordinatorOrderEntry;

  public FormMain()
  {
    InitializeComponent();

    // build everything
    workerOrderEntry = new Asap.Cars.OrderEntry.WorkerOrderEntry();
    coordinatorOrderEntry = new Asap.Cars.OrderEntry.CoordinatorOrderEntry();

    // bind everything
    workerOrderEntry.OnGetColors +=
        new GetColorsHandler(coordinatorOrderEntry.GetColors);
    workerOrderEntry.OnGetOptions +=
        new WorkerOrderEntry.GetOptionsHandler(coordinatorOrderEntry.GetOptions);
    workerOrderEntry.OnGetStyles +=
        new WorkerOrderEntry.GetStylesHandler(coordinatorOrderEntry.GetStyles);
    workerOrderEntry.OnSubmitOrder +=
        new WorkerOrderEntry.SubmitOrderHandler(coordinatorOrderEntry.SubmitOrder);
    workerOrderEntry.OnComputeCostOfOptions +=
        new WorkerOrderEntry.ComputeCostOfOptionsHandler(
                    coordinatorOrderEntry.ComputeCostOfOptions);

    coordinatorOrderEntry.OnGetColors +=
        new CoordinatorOrderEntry.GetColorsHandler(
            coordinatorOrderEntry_OnGetColors);
    coordinatorOrderEntry.OnGetOptions +=
        new CoordinatorOrderEntry.GetOptionsHandler(
            coordinatorOrderEntry_OnGetOptions);
    coordinatorOrderEntry.OnGetStyles +=
        new CoordinatorOrderEntry.GetStylesHandler(
            coordinatorOrderEntry_OnGetStyles);
    coordinatorOrderEntry.OnSubmit +=
        new CoordinatorOrderEntry.SubmitHandler(coordinatorOrderEntry_OnSubmit);

    // setup UI elements
    Controls.Add(workerOrderEntry.panelMain);
    string[] models = new string[] {"Model 1", "Model 2", "Model 3"};
    workerOrderEntry.PopulateModels(models);
  }
```

```csharp
// …

[STAThread]
static void Main()
{
    Application.Run(new FormMain());
}

private string[] coordinatorOrderEntry_OnGetModels()
{
  string[] models = new string[] {"Model 1", "Model 2", "Model 3"};
  return models;
}

private Color[] coordinatorOrderEntry_OnGetColors(string theModel,
                                                  string theStyle)
{
  Color[] colors = new Color[] {Color.White, Color.Navy, Color.Lavender};
  return colors;
}

private ArrayList coordinatorOrderEntry_OnGetOptions(string theModel,
                                                     string theStyle)
{
  ArrayList options = new ArrayList();

  ArrayList category1 = new ArrayList();
  PricedItem[] category1Items = new PricedItem[] {
    new PricedItem("Category 1", 0),
    new PricedItem("Option 1", 111),
    new PricedItem("Option 2", 222),
    new PricedItem("Option 3", 333)};
  options.Add(category1Items);

  ArrayList category2 = new ArrayList();
  PricedItem[] category2Items = new PricedItem[] {
    new PricedItem("Category 2", 0),
    new PricedItem("Option 11", 777),
    new PricedItem("Option 22", 888),
    new PricedItem("Option 33", 999)};
  options.Add(category2Items);

  return options;
}

private string[] coordinatorOrderEntry_OnGetStyles(string theModel)
{
  string[] styles = new string[] {"Style 1", "Style 2", "Style 3"};
  return styles;
}
```

```csharp
    private void coordinatorOrderEntry_OnSubmit(string theModel,
                                                string theStyle,
                                                Color theColor,
                                                PricedItem[] theOptions)
    {
      string s = string.Format("Model=[{0}] Style=[{1}] Color=[{2}]",
                               theModel, theStyle, theColor);
      for (int i = 0; i < theOptions.Length; i++)
        s += string.Format(" Option[{0}]=[{1}]", i, theOptions[i].Name);

      MessageBox.Show(s, "Order submitted");
    }
}
```

VB .NET Code

The OrderEntry Component

```vbnet
'   App.config

<configuration>
    <system.runtime.remoting>
        <application>
            <service>
                <wellknown
                    type="OrderProcessor.OrderSystem, OrderProcessor"
                    mode="Singleton" url="tcp://localhost:8011/AsapOrders"/>
            </service>
        </application>
    </system.runtime.remoting>
</configuration>

' class FormMain

Public Class FormMain
  Inherits System.Windows.Forms.Form

  Private _workerOrderEntry As WorkerOrderEntry
  Private _coordinatorOrderEntry As CoordinatorOrderEntry
  Private _router As Router

  Sub Build()
    _workerOrderEntry = New WorkerOrderEntry
    _coordinatorOrderEntry = New CoordinatorOrderEntry
    _router = New Router
  End Sub
```

```vbnet
Sub Bind()
  _workerOrderEntry.OnGetColors = _
          AddressOf _coordinatorOrderEntry.GetColors 'delegate
  _workerOrderEntry.OnGetOptions = _
          AddressOf _coordinatorOrderEntry.GetOptions 'delegate
  _workerOrderEntry.OnGetStyles = _
          AddressOf _coordinatorOrderEntry.GetStyles 'delegate
  AddHandler _workerOrderEntry.OnSubmitOrder, _
          AddressOf _coordinatorOrderEntry.SubmitOrder 'event
  _workerOrderEntry.OnComputeCostOfOptions = _
          AddressOf _coordinatorOrderEntry.ComputeCostOfOptions 'delegate

  _coordinatorOrderEntry.OnGetColors = AddressOf _router.GetColors 'delegate
  _coordinatorOrderEntry.OnGetOptions = AddressOf _router.GetOptions 'delegate
  _coordinatorOrderEntry.OnGetStyles = AddressOf _router.GetStyles 'delegate
  AddHandler _coordinatorOrderEntry.OnSubmit, AddressOf _router.SubmitOrder event
End Sub

Sub SetupUi()
  Controls.Add(_workerOrderEntry.PanelMain)
  PopulateModels()
End Sub

Sub PopulateModels()
  Try
    Dim models As String() = _router.GetModels()
    _workerOrderEntry.PopulateModels(models)
  Catch ex As Exception
    Dim msg As String = _
    String.Format("The server must be running before " +_
                  "starting the Order Entry program. " + _
                  "To run the server, start OrderProcessingHostProgram.exe.\n" +
                  "Exception Details: [{0}]", ex.Message)
    MessageBox.Show(msg, "An exception occurred while connecting to server")
    Throw ex
  End Try
End Sub

Public Sub New()
  MyBase.New()

  'This call is required by the Windows Form Designer.
  InitializeComponent()

  Build()
  Bind()

  SetupUi()
End Sub

  ' …
```

```vb
  Shared Sub Main()
    Dim _formMain As FormMain = Nothing
    Try
      _formMain = New FormMain
    Catch ex As Exception
      ' exceptions typically occur if the client can't connect to the server
      MessageBox.Show(ex.Message, "An exception occurred")
      Return
    End Try

    Application.Run(_formMain)
  End Sub

End Class


' class WorkerOrderEntry


Public Class WorkerOrderEntry
  Inherits System.Windows.Forms.UserControl

  Public Sub New()
    MyBase.New()

    'This call is required by the Windows Form Designer.
    InitializeComponent()
  End Sub

    ' ...


  Private Sub ComboBoxModel_SelectedIndexChanged(_
                    ByVal sender As Object, e As System.EventArgs)  _
                    Handles ComboBoxModel.SelectedIndexChanged
    ComboBoxStyle.Items.Clear()
    Dim model As String = ComboBoxModel.Text
    Dim styles As String() = FireGetStyles(model)
    If styles Is Nothing Then Return
    If styles.Length = 0 Then Return
    ComboBoxStyle.Items.AddRange(styles)
    ComboBoxStyle.SelectedIndex = 0
  End Sub

  Private Sub ComboBoxStyle_SelectedIndexChanged( _
                    ByVal sender As Object, ByVal e As System.EventArgs) _
                    Handles ComboBoxStyle.SelectedIndexChanged
    TreeViewOptions.Nodes.Clear()
    Dim model As String = ComboBoxModel.Text
    Dim style As String = ComboBoxStyle.Text
    Dim options As ArrayList = FireGetOptions(model, style)
    If Not options Is Nothing Then
      PopulateOptions(options)
    End If
```

```vbnet
    Dim colors As Color() = FireGetColors(model, style)
    ComboBoxColor.Items.Clear()
    If colors Is Nothing Then Return
    If colors.Length = 0 Then Return
    For Each clr As Color In colors
      ComboBoxColor.Items.Add(clr.ToKnownColor().ToString())
    Next
    ComboBoxColor.SelectedIndex = 0
End Sub

' each entry in the Options is a PricedItem array. In each array, the
' first element is the option category, the remaining elements
' are the options for the given category
Sub PopulateOptions(ByVal theOptions As ArrayList)
  If theOptions Is Nothing Then Return

  For Each options As PricedItem() In theOptions
    PopulateOption(options)
  Next

  TreeViewOptions.ExpandAll()
End Sub

' first item is category, remainders are options
Sub PopulateOption(ByVal theOptions As PricedItem())
  If theOptions.Length = 0 Then Return

  Dim category As PricedItem = theOptions(0)
  Dim categoryNode As New TreeNode(category.Name)
  categoryNode.Tag = category
  TreeViewOptions.Nodes.Add(categoryNode)

  For i As Integer = 1 To theOptions.Length - 1
    Dim opt As PricedItem = theOptions(i)
    Dim node As New TreeNode(opt.Name)
    node.Tag = opt
    categoryNode.Nodes.Add(node)
  Next
End Sub

Sub PopulateOption(ByVal theNode As TreeNode, ByVal theOptions As PricedItem())
  For Each opt As PricedItem In theOptions
    Dim node As New TreeNode(opt.Name)
    theNode.Nodes.Add(node)
  Next
End Sub

Public Sub PopulateModels(ByVal theModels As String())
  ComboBoxModel.Items.Clear()
  If theModels Is Nothing Then Return
  If theModels.Length = 0 Then Return
  ComboBoxModel.Items.AddRange(theModels)
  ComboBoxModel.SelectedIndex = 0
End Sub
```

```vb
    Private Sub TreeViewOptions_AfterCheck( _
                        ByVal sender As Object, _
                        ByVal e As System.Windows.Forms.TreeViewEventArgs) _
                        Handles TreeViewOptions.AfterCheck
      Dim node As TreeNode = e.Node
      If node Is Nothing Then Return

      If IsCategoryNode(node) Then
        ' check or uncheck all the child options
        For Each childNode As TreeNode In node.Nodes
          childNode.Checked = node.Checked
        Next
      Else
          ' must be an Options node
          UpdateOptionsCost()
      End If
    End Sub

    Function IsCategoryNode(ByVal theNode As TreeNode) As Boolean
      ' category nodes are at the root level
      Return theNode.Parent Is Nothing
    End Function

    Sub UpdateOptionsCost()
      Dim optionsSelected As New ArrayList

      ' get a list of all the selected options
      For Each categoryNode As TreeNode In TreeViewOptions.Nodes
        For Each optionNode As TreeNode In categoryNode.Nodes
          If optionNode.Checked Then
            optionsSelected.Add(optionNode.Tag)
          End If
        Next
      Next

      ' get total cost of options and show result
      Dim options As PricedItem() = _
            DirectCast(optionsSelected.ToArray(GetType(PricedItem)), PricedItem())
      Dim totalPrice As Decimal = FireComputeCostOfOptions(options)
      LabelTotalPrice.Text = totalPrice.ToString("C")  ' display as a currency
    End Sub

    Private Sub ButtonSubmit_Click(ByVal sender As Object, _
                            ByVal e As System.EventArgs) _
                      Handles ButtonSubmit.Click
      Dim options As New ArrayList
      For Each categoryNode As TreeNode In TreeViewOptions.Nodes
        For Each optionNode As TreeNode In categoryNode.Nodes
          If optionNode.Checked Then
            options.Add(optionNode.Tag)
          End If
        Next
      Next
```

```vb
    Dim items As PricedItem() = DirectCast(options.ToArray(GetType(PricedItem)), _
                                           PricedItem())
    Dim clr As Color = Color.FromName(ComboBoxColor.Text)
    FireSubmitOrder(ComboBoxModel.Text, ComboBoxStyle.Text, clr, items)
End Sub

Public Delegate Function GetStylesHandler(ByVal theModel As String) As String()
Public OnGetStyles As GetStylesHandler
Function FireGetStyles(ByVal theModel As String) As String()
  If OnGetStyles Is Nothing Then Return Nothing
  Return OnGetStyles(theModel)
End Function

Public Delegate Function GetColorsHandler(ByVal theModel As String, )
                                          ByVal theStyle As String) As Color()
Public OnGetColors As GetColorsHandler
Function FireGetColors(ByVal theModel As String,
                       ByVal theStyle As String) As Color()
  If OnGetColors Is Nothing Then Return Nothing
  Return OnGetColors(theModel, theStyle)
End Function

Public Delegate Function GetOptionsHandler(ByVal theModel As String, _
                                           ByVal theStyle As String) _
                                           As ArrayList
Public OnGetOptions As GetOptionsHandler
Function FireGetOptions(ByVal theModel As String, _
                        ByVal theStyle As String) As ArrayList
  If OnGetOptions Is Nothing Then Return Nothing
  Return OnGetOptions(theModel, theStyle)
End Function

Public Event OnSubmitOrder(ByVal theModel As String, _
                           ByVal theStyle As String, _
                           ByVal theColor As Color, _
                           ByVal theOptions As PricedItem() )

Sub FireSubmitOrder(ByVal theModel As String, _
                    ByVal theStyle As String, _
                    ByVal theColor As Color, _
                    ByVal theOptions As PricedItem() )
  RaiseEvent OnSubmitOrder(theModel, theStyle, theColor, theOptions)
End Sub

Public Delegate Function ComputeCostOfOptionsHandler( _
                       ByVal theOptionsSelected As PricedItem() ) As Decimal
Public OnComputeCostOfOptions As ComputeCostOfOptionsHandler
Function FireComputeCostOfOptions(ByVal theOptionsSelected As PricedItem()) _
        As Decimal
  If OnComputeCostOfOptions Is Nothing Then Return Nothing
  Return OnComputeCostOfOptions(theOptionsSelected)
End Function

End Class
```

```vbnet
' class CoordinatorOrderEntry

Public Class CoordinatorOrderEntry

  Public Function GetColors(ByVal theModel As String, _
                            ByVal theStyle As String) As Color()
    Return FireGetColors(theModel, theStyle)
  End Function

  ' each entry in the returned ArrayList is a PriceItem[]
  Public Function GetOptions(ByVal theModel As String, _
                             ByVal theStyle As String) As ArrayList
    Return FireGetOptions(theModel, theStyle)
  End Function

  Public Function GetStyles(ByVal theModel As String) As String()
    Return FireGetStyles(theModel)
  End Function

  Public Sub SubmitOrder(ByVal theModel As String, ByVal theStyle As String, _
                         ByVal theColor As Color, ByVal theOptions _
                         As PricedItem() )
    FireSubmit(theModel, theStyle, theColor, theOptions)
  End Sub

  Public Function ComputeCostOfOptions(ByVal theOptions As PricedItem() ) _
                  As Decimal
    Dim totalPrice As Decimal = 0

    For Each opt As PricedItem In theOptions
      totalPrice += opt.Cost
    Next

    Return totalPrice
  End Function

  Public Delegate Function GetStylesHandler(ByVal theModel As String) As String()
  Public OnGetStyles As GetStylesHandler
  Function FireGetStyles(ByVal theModel As String) As String()
    If OnGetStyles Is Nothing Then Return Nothing
    Return OnGetStyles(theModel)
  End Function

  Public Delegate Function GetColorsHandler(ByVal theModel As String, _
                                            ByVal theStyle As String) As Color()
  Public OnGetColors As GetColorsHandler
  Function FireGetColors(ByVal theModel As String, _
                         ByVal theStyle As String) As Color()
    If OnGetColors Is Nothing Then Return Nothing
    Return OnGetColors(theModel, theStyle)
  End Function
```

```vbnet
' each entry in the returned ArrayList is a PriceItem
Public Delegate Function GetOptionsHandler(ByVal theModel As String, _
                                           ByVal theStyle As String) _
                                      As ArrayList
Public OnGetOptions As GetOptionsHandler
Function FireGetOptions(ByVal theModel As String, ByVal theStyle As String) _
       As ArrayList
   If OnGetOptions Is Nothing Then Return Nothing
   Return OnGetOptions(theModel, theStyle)
End Function


Public Event OnSubmit(ByVal theModel As String, ByVal theStyle As String, _
                  ByVal theColor As Color, _
                  ByVal theOptions As PricedItem() )
Sub FireSubmit(ByVal theModel As String, ByVal theStyle As String, _
           ByVal theColor As Color, ByVal theOptions As PricedItem() )
   RaiseEvent OnSubmit(theModel, theStyle, theColor, theOptions)
End Sub
End Class

' class Router

Public Class Router
   Private _orderSystem As OrderProcessor.OrderSystem

   Public Sub New()
      EstablishConnectionToServer()
   End Sub

   Sub EstablishConnectionToServer()
      Try
         Dim configFile As String = _
            System.Windows.Forms.Application.ExecutablePath + ".config"
         RemotingConfiguration.Configure(configFile)

         _orderSystem = _
            DirectCast(Activator.GetObject(GetType(OrderProcessor.OrderSystem), _
                    "tcp://localhost:8011/AsapOrders"), _
                    OrderProcessor.OrderSystem)
      Catch ex As Exception
         Throw New Exception("Couldn't connect to Order Processing server. " +_
                                       "Details:\n\n" + ex.Message)
      End Try
   End Sub

   Public Sub SubmitOrder(ByVal theModel As String, ByVal theStyle As String, _
                     ByVal theColor As Color, ByVal theOptions As PricedItem() )
      _orderSystem.SubmitOrder(theModel, theStyle, theColor, theOptions)
   End Sub
```

```vb
    Public Function GetModels() As String()
      Return _orderSystem.GetModels()
    End Function

    Public Function GetStyles(ByVal theModel As String) As String()
      Return _orderSystem.GetStyles(theModel)
    End Function

    Public Function GetColors(ByVal theModel As String, ByVal theStyle As String) _
                As Color()
      Return _orderSystem.GetColors(theModel, theStyle)
    End Function

    ' each entry in the returned array is a PricedItem[]
    Public Function GetOptions(ByVal theModel As String, ByVal theStyle As String) _
                As ArrayList
      Return _orderSystem.GetOptions(theModel, theStyle)
    End Function
End Class
```

The OrderEntry Test Fixture Component

```vb
Public Class FormMain
  Inherits System.Windows.Forms.Form

  Private _workerOrderEntry As WorkerOrderEntry
  Private _coordinatorOrderEntry As CoordinatorOrderEntry

  Public Sub New()
    MyBase.New()

    'This call is required by the Windows Form Designer.
    InitializeComponent()

    ' build everything
    _workerOrderEntry = New WorkerOrderEntry
    _coordinatorOrderEntry = New CoordinatorOrderEntry

    ' bind everything
    _workerOrderEntry.OnGetColors = _
                AddressOf _coordinatorOrderEntry.GetColors 'delegate
    _workerOrderEntry.OnGetOptions = _
                AddressOf _coordinatorOrderEntry.GetOptions 'delegate
    _workerOrderEntry.OnGetStyles = _
                AddressOf _coordinatorOrderEntry.GetStyles 'delegate
    AddHandler _workerOrderEntry.OnSubmitOrder, _
                AddressOf _coordinatorOrderEntry.SubmitOrder 'event
    _workerOrderEntry.OnComputeCostOfOptions = _
                AddressOf  _coordinatorOrderEntry.ComputeCostOfOptions 'delegate
```

```vb
        _coordinatorOrderEntry.OnGetColors = _
                    AddressOf coordinatorOrderEntry_OnGetColors 'delegate
        _coordinatorOrderEntry.OnGetOptions = _
                    AddressOf coordinatorOrderEntry_OnGetOptions 'delegate
        _coordinatorOrderEntry.OnGetStyles = _
                    AddressOf coordinatorOrderEntry_OnGetStyles 'delegate
        AddHandler _coordinatorOrderEntry.OnSubmit, _
                    AddressOf coordinatorOrderEntry_OnSubmit 'event

      ' setup UI elements
      Controls.Add(_workerOrderEntry.PanelMain)
      Dim models As String() = New String() {"Model 1", "Model 2", "Model 3"}
      _workerOrderEntry.PopulateModels(models)
End Sub

' ...


Private Function coordinatorOrderEntry_OnGetModels() As String()
    Dim models As String() = New String() {"Model 1", "Model 2", "Model 3"}
    Return models
End Function


Private Function coordinatorOrderEntry_OnGetColors( _
                        ByVal theModel As String, _
                        ByVal theStyle As String) As Color()
    Dim colors As Color() = New Color() {Color.White, Color.Navy, Color.Lavender}
    Return colors
End Function


Private Function coordinatorOrderEntry_OnGetOptions( _
                        ByVal theModel As String, _
                        ByVal theStyle As String) As ArrayList
    Dim options As New ArrayList

    Dim category1 As New ArrayList
    Dim category1Items() As PricedItem = New PricedItem() _
    {New PricedItem("Category 1", 0), _
     New PricedItem("Option 1", 111), _
     New PricedItem("Option 2", 222), _
     New PricedItem("Option 3", 333)}
    options.Add(category1Items)

    Dim category2 As New ArrayList
    Dim category2Items() As PricedItem = New PricedItem() _
     {New PricedItem("Category 2", 0), _
      New PricedItem("Option 11", 777), _
      New PricedItem("Option 22", 888), _
      New PricedItem("Option 33", 999)}
    options.Add(category2Items)

    Return options
End Function
```

```
Private Function coordinatorOrderEntry_OnGetStyles(ByVal theModel As String) _
                As String()
  Dim styles As String() = New String() {"Style 1", "Style 2", "Style 3"}
  Return styles
End Function

Private Sub coordinatorOrderEntry_OnSubmit(ByVal theModel As String, _
                                ByVal theStyle As String, _
                                ByVal theColor As Color, _
                                ByVal theOptions As PricedItem() )
  Dim s As String = String.Format("Model=[{0}] Style=[{1}] Color=[{2}]", _
                                theModel, theStyle, theColor)
  For i As Integer = 0 To theOptions.Length - 1
    s += String.Format(" Option[{0}]=[{1}]", i, theOptions(i).Name)
  Next
  MessageBox.Show(s, "Order submitted")
End Sub

End Class
```

The Server Components

The server side of the system consists of four main components, as shown in the coupling diagram back in Figure 13-3. I distributed the logic across four different components, because a real system might run each component on a different computer in a LAN or WAN environment. The only server component that the client accesses directly is called Order Processing. It contains a class called OrderSystem that is called from the client side over a .NET remoting TCP/IP connection. The other server components are hidden from the client. Each component is associated with its own MSMQ queue. Figure 13-10 shows the queues related to each server component.

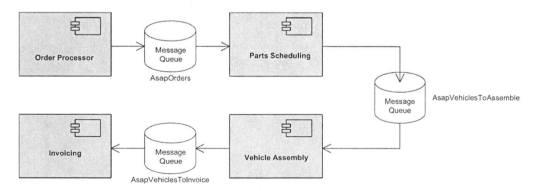

Figure 13-10. *The server-side components and message queues*

The overall process is like a pipeline, with messages flowing from one message queue to the next after being processed. All the server components are implemented as separate standalone programs, with exception of the Order Processor component, which is implemented as a DLL. The reason for the DLL is that Order Processor is called using RPCs from a remote client using .NET remoting, which requires the server component to be packaged as a DLL.

■**Implementation Note** The code uses embedded literals for the queue paths. Besides the name of the queue, the queue path identifies the name of machine on which the queue resides. To run the code, you need to create the MSMQ queues on your machine or machines and set the embedded machine names in the source code accordingly. I used embedded literals to keep the code simple. A production system might have used a directory service to hold the various queue paths.

Each standalone server component is notified of incoming messages by a message queue notification. Let's look at each component in more detail.

The Order Processor Component

The job of the Order Processor component is to handle orders submitted by clients, create a `WorkOrder` object describing the order, and post the object to the AsapOrders queue. The `WorkOrder` class is a user-defined type contained in the CommonTypes component. The class encapsulates the model, style, color, and options of the car being ordered. The class is serializable, so you can pass it as the notification payload to the message queue of each server component. `WorkOrder` also contains a unique identifier for each order. Although this simplified case study doesn't use a database, a real system would probably save all the data related to a car order in a database. It would then use the WorkOrder ID to identify the database elements associated with the order, such as the list of parts, the paint color codes, supplier information, and so on. As mentioned earlier, Order Processor is implemented as a DLL, to allow remote client components to make calls to it using the .NET remoting framework. Figure 13-11 shows the wiring diagram of the Order Processor system.

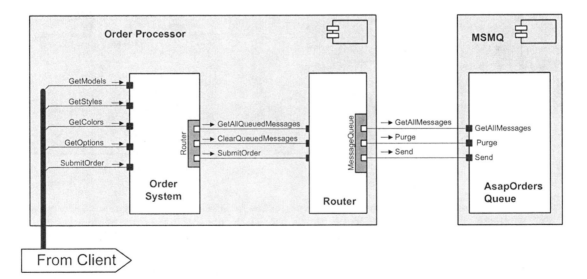

Figure 13-11. *The wiring diagram of the Order Processor system*

You load the Order Processor DLL by running a standalone executable program called Order Processor Host Program, which also acts as an administrative console showing details about the running Order Processor component. The main purpose of the host program is to set up the communication channel for clients to use when making .NET remoting RPCs. Figure 13-12 shows the UI of the host program.

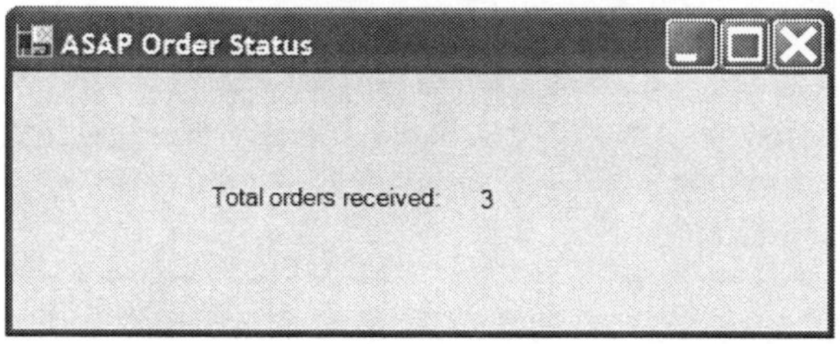

Figure 13-12. *The UI of the Order Processor host program*

The UI is deliberately kept very simple. The host program doesn't use .NET remoting to access the Order Processor component, because the host program runs on the same machine as the Order Processor.

The Test Fixture

The Order Processor component has five main methods that need testing: GetModels, GetStyles, GetColors, GetOptions, and SubmitOrder. The test fixture project exercises the server methods by making local calls into the OrderSystem class of the Order Processor component. Figure 13-13 shows the test fixture's UI.

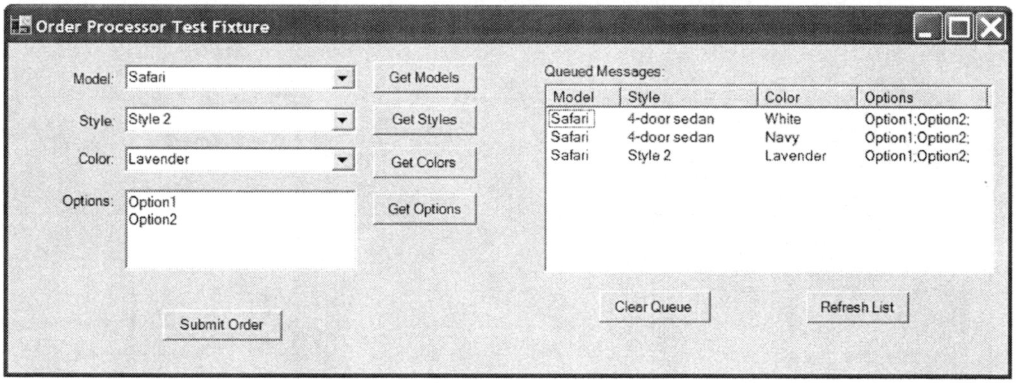

Figure 13-13. *The Order Processor test fixture UI*

Since orders are saved in a message queue, the test fixture also shows the contents of the queue. When the user clicks the Submit Order button, a new order appears in the Queued Messages list. Under the list are two buttons, one for clearing the queue and one for refreshing the display with the queue contents.

C# Code

The OrderProcessor Component

```
// class OrderSystem

public class OrderSystem: MarshalByRefObject
{
  static int ordersReceived;
  static public int OrdersReceived
  {
    get {return ordersReceived;}
  }

  public OrderSystem()
  {
  }

  Router router;
  public Router Router
  {
    get
    {
      if (router == null)
        router = new Router();
      return router;
    }
  }

  public string[] GetModels()
  {
    // the following data would probably be fetched from a database
    string[] models = new string[] {"Model 1", "Model 2", "Model 3"};
    return models;
  }

  public string[] GetStyles(string theModel)
  {
    // the following data would probably be fetched from a database
    string[] styles = new string[] {"Style 1", "Style 2", "Style 3"};
    return styles;
  }

  public Color[] GetColors(string theModel, string theStyle)
  {
    // the following data would probably be fetched from a database
    Color[] colors = new Color[] {Color.White, Color.Navy, Color.Lavender};
    return colors;
  }
```

```csharp
    // each entry in the returned array is a PricedItem[]
    public ArrayList GetOptions(string theModel, string theStyle)
    {
      // the following data would probably be fetched from a database
      ArrayList options = new ArrayList();

      ArrayList category1 = new ArrayList();
      PricedItem[] category1Items = new PricedItem[] {
        new PricedItem("Category 1", 0),
        new PricedItem("Option 1", 111),
        new PricedItem("Option 2", 222),
        new PricedItem("Option 3", 333)};
      options.Add(category1Items);

      ArrayList category2 = new ArrayList();
      PricedItem[] category2Items = new PricedItem[] {
        new PricedItem("Category 2", 0),
        new PricedItem("Option 11", 777),
        new PricedItem("Option 22", 888),
        new PricedItem("Option 33", 999)};
      options.Add(category2Items);

      return options;
    }

    public void SubmitOrder(string theModel, string theStyle, Color theColor,
                                          PricedItem[] theOptions)
    {
      WorkOrder workOrder = new WorkOrder(theModel, theStyle, theColor, theOptions);
      Router.SubmitOrder(workOrder);
      ordersReceived++;
    }

    public System.Messaging.Message[] GetAllQueuedMessages()
    {
      return Router.GetAllQueuedMessages();
    }

    public void ClearQueuedMessages()
    {
      Router.ClearQueuedMessages();
    }
}


// class Router

public class Router : System.ComponentModel.Component
{
  public System.Messaging.MessageQueue messageQueueOrders;

  // …
```

```csharp
public void SubmitOrder(WorkOrder theWorkOrder)
{
  messageQueueOrders.Send(theWorkOrder);
}

public System.Messaging.Message[] GetAllQueuedMessages()
{
  return messageQueueOrders.GetAllMessages();
}

public void ClearQueuedMessages()
{
  messageQueueOrders.Purge();
}
}
```

The OrderProcessor Test Fixture Component

```csharp
public class FormMain : System.Windows.Forms.Form
{

  // …

  OrderSystem orderSystem = new OrderSystem();

  public FormMain()
  {
      InitializeComponent();

      comboBoxColors.Items.Add("White");
      comboBoxColors.SelectedIndex = 0;

      columnHeaderOptions.Width = -2;  // auto size last column

      DisplayQueuedMessages();
  }


  [STAThread]
  static void Main()
  {
      Application.Run(new FormMain());
  }

  private void buttonGetModels_Click(object sender, System.EventArgs e)
  {
    string[] models = orderSystem.GetModels();
    comboBoxModels.Items.Clear();
    if (models == null) return;

    foreach (string model in models)
      comboBoxModels.Items.Add(model);
    comboBoxModels.SelectedIndex = 0;
  }
```

```csharp
private void buttonGetStyles_Click(object sender, System.EventArgs e)
{
  string[] styles = orderSystem.GetStyles(comboBoxModels.Text);
  comboBoxStyles.Items.Clear();
  if (styles == null) return;

  foreach (string style in styles)
    comboBoxStyles.Items.Add(style);
  comboBoxStyles.SelectedIndex = 0;
}

private void buttonGetColors_Click(object sender, System.EventArgs e)
{
  Color[] colors = orderSystem.GetColors(comboBoxModels.Text,
                                         comboBoxStyles.Text);
  comboBoxColors.Items.Clear();
  if (colors == null) return;

  foreach (Color color in colors)
    comboBoxColors.Items.Add(color.Name);
  comboBoxColors.SelectedIndex = 0;
}

ArrayList options = new ArrayList();
private void buttonGetOptions_Click(object sender, System.EventArgs e)
{
  options = orderSystem.GetOptions(comboBoxModels.Text, comboBoxStyles.Text);
  textBoxOptions.Text = "";
  if (options == null) return;

  ArrayList items = new ArrayList();
  foreach (PricedItem[] pricedItems in options)
    foreach (PricedItem pricedItem in pricedItems)
      items.Add(pricedItem);

  // show options in the textbox
  string[] lines = new string[items.Count];
  for (int i = 0; i < items.Count; i++)
    lines[i] = (items[i] as PricedItem).Name;
  textBoxOptions.Lines = lines;
}

private void buttonSubmitOrder_Click(object sender, System.EventArgs e)
{
  PricedItem[] requestedOptions;
  if (options.Count > 0)
  {
```

```csharp
      // convert an array of PriceItem arrays into a PricedItem array
      ArrayList items = new ArrayList();
      foreach (PricedItem[] pricedItems in options)
        foreach (PricedItem pricedItem in pricedItems)
          items.Add(pricedItem);
        requestedOptions = items.ToArray(typeof(PricedItem)) as PricedItem[];
      }
      else
        requestedOptions = new PricedItem[] {new PricedItem("Option1", 11),
                                   new PricedItem("Option2", 22) };

      Color color = Color.FromName(comboBoxColors.Text);
      orderSystem.SubmitOrder(comboBoxModels.Text, comboBoxStyles.Text,
                          color, requestedOptions);
      DisplayQueuedMessages();
    }

    private void DisplayQueuedMessages()
    {
      listViewQueuedMessages.Items.Clear();

      System.Messaging.Message[] messages = orderSystem.GetAllQueuedMessages();
      System.Messaging.XmlMessageFormatter formatter;
      formatter = new System.Messaging.XmlMessageFormatter(new Type[]
                                          {typeof(WorkOrder)});

      foreach (System.Messaging.Message message in messages)
      {
        message.Formatter = formatter;
        WorkOrder workOrder = message.Body as WorkOrder;
        ListViewItem item = new ListViewItem(workOrder.Model);
        item.SubItems.Add(workOrder.Style);
        item.SubItems.Add(workOrder.Color);
        string options = string.Empty;
        foreach (PricedItem option in workOrder.Options)
          options += option.Name + ";";
        item.SubItems.Add(options);
        listViewQueuedMessages.Items.Add(item);
      }
    }

    private void buttonClearQueue_Click(object sender, System.EventArgs e)
    {
      orderSystem.ClearQueuedMessages();
      DisplayQueuedMessages();
    }

    private void buttonRefreshList_Click(object sender, System.EventArgs e)
    {
      DisplayQueuedMessages();
    }
}
```

The OrderProcessor Hosting Component

```
// app.config

<configuration>
    <system.runtime.remoting>
        <application>
            <service>
                <wellknown type="OrderProcessor.OrderSystem,
                            OrderProcessor " mode="Singleton"
                            url="tcp://localhost:8011/AsapOrders"/>
            </service>
        </application>
    </system.runtime.remoting>
</configuration>

// class FormMain

public class FormMain : System.Windows.Forms.Form
{
  public FormMain()
  {
    InitializeComponent();

    // configure the server component to listen for orders
    TcpChannel channel = new TcpChannel(8011);
    ChannelServices.RegisterChannel(channel);
    RemotingConfiguration.RegisterWellKnownServiceType(
                                    typeof(OrderSystem),
                                    "AsapOrders",
                                    WellKnownObjectMode.Singleton);
  }

  // …

  [STAThread]
  static void Main()
  {
      Application.Run(new FormMain());
  }

  private void timerOrdersReceived_Tick(object sender, System.EventArgs e)
  {
    UpdateOrdersReceived();
  }

  int ordersReceived;
  void UpdateOrdersReceived()
  {
    int c = OrderSystem.OrdersReceived;
    if (c == ordersReceived) return;
```

```
    labelTotalOrdersReceived.Text = c.ToString();
    ordersReceived = c;
  }
}
```

VB .NET Code

The OrderProcessor Component

```vb
' class OrderSystem

Public Class OrderSystem
  Inherits MarshalByRefObject

  Private Shared _ordersReceived As Integer
  Public Shared ReadOnly Property OrdersReceived() As Integer
    Get
      Return _ordersReceived
    End Get
  End Property

  Public Sub New()
  End Sub

  Private _router As Router
  Public ReadOnly Property Router() As Router
    Get
      If _router Is Nothing Then
        _router = New Router
      End If
      Return _router
    End Get
  End Property

  Public Function GetModels() As String()
    ' the following data would probably be fetched from a database
    Dim models As String() = New String() {"Model 1", "Model 2", "Model 3"}
    Return models
  End Function

  Public Function GetStyles(ByVal theModel As String) As String()
    ' the following data would probably be fetched from a database
    Dim styles As String() = New String() {"Style 1", "Style 2", "Style 3"}
    Return styles
  End Function
```

```vbnet
    Public Function GetColors(ByVal theModel As String, _
                              ByVal theStyle As String) As Color()
      ' the following data would probably be fetched from a database
      Dim colors As Color() = New Color() {Color.White, Color.Navy, Color.Lavender}
      Return colors
    End Function


    ' each entry in the returned array is a PricedItem[]
    Public Function GetOptions(ByVal theModel As String, _
                               ByVal theStyle As String) As ArrayList
      ' the following data would probably be fetched from a database
      Dim options As New ArrayList

      Dim category1 As New ArrayList
      Dim category1Items As PricedItem() = New PricedItem() _
      {New PricedItem("Category 1", 0), _
        New PricedItem("Option 1", 111), _
        New PricedItem("Option 2", 222), _
        New PricedItem("Option 3", 333)}
      options.Add(category1Items)

      Dim category2 As New ArrayList
      Dim category2Items As PricedItem() = New PricedItem() _
      {New PricedItem("Category 2", 0), _
        New PricedItem("Option 11", 777), _
        New PricedItem("Option 22", 888), _
        New PricedItem("Option 33", 999)}
      options.Add(category2Items)

      Return options
    End Function

    Public Sub SubmitOrder(ByVal theModel As String, ByVal theStyle As String, _
                           ByVal theColor As Color, ByVal theOptions As PricedItem() )
      Dim wo As New WorkOrder(theModel, theStyle, theColor, theOptions)
      Router.SubmitOrder(wo)
      _ordersReceived += 1
    End Sub

    Public Function GetAllQueuedMessages() As System.Messaging.Message()
      Return Router.GetAllQueuedMessages()
    End Function

    Public Sub ClearQueuedMessages()
      Router.ClearQueuedMessages()
    End Sub
End Class

' class Router

Public Class Router
    Inherits System.ComponentModel.Component
```

```vb
Public Sub SubmitOrder(ByVal theWorkOrder As WorkOrder)
  MessageQueueOrders.Send(theWorkOrder)
End Sub

Public Function GetAllQueuedMessages() As System.Messaging.Message()
  Return MessageQueueOrders.GetAllMessages()
End Function

Public Sub ClearQueuedMessages()
  MessageQueueOrders.Purge()
End Sub

  ' …

End Class
```

The OrderProcessor Test Fixture Component

```vb
Public Class FormMain
  Inherits System.Windows.Forms.Form

  Private _orderSystem As New OrderSystem

  Public Sub New()
    MyBase.New()

    'This call is required by the Windows Form Designer.
    InitializeComponent()

    ComboBoxColors.Items.Add("White")
    ComboBoxColors.SelectedIndex = 0

    columnHeaderOptions.Width = -2    ' auto size last column

    DisplayQueuedMessages()
  End Sub

  ' …

  Private Sub ButtonGetModels_Click(ByVal sender As Object, _
                                    ByVal e As System.EventArgs) _
                                    Handles ButtonGetModels.Click
    Dim models As String() = _orderSystem.GetModels()
    ComboBoxModels.Items.Clear()
    If models Is Nothing Then Return

    For Each model As String In models
      ComboBoxModels.Items.Add(model)
    Next
    ComboBoxModels.SelectedIndex = 0
  End Sub
```

```vbnet
  Private Sub ButtonGetStyles_Click(ByVal sender As Object, _
                              ByVal e As System.EventArgs) _
                              Handles ButtonGetStyles.Click
    Dim styles As String() = _orderSystem.GetStyles(ComboBoxModels.Text)
    ComboBoxStyles.Items.Clear()
    If styles Is Nothing Then Return

    For Each style As String In styles
      ComboBoxStyles.Items.Add(style)
    Next
    ComboBoxStyles.SelectedIndex = 0
  End Sub

  Private Sub ButtonGetColors_Click(ByVal sender As Object, _
                              ByVal e As System.EventArgs) _
                              Handles ButtonGetColors.Click
    Dim colors As Color() = _orderSystem.GetColors(ComboBoxModels.Text, _
                                        ComboBoxStyles.Text)
    ComboBoxColors.Items.Clear()
    If colors Is Nothing Then Return

    For Each clr As Color In colors
      ComboBoxColors.Items.Add(clr.Name)
    Next
    ComboBoxColors.SelectedIndex = 0
  End Sub

  Private _options As New ArrayList

  Private Sub ButtonGetOptions_Click(ByVal sender As Object, _
                              ByVal e As System.EventArgs) _
                              Handles ButtonGetOptions.Click
    _options = _orderSystem.GetOptions(ComboBoxModels.Text, ComboBoxStyles.Text)
    TextBoxOptions.Text = ""
    If _options Is Nothing Then Return

    Dim items As New ArrayList
    For Each pItems As PricedItem() In _options
      For Each pItem As PricedItem In pItems
        items.Add(pItem)
      Next
    Next

    ' show options in the textbox
    Dim lines(items.Count) As String
    For i As Integer = 0 To items.Count - 1
      lines(i) = DirectCast(items(i), PricedItem).Name
    Next
    TextBoxOptions.Lines = lines
  End Sub
```

```vb
    Private Sub ButtonSubmitOrder_Click(ByVal sender As Object, _
                                  ByVal e As System.EventArgs) _
                                  Handles ButtonSubmitOrder.Click
      Dim requestedOptions As PricedItem()
      If _options.Count > 0 Then
        ' convert an array of PriceItem arrays into a PricedItem array
        Dim items As New ArrayList
        For Each pItems As PricedItem() In _options
          For Each pItem As PricedItem In pItems
            items.Add(pItem)
          Next
          requestedOptions = DirectCast(items.ToArray(GetType(PricedItem) ), _
                                  PricedItem())
        Next
      Else
        requestedOptions = New PricedItem() {New PricedItem("Option1", 11), _
                                  New PricedItem("Option2", 22) }
      End If
      Dim clr As Color = Color.FromName(ComboBoxColors.Text)
      _orderSystem.SubmitOrder(ComboBoxModels.Text, ComboBoxStyles.Text, _
                                  clr, requestedOptions)
      DisplayQueuedMessages()
    End Sub

    Private Sub DisplayQueuedMessages()
      ListViewQueuedMessages.Items.Clear()

      Dim messages As System.Messaging.Message() = _orderSystem.GetAllQueuedMessages()
      Dim formatter As System.Messaging.XmlMessageFormatter
      formatter = New System.Messaging.XmlMessageFormatter( _
                            New Type() {GetType(WorkOrder)})

      For Each message As System.Messaging.Message In messages
        message.Formatter = formatter
        Dim wo As WorkOrder = DirectCast(message.Body, WorkOrder)
        Dim item As New ListViewItem(wo.Model)
        item.SubItems.Add(wo.Style)
        item.SubItems.Add(wo.Color)
        Dim options As String = String.Empty
        For Each opt As PricedItem In wo.Options
          options += opt.Name + ";"
        Next
        item.SubItems.Add(options)
        ListViewQueuedMessages.Items.Add(item)
      Next
    End Sub

    Private Sub ButtonClearQueue_Click(ByVal sender As Object, _
                                  ByVal e As System.EventArgs) _
                                  Handles ButtonClearQueue.Click
      _orderSystem.ClearQueuedMessages()
      DisplayQueuedMessages()
    End Sub
```

```vbnet
Private Sub ButtonRefreshList_Click(ByVal sender As Object, _
                                    ByVal e As System.EventArgs) _
                                    Handles ButtonRefreshList.Click
    DisplayQueuedMessages()
End Sub
End Class
```

The OrderProcessor Hosting Component

```vbnet
'   app.config
```

```xml
<configuration>
    <system.runtime.remoting>
        <application>
            <service>
                <wellknown type="OrderProcessor.OrderSystem,
                            OrderProcessor " mode="Singleton"
                            url="tcp://localhost:8011/AsapOrders"/>
            </service>
        </application>
    </system.runtime.remoting>
</configuration>
```

```vbnet
'   class FormMain

Public Class FormMain
  Inherits System.Windows.Forms.Form

  Public Sub New()
    MyBase.New()

    'This call is required by the Windows Form Designer.
    InitializeComponent()

    'configure the server component to listen for orders
    Dim channel As New TcpChannel(8011)
    ChannelServices.RegisterChannel(channel)
    RemotingConfiguration.RegisterWellKnownServiceType( _
                                GetType(OrderSystem), _
                                "AsapOrders", _
                                WellKnownObjectMode.Singleton)
  End Sub

  '  …

  Private Sub TimerOrdersReceived_Tick(ByVal sender As Object, _
                                ByVal e As System.EventArgs) _
                                Handles TimerOrdersReceived.Tick
    UpdateOrdersReceived()
  End Sub
```

```
Private _ordersReceived As Integer
Sub UpdateOrdersReceived()
  Dim c As Integer = OrderSystem.OrdersReceived
  If c = _ordersReceived Then Return

  LabelTotalOrdersReceived.Text = c.ToString()
  _ordersReceived = c
End Sub

End Class
```

The Parts Scheduling Component

When a WorkOrder is posted to the AsapOrders queue, MSMQ sends a notification to the Parts Scheduling queue. The notification's payload contains a WorkOrder object. The Parts Scheduling component uses the WorkOrder to determine which parts are required to build the vehicle. Class ScheduledPart contains a WorkOrder object and a date indicating when the given part will be available. Figure 13-14 shows the details of the ScheduledPart, WorkOrder, and PricedItem classes.

When an order arrives in the Parts Scheduling queue, the Part Scheduler puts the order in a local Hashtable using the Order ID as the key and an ArrayList as the value. The ArrayList contains all the parts related to the order. See Figure 13-15.

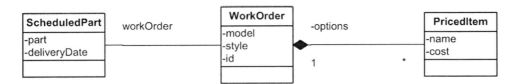

Figure 13-14. *The WorkOrder and PricedItem classes*

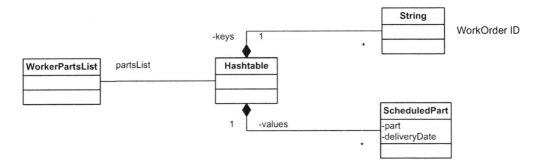

Figure 13-15. *The data structures used to manage WorkOrder with pending parts*

The sample code assumes there are three parts for each order, with hard-coded delivery dates. From a scheduling standpoint, you only care about the delivery date of the part that will be delivered last. Only when this part arrives can the system schedule the vehicle to be assembled. This date is the vehicle assembly date. I'll assume a vehicle can be assembled immediately when all its parts are delivered. To expedite testing, the delivery date for each part is hard-coded to a time in the immediate future.

The Parts Scheduler runs a background thread, keeping an eye on the parts list, to detect when a WorkOrder is ready for assembly. When it finds a WorkOrder that is ready, it is written to the AsapVehiclesToAssembly queue, where it will subsequently be picked up by the next workflow process, which is the VehicleAssembly component. Figure 13-16 shows the UI of the Parts Scheduling component.

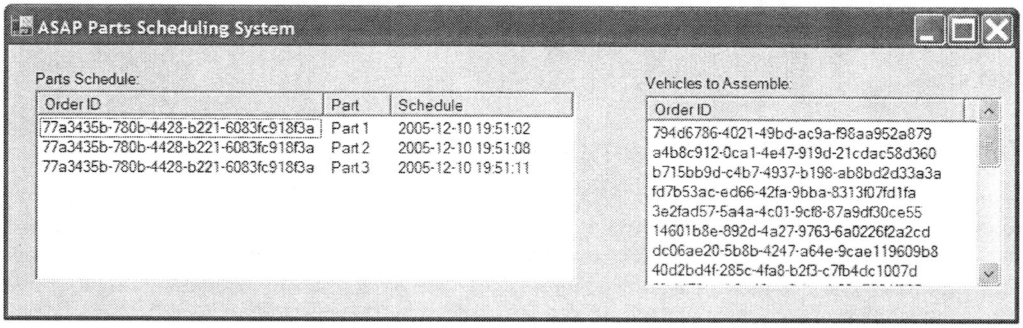

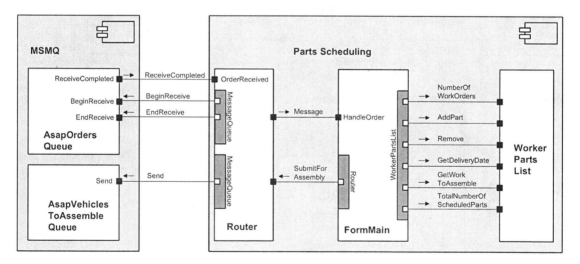

Figure 13-16. *The UI of the Parts Scheduling component*

Figure 13-17 shows the wiring diagram for the Parts Scheduling system.

Figure 13-17. *The wiring diagram of the Parts Scheduling system*

The system uses class Router to encapsulate access to the remote message queues. Router contains no business logic. When an incoming message is posted to the AsapOrders queue, Router fires an event to FormMain. The event notification is sent on a background thread and contains a WorkOrder as the payload. FormMain gives the WorkOrder to WorkerPartsList, which stores the order in a Hashtable. FormMain runs a timer with one-second ticks. On each tick, FormMain checks WorkerPartsList for new orders. If any are found, they are added to the ListView on the right side of FormMain.

C# Code

```
// class FormMain

public class FormMain : System.Windows.Forms.Form
{
  // …

  // manages connections to incoming and outgoing message queues
  Router router;

  // manages a list of scheduled parts
  WorkerPartsList partsList = new WorkerPartsList();

  public FormMain()
  {
    InitializeComponent();

    System.Threading.Thread.CurrentThread.Name = "User Interface";

    router = new Router();
    router.OnMessage += new Router.MessageHandler(HandleOrder);

    Thread partsListMonitor = new Thread(new ThreadStart(CheckPartsList));
    partsListMonitor.IsBackground = true;
    partsListMonitor.Name = "PartsListMonitor";
    partsListMonitor.Start();

    DisplayScheduledParts();
    ShowVehiclesReadyForAssembly();
  }

  bool removingPartsFromPartsList;
  void CheckPartsList()
  {
    while (true)
    {
      ArrayList workOrdersReady = partsList.GetWorkToAssemble();
      if (workOrdersReady == null)
      {
        Thread.Sleep(100);
        continue;
      }
      else
      {
        // lock out DisplayScheduledParts from running temporarily
        removingPartsFromPartsList = true;
        // send all ready WorkOrders to next queue
        foreach (WorkOrder workOrder in workOrdersReady)
        {
          partsList.Remove(workOrder);
          router.SubmitForAssembly(workOrder);
        }
```

```
          removingPartsFromPartsList = false;
        }
      }
    }

    //  ...

    [STAThread]
    static void Main()
    {
        Application.Run(new FormMain());
    }

    private void HandleOrder(WorkOrder theWorkOrder)
    {
      // a WorkerOrder has arrived. Add three parts for it, with
      // hard-coded delivery dates

      if (theWorkOrder == null) return;

      // pretend the work order has three parts
      partsList.AddPart(theWorkOrder, "Part 1", DateTime.Now.AddSeconds(3));
      partsList.AddPart(theWorkOrder, "Part 2", DateTime.Now.AddSeconds(6));
      partsList.AddPart(theWorkOrder, "Part 3", DateTime.Now.AddSeconds(9));
    }

    private void timerUpdatePartsScheduled_Tick(object sender, System.EventArgs e)
    {
      DisplayScheduledParts();
      ShowVehiclesReadyForAssembly();
    }

    int scheduledPartsDisplayed = 0;

    private void DisplayScheduledParts()
    {
      if (removingPartsFromPartsList)
        return; // can't display the list while it's being changed

      if (scheduledPartsDisplayed == partsList.TotalNumberOfScheduledParts)
        return;

      listViewPartsSchedule.Items.Clear();

      foreach (ArrayList parts in partsList.List.Values)
      {
        foreach (ScheduledPart part in parts)
        {
          ListViewItem item = new ListViewItem(part.workOrder.Id);
          item.SubItems.Add(part.part);
          item.SubItems.Add(part.deliveryDate.ToString("yyyy-MM-dd HH:mm:ss"));
          listViewPartsSchedule.Items.Add(item);
        }
```

```csharp
      scheduledPartsDisplayed = partsList.TotalNumberOfScheduledParts;
    }
  }

  int vehiclesToAssembleDisplayed = 0;

  void ShowVehiclesReadyForAssembly()
  {
    System.Messaging.Message[] messages = router.GetVehicleAssemblyMessages();

    if (vehiclesToAssembleDisplayed == messages.Length)
      return;

    System.Messaging.XmlMessageFormatter formatter;
    formatter = new System.Messaging.XmlMessageFormatter(new Type[]
                                                {typeof(WorkOrder)} );

    listViewVehiclesToAssemble.Items.Clear();

    foreach (System.Messaging.Message message in messages)
    {
      message.Formatter = formatter;
      WorkOrder workOrder = message.Body as WorkOrder;
      ListViewItem item = new ListViewItem(workOrder.Id);
      listViewVehiclesToAssemble.Items.Add(item);
    }
    vehiclesToAssembleDisplayed = messages.Length;
  }
}

// class ScheduledPart

public class ScheduledPart
{
  public WorkOrder workOrder;
  public string part;
  public DateTime deliveryDate;

  public string Id
  {
    get {return workOrder.Id;}
  }

  public ScheduledPart(WorkOrder theWorkOrder, string thePart,
                       DateTime theDeliveryDate)
  {
    workOrder = theWorkOrder;
    part = thePart;
    deliveryDate = theDeliveryDate;
  }
}
```

```csharp
// class WorkerPartsList

public class WorkerPartsList
{
  // key is WorkOrder ID, value is an ArrayList of ScheduledParts
  Hashtable partsList = new Hashtable();
  public Hashtable List
  {
    get {return partsList;}
  }

  // number of WorkOrders that are waiting for parts
  public int NumberOfWorkOrders
  {
    get {return partsList.Count;}
  }

  // number of WorkOrders that are waiting for parts
  public int TotalNumberOfScheduledParts
  {
    get
    {
      int count = 0;
      foreach (ArrayList scheduledParts in partsList.Values)
        count += scheduledParts.Count;
      return count;
    }
  }

  public void AddPart(WorkOrder theWorkOrder, string thePart,
                      DateTime theDeliveryDate)
  {
    ScheduledPart part = new ScheduledPart(theWorkOrder, thePart, theDeliveryDate);

    // see if this WorkOrder already has pending parts
    ArrayList pendingParts = partsList[theWorkOrder.Id] as ArrayList;
    if (pendingParts == null)
    {
      // no: create a new list and add it to the list
      pendingParts = new ArrayList();
      partsList.Add(theWorkOrder.Id, pendingParts);
    }

    pendingParts.Add(part);
  }

  public void Remove(WorkOrder theWorkOrder)
  {
      partsList.Remove(theWorkOrder.Id);
  }
```

```
// find the date of the latest part to
// be delivered for a given WorkOrder
public DateTime GetDeliveryDate(string theWorkOrderId)
{
  ArrayList scheduledParts = partsList[theWorkOrderId] as ArrayList;
  if (scheduledParts == null) return DateTime.MinValue;

  DateTime latestDate = DateTime.MinValue;
  foreach (ScheduledPart part in scheduledParts)
  {
    if (part.deliveryDate > latestDate)
      latestDate = part.deliveryDate;
  }
  return latestDate;
}

// returns an ArrayList of WorkOrders whose parts are available now
public ArrayList GetWorkToAssemble()
{
  ArrayList workOrdersReady = null;

  foreach (string workOrderId in partsList.Keys)
  {
    DateTime deliveryDate = GetDeliveryDate(workOrderId);
    if (deliveryDate == DateTime.MinValue) continue;
    if (deliveryDate <= DateTime.Now)
    {
      // WorkOrder is ready
      if (workOrdersReady == null)
        workOrdersReady = new ArrayList();
      ArrayList parts = partsList[workOrderId] as ArrayList;
      if (parts.Count > 0)
      {
        // if there is at least one scheduled part, get its WorkOrder
        // parent. All the parts are for the same WorkOrderID
        ScheduledPart part = parts[0] as ScheduledPart;
        workOrdersReady.Add(part.workOrder);
      }
    }
  }
  return workOrdersReady;
}
}


// class Router

public class Router : System.ComponentModel.Component
{
  private System.Messaging.MessageQueue messageQueueVehiclesToAssemble;
  private System.Messaging.MessageQueue messageQueueOrders;
```

```csharp
// …
public Router(System.ComponentModel.IContainer container)
{
  // …
  // start waiting for the first incoming message
  messageQueueOrders.BeginReceive();
}

public Router()
{
  InitializeComponent();

  // start waiting for the first incoming message
  messageQueueOrders.BeginReceive();
}

private void InitializeComponent()
{
  this.messageQueueVehiclesToAssemble = new System.Messaging.MessageQueue();
  this.messageQueueOrders = new System.Messaging.MessageQueue();
  //
  // messageQueueVehiclesToAssemble
  //
  this.messageQueueVehiclesToAssemble.Path =
        "alessandra\\Private$\\AsapVehiclesToAssemble";
  //
  // messageQueueOrders
  //
  this.messageQueueOrders.Path = "alessandra\\Private$\\AsapOrders";
  this.messageQueueOrders.ReceiveCompleted +=
      new System.Messaging.ReceiveCompletedEventHandler(this.OrderReceived);

}

public void SubmitForAssembly(WorkOrder theWorkOrder)
{
  messageQueueVehiclesToAssemble.Send(theWorkOrder);
}

public System.Messaging.Message[] GetVehicleAssemblyMessages()
{
  return messageQueueVehiclesToAssemble.GetAllMessages();
}

private void OrderReceived(object sender,
                          System.Messaging.ReceiveCompletedEventArgs e)
{
  System.Messaging.XmlMessageFormatter formatter =
    new System.Messaging.XmlMessageFormatter(new Type[] {typeof(WorkOrder)});
  System.Messaging.Message msg = messageQueueOrders.EndReceive(e.AsyncResult);
  msg.Formatter = formatter;

  WorkOrder workOrder = msg.Body as WorkOrder;
```

```csharp
  // start waiting for the next message
  messageQueueOrders.BeginReceive();

  FireMessage(workOrder);
}

public delegate void MessageHandler(WorkOrder theWorkOrder);
public event MessageHandler OnMessage;
void FireMessage(WorkOrder theWorkOrder)
{
  if (OnMessage != null)
    OnMessage(theWorkOrder);
}
}
```

VB .NET Code

```vbnet
' class FormMain

Public Class FormMain
  Inherits System.Windows.Forms.Form

  ' manages connections to incoming and outgoing message queues
  Private _router As Router

  ' manages a list of scheduled parts
  Private _partsList As New WorkerPartsList

  Private _removingPartsFromPartsList As Boolean

  Private Sub CheckPartsList()
    While (True)
      Dim workOrdersReady As ArrayList = _partsList.GetWorkToAssemble()
      If workOrdersReady Is Nothing Then
        System.Threading.Thread.Sleep(100)
      Else
        ' lock out DisplayScheduledParts from running temporarily
        _removingPartsFromPartsList = True
        ' send all ready WorkOrders to next queue
        For Each wo As WorkOrder In workOrdersReady
          _partsList.Remove(wo)
          _router.SubmitForAssembly(wo)
        Next
        _removingPartsFromPartsList = False
      End If
    End While
  End Sub

  Private Sub HandleOrder(ByVal theWorkOrder As WorkOrder)
    ' a WorkerOrder has arrived. Add three parts for it, with
    ' hard-coded delivery dates

    If theWorkOrder Is Nothing Then Return
```

```vb
    ' pretend the work order has three parts
    _partsList.AddPart(theWorkOrder, "Part 1", DateTime.Now.AddSeconds(3))
    _partsList.AddPart(theWorkOrder, "Part 2", DateTime.Now.AddSeconds(6))
    _partsList.AddPart(theWorkOrder, "Part 3", DateTime.Now.AddSeconds(9))
End Sub

Public Sub New()
  MyBase.New()

  'This call is required by the Windows Form Designer.
  InitializeComponent()

  System.Threading.Thread.CurrentThread.Name = "User Interface"

  _router = New Router
  AddHandler _router.OnMessage, AddressOf HandleOrder

  Dim partsListMonitor As New System.Threading.Thread(AddressOf CheckPartsList)
  partsListMonitor.IsBackground = True
  partsListMonitor.Name = "PartsListMonitor"
  partsListMonitor.Start()

  DisplayScheduledParts()
  ShowVehiclesReadyForAssembly()
End Sub

' …


Private Sub TimerUpdatePartsScheduled_Tick( _
                  ByVal sender As Object, _
                  ByVal e As System.EventArgs) _
                  Handles TimerUpdatePartsScheduled.Tick
  DisplayScheduledParts()
  ShowVehiclesReadyForAssembly()
End Sub

Private _scheduledPartsDisplayed As Integer = 0

Private Sub DisplayScheduledParts()
  If _removingPartsFromPartsList Then
    Return ' can't display the list while it's being changed
  End If

  If _scheduledPartsDisplayed = _partsList.TotalNumberOfScheduledParts Then
    Return
  End If

  ListViewPartsSchedule.Items.Clear()

  For Each parts As ArrayList In _partsList.List.Values
    For Each part As ScheduledPart In parts
      Dim item As New ListViewItem(part._workOrder.Id)
      item.SubItems.Add(part._part)
      item.SubItems.Add(part._deliveryDate.ToString("yyyy-MM-dd HH:mm:ss"))
      ListViewPartsSchedule.Items.Add(item)
```

```vbnet
      Next
        _scheduledPartsDisplayed = _partsList.TotalNumberOfScheduledParts
    Next
  End Sub


  Private _vehiclesToAssembleDisplayed As Integer = 0

  Sub ShowVehiclesReadyForAssembly()
    Dim messages As System.Messaging.Message() = _
        _router.GetVehicleAssemblyMessages()

    If (_vehiclesToAssembleDisplayed = messages.Length) Then
      Return
    End If

    Dim formatter As System.Messaging.XmlMessageFormatter
    formatter = New System.Messaging.XmlMessageFormatter( _
                    New Type() {GetType(WorkOrder)})

    ListViewVehiclesToAssemble.Items.Clear()

    For Each message As System.Messaging.Message In messages
      message.Formatter = formatter
      Dim wo As WorkOrder = DirectCast(message.Body, WorkOrder)
      Dim item As New ListViewItem(wo.Id)
      ListViewVehiclesToAssemble.Items.Add(item)
    Next
    _vehiclesToAssembleDisplayed = messages.Length
  End Sub

End Class

' class ScheduledPart

Public Class ScheduledPart
  Public _workOrder As WorkOrder
  Public _part As String
  Public _deliveryDate As DateTime

  Public ReadOnly Property Id() As String
    Get
      Return _workOrder.Id
    End Get
  End Property

  Public Sub New(ByVal theWorkOrder As WorkOrder, ByVal thePart As String, _
                     ByVal theDeliveryDate As DateTime)
    _workOrder = theWorkOrder
    _part = thePart
    _deliveryDate = theDeliveryDate
  End Sub
End Class
```

```vbnet
' class WorkerPartsList

Public Class WorkerPartsList
  ' key is WorkOrder ID, value is an ArrayList of ScheduledParts
  Private _partsList As New Hashtable
  Public ReadOnly Property List() As Hashtable
    Get
      Return _partsList
    End Get
  End Property

  ' number of WorkOrders that are waiting for parts
  Public ReadOnly Property NumberOfWorkOrders() As Integer
    Get
      Return _partsList.Count
    End Get
  End Property

  ' number of WorkOrders that are waiting for parts
  Public ReadOnly Property TotalNumberOfScheduledParts() As Integer
    Get
      Dim count As Integer = 0
      For Each scheduledParts As ArrayList In _partsList.Values
        count += scheduledParts.Count
      Next
      Return count
    End Get
  End Property

  Public Sub AddPart(ByVal theWorkOrder As WorkOrder, ByVal thePart As String, _
                 ByVal theDeliveryDate As DateTime)
    Dim part As New ScheduledPart(theWorkOrder, thePart, theDeliveryDate)

    ' see if this WorkOrder already has pending parts
    Dim pendingParts As ArrayList = _
        DirectCast(_partsList(theWorkOrder.Id), ArrayList)
    If pendingParts Is Nothing Then
      ' no: create a new list and add it to the list
      pendingParts = New ArrayList
      _partsList.Add(theWorkOrder.Id, pendingParts)
    End If

    pendingParts.Add(part)
  End Sub

  Public Sub Remove(ByVal theWorkOrder As WorkOrder)
    _partsList.Remove(theWorkOrder.Id)
  End Sub
```

```vbnet
' find the date of the latest part to
' be delivered for a given WorkOrder
Public Function GetDeliveryDate(ByVal theWorkOrderId As String) As DateTime
    Dim scheduledParts As ArrayList = _
        DirectCast(_partsList(theWorkOrderId), ArrayList)
    If scheduledParts Is Nothing Then Return DateTime.MinValue

    Dim latestDate As DateTime = DateTime.MinValue
    For Each part As ScheduledPart In scheduledParts
      If DateTime.op_GreaterThan(part._deliveryDate, latestDate) Then
        latestDate = part._deliveryDate
      End If
    Next
    Return latestDate
End Function

' returns an ArrayList of WorkOrders whose parts are available now
Public Function GetWorkToAssemble() As ArrayList
    Dim workOrdersReady As ArrayList = Nothing

    For Each workOrderId As String In _partsList.Keys
      Dim deliveryDate As DateTime = GetDeliveryDate(workOrderId)
      If DateTime.op_GreaterThan(deliveryDate, DateTime.MinValue) AndAlso _
        DateTime.op_LessThanOrEqual(deliveryDate, DateTime.Now) Then
        ' WorkOrder is ready
        If workOrdersReady Is Nothing Then
          workOrdersReady = New ArrayList
        End If
        Dim parts As ArrayList = DirectCast(_partsList(workOrderId), ArrayList)
        If (parts.Count > 0) Then
          ' if there is at least one scheduled part, get its WorkOrder
          ' parent. All the parts are for the same WorkOrderID
          Dim part As ScheduledPart = DirectCast(parts(0), ScheduledPart)
          workOrdersReady.Add(part._workOrder)
        End If
      End If
    Next
    Return workOrdersReady
  End Function
End Class


' class Router

Public Class Router
  Inherits System.ComponentModel.Component

  Public Sub SubmitForAssembly(ByVal theWorkOrder As WorkOrder)
    MessageQueueVehiclesToAssemble.Send(theWorkOrder)
  End Sub
```

```vb
    Public Function GetVehicleAssemblyMessages() As System.Messaging.Message()
      Return MessageQueueVehiclesToAssemble.GetAllMessages()
    End Function

    Public Sub New(ByVal Container As System.ComponentModel.IContainer)
      MyClass.New()

      'Required for Windows.Forms Class Composition Designer support
      Container.Add(Me)

      ' start waiting for the first incoming message
      MessageQueueOrders.BeginReceive()
    End Sub

    Public Sub New()
      MyBase.New()

      'This call is required by the Component Designer.
      InitializeComponent()

      ' start waiting for the first incoming message
      MessageQueueOrders.BeginReceive()
    End Sub

    Private Sub InitializeComponent()
      Me.MessageQueueOrders = New System.Messaging.MessageQueue
      Me.MessageQueueVehiclesToAssemble = New System.Messaging.MessageQueue
      '
      'MessageQueueOrders
      '
      Me.MessageQueueOrders.Path = "alessandra\Private$\AsapOrders"
      '
      'MessageQueueVehiclesToAssemble
      '
      Me.MessageQueueVehiclesToAssemble.Path = _
            "alessandra\Private$\AsapVehiclesToAssemble"

    End Sub

#End Region

    Private Sub MessageQueueOrders_ReceiveCompleted( _
                      ByVal sender As Object, _
                      ByVal e As System.Messaging.ReceiveCompletedEventArgs) _
                      Handles MessageQueueOrders.ReceiveCompleted
      Dim formatter As New System.Messaging.XmlMessageFormatter( _
                        New Type() {GetType(WorkOrder)})
      Dim msg As System.Messaging.Message = _
                        MessageQueueOrders.EndReceive(e.AsyncResult)
      msg.Formatter = formatter
```

```
    Dim wo As WorkOrder = DirectCast(msg.Body, WorkOrder)

    ' start waiting for the next message
    MessageQueueOrders.BeginReceive()

    FireMessage(wo)
  End Sub

  Public Event OnMessage(ByVal theWorkOrder As WorkOrder)
  Private Sub FireMessage(ByVal theWorkOrder As WorkOrder)
    RaiseEvent OnMessage(theWorkOrder)
  End Sub

End Class
```

The Vehicle Assembly Component

When a WorkOrder is posted to the AsapVehiclesToAssemble queue, a notification is sent to the Vehicle Assembly component. In a production system, the Vehicle Assembly component interacts with the manufacturing floor, downloading instructions to the assembly robots. After completing the vehicle assembly, the WorkOrder is sent to the next stop in the workflow process to generate the customer's invoice. In this case study, I ignore the details regarding the physical vehicle assembly and simply pass the WorkOrder to the AsapVehiclesToInvoice queue directly. The Vehicle Assembly component uses a Router to interact with the MSMQ message queues, as the Parts Scheduling component did. Figure 13-18 shows the design of the simple Vehicle Assembly system.

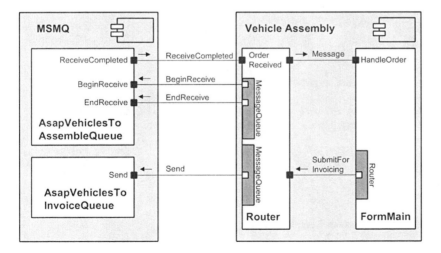

Figure 13-18. *The wiring diagram of the Vehicle Assembly system*

FormMain is the UI component of Vehicle Assembly. In a production system, the UI would show all the details about the vehicle assembly process. In this example, the UI is just a blank form.

C# Code

// class FormMain

```csharp
public class FormMain : System.Windows.Forms.Form
{
  // …

  // manages connections to incoming and outgoing message queues
  Router router;

  public FormMain()
  {
    InitializeComponent();

    router = new Router();
    router.OnMessage += new Router.MessageHandler(HandleOrder);
  }

  private void HandleOrder(WorkOrder theWorkOrder)
  {
    // a WorkerOrder has arrived. Skip the actual vehicle
    // assembly details and just issue an invoice
    router.SubmitForInvoicing(theWorkOrder);
  }

  // …
}
```

// class Router

```csharp
public class Router : System.ComponentModel.Component
{
  private System.Messaging.MessageQueue messageQueueVehiclesToAssemble;
  private System.Messaging.MessageQueue messageQueueVehiclesToInvoice;

  // …

  public Router()
  {
    // …
    messageQueueVehiclesToAssemble.BeginReceive();
  }

  private void InitializeComponent()
  {
    this.messageQueueVehiclesToAssemble = new System.Messaging.MessageQueue();
    this.messageQueueVehiclesToInvoice = new System.Messaging.MessageQueue();
    //
    // messageQueueVehiclesToAssemble
    //
    this.messageQueueVehiclesToAssemble.Path =
        "FormatName:DIRECT=OS:alessandra\\private$\\asapvehiclestoassemble";
```

```csharp
    this.messageQueueVehiclesToAssemble.ReceiveCompleted +=
            new System.Messaging.ReceiveCompletedEventHandler(this.OrderReceived);
    //
    // messageQueueVehiclesToInvoice
    //
    this.messageQueueVehiclesToInvoice.Path =
            "FormatName:DIRECT=OS:alessandra\\private$\\asapvehiclestoinvoice";

}

public void SubmitForInvoicing(WorkOrder theWorkOrder)
{
  messageQueueVehiclesToInvoice.Send(theWorkOrder);
}

private void OrderReceived(object sender,
                          System.Messaging.ReceiveCompletedEventArgs e)
{
  System.Messaging.XmlMessageFormatter formatter =
            new System.Messaging.XmlMessageFormatter(new Type[]
                                                {typeof(WorkOrder) } );
  System.Messaging.Message msg =
              messageQueueVehiclesToAssemble.EndReceive(e.AsyncResult);
  msg.Formatter = formatter;

  WorkOrder workOrder = msg.Body as WorkOrder;

  // start waiting for the next message
  messageQueueVehiclesToAssemble.BeginReceive();

  FireMessage(workOrder);
}

public delegate void MessageHandler(WorkOrder theWorkOrder);
public event MessageHandler OnMessage;
void FireMessage(WorkOrder theWorkOrder)
{
  if (OnMessage != null)
    OnMessage(theWorkOrder);
}
}
```

VB .NET Code

```vbnet
'  class FormMain

Public Class FormMain
  Inherits System.Windows.Forms.Form

  ' manages connections to incoming and outgoing message queues
  Private _router As Router

  Public Sub New()
    MyBase.New()
```

```
    'This call is required by the Windows Form Designer.
    InitializeComponent()

    _router = New Router
    AddHandler _router.OnMessage, AddressOf HandleOrder
  End Sub

  Private Sub HandleOrder(ByVal theWorkOrder As WorkOrder)
    ' a WorkerOrder has arrived. Skip the actual vehicle
    ' assembly details and just issue an invoice
    _router.SubmitForInvoicing(theWorkOrder)
  End Sub

  ' ...

End Class


'  class Router

Public Class Router
  Inherits System.ComponentModel.Component

  Public Sub New(ByVal Container As System.ComponentModel.IContainer)
    MyClass.New()

    'Required for Windows.Forms Class Composition Designer support
    Container.Add(Me)

    MessageQueueVehiclesToAssemble.BeginReceive()
  End Sub

  Public Sub New()
    MyBase.New()

    'This call is required by the Component Designer.
    InitializeComponent()

    MessageQueueVehiclesToAssemble.BeginReceive()
  End Sub

  ' ...

  Private Sub InitializeComponent()
    Me.MessageQueueVehiclesToInvoice = New System.Messaging.MessageQueue
    Me.MessageQueueVehiclesToAssemble = New System.Messaging.MessageQueue
    '
    'MessageQueueVehiclesToInvoice
```

```vbnet
        Me.MessageQueueVehiclesToInvoice.Path = _
            "FormatName:DIRECT=OS:alessandra\private$\asapvehiclestoinvoice"

        'MessageQueueVehiclesToAssemble

        Me.MessageQueueVehiclesToAssemble.Path = _
            "FormatName:DIRECT=OS:alessandra\private$\asapvehiclestoassemble"

    End Sub

#End Region

    Public Sub SubmitForInvoicing(ByVal theWorkOrder As WorkOrder)
        MessageQueueVehiclesToInvoice.Send(theWorkOrder)
    End Sub

    Private Sub MessageQueueVehiclesToAssemble_ReceiveCompleted( _
                        ByVal sender As Object, _
                        ByVal e As System.Messaging.ReceiveCompletedEventArgs) _
                        Handles MessageQueueVehiclesToAssemble.ReceiveCompleted
        Dim formatter As New System.Messaging.XmlMessageFormatter( _
                            New Type() {GetType(WorkOrder)})
        Dim msg As System.Messaging.Message = _
                        MessageQueueVehiclesToAssemble.EndReceive(e.AsyncResult)
        msg.Formatter = formatter

        Dim wo As WorkOrder = DirectCast(msg.Body, WorkOrder)

        ' start waiting for the next message
        MessageQueueVehiclesToAssemble.BeginReceive()

        FireMessage(wo)
    End Sub

    Public Event OnMessage(ByVal theWorkOrder As WorkOrder)
    Private Sub FireMessage(ByVal theWorkOrder As WorkOrder)
        RaiseEvent OnMessage(theWorkOrder)
    End Sub

End Class
```

The Invoicing Component

When the Vehicle Assembly component posts a WorkOrder to the AsapVehiclesToInvoice queue, a notification is sent to the Invoicing component, which in a production system would generate the invoice, print it, and send it to the customer. In this simplified case study, the Invoicing component limits itself to displaying some information on the screen about the vehicle ordered, as shown in Figure 13-19.

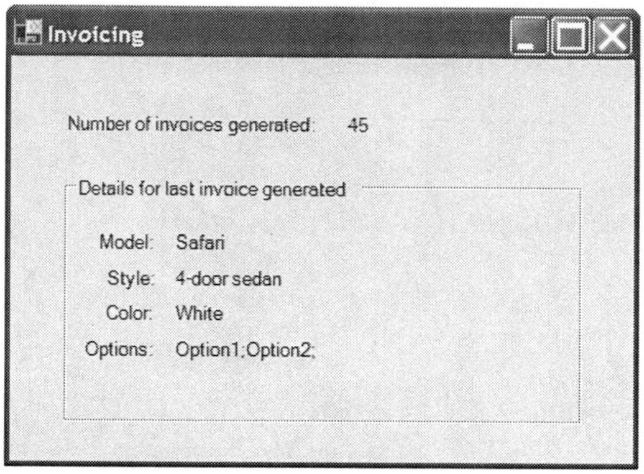

Invoicing

Number of invoices generated: 45

Details for last invoice generated

Model: Safari

Style: 4-door sedan

Color: White

Options: Option1;Option2;

Figure 13-19. *The UI of the Invoicing component*

The details regarding the actual generation of an invoice are not of particular interest here and were omitted. The design of the Invoicing component is fairly straightforward and has much in common with the Vehicle Assembly system, as you can see from the wiring diagram in Figure 13-20.

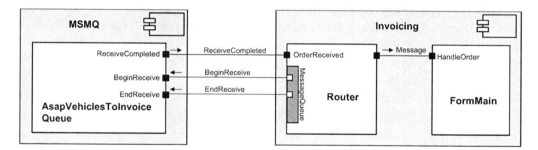

Figure 13-20. *The wiring diagram of the Invoicing component*

C# Code

```csharp
// class FormMain

public class FormMain : System.Windows.Forms.Form
{
  // …

  // manages connections to incoming and outgoing message queues
  Router router;

  public FormMain()
  {
    InitializeComponent();
    System.Threading.Thread.CurrentThread.Name = "User Interface";
```

```
      router = new Router();
      router.OnMessage += new Router.MessageHandler(HandleOrder);
    }

    delegate void WorkOrderHandler(WorkOrder theWorkOrder);
    private void HandleOrder(WorkOrder theWorkOrder)
    {
      // process order on the UI thread
      this.Invoke(new WorkOrderHandler(DoHandleOrder), new object[] {theWorkOrder});
    }

    int invoiceCount = 0;
    private void DoHandleOrder(WorkOrder theWorkOrder)
    {
      // just update the displayed info
      invoiceCount++;
      labelInvoicesGenerated.Text = invoiceCount.ToString();
      labelModel.Text = theWorkOrder.Model;
      labelStyle.Text = theWorkOrder.Style;
      labelColor.Text = theWorkOrder.Color;

      string options = string.Empty;
      for (int i = 0; i < theWorkOrder.Options.Length; i++)
        options += string.Format("{0};", theWorkOrder.Options[i].Name);
      labelOptions.Text = options;
    }


    [STAThread]
    static void Main()
    {
        Application.Run(new FormMain());
    }
  }
}


// class Router

public class Router : System.ComponentModel.Component
{
    private System.Messaging.MessageQueue messageQueueVehiclesToInvoice;

    // ...


    public Router(System.ComponentModel.IContainer container)
    {
      // ...
      messageQueueVehiclesToInvoice.BeginReceive();
    }
```

```
    public Router()
    {
      // …
        messageQueueVehiclesToInvoice.BeginReceive();
    }

    private void InitializeComponent()
    {
        this.messageQueueVehiclesToInvoice = new System.Messaging.MessageQueue();
        //
        // messageQueueVehiclesToInvoice
        //
        this.messageQueueVehiclesToInvoice.Path =
            "FormatName:DIRECT=OS:alessandra\\private$\\asapvehiclestoinvoice";
        this.messageQueueVehiclesToInvoice.ReceiveCompleted +=
            new System.Messaging.ReceiveCompletedEventHandler(this.OrderReceived);

    }

    private void OrderReceived(object sender,
                              System.Messaging.ReceiveCompletedEventArgs e)
    {
      System.Messaging.XmlMessageFormatter formatter =
        new System.Messaging.XmlMessageFormatter(new Type[] {typeof(WorkOrder)});
      System.Messaging.Message msg =
                  messageQueueVehiclesToInvoice.EndReceive(e.AsyncResult);
      msg.Formatter = formatter;

      WorkOrder workOrder = msg.Body as WorkOrder;

      // start waiting for the next message
      messageQueueVehiclesToInvoice.BeginReceive();

      FireMessage(workOrder);
    }

    public delegate void MessageHandler(WorkOrder theWorkOrder);
    public event MessageHandler OnMessage;
    void FireMessage(WorkOrder theWorkOrder)
    {
      if (OnMessage != null)
        OnMessage(theWorkOrder);
    }
  }
```

VB .NET Code

```
' class FormMain

Public Class FormMain
  Inherits System.Windows.Forms.Form

  ' manages connections to incoming and outgoing message queues
  Private _router As Router
```

```vb
  Public Sub New()
    MyBase.New()

    'This call is required by the Windows Form Designer.
    InitializeComponent()

    _router = New Router
    AddHandler _router.OnMessage, AddressOf HandleOrder
  End Sub

  Private Sub HandleOrder(ByVal theWorkOrder As WorkOrder)
    ' a WorkerOrder has arrived. Skip the actual vehicle
    ' assembly details and just issue an invoice
    _router.SubmitForInvoicing(theWorkOrder)
  End Sub

  ' …
End Class


' class Router

Public Class Router
  Inherits System.ComponentModel.Component

  Public Sub New(ByVal Container As System.ComponentModel.IContainer)
    MyClass.New()

    'Required for Windows.Forms Class Composition Designer support
    Container.Add(Me)

    MessageQueueVehiclesToAssemble.BeginReceive()
  End Sub

  Public Sub New()
    MyBase.New()

    'This call is required by the Component Designer.
    InitializeComponent()

    MessageQueueVehiclesToAssemble.BeginReceive()
  End Sub

      ' …
Private Sub InitializeComponent()
    Me.MessageQueueVehiclesToInvoice = New System.Messaging.MessageQueue
    Me.MessageQueueVehiclesToAssemble = New System.Messaging.MessageQueue
    '
    'MessageQueueVehiclesToInvoice
    '
    Me.MessageQueueVehiclesToInvoice.Path = _
        "FormatName:DIRECT=OS:alessandra\private$\asapvehiclestoinvoice"
```

```
        '
        'MessageQueueVehiclesToAssemble
        '
        Me.MessageQueueVehiclesToAssemble.Path = _
            "FormatName:DIRECT=OS:alessandra\private$\asapvehiclestoassemble"

    End Sub

    Public Sub SubmitForInvoicing(ByVal theWorkOrder As WorkOrder)
        MessageQueueVehiclesToInvoice.Send(theWorkOrder)
    End Sub

    Private Sub MessageQueueVehiclesToAssemble_ReceiveCompleted( _
                        ByVal sender As Object, _
                        ByVal e As System.Messaging.ReceiveCompletedEventArgs) _
                        Handles MessageQueueVehiclesToAssemble.ReceiveCompleted
        Dim formatter As New System.Messaging.XmlMessageFormatter( _
                            New Type() {GetType(WorkOrder)})
        Dim msg As System.Messaging.Message = _
                        MessageQueueVehiclesToAssemble.EndReceive(e.AsyncResult)
        msg.Formatter = formatter

        Dim wo As WorkOrder = DirectCast(msg.Body, WorkOrder)

        ' start waiting for the next message
        MessageQueueVehiclesToAssemble.BeginReceive()

        FireMessage(wo)
    End Sub

    Public Event OnMessage(ByVal theWorkOrder As WorkOrder)
    Private Sub FireMessage(ByVal theWorkOrder As WorkOrder)
        RaiseEvent OnMessage(theWorkOrder)
    End Sub

End Class
```

Common Types Used in the System

The ASAP Cars system, like most systems, relies on a series of UDTs that are used in many of the components. There are only two such UDTs in this case study, but a typical system contains many more. All these types are packaged together in a component called CommonTypes, as shown in Figure 13-21.

By packaging all the commonly used types in a single component, the overall system's coupling is kept at a minimum. The coupling diagram in Figure 13-22 shows the components that are type-coupled to CommonTypes.

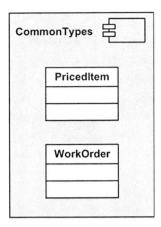

Figure 13-21. *The common user-defined types in CommonTypes*

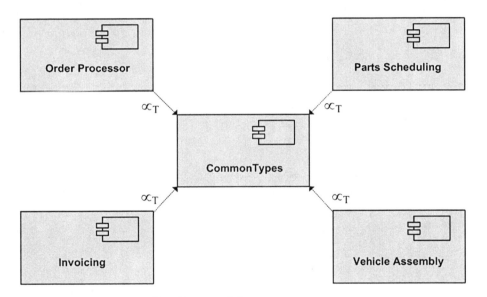

Figure 13-22. *The type-coupling diagram of the system*

The star pattern shows that the system has ideal coupling. None of the outer components are coupled to each other. It is very important to note that the CommonTypes component is not coupled to any other components in the system. Since many components in the system are coupled to the component containing the shared UDTs, circular coupling may occur if a type were added to CommonTypes that type-coupled CommonTypes to other components.

C# Code

```csharp
// class PricedItem

[Serializable]
public class PricedItem
{
  string name;
  public string Name
  {
    get {return name;}
    set {name = value;}
  }

  decimal cost;
  public decimal Cost
  {
    get {return cost;}
    set {cost = value;}
  }

  public override string ToString()
  {
    return name;
  }

  // public default constructor is required in serializable classes
  public PricedItem()
  {
  }

  public PricedItem(string theName, decimal theCost)
  {
    name = theName;
    cost = theCost;
  }
}

// class WorkOrder

[Serializable]
public class WorkOrder
{
  string model;
  public string Model
  {
    get {return model;}
    set {model = value;}
  }
```

```csharp
  string style;
  public string Style
  {
    get {return style;}
    set {style = value;}
  }

  string color;
  public string Color
  {
    get {return color;}
    set {color = value;}
  }

  PricedItem[] options;
  public PricedItem[] Options
  {
    get {return options;}
    set {options = value;}
  }

  string id;
  public string Id
  {
    get {return id;}
    set {id = value;}
  }

  // public default constructor is required in serializable classes
  public WorkOrder()
  {
  }

  public WorkOrder(string theModel, string theStyle,
                   Color theColor, PricedItem[ ] theOptions)
  {
    model = theModel;
    style = theStyle;
    color = theColor.Name;
    options = theOptions;

    id = Guid.NewGuid().ToString();
  }
}
```

VB .NET Code

```vbnet
' class PricedItem

<Serializable()> _
Public Class PricedItem
```

```vbnet
    Private _name As String
    Public Property Name() As String
      Get
        Return _name
      End Get
      Set(ByVal Value As String)
        _name = Value
      End Set
    End Property

    Private _cost As Decimal
    Public Property Cost() As Decimal
      Get
        Return _cost
      End Get
      Set(ByVal Value As Decimal)
        _cost = Value
      End Set
    End Property

    Public Overrides Function ToString() As String
      Return _name
    End Function

    ' public default constructor is required in serializable classes
    Public Sub New()
    End Sub

    Public Sub New(ByVal theName As String, ByVal theCost As Decimal)
      _name = theName
      _cost = theCost
    End Sub
End Class

'   class WorkOrder

<Serializable()> _
Public Class WorkOrder

  Private _model As String
  Public Property Model() As String
    Get
      Return _model
    End Get
    Set(ByVal Value As String)
      _model = Value
    End Set
  End Property

  Private _style As String
  Public Property Style() As String
    Get
      Return _style
    End Get
```

```vbnet
      Set(ByVal Value As String)
        _style = Value
      End Set
    End Property

    Private _color As String
    Public Property Color() As String
      Get
        Return _color
      End Get
      Set(ByVal Value As String)
        _color = Value
      End Set
    End Property

    Private _options As PricedItem()
    Public Property Options() As PricedItem()
      Get
        Return _options
      End Get
      Set(ByVal Value As PricedItem())
        _options = Value
      End Set
    End Property

    Private _id As String
    Public Property Id() As String
      Get
        Return _id
      End Get
      Set(ByVal Value As String)
        _id = Value
      End Set
    End Property

    ' public default constructor is required in serializable classes
    Public Sub New()
    End Sub

    Public Sub New(ByVal theModel As String, _
                   ByVal theStyle As String, _
                   ByVal theColor As System.Drawing.Color, _
                   ByVal theOptions As PricedItem())
      _model = theModel
      _style = theStyle
      _color = theColor.Name
      _options = theOptions

      _id = Guid.NewGuid().ToString()
    End Sub
End Class
```

Testing the Complete System

The central notification server that ties the whole system together in this case study is Microsoft MSMQ. You won't be able to run the case study unless you have MSMQ in your local environment somewhere. Before you try to run the code, you need to configure the Microsoft MSMQ queue paths. If you download the book's code, the server-side components by default reference MSMQ queues that won't exist in your system (barring a miracle). In my environment, MSMQ runs on a server named "Alessandra." On this server, I configured a number of private MSMSQ queues with various names. You need to set up equivalent private queues on your MSMQ server. Each Router component in the server-side projects has one or more MessageQueue objects. Each object points to a given MSMQ queue. To change a queue path, open a Router in the Forms Designer and select the MessageQueue object, as shown in Figure 13-23.

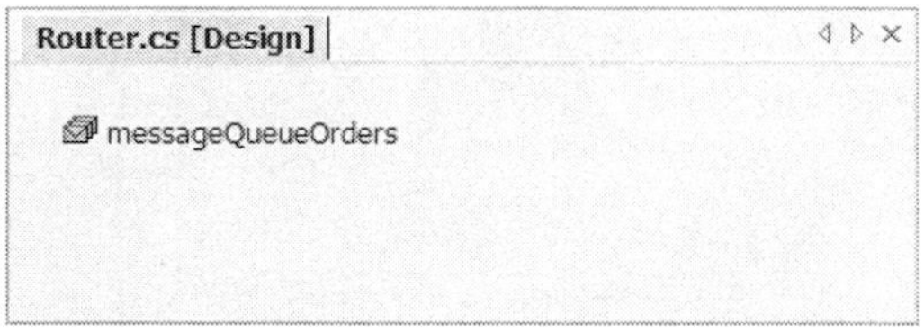

Figure 13-23. *Selecting a MessageQueue object*

The MessageQueue properties will appear something like Figure 13-24.

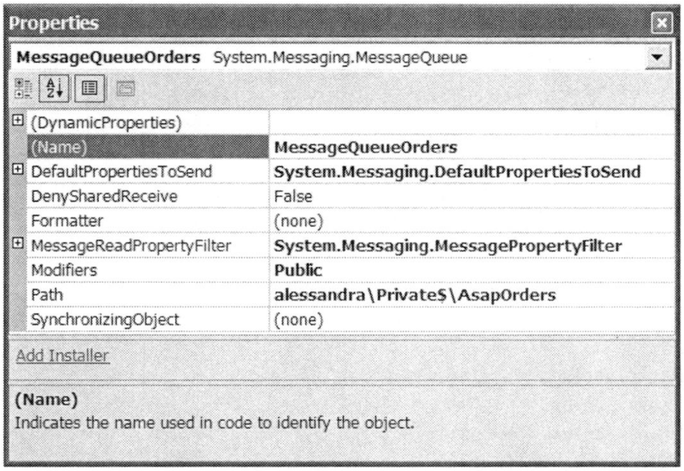

Figure 13-24. *The default properties of a MessageQueue*

Change the Path property to reference the computer on which you're running MSMQ. Make sure the queue name you choose corresponds to one you created in MSMQ. Also, make sure you change the paths of all the MessageQueue objects on all the various Router components. If you configure a path incorrectly, errors occur at run time.

To test the system, you need to run several programs at once. Visual Studio allows you to designate more than one program as the Startup Project. You can also control the order in which the various programs start. To designate multiple Startup Projects, right-click on the Solution node in the Solution Explorer. From the context menu, select the command Set Startup Projects. You'll see the dialog shown in Figure 13-25.

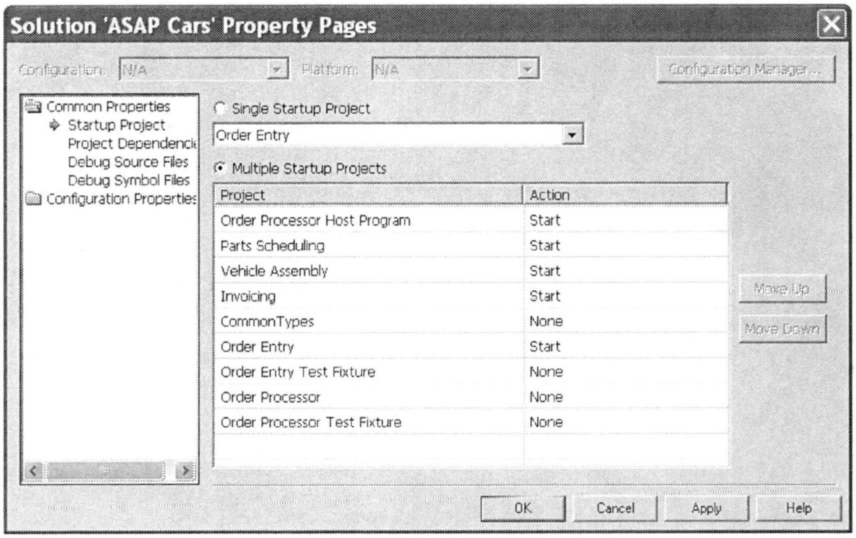

Figure 13-25. *Configuring the Startup Projects in Visual Studio*

Using the Move Up and Move Down buttons, reorder the projects as shown in the figure. For each project you want to run, use its drop-down box and set the Action parameter to Start. Close the dialog box and click the Run button on the toolbar. All the selected programs will start in the designated order, and you can experiment with the various components in the case study.

Summary

In this case study, I've shown a fairly small distributed system, whose individual components are all very simple. The complexity of the overall system—like most distributed systems—is due mainly to the interactions between the various parts. While class diagrams are useful to describe the design of individual components, wiring diagrams are generally more helpful in depicting the whole system.

Software development is one of those activities that just seems to be inherently complicated, so anything you can do to simplify the job is useful. Using events to avoid coupling between the key parts of a system is often a great way to simplify design, testing, and maintenance. My hope is that you finish reading this book feeling that event-based programming is not just a fad, but also a reasonable way to create software in today's world of shrinking budgets, timelines, and product shelf lives. Go for it!

APPENDIX A

■■■

Glossary

ADL	Architecture Description Language
AI	artificial intelligence
ALC	algorithmic logic coupling
AMI	asynchronous method invocation
API	Application Programming Interface
ATC	ambiguous type coupling
BBM	break before make
CBD	component-based development
CLI	Common Language Infrastructure
COM	Component Object Model
CORBA	Common Object Request Broker Architecture
CR/LF	carriage-return/line-feed
DCE	Distributed Computing Environment
DCOM	Distributed Component Object Model
DNS	Domain Name System
DS	Dispatching Server
DSM	Distributed Shared Memory
EAI	enterprise application integration
EBS	event-based system
EIS	Enterprise Information System
EJB	Enterprise JavaBeans
FIFO	First In, First Out
GIOP	General Inter-ORB Protocol

GPS	Global Positioning System
GUI	graphical user interface
GUID	Globally Unique Identifier
HTTP	HyperText Transfer Protocol
IANA	Internet Assigned Numbers Authority
IC	integrated circuit
IDL	interface definition language
IETF	Internet Engineering Task Force
IIOP	Internet Inter-ORB Protocol
IP	Internet Protocol
J2EE	Java 2 Platform, Enterprise Edition
JDK	Java Development Kit
JIT	Just In Time
JMS	Java Message Service
JTA	Java Transaction API
JTS	Java Transaction Service
LC	logic coupling
LCE	loosely coupled event
LLC	literal logic coupling
LPC	local procedure call
MBB	make before break
MDB	message-driven bean
MIL	module interconnection language
MOM	message-oriented middleware
MSMQ	Microsoft Message Queuing
OMG	Object Management Group
OO	object-oriented
OOP	object-oriented programming
OS	operating system
P2P	peer-to-peer
PC	procedure call
PCB	printed circuit board
PGM	Pragmatic General Multicast

PTP	point-to-point
QoS	Quality of Service
RAD	rapid application development
RFC	Request For Comments
RMI	Remote Method Invocation
RPC	remote procedure call
SAF	store-and-forward
SC	signature coupling
SDL	Specification and Description Language
SM	shared memory
SMP	symmetric multiprocessor
SOAP	Simple Object Access Protocol
SR	shared resource
SRMP	SOAP Reliable Messaging Protocol
TC	type coupling
TCP/IP	Transmission Control Protocol / Internet Protocol
UDT	user-defined type
UI	user interface
UMA	Uniform Memory Access
UML	Unified Modeling Language
UNC	Universal Naming Convention
UTC	unambiguous type coupling
W3C	World Wide Web Consortium
XML	Extensible Markup Language

APPENDIX B

■■■

References

Agha, Gul, *ACTORS: A Model of Concurrent Computation in Distributed Systems* (Cambridge, MA: The MIT Press, 1986).

Alexander, Christopher, *The Timeless Way of Building* (New York: Oxford University Press, 1979).

Alexander, Christopher, Sara Ishikawa, and Murray Silverstein, *A Pattern Language: Towns, Buildings, Construction* (New York: Oxford University Press, 1977).

Allen, Robert and David Garlan, "A Formal Basis for Architectural Connection," *ACM Transactions on Software Engineering and Methodology*, July 1997.

Allen, Robert and David Garlan, "Formalizing Architectural Connection" (proceedings of the 16th International Conference on Software Engineering, Sorrento, Italy, May 1994).

Arnold, Matthew, Michael Hind, and Barbara Ryder, "An Empirical Study of Adaptive Optimization" (proceedings of the 13th International Workshop on Languages and Compilers for Parallel Computing, Yorktown Heights, NY, August 2000).

Bacon, Jean, Ken Moody, John Bates, Richard Hayton, Chaoying Ma, Andrew McNeil, Oliver Seidel, and Mark Spiteri, "Generic Support for Distributed Applications," *IEEE Computer*, March 2000.

Bala, Vasanth, Evelyn Duesterwald, and Sanjeev Banerjia, "Dynamo: A Transparent Dynamic Optimization System"(proceedings of the SIGPLAN 2000 Conference on Programming Language Design and Implementation, Vancouver, British Columbia, Canada, June 2000).

Banerjee, Suman, Bobby Bhattacharjee, and Christopher Kommareddy, "P2P and Multicast" session, "Scalable Application Layer Multicast" (proceedings of the 2002 conference on Applications, Technologies, Architectures, and Protocols for Computer Communications, Pittsburgh, August 2002).

Barrett, Daniel J., Lori A. Clarke, Peri L. Tarr, and Alexander E. Wise, "A Framework for Event-Based Software Integration," *ACM Transactions on Software Engineering and Methodology*, October 1996.

Bergstra, Jan A. and Paul Klint, "The Discrete Time ToolBus: A Software Coordination Architecture," *Science of Computer Programming*, July 1998.

Berners-Lee, Tim, Roy Fielding, and Henrik Frystyk Nielsen, "Hypertext Transfer Protocol -- HTTP/1.0," www.w3.org/Protocols/rfc1945/rfc1945 (technical report, 1996).

Birman, Kenneth P., "The Process Group Approach to Reliable Distributed Computing," *Communications of the ACM*, December 1993.

Blakeley, Burnie, Harry Harris, and Rhys Lewis, *Messaging and Queuing Using the MQI* (Columbus, OH: McGraw-Hill, 1995).

Borland, "What are events?," online help documentation for Borland Delphi 5, 1997.

Box, Don, *Essential COM* (Boston: Addison-Wesley Professional, 1997).

Box, Don, David Ehnebuske, Gopal Kakivaya, Andrew Layman, Noah Mendelsohn, Henrik Frystyk Nielsen, Satish Thatte, and Dave Winer, "Simple Object Access Protocol (SOAP) 1.1," www.w3.org/TR/2000/NOTE-SOAP-20000508/, 2000.

Briand, Lionel C., John W. Daly, and Jurgen K. Wüst, "A Unified Framework for Coupling Measurement in Object-Oriented Systems," *IEEE Transactions on Software Engineering*, January/February 1999.

Bruening, Derek, Timothy Garnett, and Saman Amarasinghe, "An Infrastructure for Adaptive Dynamic Optimization" (proceedings of the 1st International Symposium on Code Generation and Optimization, San Francisco, CA, March 2003).

Cabrera, Luis Felipe, Michael B. Jones, and Marvin Theimer, "Herald: Achieving a Global Event Notification Service" (proceedings of the Eighth Workshop on Hot Topics in Operating Systems, Elmau/Oberbayern, Germany, May 2001).

Cain, James Westland and Rachel Jane McCrindle, "An Investigation into the Effects of Code Coupling on Team Dynamics and Productivity" (proceedings of the IEEE 26th Annual International Computer Software and Applications Conference, Oxford, England, August 26–29, 2002).

Carnegie Mellon University, School of Computer Science, "An Overview of Acme," www-2.cs.cmu.edu/~acme/language_overview.html.

Carnegie Mellon University, School of Computer Science, "The Acme Architectural Description Language," www-2.cs.cmu.edu/~acme.

Carzaniga, Antonio, David S. Rosenblum, and Alexander L. Wolf, "Design and Evaluation of a Wide-Area Event Notification Service," *ACM Transactions on Computer Systems*, August 2001.

Chatty, Stephane, "The Ivy Software Bus," www.tls.cena.fr/products/ivy/documentation/ivy.pdf (white paper, 2003).

Consel, Charles, Luke Hornof, Julia L. Lawall, Renaud Marlet, Gilles Muller, Jacques Noye, Scott Thibault, and Eugen-Nicolae Volanschi, "Tempo: Specializing Systems Applications and Beyond," *ACM Computing Surveys, Symposium on Partial Evaluation*, September 1998.

Cox, Brad J., *Object-Oriented Programming: An Evolutionary Approach* (Boston: Addison-Wesley Professional, 1986).

Cugola, Gianpaolo, Elisabetta Di Nitto, and Alfonso Fuggetta, "The JEDI Event-Based Infrastructure and Its Application to the Development of the OPSS WFMS," *IEEE Transactions of Software Engineering*, September 2001.

Deering, Stephen E. and David R. Cheriton, "Multicast Routing in Datagram Internetworks and Extended LANs," *ACM Transactions on Computer Systems*, May 1990.

DeRemer, Frank and Hans Kron, "Programming-in-the-Large Versus Programming-in-the-Small," *IEEE Transactions on Software Engineering*, June 1976.

D'Souza, Desmond Francis and Alan Cameron Wills, *Objects, Components, and Frameworks with UML: The Catalysis Approach* (Boston: Addison-Wesley Professional, 1998).

Eder, Johann, Gerti Kappel, and Michael Schrefl, "Coupling and Cohesion in Object-Oriented Systems" (technical report, University of Klagenfurt, Austria, 1994).

Ellsberger, Jan, Dieter Hogrefe, and Amardeo Sarma, *SDL: Formal Object-Oriented Language for Communicating Systems* (Upper Saddle River, NJ: Prentice Hall, 1997).

Engelmore, Robert and Tony Morgan, *Blackboard Systems* (Boston: Addison-Wesley Professional, 1988).

Eugster, Patrick Th., Pascal A. Felber, Rachid Guerraoui, and Anne-Marie Kermarrec, "The Many Faces of Publish/Subscribe," *ACM Computing Surveys*, June 2003.

Eugster, Patrick Th., Rachid Guerraoui, and Christian Heide Damm, "On Objects and Events" (proceedings of the Conference on Object-Oriented Programming, Systems, Languages, and Applications [OOPSLA], Tampa Bay, FL, October 2001).

Faison, Ted, *Component-Based Development with Visual C#* (Indianapolis, IN: John Wiley & Sons, 2002), p. 40.

Faison, Ted, "Interaction Patterns for Communicating Processes" (proceedings of PLoP98, Pattern Languages of Programs, Monticello, IL, August 1998, http://citeseer.ist.psu.edu/faison98interaction.html).

Faison, Ted, "Interactive Component-Based Software Development with Espresso" (proceedings of the International Conference on Automated Software Engineering, Lake Tahoe, NV, November 1997).

Faison, Ted, "Object-Oriented State Machines," *Software Development Magazine*, September 1993.

Feynman, Richard P., "He Fixes Radios by Thinking!," "*Surely You're Joking, Mr. Feynman!*" *Adventures of a Curious Character* (New York: W. W. Norton & Company, 1984).

Fleisch, Brett D., "Distributed Shared Memory in a Loosely Coupled Distributed System," *Proceedings of the ACM Workshop on Frontiers in Computer Communications Technology* (New York: ACM Press, 1987).

Floyd, Sally, Van Jacobson, Ching-Gung Liu, Steven McCanne, and Lixia Zhang, "A Reliable Multicast Framework for Lightweight Sessions and Application Level Framing," *IEEE/ACM Transactions on Networking*, December 1997.

Freeman, Eric, Susanne Hupfer, and Ken Arnold, *Javaspaces Principles, Patterns, and Practice* (Boston: Addison-Wesley Professional, 1999).

Gamma, Erich, Richard Helm, Ralph Johnson, and John Vlissides, *Design Patterns: Elements of Reusable Object-Oriented Software* (Boston: Addison-Wesley Professional, 1995).

Garlan, David and Curtis Scott, "Adding Implicit Invocation to Traditional Programming Languages" (proceedings of the 15th International Conference on Software Engineering, Baltimore, MD, May 1993).

Garlan, David, Robert Monroe, and David Wile, "ACME: An Architectural Interconnection Language" (technical report, Carnegie Mellon University, Pittsburgh, November 1995).

Garlan, David, Robert Monroe, and Dave Wile, "Acme: An Architecture Description Interchange Language" (proceedings of IBM Centers for Advanced Studies Conference, Toronto, Ontario, Canada, November 1997).

Gelernter, David, "Generative Communication in Linda," *ACM Transactions on Programming Languages and Systems*, January 1985.

Gemmell, Jim, Todd Montgomery, Tony Speakman, Nidhi Bhaskar, and Jon Crowcroft, "The PGM Reliable Multicast Protocol," *IEEE Network*, January/February 2003.

Geraghty, Ronan, Sean Joyce, Tom Moriarty, and Gary Noone, *COM-CORBA Interoperability* (Upper Saddle River, NJ: Prentice Hall, 1998).

Grundy, John C., John G. Hosking, and Warwick B. Mugridge, "Supporting Flexible Consistency Management via Discrete Change Description Propagation, Software," *Practice and Experience*, September 1996.

Haahr, Mads, Rene Meier, Paddy Nixon, Vinny Cahill, and Eric Jul, "Filtering and Scalability in the ECO Distributed Event Model" (proceedings of the 5th International Symposium on Software Engineering for Parallel and Distributed Systems, Limerick, Ireland, June 2000).

Hapner, Mark, Rich Burridge, Rahul Sharma, Joseph Fialli, Kim Haase, *Java Message Service API Tutorial and Reference: Messaging for the J2EE Platform* (Boston: Addison-Wesley Professional, 2002).

Harel, David, "Statecharts: A Visual Formalism for Complex Systems," *Science of Computer Programming*, June 1987.

Hayes-Roth, Barbara, "A Blackboard Architecture for Control," *Artificial Intelligence*, July 1985.

Heineman, George T. and William T. Councill, *Component-Based Software Engineering: Putting the Pieces Together* (Boston: Addison-Wesley Professional, 2001).

Henning, Michi and Steve Vinoski, *Advanced CORBA Programming with C++* (Boston: Addison-Wesley Professional, 1999).

Hitz, Martin and Behzad Montazeri, "Measuring Coupling and Cohesion in Object-Oriented Systems" (proceedings of the International Symposium on Applied Corporate Computing, Monterrey, Mexico, October 1995).

IBM Corporation, "IBM WebSphere Business Integration Connect: Architecture Overview," www-3.ibm.com/software/integration/wbiconnect/library/doc/wbic420/pdf/architecture.pdf.

Institute for Energy Technology, "SWBus Technical Overview," www2.hrp.no/swbus/overview/overview.html, 2000.

Jagannathan, Vasudevan, Rajendra Dodhiawala, and Lawrence S. Baum, *Blackboard Architectures and Applications (Perspectives in Artificial Intelligence)* (Burlington, MA: Academic Press, 1989).

Jin, Yuhui and Rob Strom, "Relational Subscription Middleware for Internet-Scale Publish-Subscribe" (proceedings of the Second International Workshop on Distributed Event-Based Systems, San Diego, CA, June 2003).

Kaiser, Joerg, Cristiano Brudna, and Carlos Mitidieri, "A Real-Time Event Channel Model for the CAN-Bus" (proceedings of the "Workshop on Parallel and Distributed Real-Time Systems," 17th International Symposium on Parallel and Distributed Processing, Nice, France, April 2003).

Kazaa, "Peer-To-Peer (P2P) and How Kazaa Works," www.kazaa.com/us/help/glossary/p2p.htm, 2003.

Kielmann, Thilo, "Object-Oriented Distributed Programming with Objective Linda" (proceedings of the First International Workshop on High Speed Networks and Open Distributed Platforms, St. Petersburg, Russia, June 1995).

Krall, Andreas, "Efficient JavaVM Just-in-Time Compilation" (proceedings of the International Conference on Parallel Architectures and Compilation Techniques, Paris, France, October 1998).

Krasner, Glenn E. and Stephen T. Pope, "A Cookbook for Using the Model-View-Controller User Interface Paradigm in Smalltalk-80," *Journal of Object-Oriented Programming*, August/September 1988.

Kulik, Joanna, "Fast and Flexible Forwarding for Internet Subscription Systems" (proceedings of the Second International Workshop on Distributed Event-Based Systems, San Diego, CA, June 2003).

Lamport, Leslie, "Time, Clocks, and the Ordering of Events in a Distributed System," *Communications of the ACM*, July 1978.

Lin, John C. and Sanjoy Paul, "A Reliable Multicast Transport Protocol" (proceedings of IEEE INFOCOM'96, San Francisco, CA, March 1996).

Luckham, David C. and James Vera, "An Event-Based Architecture Definition Language," *IEEE Transactions on Software Engineering*, September 1995.

Luckham, David C., John J. Kenney, Larry M. Augustin, James Vera, Doug Bryan, and Walter Mann, "Specification and Analysis of System Architecture Using Rapide," *IEEE Transactions on Software Engineering*, April 1995.

Maffeis, Silvano, "Components Need Software Bus Middleware" (proceedings of the CHOOSE Forum on Object-Oriented Software Architecture, University of Bern, Bern, Switzerland, March 1999, www.riehle.org/community-service/choose/1999-forum/maffeis.pdf).

Mansouri-Samani, Masoud and Morris Sloman, "GEM: A Generalized Event Monitoring Language for Distributed Systems," *IEE/IOP/BCS Distributed Systems Engineering Journal*, June 1997.

Martin, James and James J. Odell, *Object-Oriented Methods: A Foundation—UML Edition* (Upper Saddle River, NJ: Prentice Hall, 1995).

Medvidovic, Nenad, David S. Rosenblum, and Richard N. Taylor, "A Language and Environment for Architecture-Based Software Development and Evolution" (proceedings of the 21st International Conference on Software Engineering, Los Angeles, CA, May 1999).

Medvidovic, Nenad and Richard N. Taylor, "A Classification and Comparison Framework for Software Architecture Description Languages," *IEEE Transactions on Software Engineering*, January 2000.

Medvidovic, Nenad, Richard N. Taylor, and E. James Whitehead, Jr., "Formal Modeling of Software Architectures at Multiple Levels of Abstraction" (proceedings of the California Software Symposium, Los Angeles, CA, April 1996).

Meier, Rene and Vinny Cahill, "Taxonomy of Distributed Event-Based Programming Systems," *The Computer Journal*, June 24, 2005.

Microsoft, "Microsoft Message Queuing," www.microsoft.com/windowsserver2003/technologies/msmq/default.mspx (technical report).

Milojicic, Dejan S., Vana Kalogeraki, Rajan Lukose, Kiran Nagaraja, Jim Pruyne, Bruno Richard, Sami Rollins, and Zhichen Xu, "Peer-to-Peer Computing," www.hpl.hp.com/techreports/2002/HPL-2002-57R1.html (HP Labs technical report, 2002).

Minsky, Naftaly H. and David Rozenshtein, "A Software Development Environment for Law-Governed Systems," *ACM SIGPLAN Notices*, February 1989.

Mitidieri, Carlos and Jörg Kaiser, "Attribute-Based Filtering for Embedded Systems" (proceedings of the Second International Workshop on Distributed Event-Based Systems, San Diego, CA, June 2003).

MSDN, "Events and Delegates," http://msdn.microsoft.com/library/default.asp?url=/library/en-us/cpguide/html/cpconeventsdelegates.asp, 2004.

MSDN, "Inside the .NET Framework," http://msdn.microsoft.com/library/default.asp?url=/library/en-us/cpguide/html/cpconinsidenetframework.asp.

Murata, Tadao, "Petri Nets: Properties, Analysis and Applications," *Proceedings of the IEEE*, April 1989.

Nielsen, Henrik Frystyk and Satish Thatte, "Web Services Routing Protocol (WS-Routing)," http://msdn.microsoft.com/library/default.asp?url=/library/en-us/dnglobspec/html/ws-routing.asp (technical report, 2001).

Oberleitner, Johann, Thomas Gschwind, and Mehdi Jazayeri, "The Vienna Component Framework Enabling Composition Across Component Models" (proceedings of the 25th International Conference on Software Engineering, Portland, OR, May 2003).

Object Management Group, "Common Object Request Broker Architecture: Core Specification," www.omg.org/docs/formal/02-12-06.pdf (technical report, 2002).

Object Management Group, CORBA Event Service Specification, www.omg.org/technology/documents/formal/event_service.htm, 2001.

Object Management Group, "CORBA Messaging," www.omg.org/docs/formal/02-12-09.pdf (technical report, 2002).

Object Management Group, "Event Service Specification," www.omg.org/docs/formal/01-03-01.pdf (technical report, 2001).

Object Management Group, "Notification Service Specification," www.omg.org/cgi-bin/apps/doc?formal/02-08-04.pdf (technical report, 2002).

Oracle, "Advanced Oracle Queuing," www.oracle.com/technology/products/aq/htdocs/9iaq_ds.html (technical report).

Perry, Mark, Manesh Balachandran, Jorge Plata, Paul Solano, and Phillip Thomas, *MQSeries Programming Patterns* (White Plains, NY: IBM Redbooks, 2002, http://publib-b.boulder.ibm.com/Redbooks.nsf/RedbookAbstracts/sg246506.html?Open).

Pietzuch, Peter R. and Jean Bacon, "Hermes: A Distributed Event-Based Middleware Architecture" (proceedings of the International Conference on Distributed Computing Systems, Vienna, Austria, July 2002).

Platt, David S., *Understanding COM+* (Redmond, WA: Microsoft Press, 1999).

Prem, Jatinder, Bernard Ciconte, Peter Go, Scott Dunbar, and Manish Devgan, *BEA WebLogic Platform 7* (Indianapolis, IN: Sams, 2003).

Protic, Jelica, Milo Tomasevic, and Veljko Milutinovic, "Distributed Shared Memory: Concepts and Systems," *IEEE Parallel And Distributed Technology*, Summer 1996.

Purtilo, James M., "The Polylith Software Bus," *ACM Transactions on Programming Languages and Systems*, January 1994.

Rajagopalan, Mohan, Saumya K. Debray, Matti A. Hiltunen, and Richard D. Schlichting, "Profile-Directed Optimization of Event-Based Programs" (proceedings of the ACM Special Interest Group on Programming Languages [SIGPLAN], Berlin, Germany, June 2002).

Reiss, Steven P., "Connecting Tools Using Message Passing in the Field Environment," *IEEE Software*, July/August 1990.

Rowstron, Antony, Anne-Marie Kermarrec, Miguel Castro, and Peter Druschel, "Scribe: The Design of a Large-Scale Event Notification Infrastructure" (proceedings of the Third International Workshop on Networked Group Communications, London, UK, November 2001).

Rowstron, Antony and Peter Druschel, "Pastry: Scalable, decentralized object location and routing for large-scale peer-to-peer systems" (proceedings of the IFIP/ACM International Conference on Distributed Systems Platforms, Heidelberg, Germany, November 2001).

Schmidt, Douglas C., Timothy H. Harrison, and Irfan Pyarali, "Asynchronous Completion Token - An Object Behavioral Pattern for Efficient Asynchronous Event Handling" (proceedings of the 3rd Annual Pattern Languages of Programs Conference, Allerton Park, IL, September 1996).

Shaw, Mary, Robert DeLine, and Gregory Zelesnik, "Abstractions and Implementations for Architectural Connections" (proceedings of the Third International Conference on Configurable Distributed Systems, Annapolis, MD, May 1996).

Shereshevsky, Mark, Habbib Ammari, Nicholay Gradetsky, Ali Mili, and Hany H. Ammar, "Information Theoretic Metrics for Software Architectures" (proceedings of the IEEE 25th Annual International Computer Software and Applications Conference, Chicago, IL, October 8–12, 2001).

Stevens, Wayne, Glenford J. Myers, and Larry Constantine, "Structure Design," *IBM Systems Journal*, May 1974.

Stoica, Ion, Robert Morris, David Karger, M. Frans Kaashoek, and Hari Balakrishnan, "Chord: A Scalable Peer-to-peer Lookup Service for Internet Applications" (proceedings of the ACM SIGCOMM Conference, San Diego, CA, August 2001).

Strom, Rob, Guruduth Banavar, Tushar Chandra, Marc Kaplan, Kevan Miller, Bodhi Mukherjee, Daniel Sturman, and Michael Ward, "Gryphon: An Information Flow Based Approach to Message Brokering" (technical report, Hawthorne, NY, IBM T.J. Watson Research Center, 1998).

Sun Microsystems, "Java Client Developer's Guide: Sun ONE Message Queue," http://docs-pdf.sun.com/817-3728/817-3728.pdf (technical report, 2003).

Sun Microsystems, "ToolTalk User's Guide," http://docs-pdf.sun.com/801-6647/801-6647.pdf.

Swan, R.J., A. Bechtolsheim, Kwok-Woon Lai, and John Ousterhout, "The Implementation of the Cm* Multi-Microprocessor" (proceedings of the National Computer Conference, Dallas, TX, June 1977).

Szyperski, Clemens, *Component Software: Beyond Object-Oriented Programming* (Boston: Addison-Wesley Professional, 2002).

Tarkoma, Sasu, Jaakko Kangasharju, and Kimmo Raatikainen, "Client Mobility in Rendezvous-Notify" (proceedings of the Second International Workshop on Distributed Event-Based Systems, San Diego, CA, June 2003).

Taylor, Richard N., Nenad Medvidovic, Kenneth M. Anderson, E. James Whitehead Jr., and Jason E. Robbins, "A Component- and Message-Based Architectural Style for GUI Software" (proceedings of the 17th International Conference on Software Engineering, Seattle, WA, April 1995).

Teixeira, Steve and Xavier Pacheco, *Delphi 5 Developer's Guide* (Indianapolis, IN: Sams, 1999).

The Open Group, "DCE 1.1: Remote Procedure Call," www.opengroup.org/onlinepubs/009629399/toc.pdf, 1997.

TIBCO, "TIBCO Rendezvous," http://cf.tibco.com/eval/tibrv.cfm (technical report).

TIBCO, "TIBCO SmartSockets," http://cf.tibco.com/eval/tibss.cfm (technical report).

Toinard, Christian, Gerard Florin, and C. Carrez, "A Formal Method to Prove Ordering Properties of Multicast Systems," *ACM SIGOPS Operating Systems Review*, October 1999.

VITA, VMEbus specifications, www.vita.com.

Weber, Herbert, *The Software Factory Challenge: Results of the Eureka Software Factory Project* (Amsterdam, The Netherlands: IOS Press, 1997).

Wikipedia, "Morpheus (computer program)," http://en.wikipedia.org/wiki/Morpheus_(computer_program), 2003.

Wilhelm, Uwe and Andre Schiper, "A Hierarchy of Totally Ordered Multicasts" (proceedings of the 14th IEEE Symposium on Reliable Distributed Systems, Bad Neuenahr, Germany, September 1995).

Wollrath, Ann and Jim Waldo, "Trail: RMI," http://java.sun.com/docs/books/tutorial/rmi/ (technical report).

Wulf, W., E. Cohen, W. Corwin, A. Jones, R. Levin, C. Pierson, and F. Pollack, "HYDRA: The Kernel of a Multiprocessor Operating System," *Communications of the ACM*, June 1974.

van der Aalst, W.M.P., "Formalization and Verification of Event-Driven Process Chains," *Information and Software Technology*, July 1999.

Zhao, Ben Y., John Kubiatowicz, and Anthony D. Joseph, "Tapestry: An Infrastructure for Fault-tolerant Wide-area Location and Routing" (technical report, University of California, Berkeley, Berkeley, CA, April 2001).

Index

CPSIA information can be obtained at www.ICGtesting.com
Printed in the USA
LVOW100458250412

279042LV00006B/2/P

9 781430 243267